On What Matters

'the most significant work in ethics since Sidgwick's masterpiece was published in 1874.'

Peter Singer, *Times Literary Supplement*

'Parfit's arguments are of extraordinary brilliance and clarity, and by any standards *On What Matters* is an immensely powerful achievement . . . undoubtedly the work of a philosophical genius.'

John Cottingham, *The Tablet*

'one of the richest, most exciting contributions to moral philosophy in decades . . . Its originality is often striking and its arguments profound . . . the most perceptive, enlightening introduction to moral theory I know. I say 'introduction' not because the treatment is simplistic—on the contrary, it is extraordinarily subtle—but because it is so clearly written, so carefully argued, and so sharply focused on the most essential points . . . Along the way, he makes countless original and constructive moves.'

Kieran Setiya, *Mind*

'Does Parfit, then, succeed in his grand argument that Kant and Sidgwick lead toward one summit? . . . I myself think he succeeds beautifully . . .'

Allan Gibbard, *London Review of Books*

'a great achievement . . . a vast structure of philosophical argument which is remarkable for its clarity, persistence and charm.'

James Alexander, *Philosophy Now*

'*On What Matters* dryly sets forth countless arguments, but its author is passionate in his conviction that there must be objective values that give meaning to our lives in a godless world. It is rare to find an academic philosophical treatise that sincerely grapples with such cosmic questions as "whether human history has been worth it," given all the suffering that has existed in the world.'

Samuel Freeman, *New York Review of Books*

'Time and time again, one is impressed, even moved, by Parfit's enthralling and indefatigable resourcefulness.'

Gerald Lang, *Utilitas*

'Parfit's intellectual personality radiates throughout *On What Matters*, which as a whole presents a gripping and illuminating picture . . . of the moral outlook—both normative and metaethical—of one of the greatest moral thinkers of our time.'

Mark Schroeder, *Notre Dame Philosophical Reviews*

Derek Parfit is an Emeritus Fellow at All Souls College, Oxford, and a Regular Visiting Professor at New York University, Harvard, and Rutgers.

The Berkeley Tanner Lectures

The Tanner Lectures on Human Values were established by the American scholar, industrialist, and philanthropist Obert Clark Tanner; they are presented annually at nine universities in the United States and England. The University of California, Berkeley became a permanent host of annual Tanner Lectures in the academic year 2000–2001. This two-volume work is the sixth in a series of books based on the Berkeley Tanner Lectures. The volumes include a substantially revised and expanded version of the lectures that Derek Parfit presented at Berkeley in November of 2002, together with the responses of the three invited commentators on that occasion, T. M. Scanlon, Susan Wolf, and Allen Wood; there is also a fourth set of comments, by Barbara Herman, as well as replies to the comments and additional material by Derek Parfit. The volumes are edited by Samuel Scheffler, who also contributes an introduction. The Berkeley Tanner Lecture Series was established in the belief that these distinguished lectures, together with the lively debates stimulated by their presentation in Berkeley, deserve to be made available to a wider audience. Additional volumes are in preparation.

Martin Jay
R. Jay Wallace
Series Editors

Volumes Published in the Series:

Joseph Raz, *The Practice of Value*
Edited by R. Jay Wallace
With Christine M. Korsgaard, Robert Pippin, and Bernard Williams

Frank Kermode, *Pleasure and Change: The Aesthetics of Canon*
Edited by Robert Alter
With Geoffrey Hartman, John Guillory, and Carey Perloff

Seyla Benhabib, *Another Cosmopolitanism*
Edited by Robert Post
With Jeremy Waldron, Bonnie Honig, and Will Kymlicka

Axel Honneth, *Reification: A New Look at an Old Idea*
Edited by Martin Jay
With Judith Butler, Raymond Geuss, and Jonathan Lear

Allan Gibbard, *Reconciling Our Aims*
Edited by Barry Stroud
With Michael Bratman, John Broome, and F. M. Kamm

On What Matters

VOLUME TWO

DEREK PARFIT

Edited and Introduced by
Samuel Scheffler

OXFORD
UNIVERSITY PRESS

OXFORD

UNIVERSITY PRESS

Great Clarendon Street, Oxford OX2 6DP

Oxford University Press is a department of the University of Oxford.
It furthers the University's objective of excellence in research, scholarship,
and education by publishing worldwide. Oxford is a registered trade mark
of Oxford University Press in the UK and in certain
other countries

Portions of 'On What Matters' by Derek Parfit were delivered as a Tanner Lecture
on Human Values at the University of California, Berkeley, November 2002.
Printed with permission of the Tanner Lectures on Human Values, a Corporation,
University of Utah, Salt Lake City, Utah, USA.

First published 2011
First published in paperback 2013

Published in the United States of America by Oxford University Press
198 Madison Avenue, New York, NY 10016, United States of America

British Library Cataloguing in Publication Data
Data available

Library of Congress Cataloging in Publication Data
Parfit, Derek.
On what matters / Derek Parfit.
p. cm.
Includes bibliographical references and index.
ISBN 978-0-19-957280-9
1. Ethics. I. Title.
BJ1012.P37 2009
170—dc22   2009029662

Typeset by Laserwords Private Limited, Chennai, India
Printed in Great Britain
on acid-free paper by
Clays Ltd., St Ives plc

ISBN 978-0-19-968103-7 (Vol. 1)
978-0-19-968104-4 (Vol. 2)

Cover photograph, by the author, of the University Embankment in St. Petersburg.

To Tom Nagel and Tim Scanlon

On What Matters

VOLUME ONE

List of Contents
Introduction
Preface
Summary
PART ONE   Reasons
PART TWO   Principles
PART THREE   Theories
APPENDICES
Notes to Volume One
References
Bibliography
Index

VOLUME TWO

List of Contents
Preface
Summary
PART FOUR   Commentaries
PART FIVE   Responses
PART SIX   Normativity
APPENDICES
Notes to Volume Two
References
Bibliography
Index

Contents

VOLUME TWO

PREFACE   xiv

SUMMARY   1

PART FOUR

COMMENTARIES

HIKING THE RANGE   SUSAN WOLF   33

HUMANITY AS END IN ITSELF   ALLEN WOOD   58

A MISMATCH OF METHODS   BARBARA HERMAN   83

HOW I AM NOT A KANTIAN   T. M. SCANLON   116

PART FIVE

RESPONSES

18   ON HIKING THE RANGE   143

    65   Actual and Possible Consent   143

    66   Treating Someone Merely as a Means   145

    67   Kantian Rule Consequentialism   147

    68   Three Traditions   152

19   ON HUMANITY AS AN END IN ITSELF   156

    69   Kant's Formulas of Autonomy and of Universal Law   156

70 Rational Nature as the Supreme Value   159
71 Rational Nature as the Value to be Respected   164

20   ON A MISMATCH OF METHODS   169

72 Does Kant's Formula Need to be Revised?   169
73 A New Kantian Formula   174
74 Herman's Objections to Kantian Contractualism   179

21   HOW THE NUMBERS COUNT   191

75 Scanlon's Individualist Restriction   191
76 Utilitarianism, Aggregation, and Distributive Principles   193

22   SCANLONIAN CONTRACTUALISM   213

77 Scanlon's Claims about Wrongness and the Impersonalist
    Restriction   213
78 The Non-Identity Problem   217
79 Scanlonian Contractualism and Future People   231

23   THE TRIPLE THEORY   244

80 The Convergence Argument   244
81 The Independence of Scanlon's Theory   254

PART SIX

NORMATIVITY

24   ANALYTICAL NATURALISM AND SUBJECTIVISM   263

82 Conflicting Theories   263
83 Analytical Subjectivism about Reasons   269
84 The Unimportance of Internal Reasons   275
85 Substantive Subjective Theories   288
86 Normative Beliefs   290

25   NON-ANALYTICAL NATURALISM   295

87 Moral Naturalism   295

88 Normative Natural Facts   305
89 Arguments from 'Is' to 'Ought'   310
90 Thick-Concept Arguments   315
91 The Normativity Objection   324

26 THE TRIVIALITY OBJECTION   328

92 Normative Concepts and Natural Properties   328
93 The Analogies with Scientific Discoveries   332
94 The Fact Stating Argument   336
95 The Triviality Objection   341

27 NATURALISM AND NIHILISM   357

96 Naturalism about Reasons   357
97 Soft Naturalism   364
98 Hard Naturalism   368

28 NON-COGNITIVISM AND QUASI-REALISM   378

99   Non-Cognitivism   378
100 Normative Disagreements   384
101 Can Non-Cognitivists Explain Normative
     Mistakes?   389

29 NORMATIVITY AND TRUTH   401

102 Expressivism   401
103 Hare on What Matters   410
104 The Normativity Argument   413

30 NORMATIVE TRUTHS   426

105 Disagreements   426
106 On How We Should Live   430
107 Misunderstandings   433
108 Naturalized Normativity   439
109 Sidgwick's Intuitions   444
110 The Voyage Ahead   448
111 Rediscovering Reasons   453

31   METAPHYSICS   464

    112 Ontology   464
    113 Non-Metaphysical Cognitivism   475

32   EPISTEMOLOGY   488

    114 The Causal Objection   488
    115 The Validity Argument   498
    116 Epistemic Beliefs   503

33   RATIONALISM   511

    117 Epistemic Reasons   511
    118 Practical Reasons   525
    119 Evolutionary Forces   534

34   AGREEMENT   543

    120 The Argument from Disagreement   543
    121 The Convergence Claim   549
    122 The Double Badness of Suffering   565

35   NIETZSCHE   570

    123 Revaluing Values   570
    124 Good and Evil   582
    125 The Meaning of Life   596

36   WHAT MATTERS MOST   607

    126 Has It All Been Worth It?   607
    127 The Future   612

APPENDICES   621

D   WHY ANYTHING? WHY THIS?   623
E   THE FAIR WARNING VIEW   649
F   SOME OF KANT'S ARGUMENTS FOR HIS
    FORMULA OF UNIVERSAL LAW   652
G   KANT'S CLAIMS ABOUT THE GOOD   672

H   AUTONOMY AND CATEGORICAL IMPERATIVES   678
I   KANT'S MOTIVATIONAL ARGUMENT   690
J   ON WHAT THERE IS   719

Notes to Volume Two   750
References   775
Bibliography   799
Index   809

Preface

Though the first quarter of this volume is partly about Volume One, the remaining three quarters are entirely self-standing.

Of those who gave me comments on this volume, I was helped most by Robert Adams, Robert Audi, Selim Berker, Paul Boghossian, Laurence Bonjour, Nicholas Bostrom, Philip Bricker, John Broome, Ruth Chang, Eugene Chislenko, Roger Crisp, Garrett Cullity, Terence Cuneo, Jonathan Dancy, Cian Dorr, David Enoch, Kit Fine, Stephen Finlay, William Fitzpatrick, Alvin Goldman, Bob Hale, Michael Jubien, Shelly Kagan, Guy Kahane, Thomas Kelly, Samuel Kerstein, Patricia Kitcher, Niko Kolodny, Brian Leiter, William Lycan, Tim Maudlin, Brian McLaughlin, Charles Parsons, Ingmar Persson, Thomas Pogge, Peter Railton, Simon Rippon, Jacob Ross, Stephen Schiffer, Mark Schroeder, Russ Shafer-Landau, Peter Singer, Knut Skarsaune, Robert Stalnaker, Larry Temkin, Brian Weatherson, Ralph Wedgwood, and Timothy Williamson.

SUMMARY

PART FOUR   COMMENTARIES

PART FIVE   RESPONSES

CHAPTER 18 ON HIKING THE RANGE

65 *Actual and Possible Consent*

According to what I call Kant's *Consent Principle*, we ought to treat people only in ways to which they could rationally consent. Wolf suggests that, by interpreting Kant in this way, I abandon the Kantian idea of respect for autonomy, which often requires us to treat people only in ways to which they *actually* consent. But the Consent Principle does not abandon this idea, since people could seldom rationally consent to being treated in some way without their actual consent. And when such treatment would be wrong, this principle would not require such acts.

66 *Treating Someone Merely as a Means*

It is wrong to impose certain harms on people, Wolf claims, if we are treating these people merely as a means. It may be wrong, I claim, to harm people *as a means* even if we are *not* treating these people *merely* as a means. On this second view, harming people as a means would more often be wrong.

67 *Kantian Rule Consequentialism*

According to the Kantian Contractualist Formula, everyone ought to follow the principles whose universal acceptance everyone could rationally choose. This formula requires us, I argue, to follow optimific Rule Consequentialist principles. Wolf objects that everyone could rationally choose certain *non*-optimific *autonomy-protecting* principles. If everyone could rationally choose these principles, however, these principles must be optimific. But Wolf may be right to claim that everyone could rationally choose these principles.

68 *Three Traditions*

As Wolf claims, it would not be a tragedy if there is no single supreme moral principle. But it would be a tragedy if there is no single true morality.

CHAPTER 19 ON HUMANITY AS AN END IN ITSELF

69 *Kant's Formulas of Autonomy and of Universal Law*

The 'most definitive form' of Kant's supreme principle, Wood claims, is Kant's Formula of Autonomy. When revised in the way that is clearly needed, this formula becomes another version of my proposed Kantian Contractualist Formula.

70 *Rational Nature as the Supreme Value*

On Wood's interpretation of Kant's view, humanity or rational nature has the supreme value that both grounds morality and gives us our reason to obey the moral law. The supreme value of rational beings is not a kind of goodness, however, but a kind of moral status. This moral status could not be what grounds morality and gives us our reason to obey the moral law. Nor could such a ground be provided by the value of non-moral rationality. But Kant sometimes uses 'humanity' to refer to our capacity for morality and for having good wills. The supreme goodness of good wills might be the value that grounds morality. Wood's arguments against this view are not decisive.

71 *Rational Nature as the Value to be Respected*

Our acts are wrong, Wood suggests, when and because they fail to respect the value of non-moral rationality. Herman makes a similar suggestion. These suggestions seem open to strong objections. And respect for persons should be respect, not for their non-moral rationality, but for *them*.

CHAPTER 20 ON A MISMATCH OF METHODS

72 *Does Kant's Formula Need to be Revised?*

According to Kant's Formula of Universal Law, it is wrong to act on any maxim that we could not rationally will to be universal. This formula fails, I argued, because there are many maxims on which it is sometimes but not always wrong to act. Two examples are the Egoistic maxim 'Do whatever would be best for me' and the maxim 'Never lie'. We could not rationally will these maxims to be universal. But my imagined Egoist does not act wrongly when he acts on his maxim by keeping his promises, paying his debts, and saving a drowning child. Nor would it be wrong to act on the maxim 'Never lie' by telling someone the correct time.

Herman suggests that my Egoist does, in several senses, act wrongly. But Kant intends his formula to answer questions about which acts are wrong in the sense of being *contrary to duty*, and Kant would agree that my Egoist's acts are not in *this* sense wrong. And it would seldom be in this sense wrong to act on the maxim 'Never lie'. So Kant's Formula needs to be revised.

73 *A New Kantian Formula*

Kant's Formula might be claimed to tell us when acts are in certain other senses wrong. But this version of Kant's Formula would fail.

74 *Herman's Objections to Kantian Contractualism*

Herman earlier wrote that, despite a sad history of attempts, no one has been able to make Kant's Formula work. I argue that, if we revise Kant's Formula in two wholly Kantian ways, we can make this formula work.

Herman objects that, in applying both Kant's original formula and my proposed revision, I abandon one of the most distinctive parts of Kant's moral theory. I appeal to our reasons to care about our own and other people's well-being, and to the facts that give us other non-moral reasons to care about what happens. It is deeply un-Kantian, Herman suggests, to appeal to such reasons. That is not, I believe, true. And it is only by appealing to such reasons that we can make Kant's Formula work.

CHAPTER 21   HOW THE NUMBERS COUNT

75 *Scanlon's Individualist Restriction*

According to Scanlon's *Contractualist Formula*, we ought to follow the principles that no one could reasonably reject. Scanlon makes various claims about what are admissible grounds for rejecting principles. According to Scanlon's

> *Individualist Restriction*, in rejecting principles, we must appeal to their implications only for ourselves, or for other *single* people.

This restriction is given some support by Scanlon's appeal to the idea of justifiability to *each* person. But this part of Scanlon's view also has, I shall argue, some unacceptable implications.

76 *Utilitarianism, Aggregation, and Distributive Principles*

In proposing his Individualist Restriction, one of Scanlon's aims is to avoid certain Utilitarian conclusions. Utilitarians believe that it can be right to impose a great burden on one person, if we can thereby give small benefits to a large enough number of other people. Utilitarians go astray, Scanlon assumes, by adding together these people's benefits. On Scanlon's view, in such cases, the numbers don't count.

Scanlon, I suggest, misdiagnoses how Utilitarians reach such unacceptable conclusions. Their mistake is not their belief that the numbers count, but their belief that it makes no moral difference how benefits and burdens are distributed between different people. To illustrate this distinction, we should consider cases in which, if we don't intervene, everyone will be equally badly off. In some cases of this kind, Scanlon's view would imply that we ought to benefit one of many people rather than giving to all these people a much greater total benefit that would be shared equally between them. If we are doctors, for example, we ought to lengthen a single person's life from 30 years to 70 rather than lengthening a million people's lives from 30 years to 35. That is clearly the wrong conclusion.

These cases show, I believe, that Scanlon ought to drop his Individualist Restriction. For Scanlon's Formula to apply successfully to such cases, Scanlon must allow that we can sometimes reasonably reject some principle by appealing to this principle's implications not only for us but also for the other people in some group. In the case that I have just described, each of the million people could reasonably reject any principle that did not require us to give them all five more years of life. These people could reasonably appeal to the facts that they are just as badly off as the single person, and that they together would receive a much greater total sum of benefits, which would also be more fairly shared between all these people.

Scanlon suggests that, if he gave up his Individualist Restriction, his view would cease to provide a clear alternative to Utilitarianism. That is not so. Rather than denying that the numbers count, Scanlon should return to a stronger version of one of his earlier claims, which we can call *the Contractualist Priority View*. People have stronger grounds to reject some principle, Scanlon should claim, the worse off these people are. This revised version of Scanlon's view would often conflict with Utilitarianism, and in ways that avoid implausible conclusions.

CHAPTER 22 SCANLONIAN CONTRACTUALISM

77 Scanlon's Claims about Wrongness and the Impersonalist Restriction

In his book, Scanlon claimed that his Contractualism gives an account of wrongness itself, or what it is for acts to be wrong. Scanlon should claim instead that, when acts are wrong in his Contractualist sense, that makes these acts wrong in other, non-Contractualist senses. He might, for example, claim that, when some act is disallowed by some principle that no one could reasonably reject, this fact makes this act unjustifiable to others, blameworthy, and an act that gives its agent reasons for remorse, and gives others reasons for indignation. Scanlon now accepts that his Contractualist theory should take some such form.

According to Scanlon's

> *Impersonalist Restriction*: In rejecting some moral principle,
> we cannot appeal to claims about which outcomes would
> be impersonally better or worse, in the impartial reason-
> involving sense.

When Scanlon describes what it is for acts to be wrong in his proposed Contractualist sense, he can claim that, *by definition*, appeals to such impartial reasons are irrelevant. But if Scanlon claims that such acts are wrong in other senses, he could not defend his Impersonalist Restriction in this way. Nor could he defensibly claim that, when acts are wrong in his Contractualist sense, this fact has absolute moral priority over facts about what is impersonally better or worse. If Scanlon keeps his Impersonalist Restriction, he would have to retreat to the weaker claim that, when acts are wrong in his Contractualist sense, that makes these acts *prima facie* wrong in other senses. If Scanlon dropped this restriction, he could make the stronger claim that acts are wrong in other senses *just when*, and in part because, such acts are wrong in his Contractualist sense. If that were true, Scanlon's Contractualism would unify, and help to explain, all of the more particular ways in which some acts are wrong. That gives Scanlon a reason to make this bolder claim.

78 *The Non-Identity Problem*

Scanlon has other reasons to drop his Impersonalist Restriction. When he describes what we owe to others, Scanlon intends these *others* to include all future people. Many of our acts or policies affect the identity of future people, or *who it is* who will later live. We can often know both that

> (A) if we act in one of two ways, or follow one of two policies,
> we would be likely to cause some of the lives that are later lived
> to be less worth living,

and that

> (B) since it would be different people who would live these
> lives, these acts or policies would not be worse for any of
> these people.

We can ask whether and how (B) makes a difference. I have called this
the Non-Identity Problem.

On one view, one of two outcomes cannot be worse, nor can one of two
acts be wrong, if this outcome or act would be worse for no one. Even if
such acts or policies would greatly lower the quality of future people's
lives, we have no reason not to act in these ways.

According to another, better view, it would be in itself worse if some of
the lives that will be lived will be less worth living, and we have reasons
not to act in ways that would have such effects. If these effects would
be very bad, and we knew that we could avoid them at little cost to
ourselves, such acts would be wrong. This view could take two forms.
According to

> *the No Difference View*: It makes no difference whether,
> because these future lives would be lived by the same people,
> these acts would be worse for these people.

According to

> *the Two-Tier View*: This fact does make a difference. Though
> we always have some reasons not to cause future lives to be
> less worth living, these reasons would be weaker if, because
> these lives would be lived by different people, these acts would
> not be worse for any of these people.

The Two-Tier View has some unacceptable implications. We ought to
accept the No Difference View.

79 *Scanlonian Contractualism and Future People*

When applied to acts that affect future people, Scanlon's present view
also has unacceptable implications. As before, Scanlon should drop his

Impersonalist Restriction, and allow us to appeal to impartial reasons. When our acts will affect future people, we must consider the different possible people who might later be actual. To explain why certain acts would be wrong, we must appeal to the better lives that would have been lived by the people who, if we had acted differently, *would* have later existed. We cannot defensibly claim that these acts are wrong because these people could reasonably reject any principle that permits such acts. If we acted in these ways, these people would never exist, and we cannot defensibly appeal to claims about what could be reasonably rejected by people who are merely possible. Since we cannot appeal to the *personal* reasons that are had by people who never exist, we should appeal to the *impartial* reasons that are had by people who do exist.

On this version of Scanlon's view, when we ask which are the principles that no one could reasonably reject, we would sometimes have to compare the moral weight of such conflicting personal and impartial reasons. We would have to use our judgment about which of these reasons would, in different kinds of case, provide stronger grounds for rejecting principles. As Scanlon points out, however, all claims about reasonable rejection require such comparative judgments.

Such judgments could go either way. When some act would make things go best, we would all have impartial reasons to reject principles that did not require such acts. In some cases, these impartial reasons would be decisive, and Scanlon's Formula would require us to do what would make things go best. In some other cases, some people could reasonably reject any principle that required such acts, since everyone's impartial reasons would be morally outweighed by these people's conflicting personal reasons.

There are, I have claimed, two reasons why Scanlonian Contractualism should allow us to appeal to impartial reasons. If we cannot appeal to such reasons,

> Scanlon's Formula could not be defensibly applied to many of the acts or policies with which we affect future people,

and, as I argued earlier,

Scanlon could claim only that, when acts are wrong in his Contractualist sense, that makes these acts *prima facie* wrong in other, non-Contractualist senses.

If we can appeal to impartial reasons, Scanlon's Formula can be defensibly applied to all of our acts, and can be claimed both to tell us which acts are wrong, and to help to explain why such acts are wrong. Scanlonian Contractualism should, I believe, take this stronger form.

CHAPTER 23 THE TRIPLE THEORY

80 *The Convergence Argument*

When we apply the Kantian Contractualist Formula, I argued, it is only the optimific principles whose universal acceptance everyone could rationally choose. These principles might require us to impose a great burden on one person, for the sake of small benefits to many others. It may seem that, in some of these cases, the person who would bear this great burden could not rationally choose that everyone accepts these principles. Such cases would count against my claim that Kantian Contractualism implies Rule Consequentialism. This objection, I argue, fails.

I also argued that Kantian Rule Consequentialism could be combined with Scanlonian Contractualism. Scanlon objects that, even if the person who would be greatly burdened could rationally choose the optimific principles, this person could also reasonably reject these principles. In most cases, I believe, that is not so.

81 *The Independence of Scanlon's Theory*

In some cases, however, Scanlon's objection may succeed. Compared with Kantian Rule Consequentialism, Scanlonian Contractualism more strongly supports certain distributive principles, and may support some stronger principles. The three parts of the Triple Theory may also conflict in some other ways.

If there are such conflicts, that may seem to show that we should reject this theory. But that is not, I believe, true. All of our theories need to be revised. We are still climbing this mountain. And a team of mountaineers may do better if they have different abilities and strengths, and they sometimes try different routes. It would be only at the mountain's peak that we, or those who follow us, would have all the same true beliefs.

PART SIX NORMATIVITY

CHAPTER 24 ANALYTICAL NATURALISM AND SUBJECTIVISM

82 *Conflicting Theories*

By asking certain questions, we can distinguish several kinds of meta-ethical view. We ought, I shall argue, to reject Non-Cognitivism and two forms of Naturalism. These views are close to Nihilism. Normativity is either an illusion, or involves irreducibly normative truths. I shall then defend one form of Non-Naturalist Cognitivism.

Words, concepts, and claims may be either normative or naturalistic. Some fact is natural if such facts are investigated by people who are working in the natural or social sciences. According to *Analytical Naturalists*, all normative claims can be restated in naturalistic terms, and such claims, when they are true, state natural facts. According to *Non-Analytical Naturalists*, though some claims are irreducibly normative, such claims, when they are true, state natural facts. According to *Non-Naturalist Cognitivists*, such claims state irreducibly normative facts.

On the rule-involving conception, normativity involves rules, or requirements, which distinguish between what is or is not *allowed* or *correct*. On the reason-involving conception, normativity involves reasons or apparent reasons. On the motivational, attitudinal, and imperatival conceptions, normativity involves actual or possible motivation, or certain kinds of attitude, or commands. The reason-involving conception is, I believe, the best.

83 *Analytical Subjectivism about Reasons*

When we claim that someone has an *internal* reason to act in some way, we mean that this act would fulfil one of this person's present fully informed telic desires, or that after informed and procedurally rational deliberation this person would be motivated or would choose to act in this way. When we claim that someone has an *external* reason to act in some way, we use a fundamental, irreducibly normative concept that cannot be helpfully explained in other terms, but can also be expressed with the phrase 'counts in favour'. Though it is clear that we often have internal reasons for acting, some people believe that there are no external reasons. If we have both kinds of reason, as I believe, it is only external reasons that are important.

84 *The Unimportance of Internal Reasons*

If we used the words 'reason', 'should', and 'ought' in their internal senses, Subjectivism about Reasons would not be a substantive normative view, but a concealed tautology. If we used such words only in their *Naturalist internal* senses, we could not even have normative beliefs. If we used such words only in their *normative internal* senses, we could have some substantive normative beliefs, but we could not have distinct normative beliefs about what we have reasons to do, or what we should or ought to do.

85 *Substantive Subjective Theories*

For Subjectivists to make substantive claims, they should use these normative words in their external, irreducibly normative senses. The concept of an *internal reason* does no useful work.

86 *Normative Beliefs*

We can defensibly assume that normative words have such external senses, and can be used to make irreducibly normative claims.

CHAPTER 25 NON-ANALYTICAL NATURALISM

87 *Moral Naturalism*

It is sometimes claimed that, if normative and naturalistic concepts necessarily apply to all and only the same things these concepts must refer to the same property. That is not so.

Some normative concepts might refer to natural properties. But this does not show, as many Naturalists assume, that some normative claims might state natural facts. Some of these people ignore the important distinction between the properties that *make* acts right and the property of *being* right.

If Naturalism were true, Sidgwick, Ross, I, and others would have wasted much of our lives.

88 *Normative Natural Facts*

Some normative fact is *natural* in the *reductive* sense if this fact could be restated by making some non-normative, naturalistic claim. Naturalists believe that all normative facts are in this sense natural. Non-Naturalist Cognitivists believe that there are some irreducibly normative facts. We can ignore the question whether such normative facts might be, in some wider sense, natural facts.

If we use 'normative' in the rule-involving sense, we can defensibly claim that certain facts are both normative and natural. We can give Naturalistic accounts, for example, of what it is for certain acts to be illegal, dishonourable, or bad etiquette, or for the uses of certain words to be incorrect. Natural facts can also be normative in motivational and attitudinal senses. But no such facts can be normative in the reason-implying sense. There is a deep distinction between all natural facts and irreducibly normative reason-involving facts.

89 *Arguments from 'Is' to 'Ought'*

Searle argues that, if we accept certain natural, institutional facts, we must accept certain normative conclusions. Such arguments cannot succeed. We can recognize rule-implying normative facts but coherently deny that these facts give us any reasons.

90 *Thick-Concept Arguments*

Some writers similarly claim that, by appealing to *thick* normative concepts, such as *chaste* or *unpatriotic*, we can give sound arguments from *facts* to *values*. On one such argument, if we admit that someone has not committed any crime, we must accept that this person's punishment would be retributively unjust, and therefore likely to be wrong. But we can coherently deny that any way of treating people could be either retributively just or retributively unjust. These *thick-concept arguments* make a serious meta-ethical mistake. We cannot derive moral conclusions from the meanings of our words. Just as we cannot prove that God exists by appealing to what we mean by 'God', we cannot give linguistic or conceptual proofs of any positive substantive normative truth.

91 *The Normativity Objection*

Normative claims could not state natural facts because such claims are in a separate, distinctive category. This objection to Normative Naturalism would also be accepted, though for partly different reasons, by those *Metaphysical* Naturalists who are Nihilists or Non-Cognitivists.

CHAPTER 26 THE TRIVIALITY OBJECTION

92 *Normative Concepts and Natural Properties*

When irreducibly normative concepts refer to natural properties, they do that by also referring to some other, normative property, so we should not expect that we could use such concepts to make normative claims that state natural facts.

93 *The Analogies with Scientific Discoveries*

Many Naturalists appeal to analogies with scientific discoveries, such as the discovery that water is H2O or that heat is molecular kinetic energy. When looked at more closely, such analogies partly fail.

94 *The Fact Stating Argument*

According to Non-Analytical Naturalists, any true normative claim states some fact that is both normative and natural. If this fact were natural, it could also be stated by some non-normative claim. If these claims stated the same fact, they would give us the same information. Since the non-normative claim could not state a normative fact, nor could the normative claim. So such claims could not, as these Naturalists believe, state facts that are both normative and natural.

95 *The Triviality Objection*

When we say that we ought to act in some way, we are making a substantive claim, which might state a positive substantive normative fact. If these forms of Naturalism were true, such claims would not be substantive, but would be trivial. So these forms of Naturalism cannot be true.

Naturalists claim that, when some act would have certain natural properties, this fact is the same as this act's being what we ought to do. Such claims, some Naturalists believe, might tell us what we ought to do. That is not so. And what makes such claims seem informative also ensures that they could not be true.

For such normative claims to be substantive, they cannot merely refer to the same property in two different ways, but must tell us about the relation between two or more different properties, one of which is normative.

CHAPTER 27 NATURALISM AND NIHILISM

96 *Naturalism about Reasons*

The Triviality Objection also applies to Non-Analytical Naturalism about reasons.

97 *Soft Naturalism*

According to some Naturalists, though all facts are natural, we need to make some irreducibly normative claims. This view could not be true.

98 *Hard Naturalism*

Other Naturalists believe that, since all facts are natural, we could replace our normative concepts with naturalistic substitutes. This view is close to Nihilism.

CHAPTER 28 NON-COGNITIVISM AND QUASI-REALISM

99 Non-Cognitivism

According to *Non-Cognitivists*, normative claims are not intended to state facts, except perhaps in some minimal sense. Morality essentially involves certain kinds of desire, or other conative attitude. According to *Expressivists*, moral claims express such attitudes.

According to the *Humean Argument for Non-Cognitivism*, if moral convictions were beliefs, we might have moral convictions that did not motivate us. Since that is inconceivable, moral convictions cannot be beliefs, but must be desires or other conative attitudes. According to the *Naturalist Argument for Non-Cognitivism*, since moral claims could not state facts, but we can justifiably make such claims, these claims are not intended to state facts. According to the *Naturalist Argument for Nihilism*, since moral claims could not state facts, as they are intended to do, these claims are all false. We can reject these arguments.

100 Normative Disagreements

Expressivists cannot explain how we can have moral disagreements. We cannot disagree with other people's conative attitudes, or acts. Gibbard claims that, to understand our normative concepts and beliefs, it is enough to understand what is involved in deciding what to do, and in disagreeing with our own and other people's plans. That is not so.

101 Can Non-Cognitivists Explain Normative Mistakes?

Blackburn argues that, though our moral judgments express desires or other conative attitudes, these judgments and attitudes can be true or false, correct or mistaken. Expressivist Non-Cognitivists can thus be *Quasi-Realists*, who can claim all or nearly all that Cognitivists or *Realists* claim.

This ambitious project does not, I believe, succeed. Non-Cognitivists cannot explain what it would be for our moral judgments and conative attitudes to be correct or mistaken. Blackburn suggests that such attitudes might be mistaken in the sense that we would not have these attitudes if our standpoint were improved in certain ways. But to explain the sense in which this standpoint would be improved, Blackburn would have to claim that, if we had this standpoint, our attitudes would be less likely to be mistaken. This explanation would fail because it would have to use the word 'mistaken' in the sense that Blackburn is trying to explain. We might similarly claim that our headaches might be mistaken in the sense that we would not have these headaches if we had some standpoint in which our headaches would not be mistaken. That would not explain a sense in which our headaches might be mistaken.

In defending Quasi-Realism, Blackburn also claims that some apparently external meta-ethical questions are really internal moral questions. That may be so. If we ask Expressivists whether it is really true that acts of a certain kind are wrong, they can consistently answer Yes. But we are asking what it would *be* for conative attitudes and moral judgments to be true or false, correct or mistaken. This is not an internal moral question. Though Blackburn suggests that he need not answer this question, that is not so.

To defend their Non-Cognitivist Expressivism, Quasi-Realists must claim that our conative attitudes cannot be correct or mistaken. To defend their Quasi-Realism, these people must claim that these attitudes can be correct or mistaken. These people must therefore claim that these attitudes both cannot be, and can be, correct or mistaken. Since that is impossible, no such view could be true.

CHAPTER 29 NORMATIVITY AND TRUTH

102 *Expressivism*

Gibbard's Expressivist account of the concept *rational* does not achieve Gibbard's aims, since it could not help us to decide how it is rational for us to live.

103 *Hare on What Matters*

In his account of the word 'matters', Hare denies that anything could matter.

104 *The Normativity Argument*

According to a third argument for Non-Cognitivism, normative truths would not really be normative, since no truth could answer a normative question. That is not so. Only truths could answer such questions.

CHAPTER 30 NORMATIVE TRUTHS

105 *Disagreements*

When we disagree with other people, we cannot rationally keep our beliefs unless we can justifiably assume that there is some asymmetry between us and these other people, making us more likely to be right. In most of my disagreements with other people, there are, I believe, such asymmetries. My main example will be Williams, the person from whom, in several disagreements, I have learned most. If there seemed to be no asymmetries between us, I could not rationally believe that, in these disagreements, it was Williams who was less likely to be right.

106 *On How We Should Live*

Socrates asked which kind of life is intrinsically best, by being the life that we have most reason to want to live. Williams denies that some ways of living could be, in this sense, intrinsically better than others. Rather than asking Socrates' question, Williams suggests, we should ask 'What do I basically want?'

107 *Misunderstandings*

When we claim that we have a reason to want something, we are using the phrase 'a reason' in the indefinable normative sense that we can also express with the phrase 'counts in favour'. Williams believes that the phrase 'a reason' has no such intelligible purely normative sense. When Williams makes claims about reasons, these claims are about what might motivate us. That is why Williams rejects the view that some lives are intrinsically better than others. If the phrase 'a reason' can have this purely normative sense, as I believe, Williams does not fully understand the view that he rejects. When people disagree about whether some view is true, those who fully understand this view are more likely to be right.

108 *Naturalized Normativity*

Since Williams uses the phrase 'a reason' in a motivational sense, and he assumes that normativity involves reasons, Williams's normative claims are all psychological claims, which are at most weakly normative. Suppose I say: 'I *must* keep my promise to my wife. I *cannot* let her down.' This use of 'cannot', Williams claims, is a prediction. If I later give in to temptation, and break my promise to my wife, Williams might say: 'You were mistaken. As you found out, you didn't *have* to keep your promise. You *could* let her down.' But this remark would misunderstand my earlier claim. That claim was normative, and could be true whatever I later did.

Williams's view has unwelcome implications. Most of us believe, for example, that it would be wrong for anyone to torture other people for his own amusement. On Williams's view, given some sadist's motivations, this person may have no reason to act differently. This person's torturing of other people would not then be wrong.

109 *Sidgwick's Intuitions*

On Sidgwick's view, we have equal reason to be concerned about all parts of our conscious life. We have no reason, for example, to postpone some ordeal, when we know that this postponement would only make this ordeal worse. Sidgwick also claims that, from an impartial point of view, what happens to each person is equally important. Williams misunderstood these claims.

110 *The Voyage Ahead*

When I talked to Williams, I misunderstood his claims. I failed to see that these claims were psychological. I also misunderstood Mackie's claims. When Mackie denied that there are *objectively prescriptive values*, he was not denying a normative claim. Mackie meant that there are no normative beliefs that would *necessarily motivate* us. Since I knew these people well, I am puzzled and disturbed by our failures to understand each other.

111 *Rediscovering Reasons*

Hume is often assumed to be a Subjectivist, who believes that reasons for acting are given by facts about our present desires, and that we have no reasons to have our desires. But Hume's *stated* view is not Subjectivist, since Hume never discusses whether we have reasons for acting. Nor is Hume's *real* view Subjectivist. As many of his remarks show, Hume really believed that, as well as having reasons for acting, we have value-based object-given reasons to have particular desires, preferences, and aims.

Since Hume was really an Objectivist about reasons, that might be true of some other Humeans. The way a red hot iron feels, Mackie claims, gives him a powerful reason to try to end such pain. Mackie seems to be using the phrase 'a reason' in the motivational sense that is compatible with his Metaphysical Naturalism. But if Mackie had considered some of the distinctions I have drawn, he might have moved to a different view. The way a red hot iron *would* feel, Mackie might have believed, counts in favour of his trying to avoid this future pain. In coming to have this belief, Mackie would have abandoned both Naturalism and Subjectivism.

CHAPTER 31 METAPHYSICS

112 *Ontology*

In believing that some things matter in the reason-implying sense, I am believing that there are some irreducibly normative truths. That is denied by Metaphysical Naturalists, who believe that all properties and facts must be natural properties and facts. Irreducibly normative truths, these people assume, would involve the existence of strange metaphysical entities, which are too queer to be part of the fabric of the Universe.

On one widely held view, to be or to exist is to be actual, so there cannot be anything that is merely possible. If this *Actualist* view were true, much of our thinking would be undermined. We could never choose between different possible acts, or compare their possible outcomes, nor could we ever have reason to regret having acted as we did, since there would never be something else that we could have done instead. On the true view, which we can call *Possibilism*, there are some things that are never actual, but are merely possible. We should draw some other distinctions between the kinds of thing that do or might exist, and their ways of existing, or the senses in which they exist.

113 *Non-Metaphysical Cognitivism*

There are some abstract entities, properties, and truths that are not mind-dependent, nor created by us. Some examples are mathematical entities and truths. Some people ask

> Q2: Do numbers really exist in a fundamental, ontological
> sense, though they do not exist in space or time?

Platonists answer Yes. *Nominalists* answer No. According to a third view, which we can call the *No Clear Question View*, Q2 is too unclear to have an answer.

There is another kind of view, which we can call *Non-Metaphysical Cognitivism*. On such views:

> (F) There are some claims that are, in the strongest sense, true,
> but these truths have no ontological implications.

> (G) When such claims assert that there are certain things, or
> that these things exist, these claims do not imply that these
> things exist in some ontological sense.

Some examples are arithmetical truths. This view is not a form of Possibilism. Compared with actual events, merely possible events have a *lesser* ontological status. When we consider entities like numbers, this distinction does not apply. These entities have *no* ontological status. They are neither actual nor merely possible, and neither real nor unreal.

Here is one way to argue that the phrase 'there are' and the word 'exist' have an important non-ontological sense. We can claim that

> (O) it might have been true that nothing ever existed: no living
> beings, no stars, no atoms, not even space or time.

Someone might say: '(O) could not have been true. If it had been true that nothing ever existed, there would have been the truth that nothing existed. That is a contradiction.' We can reply: 'Truths do not have to exist, or be real, in an ontological sense. Truths need only be true. If it had been true that nothing ever existed, there would have *been* this truth, but this truth would not have existed in an ontological sense.' Similar claims apply to many other abstract entities. Even if nothing had ever existed, there would have been prime numbers greater than 100. It would also have been true that things like rocks, stars, and living beings might have existed. There would have been these possibilities.

There would also have been some irreducibly normative truths. Compared with nothing's ever existing, it would have been much better if blissfully happy beings had existed, and it would have been much worse if there had existed conscious beings whose lives involved unrelieved suffering. According to *Non-Metaphysical Non-Naturalist Normative Cognitivism*—which I shall call *Rationalism*—there are some claims that are irreducibly normative in the reason-involving sense, and are in a strong sense true. These truths have no ontological implications. For such claims to be true, it need not be true that reason-involving properties exist either as natural properties in the spatio-temporal world, or in some non-spatio-temporal part of reality.

CHAPTER 32 EPISTEMOLOGY

114 *The Causal Objection*

It is often objected that, since we could not be causally affected by irreducibly normative properties, we could not have any way of knowing about them. But we can have other ways of knowing about non-natural properties and truths. Though our computers cannot be causally affected by numbers or their properties, their internal circuitry enables them to produce true answers to mathematical questions. God might have designed our brains so that we could answer such questions, and could also respond to reasons. If God does not exist, natural selection could explain how we came to have such brains. Just as cheetahs were selected for their speed, and giraffes were selected for their long necks, human beings were selected for their rationality, which chiefly consists in their ability to respond to reasons. By responding to epistemic reasons, our ancestors were able to form many true beliefs which helped them to survive and reproduce.

115 *The Validity Argument*

When we ask how computers work, there are two kinds of event or fact that we need to explain. At the *micro-level*, there are many physical changes in the chips, circuits, and other small components of these computers. These events can each be fully explained by the laws of physics. But the laws of physics cannot explain the higher level fact that these computers reliably produce true answers to these many mathematical questions. This fact needs to be explained, since it would otherwise involve a highly implausible coincidence. These computers have this ability only because their calculations correspond to *valid reasoning*. Similar claims apply to us. Though the laws of physics may fully explain the neurophysiological events in our brains, these laws cannot explain how we can form so many true mathematical beliefs. We can form these beliefs only *because* we reason in valid ways. Though we cannot be causally affected by the property of validity, our mental processes involve a *non-causal response* to this validity. Metaphysical Naturalists believe that all properties and facts are natural. Validity is not, in the relevant sense, a natural property. Since the explanation of these mathematical abilities must appeal to non-natural truths about validity, we should reject this form of Naturalism. And though validity is not a normative property, these facts show that we might be able to respond, in similar non-causal ways, to non-natural normative properties and truths.

116 *Epistemic Beliefs*

The words 'probable', 'likely', and 'certain' can be used in non-normative, *alethic* senses. According to *Analytical Naturalists*, epistemic normative concepts can be explained in alethic terms, and refer to alethic properties. According to *Epistemic Rationalists*, these concepts are irreducibly normative, and refer to irreducibly normative properties. According to *Non-Analytical Naturalists*, though these concepts are irreducibly normative, they refer to alethic properties. According to Rationalists, for example, when certain facts make it likely that P is true, that makes these facts have the different property of giving us some reason to believe P. According to Non-Analytical Naturalists, when certain facts make it likely that P is true, that's *what it is* for these facts to give us such a reason.

CHAPTER 33 RATIONALISM

117 *Epistemic Reasons*

Some normative skeptics argue:

(1) Our normative epistemic beliefs were often advantageous, by causing us to have true worldly beliefs which helped us to survive and reproduce.

(2) Because these normative beliefs were advantageous, natural selection made us disposed to have them.

(3) These beliefs would have had the same effects whether or not they were true.

Therefore

(4) These beliefs would have been advantageous whether or not they were true.

Therefore

(5) Natural selection would have disposed us to have these beliefs whether or not they were true.

(6) We have no empirical evidence for the truth of these beliefs.

(7) We have no other way of knowing whether these beliefs are true.

Therefore

We cannot justifiably believe that these beliefs are true.

We can call this the *Naturalist Argument for Normative Skepticism*. When we consider normative beliefs that are grounded on alethic beliefs about what is certain or likely to be true, we should accept (3), (4), (5), and (6). But we can reject (1) and (7), as similar claims about our modal beliefs help to show.

118 *Practical Reasons*

When this skeptical argument is applied to our practical and moral beliefs, we can respond in similar ways.

119 *Evolutionary Forces*

We have many practical and moral beliefs that were not produced by natural selection, or other evolutionary forces. Though we cannot have empirical evidence for the truth of these beliefs, we do not need such evidence. We have strong reasons to believe that we can have both epistemic and practical reasons, some of which are moral reasons. In defending these claims, however, there is a further challenge that we must meet.

CHAPTER 34 REACHING AGREEMENT

120 *The Argument from Disagreement*

When people deny that there are moral truths, many appeal to the facts of widespread moral disagreement, and to the cultural origin of many moral beliefs. Similar claims apply to other normative beliefs. In response to this argument, we should ask whether we can defend the claim that, in *ideal conditions*, we would nearly all sufficiently agree. According to this

> *Convergence Claim*: If everyone knew all of the relevant
> non-normative facts, used the same normative concepts,
> understood and carefully reflected on the relevant arguments,

and was not affected by any distorting influence, we would
nearly all have similar normative beliefs.

Metaphysical Naturalists believe that there could not be any irreducibly
normative truths. When we consider the Convergence Claim, we should
ignore such meta-ethical beliefs. We should ask what these Naturalists
would believe if they believed that there could be such truths. According
to Error Theorists, for example, there could not be any moral truths,
not even the truth that torturing children merely for fun is wrong. But
these people would agree that, if any acts could be wrong, these acts
would be wrong.

121 *The Convergence Claim*

There are many ways in which, when different people seem to have
conflicting normative beliefs, these cases may not involve pure normative disagreements. These people may be considering borderline
cases, or have conflicting non-normative or meta-ethical beliefs, or they
may not know all of the relevant facts, or they may not understand
the relevant arguments, or they may be using different concepts, or be
affected by some distorting influence, or they may fail to realize that
many normative truths are matters of degree, that many of these truths
are very imprecise, and that some normative questions may not have
answers. We can also plausibly believe that we have made normative progress. These facts do not show that, in ideal conditions, we would nearly
all have sufficiently similar normative beliefs. But when we consider
most actual disagreements, these cases do not count strongly against
this prediction. We can add that, when we consider certain important
questions, we *already* have sufficiently similar normative beliefs.

122 *The Double Badness of Suffering*

Nearly everyone believes that it is in itself bad to suffer, and that it
is bad when people suffer in ways that they do not deserve. Though
some people have seemed to deny these beliefs, they were either not
really doing that, or were under the influence of some distorting factor,
or both.

CHAPTER 35 NIETZSCHE

123 *Revaluing Values*

It may seem implausible to claim that, even in ideal conditions, we and Nietzsche would have had sufficiently similar normative beliefs. In defending the Convergence Claim, we cannot ignore Nietzsche, who is the most admired and influential moral philosopher of the last two centuries. Though Nietzsche sometimes denies that suffering is bad, and that happiness is good, that is not his real view; and Nietzsche's rejection of pity depended on false beliefs. Nietzsche's thinking was often distorted in certain other ways.

124 *Good and Evil*

The German word 'sollen' can be used both to express commands, such as 'Thou shalt not kill', and to express moral claims, such as 'You ought not to kill'. Some Germans have overlooked this distinction. Nietzsche assumes that morality consists of commands, and that only God would have sufficient authority to give such commands. Since God does not exist, Nietzsche concludes, there is nothing that we ought morally to do. If we believe that moral claims are not commands, Nietzsche's claims do not straightforwardly conflict with our beliefs about what we ought to do.

Nietzsche makes some other claims which might have led him to reject our beliefs. But Nietzsche contradicts many of these claims. When Nietzsche disagrees with himself, he does not clearly disagree with us. Other conflicts are less deep than they seem.

125 *The Meaning of Life*

Nietzsche's main questions were not about what we ought to do, or what is good or bad, but about *why* humanity exists, and whether the answer can give meaning to our lives. When Nietzsche lost his belief in God, he sometimes believed that we were created by Life or Nature to achieve some purpose. When Nietzsche recognized that Life or Nature had no such purpose, he hoped that we ourselves could create new values, thereby giving our lives meaning. Since Nietzsche's normative concepts were not reason-involving, but imperatival or command-implying, his attempt to avoid Nihilism failed.

CHAPTER 36 WHAT MATTERS MOST

126 *Has It All Been Worth It?*

The badness of suffering casts doubt on the goodness of the world. When we consider the horrors of the past, we can ask whether human history has been worth it. Some believe the answer to be No. On this view, it would have been better if no human beings had ever existed.

127 *The Future*

Even if the past has been in itself bad, the future may be good, and this goodness might outweigh the badness of the past. Human history would then be, on the whole, worth it. In deciding what we ought to do, we can ignore the badness of the past. Even if history could not be, on the whole, good, the future might be good. Since the further future might be very good, what now matters most is that we avoid ending human history, by overheating the atmosphere, or in other ways. If there are no rational beings elsewhere, it may depend on us and our successors whether it will all be worth it, because the existence of the Universe will have been on the whole good.

APPENDICES

APPENDIX D WHY ANYTHING? WHY THIS?

Why does the Universe exist? There are two questions here. First, why is there a Universe at all? It might have been true that nothing ever existed: no living beings, no stars, no atoms, not even space or time. When we think about this possibility, it can seem astonishing that anything exists. Second, why does *this* Universe exist? Things might have been, in countless ways, different. So why is the Universe as it is?

Many people have assumed that, since these questions cannot have causal answers, they cannot have any answers. Some therefore dismiss these questions, thinking them not worth considering. Others conclude that they do not make sense.

These assumptions are, I believe, mistaken. Even if these questions could not have answers, they would still make sense, and be worth considering. Nor should we assume that answers to these questions must be causal. Even if reality cannot be fully explained, we may still make progress, since what is inexplicable may become less baffling than it now seems.

APPENDIX E THE FAIR WARNING VIEW

Though punishments cannot be just or unjust in the desert-implying sense, such penalties can be fair or unfair. But when we justifiably impose fair punishments, we should greatly regret what we are doing.

APPENDIX F SOME OF KANT'S ARGUMENTS FOR HIS FORMULA OF UNIVERSAL LAW

Kant argues:

> All principles or imperatives are either *hypothetical*, requiring us to act in some way as means of achieving some end that we have willed, or *categorical*, requiring us to act in some way as an end, or for its own sake only, rather than as a means of achieving any other end.

> Categorical imperatives impose only a formal constraint on our maxims and our acts, since these imperatives require only conformity with the universality of a law as such.

Therefore

> There is only one categorical imperative, which requires us to act only on maxims that we could will to be universal laws.

Kant's premises are false, and, even if they were true, Kant's conclusion would not follow. Kant also argues:

> (1) When our motive in acting is to do our duty, we must be acting on some principle whose acceptance motivates us without the help of any desire for our act's effects.

> (2) For some principle to have such motivating force, it must be purely formal, requiring only that our acts conform with universal law.

> (3) Such a principle must require that we act only on maxims that we could will to be universal laws.

Therefore

> This requirement is the only moral law.

Premises (2) and (3) are false. Kant gives other arguments that seem to fail.

APPENDIX G KANT'S CLAIMS ABOUT THE GOOD

In several passages, Kant seems to overlook the sense in which happiness and suffering are non-morally good and bad, and to ignore our other non-moral reasons to care about what happens.

APPENDIX H AUTONOMY AND CATEGORICAL IMPERATIVES

According to Kant's *Autonomy Thesis*, we are subject only to principles that we give to ourselves as laws, and obligated only to act in conformity with our own will. This thesis seems to be either indefensible or trivial. In his claims about heteronomy, Kant seems to conflate two very different things: motivation by desire, and strongly categorical requirements.

APPENDIX I KANT'S MOTIVATIONAL ARGUMENT

Kant seems to argue:

True moral laws must be both universal and normatively categorical, applying to all rational beings whatever they want or will.

No principle could be such a moral law unless the acceptance of this principle would necessarily motivate all rational beings.

No principle could have such necessary motivating force, and thus be able to be a true moral law, unless this principle can motivate us all by itself, without the help of any desire.

Only Kant's Formal Principle has such motivating force.

There must be some true moral law.

Therefore

Kant's Formal Principle is the only true moral law, and is thus the supreme principle of morality.

This argument could not succeed.

APPENDIX J ON WHAT THERE IS

There are some things that are actual, and others that are merely possible. Some Actualists claim that, when we decide what to do, we are not choosing different possible acts, but merely choosing which way in which we shall act. But if I act in one way, by saving your life, this act would be one future event. If instead I let you die, this act would be a different event. There are here two possible events, one of which would be merely possible. Such events exist, however, in a different, ontologically thinner sense. There are also various other entities and truths that exist in a non-ontological sense. These include some irreducibly normative truths.

PART FOUR

COMMENTARIES

Hiking the Range

Susan Wolf

On What Matters is a *tour de force*—a fast-paced ride across the territory of philosophical ethics, filled with challenging and provocative discussions of an astonishing number of philosophical positions and problems. All of these discussions are at least loosely presented as being in the service of the search for the supreme principle of morality. To top it off, Parfit concludes the first volume of this work with what he takes to be a good candidate for such a principle—the Kantian Contractualist Formula, which tells us that

> Everyone ought to follow the principles whose universal acceptance everyone could rationally will, or choose (Volume One, *342*).*

From this principle, he argues, it follows that everyone ought to follow the principles that are optimific, thus yielding the view he calls Kantian Rule Consequentialism (*411*).

One way to approach the book is to see it as displaying the thought of one philosopher picking and choosing what he takes to be the best and most insightful aspects of several different ethical theories, and putting them together to come up with a different view of his own. As such, it represents a fine way to do moral philosophy—not the only way, but a fine way—and there is much in the particular view that Parfit arrives at, as well as in the particular assessments of other views which he offers and defends along the way, that I find attractive. Another, even more ambitious way of reading the book, however, is suggested in the way Parfit presents his thought, and especially by the concluding remarks of Volume One, which give the volume's final section its

* Page numbers in italics refer to Volume One.

name. As he notes, Kantian Contractualism has a claim to being at once Kantian, contractualist and (at least one-third) consequentialist. Though these three great moral philosophical traditions are often seen as expressing deeply contrasting and mutually incompatible ethical perspectives, Parfit suggests that the plausibility of his proposed formula, in conjunction with the arguments by which he has arrived at it, gives us reason to see these traditions differently. 'It has been widely believed that there are . . . deep disagreements between Kantians, contractualists, and consequentialists,' he writes. 'That, I have argued, is not true. These people are climbing the same mountain on different sides' (*419*).

The suggestion, if I am interpreting it correctly, is that there is a single true morality, crystallized in a single supreme principle which these different traditions may be seen to be groping towards, each in their own separate and imperfect ways.

It is this suggestion — or, as one might say, this ambition — with which I shall take issue in this paper. The suggestion has both a metaethical and a normative aspect. Metaethically, Parfit's work seems to embody the assumption that there are very strong reasons for wanting or hoping for there to be a single supreme, and presumably universal and timeless, principle of morality, to which all other moral principles would be subsidiary. Parfit shares this assumption with many if not all of the major figures associated with the traditions he claims to combine. However, insofar as the remarks quoted above are meant to suggest that the values these different traditions emphasize can be interpreted and ordered in such a way as to eliminate tensions among them, or that it would be in the spirit of these traditions' greatest exponents to accept revisions and qualifications to their stated views that would ultimately reconcile them with their opponents, Parfit departs from the explicit positions of any of the philosophers whose work he discusses, in a way that seems to me both interpretively implausible and normatively regrettable.

Like Parfit, I see the Kantian, consequentialist, and contractualist traditions as each capturing profound and important insights about value. Using Parfit's metaphor, we might say that each contains, not just a grain, but rather something more like a mountain of truth. Each makes a profound contribution to our appreciation of what we have reasons to do and to care about, and to what morality should express, protect, and promote. For Parfit, appreciation of the different evaluative perspectives poses a challenge which he aims in this book to meet: to unify, systematize, or otherwise combine the insights gleaned from these perspectives to reach a single coherent moral view that can guide our actions in a way that is free of moral remainders and normative tensions. Though I think I understand the wish to reconcile the different traditions and transform their ideas into a single unified whole, I am less gripped by it than many other moral philosophers.

Of course there are reasons for hoping that there is, or wishing that there were, a single supreme principle of morality, and if it turns out that there is such a principle, it would be good to know what it is. However, in the absence of a particular metaethical account of what morality is, there is no reason to assume that there will be such a principle, and it would not be a moral tragedy if it turned out that morality were not so cleanly structured as to have one. Moreover, on my own understanding and assessment of the contributions of the Kantian, consequentialist, and contractualist traditions, the values these different theoretical stances express continue to elude such complete unification. As it seems to me, there are fairly frequent occasions when the world presents us with choices for which there is no easy or unique moral answer: there are good moral reasons to favor one alternative and good moral reasons to favor another—and no overarching or further reason to settle the issue between these alternatives without begging the question.

There may be reasons, at the level of concrete social practice, to adopt a conventional ordering of values or a decision procedure that has the effect of a compromise between the realization and expression of competing values. Still, it seems to me important that in moral philosophical contexts, compromises and conventions be recognized as such. We should not allow our interest in reaching agreement on universal principles, much less on a single fundamental principle, to distort our understanding of the individual values on which such principles are based or to suppress our acknowledgment of the tensions that may exist among them.

In any case, it seems to me that there *are* tensions in our common moral thought at least some of which are reflected in the differences among Kantian, contractualist, and consequentialist perspectives. (I thus share the common view, which Parfit rejects, that these views are in deep disagreement.) As Parfit critically interprets and revises Kant's theory so as to reconcile it with contractualist and consequentialist insights, some of these tensions get lost, and some of what seems to me most compelling and distinctive about Kant's own moral perspective gets diluted.

In this paper, I shall focus especially on one such tension, which is frequently associated with the difference between Kantian and consequentialist ethics, namely, that between respect for autonomy and concern for optimific results. It will be instructive to see how Parfit's transformation of Kant's theory makes this tension disappear, and what might be said in favor of a different interpretation of Kant. Following that, I will also have some things to say about tensions between contractualist and noncontractualist theories, and about the importance (or unimportance) of finding a supreme principle of morality.

Not being a Kant scholar, I do not wish to make claims about what Kant really meant or what is truly Kantian in spirit. My concern is normative rather than interpretive. Still, it seems to me there is an interpretation of Kant, or, at least, a moral perspective inspired by Kant, according to which some of Parfit's suggested revisions take us away from rather than toward a more persuasive moral theory.

Respect for Autonomy

Though Kant himself used the term 'autonomy' to refer to a metaphysical property that Parfit and probably most contemporary philosophers don't believe humans possess, there is a nonmetaphysical understanding of the term that still retains much of what Kant was concerned with. Specifically, we may understand autonomy to refer to the possession of practical reason, which gives its possessor the ability to think and decide for herself what to value, what to do, and how to live. To say that we should respect autonomy, or that we should respect people as autonomous beings, is to say that we should take this feature of persons to heart, as calling for a response, limiting our behavior toward them in certain ways, and perhaps demanding types of behavior in others. Roughly, the idea is that respecting autonomy involves honoring people's ability to govern their own lives, refraining from interfering with their choices for themselves, and from imposing burdens on them that they would not themselves endorse. The tension between this value and concern for good results stems from the fact that people do not always know what is good, even for themselves, and they do not always know or care very much about what is good for the world at large. This tension is evident in our possibly mixed reactions to cases of paternalism, as well as in our reactions to cases like Parfit's *Bridge* (218) and *Means* (201), in which one must choose whether to impose a burden on one person (or group) in order to save another person (or group) from even greater harm. Arguably, respect for autonomy urges us to let people decide for themselves whether they want to sacrifice their own welfare for the greater good. If they do not so choose, respect for their autonomy urges us to leave them alone.

In his writings, Kant's respect for autonomy, even of this nonmetaphysical sort, is quite pronounced, and seems to many readers built into his injunction never to treat a person as a means only. It is even more obviously connected with the importance of consent in legitimating one's treatment of another human being. Yet Parfit's interpretation of Kant's Consent Principle and his interpretation of what it is to treat someone as a mere means seem to leave respect for autonomy behind. Parfit's derivation of Kantian Consequentialism from Kantian Contractualism seems also to reflect a lack of appreciation for the value of respect for autonomy. Let us see how one who is deeply impressed with that value might respond to Parfit's arguments.

Consent

We may begin with Parfit's discussion of Kant's claims about consent, which Parfit restates as '(A) It is wrong to treat people in any way to which they cannot possibly consent' (180). As Parfit notes, on at least one natural interpretation of (A), the claim is too strong to represent what might most charitably be understood as Kant's considered view.[1]

---

[1] Parfit objects, more specifically, to Korsgaard's and O' Neill's interpretation of Kant's claims, according to which '(B) It is wrong to treat people in any way

It is also too strong, we might add, to represent a reasonable view of a constraint that is meant to embody respect for autonomy. Situations may arise, for example, when one must take action but cannot obtain consent because the person is unconscious, or unable to communicate, or because there is no time to stop and ask. There may be other cases when a person explicitly refuses to consent to action because he is in the midst of a psychotic episode or is seriously misinformed. In cases like these, taking action to save someone from serious harm in the absence of consent seems neither wrong nor disrespectful. If one is reasonably assured that the person *would* consent if he were conscious, in his right mind, and so on, that would seem enough to make the action meet the standards the spirit of the consent principle demands.[2]

Parfit's own suggested redescription of Kant's claim might appear at first glance merely to be a way to build these sorts of qualifications into the statement of the position. According to Parfit, we should understand Kant's Consent Principle to say 'It is wrong to treat people in any way to which they could not *rationally* consent' (181). However, Parfit's version takes us much further from the original idea of consent than first meets the eye. Because Parfit employs a value-based theory in his interpretation of reasons and rationality, and because his suggested principle concerns what a person *could* rationally consent to, Parfit's version of the Consent Principle might allow us to do things to someone even if we had no reason whatsoever to suppose that the person affected by it *would* consent to it—indeed, it would allow us to do things to a person even if he explicitly refuses to consent to it under conditions of full rationality and information.[3]

---

to which they cannot possibly consent, because we have not given them the possibility of giving or refusing consent' (179).

[2] This is meant only as a rough statement of a plausible revision to the Consent Principle that would not violate the spirit of respect for autonomy. It would need to be fine-tuned, however. A Jehovah's Witness who refuses life-saving medical treatment because he believes such treatment would be against God's will, might be thought by his doctor to be seriously misinformed, yet it is arguably incompatible with respect for the patient's autonomy in this case to waive the consent condition despite the doctor's (well-grounded) belief.

[3] Parfit is careful to point out that the Consent Principle is not offered as the supreme or sole principle of morality. As he notes, 'The Consent Principle

Consider, for example, *Means*, the variant of Parfit's *Earthquake* case, in which you may save White's life, but only by moving Grey in such a way that he would lose his leg. (Both are trapped in the wreckage so that neither can move themselves.) According to Parfit's wide value-based theory of reasons, Grey could rationally choose that you move him, causing him to lose his leg in order to save White's life, but he could also rationally choose that you leave him alone, thus letting him keep his leg, but allowing Grey to die. Since Parfit's Consent Principle requires you to restrict your action to what affected parties *could* (but not necessarily would) rationally choose, that principle permits you either to move Grey or not, at least so far as Grey is concerned.

We may further imagine, however, that you happen to know Grey, and know that he is not the kind of person to voluntarily sacrifice a limb to help a stranger. Just last week, we may suppose, he refused to donate his kidney to help save his own brother. Indeed, we may imagine that Grey, though trapped in the rubble, is still alert enough to size up the situation he and White are in, and is yelling at you, 'Stay away from me, you self-righteous, do-gooding consequentialist.'

I do not want to argue one way or the other about what one *ought* to do in a situation like this. There seems to me to be something to be said for refraining from moving Grey if he refuses to consent, and something to be said for moving Grey anyway, in order to save White's life. But if one chooses the latter over Grey's protests, it seems odd to say that one has satisfied a Consent Principle.[4] It seems much more natural

does not claim that acts are wrong *only if* people could not rationally consent to them . . . This principle allows that acts can be wrong in other ways, or for other reasons.' My point is simply that Parfit's Consent Principle *itself* does not condemn or otherwise discourage treating someone in a way to which he, under conditions of full rationality and information, has explicitly refused consent.

[4] There is a way of thinking about this case in which it might satisfy a Consent Principle: if one thinks the level at which consent principles should operate is the level of general principles rather than particular actions, it is possible that under certain plausible conditions, Grey would consent to a principle that allowed you to move his leg, even though at the moment of crisis, he does not care about principles, and does not consent to the particular action. I'll discuss this very significant complication later in the paper.

to think of this as a case in which the value of restricting oneself to what someone would consent to is overridden by the value of saving a life.

Insofar as respect for autonomy—understood, as I suggested, as an injunction to try, so far as possible, to let a person decide for herself what to do—is the value motivating a principle that appeals to consent, Parfit's own Consent Principle is wholly beside the point. Respect for Grey's autonomy would require us to take Grey's values and choices into account, or, failing that, to take into account the values Grey would have and the choices Grey would make if he were in a position to consider the relevant questions, with relevant information, and so on. The fact that Grey *could* choose to give up his leg—that it would not be irrational were Grey to do so—has very little to do with Grey himself, and nothing at all to do with Grey's exercise of his own practical reason.

In his chapter on consent, Parfit considers some versions of the Consent Principle—namely, the Choice-Giving Principle and the Veto Principle—that would require a person to refrain from actions to which the affected party, under conditions of rationality and information, would not consent. He rejects these principles, at least partly because it is clear that if one were to try to restrict one's actions to ones to which all affected parties *would* consent (under conditions of full rationality and information), one would fail in one's aspirations. Frequently, we would find that one party would only consent to one action, while another party would only consent to another. Grey might not consent to losing his leg; White might not consent to losing his life. In Parfit's terms, such principles would fail to meet the Unanimity Condition (*188*).

For Parfit, searching as he is, for a supreme principle of morality, and, even short of that, for principles that will give us decisive reasons for narrowing down the range of permissible actions, the Unanimity Condition will understandably carry a lot of weight. To meet this condition, one must move beyond the interpretations of the Consent Principle that would forbid actions that would affect parties in ways to which they would rationally not consent. One way to do this, connected to philosophical positions Parfit considers later in the book, would be to 'move up a level' by asking not which particular acts a person would consent to, but rather what general principles of action would be agreed on under relevant conditions. In his discussion of the Consent

Principle, however, Parfit seems to take a different path—namely that of a restriction based on what people *could* rationally consent to, rather than on what they *would* rationally consent to.

The problem with this suggestion, as I have argued, is that it leaves what may be considered the moral point behind a consent principle behind. It leaves consent behind, and the respect for autonomy, from which the value of consent might be thought to derive. If one is concerned in the first instance not in formulating a supreme or decisive moral principle, but rather in registering and articulating important (but possibly competing) moral considerations, the need for unanimity would not be allowed to transform one's principles in this way.

Treating Someone as a Means Only

In any event, the search for a single comprehensive principle that will distinguish right from wrong action leads Parfit to dismiss even his own form of the Consent Principle, as too weak for the job (*211*). He moves on to consider the possibility of finding such a principle in the development of another aspect of Kant's Formula of Humanity. Here, too, however, as I shall argue, Parfit's interpretation fails to capture at least part of that formula's strength. The formula tells us always to treat rational agents as ends-in-themselves, and never as a means only. Tellingly, Parfit chooses to focus on the second idea, that of treating someone as a means only, rather than on the first idea, that of treating someone as an end in itself, in understanding what that principle might mean.

What does it mean to say of someone that he treats another as a means only? As Parfit shows us, if one pays special attention to the qualification 'only', and offers no context by which to interpret what that qualification might be intended to rule out, it is possible to understand treating someone as 'a means only,' or, as Parfit puts it, as 'a mere means,' as follows: You treat someone as a means only when, and only when you 'make use of a person's abilities, activities, or body, and . . . we also regard him as a mere instrument or tool: someone whose well-being and moral claims we ignore, and whom we would treat in whatever way would best achieve our aims' (*213*). By contrast, on Parfit's reading, 'we do not treat someone merely as a means, nor are we even close to doing that, if either (1) our treatment of this person is governed or guided in sufficiently important ways by some relevant moral belief or concern or (2) we do or would relevantly choose to bear some great burden for this person's sake' (*214*).

On this interpretation, as Parfit notes, a rabbit bred and used for experiments, a woman who is robbed of her engagement ring but not of her wedding ring, a man pushed over a bridge to prevent a greater number of deaths to other men, is not treated as a means only, so long as the treatment in question is shaped or even counterfactually constrained by restrictions on what kinds and extent of harm and suffering the agent is willing to inflict on her charge.[5]

A different way to understand the idea of treating someone as a means only might pay more attention to the formula of humanity as a whole, taking note that treating someone as a means only is contrasted

---

[5] As an aside, it might be noted as a point in favor of Parfit's understanding of the principle that it may be applied not only to rational agents but to nonrational animals, such as rabbits, as well. It seems to me to have broader application still, for I may also refrain from treating inanimate objects in certain ways in order to avoid damaging or destroying them. I may refrain from placing my favorite oil painting in the spot where I would get the most pleasure from it, because the sunny location would harm the painting in the long run. In similar ways, I might 'take care of' my home, my car, my breakfast dishes, and my tool kit — refraining from doing some things to them because it would damage them, and making efforts to preserve and maintain them even when, given my busy schedule, I have better things to do for myself. True, some of these activities might be justified by the fact that by keeping these objects in good shape they will be more useful to me in the long run. Insofar as this thought motivates me, I would still be treating them as means only, just being careful to consider the long view of these objects' value to me as means. But many people — and, for better or worse, I am among them — are in the habit of taking care of their possessions (and the possessions of others, too) whether it is in their interest or not. They are reluctant to destroy or damage objects of beauty or potential use, even when it is no good to them, and no known or certain good to anyone else. Though we treat these objects as means, we do not, on Parfit's interpretation, treat them as *mere* means. We would not do just anything to them as long as it suits our purposes. But this means that we do not treat even things that are first and foremost and essentially means, or tools, as mere means on Parfit's interpretation.

with treating someone as an end in itself. As I have always thought, the qualification 'only' serves as a way of recognizing that it is possible to treat people as means where this is not at all in tension with regarding them as ends-in-themselves. Indeed, we do this all the time: I treat my hairdresser as a means for securing a decent haircut; I treat my friend as a means for getting a ride to the airport; my students treat me as a means for getting training in philosophy; and my children treat me as a means for a home-cooked meal. There is nothing objectionable in any of these forms of interaction, at least in part because we offer ourselves up for such treatment. We do not treat each other in these cases as means only, or as mere means, because one of us is not using the other for his purposes *as opposed to*, or in negligence of, her own.

If we understand the Formula of Humanity along these lines, we will see it as instructing us to see rational beings, beings with purposes and plans of their own, as beings whose status forbids our using them in a way that neglects or ignores these purposes. On such an interpretation, one who pushes someone over a bridge in order to save several others from harm (assuming that he has not consented to being pushed, or shown himself about to jump anyway) is very definitely treating him as 'a means only'.[6] On this interpretation, the Formula is closely related in spirit to a principle that demands that we act only in ways to which affected parties do or would consent. Both such principles are ways of expressing the value of respect for other agents' autonomy.

However plausible and attractive we may find such principles as capturing *a* morally important perspective, however, they are highly problematic when considered as candidates for an absolute and supreme principle of ethics. For, as we noted before, many people are relatively uninterested and unwilling to sacrifice themselves or their loved ones for the sake of strangers or the common good—nor, as Parfit agrees, need they be irrational in being so. If we must respect their own actual choices and values, at least insofar as they are rational, then we will be frequently blocked from doing things that many will think we have strong moral reasons to do. We cannot, for example, save five or perhaps even five

---

[6] I should have thought that this would speak in favor of the interpretation insofar as one aims to capture an ordinary sense of the phrase (see Parfit, *227*).

thousand people by sacrificing one who does not want to be sacrificed. If we remove the qualification that their choices must be rational, or interpret rationality as ranging more widely, we will be even more tightly constrained—prevented, for instance, from smashing someone's toe in order to save a child's life. With Parfit, I agree that this is an unacceptable conclusion. So strong a principle of respect for autonomy cannot be an absolute, unconditional principle of morality. What is less clear to me, however, is that this implies that we must either interpret the *idea* of treating someone as a means only (that is, as a mere means) differently or else reject the suggestion that treating someone as a means only has direct and fundamental relevance to morality. An alternative approach would reject this dilemma. Rather, it would register the thought that, other things being equal, treating someone as a means only is to be avoided, and that it is always to be regretted, while yet allowing that it may sometimes be overridden by other moral considerations.

Parfit does not choose this alternative. Instead he moves on to discuss a different formulation of the Categorical Imperative, the Formula of Universal Law, to suggest that it be revised in a way that is more explicitly contractualist than Kant's own writings are, arriving at the principle he calls Kantian Contractualism. This principle, which I mentioned at the beginning of this paper, states that' everyone ought to follow the principles whose universal acceptance everyone could rationally will, or choose' (*342*).

This formula, like Parfit's so-called Consent Principle, asks us to constrain our actions not according to what everyone (under certain ideal conditions) *would* choose, but rather to what everyone rationally *could* choose. As such, one might think that this formula is as far from embracing the Kantian value of respect for autonomy as the Consent Principle we discussed earlier. It is possible, however, for a contractualist to defend this principle against such a complaint is a way that is not open to a defender of an analogous principle (like Parfit's Consent Principle) in a noncontractualist context. Specifically, contractualists aim at finding principles that all people, if they are reasonable, can agree on. As Rawls and Scanlon have pointed out, finding any such principles requires that we imagine people deliberating under certain ideal conditions. In particular, they suggest, not implausibly, that the deliberators be thought to be under some pressure to try to reach agreement. Because of this, a deliberator might choose principles even though they are not her favorite ones because, unlike her favorite principles, these might be chosen by everyone, and the deliberator recognizes that some principles (or, at any rate, these principles) that everyone can agree on are better than none at all.

In other words, under the conditions relevant to contractualism (in which one is looking for principles that everyone can accept), the recognition that everyone rationally *could* accept a principle may count as a reason for someone *to* accept that principle. That is, that everyone could accept a principle may contribute to its making it true that, under certain ideal conditions, everyone would accept the principle.

Kantian Contractualism

Even if the Kantian Contractualist Formula is plausibly Kantian in embodying a respect for autonomy that is one of the hallmarks of Kantian ethics, what Parfit goes on to do with this formula once again bespeaks a failure to appreciate the value of autonomy and its power to generate reasons. Specifically, Parfit argues that Kantian Contractualism should lead us to accept a version of Rule Consequentialism. That is, he thinks Kantian Contractualists should ultimately see their view as committing them to the claim that 'Everyone ought to follow the principles whose universal acceptance would make things go best' (Chapter 16). Here is perhaps the most dramatic argument for the idea that the major traditions of Kantianism, contractualism, and consequentialism can be synthesized. Here again, however, it is open to question whether a defender of the Kantian tradition, or of combined Kantian and contractualist traditions, would agree.

As the shorter form of the argument (*400*) makes especially clear, the derivation that Parfit offers is very simple. Since, on Parfit's view, everyone *could* rationally choose that everyone act on optimific principles (principles, that is, whose acceptance by everyone would make things go best), and since, as he also thinks, there are no other principles that everyone could rationally choose, Kantian Contractualists should embrace the optimific principles. But it is not clear to me that there are no other principles that everyone could rationally choose.

It will be easiest to explain my reasons for doubt by considering one of the controversial consequences that Parfit thinks his argument implies—viz., that Kantian Contractualists should support principles that would require an agent faced with *Means* (the variation of *Earthquake* referred to earlier) to sacrifice Grey's leg in order to save White's life, and that may well require an agent faced with *Bridge* to push one man over the bridge to prevent the runaway trolley from killing five others who are in the trolley's path.

Parfit realizes that insofar as one imagines oneself in the positions of Grey or the man on the bridge, one may rationally want such principles not to be followed. One may rationally want a principle that would forbid one person from deciding to sacrifice another person's life or limb without his consent for the greater good of all. However, Parfit suggests, if you imagine yourself in the positions of White or of the five people stranded on the trolley track, you cannot rationally accept such a principle, for from these points of view the principle would lead to results that are both personally and impartially worse. I am not so sure.

It seems to me that what makes people resistant to endorsing a principle that would require, or even allow, someone to push the man off the bridge in the relevant case is not just the idea that the man, who is innocently minding his own business, would lose his life.[7] After all, we can assume that the five who are stranded on the trolley tracks are innocently minding their own business, too. Rather, what is distressing has to do with the fact that someone else, a third party, another human agent, is taking it into his own hands to sacrifice this man for the greater good. Imagining oneself in the position of this man, one might want it to be the case that insofar as it is anyone's decision whether he should give up his life to save the five, it should be *his* decision. And this thought seems to me one that can be entertained and supported even if one is not in his position.

---

[7] Strictly speaking, the agent in Parfit's *Bridge* case is not in a position literally to *push* White off the bridge, but rather to use a remote control device to cause White to fall onto the track. This variation, constructed so as to eliminate the possibility that the agent in the case had the option of jumping from the bridge himself, does not, so far as I can tell, make a difference to the train of thought I am discussing here.

In other words, it seems to me that many people have a strong preference for being in control of their own lives—that is, for being in control of their own lives insofar as anyone is in control of it.[8] They want to be the ones calling the shots, at a fairly local level, about what happens to their bodies, not to mention their lives. Moreover, this preference does not seem to have the character of a mere preference, as opposed to a value. It may well persist even in the face of the recognition that by retaining such control, one may lower one's overall security against the loss of life and limb. Indeed, it seems to me this concern is more on the surface of people's resistance to organ-transplant schemes that would allow a doctor to secretly kill a patient whose organs could be used to save five people than any concern about the anxiety and mistrust of doctors and hospitals that such a scheme would breed (363).

This preference does not seem to depend on any features of the agent that are not potentially universal. It does not depend, for example, on one's social status or one's wealth or gender. It seems rather a matter of taste or temperament. If this is right, then in principle *anyone* could have such a preference. If, in addition, we allow that this preference is rational—that is, *as* rational as a preference for a principle that would permit people to intervene in one's life in (nonmedical) emergency situations where the intervention would bring about a greater impartial good—then it follows that anyone *could* rationally accept the principle that favors leaving the man on the bridge alone to the principle that favors pushing him.[9]

If it be granted, therefore, that a person may rationally prefer to maintain immediate control over his body and his life to minimizing his risk of loss of life and limb, then Parfit's argument that Kantian

---

[8] This last clause is meant as a preemptive response to the objection that we are not in control of whether we find ourselves in the path of a runaway trolley or pinned down by an avalanche or subject to organ failure either.
[9] Or using remote control to cause him to fall off the bridge. These remarks are suggestive of a defense of the more general principle Parfit calls the Harmful Means Principle, according to which 'It is wrong to impose a serious injury on one person as a means of benefiting others' (361). According to Parfit, 'the Harmful Means Principle is best defended by appealing to our intuitive beliefs about which acts are wrong (362). My remarks do not appeal to such intuitions, however.

Contractualists must support a form of Rule Consequentialism will not go through. Even if we grant Parfit's claim that everyone *could* rationally accept optimific principles, as I am happy to do, we would also have to admit that everyone could rationally accept nonoptimific principles, in particular principles which would more strongly protect people against interference from others in the control of their own bodies and lives.

It will by now have occurred to many readers that the preference I have been describing as competitive with a preference for welfare — the preference for control over one's own life and limbs, the preference to be calling the shots with respect to one's own life — is closely related to the value of autonomy. Indeed, it might be described as a preference for the ability to exercise one's autonomy at the level of concrete action or of direct and immediate control.

Some Kantians or Kantian Contractualists might go farther, taking the preference for principles protecting the exercise of autonomy over principles that would bring optimific results to be *uniquely* rational. For them, Kantian Contractualism not only fails to imply what Parfit calls Kantian Consequentialism, it implies principles that are very likely, if not certain, to conflict with it. My remarks are not aimed at so strong a normative conclusion, however. Rather, they are meant to suggest that in failing to notice or address the challenge to his argument that is posed by a preference for autonomy over welfare, Parfit reveals once again a failure to recognize and appreciate the value of autonomy and the point of view of someone for whom that value is irreducibly important. Insofar as the expression of that point of view and of its fundamental relevance to morality is considered a major component and contribution of the Kantian tradition, Parfit's interpretation of that tradition seems inadequate, and the suggestion that a Kantian might come to support Parfit's 'Triple Theory' without violating or abandoning the spirit that led him to be a Kantian in the first place is open to doubt. A Kantian form of contractualism does not lead so quickly or so clearly to any form of consequentialism.

Other Tensions

I began this paper by quoting some remarks from the final paragraphs of Volume One of *On What Matters*, in which Parfit questions the widely held view that Kantians, contractualists, and consequentialists disagree in certain sorts of deep and especially recalcitrant ways. Rather, he suggests, these three types of ethical theorists are all climbing the same mountain on different sides. In supporting the widely held view that Parfit rejects, I have focused on an aspect of Kantian ethics that, it seems to me, Parfit fails to capture and address in his interpretations and suggested revisions of Kant—namely, the central role Kant and Kantians accord to the idea of respect for autonomy. As is widely recognized, this aspect of Kantian ethics is especially in tension with consequentialism. Since Parfit talks not just of two but of three traditions that he aims to integrate and synthesize, however, a full discussion of his final claim would look also at the relations between contractualist and noncontractualist theories. Are there tensions between Kantianism and contractualism and between contractualism and consequentialism as deep as the tension between Kantianism and consequentialism?

These questions are difficult, in part because of the slipperiness of the term 'contractualism', understood as a label for a type of theory, or of a moral philosophical tradition. It is not clear whether the important ethical theories that appeal in one way or another to the idea of a contract all ought to be considered part of the same ethical tradition, and even when one is focusing on a single view or closely related set of views that have been identified as contractualist, one may be uncertain about which features of these views mark them out as distinctively deserving of that label.

If we accept Scanlon's characterization of contractualism, which associates it with the view that morality is fundamentally concerned with being able to justify oneself and one's actions to others, we should not be surprised to see a kind of harmony between Kantianism and contractualism. The restriction that one's actions must be justifiable to others seems close to the idea that one must act only in ways to which affected parties would, under specified conditions, consent. As such, it might be seen as another way to capture the view that morality requires us to respect other agents' autonomy that I have been identifying as a hallmark of Kantianism. Whether there are also plausible forms of Kantianism that would oppose contractualism is an interesting question, but I shall not pursue it here.

The relations between contractualism and consequentialism seem to me more complicated, and, more specifically, asymmetrical. Even though I argued above that a Kantian Contractualist need not accept Parfit's claim that her position leads to a kind of consequentialism (and for reasons that might apply to any contractualist, Kantian or otherwise), the argument was not meant to show a tension between the very idea of contractualism and that of consequentialism. To the contrary, as I understand them, contractualists are committed to the view that the right principles of morality are *whatever* principles satisfy the condition that is identified with 'being justifiable to everyone.' If those principles turn out to be the principles whose universal acceptance would make everything go best, then contractualism and this sort of Rule Consequentialism will coincide. On the other hand, there is a powerful form of consequentialism that would reject any form of contractualism. Specifically, consequentialists like Sidgwick, Smart, and Kagan, who take the sole fundamental value in morality to be that of making the world as good a place as possible, will not acknowledge moral reasons to limit themselves to acting within the limits of principles everyone could rationally accept if contradicting such principles would make things go better from an impartial point of view. Moreover, they will not acknowledge such reasons even if the principles in question are optimific principles (principles, that is, whose universal acceptance would make everything go best).

This point has often been made in discussions of Rule Consequentialism, a view which is rationally unstable from a purely consequentialist point of view. It has often been noted that if obedience to optimific rules always produces the best outcome, then Rule Consequentialism 'collapses' into Act Consequentialism, and if such obedience doesn't always produce the best outcome, then a strict consequentialist will have reason on occasion to violate the rules. Either way, a strict consequentialist will not have reason to adopt Rule Consequentialism over Act Consequentialism. Parfit himself seems to recognize this when he acknowledges, quite sensibly, that his Triple Theory, which includes an identification of moral wrongness with a violation of optimific principles, is 'only one-third consequentialist' (*418*).

Moreover, even if one is not a consequentialist, one may well think that consequences matter morally (indeed, it is hard not to think this).

The fact that you can save more lives or alleviate more misery by taking one course of action rather than another may count morally in favor of that action even if it is does not count decisively. Though adherents of Parfit's Triple Theory will support acting always according to optimific principles, occasions will arise in which one can be reasonably confident that one can do more good—save more lives, for example—by acting in ways that these principles forbid. Why should one follow the principles in this case? Strict consequentialists will think there is no reason, thus rejecting the Triple Theory, and Rule Consequentialism, completely. But even a pluralist, who acknowledges *some* reason to follow the rules at the cost of utility, reasons having to do perhaps with being able to justify oneself to others or to act consistently with the ideal of the kingdom of ends, may question whether, and if so why, these nonconsequentialist reasons *always* trump considerations of utility.

Conclusion—Hiking the Range

An answer might be forthcoming if one holds paramount the goal of reaching agreement on a supreme principle of morality. Parfit's Triple Theory does after all recognize both consequentialist and non-consequentialist (e.g., contractualist) values and fits them together in a systematic way. If one is looking for a single principle, or even a well-ordered set of principles, that assigns some importance to considerations of overall utility as well as to considerations of making oneself justifiable to others, Parfit's Triple Theory may be the best candidate for the job.

However, the commitment to reaching agreement on a single principle and on identifying that principle with the true morality can be questioned. That commitment itself is supported by only some values among others, and the idea that it can on occasion be morally better to act in a way that would *not* be supported by principles that everyone should accept is not, at least not plainly or obviously, self-contradictory.

Insofar as we can identify individual moral theorists as exponents of distinctively Kantian, contractualist, and consequentialist traditions, we can think of them as forming so many different hiking parties hiking along different trails. Along the way, each party will come to various trail junctions, and have to decide on which branch to continue.

There will be some reasons favoring the choice of continuing along one trail, and other reasons supporting the choice of another. Making one choice will give the hikers a better chance of arriving at a theory whose principles will yield more definite results, or which will be more likely to be agreeable to a greater variety of others. The other path, however, may, have more of what attracted the hikers to that particular trail in the first place.

Some members of each party may choose the path that has the advantages of the first sort. Parfit's book gives us reasons to think and to hope that the members of each party who make this choice will indeed be climbing the same mountain and will meet at the top.

As I have meant to show, however, others will comprehensibly choose other paths. Some Kantians will choose to forgo principles obedience to which would allow greater benefits in order to more faithfully respect autonomy—for example, they will choose principles that would forbid pushing bystanders off bridges even to save more people. Some consequentialists will sacrifice the ability to justify themselves to everyone in order to bring about a greater good—for example, they may approve of the doctor who surreptitiously kills one healthy person to use his organs to save five others. These paths will presumably take them up different mountains.

Parfit's reading of Kant makes me speculate that insofar as Parfit imagines himself to be a member of the Kantian party, his own methodological commitment to finding a supreme principle of morality illuminates one path so much more brightly than others that he fails to so much as notice some of the junctures where there may be more than one plausible way to go on. My main purpose in this paper has been to more accurately represent the landscape, so as at least to register the fact that, however good the reasons are for choosing one route, and ultimately, one mountain, over another, one who does so will inevitably miss benefits or beauties that lie along the paths not taken.

If one conceives of the enterprise of moral theorizing as the single-minded pursuit of a supreme principle of morality, then perhaps there is only one choice to make, and only one mountain worth climbing. One might instead, however, think of moral theorizing as an activity with a number of aims, including the articulation and appreciation of the values that are fundamental to moral action and moral reasoning, and the exploration of how far these values can be jointly realized and expressed. If one does not assume that these values can be jointly realized to a maximum degree, then one will think that in order to get the most out of moral theory, one must hike the whole range.

Is there a right way to conceive of the task of moral theorizing? This is one way of asking how important it is to find, or agree on, a supreme principle (or a well-ordered set of principles) of morality. How valuable is it to find or agree on a unified set of principles that is comprehensive and that yields definite answers to questions that, at first glance, require balancing different and incommensurable values? What is to be gained by identifying such principles? What, if anything, might be lost? And what practical implications would or should the identification of such principles have?

As I mentioned at the beginning of this paper, philosophers have been searching for the supreme principle of morality since moral philosophy began. The desire for such a principle is so natural and its value so apparently obvious as to hardly call for explicit defense. Still, before concluding, I want to raise doubts about two reasons for thinking that the determination of such a principle would be as valuable and important as moral philosophers have tended to think.

One pattern of thought that makes the goal of finding a supreme principle of morality seem very desirable has to do with the ideal of social harmony, the appeal of achieving social consensus. If there is a supreme principle of morality, one might think, then everyone ought rationally to recognize and accept it, and acting according to it would be justifiable to all.[10] And wouldn't it be great to know how to live, or to act, in a way that everyone would approve?

Indeed, it would. However, there is a slide in this line of thought from the prospect of reaching the *theoretical* goal of identifying a principle that all reasonable people ought to accept and the imagined consensus of real human beings in our diverse and fractured world. While doing moral theory, we naturally take ourselves to be reasonable people, and

[10] Contractualists think the fact that a principle is justifiable to all is what makes it a supreme principle of morality; noncontractualists may think the order of explanation is reversed.

tend perhaps implicitly to assume that everyone else (everyone else in the world, that is) is equally reasonable and equally interested enough in discovering the true morality to engage in the kind of moral reflection that would be necessary for coming to see that the principle one has identified as the supreme moral principle deserves to be treated as such. But this assumption is crazy.

Even if there were a principle that it would be reasonable for everyone to accept, not everyone would accept it. Not everyone *is* reasonable, and not every reasonable person *will* accept a principle that, were they perfectly reasonable and also perfectly attentive to a set of complicated moral arguments, they should accept. The social harmony that would be achieved by identifying a supreme principle of morality and acting according to it, would, in other words, be purely hypothetical. Even if one acted according to that principle, one would be likely to find herself acting on occasion in a way to which an affected party would not consent, or in a way in which an affected party would feel himself treated unacceptably as a means, in a way that he did not regard as justifiable to him.

A second, perhaps even more powerful, reason for being deeply attracted to the goal of finding a supreme principle of morality, has to do with the desire for practical moral guidance, a wish to be given definite answers to hard moral questions. Like the desire for social consensus, this wish is reasonable, too. A lot is at stake in situations like *Earthquake, Means, Bridge*, and *Transplant*, for example, and it would be nice to have a principle to apply that would assure one of doing the right thing. To be told that there are reasons for doing one thing and reasons for doing the other, is to tell us nothing new, nothing helpful. We want more from moral theory than that.

I agree. However, it is not obvious that searching for, or even succeeding in finding, a supreme principle will give us the moral guidance we seek. The principles that Parfit defends are of less practical usefulness than might be supposed.

To be sure, these principles can be given as answers, in a sense, to any question of what to do. I find myself beside a man on a bridge, and see a runaway trolley speeding below on its way to kill five people if nothing is done to interfere. If I push the man over, he will die but halt the trolley, saving the five other people's lives. What should I do?

Kantian Contractualism has an answer of sorts: Act according to those principles whose universal acceptance everyone could rationally will, or choose. In an earlier section, I gave some reason for doubting that that principle would yield any determinate advice. Even if all rational people could accept principles whose universal acceptance would make things go best, I suggested, they might also be able to accept principles that gave higher priority to respecting autonomy.

Moreover, even if I am wrong about this and Parfit is right that Kantian Contractualism gives exclusive support to optimific principles, the question would remain which principle, in cases like this, is optimific. Parfit suggests that there is a difference between medical cases and cases that in other respects are structurally similar. But I can construct an argument concerning the *Bridge* case, too, that suggests that it would be optimific in the long run to refrain from pushing people off bridges. Between Parfit's defense of the Emergency Principle (365–6) and my imagined argument that suggests that the adoption of something closer to the Harmful Means Principle would lead to better results, I have no idea which argument is stronger. There is so much to consider about which it is difficult to be certain. What seems most reasonable here is to mistrust one's ability to be objective enough, imaginative enough, and thorough enough to reach reliable conclusions about such matters.

The point is that any plausible candidate for a supreme principle of morality would have to be so abstract or so complicated or both that the principle would be difficult to apply. Though such a principle may be helpful in suggesting a way to explain to ourselves why acts that we think are right really are right, or in suggesting a way to respond to concerns that some other action would be better, it is unlikely to give us practical guidance for morally difficult situations in which we don't know what to do before consulting the principle.

Although I have, in the last few paragraphs, offered reasons to question the preeminent place that Parfit and others have accorded the search for a supreme principle of morality as the aim of moral theorizing, I do not mean to suggest that the search is a worthless or a futile one. To the contrary, there is much to be gained — much indeed, that has been gained — even if we do not agree that the search has, or has yet, been entirely successful. We will gain even more if we actually find, or, alternatively, choose to agree on, such a principle. However, I suspect that if we find or choose such a principle, acting according to it will not capture or realize all the values that are traditionally regarded as moral values without remainder. Maximizing utility does conflict sometimes with respecting autonomy, and for all I know each may conflict sometimes with obedience to principles that no one can reasonably reject. Contrary to what Parfit seems to suggest at the end of Volume One, you cannot please all the moral theorists all the time.

If that is right, then were we to find or agree on a supreme principle of morality, it would embody some degree of compromise among values, reached presumably for the sake of gaining the benefit of having some supreme principle of morality rather than none at all. In the interest of moral clarity, we ought to recognize that fact, and so acknowledge that even if an act is supported by what we have come to regard as the supreme principle, and so is, strictly speaking, morally right, that would not mean that there can be nothing to regret or to apologize for in the doing of it, and even if an act is forbidden by the supreme principle and so is, strictly speaking, morally wrong, that would not mean that there is nothing to be said in its or its agent's defense. These thoughts in turn may raise questions about what the claim that an act is morally wrong really means. Does it mean, or imply, that an agent who performs such an act ought to feel guilty, or that a third party who recognizes that the agent behaved wrongly is justified in blaming the agent? How strongly or consistently should we want people to be constrained by the principles — and in particular, by the supreme principle of morality, if there is one? How strongly should we be guided by them (or it) ourselves?

These are metaethical questions of a kind Parfit points toward in Chapter Seven, section 22. Noting that different senses of 'wrong' are associated variously with blameworthiness, with the appropriateness of reactive attitudes, and with justifiability to others, he explains that 'in the rest of this book, [he] shall use "ought morally" and "wrong" vaguely, in some combination of these senses' (*174*). 'Except in Part Six,' he continues, 'I shall say little about these *meta-ethical* questions. Such questions will be easier to answer when we have made more progress in our thinking about practical and epistemic reasons, and about morality.' An assessment of Parfit's discussion in Part Six is beyond the scope of this essay. It is both striking and impressive how well Parfit characterizes the range of these meta-ethical questions (geographical pun unintended) even here, before he subjects them to thorough examination, and much to his credit that he recognizes their significance for a satisfactory understanding of what the arguments of Volume One can be said to have accomplished. Whether they have taken us closer to a supreme principle of morality, whatever that means, is open to doubt. But even if they do not, they have surely led us on a trail worth following, full of intellectual attractions and moral philosophical insights along the way.

Humanity as End in Itself

Allen Wood

Part One: Rational Consent, Practical Reason, and Humanity as End in itself

There is a great deal in Parfit's chapters, especially in Chapters 8 to 10 (on which I am going to concentrate these comments) with which I strongly agree. I think Parfit provides a better account than O'Neill and Korsgaard do of what Kant meant in saying that for me to treat another as an end in itself, the other must be able to 'contain in himself the end of my action' (G4: 429 – 30),[11] and also a better account of the relation of this idea to issues surrounding hypothetical rationally consent. I also find very illuminating Parfit's remarks about the relation of possible rational consent to actual consent and how each bears on the morality of actions.

At a deeper level, too, I think I favor a reading of Kant that puts him closer to what Rawlsian style Kantians would regard as 'dogmatic rationalist' views in ethics — and I think this means closer to the position Parfit wants to defend. Thus I would accept, as good Kantianism, what Parfit calls a 'value-based' theory of reasons; Parfit's rejection of 'desire-based' theories therefore seems to me nothing but good Kantianism. I therefore also accept his thesis that 'no reasons are provided by our desires and aims.' But to this I would want to add two other things (which I don't think Parfit means to deny): first, that our desires and aims are often merely the rational expression of value-based reasons,

---

[11] Kant, *Groundwork for the Metaphysics of Morals*, ed. and tr. Allen W. Wood (New Haven: Yale University Press, 2002), abbreviated as 'G' and cited by volume: page number in the Akademie-Ausgabe of Kants *Schriften* (Berlin: W. de Gruyter, 1902–). Other writings of Kant will be cited by volume: page number in that edition.

and second, that our desires might constitute a crucial aspect of some of our reasons, as long as they stand in the right relation to values.

Where I think I part company with Parfit is on certain questions of method in ethical theory. He seems to prefer a method descending (as I see it) from Sidgwick—a method that involves appeal to what Sidgwick called 'the common moral opinions of mankind' (or just 'Common Sense') in the formulation and testing of moral principles. By contrast, I favor a method, which I find not only in Kant but also in utilitarians such as Bentham and Mill, that would draw the fundamental moral principle from very general and fundamental considerations about the nature of rational desire and action, and would then attempt to reconcile these principles with common moral opinions only insofar as those opinions can be seen as applications of the principles. Sidgwick seems to have thought that what he called 'primary intuitions of Reason' are to be used only to systematize and correct Common Sense,[12] which continues to exercise authority within moral theory independently of first principles, and might even help to shape the formulation of moral principles.[13]

The Kantian and Millian method that I favor, by contrast, involves a fundamental principle whose ground is independent of moral intuitions or Common Sense, and then the derivation from the fundamental principle of various moral rules or duties. Conclusions about particular cases are not inferred directly from the first principle at all, but rest on it only mediately, through what Mill calls 'secondary principles' and Kant calls 'duties' (of various kinds, of which he provides a taxonomy). The derivation of moral rules or duties from the first principle, moreover, is also not deductive. The first principle is instead fundamentally an articulation of a basic value (that of rational nature for Kant, that of happiness for Mill). The rules or duties represent an interpretation of the normative principles applying that basic value under the conditions of human life. In their application, moreover, the rules or duties themselves require interpretation, and admit of exceptions, by reference to the first

[12] Henry Sidgwick, *The Methods of Ethics* (Indianapolis: Hackett, 1981), 373–4.

[13] In this respect, Rawls's method of 'reflective equilibrium' owes more to Sidgwick than it does to Kant.

principle.[14] More recent (Sidgwickian) theory sets itself the goal of providing a precise principle or set of principles which, along with a set of facts, enable one to deduce the 'right' conclusion about what to do under any conceivable situation. That's what it is for Sidgwick to make ethics 'scientific'.[15] For Kantian or Millian theory, as I understand them, this is such a hopeless goal that it would be wrongheaded to orient your theoretical method to it.

[14] This interpretation of Mill might be controversial, but I would defend it based on the following things: (1) the account he gives of the relation of the rules of morality to the principle of utility, as social 'direction-posts,' giving us some guidance regarding the social pursuit of the general happiness, which he regards as a standard exercising only a very general (and even largely unacknowledged) influence on the content of such rules (Mill, *Utilitarianism*, ed. G. Sher, 2nd edn. (Indianapolis: Hackett, 2001), 24–6); (2) Mill responds to the charge that there is not enough time prior to each action to weigh all the utilities on every side by comparing the application of the principle of utility to the application, by Christian ethics, of the Old and New Testaments — which would involve the *interpretation* of the scriptures in the light of human experience — so likewise, I suggest, Mill regards moral rules as resulting from the interpretation of the principle of utility in the light of experience (p. 23); and (3) the fact that Mill's formulation of the first principle itself — that 'actions are right in proportion as they tend to promote happiness; wrong as they tend to produce the reverse of happiness' (p. 7) — is a rather loose one, not a formulation from which anyone could justifiably think that we could directly determine what to do in particular cases. It may also be controversial (though it should not be) that Kantian duties always in principle admit of exceptions. 'Exceptivae' constitutes one of the twelve basic 'categories of freedom' Kant presents (analogously to the twelve theoretical categories) in the *Critique of Practical Reason* (5: 66). Most of the twenty-odd 'casuistical questions' Kant discusses in the Doctrine of Virtue concern possible exceptions to the duty in question. The general purpose of these discussions is described by Kant as 'a practice in how to *seek* truth' regarding 'questions that call for judgment' – and judgment (the correct application of a rule to particular circumstances) is something Kant insists can never be reduced to maxims, rules or principles since 'one can always ask for yet another principle for applying this maxim to cases that may arise' (6: 411). Thus casuistry, the interpretation and application of moral rules or duties to particular cases, always involves a distinct stage of thinking that cannot be made a matter of rules or principles.

[15] Sidgwick, *Methods of Ethics*, 359–61.

The system of moral philosophy, following the Kantian conception, consists of three different things: first, a fundamental principle or value (which Kant thought was *a priori*); second, a body of empirical information and theory about human beings and their situation (which in the Groundwork Kant called 'practical anthropology' (G4:388) and later described as 'empirical principles of application' for the moral principles (MS 6:217)); and finally a set of rules, duties, or other moral conclusions resulting from the interpretation of the former principle or value in light of the latter information. This third part of Kantian ethical theory is the taxonomy or system of duties expounded in the *Metaphysics of Morals* (the *ethical* part in the Doctrine of Virtue). It corresponds roughly to the set of moral rules that Mill regards as involved in every case of moral obligation, and relates only loosely to the principle of utility, which he does not regard as imposing on us any obligations directly, and from which Mill immediately derives (even together with facts about the consequences of actions) no substantive conclusions about what to do in particular cases.[16]

I think this way of conceiving of moral theory, and the fact that Parfit favors a different theoretical method, accounts for some of the ways Parfit disagrees with my interpretation of Kant at the beginning of Chapter 10. He quotes me interpreting Kant's Formula of Humanity as End in Itself (FH) as saying that 'we must always treat people in ways that express respect for them' and then objects that 'most wrong acts do not treat people in disrespectful ways.' The remark he quotes here

---

[16] Thus Mill is neither an 'act utilitarian' nor any member of the large species of 'rule utilitarian' whose procedure takes the form of stating a utilitarian principle from which, along with a set of facts, conclusions about what to do could be drawn. For Mill, the main functions of the first principle seem to be three: (*a*) to provide the basic value-orientation of ethics, whose interpretation provides the basis for accepted moral rules; (*b*) to provide a standard through which the accepted moral rules can be corrected and improved, and (*c*) to provide a ground on which exceptions to these rules may be admitted. None of these functions, however, takes the form of a decision procedure through which specific rules or the making of exceptions to them is to be arrived at by deductive inferences. In this way, Mill seems to me the most sensible (and incidentally, despite the gross misunderstandings of Kant displayed in *Utilitarianism*, also the most Kantian) of the great historical utilitarians.

occurs in the context of a more systematic exposition of Kant's theory, which, as I read it, is what Parfit would call a 'narrow' or 'monistic' value-based theory. For this theory, all reasons are grounded, directly or indirectly, on the single value of rational nature, which Kant expresses in two ways: as the objective worth of humanity as end in itself, and the dignity of personality as universally legislative.

Respect, as I understand it, is first of all a feeling or emotion. Contrary to the Stoics (and to some grossly mistaken misinterpretations of Kantian ethics), Kant thought it impossible for a finite rational being to act rationally at all without having certain feelings and emotions and manifesting them in its actions. In the *Metaphysics of Morals*, Kant specifies four such feelings (moral feeling, conscience, love of human beings, and respect). These feelings are rational rather than empirical in origin, and susceptibility to them is a condition for being a moral agent at all (MS 6:400). I would describe *respect* in general as the feeling appropriate to the rational recognition of objective value.[17]

Respect is something we not only feel but also show in actions that express it. It is the active expression of respect rather than the mere feeling that matters for moral conduct. On Kant's monistic value-based theory of practical reasons, all reasons for action are based directly or indirectly on the objective value of rational nature, and this is especially true of moral reasons that take the form of categorical imperatives. Obedience to every categorical imperative thus involves showing respect for the objective value of rational nature. In that sense, what morality demands most fundamentally is that we show respect for that value, and violations of morality all involve treating that value—often, the value of rational nature in the person of rational beings—with disrespect. Many morally wrong actions do not 'display disrespect for people' in any conventional sense of that phrase, but if Kant's theory is correct,

---

[17] From this observation about respect I immediately infer that all metaethical antirealists, who deny there is such a thing as objective value, are either radically defective specimens of humanity who are incapable of feeling respect for anyone or anything, or else every time they do feel it they commit themselves to contradict their own metaethical theories—theories which are often ravishingly subtle and sophisticated in execution, but must nevertheless be recognized from the start by all rational agents as obviously and brutally false.

the moral wrongness of these actions always consists fundamentally in the way they show disrespect for the objective value of rational nature.

Parfit recognizes the Kantian distinction between values to be respected and values to be promoted. But he is worried that the claim that dignity is a value above all price may commit Kantians to the view that rational nature as a value to be promoted must take absolute priority over other values to be promoted. This is, for instance, the way Parfit reads the following statement by Thomas Hill: 'Kant's view implies that pleasure and the alleviation of pain, even gross misery, have mere price, never to be placed above the value of rationality in persons.'[18] That fear seems to me based on a misunderstanding. Promoting rational nature (as one value that can be promoted) is grounded in respect for rational nature (as the basic value to be respected). It is the latter value that has a dignity that is beyond all price, and it must be given priority over all competing values. But equally, concern for the alleviation of human suffering (as a value to be promoted) is grounded in this same fundamental value. But this implies no absolute priority of the value of developing rational nature (as one of the values to be promoted) over other values to be promoted that are also grounded in respect for rational nature. If the above quotation from Hill is correctly read as asserting *that* priority, then his position is not a correct interpretation of Kantian doctrines.

In Kant's view, the objective value of rational nature grounds two general kinds of ends which are duties: our own perfection and the happiness of others. (The value of our own happiness, except as an indirect duty, is for Kant an object of prudential rather than moral reason; and the perfection of others is a duty for us only insofar as we contribute to perfections they want to acquire, and therefore falls under the heading of their happiness.) Perfection prominently includes our rational nature (both moral and nonmoral) as a value to be promoted. Both kinds of duty are wide or imperfect. Thus for Kant there is no systematic priority of perfection over happiness as ends or values to be promoted.

[18] Thomas E. Hill, *Dignity and Practical Reason* (New York: Cornell University Press, 1992), 56–7.

Parfit is also in danger of misunderstanding Kant when he says that the 'humanity' which has dignity cannot refer to non-moral rationality. Kant says that humanity, as the capacity to set ends according to reason, is an end in itself and that humanity insofar as it is capable of morality has dignity. As I interpret him, Kant holds that it is our *humanity* that is an end in itself—where 'humanity' has a technical sense, referring to our capacity to set ends (which includes both instrumental rationality and prudential rationality—the capacity to frame a concept of happiness and to give our happiness priority over more limited aims of inclination). We should therefore include the permissible ends of others, especially their happiness (as the general and comprehensive conception of those ends), among our ends as well (though there are no strict rules in general regarding the priority we must give all these ends among one another). *Dignity*—by which Kant means that supreme worth which must never be sacrificed or traded away—belongs to rational nature not in its capacity to set ends, but only in its capacity of giving (and obeying) moral laws (G 4:435).

It is the *capacity* for morality, however, not its successful exercise, that has dignity.[19] Thus I agree with Parfit when he interprets Kant as saying that even the morally worst people have dignity, and in that sense they have exactly the same worth as even the morally best people. I also agree with Parfit when he says that this view of Kant's expresses a 'profound truth.' Parfit is further correct to point out that none of this implies that my having dignity as a human being makes me a *good human being*. Not everything having value is thereby something *good*, especially good of its kind. For Kant, the *good* is that which is recognized as practically necessary independently of inclination (G 4:412). Having a character like that of a bad person is the direct reverse of what is practically necessary, though it is also practically necessary to treat even

[19] Parfit concludes that Kant's uses of 'humanity' are 'shifting and vague'. I think this is right insofar as he speaks of the 'dignity of humanity', whereas, to be strictly accurate, it is personality (the capacity to give universal law and obey it) rather than humanity (the capacity to set ends according to reason) that has dignity. But if, as I believe, Kant does hold (and must hold) that humanity and personality in these senses are necessarily coextensive, then no serious error is involved in his use of the phrase 'dignity of humanity'.

the worst person with the respect due to the dignity of rational nature, and so it is that treatment of the bad person, and not the bad person, that is good.

Parfit denies that FH—the principle that we should always respect humanity as an end in itself—is a practically useful principle. In response to my claims that it provides us with the right value-basis for settling difficult issues and that on many difficult issues, it is an advantage of FH that different sides can use it to articulate their strongest arguments, Parfit asserts that on a wide range of disputed issues appeals to FH do not in fact constitute the strongest arguments of each side. I think we may be talking past each other here, because we are beginning from different assumptions (which I have tried to clarify above) about the aims and structure of moral theory and the relation of a theory's basic principle to conclusions about what to do. Kantian theory is grounded on a supreme principle, which is then applied interpretively to a body of empirical information and theory about human nature and human life, yielding a set of moral rules or duties. These in turn are applied to particular circumstances, through practical judgment, in determining what to do.

FH is one of Kant's formulations of the supreme principle, the one he uses most often in deriving his system of duties in the *Metaphysics of Morals*. That is the role FH is playing when I make the claims about which Parfit is skeptical. I suspect that Parfit, on the other hand, thinks of moral theory as the attempt to formulate precise principles from which we can rigorously derive a set of conclusions about what to do in all actual or imaginary cases. The acceptability of these principles, for Parfit, depends on how the conclusions derivable from them match up with Sidgwick's 'Common Sense' or 'common moral opinions of mankind'. Principles well-grounded might in difficult cases give us reasons for revising our conclusion about particular cases, but flagrant and systematic conflict of a candidate principle with our intuitions is regarded as invalidating that principle. Parfit is treating FH as a principle to be evaluated by these criteria, and he is rejecting it as too indeterminate to yield the specific conclusions such a principle is supposed to yield, and hence also incapable of providing adequate arguments on different sides of a moral controversy that would be required by this conception of moral theory.

When FH is regarded in this way, I think Parfit is right, but not when it is regarded in the way I regard it—which is also the way I think Kant regarded it. (My way of reading Kant obviously involves reading his four famous illustrations of the Formula of Universal Law in quite a different way from that in which they are customarily read—including, I think, the way Parfit chooses to read them in Chapters 12 and beyond. But that difference will not be pursued further in these comments.)

Part Two: 'Trolley Problems'

The rest of my comments here will contain some general reflections on some of the examples Parfit uses, especially in Chapters 8 and 9. I think these comments are relevant to the theoretical differences I have tried to sketch above, for they concern one now fashionable way of executing the methodological strategy I have suggested that Parfit draws broadly from Sidgwick. I don't think the following remarks do anything at all to discredit the Sidgwickian program broadly conceived. Like many ambitious philosophical projects, it is too formidable in its conception ever to be refuted by a few clever arguments or examples. But I do intend to challenge some fashionable ways of carrying out such a program. My comments also relate to FH, in that they help to illustrate the way in which I think it can figure productively in moral reasoning. I should also frankly admit that these comments give me the opportunity to get off my chest some complaints about what many moral philosophers do nowadays.

In May of 2001, the Tanner lecturer at Stanford University was Dorothy Allison, author of the novel *Bastard Out of Carolina*. Allison didn't talk much about moral philosophy as such, but she did discuss a 'lifeboat problem' that she had heard about from a philosopher. Her reaction was to *reject* the problem—to refuse to answer it at all—on the ground that we should refuse on principle to choose between one life and five lives. Even to pose the question in those terms, she said, is already immoral. The only real moral issue raised by such examples, she thought, is why provision had not been made for more or larger lifeboats. To many philosophers her remarks would no doubt seem naïve or even unreasonable. Yet I think Allison's reaction to the lifeboat problem is far more sensible and right-minded than what we usually get from most of the philosophers who make use of such examples.

I am going to refer to these kinds of examples not as 'lifeboat problems' but as 'trolley problems'. (None of Parfit's examples are actually about trolleys, though two of them are about trains.) They are all examples where the main point is that you must choose between saving more people from death and saving fewer. Since we think a human death is in general something very bad, it is natural also to think that the option involving fewer deaths must be preferable to the one involving more deaths. The examples gain their poignancy from the fact that this apparently obvious point suddenly begins to seem questionable or even counterintuitive when the fewer deaths are *caused* in the wrong way. The intent of the examples is usually to incite us to formulate principles that correspond to, or even justify, our moral intuitions (or deliverances of Sidgwickian 'Common Sense') about the difficult or problematic cases presented in the examples. The hope is apparently that principles arrived at in this way will help us decide difficult cases in real life with Sidgwickian scientific precision.

Some might think that if FH regards every rational being as having dignity (or worth that cannot be rationally traded away to get anything else), then it might very well not only support Allison's judgments about the lifeboat problem, but also entail that there could be no rational way of choosing between one life and five lives, or if it comes to that, five billion lives. If so, then FH would appear to have consequences that seem plainly unacceptable according to our intuitions. We apparently could never permit even a single death, not even to save the whole human race.

No doubt the fact that rational nature has dignity or incomparable worth *does* mean that the lives of beings having rational nature are valuable and important. But merely from the fact that the value of *rational nature* cannot be rationally sacrificed or traded away, it clearly *does not* follow that the *lives* of rational beings can never be rationally sacrificed. If a person heroically sacrifices her life to save others, or to uphold some important moral principle, that is not a case of undervaluing her own rational nature. Depending on the circumstances and the principle involved, it might even be a case of *preferring* the value of her *rational nature* to the value of her *life*, and Kantian ethics might even require it. Nor does FH lend unambiguous support to the vague idea of the 'sanctity of human life'—an idea that, in its popular and political application, usually involves a lot of self-deceptive rhetorical posturing, and is sometimes put in the service of some of the most pernicious moral superstitions currently on sale in the marketplace of moral ideas (for instance, dreadful superstitions about the unexceptionable wrongness of euthanasia, or the right to life of human embryos and fetuses). I strongly caution against associating FH with morally obscene popular prejudices such as these.

The bearing of FH on trolley problems is therefore also not entirely clear. One thing I hope is clear by now is that for Kantian ethics, the point of a moral principle such as FH is not directly to tell us what we should *do*. It is rather to ground a set of rules or duties, and more generally to orient us as to how we should and should not *think* about what we should do. We would be right to conclude from FH, for instance, that we should be reluctant to treat human lives as having the sort of value that can be measured and reckoned up. That is what I think Dorothy Allison was getting right. It would follow that answers to problems like Parfit's *Lifeboat*, *Tunnel* and *Bridge*, therefore, can never be as clear (or as trivial) as the arithmetical fact that five is greater than one. The tendency of some moral philosophers to draw such inferences is due to their bad habit of thinking that the canonical form of every moral principle must consist in the scientifically precise way it preferentially ranks states of affairs (as the outcomes of actions). But what FH tells us is that the fundamental bearers of value are not states of affairs at all, but persons and the humanity or rational nature in persons. This is not a kind of value that translates easily into preferential rankings of states of affairs.

FH does not imply that it is always immoral to choose five lives instead of one, but I think it does imply that we should be reluctant to think about such choices in those terms, or indeed in terms of any preferential rankings of states of affairs. FH rather implies that we ought to arrange things in the world so that agents are not faced with choices of that kind. Of course this means arranging things, as far as possible, so that one life need not be sacrificed to save five. But it also means arranging things—including our moral deliberations—so that when numbers of lives are at stake, the choices dictated by our moral principles are not based merely on the numbers, as trolley problems — in the very way they are posed, through the careful selection of information included in and excluded from them — often suggest they have to be.

I have long thought that trolley problems provide misleading ways of thinking about moral philosophy. Part of these misgivings is the doubt that the so-called 'intuitions' they evoke even constitute trustworthy data for moral philosophy. As Sidgwick was fully aware, regarded as indicators of which moral principles are acceptable or unacceptable, our intuitions are worth taking seriously only if they represent reflective reactions to situations to which our moral education and experience might provide us with some reliable guide.[20] Poll-takers are well aware that the way a question is framed often determines the answer most people will give to it. What might seem to us genuine intuitions are unreliable or even treacherous if they have been elicited in ways that lead us to ignore factors we should not, or that smuggle in theoretical commitments that would seem doubtful to us if we were to examine them explicitly.

Most of the situations described in trolley problems are highly unlikely to occur in real life and the situations are described in ways that are so impoverished as to be downright cartoonish. (In imagining *Bridge*, for instance, I can't help casting my favorite cartoon superhero, Wile E. Coyote, in the role of the hapless single person who may be toppled onto the track.) But this by itself is surely not a problem. It is extremely rare for a man to lure teenage boys into his apartment, then kill, dismember and eat them; and at this writing, at any rate, it remains an utterly unique occurrence for a group of terrorists to hijack airliners and crash them into skyscrapers filled with innocent people going about their daily lives. But the rarity of such cases does not lead us to mistrust our moral intuitions about these cases. Nor do we mistrust our moral reactions to the absurdly fantastic villainy sometimes depicted in comic books and action movies.[21]

[20]   Sidgwick, *Methods of Ethics*, 96 – 103, 374, 421 – 2.

[21]   We ought, however, to mistrust its dramatic purpose, which is typically to render morally acceptable to us the fantastic brutality and violence practiced by the heroes of such stories. It seems to me by no means implausible to think that the currency of such dramatic situations has helped create a climate in

The deceptiveness in trolley problems is indirectly related to their cartoonishness, however, in that it consists at least partly in the fact that we are usually deprived of morally relevant facts that we would often have in real life, and often just as significantly, that we are required to stipulate that we are certain about some matters which in real life could never be certain. The result is that we are subtly encouraged to ignore some moral principles (as irrelevant or inoperative, since their applicability has been stipulated away). And in their place, we are incited to invoke (or even invent) quite other principles, and even to regard these principles as morally fundamental, when in real life such principles could seldom come into play, or even if they did, they would never seem to us as compelling as they do in the situation described in the trolley problem.

Trolley problems focus primary attention on the value or disvalue of certain consequences or states of affairs (usually, more human deaths or fewer). But trolley problem philosophers are by no means all consequentialists. Trolley problems are quite frequently used, in fact, to support anti-consequentialist conclusions in moral philosophy, and many of them appear to do so. But in these problems, attention is directed exclusively to the consequences of certain actions for the weal or woe of individuals and also the way those actions relate causally to those consequences. Typically, the circumstantial rights, claims and entitlements people would have in real life situations are put entirely out of action (ignored or stipulated away). In the process, an important range of considerations that are, should be, and in real life would be absolutely decisive in our moral thinking about these cases in the real world is systematically abstracted out. The philosophical consequences of doing this seem to me utterly disastrous, and to render trolley problems far worse than useless for moral philosophy. I would like to illustrate these general points by briefly discussing three problems used by Parfit in Chapters 8 and 9.

which a great many people can find morally acceptable the monstrous conduct, domestic as well as foreign, of the utterly evil regime that ruled the U.S. from 2001 to 2009.

1 Lifeboat

It seems to me that when faced with a situation like *Lifeboat*, there is only one morally defensible policy: You must seek to rescue all six people as quickly and efficiently as possible. It might very well be true that, following this policy, you should first set about rescuing the five and only then try to rescue the single person, because in that way you will go farther, faster and with greater certainty toward achieving your only legitimate goal (which is rescuing all six). But if you thought you could go farther faster and with greater certainty toward the goal of saving all six by rescuing the single person first (say, because this person's rock is right on your way to the rock with the other five on it), then you obviously should do that.

It is relevant here — even decisive — that in the real world, if both rocks are in imminent danger of being swept under the water, then you would very likely not know for certain that you must choose between saving the single person and saving the five. (The stipulation that you are certain about this ruins the real moral issue just as certainly as it would ruin some issue in rational choice theory to stipulate that you are sure which box being offered you contains the larger amount of money.) Rather, in real life there would always be some chance that you would save all six, and if both rocks were about to go under there would also probably be a significant chance that no matter what you did, all six people would drown. When a philosopher simply stipulates that we are certain you can save all and only the inhabitants of exactly one rock, then we should be clear that he is posing a problem so different from otherwise similar moral problems you might face in real life that any 'intuitions' we have in response to the philosopher's problem should be suspect.

There is one intuition about a situation such as *Lifeboat* that is perfectly clear and not the least suspect. It is this: if any of the six drown, the result is tragic — it is unacceptable. You will regard yourself as having failed significantly in your rescue efforts no matter what you did, even if you know your failure was inevitable and not your fault. Another vivid and reliable intuition is that all concerned have an urgent obligation to call to account whoever is to blame for the fact that there were not enough lifeboats. They should try to find out why this happened, and take steps to minimize the chances of its happening ever again. We saw this point illustrated dramatically several years ago in the universal reaction to the utter incompetence of federal authorities to hurricane Katrina.

These intuitions are at least as strong and certain as any intuition we might have about what you should actually do about the single person and the five. To many trolley problems, as they are posed,[22] I think the right reaction is to regard it as simply indeterminate what the agent should do, and the only real moral issue raised by the problem is (as Dorothy Allison rightly said), how the situation in question was permitted to arise in the first place. The fact that lives are at stake is intended to compel us to reject this correct reaction, and make us feel that we simply must decide to do *something*—hence to decide that something is morally right and something else is morally wrong.

Yet trolley problem philosophers would regard us as missing the whole point of the problem if we even bothered to express any of the moral intuitions that don't directly involve saying what the agent should do. These philosophers are focusing our attention shortsightedly, even compulsively, solely on the question about what you should do in the immediate situation, as if that were the only thing moral philosophy has any reason to care about. In the context of the moral epistemology that goes with Sidgwickian style moral theory, the reasons for this restriction of attention are clear enough. But the fact that the clearer and more compelling intuitions about such a case are irrelevant to what interests them ought all by itself to make us distrust the philosophical value of the questions these philosophers are posing.[23]

---

[22] Here the qualification 'as they are posed' is also important, since I will be arguing that in the real world there would *always* be other facts that the philosopher is not permitting us to consider, and these would frequently determine what should be done. Often enough, these facts would dictate an answer directly contrary to the one the philosopher thinks our intuitions would dictate to the problem as he has posed it.

[23] This is a problem with much of moral philosophy generally, which behaves as if every moral problem must have a single right answer and as if it is moral philosophy's only job to say what it is. In real life, if a friend of yours faced a serious moral dilemma—for instance, whether to turn a guilty child in to the police or to lie to the police and let the child escape—I think most of us

2 Why trolley problems mislead

In real life, people go to a lot of trouble to arrange things so that no one will ever be placed in the position that, for example, the bystander in the train examples is placed. There are sound *moral* reasons why this is so, reasons that could be derived from FH and that are closely connected to Dorothy Allison's reaction that it is already immoral to ask anyone to decide between one person's life and five people's lives. The way I would put the point is to say that even if some choices do inevitably have the consequence that either one will die or five will die, there is nearly always something wrong with looking at the choice only in that way. But trolley problems are posed so that you know from the start that you are not supposed to look at them in any other way. You are given virtually no facts about the choice facing you except how many people will die if we choose each option and how you will bring about these deaths. Sometimes you even have it *stipulated* for you that there *are* no other relevant facts.

Such a stipulation cannot be regarded as either theoretically neutral or morally innocent. Suppose a moral philosopher posed for you the following problem: 'A group of white people are stranded on one rock and a group of black people are stranded on another. Before the rising tide covers both rocks, we could use a lifeboat to save either the white people or the black people. It is stipulated that there are no other relevant facts. Which group should we save?' Since the philosopher has told you nothing about how many people are in each group, nor even anything else about them except their skin color, I would hope that you would resist giving any answer at all to the philosopher's question. If you did have the 'intuition' that you should save the group whose skin color is the same as your own, then I would hope that you would resist answering on the basis of that 'intuition', and also that you would

would respect whatever choice the friend made, as long as we were sure that the friend had thought about the situation the right way, weighing appropriately both society's and their own child's moral claims on them. Any moral principle that dictated a single, unambiguous answer to the question what such a parent should do would be unacceptable simply because it did so. This is the valid point Sartre is making in his famous example of his student who had to choose between staying with his mother and joining the Resistance.

be heartily ashamed of yourself for having had that 'intuition' at all. Certainly you should not think that agreement with such an 'intuition' ought to serve as a test all moral principles ought to pass.

What is most objectionable here is the conversational implicature of the philosopher's question itself, in light of his outrageous stipulation that there are no other relevant facts. The question implies, namely, that you have been given enough information to answer the question as posed, or at least enough to have some 'intuition' worth reflecting on about what the answer should be. In this example, that implicature is morally offensive all by itself in a very obvious way. But most trolley problems differ from that example in that in them we have been given information about the situation that is at least *prima facie* morally relevant: the number of people on each rock is at least not so obviously and offensively irrelevant. Yet it may still be true that in trolley problems we have typically not been given enough information or the right information, to evoke intuitions that are worth anything. In the cases of *Tunnel* and *Bridge*, for example, in the real world there would simply *have* to be relevant facts about the situation beyond those we have been given, and in the real world what we should do would turn far more on those facts than they do on the facts we have been given. So the stipulation that these are the only relevant facts is not one we should accept at face value.

3 *Tunnel*

Here's what I mean: Trains and trolley cars are either the responsibility of public agencies or private companies that ought to be, and usually are, carefully regulated by the state with a view to ensuring public safety and avoiding loss of life. There ought to be, and usually are, provisions for physically preventing anyone from being in places where they might be killed or injured by a runaway train or trolley. If either the five or the single person in *Tunnel* are disobeying such rules by entering such dangerous areas, then they are behaving recklessly and are present there entirely at their own risk. Their claim to protection from harm is obviously far less than that of anyone who is in a permitted area. The claim of interlopers to protection in comparison to the claim of people in permitted areas is not increased proportionately (I submit it is not increased at all) just because there are more of the interlopers. Further, mere bystanders ought to be, and usually are, physically prevented from getting at the switching points of a train or trolley. They would be strictly forbidden by law from meddling with such equipment for any reason, and they would be held criminally responsible for any death or injury they cause through such meddling.

These facts, if we were allowed to take account of them, would be decisive in a case like *Tunnel*: As mere bystanders, we would be forbidden by law to touch the switching points. (Unless railway officials have been criminally derelict in their duty, we would probably also be physically prevented from touching them.) In the real world there are not only good reasons for the existence of such laws, but in the real world there would also always be overwhelmingly good reasons for us to obey them. In real life, we would most likely not be sure we know how to operate the mechanism properly. For all we could know, our attempt to save the five might result in wrecking the runaway train and killing dozens of people on board. Further, if in real life we see five people in one tunnel and one person in another tunnel, we would have no way of knowing whether just a bit farther down the track from the one there are not many more people we would also be killing by switching the points. For all a mere bystander could know, the five people are interlopers, present on the track illegally and entirely at their own risk, while the single person is an employee of the railway who is there on the job. In the real world, these uncertainties would always be present, and the likelihood of their applying would never be merely negligible. That is an important reason why bystanders would be, and why they always should be, strictly forbidden by law from meddling with switching mechanisms.

Of course if in the situation as just described I were the bystander who correctly did nothing, I might nevertheless second-guess myself in my nightmares for years afterward, tormenting myself with the thought that there might have been something I could have done to save the five. This would be a natural human reaction to the horrible scene I had witnessed. But my feelings of guilt and self-reproach, though perhaps understandable, would be irrational. Far worse, however, and far more irrational, would be the truly monstrous state of mind of the bystander who switched the points, killing the single person but saving the five, and then thought for the rest of his life that he had been treated unjustly when he was sentenced to prison for manslaughter — as he obviously should be.

4 *Bridge*

Many of the same observations apply here as apply to *Tunnel*, except that here the criminal wrongdoing of the bystander who acts to save the five is obviously far graver. For here the bystander surely must suppose that the single person, in walking on the *Bridge* over the train, is in a place where people have a perfect right to walk and to regard themselves as free from risk of harm from the deeds either of railway employees or meddling bystanders. The five, however, can be presumed to have entered a forbidden zone at their own risk. To kill the single person to save the five would in this case not be merely manslaughter but murder. The meddling bystander, sitting in his cell during the long years of his prison sentence, might have the consolation that many prestigious professors of moral philosophy at the world's leading universities think it worthwhile to reflect on the moral intuitions that put him where he is. I hope I may be forgiven for the ungenerous wish to deprive him of this one last consolation.

If a case such as *Tunnel* or *Bridge* were to occur in the real world, there would surely be an enraged public outcry against the railway system. The question whether one died or five died would be (and should be) of far less importance to the protesters than the fact that a runaway train had caused death. If it were further to come to light that the choice of who died had been at the mercy of a mere bystander, acting solely on his or her moral intuitions, this would only be further ground for public outrage. Relatively little attention would (or should) be paid to whether the bystander had chosen the death of one or the death of five. The protesters, in other words, would — and rightly so — care far less about the question that obsessively concerns the trolley problem philosophers than about relevant facts that these philosophers have lightheartedly stipulated away.

5 Rights and entitlements

Trolley problem philosophers seldom consider the kinds of entitlements to protection the people on the tracks might have, or might have forfeited, nor do they ever worry about our claim to be entitled, as mere bystanders, to choose who is to live and who is to die based only on our moral intuitions.[24]

Do they think the people on the tracks all necessarily have the same right to protection from harm, no matter how they came to be where they are? Are they supposing that the switches ought to be conveniently located where the general public can get at them, so as to have maximal opportunity to act on their moral intuitions in cases of emergency? Or, on the other hand, are they supposing instead that we know we are behaving both recklessly and illegally by touching the switches, but assuming that we would be justified nonetheless arrogating to ourselves the decision who should live and who should die (even when we can't be sure we aren't killing many others besides those we intend to kill)? In that case, the moral assumptions they are tacitly taking for granted are surely far more doubtful than any moral intuitions they could possibly hope to evoke in us.

One reason some philosophers might wish to abstract from every consideration of people's claims to protection from harm or entitlement to operate the switching mechanism is that they are tacitly assuming as a fundamental moral principle that all rights and claims must be derivative from the very moral principles they intend to use trolley problems to test. In that way, trolley problems seem theory-driven to the extent that they appear to assume that the basic subject matter of normative ethics consists solely in reckoning up the goodness and badness of states of affairs for particular people—though they also take into account the various causal relations human actions may have to those states of affairs. Some trolley problems seem little more than vehicles for representing certain abstract moral principles that are based

---

[24] A notable exception is Judith Thomson, *The Realm of Rights* (Cambridge: Gauthier, 1986; Harvard University Press, 1990), ch. 7, who does discuss the relevance of the question whether the people on the track are entitled to be there or have ignored some notice telling them to keep off the track. I thank Parfit for bringing this reference to my attention.

on that unargued assumption.[25] But the assumption is never stated, and one suspects that one aim of trolley problems might be to sneak the assumption past people's critical faculties as though *it* were simply given along with our moral intuitions about the problems themselves.

Clearly, however, it is defensible to hold that the value we attach to states of affairs is derivative from other values (such as the dignity of rational nature) which may also place significant constraints on when we value states of affairs and also the ways we compare and rank the value of states of affairs. For example, at least part of the value of the state of affairs consisting in a promise being kept is derivative from the obligatoriness of the principle that promises should be kept. The value of the state of affairs of the single person's being protected from harm by others is likewise derivative from this person's right to such protection, which (for someone who grounds rights on FH) is in turn derivative from the dignity of this person's humanity as an end in itself. It is so far from being true that all rights and entitlements are based on calculations about welfare that one excellent reason for arranging things so that people have rights and entitlements is simply to *make it false* that moral issues can ever be reduced to such calculations. FH is one moral principle, though by no means the only principle, that could provide such a reason.

Some people mistrust rights not based on welfare considerations because they think that such rights are typically appealed to only by privileged minorities (such as wealthy property owners) to justify prevailing social systems (such as those involving manifestly unequal distribution). These people may think that the assumptions built into trolley problems are right-headed, and my rejection of them is necessarily pernicious. But it would be naïve to think that this is the only meaning such rights could have. In the real world, policies favoring the welfare of

[25] It is true that the philosophers who use trolley problems do not necessarily accept this assumption, and some, such as Thomson and Philippa Foot, explicitly reject the idea that it is necessarily worse if more people die. As I have already mentioned, trolley problems sometimes seem to be designed to make the point that whether an action is morally right depends not only on the value of the states of affairs it produces, but also on the causal process through which it produces them. Still, the problems seem to assume a theory in which those two factors are the only relevant ones.

a majority ('the taxpayers') are often used to rationalize the oppression of underprivileged minorities ('the underclass'). Appeals to rights and appeals to welfare are equally open to abuse. Hence from the standpoint of moral theory, surely the best course is to keep an open mind about what rights people have and what considerations might ground them. If it is an unargued assumption of trolley problems, and hence of the moral intuitions they evoke, that all such rights must be based solely on the considerations on which these problems focus, then that is a reason for doubting that these intuitions provide reliable data for moral theorizing.

6 Extreme situations

To others, trolley problems may appeal because it seems to them that the only honest way to confront many social policy decisions is to see them as frank trade-offs between the deepest interests of different people. It is simply a fact about many social policy decisions that if they are made one way, then *these* people will be hurt and if they are made the other way, then *those other people* will be hurt. But it does not follow from this fact that the correct way to view all such situations is to see them simply, or even primarily, in this light. One important reason why people are regarded as having rights or entitlements — and why most people are forbidden or even prevented from directly choosing between the competing interests of others — is that it is in general *evil* to decide between competing interests merely on such a basis. That is the real reason why, for instance, doctors are not permitted to carve up a healthy person in order to distribute their vital organs among five people needing organ transplants. It is also why railway workers and people walking across bridges have rights to be protected that interlopers on tracks do not have, and why bystanders are not permitted to switch the points on trains or operate trapdoors in bridges in order save five by killing one.

There are some extreme and desperate situations in human life — such as war or anarchy, or sometimes pestilence, famine or natural disaster — in which it can look as if the only way to think rationally about them is simply to consider coldly and grimly the numbers of people, the amounts of benefit and harm, and the kind of actions available to you that will produce the benefit and harm. But it is significant that we should think of such decisions as being made coldly and grimly, calculating consequences with a kind of economist's tunnel-vision while totally denying all our normal human thoughts and feelings. For those are situations in which human beings have been deprived of humanizing social institutions (like those that should provide enough lifeboats, prevent runaway trains and trolleys, keep interlopers off tracks and bystanders away from switches, and so forth) that make it rationally possible *not* to look at matters in that way. I grant you that trolley problems might help you to think in a rational (if dehumanized) fashion about situations in which that is the only way left to think about them because the situations themselves have already been dehumanized. That is a powerful argument *against* using trolley problems in moral philosophy.

We think of war as a morally unacceptable condition, in large part because in war it can indeed seem rational for people to think about their lives and the lives of others in truly monstrous ways. One of our primary tasks as human beings is to view things in better ways, and if necessary to make changes in the world (regulating the behavior of doctors and trolley systems) so as to bring it about that there are other ways of viewing things rationally. If you take some part of human life (such as health care delivery) which is not inherently as barbarous as war, and come to regard this as the only rational way to think about it—or especially if you come to regard this as the only rational way to think about the fundamental principles of morality generally—then that amounts to a voluntary decision on your part to turn health care, or even human life as a whole, into something horrible and inhuman, something like war, that ought never to exist.

7 *The realm of ends*

FH, the principle that humanity in every person has dignity as an end in itself, may give us reasons refusing to look at the world in the way trolley problems tend to induce us to look at it. But perhaps the Kantian ideal of a realm of ends provides an even more direct route to the same conclusions. It implies that we should not think about moral problems in terms of trade-offs between competing human ends, but should try to understand the answer to every problem as one that treats all people as ends, and leaves out no human ends except those that exclude themselves from the harmonious system (or realm) of all rational ends. For in a realm of ends, no one would have to choose between one life and five simply on the basis of numbers—since every life, considered simply as such, would have equal dignity as part of the realm of ends. Thus no one's life would have to be sacrificed unless their actions excluded its preservation from the harmonious system of ends.

No doubt human vulnerability to nature, and even more human wickedness, will forever prevent there actually being such a realm of ends. That is why there will probably always be such things as hurricanes, shipwrecks, unjust economic systems and wars. That is why there are problems about the distribution of such things as healthcare that (especially in a fundamentally unjust and inhuman society like ours) seem to come down to stark trade-offs between the deepest interests of different people and groups. Consequently, there will always be a place for the kinds of issues trolley problems are meant to address. That is my one concession to those philosophers who like to think about trolley problems. It is a significant concession, but a much more limited one than it might at first seem. For because people can, to some extent, create a realm of ends in their relations with each other and in their ways of thinking about these relations, it also means that these problems are not as universal in their moral significance as many philosophers think. Because the actual operation of trains and trolleys, for example, is subject to a considerable degree of responsible human control and regulation, runaway trolleys are not in fact very good examples of situations in which there arise the kinds of problems the trolley problem philosophers want to address.

More importantly, trolley problem cases do not represent the fundamental issues with which moral principles must deal. On the contrary, these kinds of problems mark the limits of the power of moral thought to deal with problems of human life. The kind of thinking they force on us rather constitutes the way we have to think about things precisely where our moral aspirations have essentially failed. If it ought to be our chief moral concern to make human life, as far as we can, into a realm of ends, then from the standpoint of morality preventing people from having to think about competing human interests in ways trolley problems encourage you to do always takes precedence in principle over any rule or policy about what an agent should actually *do* in a situation such as *Lifeboat*, *Tunnel* or *Bridge*. If that is true, then the use of trolley problems by moral philosophers to test fundamental moral principles involves a deep misconception about the ways of thinking that should be fundamental in moral philosophy.

Fans of trolley problems have suggested to me that these problems are intended to be philosophically useful because they enable us to abstract in quite precise ways from everyday situations, eliciting our intuitions about what is morally essential apart from the irrelevant complexities and 'noise' of real world situations that get in the way of our seeing clearly what these intuitions are. But I have already suggested why I cannot accept that. Trolley problems seem to me to abstract not from what is irrelevant, but from what is morally vital about all the situations that most resemble them in real life. At the very least, trolley problems presuppose (rather than establish) that certain things are morally fundamental, and my own view is that these presuppositions are at least highly doubtful, probably perniciously false, and that trolley problems (or people's responses to them) do nothing at all to support or confirm these presuppositions. Instead, they only provide a kind of illegitimate pseudo-support for them, as well as the opportunity to do moral philosophy in a manner that encourages us not to question them.[26]

---

[26] Other fans of trolley problems (a different kind of fan of them) admit that they do not elicit moral intuitions that would be of much use in real life, but these fans are struck by the degree of convergence among different people's intuitions about some trolley problems, since this suggests to them that the degree of agreement among people about even such weird examples that are so different from our real-life moral judgments is itself a significant datum that is of psychological interest and requires theoretical explanation. I remain skeptical that convergence among responses to trolley problems are interesting data of any sort, or that they prove anything at all, except perhaps the very general point, which seems to me to cast serious doubt on a lot of what passes for psychological and sociological research — namely that people can easily be misled in all kinds of surveys by superficial features of the way questions are posed to them. This suggestion has been made to me by John Mikhail and Marc Hauser, who both think that the convergence of responses to some trolley problems, even across differences in age, gender and culture, constitute evidence for the existence of an innate moral faculty, analogous to the Chomskian innate linguistic faculty, and further that studying responses to trolley problems can help us determine the contents of this faculty.

A Mismatch of Methods

Barbara Herman

1

Derek Parfit's *On What Matters* offers an avowedly hybrid theory of morality, or at least of the part of morality that tells us which acts are wrong. The theory is elaborated by way of an extended and inventive critical reconstruction of Kant's ethics as a kind of contractualism. What makes it hybrid is the conjunction of the contractualist framework with an account of value that is for the most part concerned with outcome effects on well-being, taken in a very wide-ranging way.[27] Despite the embrace of a Kantian contractualist framework—the fundamental aim of morality is not to make things go best, but to find principles of action that everyone could rationally will—since the values that inform rational willing are (for the most part) about what is nonmorally best, the hybrid theory winds up having a strongly consequentialist cast.

That a normative theory is hybrid is not in itself grounds for criticism. What is puzzling is a hybrid methodological approach to understanding the ambitions of Kant's moral theory, since it is anything but hybrid. The defining feature of Kant's theory is that goodness is a function of, and not independent of, moral principle.[28] While I think Parfit is often correct in rejecting some of the versions of Kantian claims and arguments that he finds in the literature, I don't think his revisionary interpretive project, which aims to elicit the best in Kant's ethics by

[27] For Parfit, reasons that bear on judgment and action are value-responsive, though, here following Sidgwick, Parfit holds that personal and impersonal reasons enter moral judgment with separate and independent weight.
[28] This is the point of the Paradox of Method (*Critique of Practical Reason* 5: 63): well-being considerations are facts that support preferences, but not values (at least not directly).

evaluating and revising its claims in terms of nonmoral good outcomes, can capture what is most distinctive about Kant's theory. The mismatch of methods is too profound.

For the mismatch of methods to be a source of serious worry, we would want to know two things. One is that it really does have far-reaching and distorting effects on moral judgment and thought; the other that there is a version of Kant's ethics as a unified (non-hybrid) theory that is plausible. These are larger projects than can be attempted here. What I aim to do instead is work through some examples that show the depth and extent of the mismatch problem, and then offer some interpretive resistance to the hybrid arguments that provides a better fit with what Kant says, and hews to the spirit of the unified project. There will not be space to fully cite or defend each and every claim I make about Kant; the claims will perforce be provisional, their value in the plausibility and distinctiveness of the interpretations they suggest. I will argue at greater length that two regions of normative worry that prompt the demand for hybrid repair — making moral space for our personal concerns and the power of good ends to justify prima facie wrong actions as means — are not problems for Kant's theory when it is not interpreted in an unnecessarily narrow way.

2

To elicit some of the elements of the mismatch, let's begin by considering the way the hybrid revisionist approaches Kant on lying.[29] First, he looks at things Kant says: that telling lies is among the morally worst things a person can do, that lying is wrong because lies fail to respect the value of rational agency (especially the liar's own agency), and, famously, that one may not lie, regardless of the consequences. Most of this is deemed obviously incorrect. But what is not thought incorrect is the Kantian idea of morality restricting actions on the grounds that a principle permitting them cannot be rationally willed (though Kant's own view of how to understand the condition of universal rational willing is

[29] This is not an exact report of Parfit's discussion of lying, but a compressed variant that captures its main elements.

regarded as mistaken or confused). Then the revisionist offers a better, although hybrid, argument. It will go something like this. Depending on circumstances, lies can be either beneficial or harmful. Most often they are attempts to secure some advantage for the liar by controlling the information available to victims (though controlling information can also be beneficial and so possibly rational). When advantage-lying is widespread, it undermines the trust conditions necessary for cooperative activity, itself a great good. Therefore, a principle of general permissiveness about lying would not be rational to will: since lying is so often a useful means, permissiveness would likely lead to more lying than trust, and so cooperation, could survive. But a principle that permitted lying when necessary to save wrongfully threatened lives would not be interfering with interests we have reason to protect and would have little or no undermining effect on trust. So advantage-lying is shown to be wrong; not all lying is wrong; and the rationale for the wrongness points not to the value of rational agency, but to the benefits of cooperation. In this way, the revisionist retains the Kantian (contractualist) spirit and get a much more plausible moral view. The consequentialism figures in the revisionary account twice — in the values appealed to and in the treatment of the universality condition as setting up a comparison between how we would fare were advantage-lying, as opposed to life-saving lying, permissible.

Now, whatever the correct view of Kant on lying is, a best version of *it* is not going to be found in the terms of costs and benefits, and not through an argument that appeals to the comparative cost/benefit value of a selectively permissive principle's general acceptance. That way takes lying (and truth-telling) out of the center of the moral theory, and regards its moral significance merely instrumentally. But if the ambition of Kant's moral philosophy is a unified theory of value and principle *within* an account of practical reason, if it's supposed not to be possible for a maxim of lying to be principle of rational willing, we ought to be looking at the relation lying creates between rational agents as one that in some way violates a principle of (or implied by) their common rational nature.[30] However such a view is laid out, well-being outcomes

---

[30] I will return to Kant's account of lying in section 8.

won't be given an independent role in the argument.[31] Granted it's not easy to say what it could mean to take rationality or rational nature to be of value,[32] and I agree that the idea of respect for persons that is supposed to follow from it risks being either empty or a container for one's preferred account of human status. Nonetheless, if there is a deep insight that Kant offers, whatever the difficulty of working it out, it is nowhere else than in the account of value and the principles of action-evaluation derived from the constitutive principles of a rational will. It may be that Kant's theory cannot realize its ambitions, but as I hope to show later on in this paper, I don't think the best interpretation of Kant has yet reached that stage of the dialectic.[33]

3

If the example of advantage-lying displays one aspect of the mismatch in methods, a different register of the divide between Kant's theory and Parfit's methodology can be seen in their treatment of the role of motives in assessments of wrongdoing. For Parfit, it is almost never the case

[31] As I read the *Groundwork* tests, they do not ask which of two hypothetical worlds would be *better* for us, but rather which principles of action are consistent with constitutive norms of rational willing. Compossibility is not the kind of outcome the hybrid theorist has in mind. Kant thinks that were we all to act morally we would realize a kingdom of ends, and our actions and maxims are to be consistent with that effect, the kingdom of ends does not represent an *outcome* value in the sense of providing an aim or reason for action. The same is true, I believe, of Kant's notion of the Highest Good: it is not an object we can aim for except in the sense that we seek our own and others' happiness in morally directed ways.

[32] Parfit's own struggles with this set of ideas are exemplary and informative (*Volume One, 239–44*)—he has an unerring feel for the wince feature of appealing but bad arguments.

[33] To be clear about this, I do not mean to suggest that there is a way to make Kant's Formula of Universal Law work after all. I don't think there is. But since I also doubt that the Formula was ever intended to do the work of establishing permissions and requirements (it can explain the wrongness in wrong action, but cannot by itself tell us which actions are wrong), other elements of Kant's theory must be brought in to do that.

that wrongness of action is determined or even affected by an agent's motive. If, as he argues, the values that justify moral principles look to outcome-events (outcomes that would come about were a principle generally accepted), then (most) wrongful actions will either generate bad outcomes directly, or they are of a kind which if (believed to be) permitted would summatively generate bad outcomes (or significantly worse outcomes when compared with the consequences of agent's acting in conformity to some competitor principle). What makes an action wrong is then directly a function of what does or would happen, not about why an action was done (the motive here regarded as a cause of action.[34] Motive may matter to other questions—about character, reliability, the kinds of relations a person acting from this or that motive can reasonably sustain—but it does not figure in the explanation of the wrongness of wrongful action.

So a selfish motive won't make a rescue wrong, and even a morally bad motive won't transfer its negative quality to a morality-conforming action that it brings about. In a related example, Parfit has us imagine a coffee-ordering gangster, motivated to do whatever it takes to make the world conform to his desires. He is ready to cause all kinds of mayhem if anyone crosses him, and regards the barista as he would a potentially recalcitrant soda machine that he will lash out at if it balks at dispensing his drink. But no one does cross him; the coffee is ordered and paid for. Since the act is one that satisfies moral principle (paying for purchases, or somesuch), nothing bad has happened. He is a nasty guy you wouldn't want to have around, but for all that, unless and until he does something impermissible, the moral problem is all a matter of potential and probabilities—of bad motives, not bad action.[35]

---

[34] Sometimes when Parfit talks about motives he means the attitude an actor has in acting: whether I regard you as a rational person, a moral subject, or as a mere means. Since quite nasty attitudes can coexist with permissible actions—the attitude's negative potential remains unrealized—the issue of relevance to wrongness is the same.

[35] The reward-motivated life-saver may seem to be a purer case since there seems to be no question that he aims to do something good; but suppose that as he is swimming to the rescue, a greater reward is announced for saving a victim downstream: what does he now have reason to do?

One might wonder whether it is true that nothing bad happened. The barista was surely put at risk in ways he ought not to have been. Were we to assume motivational transparency, it would seem odd to say that nothing wrong has happened if you escape harm only by avoiding eye-contact or placating or doing whatever is needed to avoid setting off those around you who are motivationally primed for easy violence. Making it through a minefield is not a walk in the park. But let's leave this worry aside.

One aspect of our interest in moral wrongness would seem to support the irrelevance of motive conclusion. If we are attending to wrongful action with an eye to (possibly or even in principle) interfering with it, so long as the gangster does what is in the circumstance required—he pays for his coffee—there is nothing happening that we should prevent (and in the case of the reward-seeking life-saver, we might even have reason to help him). The more general thought would be that to judge an action wrong we must also hold that it would be better (morally better?) if it didn't happen—that its happening is an occasion, at the least, for regret. And of course it is not better that the coffee not be paid for or the life not saved. Regrets about the action seem irrational here.[36]

However, the conditions for regrets about others' doings are often different from those that apply to the agent acting. A reformed gangster might reasonably look back at the coffee scene with a kind of horror: there I was, he thinks, ready to take the guy out if he said one off word to me! It's easy enough to imagine him concluding that what he had done was wrong: it was a matter of sheer luck that there was a benign outcome. It would not be inapt for him to wish it had not happened: not the paying for the coffee, of course, but the entire episode. If a sign of wrongdoing is guilt, or a sense that apology might be in order, motive or attitude can suffice to trigger it, and a change in attitude is often integral to the work of moral repair for what was done. (That the subject of one's action be aware of the wrong done to him is not necessary for apology to be in order.) These are reasons for thinking that the moral bearing of an agent's attitude or motive touches more than the quality of his character or the associated likelihood that he will

---

[36] And there are lots of things, away from the action, we get to criticize or regret about the agent.

do as morality directs. They show an agent acting in a way he should not have. They are not reasons hybrid theory wants to register in its account of wrongness, because its consequentialist account of value propels it to implicitly model wrongness on a legalistic notion of impermissibility.[37] And while impermissibility may fairly mark out the class of wrongful actions that are wrong no matter what the agent's motive, it need not, and for Kant, as far as I can tell, it does not, exhaust the category of moral wrongness in acting.[38]

So what is it in Kant's view that could make motive relevant to determinations of wrongness? Why, in the moral assessment of an action, should we care about its underlying cause? I would put it this way: for Kant, wrongness marks incorrect *ways of acting* and not merely actions that fail to conform to principles applying to action-(intended) outcome pairs. An agent who ignores or fails to respond appropriately to the morally relevant features of his circumstances acts in a way that is wrong. And this is so whether or not his external action and (intended) end are what they would be if he had acted correctly. Returning to the gangster: in a narrow (legalistic) focus, he orders and then pays for coffee — nothing is wrong. But when we widen the focus, more is going on. For one thing, he doesn't see the ordering as calling for payment; he'll pay if nothing provokes him. Nor does he see his *ordering and paying for* coffee as a required way of getting it: he would steal from the coffee seller if that was worth the trouble (*216*). So if one thought with Kant that wrongness arises from the principles of the deliberating agent and is about whether, through them, she has a sound route of

[37] I suspect the legalism is quite deep. After all, if one thinks that motives matter, in asking whether it would be rational to will the universal acceptance of acting 'this way' — acting to save *sub specie* getting a greater reward, paying the tab *sub specie* its being the path of least annoyance — wrongness would be motive-sensitive. If, on the other hand, one thinks about wrongness by analogy with what cannot be lawfully brought about, motives are not relevant. But an analogy does not provide an argument for regarding moral wrongness in this way.

With others, I read the universality condition on the Kantian side as about form: a requirement that materially conditioned practical inference satisfy a matter-independent standard of correctness.

[38] Just as acting 'according to duty' is not the same as acting as one ought.

reasoning to her action, the gangster would be in the wrong twice over.[39] Since it is the agent's motive that is responsible for the correct elements playing the correct role in the production of an action, motive matters to the wrongfulness of what is done. On Kant's view, as I understand it, avoiding impermissibility and avoiding wrongness are not the same thing; actions can be 'not impermissible' and yet wrong.[40]

4

At this point, I can imagine someone asking whether the version of Kant I'm putting forward doesn't ignore or elide his famous distinction between morally worthy and duty-conforming actions, the former requiring that the action be done from a moral motive, the latter motive-indifferent. A first thing to note is that the question already suggests a position: that moral worth is something added on, post permissibility, as it were. *Given* an action according to duty, *that same action* would have moral worth if done with a special attitude or from the motive of duty. Such a description misses the point of the distinction *moral worth* names. In looking to the moral content of the maxim on which the agent acts, Kant points to a condition of the *action's* value (not, as the question suggests, the *agent's* value). An externally conforming action that lacks moral worth is a behavior whose connection to moral correctness is conditional or accidental. It is in that sense *not* a (morally) correct action. There may be epistemic barriers to determining whether an action is correct or not (though one shouldn't exaggerate opacity: we often can tell when an agent is not acting correctly by seeing how

[39] With others, I read the universality condition on the Kantian side as about form: a requirement that materially conditioned practical inferences satisfy a matter-independent standard of correctness.

[40] Interestingly, we can speak of degrees of wrongness, though not degrees of impermissibility. When I know something untoward will happen to you as a result of what I do, but I do not value my action because of it, that is less bad (in the dimensions of wrongness) than my directly intending it, or seeing it as a positive effect or even a second-order motivating benefit (i.e. I would not act as I do for the extra benefit, but it might add to the value of my action weighed against some other option).

she responds to failures), and there are independent reasons why we might not want to interfere with actions that are in external conformity with moral principle (there are also often good reasons not to want to interrogate agents about their conforming actions unless we are in an instructional or advisory relation with them). If I am the person acted upon, if I am not intimate with the agent, or not relying on her as a moral reasoner (we engage in one-time transactions, not long-term or complex projects), then her getting things *as if* right (according to duty) may be enough. But from the point of view of the deliberating agent it is not the same: how she regards what getting it right amounts to partly determines what she is doing.[41]

I think that the tendency to think that moral worth is about something else accepts the idea that there is a clear notion of 'doing the right thing' that survives coming to do it the right way or the wrong way. We are uneasy about this sort of idea in other areas — addition, belief-formation — where we judge accidental correctness as it tracks the genuine article, and so correct, but once removed. An unjustified true belief is of course true, but it is also *qua* belief (that is, strictly) incorrect or wrong or defective. I think Kant has a similar view about moral worth and wrongness. An action that has moral worth, one done from the motive of duty, is an action arrived at under the non-accidental regulation of moral principle (that's what it is to act from a motive of duty).[42] The primary notion is not one of avoiding *getting something wrong* (acting contrary to duty), but of *getting something right*.

The doctrine of moral worth is not the only place where Kant is taken to be offering a motive-independent notion of wrongness; also noted are his views of perfect duties and duties of justice. Neither view supports the general thesis of motive-independent wrongness. In both cases, the error in thinking that they do is instructive.

---

[41] The formal requirement is that one act only on maxims through which one *can* at the same time will . . . and not, act in conformity with that principle through which one *could* at the same time will . . .

[42] That is, moral worth is not just about an attitude one has towards one's action, at least no more so than weighing evidence is just an attitude one might have about belief-formation.

Perfect duties are described in the *Groundwork* as duties 'that admit no exception in favor of inclination' (4:421n), and so seem to be motive-independent.[43] But since inclination is only one kind of motive, or source of motives, the description leaves it open whether perfect duties might admit of exceptions in favor of motives of a different sort. And this makes sense, given Kant's theory of action, where motive is an agent's source of interest in an end, and so in action as a means (mere efficacy of means doesn't justify acting). Motives range widely, from such inclination-based concerns for self, family and friends to the rational interest we have in moral ends. Since the same action-end pair can hang together quite differently for agents with different motives, it is possible that some kinds of action (deceitful promises, say) could be wrong when employed as a means for any end of self-interest, but not wrong if the end is supported by a moral interest in saving a life. (It's not the intended end qua good state of affairs that justifies; the motive condition implies that justification depends on an agent's having a morally correct conception of her end. I will have more to say about this condition later.)

Duties of justice are indeed about external actions only; motives are not relevant to their correct performance. However, duties of justice are not one of the classes of moral duties, on all fours, as it were, with duties of truth-telling or aid or respect or friendship. For Kant, they are institution-based duties whose point is to secure conditions of equal external freedom (a 'like liberty for all' condition).[44] They only come into existence through the legislative activity of a state (or civic union with the authority to compel compliance).[45] Theft, to take Kant's central example, is contrary to a duty of justice not because it's an instance of

[43] Imperfect duties impose requirements directly on ends, only indirectly on actions.

[44] For a very clear presentation of the point and nature of duties of justice, see Arthur Ripstein, 'Authority and Coercion', *Philosophy and Public Affairs*, 32:1 (Winter 2004), 2–35. There is a moral duty to enter the state so that there might be duties of justice and so morally sanctioned regulation of property and contract.

[45] They are an essential part of a complete moral theory because they provide necessary background conditions for many moral obligations. Because we have a *moral* duty to obey the law, we can fulfill duties of justice 'from duty'.

free-riding on a convention (Parfit is quite right in requiring that we be able to distinguish decent from both trivial and abhorrent conventions). Rather, for reasons having to do with the conditions of human rational agency—we must be able to rightfully exclude others from the use of some things—we are under moral compulsion to live in a state where the boundaries of property are settled by law and have a duty to abide by its laws. (This is one of the ways we show that the rules of property have a different status, a different kind authority, than the rules of a chess club.) *Given* property laws, appropriating what belongs to someone else is wrong. It is a violation of a duty of justice even if the appropriation is for a morally good end. Such a purpose may be a reason for a court to be lenient, or, perhaps, for the law to be written with something like a moral eminent domain clause to cover such cases (one might then be acting as an agent of the state in taking what's needed to save a life). The *moral* wrong in stealing involves the invasion of a region under the rightful authority of another; but its wrongness depends on the region being defined by and under the protection of a state (or other system of enforcement).[46]

In sum, neither the doctrine of moral worth, nor Kant's account of perfect duties, nor his introduction of duties of justice support the view that the fundamental category of moral wrongness for Kant is motive-independent. While this is not enough to make the case for the relevance of motives to moral wrongness, it should be enough to give us reason to think more about what's at stake here. After all, Kant's treatment of moral action need not square with a contemporary agenda that focuses on standards of impermissibility.

Where does this leave us in thinking about the challenges Parfit directs at Kant's moral theory? If the separation of the two methodologies is so wide that there is not ground for agreement even about the kind of

But in that sense, we can also obey traffic laws from duty; that doesn't make 'no right on red' a moral duty.

[46] For this reason, a violation of a duty of justice is to be regarded as an act against the state. Duties of justice (or *recht*) include requirements to pay debts and keep promises, but only as they occur in the context of contracts. The *moral* duty of promise-keeping will have a different source, and its violations may or may not be motive-independent.

thing we look to when we assess wrongness in action, then, apart from interest in specific topics, there may not be much to be gained from a point-by-point comparison of interpretations of Kant's arguments and Parfit's hybrid reconstruction. They are simply too far apart.[47] With that in mind, I propose to use the rest of this paper to do some work on the Kant side of things: since part of the appeal of the hybrid theory comes from its avoiding or transcending perceived limitations of Kant's views, if there is a better interpretation of Kant that is not limited in those ways, we may yet make some progress.

5

Although Kant's theory has a great deal to say about one aspect of morality we care about — that our pursuit of ends be constrained by rational principle — it has seemed distressingly insensitive to another — that its principles not direct us to act in ways we would find, to use Parfit's word, awful. Because the hybrid theory is directly responsive to our natural concerns and nonmoral ends, it presents itself as more reasonable — its prohibitions and permissions, if honored, would make things go better for us. Kant's theory, by contrast, can seem indifferent to what we care about, implacable in its demands, even when the outcomes it blocks are self-evidently good. Now were it true, as I suggested in the previous section it might be, that Kant's framework allows that in freighted circumstances we *can* sometimes be justified in acting in ways that we normally must not, we might conclude that there is reason to rethink the terms of Kantian moral requirement as well as its fit with ends we care about. In that spirit, I will offer a sketch of the elements of a deliberation-centered reading of Kant's moral theory, with some focus on its treatment of nonmoral ends, and then return to the case of the necessary lie to see whether the theory, so-interpreted, can do better with the moral problem of ends and means.[48]

---

[47] This takes no position on the best version of contractualist theory inspired by Kant.

[48] The first parts of this account are drawn from my 'Reasoning to Obligation', *Inquiry*, 49:1 (Feb. 2006), 44–61.

First, the sketch. Morality, for Kant, belongs to the domain of practical reason—its principle is practical reason's first principle. To speak of reason, whether practical or theoretical, is to indicate a subject-matter that is about warranted transitions from thought to thought, thought to belief, thought to intention or choice (or between the propositions or sentences that represent them). So if the categorical imperative is or expresses a principle of practical reason, then it is a principle of inference, directing (correct) reasoning from one place to another in just the sense that *modus ponens* does—though by a different rule, of course.[49]

Take one of Kant's examples.[50] Someone gives me something of value to hold for her; no one else knows I have it; she dies before it is to be returned. *Correct* practical reasoning takes me from some premise about ownership to some conclusion about what is to be done by way of a principle or rule of inference that in its most abstract form says: 'act only on that principle (maxim) that can at the same time be willed a universal law.' If my principle is instead 'to increase my property by every safe means', then it directs my reasoning to an intention to keep the object in a way that involves a contradiction in just the sense that it would if I used a principle that warranted reasoning to not q from p, and if p then q. That is, *my* principle is not a possible instance of the correct principle of reasoning-to-action. There remain, to be sure, the familiar difficulties—how to formulate maxims, the proper understanding of universalization, etc.—but, setting them aside, it seems to me most plausible that this is the right way to approach Kant's account of moral reasoning and his account therefore of what makes actions wrong.

Now if practical reasoning emulates the form of reasoning in general, it needs access to true premises, and those would have to be premises of or about ends. That many have thought Kant clearly asserts otherwise comes, I believe, from a confusion about the argument structure of the *Groundwork*, one that mistakes a claim about the condition of

[49] Part of Kant's purpose in insisting on the possibility of synthetic *a priori* judgment is to extend the domain of necessary connection between cognitions.

[50] *Critique of Practical Reason* 5: 27–8.

application of the categorical imperative (which *is* end-independent[51]) for a claim about the irrelevance of ends, or premises of ends, for moral reasoning.[52] If, as Kant thinks, reason can determine the will to action, its principle ought to tell us that there are ends we may not have as well as ends we must have.[53] Where there are ends we may not have, *no* reasoning from them can be sound. And with morally required ends, any intention correctly derived from them will have a moral content—that is, the agent's conception of her action will draw down from the end a moral point or purpose in so acting, as well as a sense of the action's material efficacy.[54] Since, as we shall see, necessary or obligatory ends offer moral housing for our nonmoral interests, they are the right kind of thing to look to if we want to see whether and how what matters to us personally also matters morally. And last, obligatory ends will, if anything can, offer resources of justification beyond the familiar universalization rule. In exploring this possibility, I will examine two cases, one where Kant clearly does think a morally necessary end justifies normally forbidden means, and one where he should. In both I will argue that the justification the end provides is not, in any ordinary sense, instrumental. Given the place of such ends within practical reasoning, this is as it should be.

[51] The possibility of a categorical imperative depends, Kant says, on 'a practical proposition that does not derive the volition of an action analytically from another volition already presupposed (for we have no such perfect will), but connects it immediately with the concept of the will of a rational being as something that is not contained in it' (*Groundwork*, 4: 420n). It follows that the practical proposition, as a rule of inference, applies a rational standard to all willed action—means taken for some end—without regard to the content of the agent's willed end.

[52] See *Groundwork*, 4: 414–15 where we are clearly set up to expect an account of objective ends or goods. It is *further* ends that are excluded. Humanity as an end in itself is an objective end, but it is a formal end, and, uninterpreted, cannot anchor deliberation.

[53] So Kant plainly argues in *Metaphysics of Morals*, 6: 385.

[54] That there need not be two equi-fundamental principles, one for actions and one for ends, is the point of Kant's 'Paradox of Method': the moral law is a positive synthetic *a priori* principle for the correct use of the faculty of free willing—in objectively determining good willing, it must be or determine the will's principle *and* its object.

6

Kant argues that there are two, and only two, obligatory ends: of our own perfection and of the happiness of others.[55] Slightly filled out they amount to this: towards ourselves we have the end of developing and maintaining our moral and rational abilities; towards others we are to attend to the agency-related effects of our actions on their pursuit of happiness. Kant's argument for these two ends is brief and obscure; for our purposes, an intuitive gloss should suffice.

We begin by asking: What, from the point of view of practical reason, demands attention? With respect to *actions*, we are not to act on any principles inconsistent with universal law-giving (that we cannot also will to become universal law). A different kind of problem arises in the normal course of adopting *ends*, whether or not they prompt us to wrongful actions, as we develop and pursue our idea of happiness. For what we pursue under this idea may not be, from the point of view of practical reason, acceptable. Sloth, greed, sloppiness about what we believe and how we reason, neglect of core abilities, can be the effect of the pursuit of happiness when it is not under the regulatory control of any higher idea than some ordered satisfaction of our inclinations.[56] These effects are not themselves ends, nor likely intended; it is rather that, given our psychology, they are examples of dangers to practical rationality that won't be averted unless we have special reason to attend to the possible effects of some of our ends on our rational functioning. If we do, some of our ends will have to

---

[55] *Metaphysics of Morals*, 6: 386. There is in fact another kind of required end that comes from the side of *Recht* that obligates us to create and support the state. But, as we shall see in section 7, these are not, strictly, possible ends for each separate individual: no one can act for them unless others do so as well.

[56] One might think that rational prudence would do the work here: the thought that we are a perduring being and that our future selves have a claim on our present attention. But many of these vices give us no reason to want the future to be different from the present. They affect the horizon of our practical imagination, leaving us with no reason to expect projects and needs that may come that should constrain how we treat ourselves now.

be abandoned; others will need to be pursued in more reason-friendly ways; ends we may not have wanted to have we may have to take on, given rational needs or rational damage that must be repaired. From the point of view of practical reason, it cannot be a matter of indifference that our psychology, which is affected by what we do, is vulnerable to disabilities that can render us less able to respond to rational requirements. The problem is not that we will then be moved to do wrong; even if, by a fluke, we never do, we would not be reasoning-to-action well, and so not willing as we ought. In this way we get the obligatory end of one's own perfection, which gives rise to various duties-to-self.

There is a parallel story for the obligatory end of the happiness of others. Although each person necessarily pursues her own idea of happiness, others have a large effect on the pursuit at almost every step of the way, from the array of ideas we are given about how to live to the provision (or not) of all kinds of help. But suppose we ask, as we did above, what can be at issue here from the point of view of practical reason? That is, why should someone else's pursuit of happiness be made, by practical reason, of concern to me? Presumably for the very same reasons we just canvassed in the obligation to self: an additional but equally fundamental fact of our psychology is that we are not monads, not autarchic systems of desire. A person's rational abilities are (partly) formed by others, (partly) sustained by them; rational abilities are vulnerable to the effects of poverty, humiliation, and sustained misdirection. At the extreme, making someone's life too hard *or* too easy can affect their ability to sustain or value rational activity. Ignoring the awkward personification, the question then is: How could impartial practical reason be indifferent to activity that undermined our own *or others'* ability to engage in reasoning?

What do obligatory ends require of us? They are to shape both our pursuit of and our idea of happiness. They do not require that when deciding between going to a concert and spending an evening with friends I should deliberate about self- (or other-) improvement; that would be absurd. But they do imply that if I work so much that I have no time for friends or pleasures, I may be neglecting myself in ways I ought not, or may have failed to understand the material conditions of healthy human agency.[57] There is something of general concern that I should not have ignored. Likewise, as my actions affect others, I may not be indifferent to costs I impose, and never casual about respect. When the norms or standards that obligatory ends provide are not met, our willing is morally faulty. That is, unless there is a course of reasoning from the obligatory end(s) to the action, it is not fully justified (regardless of whether the action is externally permissible).[58] And while the obligatory end is usually not the only premise in reasoning, and often not the active one in determining choice, it should always be one of the agent's practical premises.

Suppose, oblivious or indifferent to the effects of my plans on my (or anybody's) rational agency, I decide to spend the weekend at the beach as a happiness-promoting kind of thing. Do we really want to say that there is moral fault in doing this—in going to the beach to have some fun? There's an analogue notion of 'acting from' and 'acting according to' for ends. What made the prudent shopkeeper's action seem unobjectionable is that it was the action that would be performed by someone who willed well—that is why it is according to duty. Likewise, what makes the end of going to the beach seem all right is that it is the sort of end (seeking enjoyment) that could be an end for someone acting under the authority of the obligatory end of self-perfection. But in just the way that the prudent shopkeeper's action is morally unstable and lacks moral content (the action is not tracking anything moral), so too the simple end of going to the beach adopted without regard to obligatory ends is morally empty and therefore morally risky. It is of course not *very* risky when compared with the end of seeking enjoyment from crack cocaine; but if, for the agent acting, that difference makes no difference, then from the moral point of view, that indifference *is* very risky indeed. It then

[57] Since this is one of the regions where truths about the individual trump general claims about persons, failure to pursue characteristically healthy human goals is a serious warning sign, not necessarily a failure.

[58] Again, the extension of judgments of wrongness from action to volition is Kant's central point: if moral wrongness is about faulty reasoning, an action-centered notion of wrongness (or impermissibility) may play a pragmatic role, but it does not fully capture the nature of moral error.

might not seem so off to say that I am morally wrong in acting on my plan.[59]

Obligatory ends thus bring a wide range of ordinary human concerns inside morality. Although our ideas of happiness may have to undergo some revision and development in order to relocate, the familiar elements of self- and other-concern remain, and remain central to our purposes. In securing norms of regard for the well-being of self and other, obligatory ends make these considerations anchors for sound reasoning to action. It remains to be seen whether obligatory ends can justify actions that ordinary ends cannot. Can they show it is all right to lie or coerce or harm for their sake?

I don't mean to suggest that obligatory ends might be crucibles of moral alchemy, able to turn immoral actions into moral ones; if they provide broader justification, it is as premises that affect the moral content of the volitions that follow from them. This is true of other moral ends as well. When acting under the end of friendship, an otherwise permissible action that causes my friend concern may, for that reason, be wrong; or, given special facts of need and intimacy, some morally difficult avenues of action are opened (think about the space of jokes and teasing). The question about obligatory ends is not whether they affect morally available means (they do), but how we are to determine their justificatory scope. The obligatory end of others' happiness may justify some paternalism, but we don't expect it to justify killing one to benefit many (or any)—it can't transform the content of willing *that* action as a means. But perhaps it can reach to a lie for the sake of a life.

7

For guidance in thinking about how moral ends might justify suspect means, I am going to draw on a different region of argument where

---

[59] If actions whose maxims have moral content exhibit good willing, then it is present when ordinary actions are done for the sake of an obligatory end. Needing a break from work, I decide to go to a movie. I could do it simply for pleasure; I could also be aware that such pleasures are part of a healthy life and act for that reason as well. Since in the latter case the reasoning is, in moral terms, both valid and sound, it does seem to be an instance of good willing (though not of moral worth, since the movie-going is not itself a dutiful action).

Kant clearly does appeal to a certain kind of moral end to show how something normally forbidden is permitted—indeed is morally necessary. The argument is about coercion into political union.[60] The formation and preservation of a state that meets rule-of-law standards has a special role in Kant's moral theory since membership in such a state is a necessary condition of external freedom of action. Through its coercive and adjudicative institutions, the state secures the integrity of body from assault and makes possible sustained possession and exchange of property. Where these conditions are not met, the plurality of individuals' rational actions in and on the world, and so also their happiness, cannot be coherently pursued. Persons are therefore strongly obligated to form a state if there is none, and to sustain the one they have. The end is not one anyone can aim at alone; it is one, Kant argues, we can and must compel others to pursue with us. This sets the problem. If the argument is a moral one, it might seem that the compulsion should be forbidden. But then morality would appear to block its own real possibility. If, however, the argument is *not* moral, we would have a political and trumping contra-moral obligation. Together, these positions form what one might call an antinomy of obligation. As with any Kantian antinomy, it is best resolved by rethinking the assumptions that generate it. In this case, the problem derives from the characterization of the entitlement to compel co-citizenship: whether it can be shown consistent with the autonomy of the rational will.

It is a core feature of Kant's ethics that something's being good for you to do does not entitle me to coerce your doing it. Yet here, the fact that 'we' (including you) must (for our good) live in a state apparently entitles us to compel entry and prevent exit (from some civil state or other). Now coercion is a matter of using force or threat of force to induce another to will against her will. But if what is at stake is putting persons and their actions under the authority of the state, it is not clear that the will is forced, or forced in a way that makes coercion morally objectionable. We might think of it this way. When the police set up a road-block, they have the authority to compel me to stop; regardless

---

[60] What follows is drawn from the *Rechtslehre*, part one of the *Metaphysics of Morals*, 6: 252–61.

of what I prefer to be doing, their act is coercive, but not in a morally objectionable way. And that suggests the antinomy might also be about authority. It would be resolved if the authority to compel (into the state) is entailed by what each and every agent necessarily wills.

Kant makes just such an argument. In summary form, it goes like this. In taking possession of any object for our use, we necessarily will that others refrain from taking it (if I take the apple for eating, or plant a crop, I will that it be mine, not yours). Since we cannot live without taking possession of objects, and the condition of our effective willing that others refrain from taking what we have is, Kant argues, the state ('Only in the civil condition can something external be mine or yours'), then in taking possession of anything, we in effect will that condition, and so the state's authority, as a necessary means. In this sense the authority of the state over the will of each is willed by each, and willed by each on condition that it is reciprocally willed by others, which it necessarily is. Thus civil union, under law, arises in and through the reciprocal rational conditions of possession (property). Since it is not an authority we can rationally avoid, in being materially compelled to act in accordance with the authority of our own will, we are not wrongfully coerced.

Resolving the antinomy in this way keeps morality from blocking its expression in the world, and it does so in a way that explains why one may not do just anything to compel civil entry (or forbid exit). Since the condition of being under law is a moral status, the terms of being brought under the state's authority have to be compatible with one's standing as an equal citizen. This then explains why territorial expansion through war and colonization is impermissible. As Kant remarks, the conditions of civil union arise from the conditions of living together; a state has no authority to create the conditions artificially.

So rather than being a disturbing embrace of contra-moral action, compelled civil union provides an example of how something that has the look of justified wrongdoing turns out to be uncompromisingly moral. Moreover, although compelled citizenship is justified with respect to a moral purpose — securing the conditions of free action — it is not justified simply as a means-to-an-end, even a moral end, but as an action on a principle with moral content (as a kind of moral self-actualization). This justification then frames and shapes subsequent moral reasoning.

The sort of thing I have in mind is this. If the state is morally justified, a variety of roles that are necessary to its function will also be (police, legislator, judge, soldier, but also doctor, educator, welfare-provider). When inhabiting these roles, individuals are allowed to act in ways they would not be permitted to act in the service of their own ends (e.g., police use of coercive force; a hospital policy of triage). We can say: the roles constitute ends of reasoning, so that actions that flow from social roles are, morally speaking, not the same actions they would be if derived from private ends. Of course the justificatory reach of institutions is limited: some actions that might instrumentally promote the function of a social role are not consistent with or would undermine the moral rationale for the institution's sphere of permission. Public officials are permitted, even required, to use force to gain compliance with the law, but they may not use bribes as a means to the same purpose. The impartial use of force is a condition of free action and so is consistent with the moral purpose of the state; bribery by public officials undermines the rule of law conditions of cooperation that a state's existence is to make possible.

There is much more to be drawn from the argument for compelled civil union, but with respect to understanding the work of obligatory ends, two things are most useful: one is the way in which the value a morally necessary end represents enters reasoning about means, and the other is the idea of a common end.

The first draws on basic facts about ends and means. We act by taking means for ends; we reason from ends to means. If the ends we reasoned from were desired states of affairs, then the reasoning would be familiarly instrumental. Further checks on such reasoning tend to be lateral, about costs to other ends one is or will be seeking. The moral check on purely instrumental reasoning is on means *simpliciter*: were one to know nothing more about the end than that it is desired, we should ask: can it permissibly be brought about *this* way? The obligatory end has additional effects on downstream reasoning in at least two ways. First, because an obligatory end, or an instance of such an end, has moral content, in acting under its auspices we are to conceive of what we would do as both morally and causally sufficient for the end. One can't act for the end of 'helping persons in need' and take as one's means impoverishing Peter to aid Paul.[61] Likewise, in taking on the moral project of making oneself more focused and attentive to detail, a regimen that caused near-obsessive behavior in this regard, while effective in one sense, would undermine the value of an end which was about the enhancement of abilities of discernment and judgment. In general, the effect of the moral content of an obligatory end *narrows* the class of otherwise permissible instrumental means by requiring that they be (and be seen to be) consistent with the value the end represents.

Sometimes, however, the effect of obligatory ends on moral reasoning is a potential *widening* of the range of means, allowing us, maybe even directing us, to do things we otherwise could not. Following the lesson of compelled civil union, we will not see the moral end as having a kind of weight that private ends lack, its value simply overriding whatever consideration opposes the questionable action. Nor will these actions be justified in spare instrumental terms. Rather, the value in the morally necessary end supports reasoning to an action-type that is only externally congruent with forbidden action. In the case of compelled civil union, what looked like a brute exercise of force turned out to be an action that all are rationally required to will. It is coercion, but not wrongful coercion.

The shift in moral valence that comes with the detail of ends can be seen in more ordinary examples. Compare the situation in which your child is drowning in your pool and I can save him only by, without asking, using your life-preserver, and the situation where it's my child in my pool and I must take your life-preserver. Let's assume I am justified in using what is not my own in both cases. But the actions are not the same kind. In the first case I would say I act for you, using what is yours as an extension of your agency, so that my taking is justified by what you are obligated to will. In the second case there is the balance of harms, the reasonable imposition of burdens, an occasion for replacement and apology, none of which makes sense in the first case. What sense could there be in *apologizing* for using your stuff to save your child?

---

[61] Assuming the impoverishing is not by way of an impermissible act, this not only could be but arguably is a variant of a possible law of nature.

I don't insist on this way of describing these cases, only that it is a possible way to think about them, and a natural one, once we allow the idea that there is more going on than causal fit when reasoning from end to means from a morally required end. We are not asking, 'May I take this means to my end?' but, 'Does this end – means pair satisfy the full moral conditions on willing?' In the terms of our earlier discussion (in section 4), it is an instance of motive, reflected in an end, affecting the (moral) identity of an action.

The second lesson to be taken from the argument for political union concerns its being a *common end*: there is something necessary for each of us to do that none can effect without others having and acting for the end as well. Obligatory ends are also common ends, though not for the same reason. Because they are ends of practical reason, each of us has a duty to adopt them. But the fact that they are ends I am under obligation to have does not make what they require my project in more than a locating sense.[62] We are all rationally required to acknowledge and adopt the obligatory end of helping others or promoting their rational well-being. That here and now it's me who must help is only indirectly of moral significance. I respond to (what we would call) an impersonal reason, based in what I rightly regard as a non-optional end. (By contrast, where ends are private ends, that they are mine is not just a matter of location: they belong to me.) So there is a sense in which, like the case of compelled civil union, obligatory ends give us a common project; but unlike the case of compelled civil union, we can, indeed we must be prepared to take on parts of the project separately.[63] For an end to be a common end it need not also be a cooperative one.

8

Armed with these features of obligatory ends — their effect on the moral content of means, the widening of the range of options, and the idea of

[62] This is a point Thomas Nagel made in *The Possibility of Altruism* and John Rawls took up into his reading of Kant.

[63] Even when we act in concert, say through charitable organizations, it is our individual obligations that are being met, though more efficiently, through shared efforts.

a common end—we are in a position to make some progress with the kind of case that Kant is thought to manage so badly, where morality seems to require us to act without regard to consequences that we have compelling reason to avoid or prevent. I will focus on the 'murderer at the door' scenario, largely because of its unfortunate fame, but also because in working through it we gain some insight about why truth-telling is so important to Kant's deliberation-centered ethics.[64]

Let's set the stage in the usual way. Confronted by a murderer demanding information concerning the whereabouts your friend, his intended victim, you think you should lie to prevent the murderer's succeeding. It is natural to regard your lie as a means to misdirect the murderer and save your friend's life. This, of course, is what Kant objects to: that your purpose in lying is to provide a benefit (or avert a harm) does not make it not wrong to do. Though the principle seems true enough in the abstract, its application to this case strikes almost everyone as absurd: if the lie here is wrong at all, that wrong is surely outweighed by the greater wrong it prevents. Kant seems unable to accept this because of the great disvalue he accords lying to promote one's ends. Whereas we are not sure that the lie in these circumstances is wrong at all.

We can't finesse the issue by arguing directly from the end or even the duty of saving a life. Saving a life is not in general a morally trumping aim (we can't maim or torture in order to save); whether it is ever a trumping aim is the question. We do no better arguing from preventing wrongdoing or a wrongful harm when there is no set calculus for balancing wrongs. Indeed, the issue won't even be raised properly unless we come to terms with Kant's views about the moral significance of lying. The best place to begin, then, is with the specific objection to lying for the sake of one's own ends. We will later consider whether and how lying (and truth-telling) might be affected by obligatory ends: that is, whether and how the kind of end in question

---

[64] Allen Wood gives good reasons for thinking we have grossly misread Kant's 'Supposed Right to Lie' (in ch. 14 of his *Kantian Ethics* (Cambridge University Press, 2008)). Here I start out with the old assumptions, though my conclusion fits better with Wood's, and indeed, with other of Kant's discussions about lying. For the record, Kant does not hold that lying is always wrong.

makes a moral difference on what may be done. The route we'll follow will take us through less familiar territory about speech and reasoning, the normative import of ends, and the moral significance of different ways of preventing wrongdoing.

So why might Kant have such intense concern with speaking the truth? We start with the fact that normal communicative speech carries a truth presumption: absent good reason to believe otherwise, we have warrant to accept what is said as true (or believed to be true by the speaker), and within limits, are right to depend on it. Whatever the source of the truth presumption—be it in reason, the logic or grammar of assertion, or the conditions of trust—it is clearly in the extension of both obligatory ends. Since, for Kant, correct reasoning in general ultimately depends on our being able to reason together, the obligatory ends' requirement that we attend to the conditions of rational agency in ourselves and others makes the truth presumption a central concern of a common end. In these terms we should say that the wrong in instrumental lying arises from a deceptive employment of the invitation to believe carried by ordinary speech, reliance on which is exploited to make the victim's reasoning conform to a purpose that is not her own (or, more precisely, not her own in the right way).

If the truth presumption is essential to the well-functioning of rational agents, by-passing it, even for a good end, would seem to involve the kind of insult to persons' status as rational agents that morality prohibits. That suggests that the natural question to ask about the forced speech situation created by the murderer is whether it somehow voids the presumption. Kant made a debater's objection to the claim that the murderer had no *right* to the truth, but it's not obvious that he had to reject the idea that in some speech conditions the truth presumption might be canceled.

There are, after all, all sorts of occasions in which we indicate that our false speech should not be taken as a lie: when we tell tall-tales, or make jokes, bluff in games, write fiction, perform political satire, and so on. Social conventions mark out arenas for white lies and tactful omissions. In the would-be murderer's case, we might argue that because the speech is compelled, or would abet wrongdoing, the context of action itself signals that the truth-presumption is suspended.[65] However, unlike jokes and tall tales where we know the speech is not intended to be truthful (or where truthfulness is not its point), or conventions of tact with which all or most are familiar, in this case one of the parties, the aggressor, depends in his reasoning on the fact that the truth presumption is in play with its usual force.

In ordinary circumstances, whether or not we like the way someone would act, whether it is for or against our interests, autonomy demands respect for a person's agency and for its expression in reasoning to action. We may not undermine another's reasoning for the sake of our own ends by introducing false beliefs or misleading truths, or even by making so much noise that she cannot think. Out of respect, we may decide not to correct errors, or limit our interventions to advice. Sometimes this is because we are not certain what the agent intends, but often even when we are, we accept the authority each has to put the elements of a life together her own way. Though one person may know more than another (in general or in one case) or deliberate with greater facility, no one has privileged access to correctness in moral reasoning (moral error is not typically a result of difference in skill or epistemic position). In that sense, we have equal status as reasoners.

On the other hand, not every course of reasoning warrants respect. The aggressor's reasoning is not just faulty; it issues in a demand on *our* speech that contravenes the core value of truthfulness, and betrays the common end of reasoning well. It is part of normal speech conditions that we use one another's truthful speech for our own purposes, regardless of whether the speaker knows what our purposes are or agrees with them. Here, however, the aggressor seeks our speech in the spirit of commandeering a weapon. He would impress our speech into the service of a contra-moral purpose — one to which there is no sound deliberative route. For that reason his demand cancels, or has no claim on, the truth presumption. Our being released from a requirement of truthful speech does not, however, get us all the way to the lie. It is because, in addition to the betrayal of the truth presumption, the aim of

---

[65] Kant says we cannot impute the harmful consequences of rightful action to the agent; might this change when a rightful action abets wrongdoing?

the aggressor's unimpeded faulty reasoning is harm to another, that we have reason not to let the situation take its course. That is what makes the defensive lie a real option.

Note that if it turns out that we may lie to resist the impressment of our speech, the *first* purpose of our intervention would not be protection of the victim, but something like preventive policing of our shared moral space in response to the aggressor's betrayal of the common end. Consider a case where our forced speech will abet faulty reasoning that would, by lucky accident, produce a beneficial outcome; we would have the same basis of action against the forced speech, but good reason to let the situation take its course.

Of course, because the aggressor is no less a rational agent despite his wrongful action, he remains within the scope of morality. If he has a heart attack on our doorstep we have whatever obligation we ever have to call an ambulance (and to tell him the truth about the help that's available). Nor are we free to do just anything in the service of moral policing; its tools are subject to the same prohibitions as the actions it targets. That is why it matters that the defensive false speech not be like the altruistic lie, an attempt to redirect the aggressor (by exploiting the truth presumption as a means of taking control of his reasoning and action) for the good end of saving our friend's life.[66] But if the aggressor's own reasoning deforms the speech situation, suspending the truth presumption, we are not in the condition of the ordinary wrongful lie. Our false speech would impede him in reasoning through to his violent purpose, but it need not aim at hijacking his will, and therefore does not share the wrong of the ordinary lie. It's a lie, but perhaps not a wrongful lie.

Although it is the aggressor's creation of the forced speech situation that signals the change in presumption, if, without increasing the risk to the victim, we can manage without the lie, we should.[67]

---

[66] It is this assumption of authority over the course of the aggressor's reasoning that makes the altruistic liar partly responsible for any new risks.

[67] I am indebted here to Collin O'Neil for his insightful work on the moral differences between the lie direct and the constrained misdirection in other forms of misleading speech (see his *The Ethics of Communication*, UCLA Ph.D. Dissertation, 2007).

There is a point to being silent, or to speaking uninformatively, if one can. Such often-mocked casuistical maneuvers show respect for the truth presumption, and have the additional moral advantage of shifting the burden to the hearer, who bears responsibility for the morally compromised circumstances. Still, because the circumstances of action are not truth-demanding, and practical exigencies may leave little room for moral finesse, the straight lie may be without fault. Reasoned to from the common end, it honors rather than betrays what Kant calls 'the supreme rightful condition in statements'.[68]

We thus approach the conclusion that appropriately conceived false speech can be morally permitted, perhaps even required. It would be morally on a par with other kinds of prevention that impede the completion of bad reasoning in wrongful action. Harking back to the example of compelled civil union, we might draw on an analogy with the policing acts of the state whose justification is that they are 'a hindering of a hindrance to freedom.'

There is, however, an apparent disanalogy between the necessary end in the argument for compelled civil union and the status of the common end and so of our entitlement to address the malfeasor as its agent. In the argument for civil union, something that the agent necessarily wills (property) has civil union as its necessary (and so omnilateral) condition. But what would count here as such prior willing? While the truth presumption belongs to both obligatory ends (neither towards our own nor others' rational well-being can we be indifferent to the conditions of correct reasoning), an obligatory end is, *qua* end, an agent's end only if she adopts it. The truth presumption *is* necessary to communicative discourse, and so to (human) rational willing in general; it is not a necessary condition of speech as such and so not necessarily willed by all. What I think we should say is that since each of us has necessary and sufficient reason to adopt obligatory ends—that's part of what it is for an end to be obligatory—we are entitled to

---

[68] 'A Supposed Right to Lie', 8: 429. This is as close as I can get to making sense of Kant's claim that we may not forgo truthfulness in speech for the sake of some contingent purpose. I think it is in fact quite close.

regard everyone, and so the malfeasor, *as if* he had the end: we impute it to him.[69]

Ends have three distinct normative roles. First, as our purposes, ends mark out targets of action; they are what we deliberate *from*. Unless an agent adopts an end, he cannot reason from it to action. Second, ends represent standards, or regulative rules for action: reason itself gives a regulative end, imposing norms of consistency, order, and justification. And third, ends indicate the kinds of reasons agents can offer that shape acceptable interactions. Normally, when someone says 'no' to an end, he has reasons that warrant our respecting his decision. But someone who refuses to adopt the end of helping others isn't thereby free from moral criticism. And the murderer-at-the-door has no reasons for refusing the common end that should concern us. In imputing the common end, we engage the second and third normative elements, and take them to warrant our acting *as if* the first were true as well.

Imputing an end is not such a strange thing to do. Seeing a geyser of water erupting from the front of your house, I enter your property to shut off the main valve to prevent flooding, though I don't actually know you care to protect your house (you might be flooding it yourself to collect insurance, or turning your house into a performance piece). I act because it is reasonable to assume you do have the end it is ordinary to have in such circumstances. I regard myself as acting on your behalf, completing the reasoning to action you would make for your ends were you here. If there is a gap, it is an epistemic one. But when, as in the earlier case, I use what is yours to save your child from drowning in your pool, while again I don't know what you want or intend, the assumptions I make about your end are not bridging an epistemic gap; there is no gap. It is not just reasonable to assume you have the end, it is an end you (morally) *must* have. We are warranted in imputing it to you. If, in turning off your water, I've

---

[69] The doctrine of imputation in Kant's *Metaphysics of Morals* (6: 227–8) is about actions and their consequences, not ends. I extend the use of this term because with the idea of imputing ends I want to argue that certain moral conditions explain when it is right to say that a standard applies to a will. Imputing other content derived from obligatory ends is possible, but isn't relevant here to the justification of the defensive lie.

made a mistake about your artistic ambition, I should apologize. It's a reasonable error. Perhaps you ought to have warned me that you were doing something so unusual.[70] There's no such mistake (or warning) possible in the drowning case: your wanting the insurance from your child's accidental death does not introduce any reasons that need to be overcome when I act.

We sometimes impute an end as a way of making sense of someone's practical reasoning (as the best account of what is affecting or shaping her reasoning). We also impute hidden motives and unacknowledged ambitions; we impute meaning to speech that is not entirely from the agent, but belongs to context or a dominant ideology (in some circumstances, we impute insensitivity at the telling of a tasteless joke).[71] We hold people in various jobs and offices to standards, criticizing them for failure, without regard to their volitional commitment: that is, given a role, we may impute ends. Imputed ends are one way of explaining what entitles us to integrity in a banker, or to reasonable care in a technician handling our x-rays—regardless of what they in fact will, we are right to complain about the person when the integrity or the care are absent.[72] This is not to say that imputed ends are just as good as the real thing. Where an end is merely imputed, an agent can fail, or reason badly, but unless it actually is her end, she cannot reason well.

So I think we may properly impute the common end to the murderer. He has no reason, in this case, or in general, that would defeat the imputation: he has sufficient reason to adopt the end, and no good reason not to. We therefore do him no disrespect as a reasoner in acting towards him as if he shared the end.

[70] The more we see morality, or parts of it, as a common project, the more responsibility we have for flagging special contexts. Insurance fraud, by contrast, is not an end that warrants deference.

[71] Judgments of negligence often involve imputation, but what is imputed is knowledge of a morally relevant action-guiding fact; the end is not in dispute.

[72] Although an agent may not embrace the standard for action, we can say it belongs to her in the imputed sense, and her reasoning to action is subject to criticism if it is not consistent with what follows from the imputed end. With respect to an end that is merely imputed, an agent can fail, or reason badly, but unless it is her end, she cannot reason well.

Now, one thing I have not discussed about obligatory ends is the fact that the duties they give rise to are imperfect. Although the obligatory end that directs us to the (rational) well-being of others implies that no one's well-being can in principle be a matter of indifference to us, because the duty is imperfect, we each act for the end in different ways, on different occasions. Imperfect duties introduce a kind of division of labor — each of us has a role, set by our location, our relationships, and our resources, in the service of the end.[73] It might then seem that little can be said in advance about how we are each to act for the sake of the common end, and that suggests that the *imputed* end is idle: it could never be the basis of (even counterfactual) reasoning to action for the agent to whom it is only imputed. Indeed, it might seem hard even to mount criticism in its name.

But the common end is not idle. The same grounds that we have for imputing the end at all are sufficient to support a *general* duty of truthfulness in communication: the normal truth presumption that is a condition of human rational well-being generally. (That is, any sound reason we may have to lie will not be when the conditions of the truth presumption apply.) That is why, whether or not it causes harm, the advantage lie is wrong: it misuses the presumption as a private source of power over others. In the case at hand, the misuse occurs in the creation of a context of forced speech, when nothing the speaker can say in response is consistent with moral ends. So the standard of the common end applies. As agents of the common end we are then warranted in intervening for its sake; our targeted deception is a reassertion of its authority.

This gives us a rather distinctive account of what the justified lie accomplishes. The malfeasor is prevented from acting contrary to the conditions of an imputed end — not an end he has, but an end that we are entitled to use as a standard of judgment for his reasoning. More specifically, the intervention targets an inappropriate chain of reasoning that gives rise to an illegitimate demand on shared conditions of speech — illegitimate from both parties' points of view (one actual,

---

[73] In this way obligatory ends shape all of our lives, but don't give all lives the same shape.

one imputed). The false speech does not force the faulty reasoner into conformity with good reasoning (again, *he* has to reason correctly for that); nor can it bring him to act in light of the imputed obligatory end he has failed to adopt. The aim of the speech is to create an impediment to the completion of his reasoning. The impeding shows no disrespect, either for the reasoning or for the reasoner, because the malfeasor has no reason for what he would do that can be respected. If he were sliding on ice towards danger to himself or harm to another, I could respectfully impede his progress. In this case, we would impede an attempt to cross a boundary of protection for truthful speech.

Clearly, this is a narrow result. It does not show that we can lie to prevent harms. It does not show that there is an exception to a truth-telling principle for the sake of protecting a life. It does not justify an exception to a rule against lying. What we learn is that an end or value that normally calls for truth-telling (making it our default position) in this context does not: the factual premises in the case involve a misuse of the truth presumption that then alters the deliberative outcome. The value content of an obligatory end works down the chain of reasoning to permit or require resistance to the misuse of the truth conditions of speech. It thereby tells us how we are to understand and so justify this lie.

If the forced speech feature is absent, the reasoning to an intervention would perforce be different. Suppose one is not compelled to speak; may one volunteer a lie with the aim of sending the murderer elsewhere? Since in such a case one makes use of the truth presumption as a means to exercise power over others, then no. (Thus the claim that once one uses a lie to orchestrate events, one assumes some responsibility for bad outcomes to which the lie contributes. No such shift occurs in the forced speech situation.) An altruistic lie is not morally different than altruistic acts that involve physical detention, constraint or injury. Nothing in the content of the obligatory end yields permission to exercise intrusive power over another. With the justified lie to the murderer, by contrast, the agent acts, as he always should, as an agent of the common end, his targeted false speech a reassertion of its authority.

Reasoning from obligatory ends we *can* have moral cause to make someone's deliberation and so his action more difficult. We tell him that his action will impair our friendship in the hope that this fact will affect his deliberations, not just as a disincentive but as cause to rethink. We can stagger information in the hope that having to wait will create an occasion for clearer-headed deliberation. We prevaricate. The aim is to keep things open and avert danger; as a private agent, we are not entitled to seize another and author his future.

But suppose it all goes wrong. To stop the murderer we would have to disable, confine, or hurt him. What I would say, though can't argue for it here, is this. If an agent of the state — the police, for example — could intervene with force, we may also. Not, however, as private agents pursuing good ends, but as surrogates for public authority when it is not available, and for public ends (we would act to disable the aggressor for the sake of public order). The model is the citizen's arrest, where force is used, but not immoral means. A private agent who uses force does something wrong because there is no valid route from the moral content of his good end to the use of force; the public action, however, has its source in the work of the state which allows for the use of force. Though externally the same, the public and the private actions have different moral content. The rejoinder that the private use of force cannot be impermissible because no one could have good reason to prevent the intervention mistakes other public reasons (a prosecutor's discretion, for example) for moral justification. But these are difficult matters, and for another time.

The purpose of engaging in this lengthy casuistical exercise was to illustrate what can happen when we have obligatory ends at the head of a chain of reasoning to action: a wider range of means is morally allowed, even some we would have thought were ruled out, and consequences are shown to count without ceding ground to moral instrumentalism. Until the casuistry is more fully elaborated, we won't know whether the route through obligatory ends offers enough to accommodate the moral intuitions that Kantian theory has seemed to ignore. But even this fragment of an account is rich enough in resources to encourage the project of a unified (non-hybrid) interpretation of Kant's ethics.

How I Am Not a Kantian

T. M. Scanlon[74]

On What Matters begins with a vigorous defense of a cognitivist and value-based account of reasons. It ends with a striking claim of a convergence between Kantian, Consequentialist and Contractualist moral theories. In these comments I will concentrate on the relation between these two parts of Parfit's rich and provocative book.

Questions about reasons are fundamental to Parfit's conclusion because the theories whose convergence is in question all characterize right and wrong in terms of what people have reason to want, or could rationally do. The three theories Parfit is considering are:

> *the Kantian Contractualist Formula*: Everyone ought to follow the principles whose universal acceptance everyone could rationally will.

> *Scanlon's Formula*: An act is wrong if it would be disallowed by any principle that no one could reasonably reject.

> *Kantian Rule Consequentialism*: Everyone ought to follow the principles that are optimific, because these are the only principles that everyone could rationally will to be universal laws.

Parfit acknowledges that the two theories he labels 'Kantian' diverge from what Kant himself said. But he regards this as no objection to what he is doing. 'We are asking,' he writes, 'whether Kant's ideas can help us to decide which acts are wrong, and help to explain why these acts are

---

[74] I am grateful to Parfit for many discussions of these issues as well as for helpful comments on an earlier version of this paper.

wrong. If we can revise Kant's formulas in a way that improves them, we are developing a Kantian moral theory' (*Volume One, 298*).

I agree that it can be a valuable project to develop a moral theory that is similar to Kant's in some ways but departs from it in others. But I believe that one of the ways in which the theories Parfit lays out diverge from Kant's own view deserves attention. The degree to which Parfit's conclusion should seem surprising depends to a certain extent on how close the theories he is discussing are to Kant's. More important, an examination of one way in which these theories differ from Kant's will bring out some of the difficulties faced by an account of reasons of the kind that Parfit and I favor, and hence also by a moral theory based on such an account.

I will not engage in detailed exegesis of Kant's texts, but will base my discussion of these issues on a few broad claims about Kant's view of rationality and morality which I hope are relatively uncontroversial. For simplicity, I will concentrate on Kant's Formula of Universal Law, and on Kant's discussion of this formula in his *Groundwork of the Metaphysics of Morals*. A full discussion would need to take into account other formulations of the Categorical Imperative as well as what Kant says in other works. But this will suffice for the mainly comparative points that I want to make.

I begin with an observation about the way in which Kant sees the Categorical Imperative as authoritative for us. What he says in Section 3 of the *Groundwork* is that when we are deciding what to do we must *see* the Categorical Imperative as our highest level principle of practical reasoning insofar as we see ourselves as acting at all. If we take any other principle to be fundamental for us, then we cannot see ourselves as acting but only as the slaves of factors acting on us. This claim depends in turn on Kant's argument, in Section 2 of the *Groundwork*, that there can be only one categorical imperative (that is, that any principle other than the one he has presented could influence an agent only though its appeal to his or her inclinations.) Thus, in Kant's view it is only if one takes the Categorical Imperative as the fundamental principle of practical reasoning that one can see oneself as *deciding* what to do rather than merely being determined by one's inclinations.

Turning now from the authority of the Categorical Imperative to its content, the Formula of Universal Law says that one should act only on a maxim that one could will to be a universal law. I believe that the best interpretation of what Kant means by a maxim's being a universal law is for everyone to believe it to be permissible to act on that maxim, and to act on it when they are so inclined. The crucial questions in determining what this formula requires are thus: (1) what, in Kant's view, would prevent a maxim from even being a universal law in this sense, and (2) what would make it the case that a maxim could not be willed to be such a law.[75]

Kant's idea seems to be that a maxim 'cannot be a universal law' in the sense he has in mind if the plan of action it describes would be incoherent in the event that people's attitudes were of the kind that this universal law describes. The 'contradiction' that he is appealing to is thus between the presuppositions of the plan of action that the maxim describes and the conditions that would obtain if this maxim were a universal law. The most plausible example of this is Kant's case of the lying promise: making a promise would not be an effective way of getting the money one desires if everyone believed that having made such a promise was no constraint on anyone's future conduct. Parfit may be right that the terms 'contradiction' and 'cannot be a universal law' are not the best way to put this point. But I think it is reasonably clear what Kant has in mind.

Parfit's understanding of the idea of something's being rationally willed to be a universal law is different from Kant's as I interpret him. When Parfit asks, in interpreting the various formulae he discusses, whether an action or principle is one that someone could rationally will, he understands this as a question about the reasons that person has, and their relative strengths. One can rationally will something, on his

---

[75] Parfit discusses these questions in sections 40 and 41 respectively. My interpretations of these Kantian ideas differ slightly from his. The claim that it is wrong to act on a maxim that one could not rationally will to be a universal law in the sense I have just described is similar to what Parfit calls the *Law of Nature Formula* except that it substitutes for the phrase 'and acts on it when they can' the phrase 'and acts on it when they are so inclined'. My version of the claim differs from what Parfit calls the *Moral Belief Formula* because it requires one to be able to will not only that everyone believes it to be permissible to act on the maxim in question, but that they also act on it when they are so inclined.

view, if one has sufficient reason to do so; one cannot rationally will it
if one's reasons not to will it are stronger than one's reasons to will it
(*285*). Kant's idea of what one can will is different. When he considers
the question of whether a given maxim could or could not be willed
to be a universal law Kant seems not to appeal at all, or at least not in
a fundamental way, to reasons or their relative strength.[76] Indeed, the
idea of a reason and of the strength of a reason have at most a derivative
role in Kant's account of rational action and morality.[77]

When Kant says that a maxim could not be willed to be a universal
law, what he means is that willing such a law (willing that everyone act
on the maxim should he or she be so inclined and believe that others will
do this as well) would be incompatible with viewing oneself as a rational
agent. For example, Kant claims that a maxim of developing one's
talents only insofar as one finds this pleasant or attractive, or a maxim
of helping others only if it happens to please one, could not be willed
to be universal laws, because in willing these laws one would be willing
that one give, and that others give, no intrinsic weight to the existence of
general conditions that are necessary to the pursuit of our ends. To be a
rational agent, however, is to have ends, and one cannot (without being
irrational) have ends yet be indifferent to the conditions necessary for
their pursuit. The 'contradiction' that Kant has in mind is thus grounded
in the same thing that (as I maintained earlier) Kant believes grounds
the authority of the Categorical Imperative itself, namely the views one
must take insofar as one sees oneself as a rational agent.

Kant's claims about what the Formula of Universal law requires are
thus not based on claims about what reasons individuals have, or about
the relative strength of these reasons. When his claim is that a certain

---

[76] To act on a maxim is to act for a certain reason. So in asking whether
one could will that people act on, or be permitted to act on a maxim, the idea
of a reason for action figures in what one is asking *about*. What I am saying is
that for Kant such questions are not to be *answered* by appeal to the reasons
an agent has.

[77] In an earlier version of the manuscript that became this book, Parfit
expressed surprise that Kant seemed not to employ the idea of a reason
in the normative sense in which Parfit understands it. My point here is
that this observation was correct in a way, but less surprising than it might
at first appear.

maxim could not *be* a universal law (as in the case of the lying promise), the question of what one can will does not even arise. When his claim is that we cannot *will* a maxim to be a universal law (such as a maxim of indifference to the development of our talents, or to the needs of others), his claim is not that the reasons we have not to will such laws are stronger than those in favor of doing so. What Kant says is rather that insofar as we see ourselves as rational agents we cannot see the development of our talents or the needs of others as considerations that in themselves count for nothing. The claims that provide the basis for Kant's arguments are claims about rationality—about the attitudes we must hold insofar as we are not irrational—not claims about the reasons we have.[78] Accordingly, the *conclusions* of these arguments are also claims that we must, insofar as we are not irrational, *see* these things—the development of our talents and the needs of others—as providing reasons for action rather than substantive claims about the reasons we have.

I should note, however, that as I have interpreted Kant's arguments about what one can will to be a universal law, their conclusions make only the most minimal claim about the strength we must see certain considerations as having. The claim is just that we cannot take these considerations—the development of our own talents and the needs of others—as counting for nothing (apart from their appeal to our inclinations). If this interpretation is correct, and this minimal conclusion is all that Kant's argument yields, then it is left up to each person to determine (depending, I suppose, on his or her inclinations) how much weight to give to these considerations. But perhaps Kant's argument actually yields a stronger conclusion. Perhaps Kant could establish that a person who sees him- or herself as a rational agent cannot consistently will a maxim of not helping others or doing what

---

[78] I discuss this distinction further in 'Reasons: A Puzzling Duality?', in R. Jay Wallace, Philip Pettit, Samuel Scheffler, and Michael Smith, eds., *Reason and Value: Themes from the Moral Philosophy of Joseph Raz* (New York: Oxford University Press, 2004), 231–46, and in 'Structural Irrationality', in Geoffrey Brennan, Robert Goodin, Frank Jackson, and Michael Smith, eds., *Common Minds: Essays in Honor of Philip Pettit* (Oxford: Oxford University Press, 2007).

is required to develop his or her talents when these aims come into conflict with certain considerations of convenience or comfort.

It might seem that in order to establish such a conclusion Kant would have to appeal to premises about the relative strength of reasons: that is, it would have to rest on a claim that the possibility of enjoying the forms of convenience or comfort in question is not a sufficient reason for failing to develop one's talents in certain ways, or for failing to aid someone else in a certain way. But from the Kantian point of view as I am interpreting it this would be to get things backwards. Claims about reasons (more exactly, about what a person must see as reasons) must be grounded in claims about rational agency, claims about what attitudes a person can take, consistent with seeing herself as a rational agent. Justification never runs in the other direction, from claims about reasons to claims about what rationality requires.

This view, which I will call Kantian constructivism about reasons, seems to me to be a fundamental feature of Kantian ethical theories, distinguishing them from other views that resemble Kant's in some ways. In particular, as I have said, it distinguishes Kant's view from all of the moral views that Parfit discusses in Part Three of *On What Matters*. All of these views, including those described as Kantian, appeal to an idea of 'what one can rationally will' that presupposes an independently understandable notion of the reasons that a person has and their relative strength. So there is one sense in which none of these views is Kantian: none of them accepts Kantian constructivism about reasons. This divergence raises questions facing in two directions. Negatively, why *not* accept Kantian constructivism about reasons? Positively, what can be said in defense of the alternative conception of reasons that Parfit employs, and that I myself would also favor?

On the negative side, Parfit raises objections to what he calls Kant's Impossibility Formula, according to which it is wrong to act on maxims that could not even *be* universal laws.[79] These objections mainly take the form of arguments that Kant's remarks about what could not be a universal law cannot be interpreted in a way that avoids intuitively implausible implications about moral right and wrong. I agree with

---

[79] See Section 40.

many of the points Parfit makes here, although I would put them in a somewhat different way.

The 'contradiction in conception' test[80] is intuitively appealing because it seems to capture the idea that it is wrong to exempt oneself from the moral requirements that apply to everyone else. Many wrongs do fit this pattern: if certain constraints are needed to provide some essential public good (or to prevent some serious 'public bad'), and people are generally complying with such constraints, then it is wrong to free ride on their compliance by exempting oneself from these constraints. But Kant's test does not track this idea in a reliable way.

The class of actions that Kant's test captures are ones in which an agent's plan of action presupposes that others believe that everyone is bound by constraints that rule out action of the kind that the agent is going to perform. The problem is that by focusing on the relation between an agent's action and what that action presupposes about the beliefs and intentions of others this test bypasses the question of whether the constraints in question are indeed justified. (This may be part of the appeal of Kant's test: it seems to provide a criterion of wrongness that can be applied without asking messy questions about the relative strength of reasons.) But the question of justification is essential. If the constraint that others take to be binding is in fact groundless (a mere taboo, for example) then it may not be wrong to violate this constraint, even if the success of one's action depends on the fact that most others take that constraint seriously. On the other hand, when constraints are necessary and justified, then it is wrong to violate them whether or not the success of *this very action* depends on the fact that others take these constraints to be binding and generally observe them. Everything depends on the need for the constraints in question, not merely on whether the success of one's action depends on their being generally observed.

What is commonly called Kant's 'contradiction in the will' test might be called upon to answer this question of justification. The idea would be that to determine whether a constraint is justified we should ask

---

[80] Parfit refers to this test as 'Kant's actual version of his Impossibility Formula' (*14, 277*).

whether one could will that it be generally believed to be permissible to violate this constraint when this suits one's purposes. As Parfit says, this criterion of justifiability is similar to the version of contractualism that I myself have proposed.

One way in which Kant's criterion appears to differ from mine, and Parfit's, is in focusing simply on whether *the agent* could will a principle permitting what he or she proposes to do, rather than on whether there is anyone who could reasonably reject a principle permitting such actions, or whether everyone could will the universal acceptance of such a principle. The question here is how a mode of thinking about right and wrong is to be sensitive to the interests of other people. Different theories solve this problem in different ways.

I believe that on the best interpretation of the way Kant understands his Formula of Universal Law, when we ask whether an agent could will his maxim to be a universal law what we are asking is whether he could will that people be universally permitted to act on such a maxim, where this universality includes situations in which the agent occupies any of the positions involved — for example, situations in which the agent is a person in need of help as well as ones in which he or she is the one called upon to give it. Assuming that this idea is intelligible, and that if the agent were in one of these other positions he or she would have the same reasons as a person who is actually in that position, this test would seem to lead to the same result as asking, as Parfit suggests, whether *everyone* could will this universal permission. Even if this is so, however, I agree with Parfit that it makes things clearer to avoid counterfactuals about the agent's being in different positions and to keep clearly in view the fact that we are dealing with different persons, by asking what everyone in these other positions could will, or could reasonably reject.

Another possible divergence from Kant arises when we consider how the idea of what someone could rationally will is to be understood. One might object to Kant's account of this idea on the ground that its implications about the reasons we have are inadequate or implausible. I have mentioned two objections of this kind. The first is that Kant's account yields only conclusions about what individuals must see as reasons, insofar as they are not irrational. It seems to me, however, that there are true substantive claims about the reasons we have that are different from claims of this kind and cannot be derived from them. Second, leaving aside the difference between these two kinds of claims, I do not believe that the idea of rational agency is rich enough to yield all the claims about reasons that seem evidently correct.

Going beyond objections of this kind, however, if we are going to reject Kant's account we need to consider the deeper question of where his argument for the Categorical Imperative as the limiting ground of the reasons we have goes wrong, if it does go wrong. Here I would cite Kant's claim that accepting the Categorical Imperative as one's highest level principle of practical reasoning is the only way in which one can see oneself as acting independent of inclination. This claim strikes me as untenable. I do not see why an agent cannot see him or herself as 'active' in making judgments about which considerations constitute reasons.[81]

Kant offers a top-down conception of reasons (or at least of our states of taking things to be reasons.) In his view, claims about reasons are grounded in the requirements of rational agency. If this account is rejected, the alternative might seem to be a 'bottom up' conception, according to which practical reasoning begins with claims about particular reasons and their relative strengths and proceeds 'upward' from there to conclusions about what we have most reasons to do or to think, taking all the relevant reasons into account. A desire-based theory of reasons for action would at least appear to be of this form. Such a view holds that if doing X would promote the satisfaction of some desire that an agent has, then that agent has at least a *pro tanto* reason to do X. What an agent has most reason to do all things considered is determined by balancing these various, and possibly conflicting, reasons.

Parfit considers and rejects desire-based theories in his Chapters 3 and 4. What provides us with reasons for action, he says, are not desires but the various facts about certain aims and acts that make them relevantly good, or worth achieving. Reasons are provided by

---

[81] It might be suggested that one can avoid these problems, and also provide the basis for a more extensive set of reasons, by appealing to Kant's Formula of Humanity—ie. to the idea that each person must regard his or her own rational nature (and that of others as well) as an end in itself. I do not believe that this line of argument is any more successful than the one I have sketched, but it would take me too far afield to examine it here.

considerations such as the fact that doing X would injure someone, or would save someone's life. This seems right to me. But when we focus simply on such considerations, considered individually, as ultimate reason-providers, a bottom-up view can be made to seem implausible. Do we really want to claim, it might be asked, that such considerations, in addition to their physical and psychological properties can have the additional normative property of providing a reason of a certain strength, and that the basis of practical reasoning lies in detecting these properties? Put in this way, this does seem odd. But the oddness results, I believe, from the fact that this way of putting things ignores several crucial aspects of reasons.

One thing that seems odd about this atomistic formulation is that it leaves out the relational character of reasons, and their dependence on context. A certain consideration does not provide a reason of a certain sort, full stop. It provides a reason for an agent, in a certain situation, to take a certain action, or to have a certain attitude. The same consideration can provide different reasons in this fuller sense depending on the agent, situation, and attitude involved. Similarly, the 'strength' of a reason — that is to say, the way in which one consideration can override, undermine, or be overridden or undermined by other considerations — depends on the context within which a decision is being made.

A desire-based theory gains some of its plausibility from the fact that it has a certain relational structure built in. A desire is a desire *for* a certain content, but it is also the desire *of* a particular agent, a desire of a particular strength, and it provides reason for different actions depending on that agent's situation. One weakness of a desire-based theory is that the relational structure that it provides is too limited. Insofar as a desire is just a desire of a certain strength for a certain outcome, it provides reasons for actions that would promote that outcome. But not all reasons are goal-directed in this way, and we have reasons for things other than actions. An adequate account of reasons needs to accommodate these facts.

The contrast with the atomistic realism I mentioned earlier brings out another feature of desire-based theories that should be noted, which is that their 'bottom-up' character is more apparent than real. Desires derive their reason giving force because they are the desires of some desiring agent. In this respect a desire-based theory is similar to the Kantian view, but it focuses on a different aspect of agency and, at least as I have formulated it, yields conclusions about the reasons that an agent has, rather than about what an agent must see as a reason insofar as he or she is rational.

But even if a desire-based theory offers a top-down account of the source of reasons, its account of the process of practical reasoning remains bottom-up: it sees practical reasoning as beginning with our experience of individual desires and their strength. An atomistic realism about reasons that preserved this bottom-up character would share this implausibility. We do not experience considerations one by one as reasons with a certain strength. Rather, to regard one consideration is a stronger reason than another is to see it as more important *in regard to a certain type of decision in a certain context.* For example, whether the fact that it would be fun to make a certain remark counts as a strong reason for making it depends on the context, on what my aims and responsibilities are, and on my relation with the others present. Moreover, judgments about reasons and their importance are subject to requirements of consistency: if I judge A to be a reason for some action in one context, and a stronger reason than B, then I must judge this to be so in other contexts and for other agents as well, unless I can cite some relevant difference between these situations.

This discussion suggests several conclusions about what an adequate account of reasons must be like: It must preserve the idea that questions about reasons arise for, and are about, agents facing certain decisions. Second, it must be holistic in the way just described: judgments about particular reasons and their relative strengths depend on an overall view of the reasons we have. The strength of the Kantian view lies in its recognition of these important points. But an account of reasons must be substantive: it must include claims about the reasons that agents have, rather than merely about what they must see as reasons. And these claims cannot be derived solely from the agents' desires or from the mere fact that they are rational agents. If I am correct about this, then an adequate account of reasons will be a kind of substantive holism.

I turn now to Parfit's striking claim, in his Chapter 16, that Contractualism and Rule Consequentialism converge or, more exactly, that what he calls Kantian Contractualism will coincide with Rule Consequentialism. I hope that an examination of his careful arguments will help to bring out what is distinctive about a Contractualist theory of the kind I have proposed, and how such a theory would differ from Rule Consequentialism even if the two were to support the same principles.

I will begin with what Parfit calls *the Kantian Contractualist Formula*:

Everyone ought to follow the principles whose universal acceptance everyone could rationally will.

As I have said, Parfit understands the question of what someone could rationally will as a question about what is supported by the overall balance of reasons that that person has. In his view, an agent can rationally will that certain principles be universally accepted just in case he or she has sufficient reason to will this. So the interpretation of the Kantian Contractualist Formula depends, as Parfit says, on claims about reasons and rationality. This formula will yield definite answers about what we ought to do in a given case only if there is a single principle (applicable to our situation) which everyone has sufficient reason to will to be universally accepted. Parfit calls this the uniqueness condition (358). Given some views of the reasons a person has, this condition will not be fulfilled because there will be no principles that everyone has sufficient reason to will. Perhaps Rational Egoism is an example of such a view.[82]

Different moral theories deal with this problem in different ways. Rawls assumes that people will lack concern for how others fare (they will be 'mutually disinterested'), but requires that they choose principles behind a veil of ignorance. My own version of contractualism deals with the problem by making particular stipulations about the reasons that are relevant to the choice of principles and the ways that these are to be

[82] As Parfit argues. David Gauthier might disagree.

considered.[83] The view that Parfit calls Kantian Contractualism makes neither of these moves. On this view, what we ought morally to do depends on what everyone could rationally will, with full information about their situation and taking into account all the reasons they in fact have. Parfit believes that the uniqueness condition is fulfilled 'sufficiently often' (358) because the reasons people have include impartial reasons as well as personal and partial ones.

Impartial reasons, he says, are reasons we see that we have when we consider matters from an impartial point of view—that is to say, without considering our own place in a situation. We take such a view when, for example, we are, or suppose ourselves to be, merely an outside observer of what happens rather than one of the people whose well-being, or that of others to whom they have close ties, will be affected by it. Central among these impartial reasons are reasons to care about the well-being of others, but our impartial reasons may also include reasons to care about things other than individuals' welfare. Parfit argues that we have these same impartial reasons when we consider matters from our own personal perspective (135). What the shift to the personal perspective does is merely to add personal and partial reasons to the impartial ones.[84]

A decision about what someone can rationally will must take all of these reasons into account. In some cases, the impartial reasons may predominate: one would not have sufficient reason to do something that would lead to the death of many people just to avoid scratching one's finger. In other cases the opposite will be true: one would not have sufficient reason to sacrifice one's life to prevent the scratching of one other person's finger (or, I would say, any number of persons' fingers.)

---

[83] Restricting these to what I call 'personal reasons'. See *What We Owe to Each Other*, 218–23.

[84] This brings out the fact that the idea of a 'point of view' is merely an expository device, a way of focusing our attention. Impartial reasons are not the reasons we *have* from a certain point of view. They are reasons we have *independent of* our particular relation to their objects, in contrast to personal reasons (to care about ourselves) or partial reasons (to care about others to whom we stand in certain special relations). When we 'take up the impartial point of view' we ignore these relations, and thus are aware only of reasons that do not depend on them.

But Parfit believes that there are many cases in which neither kind of reasons predominate in this way. In such cases, he writes,

> When one of our two possible acts would make things go in some way that would be impartially better, but the other act would make things go better either for ourselves or for those to whom we have close ties, we often have sufficient reasons to act in either of these ways (137).

Parfit believes that the uniqueness condition is fulfilled 'sufficiently often' because there are certain principles that everyone has sufficient impartial reason to will to be universally accepted, even though they may have personal and partial reasons to prefer other principles.

Parfit defines the idea of 'best outcome' in terms of the idea of impartial reason. We should call an outcome 'best', he writes, just in case it is 'the outcome that, from an impartial point of view, everyone would have most reason to want' (372). He does not say very much about which outcomes will be best in the sense he defines. In particular, he leaves it open to what degree this idea of bestness will be aggregative: will an outcome containing a greater sum of well-being be better than one which contains less aggregate well-being no matter how well-being is distributed in the two situations? For example, will a situation in which there is greater total well-being count as better if this total is produced by significant costs to a few people which however bring small benefits to a very great number? As Parfit sets things up, this will depend on whether people have impartial reasons for favoring one of these states over the other. This leaves open the possibility that conception of best outcome he is defining is in important respects non-aggregative.

Using the notion of best outcome, Parfit defines universal acceptance rule consequentialism as the view that

> Everyone ought to follow the principles whose universal acceptance would make things go best.

He argues that this view is a direct consequence of

> *the Kantian Contractualist Formula*: Everyone ought to follow the principles whose universal acceptance everyone could rationally will.

His argument for this proceeds as follows:[85]

Kantians could argue:

(A) Everyone ought to follow the principles whose universal acceptance everyone could rationally will, or choose.

(B) Everyone could rationally choose whatever they would have sufficient reasons to choose.

(C) There are some optimific principles whose universal acceptance would make things go best.

(D) These are the principles that everyone would have the strongest impartial reasons to choose.

(E) No one's impartial reasons to choose these principles would be decisively outweighed by any relevant conflicting reasons.

Therefore

(F) Everyone would have sufficient reasons to choose these optimific principles.

(G) There are no other significantly non-optimific principles that everyone would have sufficient reasons to choose.

Therefore

(H) It is only these optimific principles that everyone would have sufficient reasons to choose, and could therefore rationally choose.

Therefore

These are the principles that everyone ought to follow.

I do not dispute Parfit's conclusion about the relation between his Kantian Contractualism and Rule Consequentialism. What I want to

[85] 378–9.

concentrate on here is what this connection shows about the ways in which the structure of his Kantian Contractualism differs from the version of contractualism presented in my book.

Parfit says that according to Kantian Contractualism, in order to decide whether an action is permissible we must assess a principle that would permit it by conducting a number of thought experiments, one for each person. In each of these we ask whether one of these persons could rationally will a principle that would permit such an action. This question is to be answered by considering both the person's personal and partial reasons and his or her impartial reasons. Suppose that the person's impartial reasons support accepting the principle. If the person has personal or partial reasons for not accepting the principle, the question we are to ask is whether, despite these reasons, the person nonetheless has sufficient reason to choose that everyone accept the principles that impartial reasons favor. As we have seen, Parfit holds that this might be true even if the person has sufficient reason to choose the principle that his or her personal and partial reasons favor.

According to my version of contractualism, deciding whether an action is right or wrong also involves a series of thought experiments. These consist in asking, in the case of each person considered, whether that person could reasonably reject a principle that would permit the action in question.[86] As in the previous case, suppose that one such person, call her *Green*, has personal reasons for rejecting the principle in question because of the burdens it would require her to bear. According to my version of contractualism, to decide whether Green could reasonably reject the principle we need to consider the opposing reasons that others, considered individually, have for wanting

---

[86] Parfit and I may take different views about the correct characterization of the 'individuals' whose reasons are to be considered. Although he does not say so explicitly, some of what he does say suggests that he has in mind actual persons affected by the action, or by the acceptance of the principle. In my case what we consider are not the reasons of actual persons but the 'generic' reasons that someone would have in virtue of occupying a certain role in regard to the principle in question, such as being the person who has relied on the assurance of others, or a person in need of help, or a person called upon to give it. I discuss this issue in *What We Owe to Each Other*, 202–6.

the principle to be accepted. This involves a further series of thought experiments, corresponding to the various ways that people might be affected by the principle in question. In each case we are to ask whether, given the reasons that a person in the position in question would have for wanting the principle to be accepted, it would still be reasonable for Green to reject it. The reasons that we consider here, in opposition to Green's personal reasons for rejecting the principle, *correspond* to reasons that Green would have if she took an impartial view of the situation, but there is a significant difference. In the form of contractualism that I have proposed, what we are to consider are not two kinds of reasons that Green might have (such as personal reasons and impartial ones) but, rather, the reasons that individuals in two different positions have: Green's reasons and those that a person would have who would be affected by the principle in a different way than Green would be.

The difference between these two ways of interpreting the reasons that someone might have for accepting a principle, or not rejecting it, can be illustrated by considering the way in which Parfit deals with a potential objection to his argument that Kantian Contractualism leads to Rule Consequentialism. Imagine a lifeboat case in which one is faced with the choice between saving five strangers and saving one's own child. Parfit believes that in such a case one would have decisive reason to save one's child. It may appear that optimific principles would require one to save the five strangers. If this were so then one might have decisive reason to reject these optimific principles, despite the impartial reasons in favor of willing their universal acceptance, contrary to premise (E) of Parfit's argument in the passage I have quoted above. Parfit responds as follows:

> The optimific principles would *not*, however, require you to save the strangers rather than your child. If everyone accepted and many people followed such a requirement, things would go in one way better, since more people's lives would be saved. But these good effects would be massively outweighed by the ways in which it would be worse if we all had the motives that such acts would need. For it to be true that we would

save several strangers rather than one of our own children,
our love for our children would have to be much weaker. The
weakening of such love would both be in itself bad, and have
many bad effects. Given these and some other similar facts,
the optimific principles would often permit us, and often
require us, to give some kinds of strong priority to our own
children's well-being (385).

This line of argument is familiar from the literature on consequential-ism.[87] It has a distinctively consequentialist flavor because it appeals to what would be best overall—the kind of outcome that everyone has most impartial reason to prefer. I make a similar point within my version of contractualism, but with an important difference.[88] Rather than appealing to the idea of the best outcome—what everyone has impartial reason to prefer—my argument was based on what each individual has reason to want for him- or herself. A principle requiring us always to give the needs of strangers the same weight as those of friends and family members would be one that each of us could reason-ably reject, because it would make impossible special relationships that we have strong reasons to want to have. Even if these two arguments lead to the same conclusion, and assign normative significance to the same facts about human life, they take these facts into account in different ways.

As I said above, according to my version of contractualism the considerations that we need to consider in order to decide whether it would be reasonable for Green to reject a principle take the form of reasons that others would have to want that principle to be accepted. In Parfit's Kantian Contractualism these considerations enter in the form of impartial reasons that Green has to want the principle to be accepted. But these are only some of the impartial reasons that could count in favor of Green's accepting the principle according to Parfit's Kantian Contractualism. Two differences are particularly significant. First, in addition to reasons corresponding to the reasons that other

---

[87] See e.g. Peter Railton, 'Alienation, Consequentialism, and the Demands of Morality', *Philosophy and Public Affairs*, 13 (1984), 134–71.

[88] See *What We Owe to Each Other*, 160–1.

individuals have to want things to go better for them, Green's impartial reasons as Parfit would describe them can include impartial reasons that Green has for wanting more people to be benefited rather than fewer, or for the aggregate benefit to be as great as possible. According to the version of contractualism described in my book, however, what is to be taken into account in assessing the reasonableness of a person's rejecting a principle are only the reasons that *each* affected person has for wanting that principle to be accepted. Aggregative considerations are not directly relevant. Second, my view excluded impersonal reasons such as those associated with the value of natural objects or works of art, considered apart from the benefits to individuals of being able to experience these things. But impartial reasons as Parfit describes them could include reasons of this kind.

These two differences may be seen as improvements over the view stated in my book, which seemed implausible to many because it excluded aggregative arguments and because it gave no weight to impersonal values in determining what is right or wrong. These objections could be dealt with by allowing reasons of these two kinds to be considered in determining whether a principle could be reasonably rejected.[89]

It is worth saying a little more here about the way in which the problem of aggregation is dealt with in Parfit's Kantian Contractualism, and therefore would be dealt with on this revised version of my view. The problem of aggregation is this. There are many cases in which what we should do, and even what it is permissible to do, seems to depend on the number of people who would be affected by the courses of action available to us. It seems that an adequate account of moral argument should make aggregative considerations relevant in these cases but do this in a way that does not support implausible aggregative arguments such as ones what would justify the killing or enslaving of a few people to make a huge number of people better off, each in a very small way.

[89] Parfit has previously urged that I should make this change by giving up my 'Individualist Restriction' on reasons for rejection. See his 'Justifiability to Each Person', in Philip Stratton-Lake, ed., *On What We Owe To Each Other* (Oxford: Blackwell, 2004), 67–8.

Parfit's proposal, as I understand it, is to deal with this as a problem about which outcomes are indeed 'best' (that is to say, ones that everyone has impartial reasons to prefer.) So he would say that in a case of the kind I have just considered the fact that aggregate well-being would be increased by enslaving a few people in order to benefit a great many people in small ways does not mean that a situation in which this was done would be one that we have impartial reason to prefer: the idea of 'best outcome' is sensitive to numbers, but is not strictly aggregative. I leave aside the question of how such an account of impartial reasons and 'best outcome' might be spelled out.

I have been discussing different views about the reasons that should be taken into account in deciding whether a principle is one that everyone could will to be universally accepted, or whether it is one that could reasonably be rejected. Let me turn now to the importance of the difference between these two ways of understanding the question we should ask in carrying out the thought experiments on which the rightness or wrongness of an action depends. According to Parfit's Kantian Contractualism one is to ask whether each person could rationally will that a principle permitting that action be universally accepted. On my view one is to ask whether every such principle would be one that someone could reasonably reject. How might the differences between these questions lead to different answers about which actions are right?

As we have seen, Parfit allows that there are many cases in which a person has sufficient impartial reasons to accept a principle but also sufficient self-interested reasons to refuse to do so. It seems possible that in some cases of this kind it would be reasonable for the person to reject the principle in question. It might be that the universal acceptance of the principle would involve a cost that the person would have sufficient reason to accept (it would not be like a case of losing one's life because this would prevent the scratching of someone else's finger.) But this would also be a cost that a person could reasonably refuse to make. If there are cases of this kind, then Kantian Contractualism would involve higher costs than my version of contractualism would.

It will be helpful to divide possible cases into two types. In cases of the first type, although following the optimific principle would involve a major cost to someone, another person would suffer an even graver loss if the optimific principle were not followed. In cases of the second type this is not so: the sacrifice required of one person by the optimific principle is greater than the loss that any other individual would suffer if everyone were to follow some non-optimific principle.

Here is a possible case of the first type.   Suppose that, in

> *Case One*, by giving some organ of his for transplant, *Grey* would be shortening his life by a few years. But by doing this he could give White, whom he does not know, many more years of life.

If this is so, then Grey would have sufficient impartial reason to donate the organ, and the outcome, if he were to do so, would be better in Parfit's impartial reason-involving sense. But Grey would also have sufficient self-interested reason not to make this donation. Moreover, it seems plausible to say that it would be reasonable for someone in Grey's position to reject a principle requiring this person to make such a donation.

Cases of the second type would involve two principles, P, which is optimific and imposes a high cost on people in the position of *Blue*, and Q which does not impose that high a cost on anyone (there is no one who would lose as much by a shift from universal acceptance of P to universal acceptance of Q as someone in Blue's position would gain from such a shift). If P is optimific, and everyone has impartial reasons to prefer its universal acceptance to the universal acceptance of Q, this is most likely because the aggregate benefits to various people in P is accepted outweigh the costs to people in Blue's position. Perhaps Q would permit us to save Blue's life at the cost of failing to prevent a large number of people from being paralyzed, whereas P would require the opposite. Or perhaps P would require us to prevent many people from losing a leg rather than saving Blue's life, as Q would permit. In order to know which of these cases would fit the pattern I have described, one would have to know how Parfit's notions of impartial reasons and 'best outcome' deal with aggregation. As I have said, this is not obvious. But presumably there will be some cases that fit the abstract pattern I have described.

These reflections have a bearing on Parfit's argument for the convergence of Rule Consequentialism and the two forms of Contractualism that he discusses. In this argument, he claims that everyone would have strong impartial reasons to choose that optimific principles be universally accepted, and that, because these reasons are not decisively outweighed by any conflicting reasons, everyone could rationally choose these principles. He then argues that, because there are no other significantly non-optimific principles that everyone could rationally choose, these optimific principles are the only ones whose universal acceptance everyone could rationally choose. When Parfit turns to my version of Contractualism, he then says that if certain optimific principles are the only ones whose universal acceptance everyone could rationally choose, this means that there are stronger objections to every other set of principles, and that if this is so then these optimific principles could not reasonably be rejected.

Suppose that optimific principles would require that we save many other people from smaller burdens rather than saving Blue's life. Though someone in Blue's position may have sufficient reasons to will the universal acceptance of these optimific principles, this person may also have sufficient reasons to will the acceptance of some non-optimific principle which would permit or require us to save Blue's life.

It might be that, taking only impartial reasons into account, everyone has stronger reason to will the acceptance of these optimific principles than to will the acceptance of some non-optimific principle that would require us to save Blue's life. This might also be put by saying that (considering only impartial reasons) there are 'stronger objections' to this alternative than to the optimific principle. But taking *all* reasons into account, someone in Blue's position might have a stronger objection to the optimific principle that would impose such a sacrifice on Blue than anyone would have to some non-optimific principles that did not impose such a sacrifice. If this is correct, then the fact that these alternative principles are open to stronger (impartial) objections need not mean that they are open to decisive objections and hence need not entail that the optimific principles could not be reasonably rejected.

If what I have just said is correct, then shifting from the question 'could anyone reasonably object to these principles being universally accepted' to the question 'could everyone rationally will that they be universally accepted' produces a moral theory that requires us to make significantly greater sacrifices, and permits or requires others to impose such greater sacrifices on us.

This move would, however, also solve a difficulty that arises for a contractualist view like mine in cases of the first type.[90] If someone in Grey's position could reasonably reject a principle requiring him to make the organ donation, why would it not follow that someone in the position of the proposed recipient could reasonably reject a principle permitting Grey not to make the donation? After all, the personal reason that this person has for objecting to such a principle seems at least as strong as Grey's reason for rejecting the more demanding principle, and the cost to Grey is less. This would seem to lead to a moral standoff, in which there is no right answer to the question of what one should do. Shifting to the 'what everyone could rationally will' (or concluding, with Parfit, that the reasonable rejection standard in fact collapses into this one) would solve this problem, albeit at a certain cost.[91]

Let me close by expression my agreement with a point that Parfit makes in his conclusion. Given its emphasis on impartial reasons and optimific principles, the Triple Theory that he proposes in his conclusion sounds (at least on first impression) more like consequentialism than my version of contractualism does. So one may question whether his Triple Theory is essentially a contractualist theory or a consequentialist one.

Parfit is correct, I believe, in saying that this theory is contractualist. Any plausible moral view makes what is right or wrong in many cases depend on the harms and benefits to individuals. A theory is consequentialist only if it takes the value of producing the best consequences to be the foundation of morality. Parfit's combined theory does not do this. According to that theory it matters whether the principles that would permit an action would be optimific. But this

[90] Thomas Nagel raises this problem in *The View From Nowhere* (New York: Oxford University Press, 1986), 50–1, 172.

[91] That is to say, it would solve the problem if in such situations there always is some principle that everyone could rationally will to be universally accepted (if the 'uniqueness condition' is fulfilled). This depends on the relative strength of impartial and self-interested reasons.

matters only because these are the principles that everyone has reason to will, and taking what can be justified to others—what they have reason to will—as the most fundamental moral idea is the essence of contractualism, at least as I have described it.

Recognizing the idea of justifiability to others as basic opens up a possibility that Parfit does not discuss, but which I think should not be neglected. Many people may be drawn to consequentialism because they see that there are some situations in which it the morally correct way to decide what to do is to figure out what would produce the best consequences overall. Decisions by public officials about what kind of hospitals to build may be a good example. Because producing the best consequences seems so obviously to be the right standard in these cases, people then infer that this idea is always morally basic. This seems to me to be a mistake: producing the best consequences might be the correct standard in these cases not because it is the basis of morality but because it is what is owed to people in situations of that kind, by agents who stand in a certain relation to them. Recognizing the contractualist idea of justification to others as morally basic allows us at least to raise the possibility that although what is owed to others in some situations is to follow the principles that would produce best consequences, impartially understood, this need not always be the case. In other cases our responsibilities and obligations may be different.

Of course it needs to be asked why this should be so, if it is so. And it might be responded that the cases in which it appears to be the case are in fact misleading: they are cases in which, because of the burdens of being impartial, *optimific* principles would permit people to decide what to do on a basis other than what would be impartially best. But, as I said earlier in discussing Parfit's treatment of partiality toward one's friends and relatives, there are two ways of describing such cases. Is partiality morally permitted because permitting it is impartially best? Or is it permitted because principles that demanded a higher level of impartiality would be ones that individuals could reasonably reject (for reasons that are not impartial)? The latter seems to me more plausible. In any event, this is a point where the residual tension between Rule Consequentialism and my version of contractualism seems to show itself.

PART FIVE

RESPONSES

18

On Hiking the Range

65 Actual and Possible Consent

Susan Wolf makes several claims that seem to me both true and important. And we disagree, I believe, less than she thinks.

When Kant explains the wrongness of a lying promise, he writes:

> he whom I want to use for my own purposes with such a promise cannot possibly agree to my way of treating him.

Kant then refers to this remark as 'the principle of other human beings'. Kant's principle, I suggest, is

> (A) It is wrong to treat people in any way to which they could not rationally consent.

Wolf objects that, by interpreting Kant in this way, I abandon the Kantian idea of respect for autonomy, which often condemns treating people in ways to which they do not *actually* consent (36–41). But I do not abandon this idea. Many acts, I claim, are wrong, even if people could rationally consent to them, because these people do not in fact consent. To cover such acts, I suggest, we could plausibly appeal to

> *the Rights Principle*: Everyone has rights not to be treated in certain ways without their actual consent.

Nor, I believe, do I misinterpret Kant's remarks about consent. These remarks seem intended to cover all cases. In the sentence quoted above,

Kant seems to mean, not

> (B) It is often wrong to treat people in ways to which they do
> not actually concent,

but

> (C) It is always wrong to treat people in ways to which they
> cannot possibly consent.

That is why, when I propose the Rights Principle, I do not claim to be interpreting Kant.   According to some writers, Kant means

> (D) It is wrong to treat people in ways to which they cannot
> possibly consent because we have not given them the power
> to choose how we treat them.

But as Wolf agrees, this claim is false, and is unlikely to be what Kant means.   On my proposed interpretation, more fully stated

> (E) It is wrong to treat people in ways to which they could not
> rationally consent, if these people knew the relevant facts, and
> we gave them the power to choose how we treat them.

This claim is plausible and might be true. (E) might be called *the Principle of Possible Rational Consent*, but I used the shorter and perhaps misleading name: *the Consent Principle.*

Wolf claims that this principle would allow or permit us to do certain things to someone even if this person explicitly refuses consent to these acts (38–9).   This claim could be misunderstood.   As Wolf explains in a note, she means only that the Consent Principle does not itself condemn these acts.   Since this principle does not claim to cover all wrong acts, this principle does not *allow* or *permit* these acts in the sense of implying that these acts would not be wrong.   This principle also condemns many such acts, since it would often be irrational to consent to being treated in some way without our actual consent.   And on some plausible assumptions, this principle could not conflict with the Rights Principle.   If it would be wrong to treat someone in some way without this person's actual consent, the Consent Principle would not require this act.

66 Treating Someone Merely as a Means

According to some of Wolf's other claims, which can be summed up as

Wolf's Principle: If we harm people, without their consent, as a means of achieving some aim, we thereby treat these people merely as a means, in a way that is always to be regretted, and that, if other things are equal, makes our act wrong.

As Wolf notes, I argue against a similar principle. But Wolf does not discuss my proposed alternative.   According to my proposed

Harmful Means Principle: It is wrong to impose harm on someone as a means of achieving some aim, unless

(1) our act is the least harmful way to achieve this aim,

and,

(2) given the goodness of this aim, the harm we impose is not disproportionate, or too great.

To compare these principles, consider

Fifth Earthquake: You and your child are trapped in slowly collapsing wreckage, which threatens both your lives. You could save your child's life by using *Black's* body as a shield, without Black's consent, in a way that would destroy one of her legs. You could also save your own life, by causing Black to lose her other leg. But you believe that this act would be wrong, since it is only the saving of a child that could justify imposing such an injury on someone else. Acting on this belief, you save your child's life by causing Black to lose one leg.

According to Wolf's Principle, since you are harming Black without her consent as a means of achieving one of your aims, you are treating Black merely as a means. Given what is meant by 'merely' and 'as a means', this claim seems to me false. If you were treating Black merely as a means, you would save your own life as well as your child's, by causing Black to lose both legs. We cannot be treating someone merely as a means if, in acting in some way, we are letting ourselves die rather than imposing some lesser injury on this person.

We treat people merely as a means, Wolf also claims, if we use these people in some way that 'neglects or ignores' their 'purposes and plans'. But this claim does not support Wolf's Principle. When you save your child's life by destroying one of Black's legs, you may not be ignoring Black's purposes and plans. You may believe that you ought not to destroy Black's other leg because this second injury would make it even harder for Black to achieve some of her purposes and plans. This may be why you choose to die rather than imposing this injury on Black.

Most of us would believe that, in saving your child's life by destroying one of Black's legs, you would be acting wrongly. This, I assume, would also be Wolf's view. But Wolf's Principle supports this view only if we can truly claim that you are treating Black *merely* as a means. And as I have said, that claim is false, since you are giving up your life for Black's sake.

To defend our belief that your act is wrong, we could appeal instead to my proposed Harmful Means Principle. We could claim that, though there are some lesser harms that you could justifiably impose on Black if that were the only way to save your child's life, it is wrong to achieve this aim by imposing on Black an injury as great as losing a leg. Your act is wrong, we can add, even though you are *not* treating Black merely as a means.

Return next to

> *Bridge*, in which you could save five people's lives by using
> remote control to cause me to fall in front of a runaway train.

Wolf claims that this act would 'very definitely' treat me merely as a means (43). In some versions of this case, I argued, you would *not* be treating me merely as a means. But this fact, I also claimed, would not justify your act.

Similar claims apply to other cases. Some of Wolf's remarks suggest that, on my view, there is no objection to harming someone as a means of saving others from greater harms. But that is not my view. I make the different claim that, if it would be wrong for us to impose certain harms on people *as a means* of achieving certain aims, these acts would be wrong *whether or not* we would also be treating these people *merely as a means*. If we appeal to Wolf's Principle rather than my Harmful Means Principle, it would be *harder* to defend the belief that such acts are wrong. On Wolf's view, it would not be enough to appeal to the claim that such acts harm certain people as a means, since we must also defend the claim that these acts treat these people *merely as a means*. On the view that I suggest, to condemn harming people as a means, we do not need to defend that further and often more doubtful claim.

67 Kantian Rule Consequentialism

Wolf challenges my argument that Kantian Contractualism implies Rule Consequentialism. In giving this argument, Wolf claims, I fail to 'appreciate the value of autonomy and its power to generate reasons' (45).

We respect people's autonomy, Wolf writes, by

> refraining from interfering with their choices for themselves, and from imposing burdens on them that they would not themselves endorse.

We impose a burden on someone, in Wolf's intended sense, if we act in some way that harms this person without this person's consent. Such acts may be wrong, Wolf claims, even if they would also save several other people from similar or greater burdens. Principles that condemn such acts we can call *autonomy-protecting*. Principles that require or permit some such acts we can call *autonomy-infringing*.

According to what I call the *Kantian Contractualist Formula*, we ought to follow the principles whose being universally accepted everyone could rationally will, or choose. Such principles are *optimific* if their universal acceptance would make things go best in the impartial-reason-implying sense. Wolf assumes that certain autonomy-infringing principles would be optimific, since their acceptance would save more people from death or other burdens. Wolf also claims that, when we consider such cases,

(F) everyone could rationally choose that everyone accepts
some other, *non*-optimific autonomy-protecting principle.

In Wolf's words, we could rationally prefer some principle that preserves everyone's autonomy, even if that would reduce our 'overall security against the loss of life and limb' (47). Wolf calls this a *preference for autonomy over welfare*. Wolf objects that, since everyone could rationally choose such a non-optimific principle, my argument fails to show that Kantian Contractualism requires us to follow the optimific Rule Consequentialist principles.

To assess this objection, we can again suppose that in

Tunnel, you could redirect some runaway train so that it kills me rather than five other people.

Wolf's autonomy-protecting principles would condemn your saving the five in this way, since this act would impose a great burden on me. According to Wolf's objection,

(1) everyone could rationally choose that everyone accepts some such principle,

even though

(2) this principle would not be optimific.

But these claims could not both be true. When we apply the Kantian Contractualist Formula, by asking which principles everyone could rationally choose, we suppose that everyone knows the relevant, reason-giving facts. On this assumption, people could rationally choose only what they would have sufficient reasons to choose. If the autonomy-protecting principles would not be optimific, their acceptance would make things go worse in the impartial-reason-implying sense. That is what it means to claim that these principles would not be optimific. So everyone would have impartial reasons *not* to choose any such principle. And some people would also have strong personal reasons not to choose any such principle. In *Tunnel*, for example, the five people would know that, if they chose one of Wolf's autonomy-protecting principles, you would fail to save their lives by redirecting the runaway train. Nor would the five have any relevant and strong reason to choose such a principle. Since the five would have both impartial reasons and strong personal reasons *not* to choose any such principle, and they would have no similarly strong opposing reason, these people would not have sufficient reasons to make this choice. They could not rationally choose any principle that would *both* be significantly non-optimific *and* would require you to let them die.

Wolf might object that, in making these claims, I have overlooked the rationality of a preference for autonomy over welfare. She writes:

> in failing to notice or address the challenge to his argument
> that is posed by [this] preference . . . Parfit reveals once again a
> failure to recognize and appreciate the value of autonomy . . .
> (48).

I did fail to consider what would be implied by the rationality of this particular preference. As I have just argued, however, if this preference were rational, that would be no challenge to my argument. If, as Wolf claims, everyone could rationally choose some autonomy-protecting principle, this principle must be *optimific*, since this must be one of the principles that, from an impartial point of view, everyone would have most reason to choose. Unless the five had strong impartial reasons to choose this principle, they would have decisive personal reasons *not* to choose this principle, since that choice would lead you to let them die. But my remarks above might be mistaken. Wolf might be right to claim that the five *would* have such strong impartial reasons to choose this optimific autonomy-protecting principle.

Wolf also claims that, given the fundamental value of autonomy within the Kantian tradition, it is doubtful that any Kantian could accept Rule Consequentialism 'without abandoning the spirit that led him to be a Kantian in the first place' (48). After claiming that everyone could rationally choose some *non*-optimific autonomy-protecting principle, Wolf writes that some Kantians might go further, claiming that the choice of such a principle would be '*uniquely* rational'. On this view, she comments,

> Kantian Contractualism not only fails to imply what Parfit
> calls Kantian Rule Consequentialism, it implies principles that
> are very likely, if not certain, to conflict with it (48).

For similar reasons, however, this view could not be true. For it to be uniquely rational for everyone to choose that everyone accepts some autonomy-protecting principle, it would have to be true that everyone would have decisive reasons to make such a choice. And these could not all be *personal* reasons. Some people would have strong personal reasons *not* to choose any autonomy-protecting principle, since that choice would lead others to let them die, or let them bear some other great burden. So, if we all had decisive reasons to choose that everyone accepts some autonomy-protecting principle, these decisive reasons would have to be impartial. And if we had such reasons, these principles would be optimific, since they would be the principles whose acceptance would make things go best in the impartial-reason-implying sense. These autonomy-protecting principles would then be some of the Rule Consequentialist principles that, as I argue, Kantian Contractualism requires us to follow.

When Wolf challenges my argument, she may be using 'optimific' in some sense that differs from mine. Wolf may assume that, in the cases we are considering, principles would be optimific if their acceptance would best promote everyone's well-being in certain familiar ways, by giving them the longest life-expectancy or minimizing their risk of being injured. But we should not make that assumption. If we could all rationally prefer to live in a world in which we had more autonomy, though with less 'security against the loss of life and limb', this might be truly claimed to be a world in which our lives would on the whole go better. In preferring this world, we would not then be, as Wolf claims, preferring autonomy *over welfare*. Nor should we assume that principles are optimific only if their acceptance would on the whole best promote everyone's well-being. The goodness of outcomes may in part depend on other facts, such as facts about how benefits and burdens are distributed between different people, or facts that are not even about people's well-being. If everyone could rationally choose that everyone accepts some autonomy-protecting principle, this might be one of the principles whose acceptance would make things go best, even if this principle's acceptance would not on the whole best promote everyone's well-being. Rule Consequentialism need not take this Utilitarian form, or any other wholly *welfarist* form.

Wolf may not intend her claims to apply to cases like *Tunnel*. Of those who reject Rule Consequentialism, many would believe that, in *Tunnel*, you would be morally permitted to redirect the train so that it kills me rather than the five. This may also be Wolf's view. But Wolf does discuss *Bridge*, in which you could save the five only *by* killing me.

Most of us would believe that, in *Bridge*, it would be wrong for you to save the five in this way. According to Wolf's autonomy-protecting principles, it is wrong to impose great burdens on people without their consent. Wolf's principles would not distinguish between *Tunnel* and *Bridge*. In both cases, if you save the five, your act would impose a great burden on me, by killing me without my consent.   Wolf also writes:

> many people have a strong preference for being in control of their own lives. . . . They want to be the ones calling the shots, at a fairly local level, about what happens to their bodies, not to mention their lives (47).

These claims would also apply equally to both *Tunnel* and *Bridge*. In both cases, I and the five would all have strong reasons to prefer to be the ones calling the shots, deciding what would happen to our bodies, and whether we would live or die.

If we believe that your saving the five would be wrong in *Bridge,* but permissible in *Tunnel*, we cannot appeal to Wolf's autonomy-protecting principles, which imply that both these acts would be wrong. We must appeal to something like my suggested Harmful Means Principle. In both cases, if you save the five, your act would also kill me, without my consent, but only in *Bridge* would you be killing me as a *means* of saving the five.

I assumed that, in *Bridge*, the optimific principles would require you to save the five by killing me. Wolf questions this assumption. She suggests that, if everyone accepted 'something close to the Harmful Means Principle', this might 'lead to better results' and 'be optimific in the long run' (55). As before, this suggestion might be correct. As

Wolf claims, it can be hard to judge whether some principle would be optimific, since it can be hard to predict the effects of the acceptance of different principles, and hard to assess how good or bad these effects would be. When I discussed *Transplant*, I made a similar claim. For reasons like those given by the Anxiety and Mistrust Argument, the optimific principles would require doctors never to kill or injure their patients even when they could thereby save more people's lives. If Wolf's suggestion were correct, because the optimific principles would condemn your saving the five in *Bridge* by killing me, this would be no objection to my argument that Kantian Contractualism implies Rule Consequentialism. Wolf's suggestion would merely make Rule Consequentialism in one way easier for most of us to accept. This view would not here conflict, as I assumed, with most people's moral intuitions.

68 Three Traditions

Wolf does not discuss other moral principles or kinds of case. But she makes some wider comments. In my attempts to develop a Kantian theory, Wolf claims, I depart from Kant's 'explicit positions' in ways that are 'both interpretively implausible and normatively regrettable' (34).

Wolf is partly referring here to my claim that, on Kant's view, we ought to treat people only in ways to which they could rationally consent. I believe that, for the reasons that I gave above, this claim is neither interpretively implausible nor regrettable.

I also claim that, in several passages, Kant must be appealing to what I call the *Moral Belief Formula*, which condemns our acting on some maxim unless we could rationally will it to be true that everyone believes such acts to be permitted. This interpretation is not, I believe, implausible. I then argue that this formula should be revised, so that it does not refer to maxims in the sense that covers policies, and so that it appeals, not to what the *agent* could rationally will, but to what *everyone* could rationally will. Since I am here *revising* Kant's formula, these claims cannot be *interpretively* implausible. According to my proposed revision, we ought to follow the principles whose universal acceptance everyone could rationally will. This revised formula, moreover, differs little from some of Kant's 'explicit positions'. Kant appeals, for example, to 'the idea of the will of every rational being as a will giving universal law'.

When Wolf calls some of my claims 'normatively regrettable', she is also referring to my claim that Kantian Contractualism implies Rule Consequentialism. There may be other people who would regret this claim. But we are doing philosophy. We should ask, not whether this claim is regrettable, but whether it is true. I believe that, in Sidgwick's words,

> the real progress of ethical science . . . would be benefited
> by an application to it of the same disinterested curiosity to
> which we chiefly owe the great discoveries of physics.

Even if we hope that Kantian Contractualism does not imply Rule Consequentialism, my argument for this conclusion may be sound.

Wolf also writes that, in my development of a Kantian theory, some of what seems to her 'most compelling and distinctive about Kant's own moral perspective gets diluted' (36). Wolf is partly referring here to the idea of respect for autonomy. But the Kantian Contractualist Formula would, I believe, require us to follow some version of my proposed Rights Principle, according to which we have rights not to be treated in certain ways without our actual consent. For some of the reasons that Wolf describes, this would be one of the optimific principles whose universal acceptance everyone could rationally choose. So this part of Kant's perspective would not, I believe, get diluted.

Wolf may also be thinking of my claim that, in *Bridge*, the Kantian Formula would require you to save the five by killing me. As we have seen, Wolf questions this claim, since she suggests that the optimific principles might condemn such acts. Though I believe that the optimific principles would require doctors never to kill one of their patients as a means of saving several other people's lives, I am still inclined to believe that in certain *non-medical emergencies*, such as *Tunnel* and *Bridge*, the Kantian Formula would require us to do whatever would save the most lives. This formula would then imply that, in *Tunnel*, you ought to redirect the runaway train so that it kills me rather than the five. Like most other people, I can accept that conclusion. But this formula would also imply that, in *Bridge*, you ought to save the five *by* killing me. And like Wolf, I find this claim implausible. Intuitively, this act seems to me wrong.

This intuition is not, however, strong. There are facts that seem to me to count the other way. Compared with being killed as a side-effect in *Tunnel*, it would be no worse for me to be killed as a means in *Bridge*. And the Kantian Formula provides an argument against this intuition. If we were choosing the principles that, in such non-medical emergencies, everyone would follow, we would have more reason, I believe, to choose principles that required you to save the five. Though I am still inclined to believe that it would be wrong for you to kill me as a means, this intuition is not strong enough to convince me that we ought to reject the Kantian Formula.

We have strong reasons, I believe, to accept this formula, and to act on the optimific principles of Kantian Rule Consequentialism. As I have said, however, there might be other cases in which this moral theory conflicts more strongly with our moral intuitions. If that were true, we might justifiably reject this theory.

Wolf makes another, wider claim. 'Like Parfit', Wolf writes, 'I see the Kantian, Consequentialist, and Contractualist traditions as each capturing profound and important insights about value.' When she discusses my argument that these three kinds of systematic theory can be combined, Wolf takes me to be trying to show

> that there is a single true morality, crystallized in a single
> supreme principle that these different traditions may be
> seen to be groping towards, each in their own separate
> and imperfect ways (34).

Wolf doubts that there is any such principle. Nor, she claims, do we need such a principle.   In her words:

> there is no reason to assume that there will be such a
> principle, and it would not be a moral tragedy if it turned
> out that morality were not so cleanly structured as to have
> one (35).

If there is no single supreme principle, that, I agree, would not be a tragedy. But it *would* be a tragedy if there was no *single true morality*. And conflicting moralities could not all be true. In trying to combine these different kinds of moral theory, my main aim was not to find a supreme principle, but to find out whether we can resolve some deep disagreements. As Wolf claims, it would not matter greatly if morality *turned out* to be less unified, because there are several true principles, which cannot be subsumed under any single higher principle. But if we cannot resolve our disagreements, that would give us reasons to doubt that there are *any* true principles. There might be nothing that morality *turns out to be*, since morality might be an illusion.

19

On Humanity as an End in itself

69 Kant's Formulas of Autonomy and of Universal Law

I have learnt a great deal from Allen Wood's fascinating books, and I am delighted and relieved by the fact that, in his commentary, Wood expresses agreement with several of my claims. I shall try here to resolve some of our remaining disagreements.

Though Wood believes that Kant at least roughly describes 'the supreme principle of morality', he also believes that Kant's principle cannot provide a *criterion of wrongness*, in the sense of a way of deciding which acts are wrong. Of Kant's various formulations of his supreme principle, Wood has the lowest opinion of Kant's Formula of Universal Law. Wood calls this the 'least adequate' of Kant's formulas, and the formula that most clearly fails to provide a criterion of wrongness. He also writes:

> Self-appointed defenders of Kant . . . will probably never abandon the noble, Grail-like quest for an interpretation of the universalizability test that enables it to serve this purpose, despite the history of miserable failure that has always attended the quest. I regard their attempts as worse than a waste of time, since they encourage critics of Kant's ethics to continue thinking, falsely, that something of importance turns on whether there is a universalizability test for maxims that could serve as such a general moral criterion.

These Kantians, he adds,

> desperately seek ever more creative interpretations of Kant's
> test in a passionate effort (as they see it) to save Kantian ethics
> from oblivion.

Since I have tried to show that Kant's Formula of Universal Law can give
us a plausible criterion of wrongness, I may seem to be one of these self-
appointed defenders of Kant whose noble, Grail-like quest Wood regards
as worse than a waste of time. But I cannot claim such nobility. I accept
Wood's view that no *new interpretation* of Kant's formula, however
creative, could make this formula provide a criterion of wrongness. We
ought, I argue, to *revise* this formula.   According to my proposed

> *Kantian Contractualist Formula*: Everyone ought to follow
> the principles whose universal acceptance everyone could
> rationally will.

In revising Kant's formula, my aim is the same as Wood's aim in his
latest book, *Kantian Ethics*. We are both trying to produce what Wood
calls 'the most defensible' Kantian moral theory. To achieve this aim, as
Wood notes, we may have to revise some of Kant's claims.

The Kantian theories that Wood and I propose are also, I believe,
more similar than Wood assumes. Wood appeals to Kant's Formula of
Autonomy, which Kant sums up as 'the idea of the will of every rational
being as a will giving universal law'.   This formula, Wood writes,

> tells us to think of ourselves as members of an ideal
> community of rational beings, in which each of us should
> strive to obey the moral principles by which we would choose
> that members of the community should ideally govern their
> conduct.

In a briefer statement, which we can call

> FA: Each of us should try to follow the principles that we
> would all choose to be the principles that would govern
> everyone's conduct.

Wood calls FA 'the most definitive form' of Kant's supreme principle, and the formula that we ought always to 'use for moral judgment'. But as Wood also claims, FA is not a reliable criterion of wrongness. If we ask which are the principles that people *would in fact* choose, we could not predict which principles other people would choose. Nor could we assume that everyone would choose the same principles.

Partly for this reason, we ought to revise FA, so that this formula refers to the principles that it would be *rational* for all of us to choose. We would not here be moving further away from Kant's view. On the contrary, this revised formula would better express Kant's idea of the will of every *rational* being as giving universal law. And this revision is clearly needed, since there are countless bad principles that we might all irrationally choose, and these cannot be the principles that we should try to follow.   So FA should become

> *FA2*: Each of us should try to follow the principles that it
> would be rational for all of us to choose to be the principles
> that would govern everyone's conduct.

This claim is another version of my Kantian Contractualist Formula. Though my proposed Kantian theory revises Kant's Formula of Universal Law, and Wood's proposed theory revises Kant's Formula of Autonomy, these revisions both lead us to what I have called Kantian Contractualism. That is not surprising given Kant's assertion that these different 'ways of representing the principle of morality are, fundamentally, only so many formulas of precisely the same law'.

Return now to Wood's claim that nothing of importance turns on whether there is some 'universalizability test' that provides a criterion of wrongness. This claim would be justified only if either (1) we already have some other, wholly reliable criterion, or (2) we would not be helped by having some such criterion, since we can always reliably judge, without using any criterion, whether some act would be wrong. Wood does not defend either of these implausible claims. So Wood, I believe, should agree that it matters whether Kantian Contractualism provides a good criterion of wrongness. And that, I have argued, may be true.

70 Rational Nature as the Supreme Value

Wood also discusses Kant's Formula of Humanity, which is clearly *not*, as Kant asserts, a different way of stating 'precisely the same law'. When Kant presents this formula, I suggest, Kant claims it to be wrong to treat people in any way to which they could not rationally consent. This Consent Principle, I argue, is both plausible and defensible. I am glad that, in his commentary, Wood seems to agree. Kant's Formula of Humanity includes the different claim that we must never treat rational beings merely as a means. Though this claim is also plausible, I argue that it needs to be revised, and that it adds little to Kant's view. Though it is wrong to *regard* anyone merely as a means, whether our *acts* are wrong seldom if ever depends on whether we are treating people merely as a means. Wood ignores this part of Kant's formula, because he believes that it adds nothing to Kant's view.

Wood restates Kant's formula as

> FH: We should always respect humanity, or rational nature, as an end in itself.

This version of Kant's formula, I claim, is too vague to provide a criterion of wrongness.   Wood agrees (65–6).

Unlike me, however, Wood believes that FH is the most important of all Kant's statements of his supreme moral law. This formula, Wood claims, 'is fundamentally the articulation of a basic value'. He even writes:

> Perhaps the most fundamental proposition in Kant's entire ethical theory is that rational nature is the supreme value . . .

This supreme value, Wood suggests, gives us our 'rational ground or motive' to obey the moral law. If there are categorical imperatives, Kant argues, we must have a reason to obey them. This reason would have to be provided by something that is an end in itself, having supreme and absolute worth. And this end in itself, Kant claims, is humanity or rational nature. With these claims, Wood writes, Kant gives us 'a deeply true account of the foundations of ethics'. On this interpretation of Kant's view, which I shall call

> *Wood's Foundational Thesis*: Humanity or rational nature has the supreme value that both grounds morality and gives us our reason to obey the moral law.

Herman similarly writes:

> Kant's project in ethics is to provide a correct analysis of 'the Good', understood as the determining ground of all action.

No moral theory could succeed, Herman claims, 'without a grounding concept of value'. On Kant's theory, it is the value of rational nature that gives morality its 'end or point', thereby showing how morality's demands on us 'make sense'.

These claims need to be further explained. When Kant uses the words 'humanity' or 'rational nature', he is sometimes referring to rational beings, or persons. All persons, Kant claims, have *dignity*, which he defines as absolute, unconditional, and incomparable value or worth. So the supreme value which Kant claims to ground morality might be the dignity of all persons.

Kantian dignity, many writers assume, is a kind of supreme *goodness*. For example, Herman calls the dignity of rational nature a value that is 'absolute in the sense that there is no other kind of value or goodness for whose sake rational nature can count as a means'. Wood calls rational nature 'the underivative objective good'. Kerstein similarly writes that humanity is 'absolutely and incomparably good', and Korsgaard writes that, on Kant's view, humanity must be treated 'as unconditionally good'.

As I pointed out, however, some rational beings or persons are not good. Hitler and Stalin were two examples. Wood comments:

> I agree with Parfit when he interprets Kant as saying that even the morally worst people have dignity, and in that sense they have exactly same worth as even the morally best people . . . Parfit is further correct to point out that none of this implies that my having dignity as a human being makes me a *good*

human being. Not everything having value is thereby
something *good* (64).

If the dignity of persons were a kind of supreme goodness, and Hitler
and Stalin had this kind of goodness, that would imply that Hitler and
Stalin were supremely good. Since that is clearly false, as Kant would
have agreed, we should conclude that, at least when had by persons,
dignity is not a kind of goodness. As Wood, Hill, and others claim, the
dignity of persons is a kind of 'moral status', or a 'value to be respected'.
Though Hitler and Stalin were not good, they had dignity in the sense
that, as rational beings, they had the moral status of being entities who
ought always to be treated only in certain ways.

Return now to Wood's Foundational Thesis. If we take 'rational nature'
to refer to rational beings, or persons, this thesis implies that

> (1) our reason to treat all persons only in certain ways is
> provided by the fact that persons have supreme value.

This supreme value, as we have just seen, is not a kind of goodness but
a kind of moral status.   So we can restate (1) as

> (2) our reason to treat all persons only in certain ways is
> provided by the fact that persons have the moral status of
> being entities who ought to be treated only in these ways.

In this restatement, Wood's Thesis becomes less appealing. Nor could
(2) be claimed to ground morality's requirements in what Herman calls
'a correct analysis of the Good'. (2) claims only that our reason to follow
these requirements is provided by the fact that morality requires these
acts. This claim does not give morality what Herman calls a value that
could be its end or point, showing how morality's demands make sense.

Wood suggests another version of his thesis. Kant sometimes uses
'humanity' and 'rational nature' to refer to

> our *non-moral rationality*, which Kant describes in part as
> our 'capacity to set an end—any end whatsoever', and which
> also includes, Wood claims, both instrumental and prudential
> rationality, and various other rational abilities.

These kinds of rationality, Wood writes, have 'the absolute worth that grounds morality'.

In defending this version of his thesis, Wood once claimed that, according to Kant:

> When we use our capacity to set an end, by choosing to try to fulfil some desire, we thereby make this end good.

> The source of something's goodness must itself be good.

Therefore

> Our capacity to set an end is good.

This argument involves, Wood wrote,

> an inference from the objective goodness of the end to the unconditional objective goodness of the capacity to set the end.

Wood even suggested that, on Kant's view, the 'rational choice of ends is the act through which objective goodness enters the world'.

This is not, I believe, Kant's view. Kant did not believe that our capacity to set ends is the source of all goodness, such as the goodness of good wills, or deserved happiness. And Wood now rejects, and believes that Kant rejects, this argument's first premise. Wood accepts a value-based objective theory both of reasons and of the goodness of our ends, and he calls these views 'good Kantianism'.

Our non-moral rationality may have some kinds of value, to which I shall return. But such rationality cannot be defensibly claimed to have, as Wood suggests, the supreme goodness or absolute worth that grounds morality, by giving us our reason to obey the moral law.

There is another possibility.   Kant writes

> morality, and humanity insofar as it is capable of morality, is that which alone has dignity.

In this and some other passages, as Wood notes, Kant ascribes dignity to rational nature 'not in its capacity to set ends, but only in its capacity of giving (and obeying) moral laws' (64). Surprisingly, Wood also writes

> It is the *capacity* for morality . . . not its successful exercise,
> that has dignity.

The *unexercised* capacity for morality, as had by people like Hitler and Stalin, cannot be claimed to be supremely good, or to be what grounds morality.

Wood's Foundational Thesis might appeal instead to the *exercised* capacity to give and to obey moral laws, which is roughly what Kant calls a 'good will'. Kant claims, much more plausibly, that such good wills are supremely good. So Wood's Foundational Thesis might become the claim that

> (3) Kant grounds morality on the supreme goodness of
> good wills.

Wood considers and rejects this claim. He reminds us that, on Kant's view, we cannot be certain that any actual person has a good will. Wood then writes: 'If only the good will had the dignity of an end in itself . . . the existence of such an end, and consequently the validity of categorical imperatives, would be doubtful.'

This argument is not, I believe, sound. For something's goodness or good features to give us a reason for acting, which might be decisive and categorical, this thing need not ever actually exist. Many of our acts are intended to achieve some merely possible good end. So, if Kant had stated a version of Wood's Foundational Thesis, Kant might have claimed that

> (4) the supreme goodness of good wills gives us our reason to
> try to have such a will, and to act rightly.

For us to have such a reason, it must be possible for us to have good wills, and to act rightly. But Kant believes that we know this to be possible.

Remember next Kant's claim that the Highest or Greatest Good would be a world of universal virtue and deserved happiness. Everyone,

Kant claims, ought always to strive to promote this ideal world. And Kant also writes,

> the moral law commands me to make the greatest possible good in a world the final object of all my conduct.

These claims overlap with (4). What would make this the best possible world would be the fact that everyone had good wills and acted rightly, thereby deserving their happiness. If these claims are true, their truth would be enough to give to morality what Herman calls an 'end or point', so that morality's demands 'make sense'.

71 Rational Nature as the Value to be Respected

Wood gives another argument against the view that Kant grounds morality on the goodness of good wills. On Kant's theory, Wood writes, 'all reasons for acting are based, directly or indirectly, on the objective value of rational nature'. 'What morality demands most fundamentally is that we show respect for that value', and acts that are wrong 'all involve treating that value . . . with disrespect' (62). These claims would not be plausible, Wood argues, if the value of rational nature was the goodness of good wills. When we ask what makes it wrong to injure, coerce, deceive, or otherwise mistreat people, the answer does not seem to be that such acts show disrespect for the goodness of such wills. As Wood points out, from Kant's claim that good wills are supremely good, we cannot draw any conclusions about what we ought morally to do. This claim, Wood concludes, has only 'marginal' importance in Kant's moral theory. Kant's ethics is grounded, *not* on the goodness of good wills, but on what Wood calls the 'absolute worth of rational nature'.

Though this argument has more force, its conclusion is, I believe, too simple. In discussing Kant's theory, we can distinguish between what grounds morality, and the properties or facts that make acts wrong. Wood's argument, I believe, does not count against the view that Kant's ethics is grounded on the goodness of good wills and deserved happiness. This part of Kant's theory may not be intended to help us to decide which acts are wrong. It is a separate question whether, as Wood claims, our acts are wrong when and because they show disrespect for the value of rational nature.

Kant uses 'rational nature' to refer both to rational beings and to the rationality of these beings. The value of rational nature therefore consists in part in the dignity of all rational beings, or persons. As we have seen, this dignity is not a kind of goodness, but is the moral status of being entities who ought to be treated only in certain ways. The claim that persons have this status does not help us to decide how persons ought to be treated.

When Wood refers to the supreme value of rational nature, he is more often referring to the value of non-moral rationality, such as prudential rationality. Though Wood no longer claims that our capacity to set an end confers goodness on what we choose, he still takes Kant to be claiming truly that 'the correct exercise of one's rational capacities . . . must be esteemed as unconditionally good'. On Kant's view, Herman similarly writes, 'the domain of "the Good" is rational activity and agency: that is willing'.

These claims are not, I believe, justified. Some kinds of rational activity may have great intrinsic value as achievements, and this would support Kant's claim that we ought to develop and use our various rational abilities. But unlike good wills, non-moral rationality cannot be claimed to be supremely good. The rational agency of Hitler and Stalin was *not* good. Nor, I believe, would Kant have made this claim. On Kant's view, as Herman notes, what is good is only *good* willing.

Even if rational agency is not supremely good, such agency might be claimed to have what Wood calls 'the basic value to be respected'. Our acts are wrong, Wood suggests, when and because they fail to respect the value of non-moral rationality. Herman makes similar claims. On Kant's view, she writes,

> Failure to assign correct value to rational agency—discounting the conditions of human willing—is the 'content' of morally wrong action.

Most wrong acts are wrong, Herman suggests, because of the ways in which these acts destroy, obstruct, or misuse rational agency. Coercion is wrong, for example, because it involves 'an attack on agency', deception is wrong because it frustrates rational agency, and violence is wrong because it attacks agency's 'conditions.'

These claims are, I believe, misleading.   On Kant's view, Herman also writes:

> killing is not wrong because it brings about death, and mayhem is not wrong because it brings about pain or harm . . . The kind of value . . . I have as an agent is not lost or compromised in dying.

What makes killing wrong is instead 'some erroneous valuation'. I can justifiably resist aggression, Herman writes, because

> the aggressor acts on a maxim that involves the devaluation of my agency . . . I am not acting to save my life as such, but to resist the use of my agency . . .

Rational agency seems here to be claimed to have the kind of value that some people claim for chastity, and self-defence to be like the protection of our chastity — whose value, women were often told, is not lost or compromised in dying. I doubt that this is really either Kant's or Herman's view. Aggressive violence *is* wrong, I believe, not because it devalues rational agency, but because it brings about death, pain, or other harms.

Similar claims apply to deception and coercion. What makes these acts wrong is not, I believe, their 'failure to assign correct value to rational agency'. People can act rationally when they are being deceived and coerced. Such acts are wrong for other reasons, such as the fact that people could not rationally consent to them, or the fact that such acts treat *people*, not their *agency*, with disrespect.

Return next to Wood's claim that the capacity to set ends, and the other components of non-moral rationality, have 'the absolute worth that grounds morality'. To show respect for this value, Wood writes, we must help other people to achieve their permissible ends (64). But if it was other people's non-moral rationality that had such worth, that would give us no reason to help these people to achieve their ends.

Other people could act just as *rationally*, even if less *successfully*, without our help.

Wood also claims that concern for alleviating human suffering is 'grounded' in the 'fundamental value' of non-moral rationality. That is not, I believe, true. Our concern to relieve people's suffering should be grounded, not in the value of these people's rationality, but in the ways in which suffering is bad for these people, by being a state that they have strong reasons to want not to be in. We have similar reasons to relieve the suffering of those abnormal human beings who have no rational abilities, and the suffering of non-rational animals. As Bentham said, our question should not be 'Can they reason?' but 'Can they suffer?'

Wood elsewhere writes:

> to act morally is always to act for the sake of a person, or more precisely, for the sake of humanity in someone's person.
>
> the fundamentally valuable thing . . . is a rational being, a person — or, more precisely, rational nature in a person.

These more precise claims are, I believe, mistaken. We ought to act for the *person's* sake, not for the sake of her non-moral rationality. And it is the *person*, not her rationality, who has the high moral status that Kant calls dignity.

Wood is aware of this objection.   Some of Kant's readers, Wood writes, may

> worry about the injunction to respect humanity (or rational nature) in someone's person. They fear that it means respecting only an abstraction and not the persons themselves. Kant's answer to these worries, of course, is that rational nature is precisely what makes you a person, so that respecting it *in* you is precisely what it means to respect *you*.

This suggested answer is not, I believe, true. Respecting your non-moral rationality is not the same as respecting *you*. Wood also writes that, on Kant's view,

respect for the dignity of humanity is identical with respect for
law grounding morality in general.

Kant does claim that respect for a person is, strictly speaking, respect
for the moral law. But these are not the claims that have rightly made
Kant's Formula of Humanity so widely accepted and loved.   Respect
for persons should be, precisely, respect for *them*.

20

On a Mismatch of Methods

72 Does Kant's Formula Need to be Revised?

In some of her brilliant discussions of Kant's Formula of Universal Law, Barbara Herman claimed that this formula cannot provide a criterion of wrongness. Despite 'a sad history of attempts', she wrote, '. . . no one has been able to make it work'. Herman, I have argued, was right. In its present form, Kant's Formula cannot succeed. But if we revise this formula, I claimed, we can make it work. Herman would agree, I hoped, that her 'sad history' has a happy ending.

My hopes were dashed. In her commentary, Herman seems to argue that Kant's Formula does not need to be revised. She also argues that my proposed revision could not, even if it were needed, achieve Kant's aims.

One of my arguments can be summed up as follows:

> According to Kant's Formula, it is wrong to act on any maxim that we could not rationally will to be universal.

> There are many maxims that we could not rationally will to be universal, though acting on these maxims would often not be wrong.

Therefore

> When applied to such maxims, Kant's Formula would often mistakenly condemn acts that were not wrong.

To illustrate these claims, I imagined that some Egoist has only one maxim: 'Do whatever would be best for me'. For self-interested reasons, this man pays his debts, keeps his promises, puts on warmer clothing, and risks his life to save a drowning child, hoping to get some reward. I then argued:

> (A) When this man acts in these ways, his acts have no moral worth, but he is not acting wrongly.

> (B) This man is acting on an Egoistic maxim that he could not rationally will to be universal.

Therefore

> Kant's Formula falsely implies that this man *is* acting wrongly.

In some passages, Herman seems to reject premise (A). Kant's Formula, she suggests, *truly* implies that this man is acting wrongly.

In defending this suggestion, Herman claims that, on Kant's view,

> (C) we act wrongly when we act for the wrong motive,
> or our decision about how to act was made in some morally defective way.

When my Egoist saves the drowning child because he hopes to be rewarded, this man's selfish motive, Herman suggests, makes his act wrong. And my imagined ruthless gangster acts wrongly, Herman also suggests, when this man buys his cup of coffee from a coffee seller whom he regards as a mere means.

Herman remarks that, in suggesting that these acts are wrong, she may seem to be ignoring Kant's

> famous distinction between morally worthy and duty-conforming actions, the former requiring that the action be done from a moral motive, the latter motive-indifferent (90).

She also writes:

> The doctrine of moral worth is not the only place where Kant is taken to be offering a motive-independent notion

of wrongness; also noted are his views of perfect duties
and duties of justice (91).

But she then claims:

Neither view supports the general thesis of motive-
independent wrongness. In both cases, the error
in thinking that they do is instructive.

Kant, I believe, *does* use 'a motive-independent notion of wrongness',
so there seems to be no error here. It will be enough to consider what
Kant calls 'duties of justice'. Kant claims that, unlike duties of virtue,
which require us to act for the right motive, duties of justice can be
fulfilled whatever our motive. As Herman writes, these duties

are indeed about external actions only; motives are not
relevant to their correct performance (92).

Kant includes, among duties of justice, duties to pay our debts and keep
our promises. When my Egoist acts in these ways for self-interested
motives, he fulfils these duties. So Kant, I believe, would accept my
claim that these acts are not wrong.

Herman concedes that these acts are in one sense permissible. But on
Kant's view, she claims,

avoiding impermissibility and avoiding wrongness are not
the same thing; actions can be 'not impermissible' and yet
wrong (90).

She also writes:

duties of justice are not one of the classes of moral duties, on
all fours, as it were, with duties of aid or respect or friendship.
They are institution-based duties . . . they only come into
existence through the legislative activity of a state' (92).

Herman elsewhere suggests that we ought not to 'model wrongness on a
legalistic notion of impermissibility' (89). And Kant himself writes that,

when we fulfil duties of justice for selfish motives, that gives our acts 'legality' not 'morality'.

Kant's remark could be misunderstood. Duties of justice *are*, on Kant's view, moral duties.   As Kant writes

> all duties, just because they are duties, belong to ethics.

When Kant claims that our failure to fulfil duties of justice makes our acts 'illegal', he does not mean only that such acts are against the criminal, state-based law. He often means that such acts are against the *moral* law. Kant often uses 'illegality' to refer to the kind of wrongness, or *moral* impermissibility, that is involved in failing to fulfil duties of justice. This kind of wrongness is, in Herman's phrase, *motive-independent,* since we can fulfil such duties, thereby avoiding this kind of wrongness, whatever the motive on which we act. Kant's prudent merchant does his duty when he pays his debts, even though his motive is to preserve his reputation and his profits. Kant calls such acts 'right' or 'in conformity with duty', and our failure to fulfil such duties he calls 'wrong' or 'contrary to duty'.

Despite her remarks quoted above, Herman seems to agree that Kant sometimes uses 'wrong' in this motive-independent sense. Though we have only a duty of justice not to steal, Herman refers to the 'moral wrong of stealing'.   And she writes:

> impermissibility may fairly mark out the class of wrongful
> actions that are wrong no matter what the agent's motive (89).

Herman's claim can at most be that Kant also uses 'wrong' in at least one other sense. And she does make such claims. On Kant's view, she writes:

> An externally conforming action that lacks moral worth is a
> behavior whose connection to moral correctness is
> conditional or accidental. It is in that sense *not* a correct
> action (90).

She also writes:

> An agent who ignores or fails to respond appropriately to the
> morally relevant features of her circumstances acts in a way
> that is wrong (89).

Wrongness . . . arises from the principles of the deliberating
agent and is about whether, through them, she has a sound
route of reasoning to her action.

Herman might claim that, even when some act is morally permissible
and in conformity with duty, this act may be in these other senses wrong.

If we distinguish these senses of 'wrong', my argument could become:

(D) When my Egoist pays his debts, saves the drowning child,
and puts on warmer clothing, his acts have no moral worth,
but these acts are not wrong in the sense of being morally
impermissible and contrary to duty.

(E) According to Kant's Formula, it is in this sense wrong
to act on any maxim that we could not rationally will to be
universal.

(B) When my Egoist acts in these ways, he is acting on an
Egoistic maxim that he could not rationally will to be
universal.

Therefore

Kant's Formula falsely implies that these acts are in this sense
wrong.

Though Herman seems to accept both (D) and (B), she might reject (E).
She might claim that, in proposing his formula, Kant does not intend to
provide a criterion of whether our acts are wrong, in the sense of being
morally impermissible and contrary to duty. Herman has elsewhere
made this claim. But Kant often declares or assumes that his formula
provides such a criterion.   For example, Kant writes:

to inform myself in the shortest and yet infallible way . . .
whether a lying promise is in conformity with duty, I ask
myself: would I indeed be content that my maxim . . . should
hold as a universal law?

common human reason, with this compass in hand, knows
very well how to distinguish in every case what is good and
what is evil, what conforms with duty or is contrary to duty.

As these and many other passages together show, Herman cannot
defensibly reject premise (E). My argument, I believe, is sound. When
my Egoist acts in the ways that I have described, Kant's Formula falsely
implies that these acts are wrong in the sense of being morally impermissible and contrary to duty. So this formula fails, and needs to be revised.

This objection, moreover, can take another form, to which several of
Herman's claims do not apply. There are people who are conscientious,
and who sometimes act in ways that they truly believe to be right, though
these people are acting on maxims that they could not rationally will to
be universal. One example would be Kant himself if, as we can suppose,
he accepted the maxim 'Never lie'. Kant could not have rationally willed
it to be true that no one ever tells a lie, not even to a would-be murderer
who asks where his intended victim is. So Kant's Formula would imply
that, whenever Kant acted on this maxim by telling anyone the truth,
he would be acting wrongly. That claim is clearly false. Suppose next
that we accept the maxims 'Never steal' and 'Never break the law'. We
could not have rationally willed it to be true that no one ever steals or
breaks the law, even when these acts are the only ways to save some
innocent person's life. So Kant's Formula implies that, whenever we act
on these maxims, by returning someone's property or obeying some
law, we would be acting wrongly. These claims are also clearly false. As
before, to avoid this objection, Kant's Formula must be revised.

73 A New Kantian Formula

We should revise Kant's Formula, I argued, by making this formula
refer, not to *maxims* in the sense that covers policies, but to the acts
that we are considering, described in what are, or might be, the morally
relevant ways.

Herman does not discuss my proposed revisions. But some of
Herman's claims, quoted above, suggest some other ways in which
Kant's formula might be revised.   We might distinguish between

an act's being wrong in the sense of being morally
impermissible and contrary to duty,

and

an act's being wrong in the sense that it

(1) lacks moral worth,

(2) fails to respond appropriately to the morally
relevant facts,

(3) is done for the wrong motive, or

(4) is only accidentally in conformity with duty.

We might then suggest that, on a different version of Kant's Formula,
which we can call

the New Kantian Formula: When we act on some maxim that
we could not rationally will to be universal, our act is wrong in
one or more of these other senses.

We ought, I believe, to reject this formula. Though it matters whether
our acts have the properties described by (1) to (4), it would often be
misleading to call such acts wrong. Nor would this formula be a good
criterion of whether people's acts *are*, in these various senses, wrong.

As we have seen, Herman's remarks suggest that

(1) when some morally required act lacks moral worth, this
act is in one sense incorrect or wrong.

But this would not, I believe, be a defensible or useful sense of 'wrong'.
When my Egoist pays his debts and keeps his promises for self-interested
reasons, his acts have no moral worth, but that is no reason to call these
acts wrong.

Even if we called such acts in this sense wrong, that would not give us
a reason to appeal to the New Kantian Formula. Whether our acts have
moral worth does not depend on whether we could will our maxims to
be universal. Suppose that Kant tells someone the truth, at a great cost
to himself, because he rightly believes this act to be his duty. As I have

said, this would be more than enough to give this act moral worth. It would be irrelevant whether Kant was acting on some maxim, such as 'Never lie', that he could not rationally will to be universal. So the New Formula should not assume that all such acts lack moral worth.

Consider next Herman's claim that

> (2) we act wrongly when we fail to respond appropriately to the morally relevant facts.

When my Egoist saves the drowning child, his act is not in this sense wrong. It is wholly appropriate to save drowning children. Nor is it in this sense wrong for my Egoist to pay his debts and keep his promises. These are wholly appropriate acts. Nor would Kant act inappropriately if he acted on the maxim 'Never lie' by telling someone the correct time of day. So the New Formula should not claim that, when we act on some maxim that we could not rationally will to be universal, we are failing to respond appropriately to the relevant facts. That claim would often be false.

Some of Herman's remarks suggest that

> (3) in my imagined cases, my Egoist acts wrongly in the sense that he acts for the wrong motive.

Even when my Egoist responds appropriately to the relevant facts, he might be acting for the wrong motive. But (3) is also, I believe, false. We should distinguish here between this man's *maxim*, 'Do whatever would be best for me', and the self-interested *motive* on which this man acts. Though this man's maxim is morally defective, his motive is not always wrong. In my imagined case, since no one has a duty to risk their life to save the drowning child, no one would be acting for the wrong motive if they chose, for self-interested reasons, not to risk their life. So we should similarly claim that, when my Egoist chooses, for self-interested reasons, to risk his life in an attempt to save this child, he is not acting for the wrong motive. Nor does he act for the wrong motive when he fulfils his duties of justice, by paying his debts and keeping his promises. As Herman seems to admit, we can fulfil these duties whatever our motive. Nor should the New Formula claim that, whenever we act on some maxim that we could not rationally will to be universal, we have the wrong motive. Kant would not be acting for the wrong motive if he rightly told someone the truth because he believed this act to be his duty. It would be irrelevant whether he was acting on a maxim, 'Never lie', that he could not rationally will to be universal.

Herman also suggests that

(4) when our acts are only accidentally morally permissible, or in conformity with duty, these acts are in one sense wrong.

This claim does not, I believe, describe a useful sense of 'wrong'. When some people follow certain traditional rules, or do what is required by certain religious beliefs, they are acting on incorrect principles, and using unsound moral reasoning. In such cases, when these people do their duty, their acts would be only accidentally in conformity with duty. But we should not claim that these people's acts are all, in one sense, wrong. When these people act rightly, for the right motive, truly believing that their acts are right, their acts are not in any sense wrong.

Return next to my claim that, if Kant acted on the maxim 'Never Lie' by telling someone the correct time of day, Kant's Formula would falsely imply that this act was wrong. Herman might reply that Kant's act *would be* in one sense wrong, since this act would be only accidentally in conformity with duty. Kant's maxim might have led him to act wrongly, as would be true in the possible case in which Kant told some would-be murderer where his intended victim was. But that is not enough to justify the claim that, when Kant tells someone the correct time of day, Kant's act is in one sense wrong. Our claim should be only that, *if* Kant had acted on his maxim in the very different case involving the would-be murderer, that *different* act would have been wrong.

Return now to my imagined gangster, who regards other people merely as a means, and who pays for his coffee merely because he thinks it not worth stealing from the coffee seller. Herman imagines that this man is morally reborn, and looks back with horror at his earlier life. She then writes:

> It's easy enough to imagine him concluding that what he had done was wrong: it was a matter of sheer luck that there was a benign outcome. It would not be inapt for him to wish it had not happened: not the paying for the coffee, of course, but the entire episode. If a sign of wrongdoing is guilt, or a sense that apology might be in order, motive or attitude can suffice to trigger it, and a change in attitude is often integral to the work of moral repair for what was done (88).

As Herman here claims, however, this man has no reason to wish that he had not paid for his coffee. And that is all that this man *did*; so he should not conclude that 'what he had done was wrong', nor is it true that he should apologize for what he did.   As I wrote:

> though this gangster treats the coffee seller merely as a means, what is wrong is only his *attitude* to this person. In buying his cup of coffee, he does not *act* wrongly.

Herman herself writes elsewhere:

> not all things required of the Kantian agent are required *actions* . . . we are also required to adopt a general policy: to be willing to help when the need is there.

Since we are also morally required not to regard other people merely as a means, my gangster's attitude is wrong. And we might agree that, in having this wrong attitude to the coffee seller, this gangster in one sense wrongs this person, and should apologize later for having had this attitude. But there is no useful sense in which, when this man paid for his coffee, what he did was wrong.

In the passages that I have just been discussing, and several others, Herman makes several plausible and original claims about some of the ways in which it can be morally important whether our acts have the properties described by (1) to (4). But as I have tried to show, we should not claim either that all such acts are in one sense wrong, or that our acts have these properties when we act on maxims that we could not rationally will to be universal. Both claims would often be false.

74 Herman's Objections to Kantian Contractualism

In the last two sections, I have tried to show that Herman's claims do not answer one of my objections to Kant's Formula of Universal Law, nor do these claims suggest an acceptable way to revise this formula.

I gave several other objections to Kant's Formula, none of which Herman directly discusses. These objections show, I believe, that Kant's Formula must be revised.

My proposed revision Herman calls a 'hybrid theory', which seems to her deeply un-Kantian.   This revision, she writes,

> cannot capture what is most distinctive about Kant's theory. The mismatch of methods is too profound . . . If the separation of the two methodologies is so wide . . . there may not be much to be gained from a point-by-point comparison of the best classical Kantian arguments and Parfit's hybrid reconstruction.   They are simply too far apart (94).

These remarks surprise me. Since I revise Kant's Formula in only two main ways, a point-by-point comparison is easy to make. According to one version of Kant's Formula, which I called

> *the Moral Belief Formula*: It is wrong to act on some maxim unless we could rationally will it to be true that everyone believes that such acts are morally permitted.

According to my proposed revision,

> MB5: It is wrong to act in some way unless everyone could rationally will it to be true that everyone believes that such acts are morally permitted.

One difference here is that

(F) instead of appealing to what the *agent* could rationally
will, my proposed formula appeals to what *everyone* could
rationally will.

This revision does not make these two formulas 'too far apart' to be
worth comparing. What *each* of us could rationally will, Kant and
many Kantians assume, is the same as what *everyone* could rationally
will. This assumption, I claimed, is not relevantly true. What could be
rationally willed by some people who are men, rich, or powerful could
not be rationally willed by some people who are women, poor, or weak.
Kant's Formula therefore permits some acts that are clearly wrong. To
avoid this objection, I argued, Kant's Formula should appeal to what
everyone could rationally will. No Kantian could have a deep objection
to this proposed revision. It could at most be claimed that this revision
is unnecessary.

The other difference is that

(G) unlike Kant's Formula, which applies to maxims in the
sense that covers policies, my proposed formula applies to
certain kinds of act, described in the morally relevant ways.

This revision does abandon one of the distinctive features of Kant's
moral theory, since only Kant and Kantians often use the concept of a
maxim. But as I argued, this feature of Kant's theory is a mistake, which
we should correct. It is worth restating this argument in its most general
form.   When Kant first states his formula, he writes:

I ought never to act except in such a way that I could also will
that my maxim would become a universal law.

In this and many other passages, Kant claims only that we act wrongly
if we act on maxims that we could not rationally will to be universal.
Taken strictly, this claim allows that there might be other ways in which
some acts are wrong. But Kant's Formula is one statement of what Kant
claims to be the supreme moral principle. So Kant clearly means that
we act wrongly *if and only if*, or *just when*, we act on maxims that fail
the test provided by Kant's Formula.   We can now argue:

According to Kant's Formula, we act wrongly just when we act on some maxim that fails a certain test.

Therefore

Kant's Formula implies that, if some maxim fails this test, it is always wrong to act upon it, and that, if some maxim passes this test, it is always permissible to act upon it.

There are countless maxims on which it is sometimes but not always wrong to act.

Therefore

When applied to such maxims, Kant's Formula either mistakenly condemns some acts that are morally permissible, or mistakenly permits some acts that are wrong.

As this restatement shows, nothing turns on the content of Kant's test, or on the sense in which we could not will some maxims to be universal laws. Kant's Formula fails simply because it applies to maxims, in the sense that covers policies. For Kant's Formula to succeed, it would have to be true that, if it would *ever* be wrong to act on some maxim or policy, such acts would *always* be wrong. And that is clearly false. It is sometimes but not always wrong to act on the maxims 'Do whatever would be best for me', 'Never lie', and 'Never break the law'. And there are many other *mixed maxims* of this kind.

It might be objected that, if we revise Kant's Formula so that it does not refer to maxims, we lose Kant's concern with the *principles* on which we act. For this and other reasons, I restate my proposed revision as

the Kantian Contractualist Formula: Everyone ought to follow the principles whose universal acceptance everyone could rationally will.

Herman cannot claim, I believe, that this formula is a 'hybrid reconstruction', which is deeply un-Kantian. Kant himself refers to

the idea of the will of every rational being as a will
giving universal law.

Herman's objections are not to my proposed formula, but to my way
of *applying* this formula. She has the same objections to my way of
applying Kant's own formula.

In stating these objections, Herman asks why Kant's Formula condemns
lying, and whether this formula implies that lying is always wrong.
Herman compares two principles, of which one permits us to lie
whenever that would be to our advantage, and the other permits us
to lie only when some lie is necessary to save some innocent person's
life. Like me, Herman believes that, when Kant's Formula is correctly
applied, this formula condemns lying for our own advantage, but
permits lying to save such a person's life. But Herman objects to
my way of reaching this conclusion.   She sums up my reasoning as
follows:

> When advantage-lying is widespread, it undermines the trust
> conditions necessary for cooperative activity, itself a great
> good. Therefore, a principle of general permissiveness about
> lying would not be rational to will . . . But a principle that
> permitted lying when necessary to save wrongfully threatened
> lives would not be interfering with interests we have reason
> to protect and would have little or no undermining effect
> on trust. So advantage-lying is shown to be wrong; not all
> lying is wrong; and the rationale for the wrongness points not
> to the value of rational agency, but to the benefits of
> cooperation. In this way, the revisionist retains the Kantian
> (contractualist) spirit and get a much more plausible
> moral view (85).

To my surprise, Herman rejects this way of applying Kant's Formula,
which she claims to be too *consequentialist*.   She writes:

> The consequentialism figures in the revisionary account
> twice — in the values appealed to and in the treatment of the
> universality condition setting up a comparison between how

we would fare were advantage-lying, as opposed to life-saving lying, permissible.

What Herman finds objectionable here is my appeal to certain values. On my account, she writes,

> since the values that inform rational willing are (for the most part) about what is non-morally best, the hybrid theory winds up having a strongly consequentialist cast (83).

Some possible outcome is non-morally best, in what I call the impartial-reason-implying sense, just when this outcome is the one that, from an impartial point of view, everyone would have most reason to want, or to hope will come about. When some outcome would be in this sense *impersonally* best, that is often because of the ways in which this outcome would be *best for* particular people, in a similar reason-implying sense. When I appeal to these values, I am appealing to the facts that give us personal and impartial reasons to care about our own and other people's well-being, and to the facts that may give us other non-moral reasons to care about what happens.

There are two ways in which Herman might reject my appeal to these values and reasons. She might claim that

> (H) there are no such values, since no outcomes could be either impersonally good or bad, or good or bad for particular people, in these reason-implying senses.

Or she might claim that

> (I) though outcomes can be good or bad in these reason-implying senses, when we apply Kant's Formula or any other Kantian Formula, we should not appeal to such values or reasons.

Herman elsewhere makes some claims that seem to suggest (H). For example, she writes

> states of affairs are not possible bearers of value in Kantian ethics.

But this remark is about *moral* value.   As Herman writes elsewhere:

> Things that happen are not themselves morally good or bad,
> right or wrong: only willings are.

When she discusses some outcome that involves 'loss and distress',
Herman similarly writes

> There is no point of view from which the untoward outcome
> as such makes the world morally worse.

We could all accept *these* claims. As Kant remarks when discussing the
Stoics, it is not morally bad to be in pain. But pain is bad in the different,
non-moral sense of being a state that we all have non-moral reasons to
want not to be in. And as I claimed, outcomes can be non-morally good
or bad, and good or bad for particular people, in such reason-implying
senses. It is bad when an earthquake kills many people, though this
event is not, like the act of some mass-murderer, *morally* bad.

Herman seems to have similar beliefs about these kinds of value. For
example, she writes:

> If everyone killed as they judged useful, we would have an
> unpleasant state of affairs. Population numbers would be
> small and shrinking; everyone would live in fear. These are
> bad consequences all right.

She also writes that we could not rationally

> will a world where one's life can have no value in this
> reason-giving sense.

If we accept some desire-based or aim-based subjective theory about
reasons, we could not claim that we all have such reasons to care about
our own and other people's well-being. But as these remarks suggest,
Herman seems to reject such theories, and to assume that various facts
can give us what I call value-based object-given reasons.

Though Herman seems to believe that we can have reasons of this
kind to care about what happens, she claims that, when we apply Kant's
Formula we should not appeal to such reasons. For example, when she

describes my way of applying Kant's Formula, Herman writes that my reasoning would appeal

> not to the value of rational agency, but to the
> benefits of cooperation (85).

When Herman rejects this reasoning as too Consequentialist, she must mean that our reasoning should *not* appeal to the benefits of cooperation.

We can ask: Why not? When we apply Kant's Formula, we ask whether we could rationally will it to be true either that everyone accepts some maxim and acts upon it when they can, or that everyone believes such acts to be permissible. If such a world would be bad for us and other people, and we have reasons to care about our own and other people's well-being, these facts give us reasons not to will that this maxim be universal. When we ask what we could rationally will, why should we ignore such reasons? Why should we not appeal, for example, *both* to the value of rational agency *and* to the benefits of cooperation?

Kant himself, as I remarked, does *not* ignore such reasons. When he explains why lying is wrong, Kant writes that 'a lie . . . always *harms* another, even if not another individual, nevertheless humanity generally, inasmuch as it makes the source of right unusable'. Consider next Kant's discussion of his imagined rich and self-reliant man, who has the maxim of not helping others who are in need. This man, Kant writes, could not rationally will that his maxim be a universal law,

> since many cases could occur in which one would need the
> love and sympathy of others, and in which, by such a law of
> nature arisen from his own will, he would rob himself of all
> hope of the assistance that he wishes for himself.

Kant is appealing here, not to the value of rational agency, but to this man's reasons to care about his own future well-being. As Herman writes

> It is surely no crude mistake . . . to interpret this passage as
> making some kind of prudential appeal.

But Herman then claims that this interpretation *is* a mistake. When applying Kant's Formula, she argues, we should not appeal to reasons that are *prudential* in the sense of being concerned with our own future well-being.

Herman rightly rejects one bad argument for this conclusion. Schopenhauer suggests that, since Kant here appeals to prudential reasoning, Kant undermines his claim that we ought to do our duty for moral rather than prudential reasons. That is not so. Kant does not argue that, if his imagined man helps other people in the actual world, that would in fact be better for this man, because he would thereby bring it about that other people would help him. Kant makes the quite different claim that, if this man had the power to choose how everyone would act, he could not rationally choose to live in a world in which no one would ever help others. Kant would agree that, in the actual world, we do not always have prudential reasons to help others who are in need. On Kant's view, we ought to help others for moral reasons.

Herman gives a different argument for the claim that, when we apply Kant's Formula, we should not appeal to prudential reasons. If this is how we apply Kant's Formula, Herman claims, we may be unable to show that *everyone* ought to help others who are in need. There may be some rich and self-reliant people who *could* rationally will that the maxim of not helping be a universal law.   In Herman's words:

> The problem then appears to be: can the argument in the example be construed in a way that makes it impossible for a rational agent to adopt the strategy of being willing to forgo help in order to keep his maxim of non-beneficence?

> . . . if the reasoning is prudential, then it would also be appropriate to consider the likelihood of situations arising when he would prefer help more than he prefers the policy of non-beneficence . . . any person well situated in life and of a sufficiently self-disciplined temper might have good reason to feel that the price of increased security in having the help of others is too high.

The 'price' that Herman refers to here is the fact that, if we lived in a world in which everyone helps others who are in need, we would sometimes have to help others at some cost to ourselves. Herman continues:

> there seems to be no way . . . to show that people willing to tolerate risk have a duty to help others, if they would prefer not to help.

> To salvage the argument for beneficence then, it must be possible to show that such considerations cannot legitimately be introduced. As we have so far interpreted the argument, there seems to be no way to exclude them and so no way to show that people willing to tolerate risk have a duty to help others, if they would prefer not to help.

This objection does not, however, show that we must *exclude* appeals to prudential reasons. This objection could show only that, in some cases, it may not be *enough* to appeal only to such reasons.

When Herman tries to solve this problem, moreover, she does *not* exclude appeals to prudential reasons. According to the argument that Herman regards as too weak, because it may not apply to everyone, the costs of helping others would be likely to be much less than the benefits from being helped. Rather than disallowing this prudential argument, Herman suggests a similar but stronger argument.

Herman first considers Rawls's proposed solution, which appeals to prudential reasoning from behind a veil of ignorance. If Kant's imagined man did not know that he was rich and self-reliant, Rawls claims, this man could not rationally choose to live in a world in which no one helped others who are in need. Herman rightly rejects this proposal, not because it involves prudential reasoning, but because Rawls's veil of ignorance abandons some of Kant's distinctive and plausible claims about moral reasoning.

Herman then suggests a way of applying Kant's Formula that makes no appeal to probabilities, or to the balance of likely costs and benefits. This argument claims that, even if we are rich and self-reliant, we could not rationally choose to live in a world of universal non-beneficence, in which no one helps others. No rational agent could will such a world, Herman writes

> if either of two conditions holds: (1) that there are ends that the agent wants to realize more than he could hope to benefit from non-beneficence and that he cannot bring about unaided or (2) that there are ends that it is not possible for any rational agent to forgo (ends that are in some sense necessary ends).

Though Herman claims that this argument does not involve prudential reasoning, she means only that it does not appeal to *probabilities*, or to benefits that are merely likely. This argument does appeal to our reasons to care about our future well-being, as is shown by the phrase 'hope to benefit'.

Herman considers an objection to this argument, which appeals to an imagined Stoic who chooses to adopt only ends whose achievement could not possibly require help from others. This imagined case, she argues, may be impossible, or incoherent, and she calls it 'a strength of Kant's argument that we are pushed to the edge of what we can imagine to find a potential exception'.

If this argument succeeded, however, it would show only that, according to Kant's Formula, it is wrong *never* to help others who are in need. This would be very far from a full defence of this formula. To find other objections to Kant's Formula, moreover, we are not 'pushed to the edge of what we can imagine'. There are, I argue, many actual cases in which Kant's Formula clearly fails.

The most important cases raise what I call the Non-Reversibility Objection. This objection can be summed up by comparing Kant's Formula with the Golden Rule. There are many wrong acts with which we benefit ourselves in ways that impose much greater burdens on others. As I wrote:

> The Golden Rule condemns such acts, since we would not be willing to have other people do such things to us. But when we apply Kant's formula to our acting on some maxim, we don't ask whether we could rationally will it to be true that *other* people do these things to *us*. We ask whether we could

rationally will it to be true that *everyone* does these things to *others*. And we may know that, even if everyone did these things to others, *no one* would do these things to *us*.

To stay close to Kant's example, we can return to those rich people who act on the maxim 'Give nothing to the poor'. Kant's Formula condemns these people's acts only if they could not rationally will it to be true either that they and other rich people continue to give nothing to the poor, or that everyone, including the poor, believes that their giving nothing is morally permissible. Given the restrictions on the kinds of reason to which we can here usefully appeal, we must admit, I argued, that these rich people *could* rationally will such a world. Similar claims apply to other wrong-doers, such as the men who benefit themselves by treating women as inferior, denying women certain rights and privileges, and giving less weight to women's well-being. These men could rationally will it to be true both that they and other men continue to treat women in this way, and that everyone, including women, believes their acts to be justified.

To answer this and similar objections, we cannot appeal to Herman's suggested non-probabilistic argument. Kant's Formula faces these objections because, when we apply this formula, we appeal to what the *agent* could rationally will. To avoid these objections, I believe, Kant's Formula should appeal instead to what *everyone* could rationally will.

We can now return to Herman's claims about my attempt to answer such objections to Kant's Formula of Universal Law. Herman objects to the way in which, when I apply both Kant's Formula and my proposed revision, I appeal to facts about what would be non-morally good or bad, and to our reasons to care about our own and other people's well-being. My appeal to such values and reasons, Herman claims, makes my proposed Kantian Contractualism a 'hybrid reconstruction', which departs too far from the best elements in Kant's view. When we apply Kant's Formula, Herman writes, 'such considerations cannot be legitimately introduced'.

These claims are not, I believe, true. In the second half of her Commentary, Herman gives another brilliant demonstration of what

Kantian moral reasoning can achieve even when it does not appeal to claims about well-being. As we have seen however, when Herman applies Kant's Formula, she herself sometimes appeals to such claims. So does Kant, as is shown by some of the passages I quoted above. In one of several other similar passages, Kant writes:

> if he lets his maxim of being unwilling to assist others . . . become . . . a universal permissive law, then everyone would likewise deny him assistance when he himself is in need . . . Hence the maxim of self-interest would conflict with itself if it were made a universal law . . . Consequently the maxim of beneficence towards those in need is a universal duty.

Kant also said

> I cannot will that lovelessness should become a universal law, for in that case I also suffer myself.

On Kant's view, Herman elsewhere writes, we cannot 'weigh' amounts of non-moral value, and we should reject 'principles that involving "counting heads"'. But Kant writes:

> Then two of us suffer, though the trouble really (in nature) affects only one. But there cannot be a duty to increase the ills in the world.

If we appeal to such claims about well-being, Herman writes, our theory cannot be Kantian. Anticipating Marx, Kant might have said 'Then I am not a Kantian'.

21

How the Numbers Count

75 Scanlon's Individualist Restriction

Scanlon's Commentary starts with an illuminating discussion of Kant's Formula of Universal Law and Kant's views about rationality and reasons. Since I accept all of Scanlon's main claims, I shall add only two remarks. According to what Scanlon calls 'Kantian constructivism', claims about reasons must be grounded on claims about which attitudes are consistent with regarding ourselves as rational agents (119). Scanlon asks why we ought to reject this view, and appeal instead to what Scanlon calls 'true substantive claims about reasons', (123). We ought to appeal to such claims, I believe, because they are true. I also believe that, for Kantian moral theories to succeed, they must appeal to substantive claims about reasons. It is not enough to appeal to claims about what we could will, or choose, in ways that are consistent with regarding ourselves as rational agents. Those claims would be too restricted, and too weak.

Scanlon then discusses my attempt to show that a revised version of Scanlonian Contractualism can be combined with Kantian Rule Consequentialism. Before responding to Scanlon's comments, I shall describe and defend my proposed revisions of Scanlon's view.

According to one statement of

> *Scanlon's Formula*: We are morally required to act in some way just when such acts are required by some principle that no one could reasonably reject.

Scanlon supposes that, in

> *Case One*, if Grey gave one of his organs to White, Grey
> would shorten his own life by a few years, but he would
> also give White many more years of life.

This case, as Scanlon points out, raises a 'difficulty' for his view (138). Most of us would believe that, though it would be admirable for Grey to give his organ to White, Grey is not morally required to make this gift. But if we accept Scanlon's Formula, this belief is hard to defend. This formula implies that

> (A) Grey is not required to make this gift if he could
> reasonably reject every principle that requires this act.

If we accept (A), we cannot also claim that

> (B) Grey could reasonably reject every such principle
> because he is not required to make this gift.

These claims would go round in a circle, getting us nowhere. To defend our belief that Grey is not required to make this gift, we must suggest some other ground on which Grey could reasonably reject every principle that requires this act.

Scanlon makes several claims about what are reasonable grounds for rejecting some moral principle. According to what we can call the *Greater Burden Claim*, or

> *GBC*: 'it would be unreasonable . . . to reject a principle
> because it imposed a burden on you when every alternative
> principle would impose much greater burdens on others.'

Scanlon uses the phrase 'impose a burden' in a wide sense, which covers not only harming someone but also failing to give someone some possible benefit. If some principle required me, for example, to save some stranger's life rather than your leg, this principle would impose on you the burden of losing your leg.   Suppose next that, in

> *Case Two*, I could use some scarce drug either to give Grey a
> few more years of life, or to give White many more years of

life.   Neither Grey nor White has any other claim to be
given this drug.

Scanlon's view rightly requires me to use this drug to benefit White.
As GBC implies, Grey could not reasonably reject every principle that
required this act. Though such principles would impose on Grey the
burden of losing a few years of life, any principle that did not require
this act would impose on White the much greater burden of losing
many years of life.

Case One involves the same possible benefits and burdens. Scanlon's
GBC therefore implies that Grey could not reasonably reject every
principle that required him to give his organ to White. As in *Case Two*,
though such principles would impose a burden on Grey, any principle
that did not require this act would impose a much greater burden on
White. So Scanlon's view implies, implausibly, that Grey is morally
required to shorten his life by giving his organ to White.

There is another, more serious problem. White might appeal to some
principle which permits or requires other people to take Grey's organ
by force, without Grey's consent, and give it to White. GBC seems to
imply that Grey could not reasonably reject this principle. But most of
us would believe such an act to be very wrong.

Since it is GBC which raises these problems for Scanlon's view, we should
ask whether Scanlon could reject this claim. The answer depends on
whether Scanlon should revise his view in another, wider way.

76 Utilitarianism, Aggregation, and Distributive Principles

According to what we can call Scanlon's

> *Individualist Restriction*: In rejecting some moral principle, we
> must appeal to this principle's implications only for ourselves
> and for other *single* people.

In Scanlon's words:

the justifiability of a moral principle depends only on
individuals' reasons for objecting to that principle and
alternatives to it.

We can also call such reasons *personal grounds* for rejecting some
principle. The strength of these grounds depends in part on how great
the burdens are that this principle's acceptance would or might impose
on us. This strength may also depend on certain other facts, such as how
badly off we are, and whether we are responsible for the fact that either
we or others will have to bear certain burdens. Some reasonable personal
grounds for rejecting principles, Scanlon adds, may have nothing to do
with our well-being. Such grounds might be provided, for example, by
some principle's unfairness to us. And any such list of grounds may be
incomplete, since we may come to recognize other reasonable grounds
for rejecting moral principles.

Scanlon's Individualist Restriction is given some support by one of
Scanlon's most appealing ideas, that of justifiability to *each* person. Since
we are asking which are the principles that *no one* could reasonably
reject, we must consider each person's grounds for rejecting some
principle, and we can plausibly claim that these grounds are provided
by this principle's implications for *this* person.

Scanlon also defends this claim in another way. Like Rawls, Scanlon
intends his Contractualism to provide 'a clear account of the foundations
of non-Utilitarian moral reasoning'. Act Utilitarians believe that it would
always be right to impose great burdens on a few people, if we could
thereby give small benefits to enough other people. In one of Scanlon's
imagined cases,

> *Jones* has suffered an accident in the transmitter room of a
> television station. To save Jones from one hour of severe pain,
> we would have to cancel part of the broadcast of a football
> game, which is giving pleasure to very many people.

Within a single life, pain can be *hedonically outweighed* by pleasure.
We might have decisive reasons, for example, to choose to endure one
hour of some kind of pain for the sake of many hours of some kind
of pleasure. This choice would then benefit us, by giving us a positive

net sum of pleasure minus pain. It makes no difference, Utilitarians believe, whether pain and pleasure come, not within a single life, but in different lives. On this view, it might be wrong for us to save Jones from his hour of pain. This act would be wrong if, by lessening the pleasure of the many watchers of the football game, we would reduce the total sum of pleasure minus pain. Scanlon rejects this Utilitarian conclusion, claiming instead that, whatever the number of people whose pleasure would be lessened, we ought to save Jones from his hour of pain. Many of us would agree.

Utilitarians reach such unacceptable conclusions, Scanlon suggests, because they mistakenly *add together* different people's benefits and burdens. By appealing to the Individualist Restriction, Scanlon writes, we can avoid such conclusions 'in what seems, intuitively, to be the right way'. In his words:

> A contractualist theory, in which all objections to a principle must be raised by individuals, blocks such justifications in an intuitively appealing way. It allows the intuitively compelling complaints of those who are severely burdened to be heard, while, on the other side, the sum of the smaller benefits to others has no justificatory weight, since there is no individual who enjoys these benefits . . .

On the simplest form of Scanlon's Individualist Restriction, benefits to different people cannot ever be *morally summed*. In applying Scanlon's Formula to any two conflicting principles, we should compare only the strongest personal objection that any one person would have to one of these principles, and the strongest objection that anyone else would have to the other principle. It makes no difference how many people would have these two strongest, conflicting objections, and we can ignore all other, weaker objections. Every such choice can thus be regarded as if it would affect or involve only two people. In Scanlon's phrase, *the numbers do not count*.

Scanlon qualifies this view in two ways. He suggests that, when different possible acts would impose equal burdens on different people, numbers can break ties, since we ought to impose such burdens on as few people as we can. Scanlon also suggests that, when one burden is not much smaller than another, the numbers count. To avoid these complications, we can first discuss cases in which we could either save one person from some great burden, or save many other people from *much* smaller burdens.

Scanlon's Individualist Restriction is not, I believe, the right way to avoid unacceptable Utilitarian conclusions. Scanlon misdiagnoses how Utilitarians reach these conclusions. Their mistake is not their belief that the numbers count, but their belief that it makes no moral difference how benefits and burdens are distributed between different people.

To illustrate this distinction, we can suppose that certain people have painful diseases, and that as doctors who have scarce medical resources we must decide which of these people we shall treat. None of these people has any special claims, nor do they differ in any other morally relevant way. As before, people are *burdened* in the relevant sense if they fail to receive some possible benefit.

   In some cases of this kind, if we don't intervene, some of the people whom we could benefit would be much worse off than the others. In such cases, we can say, the *baseline* is *unequal*. Suppose that, in *Case Three*, the only possible outcomes are these:

	Future days of pain for Blue	for each of some number of other people
We do nothing	100	10
We treat Blue	0	10
We treat the others	100	0

If we do nothing, Blue will be much worse off than these other people, since Blue will suffer for ten times as long as each of them. Suppose next that each day of pain is an equal burden. Utilitarians would then claim that, if we could save eleven of these other people from their 10 days of pain, we ought to treat these people rather than Blue. We would thereby save these eleven people from a combined total of 110 days of pain, which is a greater sum of benefits than the benefit to Blue of saving her from all of her 100 days of pain. Most of us would reject this Utilitarian claim, believing instead that we ought to save Blue from her great ordeal. We might even believe that we ought to save Blue from her 100 days of pain rather than saving *any* number of such other people from their much smaller burden of 10 days of pain.

Scanlon's Formula supports these beliefs. Given Scanlon's Individualist Restriction, Blue could reasonably reject every principle that required us to treat these other people, since this act would impose on Blue a burden that would be much greater than any burden that would be imposed on any other single person if instead we treated Blue.

Though Scanlon's Formula gives a plausible answer here, it does not, I believe, support this answer in the right way. If we ought to treat Blue rather than these other people, that is not because we would be saving Blue from a much greater burden. It is because, if we don't save Blue from this burden, Blue would be much worse off than these other people, since she would suffer for many more days. To show this fact to be what matters, we can turn to a version of this case in which there is no such difference, so that the *baseline* is *equal*. We can also suppose that, rather than giving Blue a very great benefit, we could give equal though much smaller benefits to everyone. Suppose that, in *Case Four*, the only possible outcomes are these:

	Future days of pain for Blue	for each of some number of other people
We do nothing	100	100
We do A	0	100
We do B	90	90

If we do nothing, Blue and the others would all be equally badly off, since they would all have 100 days of pain. If we do B, we would give equal benefits to all these people. According to Scanlon's Individualist Restriction, benefits to different people cannot be morally summed, so we ought again to do A, thereby saving Blue from all of her 100 days of pain. We would thereby give Blue a much greater benefit than we could give to any of the other people by saving this person from only 10 of her 100 days of pain. On Scanlon's view, it makes no moral difference how many of these other people we could save from 10 of their days of pain. We ought to give Blue her 100 pain-free days rather

than giving 10 pain-free days to Blue and as many as a *million* of these
other people.

These claims are clearly false. If we gave Blue her 100 pain-free days,
we would not merely be failing to save the other people from a total of ten
million days of pain. This vastly greater sum of pain would be suffered
by people who would all, without our help, suffer just as much as Blue.
We ought instead to give 10 pain-free days to each of these many people.

In cases of this kind, Scanlon's view conflicts with all plausible views
about the distribution of benefits and burdens. According to one such
view,

> *Telic Egalitarianism*: It would always be in one way better if
> benefits and burdens were more equally distributed between
> different people.

This view implies that, compared with Blue's being saved from all of
her 100 days of pain, it would be better if Blue and nine other people
were saved from 10 of their 100 days of pain. The same total sum of
benefits would then be shared equally between Blue and these other
people. Since there are no other morally relevant facts, this would be
the outcome that, by doing B, we ought to produce. It might also be
better if a *smaller* sum of benefits were shared more equally between
different people. But such cases raise questions that we can here ignore.
Egalitarianism can also be a purely deontic view, which is not about the
goodness of outcomes, and claims only that, in many cases, we ought to
distribute benefits more equally between different people. When applied
to our examples this view would have the same implications.

According to another, less familiar view, which we can call

> *the Telic Priority View*: It would always be in one way better if
> benefits came to people who are worse off.

This view also implies that, compared with Blue's being saved from all
of her 100 days of pain, it would be better if Blue and nine other people
were saved from 10 of their 100 days of pain. But this outcome would
be better, not because there would be no inequality, but because more
of these benefits would come to people who were worse off. Suppose

that we first ensure that Blue will be saved from 10 of her 100 days of pain. On the Priority View, since the other people would then face a longer ordeal than Blue, we would do more good by giving 10 further pain-free days, not to Blue, but to any of these other people. Compared with reducing any of these people's burdens from 100 days of pain to 90, we would do less good by reducing Blue's burden from 90 days to 80, and even less good by making a further reduction from 80 to 70, and so on. Since there are no other morally relevant facts, we ought to do B, saving Blue from only 10 of her days of pain so that we can also give the same benefit to these nine other people. This view could also take a non-telic, deontic form, which claimed only that, in many cases, we ought to give priority to benefiting those who are worse off.

It may help to vary our example. Suppose that Blue and several other people are all aged 25, and have life-shortening medical conditions. With our scarce medical resources, we cannot treat all these people. In *Case Five*, the only possible outcomes are these:

	Blue will live to the age of	Each of some number of other people will live to
We do nothing	30	70
We treat Blue	70	70
We treat the others	30	75

Scanlon's view implies that we ought to give Blue her 40 more years of life, whatever the number of other people to whom we could instead give 5 more years. If the number of the other people would be very large, this view would, I believe, be too extreme. But it would be fairly plausible to claim that we ought to give Blue her 40 more years of life rather than giving 5 more years to each of eight, twelve, twenty, or even more of these people.

What makes this claim plausible, however, is the fact that, without her extra 40 years, Blue's life would be so much shorter than the lives of all these other people. As before, to show this fact's importance, we can change this feature of this case. We can again suppose that, rather than giving Blue her great benefit, we could give equal though much smaller benefits to everyone. Suppose that, in *Case Six*, the only possible alternatives are these:

	Blue will live to the age of	Each of some number of other people will live to
We do nothing	30	30
We do A	70	30
We do B	35	35

On Scanlon's view, we ought to give Blue her 40 more years of life rather than giving 5 more years to Blue and to as many as a *million* of these other people. As before, that is clearly false. And what makes it false is not merely that, compared with 40 more years, 5 million more years of life would be a vastly greater total sum of benefits. These benefits would also be more fairly distributed between different people. It would be clearly better if, rather than Blue's living to the age of 70 rather than 30, Blue and a million other people each lived to 35 rather than 30. This second outcome would be better, I believe, even if these 5 extra years came to as few as seven, or six, or perhaps even fewer of these other people.

Because Utilitarians believe that the goodness of outcomes depends only on the total net sum of benefits, they deny that it would be in itself better if benefits were more equally distributed, or if benefits came to people who were worse off. Though this view is, I believe, mistaken, Utilitarians are at least neutral between different patterns of distribution. In some cases, as we have just seen, Scanlon's Formula favours the *less* equal distribution. In such cases, this formula has a built-in bias against equality, and against giving priority to benefiting those who are worse off. That is not what Scanlon intends. And, as Scanlon now agrees, we ought to reject these conclusions. In both *Cases Four* and *Six*, rather than giving Blue her great benefit, we ought to produce a greater sum of benefits that would be shared equally between Blue and many other people who are just as badly off.

These cases show, I believe, that Scanlon ought to drop his Individualist Restriction. It might be suggested that, even if Scanlon kept this restriction, he could revise his view in some other way. But it is clearly the Individualist Restriction which is making Scanlon's Formula go astray. Suppose that, in a different version of *Case Six*, we could either enable Blue to live to 70 rather than 30, or enable only *one* other person to live to 35 rather than 30. Scanlon's Formula would then rightly imply that we ought to give Blue her much greater benefit. But if instead we could enable a hundred or a million other people to live to 35 rather than 30, that would be what we ought to do. For Scanlon's Formula to give the right answer in such cases, Scanlon must allow that these many other people could reasonably reject any principle that did not require us to give these benefits to them. Since the benefits to *each* of these people would be much smaller than the benefit that we could give Blue, these people must be allowed to appeal to the fact that, as well as being as badly off as Blue, *they together* would receive a much greater total sum of benefits, in significant amounts of five years per person. Each of these people must be allowed to appeal to this fact, speaking on behalf of this group.

As these cases also show, it is not only Utilitarianism that gives weight to the numbers of people who might receive benefits or burdens. So do all plausible distributive principles. When we consider such cases, we should reject Utilitarianism, not because this view gives weight to numbers, but because it ignores distributive principles.

Scanlon claims that his Individualist Restriction

> is central to the guiding idea of Contractualism, and is also what enables it to provide a clear alternative to Utilitarianism.

This claim implies that, if Scanlon dropped this restriction, Scanlon's view would cease to provide a clear alternative to Utilitarianism. But that is not so. Even without the Individualist Restriction, Scanlonian Contractualism would provide such an alternative.

Here is one of the many ways in which that is true. According to what we can call

> *the Contractualist Priority View*: People have stronger moral claims, and stronger grounds to reject some moral principle, the worse off these people are.

Unlike the Telic Priority View, this view is not about the goodness of outcomes. In his earliest statement of his theory, Scanlon appealed to this view. When we consider a principle, Scanlon wrote,

our attention is naturally directed first to those who would
do worst under it. This is because if anyone has reasonable
grounds for objecting to the principle it is *likely* to be them.

In his book, however, Scanlon applies this view only to certain cases,
and he gives little priority to the claims of people who are worse off. As
well as dropping his Individualist Restriction, Scanlon ought to return,
I believe, to a stronger version of this Contractualist Priority View.

With these two revisions, Scanlonian Contractualism could be successfully applied to all of the cases that we have been discussing. In
these cases, we could either save a single person from some great
burden, or save many people from much smaller burdens. Scanlon
claims that, in such cases, the numbers don't count, so that we ought
to save the single person from her great burden. When applied to some
of these cases, this claim may seem acceptable. We can agree that, in
Case Three,

> (A) we ought to save Blue from her 100 days of pain rather
> than saving each of eleven other people from all of their
> 10 days of pain.

But Scanlon's view also implies that, in *Case Four*,

> (B) we ought to save Blue from her 100 days of pain rather
> than saving Blue and a million other people from 10 of their
> 100 days of pain.

And (B) is clearly false. Instead of claiming that the numbers don't
count, Scanlon should say that people have stronger moral claims, and
stronger grounds to reject some principle, the worse off these people
are. This version of Scanlon's view would still rightly imply (A). Because
Blue would suffer much more than each of the eleven other people,
Blue has a much stronger claim to be saved from most of her days of
pain. And this view would not mistakenly imply (B). Since these million
other people are as badly off as Blue, facing the same great ordeal, these
people's claims to be saved from any of their days pain are as strong as
Blue's. So they could reasonably reject any principle that did not require
us to save them from a total of ten million of their days of pain.

Similar claims apply to *Cases Five* and *Six.* This revised version of Scanlon's view would also have more plausible implications in many other kinds of case. That is in part because, unlike the claim that benefits to different people cannot be morally summed, the Contractualist Priority View can respond to differences of degree. On this view, when we compare the strength of people's grounds for rejecting some moral principle, we ought to give slightly more weight to the moral claims of people who are slightly worse off, and much more weight to the claims of people who are much worse off.

If Scanlon drops his Individualist Restriction, he might appeal instead to a similar but weaker view. Scanlon suggests one such view, according to which numbers count only when we are comparing benefits and burdens that are *close enough* in size. But this *Close Enough View* would also have unacceptable implications. Suppose this view claims that, for some benefit to be morally outweighed by many lesser benefits, these other benefits must be at least a quarter as great.   Suppose next that, in

Case Seven, we could give extra years of life to people who would otherwise die at 30. We could either

(1) give 40 more years to Blue,

or

(2) give 15 more years to each of a thousand other people,

or

(3) give 5 more years to each of a million other people.

On the Close Enough View, the great benefit to Blue would be outweighed by the lesser benefits to the thousand other people, since these benefits are close enough in their size. The benefits to the thousand would in turn be outweighed by the benefits to the million, since these benefits are also close enough. But Blue's great benefit would *not* be outweighed by the benefits to the million, since these benefits are *not* close enough. So the Close Enough View implies that we ought to do (2) rather than (1), and that we ought to do (3) rather than (2), and that we ought to do (1) rather than (3). Whatever we do, we would be acting wrongly, since we ought to have done something else instead. Even if there might be cases in which we could not avoid acting wrongly, that is not plausible here. And it is clear that we ought to do (3) rather than doing either (1) or (2).

Rather than appealing to the Close Enough View, Scanlon's claim should at most be that significant benefits and burdens cannot be morally outweighed by any number of other benefits and burdens that are insignificant, or trivial. He might, for example, claim that

> (C) we ought to give to one person one more year of life
> rather than lengthening any number of other people's
> lives by only one minute,

and that

> (D) we ought to save one person from a whole year of pain
> rather than saving any number of other people from only one
> minute of similar pain.

Though these claims are very plausible, they can have unacceptable implications. A year contains about half a million minutes. Suppose that, in

> *Case Eight*, we are in some community of slightly more
> than a million people, each of whom we could benefit
> once in the way described by (C). Each of these acts
> would give to one of these people half a million more
> minutes of life rather than giving one more minute of
> life to each of the million other people.

Since these effects would be equally distributed, these acts would be worse for everyone. If we always acted in this way, we would give everyone only one more year of life. If instead we always gave all the other people their extra minutes, we would give everyone a total of *two* more years of life. Suppose next that, in

> *Case Nine*, these people are often in pain, and we could
> benefit each person once in the way described by (D). Each
> of these acts would save one of these people from half a

million minutes of pain rather than saving each of the million
other people from one such minute.

As before, these acts would be worse for everyone. If we always acted in
this way, we would save all these people from only one rather than two
years of pain. These are clearly unacceptable conclusions. It would be
wrong to follow (C) and (D), since these people would then all die one
year sooner, and all have one more year of pain.

There are several ways in which claims like (C) and (D) can seem
to be obviously true. Most of us are bad at judging the significance of
large numbers. We may assume that, if it matters little whether one
person would bear some burden, it also matters little whether a million
people would bear such burdens. We may also assume that, if some
people would bear much greater burdens than others, or would lose
much greater benefits, these are the people who would be worst off. But
that may not be true. And when it isn't, one great loss may be morally
outweighed by many small benefits. Suppose that, if I gave a million
dollars to some aid agency, my gift would be divided equally between
ten million of the world's poorest people, so that each of these people
would get only ten cents. If I was giving away most of my wealth, the
burden to me of losing a million dollars would be much greater than
the average benefit that ten cents would give to each of these other
people. But these million benefits would *together* be much greater than
my burden. Since this sum of benefits would both be much greater, and
would come to people who are much worse off than me, it is morally
irrelevant that the average benefit to each of these people would be very
small. My million dollars, even when giving these people such small
benefits, would do much more good.

Another mistake is to consider only single acts. Some acts give
ourselves significant benefits in ways that impose tiny burdens on very
many other people. That is true, for example, of many of the acts that
add to the pollution of many people's air, food, or water. When we
consider any one such act, the tiny effects on the many other people
may seem trivial. It may seem not to matter if such an act imposes
costs on others of less than ten cents, or reduces the life-expectancy of
others by less than one minute. But when many people act in such ways,

these small effects add up. And when such effects are roughly equally distributed, these acts are worse for almost all of the affected people. In the world as it is now, such acts together impose very great burdens on very many people.

Though we should not always ignore trivial benefits and burdens, we may often be justified in doing that. That might be true in Scanlon's case in which, to spare Jones from an hour of severe pain, we would have to interrupt the pleasure of millions of watchers of a football game. It might be reasonable for Jones to reject any principle that would require or permit us to let him suffer his hour of pain. The million watchers might object that, though each of them would lose little, they together would lose a sum of pleasure that would hedonically outweigh Jones's hour of pain. But Jones would be much worse off than all these people. Given this fact, Jones might plausibly reply, his claim to be spared his pain morally outweighs their combined claims.

We can now turn to a different question. When a great benefit to one person might be morally outweighed by several lesser benefits to other people, we must ask whether the importance of these benefits would be *proportional* to their size. That would be true, for example, if some benefit to one person would have the same importance as two benefits to other people that were half as great.

Scanlon suggests that, rather than saving one person's life, we ought perhaps to save a million people from total paralysis. For most people, becoming completely paralyzed would be at least a twentieth as bad as dying. If the moral importance of these burdens were proportional to their size, one person's death would be morally outweighed by as few as thirty or forty people's becoming completely paralyzed. Since Scanlon chooses the much larger number of a million people, he seems to give these lesser burdens much less weight.   On what we can call this

> *Disproportional View*: The moral importance of lesser benefits and burdens is *less* than proportional to their size.

This view is a weaker version of Scanlon's Individualist Restriction. On that restriction, a great benefit or burden to one person cannot be morally outweighed by any number of lesser benefits or burdens to other people. On the Disproportional View, this great benefit or burden could be morally outweighed, but the lesser benefits or burdens should not be simply added together, as Utilitarians claim. Though such lesser benefits or burdens can be added together, they should be given disproportionately less weight.

Scanlon ought, I believe, to reject this view. Though a great burden to one person should often be given disproportionately greater weight, that is true, I believe, only when and because this burden would make this person much worse off than other people. When this person would *not* be worse off, the Disproportional View is mistaken. Suppose that, in

Case Ten, we could either

(1) save Blue from all of her 100 days of pain

or

(2) save each of ten other people from 10 of their 100 days of pain.

Suppose next that, because each day of pain would be an equal burden, (1) would give a benefit to Blue that is ten times as great as the benefits that (2) would give to each of these ten other people. If the importance of these lesser benefits were less than proportional to their size, we ought to give Blue her 100 pain-free days. But the *opposite* is true. It is Blue's *greater* benefit whose moral importance is less than proportional to its size. As the Priority View claims, benefits have less moral weight when they come to people who are better off. Compared with the claims of the other people to have their days of pain reduced from 100 to 90, Blue would have a weaker claim to have her days of pain reduced from 90 to 80, an even weaker claim to have a further reduction from 80 to 70, and so on. That is one reason why, rather than giving Blue her 100 pain-free days, we ought to give 10 pain-free days to as few as nine, or eight, or even fewer of these other people.

In some cases, as Temkin suggests, there is an argument the other way. Temkin claims that, though we always have more reason to spread *burdens* over many different people, we may sometimes have reasons to concentrate *benefits*, by giving them all to a single person. In *Case Seven*, for example, we may have a special reason to give Blue her extra

40 years of life, since that would allow at least one person to live a full life. Temkin here appeals to what we might call a *qualitative* reason to give benefits to a single person.

Though we may sometimes have such reasons, Temkin's view is different from and does not support the Disproportional View. Consider, for example,

> *Musical Chairs*: A hundred people will later be at a hundred levels of well-being.   There are only two possibilities:

> (A) *Person One* is at level 1, *Person Two* at level 2, *Person Three* at level 3, and so on.

> (B) Person One is at level 100, and everyone else is one level lower down.

On the Disproportional View, we ought to choose (B). If greater gains and losses had an importance that was more than proportional to their size, the single great gain to Person One of being ninety nine levels higher would clearly morally outweigh the ninety nine small losses of the other people. That is not plausible. Person One has no claim to be at the top.

Scanlon, I conclude, should not appeal to any weaker version of his Individualist Restriction. If Scanlon appeals instead to a strong version of the Contractualist Priority View, his view would provide a clear alternative to Utilitarianism, and would avoid all of the objections that we have been considering.

We can now return to an earlier objection.   Remember that, in

> *Case One*, if Grey gave one of his organs to White, Grey
> would shorten his own life by a few years, but he would also
> give White many more years of life.

There is no other way, we can add, in which White's life could be saved, since Grey is the only other person who has an organ of the right tissue-type. As we have seen, Scanlon's present view implies that Grey ought to shorten his life in this way, since Grey could not reasonably reject every principle that required him to give his organ to White. This case raises a problem, Scanlon writes, because he is inclined to believe that Grey is *not* required to make this gift. That is also what most people would believe.

As I have said, there is another, more serious problem. If some principle requires Grey to give his organ to White, this principle could also claim that Grey has a right to decide what happens to his body. Grey would then have a right to act wrongly, by deciding not to give his organ to White. But we can next consider a more extreme principle which *denies* that Grey has such a right, since this principle permits or requires other people to take Grey's organ, without Grey's consent, and give it to White. This principle conflicts even more deeply with most people's moral beliefs.

Scanlon's Formula would support these beliefs if Grey could reasonably reject this principle. When discussing a similar case, Scanlon writes

It is not unreasonable to refuse to regard one's own life and body as 'on call', to be sacrificed whenever it is needed to save others who are at risk.

As we have seen, however, Scanlon also claims

GBC: It would be unreasonable to reject some principle because it imposed a burden on you when every alternative principle would impose much greater burdens on others.

If we accept this claim, it may be hard to argue that Grey could reasonably reject every principle that permitted or required other people to take Grey's organ, without Grey's consent, and give it to White. Even if some other people acted in this way, Grey would lose only a few years of life, and that is a much smaller burden than the many years of life that, without Grey's organ, White would lose. And if Grey could not reasonably reject this principle, Scanlon's Formula would imply that it would be right for other people to take Grey's organ without Grey's consent and give it to White. Since that is much harder to believe, this implication would provide a much stronger objection to Scanlon's view.

It might be suggested that, since Grey has a right to decide what happens to his body, Grey could reasonably reject every principle that permitted others to take his organ without his consent. But in claiming that Grey has this right, we would be claiming that it would be wrong for others to act in this way. And when we are asking what Scanlon's Formula implies, we cannot appeal to our beliefs about which acts are wrong. We can appeal to these beliefs only at a later stage, when we are deciding whether, given its implications, we ought to accept this formula.

There is, however, another way in which, when we apply Scanlon's Formula, we might defend the claim that Grey has a right to decide what happens to his organ. If Scanlon drops his Individualist Restriction, as I have argued that he should, he could also reject GBC. According to this revised version of Scanlon's view, we could reasonably reject some principles by appealing to the combined force of the grounds for rejection that we and various other people *together* have. We might then claim that we could reasonably reject any principle that permitted or required others to take Grey's organ without Grey's consent and give it to White. We all have reasons to want not to live in a world in which, when people in Grey's position refuse to give their organs, these people are hunted down by the police, and have their organs taken from them by force. Each of us would know that there would be only a small chance that we ourselves would be treated in this way. Given this fact, our reasons to want not to live in such a world would be *individually* much weaker than White's reason to want not to lose many years of life. But it might be true that *we together* have stronger grounds for rejecting any principle that would permit or require some people's organs to be forcibly removed and given to others.

It may be objected that, though we might later be in Grey's position, and would then lose a few years of life if some organ were forcibly taken from us, we would be just as likely to be in White's position, and we would then gain many more years of life if someone else's organ were given to us. Since our possible benefit in White's position would be much greater than our possible loss in Grey's position, it may seem that we could *not* reasonably reject every principle that permitted or required such acts. We could plausibly reply, however, that our grounds for rejecting these principles would not be provided only by the ways in which the acceptance of these principles would affect our own and other people's life-expectancies. Since such cases would be rare, these effects would be small. If in all such cases some people's organs would be forcibly reallocated, everyone's predictable life-expectancy might rise by only a few hours or minutes. Our reasons to want such expectable benefits might be clearly outweighed by our reasons to want not to live in a world in which the police hunt some people down and take their organs by force.

Here is another, partly similar question. When we know that the lives of certain people are in danger, as would be true, for example, if some group of miners are trapped underground, we have reasons to want great efforts to be made to save these people's lives. Some economists point out that we would do more to increase people's life-expectancy if, rather than spending huge sums on trying to save known particular people in such emergencies, we spent this money on more cost-effective safety measures that would prevent a greater number of statistically predictable future deaths. But we could reasonably deny that this fact is morally decisive. We have strong reasons to want great efforts to be made to save the lives of known particular people who are in danger. By making or supporting such efforts, for example, we reaffirm and express our solidarity with, and concern for, everyone in our community. That is less true of acts that merely prevent the statistically predictable future deaths of unknown people.

We have similar reasons to want it to be true that no one would be hunted down and have their organs removed by force. And though such acts would be done to save the lives of certain known particular people, these acts would also produce much anxiety, conflict, and mistrust. We would have to admit that, compared with White's reasons to want to have many more years of life, and the similar reasons of those few other people who would be in White's position, the rest of us would have only weaker reasons to want to avoid such anxiety and mistrust. But even if these reasons were individually much weaker, the combined force of all these reasons would, I believe, give us reasonable grounds to reject any principle that required or permitted people's organs to be taken from them by force. So, if Scanlon dropped his Individualist Restriction, he could answer the objection that his view requires or permits such acts.

We can next ask whether, if Scanlon drops his Individualist Restriction and his Greater Burden Claim, he could also argue that Grey could reasonably reject any principle which required him, in *Case One*, to *give* his organ to White. This principle allows that Grey has the right to decide what happens to his body, and the right to act wrongly by refusing to give his organ to White. Given this fact, Scanlon could not reject this principle with the claims that I have just made. If we all accepted this principle, no one would be hunted down and have their organs removed by force. We might claim that we all had reasons to want not to be morally required, if we were in Grey's position, to give up a few years of life. But we would have to admit that, if we were in White's position, we would all have stronger reasons to want to be given many more years of life.

There may, however, be other grounds on which we could reasonably reject this principle. We can reasonably reject some principles, Scanlon claims, on grounds that do not appeal only to the size of the burdens that these principles would impose on us or others, and to our level of well-being, or to claims about fairness. Of such other grounds, some might appeal to certain facts about human nature. Though most of us could follow moral requirements not to kill or seriously injure other people even when such acts would save our own lives, most of us would find it very hard to give up several years of life, merely to add many more years to some stranger's life. We might claim that, given these and similar facts, it is unreasonable to expect or require people to make this kind of sacrifice for strangers. In making such claims, we would not be violating the Moral Beliefs Restriction, since we would not be appealing to the belief that no one is morally required to make this kind of sacrifice. We would instead be claiming that these facts about human nature provide reasonable grounds for rejecting principles that require such acts.

22

Scanlonian Contractualism

77 Scanlon's Claims about Wrongness and the Impersonalist Restriction

There are, I believe, two other ways in which Scanlon should revise and thereby strengthen his version of Contractualism.

In his book, Scanlon claimed that, rather than describing the facts that can *make* acts wrong, his theory gives an account of wrongness itself, or of *what it is* for some act to be wrong. This claim, I have argued, was a mistake. According to one statement of

> Scanlon's Formula: An act is wrong just when such acts are disallowed by some principle that no one could reasonably reject.

If Scanlon was here using 'wrong' in a Contractualist sense, to mean 'disallowed by such an unrejectable principle', he could truly claim that his formula gives an account of this Contractualist kind of wrongness, or of what it is for acts to be wrong in this Contractualist sense. But Scanlon's Formula would then be a concealed tautology, whose open form would be

> SF2: An act is disallowed by some principle that no one could reasonably reject just when such acts are disallowed by such an unrejectable principle.

We could all accept this trivial claim, whatever our moral beliefs. Scanlon's claim should instead be that, if some act is disallowed by such an unrejectable principle, this fact makes this act wrong in one or more other, non-Contractualist senses. Scanlon might for example claim

> SF3: When some act is wrong in this Contractualist sense, that makes this act wrong in the justifiabilist, blameworthiness, and reactive-attitude senses.

These four senses of 'wrong' are all definable abbreviations of longer phrases. So this version of Scanlon's Formula could be more fully stated as

> SF4: When some act is disallowed by some principle that no one could reasonably reject, this fact makes this act unjustifiable to others, blameworthy, and an act that gives its agent reasons for remorse and gives others reasons for indignation.

Scanlon now accepts that his Contractualist theory should take some such form.

We can turn next to another of Scanlon's claims about what are reasonable grounds for rejecting moral principles. According to what we can call Scanlon's

> *Impersonalist Restriction*: In rejecting some moral principle, we cannot appeal to claims about the impersonal goodness or badness of outcomes.

All reasons for rejecting principles, Scanlon claims, must be *personal*. Scanlon also writes:

> impersonal values are not themselves grounds for reasonable rejection.

Though Scanlon does not explicitly say that we cannot appeal to claims about the impersonal goodness of outcomes, that is implied by these other claims. Of these who reject such appeals, some claim that there is no sense in which outcomes can be impersonally good or bad. That is not Scanlon's view. Scanlon believes both that outcomes can be good or bad in the impartial-reason-implying sense, and that we can have strong reasons to try to produce or prevent such outcomes.

Scanlon gives, as one example, reasons provided by the suffering of animals. He writes

> like the pain of humans, the pain of non-human animals is something we have reason to prevent and relieve, and failing to respond to this reason is a moral fault.

Scanlon then imagines someone saying:

> If there are impersonal reasons of this kind, why should they not count as possible grounds for reasonably rejecting principles?

He replies:

> In answering this question, it is important to bear in mind the limited range of the part of morality we are trying to characterize. The Contractualist formula is meant to describe one category of moral ideas: the requirements of 'what we owe to each other'. Reasons for rejecting a principle thus correspond to particular forms of concern that we owe to other individuals. By definition, impersonal reasons do not represent forms of such concern.

When Scanlon claims that certain acts are *owed to others*, he means that failing to act in these ways would be wrong in his Contractualist sense, because there is some principle requiring such acts that no one could reasonably reject. Since Scanlon himself defines this Contractualist sense, he is entitled to claim that, when we ask which acts are in this sense wrong, we should not appeal to impersonal reasons, since by definition such reasons are irrelevant. But Scanlon now claims that, when acts are in this sense wrong, that makes these acts wrong in other, non-Contractualist senses. And Scanlon could not say that, when we ask which acts are wrong in these other senses, claims about what is good or bad in the impartial-reason-implying sense are *by definition* irrelevant.

Scanlon also suggests that, when we ask what we owe to others in his Contractualist sense, we can appeal to the importance to us of being able to respond to certain impersonal values. For example, we could reasonably reject some principle that required us to keep some fairly trivial promise rather than saving some animal from great pain. As Scanlon points out, however, what we owe to others sometimes conflicts with impersonal values. And when we ask which acts are wrong in non-Contractualist senses, we could not defensibly claim that what we owe to others always has priority over such values.

Consider for example some *Retributive Principle* which requires us to give criminals the punishment that they deserve, even when such punishment would benefit no one. When we appeal to Scanlon's Formula, this principle is hard to defend. Criminals might reasonably object that such punishment would be bad for them and good for no one. We *owe it to them*, they might claim, not to punish them in a way that benefits no one. Scanlon would reject this Retributive Principle, I believe rightly. But Retributivists might reply that it would be in itself good if people get the punishment that they deserve. In rejecting this reply, Scanlon might claim that what we owe to others has moral priority over such facts about the goodness of outcomes. But that, I believe, would not be an adequate reply. We must reject the Retributive Principle in some other way, such as by arguing that deserved punishment is not in itself good, or that no one could deserve to suffer.

Since what we owe to others cannot be plausibly claimed to have absolute moral priority over facts about the goodness of outcomes, Scanlon's view could take either of two other forms. If Scanlon keeps his Impersonalist Restriction, he might retreat to the view that, when some act is wrong in his Contractualist sense, that makes this act *prima facie* wrong in other, non-Contractualist senses. Such acts would be wrong unless they could be justified by appeals to claims about the goodness of outcomes. On this version of Scanlon's view, his formula would claim to describe only one of the facts that can make acts wrong in other senses. This version of Scanlon's view might seem disappointingly weak. But that might not be true. Scanlon might be able to defend the claim that, when acts are wrong in his Contractualist sense, that very often makes these acts wrong in other senses. And Scanlon's Formula might condemn most wrong acts. This formula might then describe one of the most important facts that can make acts wrong, and in a way that helps to explain why many other, more particular facts can also make acts wrong.

Suppose next that Scanlon drops his Impersonalist Restriction. On this version of Scanlon's view, when we claim that we could reasonably reject some principle, we are allowed to appeal to our beliefs about the goodness of outcomes. Given this revision, Scanlon could make the bolder claim that acts are wrong in other senses *just when*, and in part because, they are wrong in Scanlon's Contractualist sense. If that were true, Scanlon's Contractualism would unify, and help to explain, all of the more particular facts that can make acts wrong. That gives Scanlon a strong reason to make this bolder claim.

78 The Non-Identity Problem

Scanlon has other reasons, I believe, to drop his Impersonalist Restriction. When Scanlon asks what we owe to others, he intends these *others* to include all future people. In his words:

> contractualism provides no reason for saying that people who do not now exist but will exist in the future have no moral claims on us . . .

He also writes: 'a restriction to presently existing human beings seems obviously too narrow'. In deciding what we owe to future people, we must answer some questions that Scanlon does not discuss. So I shall now discuss these questions, returning only later to Scanlon's theory.

When our acts will affect certain people, it may be morally irrelevant that these people do not yet exist. If I leave some broken glass in a wood, and some years later a child is injured by this glass, my negligence may straightforwardly harm this child. It may be true that, if I had not left this broken glass where I did, this child would have later walked out of this wood unharmed. If that is true, my harmful act would be just as wrong whether or not, when I acted, this child already existed.

Suppose next that we must choose whether our community will continue to deplete certain scarce unrenewable resources, or continue to overheat the Earth's atmosphere. If we choose

> *Depleting* or *Overheating*, these policies would raise the
> quality of life of existing people, but the long-term effects,
> more than a century from now, would significantly lower
> the quality of future people's lives.

Such bad effects, we may assume, are like the bad effects that our policies might have on presently existing people. As Scanlon writes, 'It matters that there are, or will be, people out there with lives that will be affected by what we do.'

There is, however, a problem here that is often overlooked. As well as having effects on the quality of future people's lives, our acts and policies may affect *who it is* who will later live. Which particular children we have depends on the slightest details of our private lives. Many of our acts affect such details in our own and other people's lives, and these effects spread, like ripples in a pool, over more and more lives. Unlike ripples, moreover, these effects never fade away. Over time, there will be more and more people of whom it is true that, if we had acted differently, these people would never have been conceived. If the motor car had not been invented, for example, it is likely that none of the readers of this book would ever have existed. When we together choose whether to continue policies like *Depleting* or *Overheating*, our choice may affect the identity of most of the people who will live more than a century from now. For these reasons, we can often know that

> (A) if we act in one of two ways, or follow one of two policies,
> we would be likely to cause some of the lives that are later lived
> to be less worth living,

but that

> (B) since it would be different people who would later live
> these lives, these acts or policies would not be worse for any
> of these people.

We should ask whether and how (B) makes a difference. I have called this *the Non-Identity Problem*.

Some people believe that

> (C) one of two outcomes cannot be worse, nor can one of two acts be wrong, if this outcome or act would be worse for no one.

On this *Narrow Person-Affecting View,* even if such acts would greatly lower the quality of life in the further future, we have no reason not to act in these ways.

Most of us would rightly reject this view. We would believe that

> (D) it would be in itself worse if some of the lives that will later be lived will be less worth living,

and that

> (E) we have reasons not to act in ways that would have such effects, and if these effects would predictably be very bad, and we could avoid them at little cost to ourselves, such acts would be wrong.

There are now two possibilities. On one view,

> (F) it makes no difference whether, because these future lives would be lived by the same people, these acts would be worse for these people.

We can call this *the No Difference View.* On what we can call

> *the Two-Tier View*: This fact does make a difference. Though we always have reasons not to cause future lives to be less worth living, these reasons would be weaker if, because these lives would be lived by different people, these acts would not be worse for any of these people.

The Non-Identity Problem must be either practically or theoretically important. If the Two-Tier View is true, this problem is practically important, since our reasons and our obligations would in part depend on whether our acts would be worse for future people. If the No Difference View is true, the Non-Identity Problem has no practical importance. But this very fact would make this problem theoretically important, since many moral theories imply that the No Difference View cannot be true. On these theories, it must make a difference whether such acts would be worse for people.

In discussing these views, it will help to define a new phrase. Suppose that *Jane*, a 14-year-old girl, declares that she intends to have a child. In trying to persuade Jane to wait, we might say:

> It would be worse for your first child if you have him now, while you are so young. If you have this child later, that would be better for him, since you would be able to give him a better start in life.

When we make such remarks, we may not be using the words 'this child' and 'him' to refer to a particular person. Suppose that Jane has a child now, whom she calls *Johnny*, and whom she fails to bring up well. We may know that, if Jane had waited before having her first child, that would not have been better for Johnny, since Johnny would never have existed. It would have been a different child to whom Jane would have later given a better start in life. Such uses of 'her child' and 'him' refer, not to a particular person, but to what we can call a *general person*. This phrase is merely an abbreviation. Like *the Average American*, a general person is not a person. A general person is a large group of possible people, one of whom will be actual. Things would go worse for the general person who is *Jane's first child* if the particular person who is actually Jane's first child has a life that is less worth living than the life that would have been lived by the different particular person who, if Jane had waited, *would* have been Jane's first child.

We can now say that, according to the No Difference View, we have equal reasons to avoid doing what would be worse either for particular people, or for general people. According to the Two-Tier View, we have stronger reasons to avoid doing what would be worse for particular people. We can here suppose that, on this view, these reasons would be twice as strong, so that, compared with benefits or burdens to particular people, benefits or burdens to general people matter morally only half as much. Other versions of the Two-Tier View would require us to give either more or less priority to the interests of particular people.

When I consider policies like *Depleting* or *Overheating*, I accept the No Difference View. We always have reasons, I believe, not to act in ways that would lower the future quality of people's lives, and these reasons would be just as strong whether or not, because these lives would be lived by different people, these acts would not be worse for any particular people. When other people first become aware of the Non-Identity Problem, many respond like me, by accepting the No Difference View. After further thought, however, some of these people turn to the Two-Tier View.

In asking which view we ought to accept, it will help to consider some other cases. Suppose that, in

> the Two Medical Programs, we are doctors who must make decisions about the future policies of some National Health Service. We have planned two screening programs. In Program A, millions of women would be tested during pregnancy, so that we can identify those women who have a certain rare disease. By curing these women, we would prevent their disease from causing their unborn children to have some life-shortening condition. In Program B, millions of women would be tested when they intend to have a child, so that we can identify those women who have some other rare disease. By curing these women, we would prevent their disease from causing any children that they conceive to have a similar life-shortening condition. Since these women would be warned to postpone having a child until they had been cured, this delay would lead them to conceive different children.

Suppose next that, because our Government cuts Health Service funds, we must cancel one of these programs, and we must choose between them. We can predict that these programs would achieve results in as many cases. If we carry out either program, we would enable the same number of women to have a child who would not have some life-shortening condition. These would be different women, on the two programs. But since the numbers would be the same, the effects on these women and on other people would be morally equivalent. If there is a moral difference between these programs, this difference must depend on how these programs would affect these children.

In considering these effects, we don't need to ask what is the moral status of a foetus or unborn child. Nor do we need to ask whether we have greater obligations to existing people than we have to future people. We can suppose that it would take at least a year before either medical program could begin, so that, when we choose between these programs, none of these future children has yet been conceived. And all of the children who will be conceived will be born and become adults. So, in choosing between these programs, we can ask how our choice would affect these future people. We can also suppose that these people's lives, even if they would be shorter than most people's lives, would be happy, and well worth living.

This example could be filled out in different ways. Suppose first that, in *Case One*:

> If we choose Program A, a thousand people would be conceived who would live for 70 rather than 50 years.

> If we choose Program B, a thousand people would be conceived who would live for 70 years, rather than a thousand different people who would live for 50 years.

On the No Difference View, these programs would be equally worthwhile. Though Program A would benefit particular future people, and Program B would benefit general people, these two kinds of benefit matter morally just as much. On the Two-Tier View, Program A would be better than Program B. Program A would give to a thousand particular people the benefit of an extra 20 years of life. Program B would give this benefit to as many general people, but such benefits matter less. Suppose next that, in *Case Two*:

> The predictable effects would be in one way different.
> If we cancel Program B, the people who would be
> conceived would live for only 40 years, so this program
> would give to a thousand general people the greater
> benefit not of 20 but of 30 extra years of life.

On the No Difference View, Program A would here be worse than Program B. On the Two-Tier View, since benefits to general people matter only half as much, Program A would again be better than Program B.

When I consider these examples, I accept the No Difference View, as do many other people. But some people accept the Two-Tier View. It must make a difference, these people believe, that only Program A would give more years of life to the same particular people, thereby benefiting these people.

In some other kinds of case, the Two-Tier View is harder to accept. Suppose first that, in *Case Three*, we have only these alternatives.

If we choose A	Tom will live for 70 years,	Dick will live for 50 years,	and Harry will never exist.
If we choose B	Tom will live for 50 years,	Dick will never exist,	and Harry will live for 70 years.

This case is a smaller version of *Case One*. On the No Difference View, these programs would be equally good. On the Two-Tier View, Program B would be worse than Program A, Since B would be worse for Tom, and A would be worse, not for any particular person, but only for the general person who would here partly consist of Dick and Harry. This general person would lose 20 extra years of life if we choose A, just as Tom would lose 20 years if we choose B. Since losses to particular people count for more, the Two-Tier View here implies that we ought to choose A.

Suppose next that, in *Case Four*, another outcome would be possible. Our alternatives are these:

If we choose A	Tom will live for 70 years	Dick will live for 50 years	————
If we choose B	Tom will live for 50 years	————	Harry will live for 70 years
If we choose C	————	Dick will live for 70 years	Harry will live for 50 years

'————' means 'will never exist'.

Just as B would be worse than A for Tom and better only for a general person, A would be worse than C for Dick and better only for a general person, and C would be worse than B for Harry and better only for a general person. The Two-Tier View therefore implies that B is worse than A, which is worse than C, which is worse than B. Whichever program we choose, we shall have acted wrongly, since some other choice would have been better. On a more widely accepted view, which we can call

> *the Pareto Principle*: One of two outcomes would be worse
> if this outcome would be worse for some people, better for
> no one, and other things would be equal.

This principle implies that, of these outcomes, B would be worse than A, which would be worse than C, which would be worse than B.

These are unacceptable conclusions. Even if there are some cases in which we cannot avoid choosing and acting wrongly, that is not true in *Case Four*. These three choices, acts, and outcomes are clearly morally equivalent. If we accept the Two-Tier View, we must revise this view, so that it ceases to have these implications.

In revising this view, we should try to change this view's implications in cases like *Four*, while preserving its implications in the much more common cases that are like *Case Three*. If we did not preserve those implications, we would be abandoning the Two-Tier

View. If this view made claims about the intrinsic goodness of outcomes, as does the Pareto Principle, the Two-Tier View could not be revised in this selective way. We could not coherently claim both that

(G) outcome B would be intrinsically worse than outcome A if these are the only possible alternatives,

and that

(H) these outcomes would be equally good if C is also possible.

Whether one of two outcomes would be *intrinsically* worse cannot depend on which other outcomes are possible. Something's intrinsic goodness depends only on its intrinsic features, not its relation to other things. But the Two-Tier View might make claims that are only about what we ought to choose, and about which acts are wrong. When we ask whether one of two acts would be wrong, the answer may sometimes depend on which other acts are possible.

Suppose for example that, in *Great Risk*, two people's lives are in danger. These people are strangers to me. I could either

X: Do nothing

or

Y: Save one of these people's lives at a great risk to myself.

We can plausibly believe that, if these are my only possible acts, I would be morally permitted to act in either way. Since Y would involve a great risk to me, this heroic act would go beyond the call of duty. Suppose instead that I could also

Z: Save both these people's lives, at no extra risk to myself.

If I knew that doing Z was also possible, doing Y would be wrong. If I decide to run this risk, I ought to save both these people. But I would still be morally permitted to do X, since I would have no duty to run this risk. Whether it would be wrong for me to do Y rather than X therefore depends on whether Z is possible. We can explain why that is true by appealing to these facts about the risk to me.

In revising the Two-Tier View, we might similarly try to defend the claim that

> (I) it would be wrong for us to choose B rather than A in *Case Three*, when these are the only possible choices, but choosing B would *not* be wrong in *Case Four*, in which choice C is also possible.

Temkin suggests one way in which we might revise the Two-Tier View. On what we can here call *Temkin's View*, in cases of the kind that we are now considering, what we ought to choose depends in part on the intrinsic goodness of the outcomes of our choices, and in part on whether any of the people involved would have a *personal complaint*, because this outcome is worse for this person than some other possible outcome would have been.

In *Case Three* the only possible outcomes are these:

If we choose A	Tom will live for 70 years	Dick will live for 50 years	————
If we choose B	Tom will live for 50 years	————	Harry will live for 70 years

These outcomes are equally good, since each would involve the existence of two people, of whom one would live for 70 years and the other for 50. If we choose B, however, Tom would have a complaint, since B is worse for him. By choosing A, we could have given Tom 20 more years of life. If we choose A, Dick would have no similar complaint. On Temkin's view, since these outcomes are equally good, Tom's complaint about B breaks this tie, and is decisive. As the original Two-Tier View implies, we ought to choose A rather than B. In *Case Four*, there is also a third possible outcome:

If we choose C	————	Dick will live for 70 years	Harry will live for 50 years

Now that we could also choose C, Dick would have a complaint if we choose A, since we could have given Dick 20 more years of life by choosing C. Harry would have a similar complaint if we choose C, since we could have given Harry 20 more years by choosing B. Since these outcomes are equally good, and these three complaints would be equally strong, Temkin's View here rightly implies that these three choices are morally equivalent.

When applying Temkin's View, we must often make further decisions. When one of two outcomes would be better, but someone in this outcome would have some personal complaint, we must ask whether the greater goodness of this outcome would be morally outweighed by this personal complaint.   Suppose that, in *Case Five*:

| If we choose A | Tom will live
for 70 years | Jack will live
for 40 years | ———— |
| If we choose B | Tom will live
for 50 years | ———— | Harry will live
for 70 years |

Of these outcomes, A would be impersonally worse, since Tom and Jack would together live for 10 years fewer than Tom and Harry would live in outcome B. We can say that, if we choose A, there would be an *impersonal loss* of 10 years of life. But if we choose B, Tom would have a personal complaint, since Tom would have lived for 20 more years if we had chosen A. This choice would impose on Tom a *personal loss* of 20 years. On one version of Temkin's view, when comparing the goodness of outcomes and people's complaints, we give equal weight to personal and impersonal benefits or losses. We can call this the *Equal Weight* version of Temkin's View. On this view, we ought here to choose A, though this choice would make the outcome worse, because the impersonal loss of 10 years of life in A would be outweighed by Tom's personal loss of 20 years in B.

On other versions of Temkin's View, when comparing the goodness of outcomes and people's complaints, we give different weights to personal and impersonal benefits and losses. If we gave *less than half as much* weight to personal losses, we would reach a different conclusion in *Case Five*. The impersonal loss of 10 years of life in A would not be outweighed by Tom's discounted personal loss of 20 years in B, so we ought here to choose B, making the outcome better in a way that is worse for Tom.

If we are inclined to accept the Two-Tier View, we may find it hard to decide between these two versions of Temkin's View. Things might be different if, in outcome B, Tom would live for 65 years. Tom's personal loss of 5 years in B might then seem to us to be clearly morally outweighed by the fact that Harry would live for 30 more years in outcome B than Jack would live in outcome A.

It may seem surprising that, on some versions of Temkin's View, we give to *personal* benefits and losses *less* weight than we give to *impersonal* benefits and losses. But in assessing the impersonal goodness of outcomes A and B, we already take into account the 20 more years of life that Tom would live in A. On the Two-Tier View, Tom's possible 20 more years of life enter our moral calculations *twice*, once impersonally and once personally. This explains why we could defensibly give less weight to personal benefits and losses. We would then be merely giving such benefits and losses less *additional* weight.

Suppose next that, in *Case Six*, the possible outcomes are these:

We choose A	Adam lives for 70 years	Bernard lives for 40 years	——	——
We choose B	——	Bernard lives for 90 years	Charles lives for 10 years	——
We choose C	——	——	Charles lives for 50 years	David lives for 20 years

As I explain in a note, our original Two-Tier View here implies that it would be wrong to do A rather than B, wrong to do B rather than C, and wrong to do C rather than A. That is an unacceptable conclusion.

Temkin's version of the Two-Tier View avoids this conclusion. But this view fails, I believe, in a different way. Suppose first that we accept the Equal Weight version of Temkin's View. In outcome A, Adam and Bernard would together live for 110 years, but Bernard would have a personal complaint, since he would have lived for 50 more years in outcome B. When we deduct these 50 years, A's final score is 60. In outcome B, Bernard and Charles would together live for 100 years, but Charles would have a complaint, since Charles would have lived for 40 more years in C. When we deduct these 40 years, B's final score is also 60. In outcome C, Charles and David would together live for 70 years. Since no one would have a complaint, C's final score is 70. On this version of Temkin's view, we ought here to choose C.

This conclusion, I believe, is clearly false. To see why, we can first return to *Case Five* in which:

if we choose A	Tom will live for 70 years	and	Jack will live for 40 years

while

if we choose B	Tom will live for 50 years	and	Harry will live for 70 years.

On the Equal Weight version of Temkin's View, we ought here to choose A. This may seem an acceptable conclusion. Though our choosing B would make the outcome better, this choice would be much worse for Tom, who would live for 20 fewer years. If we choose A, in contrast, this choice would not be worse for Jack. It is not implausible to believe that it would be wrong to produce the better outcome, by choosing B, because this choice would be so much worse for Tom.

No such claim applies to *Case Six*, in which:

if we choose A	Adam will live for 70 years	and	Bernard will live for 40 years.

while

if we choose C	Charles will live for 50 years	and	David will live for 20 years

On the Equal Weight version of Temkin's View, as I have argued above, we ought here to choose C. But if we choose A, the outcome would be much better. The people who would exist in A would together live for 40 more years than the people who would exist in C. And outcome A would be *worse for no one*. We cannot plausibly believe that, rather than causing two people to exist who would live for 70 and 40 years, we ought to cause *two other, different* people to exist, who would live for only 50 and 20 years. Why would it be wrong to cause Adam and Bernard to exist, rather than Charles and David? Why ought we to cause these other two people to exist instead, who would both live for 20 fewer years?

If we accept Temkin's View, our answer might be this. We can first point out that, in some cases, whether we ought to make one of two choices, or ought to act in one of two ways, depends on which other choices or acts are possible. In *Case Six*, there is a third possible choice, since

if we choose B   Bernard will live   and Charles will live
                     for 90 years   for 10 years

We can next point out that outcome B would be much worse for Charles than outcome C, and that outcome A would be much worse for Bernard than outcome B. These facts explain, we might say, why it would be wrong to choose A rather than C. Though choosing A would produce a better outcome than choosing C, this fact is morally outweighed by these two ways in which B would be worse than C for Charles, and A would be worse than B for Bernard.

This answer does not, I believe, successfully defend this view. On the contrary, this answer helps to explain how such person-affecting views can go astray. As this answer points out, B would be worse than C for one person, and A would be worse than B for someone else. These facts may seem to imply that A would be worse than C for *two* people. But that is not true. These two person-affecting losses both disappear. Though B would be worse than C for one person, and A would be worse than B for another person, A would be worse than C for no one. It cannot here be wrong to choose and do what would both make the outcome much better and be worse for no one.

On some other versions of Temkin's View, we would give less weight to personal benefits and losses. Such views would face similar objections. As I explain in a note, if we gave to personal losses only a third of the weight that we give to impersonal losses, this version of Temkin's View would imply that it would be wrong to cause two people to exist who would live for 70 and 40 years, rather than causing two other, different people to exist, who would live for 65 and 35 years. On this view, it would again be wrong to produce the better of two outcomes in a way that would be worse for no one. That, I believe, could not be true. For impersonal benefits to be outweighed by personal losses, there must at least *be* some personal loss, because there would *be* someone who would lose.

These various cases show, I believe, that we should reject the Two-Tier View and accept the No Difference View. We should believe that, as both views imply,

> (D) it would be in itself worse if some of the lives that will be lived will be less worth living,

and

> (E) we have reasons not to act in ways that would have such effects, and if these effects would be very bad, and we could avoid them at little cost to ourselves, such acts would be wrong.

We should also believe that

> (F) it makes no difference whether, because these future lives would be lived by the same people, these outcomes would be worse for these people.

79 Scanlonian Contractualism and Future People

We can now return to Scanlonian Contractualism. Scanlon intends his formula to cover all of the acts with which we could affect future people. When applied to such acts, I shall argue, Scanlon's view needs to be revised.

According to Scanlon's Impersonalist Restriction, we cannot reject principles by appealing to claims about the goodness of outcomes. All reasons for rejecting principles must be *personal*. Scanlon also calls these reasons 'generic'. This word may suggest that such reasons could appeal to claims about what I have called *general people*. But that is not what Scanlon means. These generic personal reasons, Scanlon writes, are the reasons 'that any person would have in virtue of standing in one of the positions in a situation of the kind to which the principle applies'. And he writes

> These must be reasons that such a person would have 'on his or her own behalf'.

He also writes: 'This interpretation . . . rules out, as grounds for rejecting a principle, appeals to impersonal values . . . What it allows are reasons arising from the way a person would be affected by following the principle'. These are claims about effects on *particular* people.

Suppose that, in *Case Seven*, we must choose between two other medical programs. The predictable results would be these:

If we do A: A thousand X-people   and a thousand Y-people
               would be conceived and   would be conceived and
               live for 41 happy years,   live for 40 happy years.

If we do B: The same X-people   and a thousand different
               would be conceived and   Z-people would be conceived
               live for 40 happy years,   and live for 80 happy years.

Given Scanlon's claims about admissible grounds for rejecting principles, Scanlon's Formula seems here to require us to choose Program A. The X-people would have reasons on their own behalf to reject any principle that permitted us to choose B, since this choice would impose on the X-people the significant burden of being denied one more year of happy life. None of the other people would have reasons on their own behalf to reject any principle that requires us to choose A, since this choice would not impose any burden on any of these people. Our choice of A would not be worse for the Y-people, since if we had chosen B these people would never have existed. Nor would our choice of A be worse for any of the Z-people, since these people would never exist. Given these facts, it seems, the X-people could reasonably reject any principle that permits us to choose B, and could claim that we *owed it to them* to choose Program A.

If Scanlon's Formula requires us to choose A, as I have just claimed, that would be an objection to Scanlon's view. We ought to choose B.

This choice would be required, not only by the No Difference View, but also by any plausible version of the Two-Tier View. Program B would give to a thousand general people 40 extra years of life. These are very much greater benefits than the single extra years that Program A would give to the thousand particular X-people. Though we may believe that benefits to particular people matter more than benefits to general people, we could not plausibly believe that these benefits matter 40 times as much. Similar remarks apply to Temkin's View.

Scanlon might reject my claims about what his formula implies. I have assumed that, for one of two acts to impose a burden on someone, this act must be worse for this person than the other act would have been. We can call this the *comparative account* of benefits and burdens. Some writers claim that, when we consider acts that would cause certain people to exist, we should appeal instead to a *non-comparative* account. On this view, if we cause someone to exist who will be in some way badly off—by being deaf, for example, or having some life-shortening condition—that is enough to make it true that we are burdening or harming this person. We are imposing a burden on this person even if our act is not worse for this person, because this person's life is worth living, and having such a life is not worse than never existing.

If Scanlon appealed to this non-comparative account of burdens, he might claim that, in *Case Seven*, his formula does not require us to choose Program A. The X-people might claim that we owed it to them to choose A, since choosing B would have imposed on the X-people the burden of living for only 40 years. But if we choose A, Scanlon might say, that would impose the same burden on the Y-people, since these people would also live for only 40 years. On this non-comparative account, it is irrelevant that, while choosing B would be worse for the X-people, by denying them one extra year of life, choosing A would *not* be worse for the Y-people. On this view, it is a burden to live for only 40 years, and people have equal claims not to have this burden imposed on them whether their alternative would be living for longer, or never existing.

In some cases, this non-comparative account is plausible. Some acts can be claimed to harm people, even though these acts are not worse for the people who are harmed. But no such claim is plausible when we are considering Case Seven. If the Y-people live for only 40 happy years, that is a burden only in the sense that it would be better for these people if they lived for more than 40 happy years. We would not be imposing a burden on these people, or be harming them, if we choose A, thereby failing to prevent these people from ever existing and having their happy 40 years.

Some Scanlonian might now argue:

> If we choose B, we would impose on the X-people the burden of being denied one extra year of life. If we choose A, we would impose on the Z-people the burden of being denied 80 years of life. Since that is a much greater burden, the Z-people could reasonably reject any principle that does not require us to choose B.

Scanlonians cannot, however, make such claims. When Scanlon appeals to the principles that no one could reasonably reject, he uses 'no one' to mean 'none of the people who ever exist'. On this suggested argument, it would be wrong for us to choose Program A, because the Z-people could reasonably reject any principle that permits this choice. But if we choose A, these Z-people would never exist. We cannot defensibly claim that some act is wrong because any principle that permits such acts could be reasonably rejected by certain people who *never exist*. We could not, for example, claim that it would be wrong for any of us to choose not to have children, because any principle that permits this way of acting could be reasonably rejected by the merely possible children whom we do not have.

Though *Case Seven* is artificial, and unrealistically precise, many actual cases are relevantly similar. Many of our possible acts or policies would predictably cause some future people to be much worse off than the different future people who, if we had acted differently, *would* have existed. My examples are acts or policies that would deplete certain scarce resources, or overheat the Earth's atmosphere. When we together could avoid such acts at little cost to ourselves, these acts would be wrong. If we act in these ways, however, these different future people would never exist. When we apply Scanlon's Formula in a way that appeals only to personal reasons, we are forced to ignore the fact that, if we had acted differently, these other people *would* have existed, and would have been *much* better off. These are morally relevant facts, which might make such acts wrong. To allow us to appeal to such facts, Scanlon must revise his claims about what are admissible grounds for rejecting principles.

Scanlon might suggest that, though all reasons for rejecting principles must be, in one sense, personal, these reasons could take two forms. In most cases, we could appeal to the burdens that some principle's acceptance would impose on us, as particular people. These burdens would give us reasons on *our own behalf.* In some other cases, however, we could appeal to the burdens that would be imposed on us, when regarded as *the person to whom some description applies.*

To assess this proposal, we can return to *Case Three*, in which our alternatives are these:

If we do A *Mary* will have a child, *Kate* will have a child,
Tom, who will live for   Dick, who will live for
70 happy years   50 happy years

If we do B Tom will live for   Dick will never exist, but Kate
50 happy years   will have another child, Harry,
who will live for 70 happy years

On this revised version of Scanlon's view, we could deny that we owed it to Tom to do A. If we do B, that would be much worse for Tom, since our act would deny Tom an extra 20 happy years of life. But if we do A, that would be much worse for Dick, when Dick is regarded as *Kate's next child*. By doing A, we would also deny Dick, when so regarded, an extra 20 happy years of life.

Scanlon should not, I believe, make such claims. Phrases like 'your next child' are often used in this way, so that they refer to what I have called some *general person*. But it would be highly misleading for Scanlon to state his view in this way. Scanlon claims to be giving an account of

the particular forms of concern that we owe to other *individuals.*

General people are *not* individuals. A general person is a vast group of possible individuals, or people, one of whom will be actual. If we do A, and Dick lives for 50 happy years, Dick might agree that it would have been in one way better if we had done B, so that Dick would never have existed, and Kate would have had a different child who would have lived for 70 happy years. But there is no sense in which our doing A was worse for Dick. And if we fail to distinguish between Dick and Harry, regarding them as merely parts of a general person, we are ignoring the *separateness* of persons, which has been called 'the basic fact for ethics'.

Return next to *Case Six*, in which three of our alternatives are these:

We choose A   Adam lives   Bernard lives   ——   ——
               for 70 years   for 40 years

We choose B   ——   Bernard lives   Charles lives   ——
                              for 90 years   for 10 years

We choose C   ——   ——   Charles lives   David lives
                                     for 50 years   for 20 years

On this version of Scanlon's view, he would claim:

> It would be wrong to choose either B or C, since any principle that permits these choices could be reasonably rejected by Charles, speaking on behalf of the general person who would here in part consist of Charles and Adam.

This claim would be implausible. If we choose either B or C, Charles might later agree that we ought to have chosen A. But choosing C would give Charles 50 happy years of life, and if we had chosen A, Charles would never have existed. Charles is the person who has, not the *strongest*, but the *weakest* personal reasons to reject any principle that permits us or requires us to choose C. Nor would it help to appeal to Charles's reasons, not on his own behalf, but on behalf of the general person who would here consist in part of Charles and Adam. As I have said, there is no such person. Nor should we regard Charles and Adam *as if* they were the same person.

There is a better version of Scanlon's view. Scanlon should claim that, when we ask which are the principles that no one could reasonably reject, we should consider, and compare, two kinds of reason for rejecting principles. Each of us would have *personal* reasons for rejecting principles that permit or require certain acts. These reasons would be provided by the facts that such acts would impose burdens on us, or be unfair to us, or by other such facts about the implications for us. We would also have *impartial* reasons for rejecting principles that permit or require certain acts. These impartial reasons would be provided by the ways in which such acts would make things go worse, in the impartial-reason-implying sense.

On this version of Scanlon's view, when we ask which are the principles that no one could reasonably reject, we would sometimes have to compare the moral weight of such conflicting personal and impartial reasons. We would have to use our judgment about which of these reasons would, in different kinds of case, provide stronger grounds for rejecting principles. As Scanlon points out, however, all claims about reasonable rejection require such comparative judgments.

Such judgments could go either way. When some act would make things go best, we would all have impartial reasons to reject principles that did not require such acts. In some cases, these impartial reasons would be morally decisive, and Scanlon's Formula would require us to do what would make things go best. In some other cases, however, some people could reasonably reject any principle that required such acts, since everyone's impartial reasons would be morally outweighed by these people's conflicting personal reasons.

Scanlonian Contractualism ought, I believe, to take this form. In defending this belief, it will help first to consider why Scanlon's view does not already take this form.

One explanation is that, on Scanlon's view, all reasons for rejecting principles must be had by single people considered on their own, rather than as members of some group. Such *individuals'* reasons must also be personal reasons. If Scanlon dropped this *Individualist Restriction,* as I have argued that he ought to do, that would allow him to drop his restriction to personal reasons.

Scanlon also claims that, when we ask what we owe to each other, we need not consider certain *impersonal* reasons. Reasons are

> *impersonal*, in Scanlon's sense, when these reasons 'are not grounded in the moral claims or the well-being of individuals, either ourselves or others'.

We have such impersonal reasons, for example, to avoid acts that would inflict pain on animals, or would cause some species of animal to become extinct. Since these reasons have nothing to do with the moral claims or well-being of persons, Scanlon claims that such reasons are not relevant to what, as persons, we owe to each other.

These impersonal reasons may also be

> *impartial*, in the sense that we have these reasons whatever our personal point of view.

But we have other *impartial* reasons that are not, in Scanlon's sense, *impersonal*. We have such impartial reasons to care about the well-being of every individual or person. We may be misled here by a different sense of the word 'impersonal'. One of two outcomes would be

> *impersonally* worse in the *impartial* reason-involving sense when everyone would have impartial reasons to prefer the other outcome.

Outcomes may be in this sense impersonally bad, or bad *period*, because of the ways in which they are *personally* bad, by being *bad for* particular people. Scanlon says little about such outcomes, and such impartial reasons. But when he claims that all reasons for rejecting principles must be personal, Scanlon thereby excludes, as irrelevant to what we owe to each other, not only impersonal reasons, but also those impartial reasons that are provided by facts about the well-being or moral claims of people. These impartial reasons, we might object, *are* relevant to what we owe to each other.

Scanlon might reply that, when our impartial reasons are provided by such facts about the well-being or moral claims of people, we have no need to appeal to these reasons. We all have impartial reasons, for example, to reject any principle that would impose burdens on certain people. But since these people would have *personal* reasons to reject such principles, we have no need to appeal, as well, to these impartial reasons.

In most of the cases that Scanlon discusses, this would be a good reply. As this reply also shows, if Scanlon allowed us to appeal to impartial reasons, that would make no difference to most of the moral reasoning that his Contractualism describes. In most of our moral thinking, we could ignore the fact that our choice between different acts would affect the identity of future people. Most of our acts would not predictably cause some future people to be worse off than different future people would been. When our acts would predictably make things go worse, that is usually because these acts would be predictably *worse for* one or more particular people. Since these people could appeal to the fact that such acts would be worse for them, we need not also appeal to the fact that such acts would make things go worse, in the impartial-reason-implying sense.

Things are different, however, when we consider some of the acts or policies with which we might affect future people. In some cases, we should consider what might happen to the different possible people who might later be actual. Some of these cases involve future people who would soon be actual. In deciding when to have children, for example, we ought to ask when we would be able to give such children a good start in life. That is why Jane ought not to have her first child when she is only 14. In other cases, such as those involving policies like Depleting or Overheating, we ought to consider how these policies might affect the many different people who might exist in the further future. When we apply Scanlon's Formula to either of these kinds of case, it is not enough to ask which are the principles that no one would have sufficient personal reasons to reject. To explain why certain acts or policies would be wrong, we must appeal to the better lives that would have been lived by the people who, if we had acted differently, would have later existed. As we have seen, we cannot claim that these acts are wrong because these people could reasonably reject any principle that permits such acts. If we acted in these ways, these people would never exist, and we cannot defensibly appeal to claims about what could be reasonably rejected by people who are merely possible, and will never be actual. Since we cannot appeal to the *personal* reasons that are had by people who *never* exist, we should appeal to the *impartial* reasons that are had by people who *do* exist.

Return, for example, to *Case Seven*, in which our alternatives are these:

A: A thousand X-people   and a thousand Y-people
      would be conceived   would be conceived
      and live for 41 years,   and live for 40 years.

B: The same X-people   and a thousand different
      would be conceived   Z-people would be conceived
      and live for 40 years,   and live for 80 years.

We ought, I have claimed, to choose Program B. But the X-people would have personal reasons to reject all principles that required us to choose B, since this choice would have denied these people the significant benefit of one extra year of life. And we cannot claim that the Z-people would have stronger personal reasons to reject principles that required us to choose A. If we choose A, these people would never exist. But *we* could reasonably reject such principles. We could appeal to the fact that, if we choose A rather than B, things would go much worse in the impartial reason-involving sense. We would all have strong impartial reasons to want there to be a thousand people who would live for 80 years, rather than a thousand *different* people who would live for only 40 years. In cases of this kind, we need to appeal to such impartial reasons. If we could appeal only to personal reasons, we would have to ignore the fact that, rather than causing the X-people to live for only one year longer, we could cause there to be as many people who would live for 40 years longer.

If Scanlonian Contractualism allowed us to appeal to impartial reasons, Scanlon's Formula would be unchanged. This view would keep Scanlon's greatest contribution to our moral thinking: his appeal to principles that no one could reasonably reject. But Scanlon might have to qualify some of his other claims. Scanlon talks of what we *owe* to others, and he writes:

> The idea of justifiability to all possible beings . . . seems impossibly broad, and barely coherent . . . the beings whom it is possible to wrong are all those who do, have, or will actually exist.

Such remarks suggest that

> (K) the acts with which we affect people cannot be wrong unless there is or will exist, at some time, some actual person whom we have *wronged*, and to whom we *owed* it not to act in this way.

(K) implies that, in *Case Seven*, it would not be wrong for us to choose Program A, though we know that there would then be many people who would live for 40 years, rather than as many other people who would have lived for 80 years. We would not have wronged the people who would live for 40 years, since we did not wrong these people by failing to prevent them from being conceived. Nor did we owe it to these people to cause them never to exist. Nor would we have wronged the people who would have lived for 80 years, since we could not have wronged people who never exist, nor could we have owed it to such people to cause them to exist.

Similar claims apply to many of the acts or policies with which we can affect those people who will live in the further future. If we choose policies like Depleting or Overheating, we may greatly lower the quality of future people's lives, for the sake of much smaller benefits to ourselves. But in many cases of this kind, (K) implies that it would not be wrong to cause this great lowering in the quality of future lives. If these lives would be lived by different people, our choice of these policies may not wrong any of these people, and we may not owe it to such future people not to choose these policies. When applied to such cases, (K) conflicts not only with the No Difference View, but even with the Two-Tier View. When we see *why* (K) has these implications,

(K) ceases to seem plausible. We should expect that, in such cases, our acts or policies may be wrong, though there would not be any actual people whom we have wronged.

In making these claims, I am *not* assuming that we cannot be wronging someone if we know that our act would not be worse for this person. As I have claimed elsewhere, some of our acts might be truly claimed to wrong certain future people even if we know both that these people's lives would be worth living, and that, if we had acted otherwise, these people would never have existed. For example, we might wrong some future people by choosing policies that risk causing some catastrophe, such as using nuclear energy and failing to ensure that radio-active wastes are stored safely. And Jane might be wronging Johnny by having him when she is only 14, so that she predictably fails to give him a good start in life. Such acts might be wrong because they violate certain people's rights, or they cause people to exist with rights that cannot be fulfilled.

Such claims, however, cannot wholly solve the Non-Identity Problem. First, we are not asking only which acts or policies would be wrong. We all have reasons to care about future generations, and about how our acts or policies might affect the quality of future people's lives. It is of great importance whether these reasons would be weaker if, because these lives would be lived by different people, these acts or policies would not be worse for these people. We cannot answer this question by appealing only to claims about people's rights.

Second, if we appeal only to such claims, we shall have false beliefs about what we ought morally to do. We shall be led to ignore the fact that, if we had acted differently, the people who would have existed later would have had better lives. And if we ignore such facts, we may act wrongly. If everyone always acted in such ways, each new set of people would live worse lives. The world would be slowly wrecked.

There are, I have claimed, two reasons why Scanlonian Contractualism should allow us to appeal to impartial reasons. If we cannot appeal to such reasons,

> Scanlon's Formula could not be defensibly applied to many
> of the acts or policies with which we affect future people,

and, as I argued earlier,

> Scanlon could claim only that, when acts are wrong in his
> Contractualist sense, that makes these acts *prima facie* wrong
> in other, non-Contractualist senses.

If we can appeal to impartial reasons, Scanlon's Formula can be
defensibly applied to all of our acts, and can be plausibly claimed
both to tell us which acts are wrong, and to help to explain why such
acts are wrong. Scanlonian Contractualism should, I believe, take this
stronger form.

23

The Triple Theory

80 The Convergence Argument

We can now turn to the relation between Scanlonian and Kantian Contractualism. When we apply the Kantian Contractualist Formula, I argued, it is only the optimific principles whose universal acceptance everyone could rationally choose. Kantian Contractualism therefore implies Rule Consequentialism. In his commentary, Scanlon does not criticize this argument.

According to my Convergence Argument, since it is only the optimific principles that everyone could rationally choose, no one could reasonably reject these principles. If that is true, Kantian Rule Consequentialism could also be combined with Scanlonian Contractualism.

This second argument does not apply to the view stated in Scanlon's book, since this view includes both the Individualist and Impersonalist Restrictions. By appealing to these restrictions, Scanlon could reject some of my argument's premises. But Scanlon's view would be strengthened, I have argued, if he dropped these two restrictions, and he described his formula as giving an account, not of wrongness itself, but of a property that makes acts wrong. I shall now ask whether my Convergence Argument succeeds when applied to this revised version of Scanlon's view.

It will be enough to discuss some of those Rule Consequentialist principles that are *UA-optimific*, in the sense that their universal acceptance would make things go best. According to one version of what I call *the Triple Theory*: Everyone ought to follow these optimific principles because these are the only principles whose universal acceptance everyone could rationally choose, and the only principles that no one could reasonably reject.

In considering this theory, we have four questions:

Q1: What do these optimific principles require us to do?

Q2: Are these the only principles whose universal acceptance everyone could rationally choose?

Q3: Are these the only principles that no one could reasonably reject?

Q4: Are these the principles that everyone ought to follow?

Whether we could *rationally choose* one of two principles depends on the strength of all of our non-deontic reasons to choose these principles. Whether we could *reasonably reject* one of two principles depends instead on whether we have an objection to this principle that is relevantly stronger than anyone's objection to the other principle. My argument for the Triple Theory is, in part:

(A) If we could *not* rationally choose one of two principles, there must be facts which give us a strong objection to this principle.

(B) If everyone *could* rationally choose the other principle, no one's objection to this alternative could be as strong.

(C) Since our objection to the first principle is stronger than anyone's objection to this alternative, we could reasonably reject this principle.

(D) When there is only one relevant principle that everyone could rationally choose, no one's objection to this principle could be as strong as the strongest objections to every alternative.

(E) No one could reasonably reject some principle if there are stronger objections to every alternative.

Therefore

> (F) When there is only one relevant principle that everyone could rationally choose, no one could reasonably reject this principle.

If we add certain further plausible premises, this argument shows, I believe, that the Kantian and Scanlonian Formulas at least very often coincide, by requiring us to follow the same principles. But there may be some exceptions.

Scanlon describes one kind of possible exception. When Rawls and Scanlon propose their versions of Contractualism, they both appeal to the same kind of case.   In what we can call

> *Rawls–Scanlon Cases*, we can either save one person from some great burden, or give much smaller benefits to many other people, who are all much better off.

We can call these people *Blue* and *the Many*. Suppose that, in one such case,

> (1) everyone could rationally choose some optimific principle that required us to give the small benefits to the Many,

and that

> (2) some people could not rationally choose any conflicting principle that required us to save Blue from her great burden.

If (1) and (2) were true, the Kantian Contractualist Formula would require us to give the small benefits to the Many. But Scanlon suggests that

> (3) in some of these cases, Blue could reasonably reject every such principle, and no one could reasonably reject some principle which required us to save Blue from her great burden.

If (1) to (3) were true, the Scanlonian Formula would require us to save Blue from this burden. Kantian and Scanlonian Contractualism would here conflict.

Before deciding whether (3) is true, we must ask in which of these cases the optimific principles would require us to give the small benefits to the Many. To answer such questions, Scanlon writes, we would have to know 'how Parfit's notions of impartial reasons and "best outcome" deal with *aggregation*', or with how the goodness of outcomes might depend on the number of people who would receive benefits or burdens. My definition of this sense of 'best', he writes,

> leaves open the possibility that the conception of 'best
> outcome' . . . is in important respects non-aggregative.

This definition ought, I believe, to leave this possibility open. Some possible outcome would be best, in this impartial-reason-implying sense, if this outcome is the one that, from an impartial point of view, everyone would have most reason to want, or to hope will come about. It is a substantive question, which could not be answered by a definition, just when and how the strengths of everyone's impartial reasons would in part depend on facts about the numbers of people who might receive certain benefits or burdens.

When we ask which of two outcomes would be in this sense better, it would be very implausible to claim that the answer *never* depends on the numbers of people who might receive benefits or burdens. But we are here considering only Rawls–Scanlon Cases. For a more extreme example of this kind, we can suppose that, in *Case One*, the only possible outcomes are these:

A: Blue will have 1,000 days of pain	Each of the Many will have no pain
B: Blue will have no pain	Each of these people will have one brief period of pain

It is often assumed that, in all such cases, there must be some number of small benefits to the Many that would outweigh Blue's great burden, making outcome A better than outcome B. If the goodness of outcomes depended only on the net sum of benefits minus burdens, as Utilitarians believe, that would imply that it must be in this way possible for A to be better than B. But this conclusion is not implied by the impartial-reason-implying sense of 'better'. In our beliefs about the goodness of outcomes, we might reject this Utilitarian view. And if the benefits to each of the Many would be very small, we might plausibly believe that no number of these benefits could outweigh Blue's great burden. We might believe for example that, if Blue had her 1,000 days of pain, that would be worse than if *any* number of other people had one minute, or one hour, of pain. This belief would be true if we would all have stronger impartial reasons to want or hope that, in all such cases, the single person would be saved from her great ordeal. It is an open question, I believe, whether we would have such reasons.

When we consider acts that would give to very many people *very small* benefits, or impose very small burdens, it is easy, I have claimed, to make moral mistakes. Given the technological developments of the last two centuries, such cases now have great importance. But we can ignore such cases here. These cases raise difficult problems which are not relevant to the question whether Scanlonian Contractualism might conflict with Kantian Rule Consequentialism. If the Scanlonian Formula would require us to ignore some such very small benefits or burdens, the same might be true of the optimific Rule Consequentialist principles. And we are looking for cases in which the optimific principles would require us to give the small benefits to the Many.

Since there are several views about which outcomes would be best, there are also several views about which principles would be optimific. The important question is whether Scanlonian Contractualism *necessarily* conflicts with Kantian Rule Consequentialism, or whether there are plausible versions of these theories that do not conflict, and could therefore be combined. So I shall suppose that, in their assessments of the goodness of outcomes, Kantian Rule Consequentialists accept a strong version of what I earlier called the *Telic Priority View*. That assumption makes this form of Consequentialism closer to Scanlonian Contractualism.

Suppose that, in *Case Two*, the only possible outcomes are these:

A: Blue will have 100 days of pain   Each of the Many
will have no pain

B: Blue will have no pain   Each of these people will
have 10 days of pain

As before, and in all these cases, we should suppose that each day of pain is an equal burden. On the Telic Priority View, people's burdens matter more, doing more to make the outcome worse, the worse off these people are. Since Blue would be much worse off in outcome A than each of the Many would be in outcome B, most of Blue's days of pain would matter more than the Many's days of pain. On a strong version of this view, for outcome B to be worse than outcome A, the numbers of the Many would have to be much greater than ten. For B to be clearly worse than A, we can here suppose, there would have to be more than a hundred or a thousand other people who, in B, would each have 10 days of pain.

Similar claims apply to *Case Three*, in which the only possible outcomes are these:

A: Blue will live to the age of 30   Each of the Many will live to 75

B: Blue will live to 70   These people will live to 70

We can again suppose that, for B to be worse than A, the number of the Many would have to be more than a hundred or a thousand.

Let us say that, in such cases, moral principles are *Blue-protecting* if they require us to save Blue from her great burden, and *Blue-burdening* if they require us instead to save the Many from their much smaller burdens, thereby giving them much smaller benefits. On the views just described, the Blue-burdening principles would be optimific only when, compared with the benefit to Blue of being saved from her great burden, we could give to the Many a *much* greater total sum of benefits.

Return next to my argument that, in the thought-experiments to which the Kantian Formula appeals, it is only the optimific principles that everyone could rationally choose. My argument compares these principles with other possible principles that are *significantly* non-optimific, in the sense that their universal acceptance would make things go much worse. *Slightly* non-optimific principles raise some complications that would be best considered later.

Everyone would have strong impartial reasons to choose that everyone accepts the optimific principles, since that choice would make things go much better. And no one's impartial reasons, I argued, would be decisively outweighed by any relevant conflicting reasons. Since the optimific principles would impose great burdens on certain people, these people would have strong personal reasons *not* to choose the optimific principles. But these reasons would not, I claimed, be decisive.

Do these claims apply to the cases that we are now considering? Would Blue have sufficient reasons to choose that everyone accepts some optimific Blue-burdening principle? When I claimed that we could all rationally choose some optimific principle even if that choice would impose some great burden on us, I was discussing cases in which, by choosing such a principle, we would indirectly save many other people from *similarly great* burdens. In *Lifeboat*, for example, if I choose the Numbers Principle rather than the Nearness Principle, I would die, but my choice would indirectly save many other people's lives.

In Rawls–Scanlon Cases, no such claim is true. If Blue chooses some optimific principle, she would bear a great burden, and she would not indirectly save any number of other people from similarly great burdens. She would only save many people from *much smaller* burdens. It may seem that, given this fact, Blue would not have sufficient reasons to choose this principle. These may be the cases in which it could most plausibly be claimed that some people could not rationally choose the optimific principles.

We ought, I suggest, to reject even this claim. Return to *Case Two*, in which we could either

(1) save Blue from all of her 100 days of pain

or

(2) save some number of other people from all of their 10 days of pain.

For the reasons given above, we are supposing that, for (2) to make the outcome better, this number of other people would have to be more than a hundred or a thousand. If Blue chose some optimific principle that required us to do (2), Blue would have 100 days of pain, but her choice would save these other people from more than 1,000 or 10,000 days of pain. This choice would also have such effects in many other such cases. These facts would, I believe, give Blue sufficient reasons to make this choice. Blue would have sufficient reasons to choose to have her 100 days of pain, if her choice would save these other people from the much greater number of 1,000 or 10,000 days of pain, in significant amounts of 10 days per person.

We can next ask whether, in any of these cases, everyone could rationally choose some significantly non-optimific Blue-protecting Principle. The answer, I suggest, is No. Since any such principle would be non-optimific, the Many would have both impartial and personal reasons *not* to choose this principle. And most of us would have these impartial reasons and would have no contrary reasons. So most people would not have sufficient reasons to choose such a principle.

These cases are not, I conclude, a strong counter-example to my argument for Kantian Rule Consequentialism. For these and some of the other reasons that I give in Chapter 16, when we apply the Kantian Formula to these cases, it is only the optimific Blue-burdening Principles that everyone could rationally choose.

We can now return to my argument that Kantian Rule Consequentialism can be combined with Scanlonian Contractualism. When applied to Rawls–Scanlon Cases, my argument would in part be this:

> (G) Since the Many could *not* rationally choose any
> Blue-protecting principle, there must be facts that
> give these people strong grounds or reasons for
> rejecting these principles.

> (H) Since Blue *could* rationally choose some Blue-burdening
> principle, Blue's grounds for rejecting these principles
> cannot be as strong.

Therefore

> (I) The Many could reasonably reject any Blue-protecting
> principle, and Blue could not reasonably reject every Blue-
> burdening principle.

In his commentary above, Scanlon rejects this argument. He suggests that

(J) in some of these cases, though Blue could rationally
choose some optimific Blue-burdening principle, Blue could
also reasonably reject every such principle, and none of the
Many could reasonably reject every non-optimific
Blue-protecting principle (135–8).

If this claim is true, the Scanlonian Formula would sometimes require us
to follow these Blue-protecting principles. Scanlonian Contractualism
would here conflict with Kantian Rule Consequentialism.

Is (J) true? In *Case Two*, we could either

(1) save Blue from all of her 100 days of pain

or

(2) save some number of other people from all of
their 10 days of pain.

We are supposing that, for the optimific principles to require us to
benefit the Many rather than Blue, it would have to be true that we
could save the Many from a total of more than 1,000 or 10,000 days
of pain. Could Blue reasonably reject these principles, claiming that we
ought instead to save Blue from her 100 days of pain? And would it be
unreasonable for the Many to reject this claim?

It is not clear that our answers should be Yes. We can agree that,
since Blue would be much worse off than any of the Many if she had
her 100 days of pain, Blue's objection to any Blue-burdening Principle
has, in one way, much greater moral weight. But in our assessment
of the goodness of these outcomes, the fact that Blue would be much
worse off has already been taken into account. That is why, for the
optimific principles to require us to give the smaller benefits to the
Many, we would have to be saving more than a hundred or a thousand
of these people from all of their 10 days of pain. In our assessment
of the goodness of these outcomes, we have already given, to Blue's
pain, as much as ten or a hundred times the weight that we give to
the pains of the Many. It is not clear that Blue could reasonably claim
that, in deciding how to act, we ought to give Blue's pain *more* than
ten or a hundred times the weight that we give to these other people's

pain. Nor would it be clearly unreasonable for the Many to reject this claim.

Return next to *Case Three*, in which we could either

(3) enable Blue to live to 70 rather than 30,

or

(4) enable some number of other people to live to 75 rather than 70.

We are supposing that, for the optimific principles to require us to do (4) rather than (3), this number of other people would have to be more than a hundred or a thousand. Rather than giving to Blue her extra 40 years of life, we would then be giving to these other people more than 500 or 5,000 extra years. Could Blue reasonably reject principles which require this act? Could she reasonably claim that her 40 extra years are morally more important than these other people's total of 500 or 5,000 extra years? And would it be unreasonable for these other people to reject this claim? As before, it is not clear that our answers should be Yes.

It might be objected that, in my claims about these cases, I have taken some plausible beliefs about what we ought morally to do, or about the strength of people's moral claims, and mistakenly presented these beliefs as being about the goodness of outcomes. The Priority View, Scanlon suggests, should be regarded as making claims, not about the goodness of outcomes, but about the strength of different grounds for rejecting moral principles. These claims, Scanlon writes, are

> most naturally understood within the context of a view that
> makes conclusions about right and wrong depend on the
> relative strength of the reasons that individuals can offer
> in the process of interpersonal justification. They are less
> plausibly interpreted as claims about what it is good or bad
> to have happen.

Rawls similarly suggests that, in our assessments of the goodness of outcomes, we should not appeal to any distributive principles, since such principles make claims that are about, not what is good, but what is morally right.

These suggestions are, I believe, mistaken. Though the Priority View can take purely deontic and Contractualist forms, it can also plausibly take a telic form, which makes claims about the goodness of outcomes. There are some moral principles which cannot plausibly take such a form. Some examples would be those deontological principles which require us not to treat people in certain ways, such as harming one person as a means of benefiting others. Such an act is wrong, these principles claim, even if this act would make the outcome better by minimizing the number of acts of this kind. But distributive principles do not make any such claims. We can plausibly believe that it would be better if benefits or burdens were more equally distributed, or if more of the benefits and fewer of the burdens came to people who were worse off. We can believe for example that, if Blue has her 100 days of pain, that would be worse than if a hundred other people each had only one day of pain. This outcome would be worse, I believe, in the sense that, if these people were all strangers to us, we would have more reason to hope that Blue avoids this great ordeal.

It might next be objected that, in our assessments of the goodness of outcomes, we might reject the Telic Priority View, or we might accept only a much weaker version of this view. We would then reject the argument that I have just given for doubting Scanlon's (G). But it is not worth claiming that *some* versions of Kantian Rule Consequentialism conflict with Scanlonian Contractualism. There are also conflicts between different versions of Rule Consequentialism, such as those versions which appeal to the principles whose being universally *accepted*, or universally *followed*, would make things go best. The important question is whether plausible versions of Scanlonian Contractualism *necessarily* conflict with plausible versions of Kantian Rule Consequentialism. And the Consequentialist Telic Priority View can plausibly take a fairly strong form.

81 The Independence of Scanlon's Theory

Remember next that, on

the Contractualist Priority View: People have stronger moral claims, and stronger grounds to reject some moral principle, the worse off these people are.

Scanlon might claim that, compared with the Telic Priority View, this Contractualist view can plausibly take an even *stronger* form. That might be enough to make (J) true.

Return for example to *Case One* in which the possible outcomes are these:

A: Blue will have 1,000 days of pain   Each of the Many will have no pain

B: Blue will have no pain   Each of these people will have one brief period of pain

It is often assumed that, if all pain is bad, there must be some number of brief periods of pain that would make outcome B worse than outcome A. This assumption is, I have claimed, mistaken. We can coherently and plausibly believe that, if Blue had her 1,000 days of pain, that would be worse than if *any* number of other people had some brief period of pain, such as 1 minute, or 10 minutes. We might have stronger impartial reasons to want or hope that, in all such cases, it would be the single person who would be saved from her great ordeal.

In some other cases, however, we could not plausibly make such claims. It might be implausible to claim that, rather than Blue's having her 1,000 days of pain, it would be better if a million, or a billion, or a billion billion people each had 10 days of pain, or 50 days of pain. We may therefore have to agree that, in some such cases, the optimific principles would require us to save some great number of people from their days of pain. And Scanlon might be right to claim that, in some of these cases, Blue could reasonably reject these optimific principles, and none of the Many could reasonably reject some principle that required us to save Blue from her 1,000 days of pain. If these claims were true, Scanlonian Contractualism would here conflict with Kantian Rule Consequentialism, since these views would require us to act in different ways.

This conflict would not, however, be deep. On both these views, we ought to give strong priority to saving Blue from her great ordeal.

The difference would be only that, on Scanlonian Contractualism, this priority would be somewhat stronger.

There are other ways in which, in some kinds of case, these two views might have different implications. We can now return to the Contractualist part of Kantian Rule Consequentialism. According to the Kantian Contractualist Formula, we ought to follow the principles whose universal acceptance everyone could rationally choose. Suppose that, in

> *Case Four*, we could easily save the lives of one of two
> relevantly similar people.

According to

> *the Principle of Equal Chances*: In such cases, we ought to save
> one of these people in some way that would give each person
> an equal chance of being saved.

This is the only principle, we might claim, that both these people could rationally choose. Though this claim is plausible, it is not obviously true. Perhaps these people could also rationally choose some principle that merely required us to save one of them, leaving it up to us how we choose whom we save. The Kantian Formula would not then support the Principle of Equal Chances. The Scanlonian Formula, in contrast, decisively supports this principle. Neither of these people could reasonably reject this principle, since neither person has any claim to be given *more* than an equal chance of being saved, nor is there any other reasonable ground for rejecting this principle.

Suppose next that, in

> *Case Five*, some quantity of unowned resources can be shared
> between different people, none of whom has any special claim
> to these resources. However we distribute these resources,
> these people would together receive the same total sum of
> benefits.

When we apply the Kantian Formula, we could claim that

(K) everyone could rationally choose some principle that requires us, in such cases, to give everyone equal shares,

and that

(L) no one could rationally choose any principle that permits us, in such cases, to give them less than equal shares.

I believe that, since these claims are true, the Kantian Formula requires us to follow this *Principle of Equal Shares*. But Utilitarians might reject (L), claiming instead that

(M) everyone could rationally choose some principle that permitted us to give them unequal shares, since the total sum of benefits would be the same.

Though I believe that this claim is false, (J) is not *obviously* false. The Scanlonian Formula, in contrast, decisively supports the Principle of Equal Shares. No one could reasonably reject this principle, since no one has any claim to be given *more* than an equal share, nor is there any other possible objection to this principle.

Four and *Five* are not cases in which Kantian and Scanlonian Contractualism conflict. The difference is only that, though the Kantian Formula gives some support to the Principles of Equal Shares and Equal Chances, the Scanlonian Formula supports these principles in a stronger and decisive way. But suppose next that, in

Case Six, if some people were given unequal shares, the total sum of benefits would be much greater.

In such cases, there might be some people who could not rationally choose the Principle of Equal Shares, since an equal distribution would both be much worse for these people, and make things go worse. But it might still be true that no one could reasonably reject the Principle of Equal Shares. Kantian and Scanlonian Contractualism *would* then conflict.

We can next note what these examples have in common. When we apply the Kantian Formula, by asking which are the principles whose universal acceptance everyone could rationally choose, we take into account facts about how it would be best for things to go, in the impartial-reason-implying sense. In assessing the goodness of outcomes, I have claimed, we can plausibly give weight to some distributive principles. We can believe that one of two outcomes would be better, despite giving people a smaller total sum of benefits, if these benefits would be more equally shared, or if more of the benefits would come to people who were worse off. We can also believe that it would be better if people were given equal chances to receive some benefit. But as some of my examples show, when we apply the Scanlonian Formula, these distributive considerations can plausibly be given *greater* weight. That is not surprising. When we ask which principles everyone could *rationally* choose, the answer depends on all of our non-deontic reasons for choosing different principles. These include, not only our impartial reasons to prefer better outcomes, but also various personal, non-moral reasons, such as our reasons to choose what would benefit ourselves. The Scanlonian Formula appeals instead to claims about what are *reasonable* grounds for rejecting moral principles, in a partly moral sense of 'reasonable'. We would expect that, in answering this question, distributive principles could plausibly be given greater weight. Though things might go somewhat better if people were given equal shares, or equal chances to receive some benefit, it is much clearer that no one could reasonably reject the Principles of Equal Shares and Equal Chances.

For an example of a different kind, suppose that in

> *Case Seven*, we could either save Green from some burden, or save Grey from a much greater burden.   Grey has been negligent, and is responsible for the fact that Green and Grey are threatened with these burdens.

When we ask which principle these people could rationally choose, the answer might be some principle that would require us to save Grey from her much greater burden. Green might have sufficient reason to choose this principle. But if we ask which principle no one could reasonably reject, we might conclude that Grey could *not* reasonably reject a principle requiring her to bear this greater burden, given the fact that it was Grey's negligence which caused both her and Green to be threatened with these burdens. Kantian and Scanlonian Contractualism would then conflict.

There may be other cases in which these kinds of Contractualism conflict. And Kantian Contractualism may sometimes conflict with Rule Consequentialism. I believe that, in all or nearly all important cases, everyone could rationally choose that everyone accepts some optimific principle. But there may be cases in which everyone could also rationally choose some significantly non-optimific principle. In such cases, Kantian Contractualism would differ from Rule Consequentialism, by permitting us to act on either of these principles. And there may be other ways in which the three parts of the Triple Theory sometimes conflict.

If there are such conflicts, that may seem to show that we should reject this Triple Theory. But that is not, I believe, true. All our moral theories need to be developed further, and revised. If what seem the most plausible theories have very similar implications, this fact gives us reasons to believe that we are making progress, and that these are the theories that we should try to develop further, and revise. If these theories have some conflicting implications, that may help us to decide how these theories should be revised. We are still climbing this mountain. And a team of mountaineers may do better if they have different abilities and strengths, and they sometimes try different routes. It would be only at the mountain's peak that we, or those who follow us, would have all the same true beliefs.

PART SIX

NORMATIVITY

24

Analytical Naturalism and Subjectivism

82 Conflicting Theories

By asking some questions, we can distinguish several views:

Are normative claims intended
or believed to state truths?

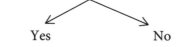

Yes   No

Semi-Cognitivism   Non-Cognitivism

Are there any
normative truths?

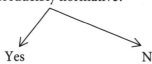

Yes   No

Cognitivism   Nihilism

Are these truths
irreducibly normative?

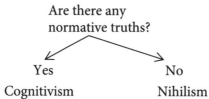

Yes   No

Non-Naturalist   Are the concepts and claims
Cognitivism   with which we state such truths
                      irreducibly normative?

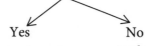

Yes   No

Non-Analytical   Analytical
Naturalism   Naturalism

These distinctions are rough, and further distinctions could be drawn. Korsgaard writes:

> The correct view is not going to be the one left standing when the contradictions and absurdities of all the others have finally been exposed. It is going to be the one that answers best to the human concerns which motivate the study of philosophy in the first place.

Korsgaard is too pessimistic. The correct view, I shall argue, is both the one left standing when we have seen how the other views fail, and the one that answers best to these human concerns. We ought to accept some form of Non-Naturalist Cognitivism.

A *concept* is what is meant or expressed by some word or phrase, and by other words or phrases with the same meaning. The words 'new' and 'nuevo', for example, both express the concept *new*. Of the concepts that we shall be considering, most refer to *properties*, such as the properties of being new, glittering, a poet, a convincing argument, the brightest star, the first man to walk on the Moon, and an act that is wrong. As these examples suggest, any true claim about something can be restated as a claim about this thing's properties. When we say that some concept *refers* to some property, we are not thereby claiming that anything *has* this property. No one has the property of being the first man to walk on the Sun, and Nihilists believe that no acts are wrong.

The same word can have different senses or meanings, thereby expressing different concepts. A genius and the brightest star are in different senses bright. We should also distinguish between some word's ordinary meaning and what some person uses this word to mean. These meanings differ when someone either misuses some word, or deliberately uses some word in something other than its ordinary sense. Some people, for example, misuse the word 'refute' to mean 'deny', and I deliberately use the word 'event' in a wide sense that covers acts and states of affairs. When many people misuse some word, what these people use this word to mean becomes one of the ordinary meanings of this word.

Consider next these two lists of words:

A: wrong, right, ought, duty, virtue, good, bad, excellent, mediocre, incorrect.

B: kill, crimson, square, electric, cause, city, marble, alive, sister, tall, unexpected.

Though I have not said what the words in either of these lists have in common, most of us would guess correctly into which list most other words should go. We would guess, for example, that 'desirable', 'rational', 'wicked', and 'blameworthy', should go in list A, and that 'desired', 'liquid', 'young', and 'sad' should go in list B.

Words in list A are *normative*, as are the concepts, claims, and facts that we can use these words to express or state. There are, as we shall see, several accounts of normativity. Words in list B are *naturalistic*, and claims that use only such words, when they are true, state natural facts. Some fact is *natural*, on one common definition, if facts of this kind are investigated or discussed by people who are working in any of the natural or social sciences. I shall suggest later how we can make these definitions more precise.

Some words are partly normative and partly naturalistic. That is true of the word 'murder' when we use it to mean 'wrongly kill', and the words 'cruel', 'rude', 'unpatriotic', and 'dishonest'. I shall say little about such words, and what are called the *thick* normative concepts that these words express. Though such concepts can add subtlety and perceptiveness to our thinking, the deepest theoretical questions are about the purely normative concepts and claims that we can express with the words in list A.

These questions are answered differently by those who accept the kinds of theory shown in my diagram above. Non-Cognitivists believe that normative claims should not be regarded as intended to be true, except perhaps in some minimal sense. Semi-Cognitivists believe that such claims *are* intended to be true. Some of these people are Nihilists, or *Error Theorists*, who believe that all positive normative claims are false.

Others are full Cognitivists, who believe that some of these claims are true, and state normative facts.

These Cognitivists are of three kinds. Normative facts, *Naturalists* believe, are also natural facts. According to *Analytical Naturalists*, normative words have meanings that can be analyzed or defined by using naturalistic words. On this view, though there is no distinction between normative and naturalistic *claims*, we can distinguish between normative and naturalistic ways of stating the same claim. This view correctly describes some uses of normative words. For example, if I said

My prediction was wrong, because my headache has got worse,

I might mean

My prediction was false, because my headache has become more painful.

These would then be different ways of stating the same claim, and the same natural fact. But Analytical Naturalism cannot be plausibly applied to many other uses of 'wrong' and 'worse', or to some uses of such words as 'irrational' and 'unjust'. If some normative concept, claim, or fact cannot be defined or restated in non-normative terms, we can call it *irreducibly* normative. According to *Non-Naturalist Cognitivists*, when such normative claims are true, they state irreducibly normative facts. According to *Non-Analytical Naturalists*, such claims state natural facts.

As examples of such theories, we can take three versions of the *Act Utilitarian* view that

(1) some act is right

just when, and because,

(2) this act maximizes happiness.

If these Utilitarians were Analytical Naturalists, they would claim that, when we say that some act is right, we mean that this act maximizes happiness. On this implausible view, since these phrases mean the same, they refer to the same property. When some act maximizes happiness, that is the same as this act's being right, or is *what it is* for this act to be right. (1) and (2) are different ways of stating the same fact, which is both normative and natural.

According to those Utilitarians who are Non-Naturalist Cognitivists, the phrase 'is right' expresses an irreducibly normative concept. When some act has the natural property of maximizing happiness, this fact makes this act have the different, irreducibly normative property of being right. (1) and (2) have different meanings, and state different facts. (2) states a natural fact, but (1) states a fact that is not natural but irreducibly normative.

According to those Utilitarians who are *Non*-Analytical Naturalists, though the phrase 'is right' expresses an irreducibly normative concept, and the phrase 'maximizes happiness' expresses a naturalistic concept, these concepts refer to the same property. Despite having different meanings, (1) and (2) state the same fact, which is both normative and natural.

Similar claims are made by other Cognitivist moral theories, and by Cognitivist theories about other normative concepts, claims, and facts. These theories can all be either Analytically or Non-Analytically Naturalist, or Non-Naturalist.

Of those who are in these ways *Normative* Naturalists, most are also *Metaphysical* Naturalists, who believe that all properties and facts are natural, so that there could not be any irreducibly normative facts. But some Metaphysical Naturalists reject Normative Naturalism, and are either Non-Cognitivists or Nihilists. I shall argue later that we ought to reject Metaphysical Naturalism. When I use the word 'Naturalism' on its own, I shall be referring to *Normative* Naturalism.

Naturalism and Non-Cognitivism are both, I shall argue, close to Nihilism. Normativity is either an illusion, or involves irreducibly normative facts.

In defending these claims, I shall also be discussing different *conceptions* of normativity. I shall use the word 'normative' both in a wide sense, and in narrower senses that express these conceptions.

On the *rule-involving* conception, normativity involves rules, or requirements, which distinguish between what is *allowed* and *disallowed*, or what is *correct* and *incorrect*. Some examples are criminal laws, the requirements of the code of honour, the rules of etiquette, and rules about spelling, grammar, and the meanings of words. Such rules or requirements are often called *norms*, and claims that state or imply such norms we can call *normative* in the *rule-implying* sense.

On the *reason-involving* conception, normativity involves reasons or apparent reasons. When I call some claim

> *normative* in the *reason-implying sense*, I mean roughly that this claim asserts or implies that we or others do or might have some reason or apparent reason.

This, I shall argue, is the best conception. To illustrate these conceptions, I might first say 'You shouldn't eat peas with a spoon', or 'You shouldn't use "refute" to mean "deny".' These claims are normative in the rule-implying sense. But I might add that, since these rules are now so often broken, you have no reason not to act in these ways. My claims would not then be normative in the reason-implying sense.

On a third conception, normativity involves actual or possible motivation. Korsgaard, for example, writes that if some argument 'cannot motivate the reader to become a Utilitarian then how can it show that Utilitarianism is normative?' Anderson similarly writes that 'any theory of the good must have normative force: we must be capable of being moved to action by the reasons it gives us.' Many other people make similar claims.

We ought, I shall argue, to reject this *motivational* conception. Normativity, we should agree, is closely related to motivation. If we are aware of facts that give us certain reasons for acting, and we are fully substantively rational, we would be motivated to act for these reasons. But that does not imply that normativity in part consists in actual or possible motivating force.

On a fourth conception, normativity involves certain kinds of attitude to our own and other people's acts such as approval or disapproval. Of those who accept this *attitudinal* conception, some are Naturalists, who believe that normative claims state beliefs about such attitudes. Others are Non-Cognitivists, who believe that these claims *express* such attitudes. On a fifth, *imperatival* conception, normativity involves commands.

These conceptions might be able to be combined. If Naturalists can successfully defend some motivational account of reasons, they could claim to give a single, unified account of both reason-involving and motivational normativity. Non-Cognitivists might similarly claim to give a unified account of motivational and attitudinal normativity. We might also apply different conceptions to different things. Some people, for example, give attitudinal or imperatival accounts of morality, motivational accounts of reasons, and rule-involving accounts of some other normative facts.

Most meta-ethical debates have been about morality. But I shall first discuss non-moral practical reasons and reason-implying oughts. Our questions here take simpler and clearer forms. These are also the most important questions if, as I believe, normativity is best understood as involving reasons or apparent reasons. Things matter only if we have reasons to care about them. In the conflict between these various theories, reasons provide the decisive battlefield. If Naturalism and Non-Cognitivism fail as accounts of reasons, these theories will also fail, I believe, when applied to morality.

83 Analytical Subjectivism about Reasons

Of those who give Naturalist accounts of normative reasons, many are *Analytical Subjectivists*, who make claims about the meaning of certain words or phrases. On Williams's account, for example, when we say that

(A) someone has a reason to act in a certain way,

we often mean something like

(B) this act would fulfil or achieve one of this person's present fully informed telic desires, or aims,

or

(C) if this person knew the relevant facts, and deliberated rationally, this person would be motivated to act in this way.

When people have reasons in what Williams calls this 'internal' sense, we can call these *internal reasons*. (B) and (C) state different claims, either of which might be true without the other's being true. But we can here combine these claims, and consider only cases in which they are both true.

Many other writers give such *Subjectivist Internalist* accounts of the concept of a reason. Falk, for example, defines a reason as a fact belief in which would motivate us. Williams, Falk, and others give similar accounts of the decisive-reason-implying senses of 'should' and 'ought'. According to this form of Analytical Subjectivism, which we can call

Analytical Internalism: When we say that

(D) someone has *decisive reasons* to act in a certain way, or *should* or *ought* to act in this way,

we often mean something like

(E) this act would best fulfil this person's present fully informed telic desires, or is what, after fully informed and procedurally rational deliberation, this person would be most strongly motivated to do, or would choose to do.

This claim defines the *internal* senses of the words 'decisive reason', 'should', and 'ought'.

According to some other people, whom Williams calls

Externalists: We often use words like 'reason', 'should', and 'ought' in other, simpler, irreducibly normative senses.

These we can call the *external* senses of these words. Most Externalists are Objectivists, who believe that we have object-given, value-based external reasons. As we shall see, however, some Externalists are *Non*-Analytical Subjectivists, who believe that we have desire-based or aim-based external reasons.

To illustrate the difference between these senses of these words, and between internal and external reasons, we can suppose that, in

Early Death, unless you take some medicine, you will later die much younger, losing many years of happy life. Though you know this fact, and you have deliberated in a procedurally rational way on this and all of the other relevant facts, you are not motivated to take this medicine.

When Williams discusses this imagined case, he claims that you have no reason to take this medicine. As he points out, you have no internal reason to act in this way. And Williams claims that there are no external reasons. I believe that there *are* such reasons. On my view, you have a decisive external reason to take this medicine, which is provided by the fact that this act would give you many more years of happy life.

This case also illustrates the reason-involving and motivational conceptions of normativity. If we use the words 'reason', 'should', and 'ought' in their internal senses, these two conceptions can be combined, since claims about someone's internal reasons are claims about what would fulfil this person's desires, or about how this person might be motivated to act. If we use these words in their external senses, claims about reasons are not even in part claims about motivation, so these conceptions are quite different, and might conflict. On the Externalist version of the reason-involving conception, normativity does not involve either actual or hypothetical motivating force. If Externalists considered *Early Death*, for example, most of them would accept my claim that you have a decisive reason to take your medicine. On this view, though you are not motivated to take your medicine even after informed and procedurally rational deliberation, this fact does not even slightly weaken this external reason, nor does it count against the claim that, in the external sense, this is what you ought to do.

In distinguishing between these views, I have assumed that we can use the phrase 'has a reason for acting' in at least two senses, which express different concepts, and refer to different kinds of reason. It might be objected that, when Internalists and Externalists discuss what we have reasons to do, these people must be using the same concept of a reason, and be disagreeing only about which are the facts that give us reasons. But these people do, I believe, use different concepts. I understand the concept of an *internal reason* as described by Williams, Falk, and others. And I accept Williams's claim that, in *Early Death*, you have no internal reason to take your medicine. Our disagreement is only about external reasons.

When Williams argues that there are no such reasons, his main claim is that Externalists cannot explain what it could mean to say that we have some external reason. I admit that, when I say that we have some reason, or that we should or ought to act in a certain way, what I mean cannot be helpfully explained in other terms. I could say that, when some fact gives us a reason to act in some way, this fact *counts in favour* of this act. But this claim adds little, since 'counts in favour of' means, roughly, 'gives a reason for'. Williams suggests that the phrase 'has a reason' does not have any such intelligible, irreducibly normative external sense. When he discusses statements about such external reasons, Williams calls these statements 'mysterious' and 'obscure', and suggests that they mean nothing. Several other writers make similar claims.

When I claim that Williams and I use different concepts of a reason, I am assuming that each of us at least knows what he himself means. But that might not be true. People sometimes fail to understand, not only what other people mean, but even what they themselves mean.

It makes a difference here whether the phrase 'has a reason for acting' has only one ordinary sense or meaning, and, if so, what that sense is. Suppose first that this phrase has only one ordinary sense, which is the internal sense. That would give some support to the view that I misunderstand my own thoughts, since I am wrong to believe that I use the phrase 'has a reason' in an intelligible external sense. When I consider *Early Death*, I believe that you have a decisive external reason to take your medicine, though I know that you have no internal reason to act in this way. I cannot see how I could be so deeply confused as to believe that it would be both true and false that you have an internal reason to act in this way. But I cannot exclude the possibility that, as Williams suggests, my use of the phrase 'has an external reason' does not really state some belief, which might be either true or false, but merely expresses some vague attitude.

Suppose next that the phrase 'has a reason' has only one ordinary sense, which is the external sense. That would give some support to the view that Williams misunderstands his own thoughts, since he does in fact use the phrase 'has a reason' in this external sense. Williams might mistakenly deny that he uses this external sense because he doubts whether we could understand and justifiably use any such irreducibly normative concept. Other people have rejected widely used concepts on similar grounds.

There are other possibilities. The phrase 'has a reason' might have two ordinary senses, which are the internal and external senses, or these senses might be used by different groups of people. Either fact would support the view that Williams and I each mean what we think we mean.

As well as distinguishing these senses, we can ask whether we have both kinds of reason. Since it is clear that we have some internal reasons, the most important possibilities can be shown as follows:

The phrase 'has a reason for acting' has only one ordinary sense which is:

	the internal sense	the external sense
We have only internal reasons	(1)	(2)
We have both internal and external reasons	(3)	(4)

If (1) were true, Externalism would completely fail, since no one would ever have external reasons, nor would Externalists correctly describe the ordinary meaning of claims about reasons.

If (2) were true, Externalists would correctly describe the ordinary meaning of such claims, but these claims would all be false, since no one would ever have external reasons. Though Internalists would misdescribe the ordinary sense of the phrase 'has a reason', these people could move to an error theory, claiming that most of us have false beliefs about reasons. Internalists could also claim that, since all reasons are internal, we should revise our normative thinking, by coming to use the phrase 'has a reason' in the internal sense.

Suppose next that (3) is true, because we have both internal and external reasons, but most people use the phrase 'has a reason' only in the internal sense. Internalists would then correctly describe what most of us mean, and would make true claims about our internal reasons. Externalists could point out that, as well as having these internal reasons, we also have external reasons. But Internalists might reply that, since most of us use the phrase 'has a reason' only in the internal sense, it is only Internalists who can help us to answer our questions about what we have reasons to do, and about what we should or ought to do in the reason-implying senses. Internalism is the more important view, these people might claim, because it is only Internalist theories that might tell us what we want to know.

These claims would not, I believe, be justified. What is most important is not whether Internalists discuss the questions that most of us ask, but whether we have external reasons. If most of us use the phrase 'has a reason' only in the internal sense, that might cast some doubt on the view that we have external reasons, since it might be unlikely that so many people have failed to recognize that they have such reasons. But if we do have external reasons, Externalism would not be a less important view if and because Externalists were not discussing the questions about reasons that most people ask. On the contrary, Externalism would then have *more* importance. Instead of merely describing the internal reasons that most of us already believe that we have, Externalists would be truly telling us that we also have external reasons, which are reasons of a kind that most of us overlook. Most of us would thereby learn new and important normative truths.

Suppose finally that (4) is true, because we have both internal and external reasons, but most of us use the phrase 'has a reason' only in the external sense. Externalists could again claim that theirs is the more important view.

Internalists might give a similar reply. These people might say that, if they are not discussing the questions that most of us ask, that would make *Internalism* the more important view. Instead of merely describing the external reasons that most us already believe that we have, Internalists would be truly telling us that we also have internal reasons, which are reasons of a kind that most of us overlook. Most of us, Internalists might say, would thereby learn new and important normative truths.

This reply, I believe, fails. As I shall now argue, if we have both internal and external reasons, it is only external reasons that are important.

84 The Unimportance of Internal Reasons

I shall first repeat some definitions. Some normative claim is

> *conceptual* or *linguistic* when this claim is about some normative concept, or the meaning of some normative word or phrase.

One example is the claim that 'morally permitted' means 'not wrong'. Some normative claim is

> *substantive* when this claim both

> (a) states that something has some normative property,

and

> (b) is *significant*, by being a claim with which we might disagree, or which might be informative, by telling us something that we didn't already know.

One example is the claim that

> (1) illegal acts are wrong.

Some other normative claims are *tautologies*, in the sense that these claims tell us only that something is what it is, or that, if something has some property this thing has this property. An *open* tautology uses the same words twice. One example is the claim that

> (2) wrong acts are wrong.

Though (2) states that acts of a certain kind would have a certain normative property, (2) is not in my sense a substantive normative claim. This claim is not significant, since we would all agree that, as we already knew, any acts that are wrong are wrong.

There are also *concealed* tautologies, which use different words or phrases with the same meaning. Such claims are deceptive, since they can seem to be substantive. If I said that

(3) illicit acts are wrong,

this might seem like the substantive claim that illegal acts are wrong. But if I were using 'illicit' to mean 'wrong', (3) would be a concealed tautology, one of whose open forms would be (2).

Let us next use 'desires' as short for 'fully informed telic desires' and 'ideal' as short for 'fully informed and procedurally rational'. We can also use the words 'should' and 'ought' in their decisive-reason-implying senses. We can then say that, according to

Subjectivism about Reasons:

(A) we have most reason to act in some way, and should or ought to act in this way,

just when

(B) this act would best fulfil our present desires, or is what after ideal deliberation we would choose to do.

According to those Subjectivists who are

Analytical Internalists: When we make claims like (A), we often mean something like (B).

If (A) and (B) meant the same, Subjectivism about Reasons would not be a substantive normative view. This view would be a concealed tautology, which told us only that

(A) we have most reason to act in some way, and should or ought to act in this way,

in the sense that

(B) this act would best fulfil our present desires, or is what after ideal deliberation we would choose to do, just when

> (B) this act would best fulfil our present desires, or is what
> after ideal deliberation we would choose to do.

This view adds nothing to Analytical Internalism. So these Internalists should say only that, when we make claims like (A), we often mean something like (B). It is not worth adding that such claims are true just when they are true.

Some Analytical Internalists have overlooked this point, since these people assume that they are defending or describing a substantive normative view. Darwall, for example, describes what he calls a 'system of rational norms', which includes the norm that

> (C) we ought rationally to do what we would be motivated
> to do if we were vividly aware of the relevant facts.

On the view that Darwall describes, however, (C) could not state a substantive norm. According to this view, when we claim that

> we ought rationally to do something

we mean that

> we would be motivated to do this thing if we were vividly
> aware of the relevant facts.

If these claims meant the same, (C) would be another concealed tautology, which told us only that

> (D) what we would be motivated to do under these conditions
> is what we would be motivated to do under these conditions.

That is true but trivial.

I have just argued that

> (E) if we used these normative words only in the senses that
> Analytical Internalists describe, Subjectivism about Reasons
> would not be a substantive normative view.

Someone might add:

> (F) Subjectivism about Reasons *is* a substantive normative
> view.

Therefore

> We do not use these words only in these senses.

But this second argument would fail. For the reasons that I have just given, Analytical Internalists should reject (F). And some of these Internalists may have already seen that they should reject (F). Williams, for example, never claims that his Analytically Internalist version of Subjectivism is a substantive normative view.

Williams does, however, believe that

> (G) for Analytical Internalism to succeed, this view must
> explain how we can use the words 'reason', 'should', and
> 'ought' to make normative claims.

In Williams's words:

> It is essential to any adequate account of 'A has reason to do
> X' that it should be normative . . .

In defending his account, Williams writes:

> Unless a claim to the effect that an agent has a reason to
> do X can go beyond what that agent is already motivated
> to do . . . then certainly the term will have too narrow a
> definition. 'A has a reason to do X' means more than 'A
> is presently disposed to do X'.

But this claim, Williams suggests, might mean that A *would be* disposed to do X if A knew some fact, or lost some false belief. In using this notion or concept of a reason, Williams writes, we would be 'adding to, or correcting', this person's factual beliefs, 'and that is already enough for this notion to be normative'.

Williams here assumes that, when we tell people that they have a reason to do something, we intend to be giving these people advice. It would seldom be advice to say 'You want to do X', since few people need to be told what they already want to do. But it might often be advice to say

If you knew what I know, you *would* want to do X.

That is enough, Williams suggests, to make such claims normative.

It is not, I believe, enough. If I said 'You would enjoy this book', or 'This is the sharpest knife', my claims might be intended as advice. But that would not make these claims, or the facts which they report, normative. For some claim to be normative, it must use at least one normative word, or concept.

Williams might reply that, though these claims are not *explicitly* normative, they would be recommendations. Similarly, if I said 'Your wine is poisoned', or 'There's an angry bull in the next field', these claims would be warnings. Such claims, Williams might say, are *implicitly* normative, since they are intended to state facts that would help people to decide what to do. On Williams's Internalist account, when we say

(G) You ought to do X,

we often mean something like

(H) X is the act that would best fulfil your present desires, or is what after ideal deliberation you would choose to do.

Since it might help you to know that (H) is true, we might similarly use this claim to give you advice. This may seem enough to show that Williams's account sufficiently preserves the normativity of claims like (G). Williams might add that, since (H) uses the normative words 'best' and 'ideal', this claim is explicitly normative.

Williams's account, I shall argue, does not succeed. We can first distinguish between facts that are *normative* and facts that have *normative importance* in the sense that these facts give us reasons. Two examples would be the facts that

(J) your wine is poisoned,

and that

> (K) the fact stated by (J) gives you a reason not to drink
> your wine.

Of these facts, (J) is natural and (K) is normative. But it is (J), the natural fact, which has normative importance, in the sense of reason-giving force. Though (K) is a normative fact, this fact has no such importance. (K) is the second-order fact *that* the fact stated by (J) gives you a reason not to drink your wine. This second-order fact about this reason does not give you any *further* reason not to drink your wine. Similar claims apply to other cases. Whenever some natural fact gives us a reason, there is also the normative fact *that* this natural fact gives us this reason.

It is easy to overlook such normative facts. This mistake is especially likely if, rather than saying that certain natural facts *give* us reasons, we say that these facts *are* reasons. These are merely different ways of saying the same things. But if we say that natural facts of certain kinds *are* reasons to act in certain ways, we may be led to assume that, to defend the view that there are normative reasons, it is enough to defend the claim that there are natural facts of these kinds. That is not so. We must also defend the claim that these natural facts each have the normative property of *being a reason*. And this second claim, property, and fact might all be irreducibly normative.

Return next to Williams's suggestion that, when we say 'You ought to do X', we often mean something like

> X is the act that would best fulfil your present desires, or is
> what after ideal deliberation you would choose to do.

As I have said, such claims are in one way like 'You would enjoy this book' or 'Your wine is poisoned'. These claims might tell you facts that would give you reasons for acting, so such claims could be used to give you advice. But to be able to use such claims in this way, we must have the concept of *advice*. We must be able to understand the thought that

> (L) certain facts can give people reasons for acting, and make
> it true that these people should or ought to act in some way.

We can now ask whether, if we used normative words only in the senses that Analytical Internalist like Williams, Falk, and others describe, we could understand such thoughts. Suppose again that, in

> *Early Death*, after ideal deliberation, you are not motivated to take the medicine that you know would give you many more years of happy life.

When Williams discusses this example, as I have said, he claims that you have no reason to take this medicine. Though Williams might hope that you will take this medicine, he could not honestly *advise* you to act in this way. We cannot claim to be advising people if we tell them to do what we believe that they have no reason to do.

Consider next

> *Revenge*: Someone insults you. After thinking about the relevant facts in a fully informed and procedurally rational way, you decide to avenge this insult by killing this person, whom you now regard as your enemy. This act would also best fulfil your present fully informed desires. You know, however, that if you kill your enemy, you would be arrested, and punished with hard labour for the rest of your life.

As I argue in Chapter 3, if we appeal to claims about *procedural* rationality, we cannot defensibly claim that such imagined cases are impossible. Nor can we claim that, because such cases are unlikely to occur, they are not worth considering. These are the kinds of case that show most clearly what Subjectivism implies.

According to those Subjectivists who are Analytical Internalists, you have decisive internal reasons to kill your enemy, and this is what in the internal sense you ought to do. As before, though these Internalists might hope that you will not kill your enemy, they could not honestly advise you not to act in this way. We cannot claim to be advising people if we tell them *not* to do what we believe that they have decisive reasons to do.

It may seem that, in appealing to these imagined cases, I am trying to show that Analytical Internalism has implausible implications. But that is not my aim. As I have said, Williams is right to claim that, in *Early Death*, you have no internal reason to take your medicine. And these Internalists would be right to claim that, in *Revenge*,

> (M) you have decisive internal reasons to kill your enemy,
> and this is what in the internal sense you ought to do.

This claim is not implausible, but *true*. (M) means that, as we have supposed,

> (N) killing your enemy is what after ideal deliberation you
> have chosen to do.

In discussing these examples, my aim is to show that such Internalist claims, though true, have no importance.

Such claims can take two forms. According to *Analytical Naturalists*, normative words or claims can be defined or restated in non-normative and naturalistic terms. Though few people now defend such accounts of morality, many people defend, or take for granted, Analytically Naturalist accounts of reasons. Some of these people claim that, when we say that

> (A) we have decisive reasons to act in a certain way,
> or that we should or ought to act in some way,

we often mean something like

> (O) this act would do most to fulfil our present fully
> informed telic desires, or is what, after deliberating
> in certain naturalistically describable ways, we would
> choose to do.

This claim describes what we can call the *Naturalist internal senses* of the words 'reason', 'should', and 'ought'. According to these Analytical Naturalists, when it is true that we have decisive reasons to act in some way, and that we should or ought to act in this way, these are natural facts of the kinds described by (O).

Several Internalists defend such a view. Falk, for example, writes:

in what I have called the motivation sense, 'ought' statements would be about a certain kind of psychological fact . . . What are here called 'natural' obligations would in one sense be facts of nature in their ordinary empirical meaning.

Darwall writes that, on this version of Internalism,

the test of whether a fact is a reason for a person is for the person rationally to consider the fact for himself and to notice whether he is motivated to prefer the act.

Describing one such test, he writes:

When I consider the fact, the motivation lapses. What seemed a reason . . . turned out on further reflection not to be one at all.

When Darwall discovers that he does not have this reason, what he discovers is the natural, empirical fact that he is not motivated to act in some way.

If we used normative words only in these Naturalist internal senses, we could not, I believe, have normative thoughts. To illustrate this point, suppose that you are in some

Burning Hotel, and you can save your life only by jumping into some canal. I am outside your hotel, which I know to be on fire, and I can see you at some window above the canal.

According to these Internalists, if I think

You ought to jump,

I would be thinking something like

(P) Jumping would do most to fulfil your present fully informed desires,

or

(Q) If you deliberated in certain naturalistically describable ways, you would choose to jump.

But these would not be normative thoughts. (P) is merely a causal claim, and (Q) is merely a psychological prediction.

These Internalists might reply:

> Since the concepts *reason*, *should*, and *ought* are all normative, any account of these concepts, if it is true, preserves their normativity.
>
> Our view gives the true account of these concepts.

Therefore

> Our view preserves their normativity.

To assess this reply, we can return to *Revenge*, and to the fact that

> (R) in the Naturalist internal sense, you ought to kill your enemy.

This fact, I have claimed, is not normative. If I agreed that, in this sense, you ought to kill your enemy, I could honestly add that I was *not* advising you to act in this way. I would mean only that this act would do most to fulfil your present desires, and is what, after deliberating in certain ways, you have chosen to do.

These Internalists might now reply that, since I would be telling you what you ought to do, I *would* be advising you to act in this way. This reply assumes that

> (S) words like 'reason', 'should', and 'ought' have only these or similar internal senses.

If (S) were true, our normative claims could only state certain natural facts, such as facts about what would fulfil our desires, or about how we might be motivated to act. There would be nothing else for normativity to be. And we would have to admit that, in *Early Death*, you have no reason to take the medicine that would save your life, and that in *Revenge* you ought to kill your enemy. But I believe that

(T) these normative words can be intelligibly used in external, irreducibly normative senses,

and that

(U) we can use these senses to make true claims.

When compared with such claims, psychological and causal claims are *not* normative. There is something else, and something better, for normativity to be. Even if I know that killing your enemy would do most to fulfil your present desires, and is what after deliberating in certain ways you have chosen to do, I can still believe that you have no external reason to kill your enemy, and that you ought, and have decisive reasons, *not* to act in this way.

Some writers, such as Williams and Darwall, defend a different form of Analytical Subjectivism or Internalism. On this view, when we say that

(A) we have decisive reasons to act in a certain way, or that we should or ought to act in this way,

we often mean something like

(V) this act would *best* fulfil our present informed desires, or is what, after fully informed and procedurally *rational* deliberation, we would choose to do.

These writers point out that, since (V) uses the normative words 'best' and 'rational', this claim cannot be restated in non-normative terms. When these people claim that (A) often means something like (V), they are describing what we can call the *normative internal senses* of the words 'reason', 'should', and 'ought'. This form of Analytical Internalism is *not* a form of Analytical *Naturalism*.

If we used these words in these normative internal senses, we could have some normative beliefs. And these beliefs might seem to be about what we have reasons to do, and what we should or ought to do. But that would not really be true.

To illustrate this point, we can first consider a new, stipulated sense of the word 'ought'. I might tell other people that, when I claim that some act is

> what someone 'ought to do' in the *unjust-world* sense, I shall mean that this act is what, in an unjust world, this person has chosen to do.

Since the concept *unjust* is normative, so is the complex concept that I could express with this new sense of 'ought'. But this new concept is only partly normative, and this concept's normative part is not about what people ought to do. Suppose again that, in *Revenge*, you have chosen to kill your enemy. Since I believe that the world is unjust, I might claim that

> (W) in the unjust-world sense, you ought to kill your enemy.

Though this claim uses the word 'ought', (W) is merely another way of saying that, in an unjust world, you have chosen to kill your enemy. Such claims are normative because they imply that the world is unjust. But these are not substantive normative claims about what people ought to do. Such claims would add nothing to the claim that these people have made their choices in an unjust world.

Similar remarks apply to the normative internal sense of 'ought' that Williams, Darwall, and others use. If we know that

> (X) you have chosen to kill your enemy after fully informed and procedurally rational deliberation,

we could truly claim that

> (Y) in this internal sense, you ought to kill your enemy.

But (Y) adds nothing to (X). (Y) merely uses different words to restate the claim that you have chosen to kill your enemy after such ideal deliberation. Since (X) is not a claim about what you ought to do, and (Y) means the same as (X), (Y) cannot be a distinct substantive normative claim about what you ought to do.

If we used the word 'ought' only in this normative internal sense, we could ask

Q1: Which ways of deliberating are procedurally rational, and in other ways ideal?

This question would be normative. We could also ask

Q2: After such a process of ideal deliberation, what would a certain person choose to do?

This question would be psychological. But we could not ask, as a further, independent question:

Q3: What ought this person to do?

Given what we meant by 'ought', Q3 would be merely another way of asking Q2. As these remarks imply,

(Z) if we used the word 'ought' only in this internal sense, we could have substantive normative beliefs about which ways of deliberating are ideal. We could also have beliefs about what, after such deliberation, we or other people *would in fact* choose to do. But we could not have any distinct substantive normative beliefs about what we or other people *ought* to choose, and *ought* to do.

I shall now summarize some of these claims. According to

Subjectivism about Reasons:

(A) we have most reason to act in some way, and should or ought to act in this way

just when

(B) this act would best fulfil our present desires, or is what after ideal deliberation we would choose to do.

According to Analytical Internalists, we often use (A) to mean something like (B). If these claims meant the same, Subjectivism about Reasons would not be a substantive normative view, but a concealed tautology, which told us only that, if we acted in the ways described by (B), we would be acting in these ways.

Analytical Internalists might reply that, when they describe the internal senses of the words 'reason', 'should', and 'ought', they are not intending to state a substantive view. Their aim is only to give a true account of some of our normative concepts and claims. These people might also claim that their Internalist account has the feature that Williams calls 'essential', since this account explains how we can use these words and concepts to have and to state substantive normative beliefs about reasons, and about what we or others ought to do.

This claim, I have argued, is not true. According to some of these Internalists, we can restate claims like (A) and (B) in wholly naturalistic terms. If we used the words 'reason', 'should', and 'ought' in these *Naturalist* internal senses, the concepts that these words express would not even be normative. If our conceptual scheme took this impoverished form, we would not be able to give people advice. Nor could we think about what, in normative senses, we ourselves had reasons to do, and should or ought to do. We could try to fulfil our desires. And there would be facts that had normative importance, and reason-giving force. But that importance would be unknown to us — as it is unknown, for example, to some active, intelligent cat.

Some other Internalists use the words 'reason', 'should', and 'ought' in irreducibly normative internal senses. I have argued that, if we used only these Internalist concepts, we could have substantive normative beliefs about what would best fulfil our desires, and about which ways of deliberating are procedurally rational, and in other ways ideal. But we could not have any distinct substantive normative beliefs about reasons, or about what we should or ought to choose, or to do.

85 Substantive Subjective Theories

Subjectivism about Reasons can take other, better forms. According to what we can call

> *the Externalist Subjective Theory*: Some possible act is
>> what we have decisive *external* reasons to do, and what
>> we should or ought in the *external* sense to do,

just when, and because,

> this act would best fulfil our present fully informed
> telic desires, or is what, after ideal deliberation, we
> would choose to do.

Unlike Analytical Subjectivism or Internalism, this form of Subjectivism is a substantive normative theory. Though I have objections to substantive subjective theories, which I present in Chapters 3 and 4, these objections are not relevant here.

Many people assume that, if we use the words 'reason', 'should', and 'ought' in these external senses, we could not accept a desire-based or choice-based subjective theory. As this Externalist Subjective Theory shows, that is not so. It is true that, if we use these words in these senses, we could coherently deny that there are any desire-based, aim-based, or choice-based reasons, thereby rejecting all subjective theories. But that is precisely why, if instead we use these external senses to state some subjective theory, we would be making substantive claims.

Subjective theories about reasons are often called 'Internalist'. But this label is misleading, since the subjective theory that I have just described makes claims about *external* reasons. Internalists might say that, according to this theory,

> we have an *external* reason to act in a certain way just when,
> and because,

> (1) we also have an *internal* reason to act in this way,

in the sense that

> (2) this act would best fulfil our present informed
> desires, or is what after ideal deliberation we would
> choose to do.

But (1) would add nothing, since (1) is merely a shorter way of stating (2). It would be clearer to drop the phrase 'an internal reason', which is now confusingly used in two different senses. When Analytical Internalists say that we have some internal reason to act in some way, these people use this phrase as an abbreviation of some claim like (2). Some other,

Non-Analytical Subjectivists use the phrase 'an internal reason' to refer to the *external* reasons that these people believe to be provided by facts of the kind that (2) describes. That is what is claimed by the Externalist Subjective Theory that I have just stated. There are also many people who have not noticed the difference between these two very different senses. To avoid confusion, we should use the phrase 'a reason' only in its external, irreducibly normative sense. If we use this phrase to refer only to external reasons, we need not call such reasons 'external' or call this sense the 'external' sense. And when we are discussing substantive theories about reasons, some of which may be subjective theories, we need not call these theories 'Externalist'.

86 Normative Beliefs

To be able to understand and accept such substantive theories, we must use words like 'reason', 'should', and 'ought' in their indefinable, irreducibly normative senses. We can now briefly reconsider whether these words have such senses.

Falk makes several relevant remarks. When we claim that we ought to do something, Falk claims, we may mean that, if we reflected on the relevant facts, we would want to do this thing. This internal *motivational* sense of 'ought', Falk argues, is the best and most useful sense. It may be objected, Falk writes

> that 'I ought' is different from 'I would want if I first stopped
> to think'. The one has a normative and coercive connotation
> which the other has not.

Falk replies that, when we use 'ought' in this sense, we may be talking, not only about what we *would* want, but also about what we would *have* to want. Such claims, Falk writes, meet Kant's criterion of normativity. According to Kant, when we say that we *ought* to do something, we mean that 'we have, contrary to our inclinations, not only a rational but a *rationally necessary* impulse or "will"' to do this thing.

This reference to rational necessity looks promisingly normative. But this promise is not fulfilled. On Falk's account, an impulse is *rational* if it is one that 'a person would have if he both acquainted himself with the facts and tested his reactions to them'. Such an impulse is *necessary* if it would not be altered 'by any repetition of these mental operations.' Falk continues:

> And this is meant by a 'dictate of reason': an impulse or will to action evoked by 'reason' and . . . one which derives a special forcibleness from [the fact that] no further testing by 'reason' would change or dislodge it . . . A conclusive reason would be one [that is] unavoidably stronger than all opposing motives.

When we ask 'Must I do that?', Falk suggests, we are asking whether there are any facts belief in which would be 'sufficiently compelling to make' us do it. Some act is *rationally necessary* when knowledge of the facts would irresistibly move us to act in this way.

There is, I believe, no normativity here. An irresistible impulse is not a normative reason. Nor is an impulse made rational by its ability to survive reflection on the facts. Even after carefully considering the facts, we might find ourselves irresistibly impelled to act in crazy ways.

Falk himself asks whether, by expanding the motivational sense of 'ought', we could make this sense of 'ought' more obviously normative. Normativity, Falk assumes, belongs most clearly to imperatives or commands. A normative utterance, he writes, 'is one like "Keep off the grass!"' Falk therefore suggests that we might use 'ought' in a sense that combined a psychological prediction and an imperative. On this suggestion, when we say, 'You ought to do X', we would mean

> If you knew the facts, you would want to do X, so do it!

Such a claim might be both normative and true, since our imperative or command would make this claim normative, and our prediction might be true.

Though Falk calls this suggestion 'tempting', he points out that it would be odd to combine such commands with 'appeals to reason'. People could ask 'Are you *advising* me to do this, or are you merely *telling* me to do it?' Some imperatives, Falk notes, do merely give advice, since we can say, 'My advice is: Do X!' But this use of imperatives, he writes, is too weak or 'anemic' to be normative.

Falk then suggests that, when we say 'You ought to do X', we are not merely claiming that you have certain reasons to do X, in the sense that there are certain facts belief in which would motivate you. We are also claiming that these facts are *good* or *valid* reasons for you to do X. On Falk's account, however, this second claim would merely repeat our psychological prediction. We would mean only that, if you knew these facts, your belief in these facts really would motivate you. In Falk's words, we want 'the hearer to have the benefit of *experiencing* what we claim'. If you find that you are *not* motivated by these beliefs, these facts would be shown *not* to be good or valid reasons for you. So this attempt to achieve normativity also fails.

It may seem surprising that, when Falk worries that his motivational sense of 'ought' is not sufficiently normative, his first response is to expand this sense of 'ought' by making it include a command, or imperative. When Falk wrote, however, it was widely believed that normative claims must either be claims about natural facts, such as psychological predictions, or be commands, or expressive utterances such as 'Lying: Boo!' or 'Keeping promises: Hurray!' Falk briefly mentions the view that we can use sentences containing 'ought' to state what we believe to be irreducibly normative truths. But this suggested sense of 'ought', Falk writes, is 'too nebulous . . . to be meaningful'.

I believe that I use 'ought' in a meaningful, irreducibly normative sense. Suppose again that I am outside your burning hotel, and I believe that you ought to jump into the canal. I would not be believing that this act would fulfil your desires, or is what after ideal deliberation you would choose to do. Nor would I be merely thinking 'Jump!' I would believe that you have *decisive reasons* to jump, and that if you don't jump you would be making a *terrible mistake*. You *should* and *must* jump.

That, at least, is what I *believe* that I would believe. We have returned to the question whether I misunderstand my own beliefs. If we claim to use some word that we cannot helpfully define, or explain by using other words, our hearers may doubt that this word means anything. But such doubts would often be unjustified. Most words cannot be helpfully explained merely by using other words, since most definitions merely use other words or phrases which have similar meanings. We learn what most words mean, not by using dictionaries, but by acting in complicated ways on the complicated surface of our planet. That is why some dictionaries contain photographs or drawings of some of the other animals or inanimate objects with which we causally interact, and to which some of our words refer. But we are also intelligent and rational animals, who can think thoughts about what we cannot see, touch, or hear. Some of these are abstract thoughts, such as thoughts about what it is for events to be in the past or the future, and thoughts about causation, possibility, necessity, or logic. The concepts that such thoughts involve cannot be helpfully explained either by using other words, or by pointing to something, or by using photographs or drawings. It would not be surprising if, as I believe, the same is true of our fundamental normative concepts, such as those expressed by the words 'a reason', 'should', and 'ought'. We cannot yet fully explain how we come to understand such words and the concepts they express, and how we can recognize any irreducibly normative truths. I shall make some suggestions later. But these gaps in our knowledge do not give us decisive reasons to believe that we have no such concepts, or that there are no such truths.

We can make another, stronger claim. We could not have decisive reasons to believe that there are no such normative truths, since the fact that we had these reasons would itself have to be one such truth. This point may not refute this kind of skepticism, since some skeptical arguments might succeed even if they undermined themselves. But this point shows how deep such skepticism goes, and how blank this skeptical state of mind would be.

I used to assume that most people have, or at least understand, such irreducibly normative beliefs about reasons and reason-implying *oughts*. That may not be true. In arguing against Externalism, for example, Williams writes:

> Blame rests, in part, on a fiction: the idea that ethical reasons
> . . . must, really, be available to the blamed agent. *He ought to*
> *have done it*, as moral blame uses that phrase . . . hopes to
> say that he had a reason to do it. But this may well be untrue:
> it was not, in fact, a reason for him, or at least not enough
> of a reason.

Given what Externalists mean by the claim that someone had a normative reason to act in a certain way, it is irrelevant to reply 'But this was *not in fact* a reason for him'. When Williams writes 'this may well be untrue', he assumes that he is denying what these Externalists are claiming. But that is not so. These people are making claims that are not even in part about this man's psychology, but are purely normative. Williams's objection should instead be that, as he often says, he doesn't understand such claims, and he doubts whether they make sense. As we have seen, Falk calls such claims too nebulous to be meaningful. And Darwall writes:

> The case for internalism is especially compelling when
> we apply it to reasons . . . Unless we suppose that a fact's
> being a reason has something to do with its capacity to
> motivate, perhaps under some kind of ideal consideration
> of it, there seems no alternative to supposing that it consists
> in some kind of non-natural property. And if we are willing
> to accept that, the resulting picture of rational motivation is
> an alien and unsatisfying one. It fails to make the desire to
> act for reasons intelligible as one that is central to us and
> not simply a superadded fascination with a non-natural
> metaphysical category.

If Darwall had my concept of a reason, he would not make such claims. When I believe that some fact gives me a decisive reason to do something, it is not *unintelligible* how I might want to act for this reason.

25

Non-Analytical Naturalism

87 Moral Naturalism

There are, I have said, two kinds of Naturalism. According to Analytical Naturalists, though we can distinguish between normative and naturalistic words and sentences, this distinction is fairly superficial. Normative words can all be defined by using purely naturalistic words, and normative and naturalistic sentences can state the same claims, which state the same facts. If we used normative words only in the senses that these Naturalists describe, we could not, I have argued, have any normative beliefs.

According to *Non*-Analytical Naturalists, we use some words to express concepts and make claims that are irreducibly normative, in the sense that these concepts and claims cannot be defined or restated in non-normative terms. When we turn to facts, however, there is no such deep distinction. All facts are natural, but some of these facts are also normative, since we can also state these facts by making irreducibly normative claims.

Most of these Naturalists make claims that are not about reasons, but about morality. We can now turn to such claims. *Normative* Naturalism is often derived from *Metaphysical* Naturalism. Most Naturalists assume that, if there are any moral properties and facts, these would have to be natural properties and facts. Sturgeon, for example, writes: 'I take natural facts to be the only facts there are. If I am prepared to recognize moral facts, therefore, I must take them, too, to be natural facts.' Smith writes that, since 'there are no non-natural properties . . . moral properties . . . must just be natural properties.' Boyd even writes that 'goodness is probably a physical property'.

Some of these writers argue that some form of Moral Naturalism must be true. Consider first those simple, *monistic* moral theories which make claims like

> (A) acts are morally right if and only if, or *just when*, these acts have a certain natural property.

If some such claim were true, the concept *right* and some other, naturalistic concept would be *necessarily co-extensive*, in the sense that these two concepts would necessarily apply to all and only the same things.   Some Naturalists claim that

> (B) when two concepts are necessarily co-extensive, these concepts refer to the same property.

When combined with (B), claims like (A) imply that moral rightness is the same as some natural property. Consider, for example, the Act Utilitarian view that

> (C) acts are right just when they maximize happiness.

If this view were true, the concepts *right* and *maximizes happiness* would apply to all and only the same acts. (B) and (C) would together imply that being an act that maximizes happiness is the same as being right, or is *what it is* for an act to be right. Similar remarks apply to other, more complex, pluralistic moral theories. When combined with (B), these theories would imply that rightness is the same as, or consists in, some set of natural properties.

This *Co-extensiveness Argument* does not, I believe, succeed. When we consider pairs of concepts that both refer to natural properties, (B) is plausible, and might be true. But when applied to some other pairs of concepts, (B) is not, I believe, true. Consider first the arithmetical concepts expressed by these phrases:

> *the only even prime number,*
> *the positive square root of 4.*

These two concepts both refer to the number 2, which is—or has the properties of being—both the only even prime number and the positive square root of 4. Consider next the concepts expressed by these deceptively similar phrases:

being the only even prime number,

being the positive square root of 4.

These concepts refer, not to the number 2, but to these two properties of this number. These two concepts are necessarily co-extensive, since they refer to properties that are necessarily had only by the number 2. But in the sense of 'property' that is relevant here, these concepts refer to different properties. Being the only even prime number cannot be the *same* as being—or be *what it is* to be—the positive square root of 4. So, when applied to these concepts, (B) is false. We can add that, if (B) were true when applied to such concepts, most of mathematics would be either impossible, or trivial.

Since (B) is false when applied to mathematics, it may also be false elsewhere. And (B) is false, I believe, when applied to pairs of concepts of which one is naturalistic but the other is normative. That is what we should expect, given the ways in which natural and normative properties are related. As I shall argue later, if (B) were true when applied to such concepts, normative theories would be either impossible or trivial. Since (B) does not apply to such concepts, we can reject this argument for Moral Naturalism. If acts were right just when they maximized happiness, this fact would not imply that being an act that maximizes happiness is the same as being right.

Other Naturalists give less ambitious arguments, which claim to show only that Moral Naturalism *might* be true, since moral rightness might be the same as some natural property, or set of properties. Some of these people argue that, if we *suppose* that certain moral claims are true, Act Utilitarianism could defensibly take a Non-Analytically Naturalist form. It is worth asking whether that is so, since similar claims would apply to the more complicated moral theories, or sets of moral beliefs, that most of us find more plausible.

According to this form of Utilitarianism,

(D) though the concept *right* is different from the concept
maximizes happiness, these concepts both refer to the
same property.

Such a claim may seem obviously mistaken. Given the difference
between these concepts, we may assume that they must refer to different
properties.

These Naturalists would reply that, though different concepts usually refer to different properties, there are some important exceptions.
Many of these people appeal to analogies taken from the history of
science. Two examples are the discoveries that water is H2O and
that heat is molecular kinetic energy. These facts had to be discovered because they were not implied by the pre-scientific meanings
of the words 'water' and 'heat'. We might similarly discover, these
Naturalists argue, that rightness is some natural property or set of
properties.

These arguments have one true premise. Naturalists can claim that

(E) some normative words and concepts might refer to natural
properties.

To defend (E), moreover, there is no need to use analogies from the
history of science. We can appeal directly to certain normative concepts.
One example is the concept expressed by the phrase:

the natural property that makes acts right.

Suppose that, as all Act Utilitarians believe,

(F) acts are right just when, and because, they maximize
happiness.

It would then be true that

(G) being an act that maximizes happiness is the natural
property that makes acts right.

This claim would use a normative concept to refer to the natural
property of maximizing happiness.

If (G) were true, however, that would not support Moral Naturalism. Though (G) would use a normative concept that referred to a natural property, this claim would be merely another way of stating the normative claim that is stated by (F). And this claim might state an irreducibly normative fact.

In making these remarks, I have used a distinction that is both of great importance and surprisingly often overlooked.   If we claim that

(H) some natural property is the property that *makes* acts right,

we are not claiming that

(I) this natural property is the property of *being* right.

In explaining this distinction, we can first note that, when some act has some natural property which makes it right, this act's having this property does not *cause* it to be right. Though there are several views about the nature of morality, no one believes that *making right* is a causal relation.

There are several ways in which, when something has some property, this fact may *non-causally* make this thing have some property. If I had a child, for example, that would make me a parent. But having a child would not cause me to be a parent. It could not do that, since causes must be different from their effects, and there are not *two* properties here. Having a child is the same as being a parent—or is *what it is* to be a parent. This truth is *analytic*, in the sense that it is directly implied by the meaning of the words 'child' and 'parent'. But some such truths are not analytic. One example is the truth that, when the molecules in some physical object move more energetically, that makes this thing hotter in the pre-scientific sense. Having such greater energy does not cause this thing to be hotter, but is the same as being hotter, or is *what it is* to be hotter. Heat *is* molecular kinetic energy.

There is another, similar pair of ways in which, when something has some property, this fact may non-causally make this thing have some property. Just as my having a child would make me a parent, so would my having a daughter. But unlike having a child, having a daughter is not the same as being a parent. These properties are different because, even if I didn't have a daughter, I could be a parent by having a son. As before, however, my having a daughter would not *cause* me to be a parent. The truth is rather that, if I had a daughter, this would *constitute* my being a parent, and if my daughter was my only child, my having a daughter would be the property in which my being a parent would *consist*. While these truths are analytic, there are also non-analytic truths of this kind. Some of the properties of genes, for example, consist in some of the properties of DNA. And mental states, many people believe, consist in states of the brain. Though having a child is the *same* as being a parent, but having a daughter is merely one of the properties in which being a parent can *consist*, these relations are very similar. And there is little metaphysical difference between the claims that mental states *are* or *consist in* states of the brain.

Return now to *making right* and *being right*. According to some writers:

> If there is only a single natural property that makes acts right,
> we could claim that, when some act has this property, that is
> the same as this act's being right, or is what it is for this act
> to be right. If instead there are several properties that can
> make acts right, the rightness of acts would consist in their
> having one of these properties. Just as my being a parent
> might consist in my having either a daughter or a son, an act's
> rightness might consist in its being an act that either saves
> someone's life, or keeps some important promise, or expresses
> gratitude, and so on.

These claims are, I believe, seriously mistaken. When having a child makes someone a parent, or having greater molecular kinetic energy makes something hotter, these relations hold between some property referred to in one way and the *same* property referred to in another way. That is not true of the relation of *making right*. More exactly, there is a trivial sense in which rightness is the property that makes acts right. This is like the sense in which redness is the property that makes things red, and legality is the property that makes acts legal. It is in a different and highly important sense that, when some act has some other property—such as that of saving someone's life—this fact can make this act right. Being an act that saves someone's life couldn't be the same as being right. Nor, I believe, could it be one of the properties in which the rightness of acts consists. When some property of an act makes this act right, this relation holds between two quite different properties. That is why, if it were true that

(G) being an act that maximizes happiness is the property that makes acts right.

this truth would not support Moral Naturalism. (G) does not imply that

(J) being an act that maximizes happiness is the same as being right.

(G) implies that

(K) when some act would maximize happiness, this fact would make this act right, by making it have the different, normative property of being right.

(K) can be used to state a *Non*-Naturalist form of Utilitarianism, of the kind that Sidgwick defends.

These remarks do not refute Moral Naturalism. These Naturalists might still argue that moral rightness is, or consists in, one or more natural properties. But these Naturalists must defend such claims in a different way. They must argue that, like the concept expressed by the phrase *the property that makes acts right*, the concept *right* might refer to certain natural properties.

This claim, however, is harder to defend. Return to the pre-scientific meaning of the word 'heat'. In the relevant sense, 'heat' means, roughly:

the property, *whichever it is*, that can have certain effects, such as those of melting solids, turning liquids into gases, causing us to have certain kinds of sensation, etc.

This concept, we can say, has an *explicit gap* that is *waiting to be filled*, since this concept refers to some property without telling us what this property is. This concept refers to this property indirectly, *as* the property that can have certain effects, such as those of melting solids, etc. This feature of the concept of *heat* allowed scientists to fill this gap, by discovering that molecular kinetic energy is the property that can have these effects.

Similar claims apply to the concept expressed by the phrase:

the natural property, *whichever it is*, that makes acts right.

This concept also has a gap that is waiting to be filled, since this concept refers to this property in a similar, indirect way, *as* the natural property that makes acts right. That is how, though this concept is normative, it might refer to some natural property, such as that of being an act that would maximize happiness.

No such claim applies, I believe, to the concept *right*, or the more fundamental concept *wrong*. We can use 'right' and 'wrong' in several definable moral senses, some of which I describe in Chapter 7. The concepts expressed by these senses do not, I believe, have similar explicit gaps that are waiting to be filled, in ways that would allow these concepts to refer to one or more natural properties. One example is the concept expressed by the word 'blameworthy'. This concept does not refer to some property indirectly, as the property of which something else is true. This concept refers directly to the property of being blameworthy. Rather than arguing that this concept might refer to some natural property, Naturalists would have to claim that blameworthiness is a natural property. And this claim would be harder to defend. Though social scientists can discover facts about which are the acts that various people judge to be blameworthy, these are not, I believe, facts about the blameworthiness of these acts.

As I have also claimed, however, there are senses of 'right' and 'wrong' that cannot be helpfully defined in other terms. When some concept is indefinable, it does not, like the pre-scientific concept of *heat*, have an explicit gap that is waiting to be filled. But some Moral Naturalists put forward arguments of a similar though looser kind. According to these people, though we cannot define the concepts that are expressed by these senses of 'right' and 'wrong', we can describe the roles or functions that these concepts have in our moral thinking. By appealing to some such functionalist theory, these people argue, we may be able to show that these concepts refer to one or more natural properties.

Though such arguments are impressive and in some ways plausible, they could not, I believe, succeed.

Before defending this belief, I shall briefly describe why this disagreement matters. Sidgwick believed that rightness is an irreducibly normative property. So did some Non-Utilitarians, such as David Ross. Suppose that Sidgwick and Ross are talking to some Utilitarian Non-Analytical Naturalist. This person claims that, though the concept *right* is irreducibly normative, this concept refers to the natural property of maximizing happiness.

Sidgwick might say:

> If your view were true, Ross and I would have wasted much of our lives. We have spent many years trying to decide which acts are right. We both believe that, when acts maximize happiness, that might always make these acts have the different property of being right. I believe that it does, Ross believes that it doesn't. If there were no such different property, as your view implies, Ross and I would both be mistaken. Morality, as we understand it, would be an illusion.

This Naturalist might reply:

> That is not so. You and Ross both asked what it is for acts to be right, and which acts have this property. My view answers both your questions. Rightness is the property of maximizing happiness, and acts are right when they have this property.

> I do claim that, when acts maximize happiness, they cannot also have some *different* property of being right. But that does not imply that these acts are not right. Maximizing happiness is the same as being right. And since identity is a symmetrical

relation, we can as truly claim that, when acts are right, they cannot also have some different property of maximizing happiness. As that shows, my view does not eliminate morality. On my view, there are certain natural properties and facts which are also *moral* properties and facts. That does not make morality an illusion.

Sidgwick might reply:

> You have not seen how deeply you and I disagree. Though you and I are both Utilitarians, and Ross rejects Utilitarianism, my view is much closer to Ross's view than it is to yours. Your view *does* eliminate morality, as Ross and I both think we understand it. Ross and I both know that some acts have the natural property of maximizing happiness. We believe that we can ask an important further question, which is whether all such acts also have the *very different*, irreducibly normative property of being right. If your view were true, *there would be no such property*, and no such further question. That would be how, in trying to decide which acts are right, Ross and I would have wasted much of our lives.

As before, these remarks do not refute Moral Naturalism. Sidgwick, Ross, I, and others may have wasted much of our lives.

I have found, to my surprise, that this imagined dialogue baffles many Naturalists. These people repeat that, since Sidgwick wanted to know both what rightness is, and which acts are right, he should be glad to discover that rightness is the property of maximizing happiness. To explain why Sidgwick would not have been glad, I shall use a crude and only partial analogy. Suppose that I believe in God, and I have spent many years trying to decide which religious texts and theologians give the truest accounts of God's nature and acts. You tell me that you also believe in God. Love exists, you say, in the sense that some people love others. God exists, because God is love. I could reply that, if your view were true, I would have wasted much of my life. I believe that God is the omniscient, omnipotent, and wholly good Creator of the Universe. If God was merely the love that some people have for others, I would have made a huge mistake, and all my years studying religious texts would have taught me almost nothing.

88 Normative Natural Facts

We shall be asking whether, as Non-Analytical Naturalists believe, irreducibly normative claims might state natural facts. We can first make this question clearer.

Some fact is natural, on one common definition, if facts of this kind are investigated or discussed by people working in any of the natural or social sciences. Rather than trying to make this definition more precise, we can add another definition, which applies only to *normative* facts. When we call any such fact

> 'natural' in the *reductive* sense, we mean that this normative fact could be restated by making some non-normative and naturalistic claim.

In applying this definition, it is often enough to ask whether some normative fact could be restated in non-normative terms. If the answer is No, this fact could not be natural in this reductive sense. We wouldn't need to ask whether this fact could be restated in naturalistic terms, so the vagueness of the word 'naturalistic' would not matter. We can now say that

> *Naturalists* believe that normative facts are all natural in the reductive sense,

and

> *Non-Naturalists* believe that some facts are not in this sense natural, but irreducibly normative.

Some Naturalists make claims that may seem not to fit these definitions. Sturgeon, for example, defends what he calls 'a naturalistic but non-reductive view of ethics'. But Sturgeon means only that his view is not *analytically* reductive, since he believes that some normative *concepts* and *claims* may not be able to be defined or restated in non-normative terms. Sturgeon claims that normative *facts* might be able to be restated in non-normative terms. He illustrates this claim in a familiar way. If one form of Utilitarianism turned out to be true, Sturgeon claims, we could define the good as pleasure and the absence of pain, and define the right as what maximizes the good. On this form of Moral Naturalism, rightness would be the natural property of maximizing the sum of pleasure minus pain.

Though Sturgeon does not reject my reductive definitions of 'natural' and 'Naturalist', other Naturalists might do that. According to what we can call

> *Wide Naturalism*: Normative facts would be natural facts even if such facts were irreducibly normative, because these facts could not possibly be restated in non-normative terms.

Since Wide Naturalists admit that certain facts might be irreducibly normative, these people would need to explain in what sense these would also be *natural* facts. It may not help to return to the claim that these facts are of a kind that could be investigated or discussed by natural or social scientists. That claim may be too vague.

Sturgeon suggests another sense of 'natural' to which these people might appeal. Normative facts might be claimed to be natural if such facts 'play a causal role in the natural world'. This *Causal Criterion* raises questions that I shall not try to answer here. It will be enough to give some reasons why we need not ask whether normative facts are in this sense natural. This criterion seems too narrow, since there are many kinds of natural fact that do not play any causal role. I shall later give some examples. Nor should we assume that all causes of natural facts must be natural. If the Universe was created by God, for example, that should not be taken to imply that God is part of the natural world.

We can also understand, I believe, how certain irreducibly normative facts might be, or might have been, part of the cause of many natural facts. Given what we know about the lives of human beings and many other animals, it is hard to believe that the actual Universe is the best possible Universe. But we can imagine how that might have been true. If the actual Universe had been the best possible Universe, in the sense that reality was as good as it could be, this fact might not have been a mere coincidence. Reality might have been this way *because* this way was the best. On the theistic version of this view, God would not merely happen to exist, as a brute fact, since God would exist because God's existing was best. On this *Axiarchic View*, facts about goodness would explain many natural facts. But this fact could not be usefully taken to imply that goodness was a natural property.

There is another, more straightforward reason why we can ignore Wide Naturalism. We shall be asking whether we ought to accept some form of Non-Naturalist Cognitivism. Such Cognitivists reject Naturalism because they believe that normative facts differ in several ways from natural facts. The most fundamental normative facts are not, these people believe, contingent, empirically discoverable facts about the actual world. These facts are necessary truths, which would be true in all possible worlds. It could not have been true, for example, that undeserved suffering was not bad. And when these people claim that such facts are irreducibly normative, they mean that these facts are in a separate, distinctive category, which cannot be restated in non-normative terms. Since Wide Naturalists would accept this claim, their views do not seriously conflict with Non-Naturalist Cognitivism. So when we consider the arguments against this form of Cognitivism, we need not ask whether there is some wider sense in which irreducibly normative facts could be claimed to be natural facts.

It is worth adding one remark. Nothing in science conflicts with the view that there are some irreducibly normative facts, such as facts about practical and epistemic reasons. Scientists make progress by responding and appealing to some of these reasons.

I shall now use 'natural' only in the reductive sense. It may seem that, in using this definition, I am begging the question against Non-Analytical Naturalism. But that is not so. These Naturalists believe that, though some concepts and claims are irreducibly normative, all normative facts are also, in the reductive sense, natural facts. That possibility is left open by my definition. And this is the form of Naturalism that is worth considering. It is not worth asking whether, even if some facts are irreducibly normative, these facts might also be natural in some other, *non*-reductive sense.

There is another way in which we can make our question clearer. According to Non-Naturalists, some normative facts are not natural in the reductive sense, but irreducibly normative. In asking whether that is true, I shall be considering facts that are normative in the reason-implying sense. Since the word 'normative' has other senses, I shall first briefly consider facts that are normative in these other senses. These other normative facts *can*, I believe, be truly claimed to be natural facts.

Facts are normative in the *rule-implying* sense when these facts are about what is correct or incorrect, or allowed or disallowed, by some rule or requirement in some practice or institution. One example are facts about which acts are illegal. The *claim* that certain acts are illegal may be irreducible, in the sense that such claims cannot be restated in non-legal terms. But when certain acts are illegal, this *fact* can be fully redescribed by making various claims that are about the law, but are not themselves legal claims. We can describe in naturalistic terms what is involved in the creation of some political community, and some legislature, and what is involved in the passing of some law which declares certain acts to be illegal. We can then claim that, when such a law is passed, that is *what it is* for these acts to be illegal. It is a straightforward empirically discoverable fact whether, in some political community, acts of some kind are illegal. The property of being illegal might thus be truly claimed to be a natural property, and facts about which acts are illegal would then be natural facts. This use of 'natural' is in part intended to imply that, from a scientific point of view, some property or fact needs no further explanation. There is nothing puzzling, or needing further explanation, in the fact that certain acts are illegal.

Similar remarks apply to many other properties and facts that are normative in the rule-implying sense. Some examples are the facts that some act would be bad etiquette, or be against some code of honour, or be an incorrect spelling, or the wrong use of a word, or an impermissible move in chess or some other game. We can describe in non-normative terms what is involved when such social rules and practices are established. We can then truly claim that, when certain acts break these rules, that's *what it is* for these acts to be disallowed or incorrect in these ways. These normative facts are also natural facts.

We cannot make such claims, I shall argue, about facts that are normative in the reason-implying sense. We cannot describe various natural facts in non-normative terms, and then truly say that, when these facts obtain, that's *what it is* for us to have some reason, or *what it is* for some act to be what we should or ought to do in some reason-implying sense.

Certain facts may be normative in both the rule-implying and the reason-implying sense. Some examples might be moral facts that depend upon, or involve, moral rules or requirements. These distinctions can overlap in other ways. Some legal theorists, for example, reject the view stated above, claiming that acts cannot be illegal if the law that forbids such acts is morally unacceptable. These people might deny that, when certain acts are illegal, these are wholly natural facts. Similar claims might be made about the requirements of the code of honour. As these remarks suggest, when we ask whether some claim is normative in the reason-implying sense, it is not enough to appeal to the words with which someone states this claim. Normative words can be used in different senses. When people say that some act is illegal, or dishonourable, or bad etiquette, or a misuse of some word, these people may or may not be intending to imply that they or others have some reason not to act in this way.

The word 'normative' is sometimes used, not in the rule-implying or reason-implying senses, but in some psychological sense. One example is the motivational sense in which some Naturalist Subjectivists call some reasons normative. Natural facts can be in this sense normative, since there are natural facts about what, after informed deliberation, we would be motivated to do.

Other Naturalists appeal to claims, not about such motivating states, but about the *attitudes* we have when we consider certain kinds of act. Three such attitudes are sympathy, approval, and disapproval. On one such view, just as jokes are funny if most people find them amusing, and works of art are beautiful if they give most people aesthetic pleasure, acts are right if most people would regard such acts with approval from an impartial point of view, and acts are wrong if these acts would arouse in most people certain sentiments of blame or indignation. Some people's moral beliefs can be fairly well described in this *response-dependent* way. Some examples are the appealing beliefs of Hume and many Humeans. There are also some plausible response-dependent accounts of well-being, and of some other normative properties and facts. But as my later arguments will imply, we cannot successfully give such response-dependent accounts of normative reasons, or of reason-implying beliefs about what we ought to want, or to do. Since these theories cannot be successfully applied to such normative reasons, they also fail, I believe, when they are applied to reason-implying moral truths. Such response-dependence theories can take many forms, which would need separate discussions. Partly for that reason, I shall not argue against these theories here, except indirectly by defending a different view.

Non-Analytical Naturalism, I have now claimed, is partly justified. Many natural facts are normative in rule-implying, motivational, or attitudinal senses. But no such facts can be normative, I shall argue, in the stronger, reason-implying sense. In what follows, I shall mostly use 'normative' in this sense. There is a deep distinction, I believe, between all natural facts and such reason-involving normative facts.

We can first consider some arguments whose validity would, I believe, challenge this distinction.

89 Arguments from 'Is' to 'Ought'

If we accept certain natural facts, some people argue, we cannot coherently or consistently deny certain normative conclusions. Consider, for example, these claims:

(A) You said to me 'I promise to help you'.

(B) You promised to help me.

(C) You put yourself under an obligation to help me.

(D) You are under an obligation to help me.

(E) If other things are equal, you ought to help me.

Searle argues that (A) states a non-normative fact, but that given certain further non-normative assumptions, (A) implies (B), which implies (C), which implies (D), which implies (E). Searle calls this an argument of a kind that Hume claimed to be impossible: one that derives an '*Ought*' from an '*Is*'.

It will be enough to consider Searle's claim that (B) implies (C). Suppose you said 'I promise to help you, but I don't believe that I am thereby putting myself under any obligation to help you'. Unless you were making a joke, or had some other unusual aim, this remark would show that you didn't understand the meaning of the word 'promise', or what is involved in the practice of making and keeping promises. You could not be sincerely promising to help me unless you believed that, in making this promise, you were thereby putting yourself under an obligation. Your promise might be insincere, since you might not intend to help me. But even insincere promises put us under obligations. Given these facts, Searle claims, no one could coherently or consistently deny that, in promising to help me, you put yourself under an obligation to act in this way.

This last claim is not, I believe, true. Consider Act Consequentialists, who believe that everyone ought always to do whatever would make things go best. When we make some promise, we might thereby make it true that keeping this promise would make things go best. That might be true, for example, if someone else would rely on us to keep this promise, so that this person would be seriously burdened if we fail to do what we have promised to do. We can suppose that, in Searle's example, no such claim is true. You could do more good if you broke your promise to me, because that would enable you to help someone else whose needs are greater than mine. Act Consequentialists could then coherently deny that you have any moral obligation to keep your promise. These people should accept Searle's claim that, if you sincerely promised to help me, you must have believed that you were thereby putting yourself under an obligation. But this belief, these Consequentialists could claim, was false. Though you *tried* to put yourself under an obligation to help me, your attempt failed.

This objection does not assume that Act Consequentialism is true. We can suppose that, as Searle claims, every promise *does* put us under an obligation. Even on that assumption, Searle's *argument* does not succeed. We cannot refute Act Consequentialism merely by appealing to the meaning of the word 'promise', or to the beliefs of those who make sincere promises.

When Searle considers a similar objection, he replies that his argument is intended to show only that we have *some* obligation to keep our promises. Act Consequentialists are free to claim that such obligations are morally overridden whenever, by breaking some promise, we could do more good. This reply comes close to abandoning Searle's view. If our obligations to keep our promises would in all such cases be overridden, these obligations would make little difference. Searle's reply is also, I believe, mistaken. Act Consequentialists can coherently deny that, in such cases, we would even have such obligations.

Searle might next reply that, as he writes, 'promises are *by definition* creations of obligations.' He might also appeal to analogies with contractual obligations. We must admit that, by signing some contract, we may put ourselves under a legal obligation to act in some way. The same is true, Searle claims, of those non-legal obligations that we create by making promises.

In response to these claims, Act Consequentialists could point out that, like the word 'ought', the word 'obligation' is ambiguous. When we claim that we have an obligation to act in some way, we may be intending to imply that we have a reason to act in this way. But we can also use the word 'obligation' in a merely rule-implying sense. We can coherently claim, for example, that our legal obligations do not in themselves give us any reasons. Act Consequentialists could similarly claim that, even if our promises always create obligations in some non-legal rule-implying sense, these obligations do not in themselves give us any reasons. When these Consequentialists claim that, in Searle's example, you would have no obligation to help me, they are claiming that you would have no obligation of the stronger, reason-implying kind.

If we are not Act Consequentialists, we may believe that you *would* have an obligation of this stronger kind. We might then doubt my claim that this obligation could be coherently denied. It may therefore help to consider some other rule-involving social practices or institutions. When Nazis joined the SS, they swore oaths of unconditional obedience. Searle's argument implies that, in swearing these oaths, these men put themselves under an obligation to obey every command, including commands to commit mass murder. Suppose that one of these men had said, 'I swear unconditional obedience, but I don't believe that I am thereby putting myself under any such obligation'. This remark would show that this man either didn't understand the practice of swearing oaths, or that his oath was not sincere. For these men to be sincerely swearing these oaths, they must have believed that they were thereby putting themselves under an obligation to obey every command. But this belief was false. Though these men tried to put themselves under such an obligation, this attempt failed. These men had no obligation to obey immoral commands.

Searle might reply that, though our promises can put us under obligations, that is not true of such sworn oaths. But this reply would undermine Searle's view. Promises and sworn oaths are, formally, very similar. If Searle's argument was sound when applied to promises, it would also be sound when applied to sworn oaths. And if promises were by definition creations of obligations, that would also be true of sworn oaths. Searle's argument, we can add, applies more easily to oaths. There are various facts that can make some promise invalid. Since it is a moral question which these facts are, this feature of promises provides another objection to Searle's argument, since it shows that this argument needs some moral premises. No such claim applies to the simpler forms of the practice of swearing oaths. If we believe that promises create obligations but that such sworn oaths do not, this would have to be a substantive moral view, which could not be true by definition.

Consider next the institution of ownership. Searle writes:

> to recognize something as someone else's property necessarily involves recognizing that he has a right to dispose of it. This is a constitutive rule of the institution of private property.

He also writes

> It is often a matter of fact that one has certain obligations, commitments, rights, and responsibilities.

There are, indeed, such rule-involving facts. It was a matter of fact that, in the Southern States of the USA before the Civil War, some people were slaves, being the legal property of slave-owners. On Searle's view, if Searle and I had been living then, and I recognized that some slave was Searle's property, I would have thereby recognized that Searle had a right to use force to control his slave in certain ways. That was a constitutive rule of the institution of slavery. But I could have recognized this rule but also coherently denied that anyone had any reason to respect Searle's right to coerce his slave in these ways.

Searle's argument appeals to facts that are normative in the rule-implying sense. These are not successful arguments from 'Is' to 'Ought', since we can coherently deny that such facts are normative in the stronger, reason-implying sense.

There is a different and deeper objection, to which we can now turn. The crucial steps in Searle's argument are all, he claims, *tautologies*: being true by definition, or implied by the meanings of certain words. No such argument, I believe, could succeed. For example, Searle claims that, from the non-evaluative premise that

> (F) some argument's premises entail or imply this argument's conclusion,

we can derive the evaluative conclusion that

> (G) this argument is valid.

When we call some argument valid, we mean that this argument's premises imply this argument's conclusion. Since (F) and (G) mean the same, we *can* derive (G) from (F). But (G) is not a *normative* claim. (G) may be in Searle's sense 'evaluative'; but this sense, as I explain in a note, is irrelevant here.

There are, however, some other, more plausible arguments of this kind.

90 Thick-Concept Arguments

Some Naturalists appeal to various *thick normative concepts*, such as the concepts expressed by the words 'cruel', 'kind', 'rude', 'unpatriotic', 'chaste', 'courageous', and 'dishonest'. These concepts are normative in the sense that we can use them to express certain kinds of praise, blame, or criticism. These concepts are *thick* in the sense that they are not purely normative, since their use implies certain non-normative facts. If we call someone cruel for example, we imply that this person intentionally inflicts pain on others, and if we call someone dishonest, we imply that this person often tells lies, cheats, or steals.

Though thick normative concepts enrich our thinking in several ways, their meta-ethical importance has been greatly overstated. Some people claim that, by appealing to such concepts, we can give other arguments from '*Is*' to '*Ought*', or from *facts* to *values*. On this view, if we accept certain non-normative facts, we must also accept certain normative conclusions.   If we know, for example, that

(A) some woman often has sexual intercourse with strangers,

we must admit that

(B) this woman is unchaste;

and if we know that

(C) some man deliberately helped to bring about the military defeat and destruction of his own nation,

we must admit that

(D) this man's act was unpatriotic.

If we denied (B) or (D), these people claim, we would be misusing the words 'unchaste' or 'unpatriotic'. Given the meaning of these words, (B) follows from (A), and (D) follows from (C). Such claims we can call *thick-concept arguments*.

Those who appealed to such arguments were mostly challenging the Non-Cognitivist view that there are no normative facts. But these arguments also challenge the Cognitivist view that there is a deep distinction between natural facts and irreducibly normative facts. Since these arguments have premises that are not normative, it would be hard to see how they could validly imply irreducibly normative conclusions. But these arguments, I believe, fail.

As before, we are not asking whether we ought to believe what these arguments are claimed to show. We are asking whether we would be contradicting ourselves, or would be making incoherent or inconsistent claims, if we accepted the premises of these arguments, but rejected their conclusions.   That, I believe, is never true.

To reject some of these arguments, it is enough to appeal to certain *thin*, or purely normative concepts, such as the concepts *virtue* and *wrong*. We can then reject the normative assumptions that some thick concepts are used to express. In response to the arguments just given, we could coherently claim that, in our opinion, chastity and patriotism are not virtues. We could add that, when people act in ways that are unchaste, or unpatriotic, these facts do nothing to support the view that these people's acts are wrong, or open to any other kind of criticism. If we made these claims, we would be using the words 'unchaste' and 'unpatriotic' in senses that are not normative. In a similar but wittier way, rather than denying that it is wrong to steal, the socialist Proudhon claimed 'Property is theft'.

There are some other, stronger thick-concept arguments. If we claimed that

> someone's punishment would be *deserved* in the *retributive* sense,

we would mean roughly that

> given certain facts about how this person has acted, this person ought to be punished, or this punishment would be in itself good.

There are various other facts which might be claimed to make it true that someone ought to be punished. This punishment might have good effects, for example, by preventing this person from committing other crimes, or by deterring other crimes. But if that is how we justify someone's punishment, we are not claiming that this punishment is *deserved*. Those who make such claims I shall call *Retributivists*. These people might similarly claim that,

> given certain facts about how someone has acted — such as the fact that this person risked his life to save some stranger — this person deserves to be rewarded.

The word 'deserve' can be used in other, non-retributive senses, such as the sense in which the best performers in some competition may deserve to win some prize, though it was merely their good luck to be able to perform so well.

We are asking whether there can be valid arguments from naturalistic premises to normative conclusions.   Some Retributivist might claim:

(E) Grey knowingly committed some crime.

Therefore

(F) Grey deserves to be punished.

But (E) does not imply (F). If Grey had broken some unjust law to save some innocent person's life, Grey might deserve only to be praised. For this argument to be valid, Retributivists must add the normative premise:

(G) Anyone who knowingly commits this kind of crime deserves to be punished.

According to another, more plausible argument:

(H) Blue has not committed any crime.

Therefore

(I) Blue could not deserve to be punished.

This argument may be valid. The concept of *retributive desert* could not be truly applied unless certain facts obtain. And we might have to admit that, for someone to deserve to be punished, this person must have committed some crime. But this argument does not support a *positive* normative conclusion. Normative Nihilists could accept (I), but defend this claim in a different way. These people might say

> (J) Since there are no positive normative truths, it could not be true that Blue deserves to be punished.

They might add

> (K) Since there are no such truths, Blue's punishment could not be wrong.

Retributivists believe that there *are* some positive normative truths, such as truths about how people deserved to be treated. These people might say:

> When we call someone's punishment *retributively unjust*, we mean that this person deserves *not* to be punished in this way.

And they might claim:

> (H) Blue has not committed any crime.

Therefore

> (L) Blue deserves not to be punished.

Therefore

> (M) Blue's punishment would be retributively unjust.

> (N) These facts would make Blue's punishment wrong.

We can call this *the Injustice Argument*. Some Retributivists might qualify (N), claiming only that Blue's punishment would be very likely to be wrong, but might be justified if it were the only way to prevent some disaster. We can here ignore this possibility.

Compared with appeals to the concepts of *chastity* and *patriotism*, this appeal to the concept of *retributive justice* is harder to reject. As I have said, we could coherently deny that patriotism is a virtue, and we could claim that, though some act was unpatriotic, that does nothing to show this act to be wrong. It seems more doubtful whether we could deny that justice is a virtue, or could claim that some act's injustice does nothing to show this act to be wrong.

Despite its plausibility, this Injustice Argument does not, I believe, succeed. First, since (L) is a positive normative claim, Nihilists could reject the inference from (H) to (L). It does not follow, from the meaning of the word 'deserved' and the truth of (H), that Blue deserves not to be punished. We cannot refute Nihilism by appealing to thick normative concepts.

It might be suggested that, for such thick-concept arguments to succeed, they do not have to refute Nihilism. This argument might claim that, if we are not Nihilists, since we believe that there are some positive normative truths, we must admit that one such truth is that Blue's punishment would be retributively unjust.

Even in this less ambitious form, this argument, I believe, fails. We might reply that, in our opinion,

(O) though there are some normative truths, some of which are moral truths, no punishment could ever be deserved in the retributive sense, or be retributively unjust.

For the Injustice Argument to fail, it is enough that (O) states a coherent moral view. Like many other people, however, I believe that (O) is not only coherent but also true. Of those who accept (O), some believe that, since all of our choices and acts are fully causally determined, we do not have the kind of free will that could make any of us deserve, in the retributive sense, to be punished. Others believe that, even if our choices are not fully caused, there is no intelligible kind of desert-implying freedom.

When Anscombe gives her version of the Injustice Argument, she writes:

If a procedure is one of judicially punishing a man for what he is clearly understood not to have done, there can be absolutely no argument about the description of this as unjust . . . Someone who attempted to dispute this would only be

pretending not to know what 'unjust' means: for this is a
paradigm case of injustice. . . . it cannot be argued that the
procedure would in any circumstances be just.

We should accept Anscombe's last claim. We should agree that, since
Blue has not committed any crime, Blue's punishment could not be
retributively just. But that does not show that, as Anscombe also claims,
such a punishment would be *unjust*. Anscombe's remarks imply that

(P) If we accept that

(H) Blue has not committed any crime,

we cannot consistently or coherently deny that

(M) Blue's punishment would be retributively unjust.

But (P), I believe, is seriously mistaken. It does not follow from the
meanings of (H) and (M) that, if (H) is true, (M) must also be true. We
could reply:

(Q) Since no one could have any kind of free will that might
justify belief in retributive desert, no punishment could be
either retributively just or retributively unjust.

We might add:

(R) It is indeed of great importance that Blue has not
committed any crime. This fact would make Blue's
punishment both unfair and wrong. But unfairness is
not the same as retributive injustice.

Since (R) is not directly relevant to Anscombe's argument, I discuss this
claim further only in Appendix E.

When I call (P) seriously mistaken, I am not rejecting Anscombe's
moral beliefs.   We ought to reject (P) even if we believe that

(M) Blue's punishment would be retributively unjust.

(P) is a serious *meta-ethical* mistake. If claims like (P) were true, we
could successfully defend moral beliefs like (M) merely by appealing to
natural facts like (H) and to the meaning of certain words. Retributivists

could dismiss any argument which claimed that no one could have any kind of desert-implying freedom. Rather than trying to answer such arguments, it would be enough for Retributivists to appeal to one meaning of the word 'unjust'. That, I believe, could not be true. Just as we cannot prove that God exists by appealing to what we mean by 'God', we cannot give linguistic or conceptual proofs of any positive substantive normative truth.

We can next ask how Anscombe might defend her claims. Anscombe writes that, if Blue is punished for something that he is known not to have done, this would be 'a paradigm case of injustice'. If we denied that this punishment would be unjust, we would be 'pretending not to know what "unjust" means'. When Anscombe makes such claims, she might be assuming that, if we said that

(M) Blue's punishment would be retributively unjust,

all we would mean is that

(S) Blue would be being punished for some crime that he is known not to have committed.

Anscombe refers, for example, to what she calls 'the mere factual description "unjust"'. If (M) and (S) meant the same, Anscombe would be right to assume that we could not coherently accept (S) but reject (M). But these claims do *not* mean the same. If they did, the concept of *retributive injustice* would not be normative. In saying that Blue's punishment would be unjust, we would be merely restating the non-normative fact that is stated by (S).

Anscombe might instead concede that, if we said that

(M) Blue's punishment would be retributively unjust,

we would mean that

(T) Blue's punishment would treat Blue in a way in which, in the retributive sense, Blue deserves not to be treated.

On this more plausible version of Anscombe's view, she could not claim that, if we accept (S) but deny (M) and (T), we would be pretending not to know—or be showing that we did not know—what the word 'unjust' means. We could coherently admit that (S) is true, but deny that (S)'s truth makes Blue's punishment retributively unjust. If we reject the belief in retributive desert in the way summed up in (Q), we shall deny that there *are* any cases of retributive injustice. That would not show that we don't know what the phrase 'retributively unjust' means. If we deny that there are any ghosts, that doesn't show that we don't know what the word 'ghost' means. We might similarly understand some normative concept but coherently deny that this concept applies to anything, because we deny that anything has the property to which this concept refers.

When we consider meta-ethical disagreements, it is sometimes hard to focus on the right question. Suppose you believe that Blue's punishment *would* be retributively unjust. It may then seem to you that, if we accept that

> (S) Blue would be being punished for some crime that he is known not to have committed,

we could *not* coherently deny that Blue's punishment would be in this sense unjust. You may also regard this meta-ethical disagreement as having little importance. But these responses would both, I believe, be mistaken. As I have said, if Anscombe's argument were valid, we could prove that certain acts were wrong merely by appealing to the meanings of certain words. Claims about wrongness could not then state substantive normative truths, but would be trivial.

Here is another way to show that this argument is not valid. When Anscombe claims that someone's punishment would be unjust, she intends this claim to imply that this punishment would be wrong. Anscombe uses 'wrong' to mean 'forbidden by God', or 'against divine law'. So Anscombe's argument could be restated as

> (U) If we accept that
>
>> (S) Blue would be being punished for some crime that he is known not to have committed,

we could not coherently deny that

> (V) this punishment would be retributively unjust, and
> would therefore be wrong in the sense that such acts
> are forbidden by God.

(U) implies that, if we admit that Blue's punishment would be of the
kind described by (S), we could not coherently deny that God exists,
and has forbidden such acts. That is clearly false. No one could prove
that God exists merely by appealing to a fact like (S) and the meaning
of the phrase 'retributively unjust'. Nor could the meaning of this word
imply that this act would be unjust and therefore wrong in some other,
non-theistic normative sense.

Some thick-concept arguments are, I have said, easy to reject. We
could coherently claim that, if certain acts are unchaste and unpatriotic,
these facts are not normative, and do not support the view that these
acts are wrong. The Injustice Argument is harder to reject. It seems
more doubtful that we can use 'unjust' in a non-normative sense, or
claim that some act's injustice does not support the view that this act
is wrong. As we have now seen, however, we can reject this argument
in a different way. We can coherently claim that there are no ways
in which people deserve to be treated, in the retributive sense. We
could therefore claim that there is no such virtue as that of retributive
justice, since no acts could be either retributively just or retributively
unjust.

For the Injustice Argument to fail, as I have said, it is enough that we
could coherently reject the view that people can deserve to be punished.
But since I believe that we ought to reject this view, I discuss briefly in
Appendix E which other view we ought to accept.

We have been asking whether, by appealing to certain natural facts
and thick normative concepts, we can validly derive positive, reason-
implying normative conclusions. If such arguments were valid, that
would challenge my claim that there is a deep distinction between
natural facts and irreducibly normative reason-involving facts.

The Injustice Argument may seem to be of this kind. But this
argument does not succeed. From the fact that someone has not

committed any crime, we cannot conclude that this person's punishment would be retributively unjust, or wrong. Such arguments must appeal to some explicitly normative claim about which ways of treating people are deserved, unjust, or wrong. Similar remarks apply, I believe, to all such arguments.

91 The Normativity Objection

According to

> *Non-Analytical Naturalists*: Though we make some irreducibly normative claims, there are no irreducibly normative facts. When such normative claims are true, these claims state facts that could also be stated by making other, non-normative and naturalistic claims. These facts are both normative and natural.

Such views, I shall now start to argue, cannot be true.   I believe that

> (A) normative and natural facts are in two quite different, non-overlapping categories.

Some beliefs like (A) have turned out to be mistaken. According to Vitalists, for example, facts about living things are in a different category from merely physical facts. This claim, we have found, is false, since the nature and activities of many mindless living things, such as amoebas or plants, can be entirely understood in physical terms. Some other similar beliefs are more controversial. There is much disagreement, for example, about whether conscious experiences could be the same as, or consist in, physical events in some brain.

Many kinds of thing, event, or fact are, however, undeniably in different categories. Rivers could not be sonnets, experiences could not be stones, and justice could not be—as some Pythagoreans were said to have believed—the number 4. To give some less extreme examples, it could not be a physical or legal fact that $7 \times 8 = 56$, nor could it be a legal or arithmetical fact that galaxies rotate, nor could it be a physical or arithmetical fact that perjury is a crime. It is similarly true, I believe, that when we have decisive reasons to act in some way, or we should or ought to act in this way, this fact could not be the same as, or consist in, some natural fact, such as some psychological or causal fact.

In defending this belief, I must appeal to what I mean when I use the words 'reason', 'should', and 'ought'. Some Naturalists would reply that they are not discussing the meanings of our words. When these people claim that normative facts might be natural facts, their claim is not intended to be analytic, or a claim whose truth is implied by what it means. These people might again cite the discoveries that water is H2O and that heat is molecular kinetic energy. When scientists made these discoveries, they were not appealing to the pre-scientific meanings of the words 'water' and 'heat'.

These analogies, I shall argue later, do not support Naturalism. We can note here that, though these discoveries were not implied by the meanings of these words, these scientists *did* appeal to these meanings. That is why these scientific discoveries were about *water* and *heat*. Of the reductive views that are both plausible and interesting, most are not analytical. But these views must still be constrained by the relevant concepts. These views are not analytical because the relevant concepts leave open various possibilities, between which we must decide on non-conceptual grounds. Many other possibilities are, however, conceptually excluded. Thus, on a wider pre-scientific version of the concept of *heat*, it was conceptually possible that heat should turn out to be molecular kinetic energy, or should instead turn out to be, or to involve, a substance, as the *phlogiston theory* claimed. But heat could not have turned out to be a shade of blue, or a medieval king. And if we claimed that rivers were sonnets, or that experiences were stones, we could not defend these claims by saying that they were not intended to be analytic, or conceptual truths. Others could rightly reply that, given the meaning of these claims, they could not possibly be true. This, I believe, is the way in which, though *much* less obviously, Normative Naturalism could not be true. Natural facts could not be normative in the reason-implying sense.

It may next be objected that normative and natural facts cannot be in different categories, since there is no sharp distinction between these two kinds of fact. It is often unclear whether some word is being used in a normative sense. And some words have complex senses that are partly normative and partly naturalistic. Some examples are the thick concepts 'dishonest', 'unpatriotic', and 'retributively unjust'. As I have just argued, however, we can distinguish between the normative and naturalistic parts of such concepts. And for Naturalism to succeed, even the claims that are most purely normative must, if they are true, state natural facts. These purely normative claims could not, I believe, state such facts. Nor do deep distinctions need sharp boundaries. Black is not white, and day is not night, though there is grey and twilight in between.

If, as I believe, reason-involving normative facts are in a separate, distinctive category, there is no close analogy for their irreducibility to natural facts. These normative facts are in some ways like certain other kinds of necessary truths. One example are mathematical truths, such as the fact that $7 \times 8 = 56$. According to some empiricists, this fact is some natural fact, such as the fact that, when people multiply 7 by 8, the result of their calculation is nearly always 56. This view misunderstands arithmetic, and the way in which mathematical claims can be true. Nor could logical truths be natural facts about the ways in which people think. In the same way, I believe, normative and natural facts differ too deeply for any form of Normative Naturalism to succeed.

To give one example, we can remember that, in *Burning Hotel*, you will die unless you jump into the canal. Since your life is worth living, it is clear that

(B) you ought to jump.

This fact, some Naturalists claim, is the same as the fact that

(C) jumping would do most to fulfil your present fully
informed desires, or is what, if you deliberated in certain
naturalistically describable ways, you would choose to do.

Given the difference between the meanings of claims like (B) and (C), such claims could not, I believe, state the same fact. Suppose that you are in the top storey of your hotel, and you are terrified of heights. You know that, unless you jump, you will soon be overcome by smoke. You might then believe, and tell yourself, that you have *decisive reasons* to jump, that you *should, ought to,* and *must* jump, and that if you don't jump you would be making a *terrible mistake.* If these normative beliefs were true, these truths could not possibly be the same as, or consist in, some merely natural fact, such as the causal and psychological facts stated by (C). We can call this *the Normativity Objection.*

This objection, we can add, could take a wider and less controversial form. In arguing against Naturalism, we need not claim that there are some irreducibly normative *facts.*   It would be enough to claim that

(D) natural facts could not be normative.

Of the people who are *Metaphysical* Naturalists, in the sense that they believe that all facts are natural facts, many would accept (D). Some of these people are Nihilists, or Error Theorists, who believe that normative claims are intended to state irreducibly normative facts, but that all such claims are false, since there are no such facts. There are also many Non-Cognitivists, who believe that normative claims should not be regarded as intended to state facts, except perhaps in some minimal sense. These people believe that, though there are no normative facts, we can justifiably make normative claims, since these claims do not state beliefs, but express certain kinds of attitude. Like Non-Naturalists, both Nihilists and Non-Cognitivists believe that normative claims are in a separate, distinctive category, so that natural facts could not be normative. These people would agree that when I say, with great passion, that you *should, ought to* and *must* jump, I cannot be stating some merely causal fact or some psychological prediction. Though most Nihilists and Non-Cognitivists are *Metaphysical* Naturalists, these two groups of people would accept my claim that *Normative* Naturalism could not be true.

26

The Triviality Objection

92 Normative Concepts and Natural Properties

Though the Normativity Objection seems to me decisive, it would not convince some Naturalists. But we have other reasons to believe that natural facts could not be normative.

We can first look more closely at one common argument for Naturalism. Gibbard writes:

> normative concepts are distinct from naturalistic concepts: on this score, Moore was right. But normative and naturalistic concepts signify properties of the same kinds: indeed a normative and a naturalistic concept might signify the very same property. What's distinctly normative, then, are not properties but concepts.

Many other people make such claims. These people argue:

(A) Some normative concepts refer to natural properties.

(B) We can use these concepts to make normative claims which are about these natural properties.

Therefore

(C) When such claims are true, they state facts that are both normative and natural.

(A) and (B), as we have seen, may be true, and the inference to (C) seems plausible. But this inference is not, I believe, justified. When we see *how* these words and concepts might refer to natural properties, we shall see that (A) and (B) do not imply or support (C). (The rest of this section is somewhat technical, however, and could be skipped.)

Consider first these phrases:

(D) the largest planet,

(E) being the largest planet.

Despite their similarity, (D) refers to Jupiter, and (E) refers to something quite different, which is the property of being the largest planet.

The same distinction applies, though in a way that is easier to miss, when we turn from the properties that are had by *objects*, such as the planet Jupiter, to the *second-order* properties that are had by *properties*. As we have just seen,

the largest planet

is different from

the property of *being the largest planet.*

In the same way,

the property that has some other property,

is different from

the property of *being the property that has this other property.*

When stated so abstractly, this second distinction is slippery, and hard to grasp. But examples may make it clear. Return to the use of 'heat' which means

the property, whichever it is, that can have certain effects, such as those of melting solids, turning liquids into gases, etc.

More fully stated, 'heat' means

the property, whichever it is, that has the *different,* second-order property of *being the property that can have certain effects*, such as those of melting solids, turning liquids into gases, etc.

When scientists discovered that

(F) heat is molecular kinetic energy,

what they discovered was that

(G) molecular kinetic energy is the property that has this different, second-order property.

Consider next the phrase

the natural property, whichever it is, that makes acts right.

More fully stated, this phrase means

the natural property, whichever it is, that has the different, second-order normative property of being the natural property that makes acts right.

Some Utilitarians claim that

(H) maximizing happiness is the natural property that makes acts right.

If (H) were true, this claim would use a normative concept to refer to the natural property of maximizing happiness. So (H) might seem to be the kind of claim for which Naturalists are looking: a normative claim which, if true, would state a natural fact. As I have said, however, (H) is not such a claim. (H) could be more fully stated as

(I) the property of maximizing happiness has the *different, second-order property of being the natural property that makes acts right*.

And this different property is normative. That is shown by the fact that both (H) and (I) are merely other ways of stating the normative claim that

(J) acts are right just when, and because, they maximize happiness.

So claims like (H) do not support Naturalism.

Naturalists might reply that, even if this example does not support their view, there may be other, better examples. There may be other ways in which, by using some normative word or concept which refers to some natural property, we could make normative claims which state natural facts.

In asking whether there could be such claims, we can first remember that, when we claim that some word or concept *refers* to some property we are not thereby claiming that anything *has* this property. The concept *witch*, for example, refers to the property of being a witch, though there have never been any witches. And Moral Nihilists could agree that the concept *wrong* refers to the property of being wrong, though they believe that no acts are wrong.

We can next distinguish two ways in which words or phrases can refer to properties. The phrase 'the property of redness' refers *explicitly* to the property of redness, or of being red. The more common word 'red', when used in a claim like 'blood is red', refers to redness *implicitly*, since this claim describes blood as having this property. Return now to the phrase

(K) the natural property, whichever it is, that makes acts right.

If there is only one natural property that makes acts right, this phrase would refer explicitly to this natural property. As we have seen, however, (K) would refer to this property indirectly, as the natural property that has the different, second-order normative property of being the natural property that makes acts right. So (K) would *also refer implicitly* to this other, normative property. And (K) would refer to this natural property only *by* also referring to this normative property. Since all claims that use this phrase would refer to this normative property, such claims could not state facts that were natural in the reductive sense.

Similar remarks apply, I believe, to all words or phrases that express irreducibly normative concepts. Some of these words or phrases, and the concepts that they express, refer to natural properties. But no such normative concept could refer *only* to some natural property, or set of properties, since such concepts can refer to some natural property only by *also* referring to some other, normative property. Such concepts might refer to some natural property either as the natural property that *has* some normative property, or as the natural property that is related to some normative property in some other, less direct way. So we can claim that

(L) irreducibly normative concepts all refer, either explicitly or implicitly, to some normative property.

This is why, though it is true that

(M) some irreducibly normative concepts might refer to natural properties,

this truth does not support Naturalism. As we have seen, Gibbard takes (M) to imply that it is only concepts, not properties, that are distinctly or irreducibly normative. That, I have argued, is not so. Since such normative concepts would refer to natural properties only by also referring to certain normative properties, (M)'s truth does not help to show that there are no irreducibly normative properties. And we have no reason to expect that, as many Naturalists assume,

(N) we could use these concepts to make irreducibly normative claims that might state natural facts.

Since such claims would also refer to certain normative properties, they would, if they were true, state what were partly normative facts. Such facts might be irreducibly normative. So this common argument for Naturalism fails.

93 The Analogies with Scientific Discoveries

Naturalists can give other arguments. Normative concepts might be

(1) definable in some way that shows how this concept might refer to some natural property,

(2) definable in some way that shows, or gives us reason to believe, that this concept could *not* refer to some natural property,

or

(3) indefinable.

We have just been discussing one concept of type (1): the concept of *the natural property that makes acts right*. As we have seen, such concepts would refer to some natural property only by also referring to some normative property, so these concepts provide no arguments for Naturalism.

As an example of type (2), I gave the concept of *being blameworthy*. Other examples are the concepts expressed by these phrases:

> *being unjustifiable to others,*
>
> *being disallowed by some principle that no one could reasonably reject,*
>
> *being an act that gives the agent reasons to feel remorse and gives others reasons for indignation.*

It would be difficult for Naturalists to argue that these concepts refer to properties that are natural in the relevant, reductive non-normative sense. These people would have to claim, for example, either that

> the concept of *being unjustifiable to others* does not refer to the property of being unjustifiable to others,

or that

> though this concept is irreducibly normative, *being unjustifiable to others* is a non-normative, natural property.

Such claims would be hard to defend. And even if some concepts of type (2) did refer to some natural property, Naturalists would have to argue that these concepts did not *also* refer to some normative property. Such claims would be harder to defend.

The most important normative concepts are, however, of type (3). These concepts are not complex and definable, but simple and not helpfully definable in other terms. Some examples are the concept of *a normative reason* and the indefinable versions of the concepts *ought morally* and *wrong*. When concepts are indefinable, it is more of an open question to which properties these concepts refer. And some Naturalists claim that, by appealing to the role or function that these concepts have in our thinking, we might be able to show that these concepts refer only to certain natural properties. Such an argument might show that irreducibly normative claims, when they are true, state facts that are both normative and natural.

Though these Naturalists make various interesting and important claims, I believe that no such argument could succeed. In explaining why, I shall first say some more about the analogies to which many Naturalists appeal. As before, it will be enough to discuss Act Utilitarianism, since our conclusions would apply to other moral views. These Utilitarians claim that

> (A) when some act would maximize happiness, this act is
> what we ought to do.

This view can take two forms. Non-Naturalists like Sidgwick claim that

> (B) when some act would maximize happiness, this fact
> would make this act have the different, normative property
> of being what we ought to do.

Utilitarian Naturalists reject (B), claiming instead that

> (C) when some act would maximize happiness, this property
> of this act is the same as the property of being what we ought
> to do.

When Gibbard argues that Utilitarian Naturalism might be true, he compares (C) with the discovery that water is the same as H2O. Other Naturalists appeal to the discovery that heat is the same as molecular kinetic energy. Such analogies can seem to support the view that some form of Naturalism is true. But if we look more closely, I believe, we find that these analogies partly fail.

True claims about the *identity* of some property use two words or phrases that refer to the same property, and tell us that this property is the same as itself. When that is *all* that such claims tell us, these claims are trivial. We already know that every property—like everything else—is the same as itself. But some of these claims use certain concepts that enable them also to state important facts. That is true of the claim that

> (D) molecular kinetic energy is the same as heat.

This claim gives us important information because the word 'heat', in its relevant sense, expresses the complex concept that can be more fully expressed with the phrase:

> *the property that can make objects have certain other*
> *properties, by turning solids into liquids, turning liquids*
> *into gases, causing us to have certain sensations, etc.*

(D) can be restated as

> (E) molecular kinetic energy is the property that can make objects have these other, different properties.

As a Non-Naturalist, Sidgwick could restate his view in the same way. Sidgwick could appeal to the concept that we can express with the phrase:

> *the natural property that makes an act have the different,*
> *normative property of being what we ought to do.*

Sidgwick's claim could become

> (F) being an act that would maximize happiness is the natural property that makes an act have this other, normative property.

Return next to Gibbard's suggestion that Utilitarian Naturalism is like the claim that

> (G) water is the same as H2O.

This claim, as Gibbard writes, has 'great explanatory power'. Unlike heat, water isn't a property but a stuff, substance, or kind of matter. But that difference is irrelevant here. In its pre-scientific sense, the word 'water' refers to

> the stuff that has the properties of quenching thirst, falling from the clouds as rain, filling lakes and rivers, etc.

'H2O' refers to

> the stuff that is composed of molecules each of which contains two hydrogen atoms and one oxygen atom.

What scientists discovered is that

> (H) the stuff that has the properties of quenching thirst, falling from the clouds as rain, etc., is the same as the stuff that has the different property of being composed of such molecules.

This claim is informative because (H) tells us about the relation between various properties. Sidgwick's (F) could be similarly restated as

> (I) the property of being an act that would maximize happiness is the same as the property that makes an act have the different property of being what we ought to do.

This claim would also be informative, by telling us about the relation between different properties. Utilitarian Naturalists claim instead that

> (C) the property of being an act that would maximize happiness is the same as the property of being what we ought to do.

Unlike Sidgwick's (F) and (I), however, (C) is *not* relevantly like the scientific claims about heat and water. (C) could not, I believe, be true. But we can try to suppose that (C) is true. We can then claim that, *if* (C) were true, (C) would not tell us about the relation between different properties. For this reason, as I shall argue further below, (C) could not be an informative claim about what we ought to do. As these remarks imply, these scientific analogies do not support Naturalism. On the contrary, these analogies remind us that substantive claims like (D) and (G) — or their fuller statements (E) and (H) — tell us about the relations between different properties. The Naturalist's (C) does *not* do that. Since it is only Sidgwick's Non-Naturalist view which is relevantly like these scientific discoveries, these analogies give us some reason to reject Naturalism.

94 The Fact Stating Argument

We can next distinguish two senses in which different claims may state the same fact. That is true

> in the *referential* sense when these claims refer to the same things and ascribe the same properties to these things,

and

> in the *informational* sense when these claims give us
> the same information.

Consider first these claims:

> (J) Shakespeare is Shakespeare.

> (K) Shakespeare and the writer of *Hamlet* are one
> and the same person.

> (L) Shakespeare wrote *Hamlet*.

In the referential sense, (J) and (K) state the same fact, since both claims refer to Shakespeare and tell us that Shakespeare has the property of being numerically identical to himself. In the informational sense, however, (J) and (K) state different facts. Unlike (J), (K) refers to Shakespeare in a way that also tells us that Shakespeare wrote *Hamlet*. In the informational sense, it is (K) and (L) that state the same fact.

Consider next:

> (M) water is water,

> (N) water is H2O.

In the referential sense, these claims state the same fact, since both claims refer to water and tell us that water is identical to itself. If this is how we think of facts, we could not say that (N) states an important scientific discovery, since this fact would be the same as the trivial fact stated by (M). To explain how (N) was an important discovery, we must point out that (M) and (N) give us different information, thereby stating different facts. Unlike (M), (N) refers to water in a way that also tells us about the atoms of which water is composed. Similar remarks apply to

> (O) heat is heat,

> (P) heat is molecular kinetic energy.

To explain how (P) states an important discovery, we must again claim that, in the relevant, informational sense, (O) and (P) state different facts. Unlike the trivial (O), (P) tells us about the relation between several different properties.

Many Naturalists claim that, just as we have discovered that water is H2O and heat is molecular kinetic energy, we might discover, or be able to show, that

> (Q) moral rightness is the same as some particular natural property.

In the referential sense, (Q) would state the same fact as

> (R) this natural property is the same as this natural property.

But (R) is as trivial as the facts that water is water, and heat is heat. To defend their claim that (Q) states an important truth, these Naturalists must therefore claim that, in the relevant, informational sense (Q) and (R) state different facts. Here is another way to make this point. To defend their claim that moral rightness is a natural property, Naturalists must discuss the information that (Q) would give us, if (Q) were true. When we discuss this information, (R) is irrelevant. Non-Naturalists would agree that any natural property is the same as itself.

We can now argue:

> (1) We make some irreducibly normative claims.

> (2) According to Non-Analytical Naturalists, when such claims are true, they state facts that are both normative and natural.

> (3) If such normative facts were also natural facts, any such fact could also be stated by some other non-normative, naturalistic claim.

Therefore

> (4) Any such true normative claim would state some fact that is the same as some fact that could be stated by some other, non-normative claim.

(5) If these two claims stated the same fact, they would give us the same information.

(6) This non-normative claim could not state a normative fact.

Therefore

If these two claims stated the same fact, by giving us the same information, this normative claim could not state a normative fact.

Therefore

Such normative claims could not, as these Naturalists believe, state facts that are both normative and natural.

These drab and dreary claims we can call *the Fact Stating Argument*.

Premise (1), I have claimed, is true, and is accepted by Non-Analytical Naturalists. (2) describes this form of Naturalism. Since we are using the word 'natural' in its reductive sense, (3) is true by definition. These premises imply (4). Since these Naturalists must use the phrase 'the same fact' in the informational sense, they must accept (5). So, if (6) is true, this valid argument would be sound. We should then accept this argument's conclusions.

To illustrate this argument, and help us to decide whether (6) is true, we can return to claims about practical reasons and decisive-reason-implying oughts. Most Naturalists accept some form of Subjectivism about Reasons. As before, it will be enough to discuss the view that

(S) we have decisive reasons to act in a certain way, and we should and ought to act in this way,

when

(T) this act would best fulfil our present fully informed desires, or is what, after fully informed and procedurally rational deliberation, we would choose to do.

Of the people who accept this view, some believe that, when we make claims like (S), we often mean something like (T). Other Subjectivists defend this view in other ways.

According to Darwall and some other Non-Analytical Naturalists, though (S) and (T) are irreducibly normative claims, such claims, when they are true, state facts that are both normative and natural. For these facts to be natural in the relevant reductive sense, they must be able to be restated by some other, non-normative, naturalistic claim. As before, we can sum up this other claim as

> (U) this act would do most to fulfil our present fully informed desires, or is what, after some process of deliberation that had certain natural properties, we would choose to do.

These natural properties are the ones that would make this process of deliberation fully informed and procedurally rational. According to these Naturalists, the fact stated by (U) is normative, because this fact could also be stated by the normative claims (S) and (T).

This view, I believe, could not be true. Consider first these claims:

> (V) You drove at a speed of 100 miles an hour,

> (W) You drove at a speed of 100 miles an hour, thereby acting illegally.

If these claims gave us the same information, thereby stating the same fact, that would have to be because your act could not have the distinct property of being illegal. Only that would make it true that (W) would not give us any further information. If your act *did* have the property of being illegal, so that (W) gave us further information, (V) and (W) would state different facts.

Similar remarks apply to (S), (T), and (U). If these claims stated the same fact, that would have to be because

> (X) no act could have the distinct normative properties of being what we have *decisive reasons* to do, or what we *should* and *ought* to do, or what would *best* fulfil our desires, or what we would choose to do after *procedurally rational* deliberation.

Only (X) would make it true that (U) would give us the same information as (S) and (T). If some acts *could* have such distinct normative properties, these claims would give us different information. But if no act could have such normative properties, as this Naturalist view implies, Naturalists would be wrong to claim that claims like (S) and (T) would state normative facts.

This objection, I conclude, succeeds. We can argue:

> If claims like (S), (T), and (U) stated the same fact, this
> fact could not be normative.

Therefore

> Such claims cannot, as these Naturalists believe, state
> facts that are both normative and natural.

Similar arguments apply to all other forms of Non-Analytical Naturalism.

95 The Triviality Objection

We can now turn to another, livelier argument, which shows more clearly how deep this disagreement goes. As before, we can discuss Hedonistic Act Utilitarianism, since our conclusions would apply to other views. These Utilitarians claim that

> (A) when some act would maximize happiness, this act is
> what we ought to do.

This view can take two forms. Non-Naturalists like Sidgwick claim that

> (B) when some act would maximize happiness, this fact
> would make this act have the different property of being
> what we ought to do.

Utilitarian Naturalists reject (B), claiming instead that

> (C) when some act would maximize happiness, that is the
> same as this act's being what we ought to do.

Suppose that you are a Utilitarian doctor. The Ethics Committee of your hospital asks you to imagine that, in

> *Transplant*, you know that, if you secretly killed one of your patients, this person's transplanted organs would be used to save the lives of five other young people, who would then live long and happy lives.

You admit that, on your view,

> (D) you ought to kill this patient, since this act would maximize happiness.

The Ethics Committee is horrified, and its legal adviser proposes that you be dismissed and debarred from any medical post. If you were a Naturalist, you might reply:

> When I claimed that I ought to kill this patient, I was only stating the fact that this act would maximize happiness. On my view, that is the property to which the concept *ought* refers. I was not claiming that this act would have some *different* property of being what I ought to do. On my view, there is no such different property. The property of maximizing happiness is the *same* as the property of being what we ought to do.

You might add:

> If I believed that killing some patient would have this property, that would not lead me to act in this way. My aim is to be a successful doctor. I want to cure my patients, whether or not my acts would maximize happiness. So my moral beliefs give you no reason to dismiss me.

These remarks might satisfy the Ethics Committee, since they might show that you do not have an unacceptable moral view.

These remarks should, however, worry Naturalists. We can object that, as your remarks suggest, you do not really have *any* moral view. Normative claims are, in my sense,

substantive and *positive* when these claims

state or imply that, when something has certain natural properties, this thing has some other, different, normative property,

and

and are significant, because we might disagree with them, or they might tell us something that we didn't already know.

When such claims are true, they state positive substantive normative facts. Utilitarian Naturalists claim both that

(A) when some act would maximize happiness, this act is what we ought to do,

and that

(C) when some act would maximize happiness, this property of this act is the same as the property of being what we ought to do.

We can argue:

(1) (A) is a substantive normative claim, which would, if it were true, state a positive substantive normative fact.

(2) If, impossibly, (C) were true, (A) could not state such a fact. (A) could not be used to imply that, when some act would maximize happiness, this act would have the different property of being what we ought to do, since (C) claims that there is no such different property. Though (A) and (C) have

different meanings, (A) would be only another way of stating the trivial fact that, when some act would maximize happiness, this act would maximize happiness.

Therefore

This form of Naturalism is not true.

We can call this *the Triviality Objection*.

This objection might be misunderstood. We are not claiming that this form of *Naturalism* is trivial. (C) is a substantive claim. And (C) is, in one way, normative, since this claim is about the property of being what we ought to do. But (C) is a *negative* normative claim, since (C) implies that, when some act would have the natural property of being an act that would maximize happiness, this act could *not* have the *different*, normative property of being what we ought to do, since there would be no such different property. Though (C) is a significant substantive claim, we are arguing that, *if* (C) were true, (A) would be trivial. Since (A) is *not* trivial, (C) cannot be true.

In response to this argument, some Naturalists would reject premise (1). These people are *Hard* Naturalists, who believe that claims like (A), even if true, would be trivial. I shall return to this view. The Triviality Objection applies only to *Soft* Naturalists, who believe that claims like (A) would, if they were true, give us positive substantive normative information. These are the people whose views I am now discussing.

Soft Naturalists might challenge premise (2). These people might say:

> (3) If (A) and (C) were true, these claims would not merely tell us that, when some act would maximize happiness, this act would maximize happiness. In telling us that we *ought* to act in this way, these claims would give us further information about such acts.

Any such information must be statable, however, as the claim that such acts would have one or more other, different properties. And these Naturalists are trying to show that (A) and (C) are substantive *normative* claims. So, to defend (3), these people would have to defend the claim that

(4) (A) and (C) would state or imply that, when some act would maximize happiness, this act would have some other, different, normative property.

It is not obvious what this other property could be. When we ask what is the best candidate for the different, normative property which (A) might tell us that such acts would have, the obvious answer is: the property of being what we ought to do. By claiming (C), however, these Naturalists lose this obvious candidate, since (C) denies that being what we ought to do is a *different* property. To defend (4), these people would have to find some other normative property to play this role. We can call this the *Lost Property Problem.*

There is another problem. If these Naturalists could find some other property to play this role, they would have to apply their Naturalism to this property. These people would have to claim that, when some act would have this other *normative* property, this fact would be the same as this act's having one or more other *natural* properties. These people would then have to defend another version of (4), which referred to some *other*, different, *normative* property. They would then have to apply their Naturalism to this other property, and so on for ever. This defence of (4) could not succeed.

These Naturalists might now challenge premise (2) in a different and more radical way. According to

(C) when some act would maximize happiness, that is the same as this act's being what we ought to do.

These people might say

(5) If (C) were true, as we believe, (A) would be a positive, substantive normative claim. (C) *itself* would be such a claim.

In his defence of Naturalism, Gibbard defends (5). Gibbard claims that

(6) if (C) were true, (C) would both tell us that we ought
to maximize happiness, and explain why we ought to act
in this way.

On this view, Utilitarians do not *need* to claim that, when some act would maximize happiness, this fact would make this act have a *different*, normative property of being what we ought to do. In Gibbard's words:

The properties are one and the same, and that explains, at
base, why to do the things we ought to do . . . A further
property of being what one ought to do would add nothing
to the explanation.

It is not clear what explanation Gibbard has in mind. If (C)'s truth explained why we ought to maximize happiness, what would this explanation be?

Utilitarian Naturalists might claim

We ought to maximize happiness because, when we use the
phrase 'what we ought to do', we are referring to the property
of being an act that would maximize happiness.

As Moore remarks, however, when we believe that we ought to do something, we are not merely believing that 'the word "ought" is generally used to denote actions of this nature'. No such fact about what this word denotes, or refers to, could tell us what we ought to do. To support this objection, we can turn to the claim that

(E) when some act has the property of being what would
maximize happiness, we can also refer to this property by
using the phrase 'being maximally felicific'.

This claim is true, because 'felicific' means 'produces happiness'. But (E) is not a substantive normative claim. It is a merely linguistic fact that the property of maximizing happiness can also be referred to with the phrase 'being maximally felicific'. These Utilitarian Naturalists appeal to the similar claim that

> (F) when some act has the property of being what would
> maximize happiness, we can also refer to this property by
> using the phrase 'being what we ought to do'.

For these Naturalists to defend their view, they must claim that (F) is relevantly *unlike* (E), since it is *not* a merely linguistic fact that the property of maximizing happiness can also be referred to with the phrase 'being what we ought to do'. Naturalists must explain how, if (F) were true, this claim would give us important normative information. Here is another way to make this point. According to these Naturalists,

> (C) being an act that would maximize happiness is the same as
> being what we ought to do.

This claim is like

> (G) being an act that would maximize happiness is the same
> as being maximally felicific.

(G) is not an important substantive claim. (G) merely refers to the same property in two different ways, and tells us that this property is the same as itself. These Naturalists must therefore claim that (C) is in one way *unlike* (G), since (C) gives us further, non-linguistic information.

There is one obvious difference to which these Naturalists might appeal. These people might say:

> (G) is trivial because this claim uses two phrases that mean
> the same. When we say that some act is maximally felicific,
> that is just another way of saying that this act would maximize
> happiness. No such claim applies to (C). When we say that we
> *ought* to do something, we do not mean that this act would
> maximize happiness. That is how, unlike (G), (C) gives us
> important, non-linguistic information.

We can reply:

> There is indeed such a difference. Because (C) uses phrases
> with quite different meanings, (C) *might* tell us about the
> relation between different properties. If that were true,
> however, we would need to be told what these different
> properties are, and how they are related. What *is* this
> important, non-linguistic information?

Since these Naturalists are discussing what we *ought* to do, they might
be tempted to answer

> (C) tells us that, when some act would maximize happiness,
> this act would have the different property of being what we
> ought to do.

But Naturalists cannot give this answer. According to (C), *there is no
such different property*. Being an act that would maximize happiness is
the *same* as being what we ought to do. So we can repeat our question.
We already know that some acts would maximize happiness. What else
do these Naturalists tell us to believe? Which *other* property would such
acts have?

This question is entirely open. As I use the concept of a *property*, any
information about such acts could be stated as the claim that these acts
would have some property. This other property might be linguistic.
But Naturalists must answer this question. We must be told what
these Naturalists are claiming, and what our new belief would be if we
accepted their view. We can then ask whether this new belief would be
important, as these Naturalists claim it to be.

These Naturalists might now return to Gibbard's claim. These people
might reply:

> For our view to be important, why do we need to make some
> claim about the relation between *different* properties? Why
> isn't it enough to learn that some acts would maximize
> happiness, and that this property is the same as that of being
> what we ought to do?

These properties could not, I believe, be the same. For this reason, as I shall argue later, it is highly misleading to ask whether, *if* these properties *were* the same, that would be an important truth. But we are now trying to suppose that these properties are the same, and asking what would then follow.

If we learnt that there was only one property here, we would indeed be learning something. We would be learning that, when some act would maximize happiness, this act could not also have the different property of being what we ought to do. Since this information would be purely negative, however, it would not make this form of Naturalism a substantive moral view. If these Naturalists are not claiming that such acts would have some other property, they are not giving us any positive information. And if their claim gives us no such information, it could not be a positive substantive claim about what we ought to do.

Though this objection seems to me decisive, some Naturalists may still not be convinced. So I shall try to explain how Naturalism can seem so plausible. Many great philosophers have believed that normative facts are natural facts. Some examples are Hobbes, Locke, Hume, Bentham, and Mill.

As I have said, Naturalists might claim:

> To learn what we ought to do, it would be enough to learn that some acts have a certain natural property, which is the same as the property of being what we ought to do.

Even to me, after many years of thinking about and disbelieving Naturalism, this claim can seem plausible. When we consider such claims, however, we can be easily misled. Utilitarian Naturalists claim

> (C) The property of maximizing happiness is the same as the property of being what we ought to do.

This claim may seem to tell us what we ought to do. (C) may seem to be a longer way of saying

> (J) Maximizing happiness is what we ought to do.

If (J) were true, this claim would tell us what we ought to do. But (C) and (J) are quite different claims. Suppose that some rude person said

Blowing your nose is what you ought to do.

This person would not mean

The property of blowing your nose is the same as the property of being what you ought to do.

That claim would be absurd. This person would mean

Blowing your nose is, or has the different property of being, what you ought to do.

In the same way, (J) means

(K) Maximizing happiness is, or has the different property of being, what we ought to do.

Since (C) implies that there is no such different property, (C) could not be a positive substantive claim about what we ought to do.

There is another, more insidious way in which we can be misled by some of the claims that Naturalists make. I believe that, given the meaning of the phrases 'being an act that would maximize happiness' and 'being what we ought to do', it could not possibly be true that

(C) being an act that would maximize happiness is the same as being what we ought to do.

These two phrases could not refer to the same property. But this very fact can make (C) *seem* informative. We may think that, if (C) were true, (C) *would* be informative, since (C) would then tell us about the relation between two different properties. It may therefore seem that, as Gibbard claims, Utilitarian Naturalism might both tell us what we ought to do, and explain why we ought to act in this way.

To illustrate this point, it may help to compare (C) with some other, less plausible claim. Our example can be

(L) Being square is the same as being blue.

This could not be an informative claim. Nor is it worth saying that, *if (L) were true, (L) would be informative*. If we were dreaming, or were only half awake, it might seem to us that (L) would be informative, because this claim would tell us about the relation between two different properties. But the fact that makes (L) seem informative also ensures that (L) is false. No claim could truly tell us that two quite different properties—such as being square and being blue—are one and the same property.

Similar remarks apply, though much less obviously, to (C). Utilitarian Naturalism may seem to be an important view, which might be informative. But what makes (C) seem informative also ensures that (C) is false.

As this comparison may also help to show, when some claim could not possibly be true, it can be misleading to *suppose* that this claim is true, and ask what would then follow.   These Naturalists might claim:

> If being an act that would maximize happiness were the same as being what we ought to do, this fact would explain why we ought to maximize happiness, since maximizing happiness would be our only way of doing what we ought to do.

As before, even to convinced Non-Naturalists like me, this claim can seem plausible.   But we could similarly claim:

> If being square were the same as being blue, this fact would explain why blue things were square, since being square would be the only way of being blue.

Such claims are not worth making. Naturalism can seem plausible because it can seem that

> if having some natural property were the same as being what we ought to do, this claim would have great importance.

But this claim seems important only because it could not be true.

I shall now summarize some of these remarks. Normative properties, Naturalists believe, are the same as certain natural properties. To explain and defend this view, many Naturalists appeal to claims about the identity of certain other properties, such as the claim that heat is molecular kinetic energy. Claims about the identity of some property are of two kinds. Some of these claims are trivial, telling us only that a certain property is the same as itself. Other such claims, if they are true, also give us important information, by telling us how the property to which they refer is related to one or more other properties. Most of these Naturalists ignore this distinction. Gibbard recognizes this distinction, but explicitly denies its importance.   As we have seen, Gibbard writes:

> The properties are one and the same, and that explains, at
> base, why to do the things we ought to do . . . A further
> property of being what one ought to do would add nothing
> to the explanation.

It is enough, Gibbard suggests, to make claims that are only about a *single* property. This view, I have argued, is seriously mistaken. For such claims to be informative, and worth making, they must tell us how the property to which they refer is related to two or more *different* properties. Only such claims could tell us what we ought to do.

This mistake is easy to make.   Utilitarian Naturalists claim

> (C) Being an act that would maximize happiness is the same
> as being what we ought to do.

This may seem to mean

> Maximizing happiness is what we ought to do.

These may seem to be claims which are about a single property, but which also tell us what we ought to do.   As I have said, however, for it to be true that

> Maximizing happiness is what we ought to do,

it would have to be true that

> Maximizing happiness is, or has the *different* property of
> being, what we ought to do.

Since (C) can easily *seem* informative, we can call this the *Single Property Illusion*.

There are some other ways in which these Naturalists might defend their view. I have claimed that, since (C) does not tell us about the relation between different properties, (C) could not give us substantive information. These Naturalists might reply that (C) might *indirectly* give us such information.

These people might first point out that, if (C) were true, Sidgwick's view would be false. Sidgwick would be wrong to claim that, when some act would maximize happiness, this fact would make this act have the different property of being what we ought to do. There would be no such different property. But since this claim is purely negative, it does not make this form of Naturalism a positive substantive normative view. These Naturalists claim to be proposing such a view.

These people might next claim that (C) would also give us positive information. Some of these people argue that, though the concept *ought morally* does not have an explicit gap that is waiting to be filled, we can give an account of the role or function that this concept plays in our moral thinking. By appealing to this account, these Naturalists might say, we can show that, if (C) were true, this claim would indirectly give us important information. For example, we might learn that

(M) when some act would maximize happiness, that is the same as this act's being justifiable to others, praiseworthy, and something that we have strong reasons to do.

As before, I believe, this claim could not possibly be true. Being an act that would maximize happiness could not be the *same* as being, or be *what it is* to be, an act that is justifiable to others, or praiseworthy, or something that we have strong reasons to do. But if we can somehow imagine or conceive that these phrases all refer to the same property, we should conclude that (M) would not then state a substantive normative fact. If *impossibly* these phrases all referred to the same property, (M) would not tell us how this property was related to any other property. So (M) could not give us important positive information.

These Naturalists might instead suggest:

> (N) Given the role of the concept *ought* in our moral thinking,
> (C) would indirectly tell us that

>> (O) when some act would maximize happiness, this act
>> would have certain other, normative properties.

> Some examples might be the properties of being justifiable
> to others, praiseworthy, and something that we have strong
> reasons to do.

If, as I believe, (C) could not be true, it is misleading to *suppose* that
(N) and (C) are true, and ask what would then follow. With that
warning, we can add that (N) could not support Naturalism. (O) is
a normative claim, and the facts stated by (O) might be irreducibly
normative. To defend their Naturalism, these Naturalists would have
to claim that these other normative properties are the same as certain
natural properties. The Triviality Objection would apply to these new
claims.   This objection would not have been answered.

There is one other possibility.   These Naturalists might suggest:

> (P) given the role of the concept *ought* in our moral thinking,
> (C) would indirectly tell us that

>> (Q) when some act would maximize happiness, this act
>> would have certain other, non-normative properties.

> Some examples might be the properties of being widely
> believed to be justifiable to others, widely praised, and believed
> to be something that we have strong reasons to do.

But (P) could not support Naturalism. Naturalists believe that substantive normative facts are also natural facts. Since (Q) is not a normative
claim, (Q) could not state a normative fact.

Similar remarks apply to other forms of Moral Naturalism. According
to what we can call any

Standard Ought Claim: When some act would have a certain natural property, this act would be what we ought to do.

There are two ways to understand such claims. According to Non-Naturalists, these claims imply that

(R) when some act would have this natural property, this fact would make this act have the different property of being what we ought to do.

According to Naturalists, these claims imply that

(S) when some act would have this natural property, this fact is the same as this act's being what we ought to do.

All such views face the Triviality Objection. We can argue:

(1) Since (S) does not tell us how this natural property is related to some other, different, normative property, (S) is not a positive, substantive normative claim.

Therefore

(2) If Naturalism were true, Standard Ought Claims would be trivial, and could not tell us positive substantive normative facts.

(3) Such claims are not trivial, and might tell us such facts.

Therefore

Naturalism cannot be true.

I have, I believe, sufficiently defended (1) and (2), here and in Section 84. And most Naturalists would accept (3).

In reply, Naturalists might claim:

(T) Given the role of the concept *ought* in our moral thinking, (S) would not be trivial, since (S) would indirectly tell us that

> (U) when some act would have this natural property, this
>   act would have certain other properties.

If, as I believe, (S) could not be true, it is misleading to suppose that (S) and (T) are true. With that warning, we can add that (T) would not support Naturalism. There are two possibilities. If these other properties were normative, Naturalists would have to claim that these properties were the same as certain natural properties. The Triviality Objection would apply to these claims, and would not have been answered. If these other properties were *not* normative, (T) would not show that (S) might indirectly tell us some substantive normative fact. So, on both possibilities, this reply fails. This argument, I believe, is sound, and shows that Naturalism cannot be true.

27

Naturalism and Nihilism

96 Naturalism about Reasons

We can now apply the Triviality Objection to claims about reasons. If normativity is best conceived as involving reasons or apparent reasons, as I believe, our main question is whether facts about reasons might be natural facts. And the Triviality Objection here takes a simpler, clearer form.

In his forceful defence of Subjectivism, Schroeder claims that

> (A) when some fact explains why some act would fulfil one of our present desires, this fact is a reason for us to act in this way.

We should distinguish, Schroeder claims, between the fact which is some reason for acting and the fact about desire-fulfilment that makes the first fact be a reason. In *Burning Hotel*, for example, if

> (B) you want to stay alive,

and

> (C) jumping into the canal would save your life,

the fact stated by (C) would be a reason for you to jump because this fact explains why this act would fulfil your desire. As a Naturalist, Schroeder also claims that

> (D) when some fact explains why some act would fulfil one of our present desires, that is the *same* as this

fact's being a reason to act in this way. That's *what it is* for some fact to be a reason.

We can argue:

(1) (A) is a positive substantive normative claim.

(2) (A) cannot be such a claim unless (A) states or implies that, when some fact explains why some act would fulfil some desire, this fact also has some other, different, normative property.

(3) If—impossibly—(D) were true, (A) could not be such a claim, since there would be no such different property. (A) would be a trivial claim, which could tell us only that, when some fact explains why some act would fulfil some desire, this fact explains why this act would fulfil this desire.

Therefore

(D) is not true.

As before, this objection might be misunderstood. We are not claiming that Schroeder's view is trivial. Schroeder's (D) is a substantive claim, which many people would reject. We are claiming that, if (D) were true, (A) would be trivial. On this objection, since (A) is not trivial, (D) cannot be true.

In response to this argument, Schroeder might challenge premise (3). When some fact explains how some act would fulfil some present desire, this fact has what we can call Schroeder's *explanatory property*. Schroeder might say:

(4) Even when combined with (D), (A) does not merely tell us that, when some fact has this explanatory property, this fact has this property. In telling us that this fact is *a reason*, (A) also gives us further information.

Any such information must be statable, however, as the claim that any such fact would have some other property. And Schroeder would be trying to show that (A) is a positive substantive *normative* claim. So Schroeder would have to defend (4) by claiming that

> (5) (A) states or implies that, when some fact has this explanatory property, this fact has some other, different, normative property.

When we ask what is the best candidate for this other property, the obvious answer is: the property of being a reason. But Schroeder cannot give this answer, since Schroeder's (D) denies that being a reason is a *different* property.   So Schroeder would have to claim that

> (6) when some fact explains why some act would fulfil some desire, this fact has some other, normative property which is different from the property of being a reason.

Schroeder would then face the Lost Property Problem. It is hard to see what this other property could be. And if Schroeder could find some other property that could be the normative property to which (6) refers, he would have to apply his Naturalism to this other property. The Triviality Objection would then apply to this other claim. This objection would not have been answered.

Since Schroeder could not successfully deny (3) by defending these other claims, he might deny (2).   Schroeder might say:

> (7) For (A) to be a positive substantive normative claim, this claim need not tell us about the relation between *different* properties. It is enough that (A) tells us when some fact is a reason.

To assess (7), we can turn to some imagined cases. According to Schroeder's

> (A) when some fact explains why some act would fulfil one of our present desires, this fact is a reason for us to act in this way.

If (A) was Schroeder's only claim, his view would have some implausible implications. As Schroeder points out, (A) implies that we might have a reason to act in some crazy way, such as trying to eat our car, since we might have some desire that this act would fulfil.   We might have similar desire-based reasons to act in other crazy ways, such as causing ourselves to be in agony for its own sake.   Such imagined cases, Schroeder assumes, cast doubt on his view, since it is hard to believe that we could have reasons to act in such crazy ways.   Schroeder therefore tries to show that such desire-based reasons would be 'of about as little weight as any reason could possibly be'.   If these reasons are extremely weak, Schroeder writes, that would reduce the 'unintuitiveness' of his view.

Schroeder also claims, however, that

> (D) when some fact explains why some act would fulfil some desire, that is the *same* as this fact's being a reason.

If we really accepted (D), we ought not to think it *unintuitive* or *implausible* to claim that, in Schroeder's imagined case, we would have a reason to try to eat our car.   Schroeder could say:

> (8) When I claim that some fact would be a reason to try to eat our car, my claim implies only that this fact explains how this act would fulfil one of our present desires.   On my view, that is the property to which the concept of *a reason* refers.   I am not claiming that this fact would have the *different*, normative property of being a reason to act in this way.   On my view, there is no such different property.   Since this fact *would* explain how this act would fulfil one of our present desires, and that is all that my view implies, this imagined case gives us no reason to reject my view.

As (8) shows, Schroeder's (D) is a *negative* normative claim, and (D)'s truth would prevent Schroeder's (A) from giving us positive normative information.   If (D) were true, (A) could not tell us that, when some fact helps to explain how some act would fulfil some desire, this fact would have some other, different, normative property.   Since Schroeder is not claiming that this fact would have any such property, his claim could not conflict with anyone's normative intuitions.   So Schroeder need not argue that, in his example, our reason to try to eat our car would be very weak. Rather than trying to defend his view's positive normative implications, Schroeder should point out that his view does not *have* any such implications.

Why does Schroeder think otherwise? Unlike Analytical Subjectivists, Schroeder uses the phrase 'a reason' in the indefinable normative sense that we can also express with the phrase 'counts in favour'. Schroeder himself writes that 'reasons count in favour of what they are reasons for'. Schroeder's use of this concept may lead him to assume that

(E) when some fact explains how some act would fulfil one of our present desires, this fact has the different property of *counting in favour* of this act.

This may be why Schroeder worries about his view's implausibility in his imagined cases. When he supposes that some fact explains how some crazy act would fulfil one of our desires, Schroeder may find it hard to believe that this fact counts in favour of this crazy act. On Schroeder's view, however, *there is only one property here.* Schroeder's view implies that

(F) when some fact explains how some act would fulfil one of our present desires, that is the *same* as this fact's counting in favour of this act. That's *what it is* for some fact to count in favour of some act.

If there was only one property here, it would not be hard to believe that, when some fact has this property, this fact has this property. Schroeder's worries seem to show that he does not really accept his own view.

This view *is* intuitively implausible. But what is implausible is not this view's positive normative implications, but the way in which, on this view, claims about reasons have no such implications.

Schroeder might defend this feature of his view. He might say:

When we believe that some fact is a reason to act in some way, we may assume that this fact has the normative property of counting in favour of this act. But this assumption is mistaken.

Since all facts and properties are natural, there could not be
any such property.

Schroeder might then reject the first premise of the Triviality Objection.
He might say that, since there could not be any such normative property,
claims about reasons *are* trivial. As we shall see, some Naturalists believe
that we have no reason to make any normative claims.

Schroeder could defend more of his beliefs, however, if he claimed
instead that certain facts do have the normative property of counting
in favour of certain acts. Though Schroeder would then cease to be a
Naturalist, he could keep his belief that claims about reasons are not
trivial. And since this version of Schroeder's view would make positive
substantive normative claims, Schroeder could also keep the impressive
arguments with which he defends the normative implications of his
desire-based subjective theory.

Other Naturalist Subjectivists should, I believe, revise their views in
similar ways.   On Darwall's view, for example, when we say that

(G) we ought to act in a certain way,

we often mean that

(H) this act is what, after fully informed and procedurally
rational deliberation, we would choose to do.

Darwall might now add that

(I) since (G) and (H) are normative claims, such claims, when
they are true, state normative and hence non-natural facts.

If Darwall gave up his Naturalism in this way, Darwall's view would
avoid the Fact Stating Argument and the Triviality Objection. But
as I have argued, if we used (G) to mean (H), that would have one
disadvantage. We could have substantive normative beliefs about which
ways of deliberating are procedurally rational, but we could not also
have distinct substantive beliefs about what we ought to do. If we
claimed that we ought to do what, after such deliberation, we would
choose to do, this claim would be a concealed tautology. For this reason,

I believe, Darwall should also give up his Analytical Subjectivism, by starting to use 'ought' in the decisive-reason-implying sense. As a Non-Naturalist and Non-Analytical Subjectivist, Darwall could then have the substantive normative belief that we ought to do whatever, after such deliberation, we would choose to do.

If Schroeder and Darwall revised their views in these ways, their subjective theories would be of the kind that I discuss in Chapters 3 and 4. Since we would then be discussing the same questions, we could learn from each other. After further discussion, we might find that we have been climbing the same mountain on different sides.

In arguing against Naturalism about reasons, I have discussed only subjective theories. We can next briefly consider Naturalist objective theories. It is not surprising that most Naturalists are Subjectivists. In Darwall's words, which are worth repeating here:

> For the philosophical naturalist, concerned to place
> normativity within the natural order, there is nothing
> plausible for normative force to be other than
> motivational force. . .

If Naturalists are Subjectivists who appeal to desire-based, aim-based, or choice-based reasons, they are appealing to facts about how we might be motivated to act, and they might thereby claim to explain the normativity of these reasons. The motivational conception of normativity is both widely accepted and fairly plausible. If Naturalists were Objectivists, who appealed instead to object-given value-based reasons, they could less plausibly claim that they could explain, in naturalistic terms, the normativity of these reasons.

There is another reason why most Naturalists are Subjectivists. If we are Objectivists, who believe that all reasons are object-given and value-based, we shall find it harder to believe that our having such a reason is always the same as, or consists in, some natural fact. This belief might seem least implausible to those Naturalists who are Hedonistic Rational Egoists. These people might believe that, when it is true that

(J) we have a reason to act in some way,

this fact is the same as the fact that

(K) this act would maximize our own happiness.

But most of us believe that facts of other kinds can give us reasons for acting. It would be implausible to claim that, when these other facts give us reasons, these facts would be the same as, or would constitute, our having these reasons.   Suppose for example that

(L) if I acted in various ways, I would relieve someone's pain, keep some promise, add to our knowledge of some significant historical event, and help to save Venice from being destroyed.

Objectivists might believe that

(M) these facts would give me reasons to act in these ways.

The normative facts to which (M) refers cannot be plausibly claimed to be the same as, or to consist in, the natural facts that are stated by (L). Of the features of Subjectivism that make such views appealing, one is the way in which subjective theories offer unified accounts of how a great variety of facts can give us reasons. On these theories, the facts stated by (L) might all give me reasons to act in these ways, since these acts might all fulfil one of my present desires, or be acts that, after some process of deliberation, I would be motivated to do, or would choose to do. If Naturalists are not Subjectivists, there is no similar way in which they could explain how such a great variety of facts could give us reasons.

Even if they could answer these objections, Naturalists could not, I believe, successfully defend any form of Objectivism about Reasons. These people could not answer the Fact Stating Argument or the Normativity and Triviality Objections.

97 Soft Naturalism

Though I believe that Naturalism cannot be true, it is worth supposing that I am mistaken. Since it is clear that some of us make some irreducibly normative claims, it could only be some form of Non-Analytical Naturalism that might be true. On these theories, such normative claims can state natural facts. But such theories can take two forms.   According to what we can call

> *Hard Naturalism*: Since all facts are natural, we don't need to make such irreducibly normative claims. The facts that are stated by such claims could all be restated in non-normative and naturalistic terms.

Sturgeon, for example, writes that, if some form of Moral Naturalism turned out to be true, we would 'be able to say, in entirely non-moral terms, exactly which natural properties moral terms refer to', and 'moral explanations would be in principle dispensable'. Jackson similarly writes that, when we have reported the facts in 'descriptive' terms,

> there is nothing more 'there' . . . There is no 'extra' feature that the ethical terms are fastening onto, and we could in principle say it all in descriptive language.

According to another view, which we can call

> *Soft Naturalism*: Though all facts are natural, we need to make, or have strong reasons to make, some irreducibly normative claims.

Railton, for example, writes that, in giving his Naturalist account of our moral thinking, he hopes to explain 'why morality matters as it does', and hopes to support our belief 'that ethics — real ethics — can be a force in the world'. Darwall is another Soft Naturalist. On Darwall's view, claims about reasons and reason-implying oughts are irreducibly normative. We have strong reasons to make such claims, Darwall assumes, even though these claims, when they are true, state natural facts.

Soft Naturalism is, I believe, an incoherent view. Unlike Non-Cognitivists, Naturalists assume that normative claims are intended to state facts. On that assumption, if we had strong reasons to make irreducibly normative claims, that would have to be because

> (A) there are some important irreducibly normative facts, which we cannot state except by making such normative claims.

If (A) is true, however, Soft Naturalism would fail. Naturalism is the view that

> (B) all normative facts are also, in the reductive sense, natural facts.

Facts are in this sense natural if they could be restated by making non-normative and naturalistic claims. So (A)'s truth would make (B) false, thereby undermining Naturalism. If instead (B) is true, (A) would be false, and Soft Naturalism would again fail. If all normative facts were also, in the reductive sense, natural facts, Hard Naturalists would be right to say that we don't need to make irreducibly normative claims, since we could state all normative facts by making non-normative and purely naturalistic claims. This objection we can call *the Soft Naturalist's Dilemma*.

To illustrate this objection, we can discuss one way in which Soft Naturalists might defend their view. If all normative facts were also natural facts, that would have to be because such facts involved normative properties that were also natural properties. Hard Naturalists would then claim that we don't need to use any normative concepts, since we could refer to all these properties by using only non-normative, naturalistic concepts. Soft Naturalists might reply that, in some cases, it is important that we can refer to some property in two different ways, by using two different concepts. For example, by discovering that

> (C) heat is the same as molecular kinetic energy,

scientists discovered how such energy is related to various other properties. Return next to the claim that

> (D) being an act that would maximize happiness is the same as being what we ought to do.

Soft Naturalists might similarly say that, if (D) were true, this claim would not merely tell us that two concepts refer to the same property. Given the difference between these concepts, (D) would also give us further information. That is how (D) would differ from the trivial claim that

(E) being an act that would maximize happiness is the
same as being an act that would maximize happiness.

(D) would give us such further information, Soft Naturalists might say,
because, unlike (E), (D) uses the normative phrase 'what we ought to do'.

There are now two possibilities.   It might be true that

(F) the further information given by (D)'s use of 'ought' is
irreducibly normative.

If (F) were true, Naturalism would be false, since (D) would state an
irreducibly normative fact.   It might instead be true that

(G) this further information consists in one or more
natural facts.

If (G) were true, Soft Naturalism would fail when applied to such claims.
As Hard Naturalists believe, we could restate these natural facts by making non-normative and naturalistic claims.   So, on both alternatives,
Soft Naturalism fails.   We can call this the *Further Information* version
of the Soft Naturalist's Dilemma.

This argument's conclusion should not be surprising.   All Naturalists
believe both that all facts are natural facts, and that normative claims
are intended to state facts.   We should expect that, on this view, we
don't need to make irreducibly normative claims.   If Naturalism were
true, there would be no facts that only such claims could state.

If there were no such facts, and we didn't need to make such claims,
Sidgwick, Ross, I, and others would have wasted much of our lives.   We
have asked what matters, which acts are right or wrong, and what we
have reasons to want, and to do.   If Naturalism were true, there would
be no point in trying to answer such questions.   Our consolation would
be only that it wouldn't matter that we had wasted much of our lives,
since we would have learnt that nothing matters.

These remarks do not imply that, if Naturalism is false, *Naturalists*
have wasted much of their lives.   When Naturalists develop theories
about *what it is* for acts to be right or wrong, we can often revise these
people's theories, so that these theories instead make claims about what

makes acts right or wrong, in one or more irreducibly normative senses. When so revised, some of these theories would make plausible and important claims.

I have now defended two main conclusions. First, Naturalism could not be true. We make some irreducibly normative claims, and these claims could not state natural facts.

Second, even if Naturalism were true, *Soft* Naturalism could not be true. There could not be any natural facts that were also important normative facts. If all facts were natural, normative claims could not give us any further information.

Naturalists are not Nihilists, since Naturalists believe that there are some normative facts. But since Soft Naturalism is incoherent, and Hard Naturalism implies that normative facts have no importance, Naturalism is close to Nihilism. So we have reasons to be glad if, as I have argued, Naturalism is not true.

98 Hard Naturalism

Some Hard Naturalists might agree that their view is close to Nihilism. According to these people, when we have reached the true moral theory, we wouldn't need to use normative concepts. As I have said, Sturgeon writes that, if some form of Moral Naturalism turned out to be true, we would 'be able to say, in entirely non-moral terms, exactly which natural properties moral terms refer to'. Jackson similarly writes 'we could in principle say it all in descriptive language'. Given their assumptions, these Naturalists are right, I have claimed, to draw this conclusion.

Of those who deny that we need normative concepts, one of the most emphatic is Brandt. Like many other people, Brandt believes that in giving someone advice we should appeal to facts about what this person would want after informed deliberation. Since our actual normative concepts do not explicitly refer to such facts, Brandt claims that we should redefine these concepts. 'The question for philosophers', he writes, 'is not how normative words are used, for they are used confusedly, but how they are best to be used.'

We can best use these words, Brandt claims, in senses that are wholly naturalistic. When we call some desire 'rational', Brandt proposes, we should mean 'fully informed', with 'no further meaning or connotation'. Our desires are in Brandt's sense rational if we would still have these desires even after full reflection on the relevant facts: or what Brandt calls *cognitive psychotherapy*. We are rational, in Brandt's sense, if our desires are in this sense rational, and the most rational thing for us to do is whatever would best fulfil our rational desires. Such an act, Brandt proposes, we can also call 'the best thing to do'.

Brandt compares his proposed senses of the words 'rational' and 'best' with what he calls their ordinary senses. I shall compare Brandt's proposed senses with the reason-implying senses of 'rational', 'best', and other such normative words. Though I am inclined to believe that these are the ordinary senses of these words, it would not matter if I am wrong. As Brandt claims, it is more important to decide how these words can best be used. Value-based objective theories are the main rival to Brandt's Naturalist, subjective theory. By comparing these theories, we can ask whether, as Hard Naturalists claim, we would lose nothing if we replaced reason-involving normative beliefs with beliefs about certain natural facts.

To illustrate his proposals, Brandt first imagines someone with some 'compulsive ambition' that would be extinguished by cognitive psychotherapy. Brandt claims that, on his account, this man's ambition would be rightly called irrational. That would be likely to be claimed by any plausible objective theory. To compare these two kinds of theory, we should turn to cases in which they disagree.

As one example, we can suppose that some young woman is afflicted with *anorexia nervosa*. Though this woman knows that she could live a long and rewarding life, her horror of gaining weight makes her prefer to starve herself to death. This preference, we can suppose, would be unaffected by cognitive psychotherapy. On Brandt's proposals, this woman's preference would then be rational, and starving herself to death would be the best thing for her to do. That is not the best way to use these words.

After explaining his proposed new senses of the words 'rational' and 'best', Brandt imagines someone who questions these proposals. This skeptic asks

Q1: Why ought I to do what is in your sense rational?

Brandt writes that, if he cannot answer this question, that would not be damaging, since any view could be challenged in the same way. 'The same puzzle arises about knowledge that one "ought" to do something.' Brandt here compares Q1 with

Q2: Why ought I to do what I know that I ought to do?

But these questions are very different. I might ask Q2 if I knew that I ought to do something, but I didn't know, or had forgotten, why this was true. Such cases raise no puzzle. Suppose next that, though I know both *that* and *why* I ought to do something, I ask why I ought to do this thing. The only puzzle here would be why I asked this question. When we know why something is true, we don't need to ask why this thing is true.

Q1 is a better question. We can ask, for example, why we should believe that our imagined anorexic woman ought to starve herself to death. Brandt might say 'Because this act would be in my sense rational'. But this would not be a good enough reply.

Brandt then imagines that his skeptic asks

Q3: 'Why should I want only those things it is rational in your sense to want?'

Brandt comments:

similar questions might be raised if we supposed it possible to know, in some other way than by determining what it is rational to want in my sense, which possible outcomes are good or worthwhile.

Brandt's 'similar' question would be

Q4: Why should I want only those things that are good or worthwhile?

This would be a similar question, Brandt writes, because 'there is no definitional connection between something's being good . . . and desire.' But there *is* a definitional connection between something's being good and this thing's being *desirable* in the reason-implying sense. Such good things have features that might give us reasons to want them. So Q4 means

> Why should I want only those things whose features might give me reasons to want these things?

Since 'Why?' asks for a reason, this means

> What reasons have I to want only those things that I might have reasons to want?

This question is easy to answer. I couldn't have reasons to want what I couldn't have reasons to want.

Brandt makes other claims that are intended to support his proposed re-definition of the word 'rational'. For example, he writes

> (1) 'a distinctive feature of knowing that a choice would be rational in this sense is that there can be no further question whether it is reasonable to make that choice.'

If (1) uses 'reasonable' in its ordinary sense, this claim's truth *would* support Brandt's proposal. But in defending (1) Brandt writes

> if a man knows what he would choose if he had vividly in mind all the relevant facts . . . the question whether it is rational for him to do this, at least in my sense of rational, is devoid of all sense.

For this remark to be relevant, Brandt's (1) must use 'reasonable' to mean 'in my sense rational'. (1) then makes the trivial claim that, if some choice is in Brandt's sense rational, there can be no further question whether this choice is in Brandt's sense rational.

Brandt also writes

> the question of what I would desire intrinsically if my desires were rational in my sense is a more important question than the question of what is intrinsically desirable, in the ordinary sense, if the two questions really are different.

Since this is Brandt's main claim, his defence of this claim is worth quoting in full.   Brandt writes:

> we have a choice as moral philosophers: Whether to recommend that a person make the best choice in the ordinary sense of 'best', or the rational choice in my sense of 'rational'. . .

> Consider an example.   Suppose I prefer to hear one orchestra program rather than another, in the situation that I know whatever facts might affect my preferences; my preference is then rational in my sense.   But suppose someone claims that the opposite preference would be better.   Perhaps this could not be shown; but since it is an empirical question how 'better' is actually used as applied to such choices, it is logically possible that the opposite preference is the better one in the ordinary sense.   The question then arises why one must recommend the preference that is 'better'.   Is the fact that it is better a reason for adopting it?   The fact that it would be better could not be a new empirical fact that would tend to move my preference in a certain way, for our definition of a 'rational' preference requires that it already have been formed in full view of *all* the relevant empirical facts, including whatever empirical fact is meant by 'the other being better'.   One might of course say that some non-natural fact is in question; but, since it is not clear what kind of fact such a non-natural fact might be, I shall ignore this possibility.   I concede that perhaps it is tautologously true that it would be better to follow the better preference rather than the rational one if there is a conflict; but this, if true, only re-raises the initial question, why one should take an interest in the better rather than the more rational.   It is also true that the expression 'is the best thing' may have *de facto* authority over conduct in the sense that when we decide that something is 'best' in the ordinary sense, our conditioned responses to the phrasing may be such that we incline to do the thing that we have judged best.   It may well be that our conditioned responses are firmer and more favourable to 'is the best thing' than to 'is the rational thing' especially when explicitly understood in my sense.   But it would be absurd for a

person to guide his conduct not by the facts but by the words which may properly be applied to it. My conclusion is that a more rational choice, in my sense, cannot in good reason take second place to a choice which is better in the ordinary sense, if there should be a conflict between the two.

This paragraph illustrates, I believe, much of what went wrong in the moral philosophy of the mid twentieth century.

Brandt first supposes that he has a well-informed preference to hear one of two musical programs. He has this preference, we can assume, because he would enjoy this program more. Brandt imagines someone claiming that, in the ordinary sense, it would be better for him to prefer to hear the other program. But we cannot plausibly suppose that, in an ordinary reason-implying sense, it would be better for Brandt to prefer the program that he would enjoy less.

Brandt then writes that, if these senses conflict, we could ask

why one must recommend the preference that is 'better.' Is the fact that it is better a reason for adopting it?

The answer to the second of these questions is, strictly, No. If some other preference is better, this fact is not itself a *further* reason for having it. But this does not support Brandt's view. If some preference is better, this fact *is* the fact that we have more reason to have it. That is what this use of 'better' means. So Brandt's first question is easy to answer. We should recommend the preference that is better because this is the preference that we have more reason to have.

If this preference would be better, Brandt continues, this could not be a new empirical fact that would cause us to have this preference. That is true. On the value-based alternative to Brandt's view, when we have more reason to have some preference, that is not an empirical fact that causes us to have this preference, but an irreducibly normative truth. Brandt mentions this other view, but merely writes that, since it is unclear what kind of fact such a truth might be, 'I shall ignore this possibility'.   We cannot defend some view by ignoring the alternatives.

Brandt then writes:

> I concede that perhaps it is tautologously true that it would be better to follow the better preference rather than the rational one if there is a conflict; but this, if true, only re-raises the initial question, why one should take an interest in the better rather than the more rational.

Brandt is here comparing what is better in the ordinary sense with what is more rational in Brandt's sense. Some preference would be better to follow, in the ordinary sense, if we have more reason to follow this preference. So Brandt's sentence should be taken to mean:

> If we have more reason to follow one of two preferences, but the other preference is in my sense rational, it may be tautologously true that we have more reason to follow the preference that we have more reason to follow. But that only returns us to the question: Why should we follow the preference that we have more reason to follow, rather than the preference that is in my sense rational?

Since 'Why?' asks for a reason, this means 'Why do we have more reason to follow the preference that we have more reason to follow?' This question answers itself.

Brandt next suggests that, if we did what we judged to be best, such acts might be merely a 'conditioned response' to the ordinary sense of 'best'. It would be absurd, he writes, for us to guide our conduct 'not by the facts, but by the words which may be properly applied to it'. As before, Brandt does not take seriously the value-based alternative to his view. Brandt is here supposing that the ordinary sense of 'best' would be '*properly* applied' to what we do. If that were true, and we did what was best because it was best in this reason-implying sense, our act would not be merely a conditioned response to the word 'best'. We would be guided, not absurdly by mere words, but by our awareness of the facts that gave us decisive reasons to act in this way.

Brandt ends:

> My conclusion is that a more rational choice, in my sense, cannot in good reason take second place to a choice which is better in the ordinary sense, if there should be a conflict between the two.

Choices are better in the ordinary sense if they are choices that we have more reason to make. Brandt is here supposing that one choice would be in this sense better, but that some other choice would be in Brandt's sense rational. So Brandt's conclusion is that, in such cases, the choice that we have less reason to make cannot be the choice that we have less reason to make.

Since Brandt was an excellent philosopher, why did he make such claims? The answer may be that, even when Brandt says he is supposing that one of two choices would be, in the ordinary sense, better, he is not really doing that. Though Brandt mentions the view that there are non-natural normative facts, he writes 'I shall ignore this possibility'.

If we ignore this possibility, and we use naturalistic substitutes for normative concepts, we can be led to make claims that seem absurd. Brandt's view implies, for example, that our anorexic woman ought rationally to starve herself to death, and that this would be the best thing for her to do.

Though these claims may seem absurd, this should not be our objection to Brandt's view. As Brandt could reply, if we use his proposed definitions, these claims would *not* be absurd. We would mean only that, in starving herself to death, this woman would be doing what, even after cognitive psychotherapy, she would most want. These claims would be true. This woman's act *would* be, in Brandt's senses, rational, and the best thing for her to do.

What makes these claims true, however, also makes them trivial. This should be our objection to Brandt's view. When Brandt claims that we ought rationally to do what would fulfil our informed desires, he means that, in doing what would fulfil these desires, we would be doing what would fulfil these desires. If we used such naturalistic substitutes for normative concepts, our claims would never be absurd because they would not be substantive normative claims. We could not significantly claim, or think, that this woman should *not* starve herself to death.

Brandt's remarks illustrate another point. Though Hard Naturalists claim that we don't need normative concepts, they use such concepts. Brandt rightly claims, for example, that philosophers should ask how normative words can *best* be used. He makes various claims about what is *more important*. And in the passage just quoted, Brandt writes that choices that are more rational in his naturalistic sense 'cannot *in good reason* take second place' to choices that are better in the ordinary sense. These are not claims about what we would want after cognitive psychotherapy.

Jackson provides some other examples. We don't need normative concepts, Jackson claims, because there are no irreducibly normative properties or facts. In his words, there is nothing else 'there'. But Jackson also writes:

> . . . it is hard to see how [such] properties could be of ethical significance. Are we supposed to take seriously someone who says, 'I see that this action will kill many and save no one, but that is not enough to justify my not doing it; what really matters is that the action has an extra property that only ethical terms are suited to pick out'? In short, the extra properties would be ethical 'idlers'.

Jackson seems to mean:

> Even if acts could have irreducibly normative properties, such as the property of being wrong, it is hard to see how such properties could have any ethical significance. If some act would kill many people and save no one, this fact is enough to justify our not acting in this way, and enough to give us a decisive reason not to act in this way. Our reason not to kill these people would not have to be given by the fact that this act would have the extra property of being wrong.

Though these last two claims are plausible, they would state irreducibly normative truths. On Jackson's view, however, there are no such truths. Jackson also writes that, if the best Naturalist theory turned out to be one form of Hedonism,

> 'we should identify rightness with maximizing expected
> hedonic value' because this would be what 'we ought
> to aim at'.

If we didn't need normative concepts, as Jackson believes, we would be able to restate this claim without using the words 'should' and 'ought'. But that would be impossible. Jackson might write that, if the best theory were this form of hedonism,

> it would maximize expected hedonic value to identify
> rightness with maximizing such value, because this
> would be what it would maximize such value to aim at.

But that is not what Jackson means, nor could it be what he ought to mean.

Normative Naturalism, I have argued, could not be true, because irreducibly normative claims could not state natural facts. But there is another way in which such claims have been held to be compatible with a wholly naturalistic view.

28

Non-Cognitivism
and Quasi-Realism

99 Non-Cognitivism

According to *Non-Cognitivists*, normative claims are not intended to state facts. When these people reject Naturalism, many of them say that, as I have argued, natural facts could not be normative. Some of these people add that, when Moore criticized what he called 'the Naturalistic Fallacy', he was only half right. Though Moore saw that normative claims could not be claims about natural properties and facts, he mistakenly assumed that such claims must be about *non-natural* properties and facts. That assumption, Non-Cognitivists believe, still underrates the distinctiveness of normative claims. According to these people, it is not merely *natural* facts that could not be normative. *No* facts could be normative, since no facts, or factual beliefs, could have the role in our lives of norms or values. These people distinguish between *facts* and *values*, assuming that there could not be evaluative or normative facts. When we claim that some act is rational or right, these people say, we are not claiming that this act has even a special, irreducibly normative non-natural property. Normativity is to be found, not in the properties of acts, but in our attitudes towards these acts. In Hume's words, we must 'look within'.

There is another, partly overlapping view. According to

> *Moral Sentimentalists*: Morality involves passion rather than reason, or the heart rather than the mind, since our moral

convictions are best understood as consisting in certain kinds
of desire, sentiment, or other *conative attitude*.

This view can take Cognitivist forms. According to those who are often
called

Moral Subjectivists: When we claim that some act is
wrong, we mean that we have some disapproving
attitude towards this act.

But this view is clearly false. If this view were true, we could not have
moral disagreements. If I said 'Stealing is wrong', and you said 'No it
isn't', these claims would not conflict, and they might both be true,
since we might each be correctly describing our own attitude to stealing.
When we make such claims, however, we *are* disagreeing.

According to some

Moral Intersubjectivists: When we claim that some act is
wrong, we mean that most people, at least in ideal conditions,
would have some disapproving attitude towards such acts.

On this view, acts can be right or wrong in the kind of way in which
apples can be red or green, jokes can be funny or feeble, and faces can
be beautiful or ugly. Apples are red if they look red to normal observers
in daylight, jokes are funny if they amuse most people, and acts are
wrong if they would arouse a sentiment or attitude of disapproval in
most well-informed and impartial observers.

Though some such *response-dependence* theory must be correct when
applied to colours, and such theories are plausible when applied to
jokes and to beauty, there are strong objections to response-dependent
accounts of morality. If I am colour-blind, for example, I might truly
claim that two apples have different colours, because they look different
to normal observers, though these apples look the same colour to me.
According to these Moral Intersubjectivists, I might similarly truly
claim that some act is wrong, because most people have disapproving
attitudes toward such acts, though I myself approve these acts. That
is not how we think about morality. If we approve some act, we cannot also believe that this act is wrong. In response to this objection,

Intersubjectivists might say that, when we claim that some act is wrong, we mean that we and most other people disapprove such acts. Though this view is more plausible, it also misdescribes how most of us think about morality. When we claim that some act is wrong, we might believe that most other people would disapprove such acts. But that is not part of what we mean. Nor would we believe such acts to be wrong because it is true that, in ideal conditions, we and most other people would disapprove these acts. We and others would disapprove, we assume, because such acts are wrong. And if we believe that some act is wrong, but learnt that most other people would not disapprove of such acts, we would not take this fact to imply that such acts are *not* wrong. As a form of Naturalism, this theory also faces the objections presented in my last four chapters.

Sentimentalism can take other, Non-Cognitivist forms.   According to

> *Moral Expressivists*: When we claim that some act is wrong,
> we are not intending to say something true, but are expressing
> our disapproving attitude toward such acts.

On the earliest and simplest view of this kind, *Emotivism*, if we claim that lying is wrong or that we ought to keep our promises, we mean something like 'Lying: Boo!' or 'Keeping promises: Hurray!' Later Expressivists, as we shall see, make more plausible suggestions.

Though Naturalist and Non-Naturalist views have been held for more than two thousand years, Non-Cognitivist views have been widely held only since the 1930s. That is not surprising, since such views are implausible. Most people assume that certain acts really are wrong, or are, at least, wrong for certain people. Though some people reject this assumption, most of these people are skeptics, or Nihilists, who believe that no acts are wrong. Moral beliefs, most of us assume, are *beliefs*, which might be true or false.

Because they recognize these facts, many Non-Cognitivists say only that moral claims can be easily misunderstood, and should not be *regarded* as intended to be true. When other people claim that some act is wrong, we might say 'That's true'. But this use of 'true', these writers suggest, is merely another way of expressing the same attitude. For example, if you said 'Milk chocolate is disgusting', I might say 'That's true' as a way of expressing the same dislike.

Since Non-Cognitivism is not plausible, such views need to be defended. Three main arguments have been given. According to what we can call *the Humean Argument*:

> (A) It is inconceivable that we might be sincerely convinced that some act was our duty, but not be in the slightest motivated to act in this way.

> (B) If moral convictions were beliefs, such a case would be conceivable.

Therefore

> Moral convictions cannot be beliefs, but must be some kind of desire, conative attitude, or other motivating state.

To defend (B), some Non-Cognitivists appeal to

> *the Humean Theory of Motivation*: No belief could motivate us unless this belief is combined with some desire.

These people claim that, if moral convictions were beliefs, it would make sense to suppose that we might believe some act to be our duty, without having the desire that would be needed to motivate us to act in this way. Since such a case is not conceivable, these Non-Cognitivists argue, moral convictions must themselves *be* desires. Only that could guarantee that, when we have moral convictions, we are motivated to act upon them.

   Some Humeans claim that, for some belief to motivate us, this belief must be combined with some *independent, pre-existing* desire. As Nagel argues, we can reject this claim. When we come to have some belief, such as the belief that we ought to act in a certain way, this belief might motivate us by causing us to have some new desire. Nor do we even need to have some new desire. Whenever we act in some voluntary way, Humeans say, we must have wanted to act as we did. But our having this desire, we can reply, might consist only in our being motivated by some belief to act in this way.

Humeans might accept this reply, and retreat to a less ambitious view. These people might claim

> (C) No belief could motivate us *all by itself*, since no belief could motivate us unless it is also true that we are *disposed* to be motivated by this belief.

Such dispositions, Humeans might say, are one of the kinds of mental state that they call desires.

This form of the Humean Theory would be undeniable, but would have little importance. Consider, for example, Kant's anti-Humean claim that pure reason can by itself motivate us. Kant would have happily agreed that, for pure reason to be able to motivate us, we must be rational beings, who are disposed to be motivated by pure reason. It is no objection to Kant's view that pure reason could not motivate a snail, or a stone.

Even in this less ambitious form, however, the Humean Theory may sufficiently support premise (B). We might have to admit that, if moral convictions are beliefs, it would be conceivable that someone might have some moral belief without being disposed to be motivated by this belief.

We can reject this argument in a different way. Premise (A) is plausible, we can point out, because we would not call someone's moral belief 'sincere', or a 'moral conviction', if this person claimed to believe that some act would be wrong but was not in the slightest motivated to refrain from acting in this way. If we ask whether such a person might *know* that such acts are wrong, our answer would often be Yes. And in knowing that such acts are wrong, this person must in one sense believe that such acts are wrong. If we revise premise (A) so that it refers merely to moral beliefs rather than to *sincere* convictions or beliefs, (A) would cease to be true, so the Humean Argument would fail.

We have other normative beliefs, such as beliefs about what we should or ought to do in the decisive-reason-implying sense. When we consider such beliefs, there is no similarly plausible Humean Argument for Non-Cognitivism. If people are deeply depressed, for example, they may believe that they have decisive reasons to do something, such as acting in some way that would protect their future well-being, without being in the slightest motivated to act in this way. It would be implausible to claim that such people cannot *sincerely believe* that they have these decisive reasons to protect their future well-being. When people are deeply depressed, what they lose may only be their motivation, not their normative beliefs. Such examples help to show that claims like (A) seem plausible only because such claims use phrases like 'sincerely convinced', or 'sincerely believe', rather than the word 'believe'.

The second main argument for Non-Cognitivism starts as follows:

> (D) Moral claims are irreducibly normative, in the sense that such claims cannot be restated in non-normative naturalistic terms.

Therefore

> (E) If these claims were true, they would state facts that were not natural but irreducibly normative.

> (F) All facts are natural.

Therefore

> (G) Moral claims could not state facts.

There are now two alternatives.   Nihilists continue:

> (H) Moral claims are intended to state facts.

Therefore

> (I) These claims are all false.

Non-Cognitivists continue:

> (J) We can justifiably make moral claims.

Therefore

> (K) These claims are not intended to state facts.

Since premise (F) assumes Metaphysical Naturalism, we can call these *the Naturalist Arguments for Nihilism* or *Non-Cognitivism*. We can reject both arguments if, as I shall later argue, we can justifiably reject Metaphysical Naturalism. But I shall first discuss Non-Cognitivism, which can be defended in other ways.

In its earliest, Emotivist form, Non-Cognitivism was close to Nihilism. I was present when the most notorious 'Boo-Hurray' Theorist, Ayer, heard Mackie present his Nihilistic Error Theory. Ayer's first comment was: 'That's what I should have said'. Ayer happily gave up his Non-Cognitivism, turning instead to the view that most people misunderstand morality, since most people mistakenly believe that there are moral truths.

Some later Non-Cognitivists firmly reject any such Error Theory. According to these writers, most of us know, or would on reflection agree, that moral claims are intended, not to state facts, but to express certain attitudes.

Some of these writers, however, make a surprising further claim. According to these Non-Cognitivists, though we do not intend our moral claims to state facts, such claims can, in a way, state facts. Two such writers are Gibbard and Blackburn, who defend similar Expressivist theories. By asking what these original and impressive theories achieve, we can reach some conclusions that apply to all forms of Non-Cognitivism.

100 Normative Disagreements

The 'key to meaning', Gibbard writes, lies 'in agreement and disagreement: we know what a thought is when we know what it would be to agree with it or disagree with it.'

Moral Subjectivism fails, as we have seen, because this view cannot explain how there can be moral disagreements. This view falsely implies that conflicting moral claims might all be true. Non-Cognitivism does not have this implication, and is in this way more plausible. But Non-Cognitivists, I shall argue, also cannot explain what is involved in moral disagreements.

On Blackburn's theory, moral claims do not fundamentally state beliefs, but express certain kinds of desire, value, or other conative attitude. These attitudes conflict whenever one person is in favour of some act or policy, and someone else is against this act or policy. Such people disagree, Blackburn claims, in the sense that their desires or other conative attitudes cannot both be fulfilled.

It is misleading, I believe, to describe such people as *disagreeing*. When two people have conflicting desires, they cannot both get what they want. These people may oppose each other, and they may even fight. But fights may not involve any disagreement. For people to disagree, they must have conflicting beliefs.

Gibbard similarly claims that we can disagree with people's preferences and acts. This claim is also misleading. If I believe that one of your preferences or acts was irrational or wrong, you and I may disagree, since you may believe that your preference or act was rational or right. But I would then be disagreeing, not with your preference or act, but with your belief.

Though Gibbard discusses our moral beliefs, his main claims are about rationality, and about what we ought to do in a practical, non-moral sense. To explain 'what *ought* assertions mean', Gibbard writes, we can say:

the concept of ought just *is* the concept of what to do.

He also writes:

The hypothesis of this book is easy to state: *Thinking what I ought to do is thinking what to do.*

Gibbard's phrase 'thinking what to do' is ambiguous. If I said that I was trying to decide what to do, I would often mean that I was trying to decide what I *ought* to do. But this is not what Gibbard means, since that would make his hypothesis trivial. Gibbard means:

Thinking about what I ought to do is thinking about what I *shall* do.

As Gibbard also writes:

If we understand concluding what to do, then we understand concluding what a person ought to do. . . . When I speak of

concluding 'what to do', understand this to mean coming to
a choice.

These claims may correctly describe how, in Gibbard's unusual phrase,
he and some other people *conclude what to do*. That Gibbard thinks in
this way is suggested by his use of this and similar phrases. Gibbard talks
of our 'disagreeing what to do', he calls one of his books *Thinking How to
Live*, he asks 'why to care?', and he writes 'what's obvious is to choose life
over death'. To some of us, these phrases seem to have a normative word
missing. Rather than asking *why to care* about something, we would ask
why we *should* care about this thing, or what *reasons* we have to care.
Rather than concluding what to do, we would reach conclusions about
what we should do. And we wouldn't think it obvious to choose life
over death. What can be obvious, we believe, isn't *to choose something*,
but only some truth or fact, such as the fact that we *should* or *ought* to
choose something, or that something is *the thing to choose*.

If we use these normative words and concepts, Gibbard's suggested
view does not, I believe, correctly describe our practical reasoning. When
we conclude that we ought to do something, we are not deciding to do
this thing, but coming to have a normative belief. Though our decisions
to act are often based on such beliefs, these decisions are not the same
as our coming to have these beliefs. We always have two questions:

Q1: What ought I to do?

Q2: What shall I do?

This distinction is clearest when we must make decisions that could not
even be based on any normative belief. Such cases take their simplest
form when we must choose between two qualitatively identical items.
Buridan's imagined donkey, or ass, was given two identical bales of
hay. Because this animal was too rigidly rational, being unable to make
decisions for no reason, he could not decide which bale to eat, since he
had no reason to prefer either bale to the other. Being unable to decide
which bale he *ought* to pick, he could not decide which bale to pick. So
he starved to death.

Return next to the case in which, to escape from the fire in your
burning hotel, you must jump into the canal. Suppose that your room

has two windows. On Gibbard's suggested view, if you decide to jump through one of these windows, you would be deciding that this is what you ought to do. That may not be true. You might know that jumping through the other window would be just as good. You wouldn't then believe that you ought to jump through one particular window. But you would still have to decide through which window you will jump.

In many cases, our decisions can based on normative beliefs. But that does not show that, when we come to believe that we ought to do something, that is the same as our deciding to do it. We may decide *not* to do what we believe that we ought to do, or decide to *do* what we believe that we ought not to do. Gibbard might qualify his view, so that it does not apply to such cases. In response to a similar objection, Gibbard writes 'we'd best look first to thinkers who are consistent', in the sense that these people's decisions always match their normative beliefs. But even when we consider such people, we should distinguish between their decisions and their beliefs. If we ignore this distinction, we shall misunderstand these people's practical reasoning.

Gibbard claims the opposite. It is *by* ignoring this distinction, he believes, that we can best understand practical reasoning. Gibbard writes:

> I the chooser don't face two clear, distinct questions, the
> question what to do and the question what I ought to do.

We can best explain the concept *ought*, Gibbard imaginatively suggests, by describing what is involved in making plans, and in disagreeing with other plans. In Gibbard's words:

> Disagreement in plan . . . is the key to explaining
> normative concepts.

We decide what we ought to do, on Gibbard's account, by choosing between possible plans, thereby deciding what to do. To explain our beliefs about what other people ought to do, Gibbard supposes that we choose between plans that would apply to some merely imaginary case. We decide what we would do if we were going to be in someone else's position, and we would be relevantly like this other person. Suppose you tell me that, if a certain person offered you a job, or proposed marriage, you would accept. I might decide that, if I were in your position and were in other ways like you, I would refuse these offers. On Gibbard's account, our plans would then disagree, and we would thereby disagree about what you ought to do.

It may be objected, Gibbard notes, that when two people make such different decisions, they may not be disagreeing. The truth may be only that these people have adopted different plans. But if such a difference between people's plans involves no disagreement, Gibbard could not explain our normative disagreements by appealing to such differences between people's plans.

In response to this objection, Gibbard first claims that, when we change some plan without some change in our factual beliefs, we thereby disagree with one of our *own* earlier normative beliefs. In Gibbard's words:

> We must count a change of plan as not only a change like a
> shave or a haircut, but as coming to disagree with one's earlier
> planning . . . [or] with what one previously thought.

This claim is not, I believe, true. As I have said, we must often choose between plans that seem to us equally good. We may adopt one of these plans, and then later change to some other plan, without any change in our factual beliefs or any disagreement with our previous normative beliefs. This might be true in *Burning Hotel*, for example, if you changed your decision about which is the window through which you will jump.

Responding to a similar objection, Gibbard qualifies his account. We disagree with some earlier normative belief, Gibbard suggests, whenever we change some plan because our preferences change. But that is not so. Suppose that when I most enjoyed climbing I planned to buy some hut in the mountains, but now that I prefer sailing I plan to buy some hut near the sea. This change of plan may involve no disagreement with my earlier normative beliefs.

Gibbard also claims that our plans must act as 'judgments' or 'determinations' to which we are committed, and with which we might later disagree. To defend this claim, Gibbard appeals to the fact that, if we don't commit ourselves to our plans, we shall be less likely to achieve our aims. But this fact does not support Gibbard's claim. In many cases, though we ought to follow *some* plan, we need not be committed to any *particular* plan, since we may know that other plans would be just as good. When you jump through one of your two windows, thereby saving your life, you wouldn't need to believe that this is the window through which you ought to jump.

When Gibbard returns to our beliefs about what other people ought to do, he concedes that different people can have different plans about how to act in some kind of case, without thereby disagreeing. But it would be better for everyone, Gibbard claims, if we all regarded such cases *as if* they involved disagreements, since that would make it easier for different people to give each other advice. 'In thinking how to live', he writes, 'we need each other's help.'

These claims do not support Gibbard's account. Gibbard is trying to explain normative disagreements by appealing to the simpler idea of disagreements between plans. On Gibbard's suggested explanation, people who have different plans thereby disagree. But such people, Gibbard concedes, may *not* be disagreeing. We cannot believe that such people *are* disagreeing merely because, if we had this belief, that would be better for us. We could at most *pretend* that such people are disagreeing. Nor could this help us to understand what is involved in real normative disagreements.

101 Can Non-Cognitivists Explain Normative Mistakes?

Even if we understand normative disagreements, there are other, more important questions. In Gibbard's words:

> Can I ever be mistaken in an *ought* judgment? . . . Do
> we discover how best to live, or is it a matter of
> arbitrary choice . . . ?

If such judgments cannot be either correct or mistaken, and merely involve arbitrary choices, there would be no point in trying to answer questions about what we ought to do, or how it would better or worse to live. Since such questions would have no answers, we could not make better decisions, thereby making our lives go better. We might as well act on impulse, consult some astrologer, or toss coins.

Gibbard and Blackburn both try to show that, though our normative judgments express desires, decisions, or other conative attitudes, these attitudes and judgments *can* be correct or mistaken. We can therefore claim, they say, that such judgments can be true or false. By making certain further claims, Blackburn suggests, Expressivist Non-Cognitivists can be *Quasi-Realists*, who can justifiably say all, or nearly all, that Cognitivists—whom he calls *Realists*—can say. As Blackburn writes:

> quasi-realism is trying to earn our right to talk of
> moral truth, while recognizing fully the subjective
> sources of our judgments inside our own attitudes,
> needs, desires, and natures.

For Gibbard and Blackburn to defend these claims, they must explain what it would *be* for our conative attitudes, and the judgments that express these attitudes, to be true or false, correct or mistaken.

According to Cognitivists, normative judgments express beliefs. When two people's judgments conflict, at least one of these judgments must be false, since contradictory beliefs cannot both be true. Non-Cognitivists, as Gibbard concedes, cannot make such a claim. On Gibbard's account, our normative judgments conflict when we make different decisions about how we would act in some situation, thereby adopting different plans. As Gibbard points out, we cannot argue that such a difference between two plans involves a contradiction, so that one of these plans must be false, or mistaken. Gibbard suggests that, if we regard such different plans as being inconsistent, so that one of them must be mistaken, this would be better for us, since we shall then get 'the benefits of normative discussion'. But as before, this fact could only give us reasons to *pretend* that, when people have different plans, one of these plans must be mistaken. This pretence could not help to show that one of these plans must be mistaken, nor could this pretence explain what it would *be* for some plan to be mistaken.

Blackburn appeals to a different kind of inconsistency. When he discusses practical conflicts, Blackburn writes:

if our attitudes are inconsistent, in that what we recommend
as policies or practices cannot all be implemented together,
then something is wrong.

But when our attitudes are in this sense inconsistent, something is wrong only in the sense that some of us will be disappointed, since some people's recommended policies will not be carried out. We cannot claim that, when two attitudes are in this sense inconsistent, one of these attitudes must be false or mistaken.

As a Quasi-Realist, Blackburn also claims that

(A) when two value judgments conflict, by being inconsistent,
at least one of these judgments must be false or mistaken.

When our value judgments express *beliefs*, which might be either true or false, we can claim that one of two conflicting judgments must be mistaken. On Blackburn's view, however, value judgments fundamentally express *desires*. The essential phenomenon, Blackburn writes,

is that of people valuing things . . . we recognize no interesting
split between values and desires . . . we call 'values' just those
desires and attitudes that stand fast when we contemplate
others and try to alter them.

When two desires cannot both be fulfilled, that does not imply that one of these desires must be in some way mistaken. We have many rational desires that cannot all be fulfilled. As Blackburn himself writes, 'desires can be faultlessly inconsistent'. Since Blackburn claims that value judgments express desires, and he believes that desires can be faultlessly inconsistent, it is hard to see how he can hope to defend (A).

Blackburn does, however, ingeniously and resourcefully defend this claim. He suggests several ways in which Non-Cognitivists might be able to explain what it would be for people's attitudes and moral judgments to be false or mistaken. Blackburn first remarks:

Of course there is no problem in thinking that *other* people
may be mistaken.

There *is*, I believe, a problem here. To explain a sense in which other people may be mistaken, it is not enough to point out that we may *think* that these people are mistaken, because we disagree with them. On Blackburn's account, we disagree with other people when we and they have different desires or other conative attitudes that cannot both be fulfilled. We cannot say that, in such cases, 'mistaken' means 'different from mine'. Here is one way to illustrate this point. As Gibbard claims,

> You can't disagree with a headache.

But suppose I reject this claim, since I believe that people's headaches can be true or false, correct or mistaken. If I was trying to explain this strange view, it would not be enough for me to claim that other people's headaches are false, or mistaken, when their mental state differs from mine, because these people have a headache and I don't.

Blackburn continues:

> The problem comes with thinking . . . that *I* may be mistaken. How can I make sense of fears of my own fallibility?

To explain such fears, Blackburn claims, he can appeal to the idea that he would cease to have some present attitude if he were in some improved state of mind. That might be true, for example, if he were better informed, or more impartial. Blackburn then writes

> the quasi-realist can certainly possess the concept of an improved standpoint from which some attitude of his appears inept, and this I suggest is all that is needed to explain his adherence to the acceptance of the apparently realist claim 'I might be wrong'.

We can call this the *Improved Standpoint Criterion.*

For this criterion to succeed, Blackburn must explain in what sense some possible standpoint might be *improved*. When we are discussing beliefs, we can describe some standpoint as improved in the sense that, if we had this standpoint, our beliefs would be less likely to be mistaken, by being false. Juries, for example, are less likely to convict innocent people if they know more of the facts, and they are not swayed by prejudice. This use of 'improved' makes sense because we already know what it would be for some jury's verdict to be mistaken.

Blackburn, however, is trying to *explain* some sense in which some of his present desires or other conative attitudes might be false, or mistaken. He suggests that

> (B) his attitudes might be false, or mistaken, in the sense
> that he would not have these attitudes if his standpoint
> were improved.

But he would also have to claim that

> (C) this standpoint would be improved in the sense that,
> if he had this standpoint, his attitudes would be less likely
> to be false, or mistaken.

And this claim would have to use the words 'false' and 'mistaken' in the very sense that Blackburn is trying to explain. So this suggested explanation fails. I might similarly claim that

> (D) my headaches might be mistaken, in the sense that I would
> not have these headaches if my standpoint were improved,

and that

> (E) my standpoint would be improved in the sense
> that, if I had this standpoint, my headaches would be
> less likely to be mistaken.

But these claims would not explain what it would be for some headache to be mistaken.

Blackburn might reply that

> (F) when we are forming our desires or other conative
> attitudes, our standpoint would be improved if we knew
> more of the relevant facts about the possible objects of our
> desires.

As I have said, however, claims like (F) assume that

> (G) the possible objects of our desires may have intrinsic features that would give us object-given reasons to have these desires, and to try to fulfil them if we can.

I believe that, because (G) is true, our standpoint would be improved if we knew more of these facts.   Because such facts can give us such reasons, our desires and other conative attitudes *can* be justified, or unjustified. Our desires are justified when, and because, we want what we have such object-given value-based reasons to want. As a Humean Non-Cognitivist, however, Blackburn rejects (G), so he cannot appeal to (F).

To explain the sense in which his conative attitudes might be false, or mistaken, Blackburn elsewhere writes:

> there are a number of things I admire: for instance, information, sensitivity, maturity, imagination, coherence. I know that other people show defects in these respects, and that these defects lead to bad opinions . . . So I can think that perhaps some of my opinions are due to [such] defects.

In claiming to know that other people have bad opinions, Blackburn again assumes what he needs to explain. In what sense are these opinions *bad*, rather than merely different from Blackburn's opinions?

We have other reasons to believe that Blackburn's appeal to an improved standpoint cannot explain any sense in which our conative attitudes might be false, or mistaken. As Blackburn notes, what he would regard as an improved standpoint depends on his present attitudes. He imagines knowing that, if he were fully informed and impartial, he would lose all of his present attitudes. If he knew this fact, Blackburn remarks, he would claim that this possible standpoint, despite being fully informed and impartial, would *not* be improved. On this version of Blackburn's view, some of our attitudes might be false, or mistaken, in the sense that we would not have these attitudes if we had less information, and we were less impartial. It would be harder to defend the claim that this more ignorant and biased standpoint would be, in some relevant sense, improved. And as these remarks imply, when we ask whether our own present attitudes might be in Blackburn's sense false, or mistaken, it is our own present attitudes that provide the answer. These attitudes would be their own judge and jury.

Blackburn might reply that, on any view, we cannot avoid giving priority to our own present point of view. As he writes,

> when I wonder how I might improve, I have to think about it deploying my current attitudes — there is no standing aside and apart from my present sensibility.

But this reply would not succeed. It is true that, even on a Cognitivist view, we must give one kind of priority to our own present beliefs. Though we know that our present beliefs might be mistaken, we cannot base our decisions on the truth rather than on what *we now believe* to be the truth. But, despite this fact, we can explain what it would be for our present beliefs to be mistaken. These beliefs would be mistaken if they were false. As a Non-Cognitivist, Blackburn cannot give this explanation. He cannot claim that our present conative attitudes might be mistaken by being false, since these attitudes are fundamentally desires, and desires cannot be false. Nor would it help to claim that our attitudes might be mistaken in the sense that we would not have these attitudes if we were in some state of mind in which our attitudes would not be mistaken. That claim, as we have seen, would have to assume the sense of 'mistaken' that Blackburn needs to explain. These objections to Blackburn's Quasi-Realism are, I believe, decisive.

Egan adds a more particular objection. Of our present moral attitudes, some are *unstable*, in the sense that we would lose these attitudes if we had what Blackburn calls some improved standpoint. These are the attitudes that, on Blackburn's view, we can regard as possibly mistaken. Our other present attitudes are *stable*, in the sense that we would keep these attitudes in any such improved state of mind. These unchangeable attitudes are deeper, or more fundamental. On Blackburn's view, we can understand what it would be for *other people's* stable attitudes to be mistaken. These other people might disagree with us, and they would then be making fundamental moral errors. But on this view, as Egan argues, we cannot intelligibly think that our *own* stable attitudes might be mistaken. So each of us can justifiably believe that we are the only person who has an *a priori* guarantee against fundamental moral error. This conclusion, Egan writes, would be at best 'very, very strange', and at worst 'incoherent'. It would, I believe, be incoherent. We could not each be entitled to be certain that we are the only person who could not make fundamental errors.

Blackburn might retreat to the view that *everyone* has a guarantee against fundamental moral error, since no one's stable moral attitudes could be false, or mistaken. But this revision would abandon Quasi-Realism, since this claim would imply that different people can have conflicting attitudes, and make conflicting judgments, none of which are false or mistaken.

Blackburn might instead reply that, on his view, each of us could still claim to know that our own judgments were true. We can talk of 'knowledge', Blackburn writes, if 'we rule out any possibility that an improvement might occur'. But we cannot turn our judgments into *knowledge* merely by claiming that we could not possibly be mistaken. And people with conflicting judgments might all make such claims.

Blackburn gives another defence of his Expressivist Quasi-Realism. When we ask what may seem to be external, *meta-ethical* questions, Blackburn claims, these may really be internal *moral* questions.

This *internalizing* response can be justifiably applied to some questions. As Blackburn says, we can use 'true' in a minimal sense, which is merely a way of repeating some claim. If you said that honey meringues were even more disgusting than milk chocolate, I would say 'That's true'. Suppose that someone asks Blackburn whether it is really true that, for example, cruelty is wrong. On Blackburn's Expressivist view, he could answer 'Yes', since this answer would express his disapproving attitude towards such acts. Someone might next object that, on Blackburn's view, cruelty isn't really in itself wrong, since what makes cruelty wrong is only Blackburn's attitude towards such acts. Blackburn could reply that, on his view, what makes cruelty wrong is not his disapproval of such acts, but the suffering that these acts cause. This reply would reflect the fact that Blackburn's attitude to cruelty is a response, not to his own attitude, but to this suffering.

As Blackburn admits, however, there are some meta-ethical questions that cannot be regarded as internal moral questions. We are now discussing one such question. We are not asking whether, on Blackburn's view, it is really true that cruelty is wrong. We are asking what it would *be*, on such Non-Cognitivist theories, for some moral judgment to be true or false, correct or mistaken. Since we are not asking whether some *particular* moral judgment is true, our question is morally neutral, and cannot be given an internal moral answer. And we may be right to conclude that Non-Cognitivists cannot answer this question, since there is no intelligible sense in which, on Non-Cognitivist theories, moral judgments might be true or false, correct or mistaken.

Blackburn tries to avoid this conclusion. Making an internalizing move, he writes:

> To think that there are no moral truths is to think that
> nothing should be morally endorsed, that is, to endorse the
> endorsement of nothing, and this attitude of indifference is
> one that it would be wrong to recommend and silly to practise.

But this claim is unjustified. When other Non-Cognitivists say that there are no moral truths, they are not making the *moral* claim that we ought not to make any moral claims. They are making the quite different *meta-ethical* claim that, even if moral claims can be said to be true in some minimal sense, such claims cannot be true or false in the strong sense to which Moral Cognitivists or Realists appeal. This, moreover, is Blackburn's own view. Blackburn writes:

> There is no problem of relativism because there is no
> problem of moral truth . . . moral opinion is not in the
> business of representing the world.
>
> . . . if realism were true . . . there would be a fact, a state of
> affairs (the wrongness of cruelty) . . . But anti-realism
> acknowledges no such states of affairs.

These, we can add, are not internal moral claims. When Non-Cogniti-vists claim that there is no property of wrongness that cruelty might have, and no such state of affairs or fact, they do not thereby reject the abhorrence of cruelty that humane Humeans like Blackburn eloquently express.

Blackburn elsewhere writes that, if some Non-Cognitivist adopts the Expressivist strategy, this person can tell us what is involved when someone *believes* that something is good. But if we

> go on to ask this strategist what it is for something to *be* good, the response is that this is not the subject of this theoretical concern—that is, not the subject of concern for those of us who, while naturalists, want a theory of ethics. Either the question illegitimately insists that trying to analyze the ethical proposition is the only possible strategy, which is not true. Or it must be heard in an ethical tone of voice. To answer it would then be to go inside the domain of ethics, and start expressing our standards.

Blackburn here suggests that we cannot legitimately ask Expressivist Non-Cognitivists what it would *be*, on their theories, for something to be good. But we *can* legitimately ask *Cognitivists* this question, and these people can give us answers. Cognitivists might tell us, for example, what it would be for something to be good in the reason-involving sense. If we ought not to ask Non-Cognitivist Expressivists what it would be, on their theories, for something to be good, this would have to be because we already know that, according to these Expressivists, nothing *could* be good, so that it would be pointless, or discourteous, to ask these people to explain how, on their view, something might be good.

Blackburn gives a similar answer to one of my earlier objections. As a Quasi-Realist Expressivist, Blackburn claims, he doesn't need to explain what it would *be*, on his view, for our conative attitudes or judgments to be false or mistaken. In his words:

> If some theorist . . . asks me what my account of moral error *itself* is, then I am not very forthcoming . . . It is much more in the spirit of quasi-realism . . . to avoid such formulations. This is not an ad hoc move, but an integral part of the package . . . the quasi-realist . . . avoids saying *what it is* for a moral claim to be true, except in boring homophonic or deflationary terms.

The only answer we should recognize to the question 'what is it for happiness to be good?' is happiness being good.

But as Blackburn earlier wrote,

> quasi-realism is trying to earn our right to talk of moral truth, while recognizing fully the subjective sources of our judgments.

As Blackburn rightly claimed, Quasi-Realists need to *earn* this right. On Blackburn's view, though our moral judgments fundamentally express certain kinds of desire or other conative attitude, such judgments can be true or false. That is a bold and surprising claim, which needs to be both explained and defended. When Blackburn applies his Quasi-Realism to some other areas of our thinking, such as our beliefs about probabilities and counterfactuals, he persuasively defends our right to call some of these beliefs true.

In the longer passage just quoted, however, Blackburn merely asserts that Quasi-Realists have this right. When we ask what it would be, on Blackburn's view, for us to judge truly that happiness is good, Blackburn replies: 'This judgment would be true if happiness is good'. We judge truly that some act is wrong, Blackburn would similarly say, if this act *is* wrong. Such claims cannot give Expressivists the right to talk of moral truth. We judge truly that some headache is mistaken, I might similarly claim, if this headache *is* mistaken. For Quasi-Realist Expressivists to *earn* their right to talk of moral truth, they must explain what it would be, on their view, for it to be true that some act is wrong. That is why I could not hope to defend Quasi-Realist Expressivism about headache judgments. I could not earn a right to call these judgments true, because I could not explain what it would *be* for it to be true that some headache is mistaken.

Return now to Blackburn's claim that, by appealing to the idea of an improved standpoint, Expressivists can explain a sense in which, like any Realist or Cognitivist, they can think 'I might be wrong'. In this way, Blackburn writes, Expressivists can both hold fast to emotivism and perfectly imitate, or 'mimic', this 'alleged realist thought'. That, I have argued, is not true. But even if these claims were justified, they would not answer our questions. We are asking whether there are truths about decisive reasons, and about what we ought to do. These are not questions about what we can perfectly mimic, or pretend to think.

Quasi-Realism could not, I believe, succeed. Suppose that, as Moral Sentimentalists believe, morality essentially involves certain desires or other conative attitudes towards our own and other people's acts. There are then two possibilities. If these attitudes can be correct or mistaken, we should be Realists or Cognitivists. On such a Cognitivist view, our moral judgments would be true whenever we judge some attitude to be correct which is in fact, as we believe, correct. Our moral judgments would be false whenever we judge some attitude to be correct which is in fact mistaken. We could justifiably reject such Cognitivist views only if these conative attitudes cannot be either correct or mistaken. Only then should we believe that our moral judgments cannot be true or false, and *merely express* such conative attitudes. Quasi-Realist Expressivists therefore face a dilemma. To defend their Non-Cognitivist Expressivism, these people must claim that our conative attitudes cannot be correct or mistaken. To defend their Quasi-Realism, these people must claim that these attitudes *can* be correct or mistaken. These people must therefore claim that these attitudes both cannot be, and can be, correct or mistaken. Since that is impossible, no such view could be true.

29

Normativity and Truth

102 Expressivism

Gibbard and Blackburn might object that, in criticizing their views, I have failed to take seriously their *Expressivism*. When I ask what it would *be* for normative judgments to be correct or mistaken, I assume that we need to know what would make such judgments true or false. This 'truth conditions approach', Blackburn objects, is not 'the only possible strategy'. Expressivists explain such judgments in a different way.

Gibbard gives an Expressivist account of rationality. His aim, he writes, is to explain 'what "rational" means'. But Gibbard does not directly answer this question. There is, he claims, no such property as that of being rational. Since that is so, we cannot explain the word 'rational' by describing what it is for something to be rational. The best we can do is to describe

> what it is for someone to *judge* that something is rational. We explain the term . . . 'rational', by saying what state of mind it expresses.

Some Expressivist claims are not worth making. We might claim that, in saying

> (A) X is good,

we *express our approval* of X. But this claim would not help if, as is likely, we use 'approve' to mean 'believe to be good'. We might similarly claim that, in saying

(B) The Earth is round,

we express our belief in the roundness of the Earth. Such claims are unhelpful in two ways. There is no difference between *stating* and *expressing* a belief. And such explanations fail when they use the concept that we are trying to explain.   Consider next

(C) Good-bye!

Here, in contrast, Expressivism helps. Since (C) does not state a belief, it is worth saying that (C) originally expressed the wish or prayer 'God be with you!', and is now conventionally used to express, to those from whom we are about to be parted, an attitude of good will.

To explain what 'rational' means, Gibbard claims that, in saying

(D) It is irrational to be angry with bringers of bad news,

we express our acceptance of a *norm* against such anger. Whether this account is helpful depends on what this norm is claimed to be. If this norm were

(E) There is no reason to be angry with such people,

this account would have both the flaws just mentioned. In expressing our acceptance of (E), we would be merely stating our belief in (E). And since (E) uses the concept of a normative reason, an appeal to (E) could not explain what 'rational' means in helpfully different, non-normative terms, as Gibbard intends to do.

Gibbard's account avoids both these flaws. Gibbard claims that, in saying (D), we express our acceptance of a norm like

(F) Don't be angry with bringers of bad news!

Like 'Good-bye!', (F) does not state some belief. And since (F) does not use any normative concept, Gibbard's claim might explain (D) in non-normative terms.

Gibbard uses the word 'norm' to 'mean simply a prescription or imperative'. Imperatives are commands, like 'Shut the door!' Such sentences cannot be either true or false. We *accept* some imperative, not by believing something, but by deciding to do what this imperative tells us to do. Imperatives are not normative, though they are sometimes used to express norms, as when we say 'Don't steal!' or 'Don't spell "committee" with only one "t"!'

There is another way in which Gibbard's account may seem to be unhelpful. Gibbard claims that, when we try to decide whether some act is rational, we are trying to decide *whether to accept* some imperative. This claim may suggest that we are trying to decide whether we have sufficient or decisive reasons to accept this imperative, or whether we ought rationally to accept it. But this account would then be using the very concepts — *reason*, *ought*, and *rational* — which it claims to explain.

As before, Gibbard avoids this objection. On Gibbard's account, we do not try to decide which imperatives we *ought* to accept, or have *reasons* to accept. We merely decide which imperatives *to accept*. Deciding what we *ought* to do, Gibbard later claims, is the same as *choosing* what to do.

Gibbard makes some other suggestions, of a socio-biological kind, about what is involved when organisms like human beings accept such imperatives. An imperative, Gibbard writes,

> is a formulation of a pattern which, in effect, controls the organism's behavior. . . . If a norm is simply an imperative, the real psychological question is what it is to internalize it. A norm prescribes a pattern of behavior, and to internalize a norm . . . is to have a motivational tendency of a particular kind to act on that pattern.

We are not the only animals, Gibbard remarks, who are subject to 'normative governance'. The capacity to 'internalize norms' is 'one we share with other mammals', such as wild dogs. But though other animals *internalize* norms, only we, because we have language, can also *accept* norms. Gibbard writes:

> The capacity to accept norms I portray as a human biological adaptation; accepting norms figures in a

peculiarly human system of motivation and control
that depends on language.

To 'accept a norm', he continues, 'is to be prepared to avow it in normative discussion'. Or more exactly, 'accepting a norm is whatever psychic state, if any, gives rise to this syndrome of avowal of the norm and governance by it.'

As these quotations show, Gibbard's account avoids circularity. If a norm is 'simply an imperative', if other animals can 'internalize' such imperatives, and if what we add to their 'system of motivation' is only the 'avowal' of these imperatives, Gibbard's account does not use materials which contain the very feature—normativity—that he is trying to explain.

Return now to Gibbard's main aim: to explain 'what 'rational' means'. If we can explain this idea, Gibbard writes, this would help us to decide 'how it is rational to conduct our lives. What are we asking? It seems the widest question in life: how to live.'

When Gibbard rejects Naturalist accounts of words like 'rational', he rightly claims that these accounts make it impossible to ask such questions.   Does Gibbard's account do better?

I believe not. If we apply Gibbard's account to these questions, we soon face a blank wall.   Gibbard writes, for example:

> What is it, then, for an act or a way of feeling to be rational?
> In what way does a person who calls something rational
> endorse it?

Our disappointment here is swift. Though Gibbard starts by asking *what it is* for some act or feeling to be rational, he turns at once to a different question. On Gibbard's view, since there isn't any property of being rational, there can't be anything *that it is* for some act or feeling to be rational. There are only endorsements of imperatives, such as, 'Do this!' or 'Dislike that!' In asking how it is rational to live, we are choosing between such imperatives. Nor could we ask which imperatives it would be rational for us to choose, since no choice could *be* rational.

Gibbard would reply that, in making these claims, I am begging the question. I am assuming that, in believing that some act or choice is rational, we are believing it to be true that this act or choice has the property of being rational. On Gibbard's view, that is not so. To believe some act to be rational isn't really to have a belief, but to accept the imperative 'Act like that!' Gibbard would say that, if his account is correct, and we accept this imperative, we *can* claim that such acts are rational. And he writes, that, on his view, we can believe that various acts

really are rational or irrational, right or wrong.

This reply, I believe, fails. Like many great philosophers, Gibbard tries to have things both ways. On Gibbard's view, acts cannot really be rational. As he writes, 'to call a thing rational is not to state a matter of fact, either truly or falsely'. But Gibbard also claims that, even if we accept his view, we can go on believing that certain acts *really are* rational. We can sometimes have things both ways. If you said 'Milk chocolate is disgusting', I could both reply 'That's true' and then consistently deny that, on my view, milk chocolate truly or really has the property of being disgusting. But that is because, in saying 'That's true', I would be merely expressing the same dislike. When we believe that some act truly is rational, or that we really do have decisive reasons to act in some way, are we using *truly* or *really* in this minimal, expressivist sense?

I believe not. Like Naturalist accounts, Gibbard's account makes it impossible to ask certain important questions. If we interpret our questions in the way that Gibbard suggests, they cease to be the questions that we wanted to ask, or thought we were asking. For example, we can't really ask what it would be rational for us to do.

As before, Gibbard would reject this claim, since he often writes of what is 'rational in the expressivistic sense'. But this phrase is misleading. There is no expressivistic sense in which acts could *be* rational. Acts can merely have the property of conforming to the imperatives that I accept, or the imperatives that you accept, or the imperatives that other people accept. If some act conforms to one of these imperatives, that is not a way of *being expressivistically rational*. It would be empty for me to claim that an act is rational in the expressivistic sense if this act conforms to *my* imperatives. You could say the same about acts that conform to *your* imperatives. The truth would be only that some acts conform to my imperatives, while others conform to yours.

Gibbard's account, he concedes, seems to leave something out. When a person calls something rational, Gibbard writes,

> he seems to be doing more than simply expressing his own
> acceptance of a system of norms . . . he claims to recognize
> and report something that is true independently of what he
> himself happens to accept or reject. Perhaps he is wrong. But
> that is the claim he is making . . . . If the person claims
> objective backing and the analysis misses the claim, then
> the analysis is defective.

Some 'claims to objectivity', Gibbard then replies, 'are well explained by norm-expressivism'. When we accept some norm, we need not regard this norm as depending on our acceptance of it.   In his words:

> If a person thinks something a matter of taste, then he does
> not think, 'This taste would be valid even if I lacked it'. In
> matters of rationality, in contrast, we do think, 'This norm
> would be valid even if I did not accept it'.

Expressivists, Gibbard argues, are able to make such claims. If I say, for example, that slavery is wrong, my attitude is a response to certain features of slavery. Since my attitude is a response to these features, I would naturally extend my attitude to an imagined case in which, though I didn't have this attitude, slavery still had these features. I might say 'Don't enslave people, even if I cease to accept this imperative!'

It is true that, as Gibbard here claims, some of our attitudes are not conditional on our continuing to have these attitudes. If we want some enemy to suffer, for example, our desire may not be conditional on its own persistence. We may want our enemy to suffer whether or not we continue to have this desire. But as this example shows, this kind of non-conditionality doesn't amount, as Gibbard claims, to a kind of *objectivity*.

Gibbard then says that, when he expresses some norm, 'I demand acceptance of what I am saying'. 'This demand', he writes,

> is part of what has been missing in the analysis. Before, I said roughly that when a person calls something 'rational' he is expressing his acceptance of norms that permit it . . . Now I say he is doing more: he is making a conversational demand. He is demanding that the audience accept what he says, that it share the state of mind that he expresses.

When we make such demands, as Gibbard notes, we are not merely issuing orders. We are making claims that we believe to have 'normative authority'. He then writes:

> To claim authority is to demand influence . . . . I say, implicitly, 'Accept these norms!'

Most of us do not, I believe, claim *authority* for ourselves. We would at most claim authority for the principles to which we are appealing. And if we did claim authority, we would not be *demanding influence*. That would be to confuse authority with power. Suppose I claim that you ought not to accept two contradictory beliefs. We would misdescribe this use of 'ought' if we said that I am *demanding* that you accept my claim.

As before, Gibbard notes this point. He writes, 'I as a speaker do not simply demand; I claim to have a basis for my demands.' When I disagree with someone, I claim 'to be "seeing" something that she doesn't: that the fundamental norms she accepts just don't make sense'. On Gibbard's account, however, there is nothing to see, since there are no truths about what 'makes sense'. And if we decide not to accept some imperative, that is not seeing that something does not make sense.

Gibbard similarly talks of our finding norms 'credible'. And he writes, 'The fact that I would enjoy something speaks in favor of doing it. I find that self-evident.' But on Gibbard's view, norms are imperatives, and when we believe that some fact 'speaks in favor' of some act, we are merely accepting some imperative, such as 'Do what I enjoy!' Unlike some belief or normative claim, imperatives like 'Do what I enjoy!' cannot be either *credible* or *self-evident*.

Gibbard might reply that, as he and Blackburn claim,

> normative judgments mimic factual judgments . . . [or] the
> search for truth.

Though the relevant norm is, really, 'Act like that!', we express this
norm in a way that mimics some factual belief, by saying 'Such acts
are rational'. Our attitude to this imperative could then similarly *mimic*
finding some belief to be credible, self-evident, or obviously true. Such
mimicry might seem, to Quasi-Realists, enough.

When Gibbard sums up his aims, he writes:

> Above all, I hope, the analysis will help us understand why it
> matters which acts and feelings are rational.

But as before, if Gibbard's view were true, there would be nothing to
understand. Since there is no expressivistic sense in which anything
could be rational, there would be no point in asking which acts and
feelings are rational. Nor could anything matter. Just as our normative
beliefs could only mimic the search for truth, things could only mimic
mattering. Since a mimic is a fake, or sham, such mimicry is not
enough.

Gibbard's analysis, he also claims,

> can transform our view of what we are doing when we ponder
> fundamental normative questions, and allow us to proceed
> more effectively in our normative thinking.

Gibbard's analysis would indeed transform the view that most of
us, or many of us, accept. If we became convinced that there are
no truths about what is rational, or about reasons, or about what
we ought to do, we would cease to believe that normative questions
could have answers. Our normative thinking would then be easier, since we would cease to worry that we might be getting things
wrong. But that would not make our thinking *more effective*, since it
would not help us to get things right. There would be nothing to get
right.

After claiming that there are no truths about what is rational, or about reasons, Gibbard writes that this claim does not leave 'normative language defective, or second rate'. That depends on whether, as Gibbard admits that our 'ordinary thought' assumes, there are truths about what is rational, and about reasons. If there are no such truths, our normative thinking *would* be defective, since we would be wrong to assume that our beliefs about rationality and reasons might be true. Accepting Gibbard's view would free us from that illusion. If instead there *are* such truths, accepting Gibbard's view would blind us to them.

Gibbard also hopes that, when we are trying to decide 'what really matters and why', his account of normativity can make some 'fruitful' answers 'seem evident and right'. If Gibbard's view were true, however, no answer could *be* right. And if we really accepted and understood this view, no answer could even *seem* to be evident or right. Phrases like 'what really matters' would be seen merely to mimic the search for truth.

As Gibbard writes, the most important question is:

> Can I ever be mistaken in an *ought* judgment? . . . Do
> we discover how best to live, or is it a matter of
> arbitrary choice . . .?

On Gibbard's view, I have argued, there would be nothing to discover. We could never be mistaken in our judgments about how it would be better or worse to live, since this *would* just be a matter of arbitrary choice.

Unlike many Non-Cognitivists, Gibbard realizes that his view cannot be restricted to practical reasons: reasons for caring and for acting. In his words, 'Norms are fundamental to thought . . . we cannot think at all without some implicit guidance by norms'. Just as 'what it is rational to do settles what to do . . . what it is rational to believe settles what to believe'. Remember finally that, on Gibbard's view, 'to call a thing rational is not to state a matter of fact, either truly or falsely'. If there could not be facts or truths about what it is rational to believe, as Gibbard's view implies, it could not be rational to believe anything, including Gibbard's view.

This bleak view is close to Nihilism.

103 Hare on What Matters

So are some other people's views. A young Swiss guest of Hare's, after reading a novel by Camus, concluded in despair that *nothing matters*. Hare suggested that his friend should ask 'what was the meaning or function of the word 'matters' in our language; what is it to be important?' His friend soon agreed, Hare writes,

> that when we say something matters or is important, what
> we are doing, in saying this, is to express our concern about
> that something . . . Having secured my friend's agreement on
> this point, I then pointed out to him something that followed
> immediately from it. This is that when somebody says that
> something matters or does not matter, we want to know *whose*
> concern is being expressed or otherwise referred to. If the
> function of the expression 'matters' is to express concern,
> and if concern is always *somebody's* concern, we can always
> ask, when it is said that something matters or does not matter,
> 'Whose concern?'

As Hare pointed out, his friend *was* concerned about several things. So is everyone—except a few fictional characters in existentialist novels. People's values differ, and may change. But since we all care about something, 'it is impossible to overthrow values as a whole'. Hare's treatment worked. 'My Swiss friend ate a hearty breakfast the next morning.'

If someone doubts whether anything matters, it may not help to ask 'Whose concern?' Hare managed to convince his friend

> that the expression 'Nothing matters' in his mouth could only
> be (if he understood it) a piece of play-acting. Of course he
> didn't actually understand it.

The word 'matters' has a meaning, I believe, which Hare did not understand. Things can matter in the sense that their nature gives us reasons to care about them.

When Hare writes that we use such words to *express* concern, he is not, he claims, using 'express' in an 'emotivist' sense. But Hare does accept an Emotivist, Expressivist, or more broadly, Non-Cognitivist view. That is why, when Hare's friend concluded in despair that nothing matters, Hare didn't remind his friend that some things, such as suffering, really do matter.   As Hare writes:

> My friend . . . had thought that mattering was something
> (some activity or process) that things did . . . If one thinks
> that, one may begin to wonder what this activity is, called
> mattering; and one may begin to observe the world closely . . .
> to see if one can catch anything doing something that could be
> called 'mattering'; and when we can observe nothing going on
> which seems to correspond to this name, it is easy for the nov-
> elist to persuade us that after all *nothing matters*. To which the
> answer is, ' "Matters" isn't that sort of word; it isn't intended
> to *describe* something . . .'

On Hare's view, it makes no sense to describe something as mattering. The truth is only that we care about some things. In saying that these things matter, we are not *claiming* that they matter, but are merely expressing our concern.

Hare assumes that, in making these claims, he is not denying anything that other people might believe. There is nothing to deny, he claims, since no other view makes sense.   Hare imagines an objector saying:

> All you have done is to show that people are *in fact* concerned
> about things. But this established only the existence of values
> in a *subjective* sense.

Hare then writes:

> I do not understand what is *meant* by the 'objectivity of
> values', and have not met anybody who does . . . suppose we

ask 'What is the difference between values being objective,
and values not being objective?' Can anybody point to any
difference? In order to see clearly that there is *no* difference,
it is only necessary to consider statements of their position by
subjectivists and objectivists, and observe that they are saying
the same thing in different words . . . An objectivist . . . says,
'When I say that a certain act is wrong, I am stating the
fact that the act has a certain non-empirical *quality* called
'wrongness' . . . A subjectivist says, 'When *I* say that a
certain act is wrong I am expressing towards it an attitude
of disapproval which I have.'

When Hare claims that there is no difference between these views,
he assumes that objectivists cannot mean what they say. There *is*
a disagreement here. As Hare writes, some objectivists believe that
there are facts about which acts have the non-empirical 'quality' or
property of being wrong. Hare's 'subjectivists'—by whom he means
Expressivists—deny that acts have any such property.

Hare continues:

> We all know how to recognize the activity which I have been
> calling 'saying, thinking it to be so, that some act is wrong'.
> And it is obvious that it is to this activity that the subjectivist
> and the objectivist are both alluding. This activity . . . is called
> by the objectivist 'a moral intuition'. By the subjectivist it is
> called 'an attitude of disapproval'. But in so far as we can
> identify anything in our *experience* to which these two people
> could be alluding by these expressions, it is the same thing—
> namely the experience which we all have when we think
> that something is wrong.

As before, Hare misdescribes what objectivists believe. When these
people claim that some acts really are wrong, they are not referring or
alluding to the experience that we all have when we believe some act
to be wrong. Their claim is about *what* we believe. More exactly, it is
about what some of us believe. Objectivists might concede that some

people—such as some Expressivists or Nihilists—do not have such beliefs.

Hare might reply that *he* has such beliefs. He is discussing the activity of 'saying, *thinking it to be so*, that some act is wrong.' Such beliefs, Hare elsewhere claims, are not like ordinary, *descriptive* beliefs. In thinking something to be wrong, we are not believing something to be true, but accepting the universal imperative 'No one ever act like that!' If Hare gave this reply, however, he would be conceding that there is a disagreement here. According to objectivists, these beliefs *are* descriptive, since they are intended to state normative truths.

Hare then considers another way in which some objectivists explain their view. These people claim that, when two moral judgments conflict, at least one of these judgments must be mistaken, since such conflicting judgments could not both be true. Subjectivists, these people argue, cannot make this claim. Hare replies that, though this claim can explain objectivity in some other areas, it does not, when applied to morality, draw any 'real distinction'. In his words:

> Behind this argument lies, I think, the idea that if it is
> possible to say that it is *right* or *wrong* to say a certain thing,
> an affinity of some important kind is established between that
> sort of thing, and other things of which we can also say this.
> So, for example, if we can say of the answer to a mathematical
> problem that it is right, and can say *the same thing* of a moral
> judgment, this is held to show that a moral judgment is in
> some way *like* the answer to a mathematical problem, and
> therefore cannot be 'subjective' (whatever that means).

That is what it means. Like answers to mathematical problems, moral judgments can be objective in the sense that they can be right or wrong, by being true or false.

104 The Normativity Argument

Hare sometimes gives a different argument. Objectivism, he claims, is self-defeating. As he writes:

> moral judgments cannot be merely statements of fact, and . . .
> if they were, they would not do the jobs that they do do, or
> have the logical characteristics that they do have. In other
> words, moral philosophers cannot have it both ways; either
> they must recognize the irreducibly prescriptive element in
> moral judgments, or else they must allow that moral
> judgments, as interpreted by them, do not guide actions in
> the way that, as ordinarily understood, they obviously do.

These claims are puzzling. Hare assumes that, if moral judgments were capable of being true, or stating facts, they could not guide actions. But if we judged truly that we ought to do something, that judgment could guide our actions.

Many other writers make such claims. There is a reason, Blackburn writes, why Expressivist Non-Cognitivism 'has to be correct'. If our normative judgments were beliefs, such as beliefs about what we have reasons to do or what we ought to do, these beliefs could not, even if they were true, answer practical questions. For any such alleged normative truth, 'there is a question of what to do about it'. To provide answers to practical questions, normative judgments cannot be beliefs about some normative truth, but must express some kind of desire or other conative attitude.

Gibbard similarly claims that, when applied to the judgments with which we make decisions, 'expressivism has to be right'. According to Non-Naturalists like Sidgwick, asking what we *ought* to do is different from asking *what to do*. Gibbard claims that, if these were different questions, asking what we *ought* to do could not help us to decide what to do. Non-Naturalists, Gibbard writes:

> just change the subject. We ask what to do, and they hand
> us analyses of a different question.

Like Blackburn, Gibbard here assumes that normative truths or facts could not answer practical questions. To illustrate this assumption, suppose that, in *Burning Hotel*, you decide that you ought to jump into the canal, because that is your only way to save your life. On Gibbard's view, if it was merely a normative fact that you ought to jump, and your coming to believe this fact was not a decision to jump, your belief that you ought to jump could not help you to decide whether to jump. That is clearly false.

Gibbard makes another, more cautious claim. He supposes that, as Non-Naturalists believe, possible acts can have the non-natural property of being what we ought to do, and that when some act has this property that would 'settle' the question of what to do. Even on these assumptions, Gibbard writes, we would never need to ask what we ought to do. It would always be enough to consider the natural facts about our different possible acts, and then decide to act in one of these ways. Nothing would be gained by our having true beliefs about what we ought to do.

Nowell-Smith similarly writes: 'Moral philosophy is a practical science; its aim is to answer questions of the form 'What shall I do?' But he then warns that 'no general answer can be given to this type of question'. That is an understatement. As Nowell-Smith notes, the word 'shall' is ambiguous. If we ask 'What shall I feel?', for example, the answer would be a prediction, which other people might correctly give. But when we ask 'What shall I do?', we are not trying to predict our acts. We are trying to make a decision. If moral philosophy had the aim of answering such questions, it could not possibly succeed. Moral philosophy cannot make our decisions.

Nor can other people. When we ask 'What shall I do?', that is not a question to which even the wisest adviser could give an answer. If I say, 'That's what I shall do', others might say, 'No you shan't', or 'No you won't.' But these claims would not make my decision. They would be either a prediction, or the expression of a contrary decision—as when a parent says to a child 'You *will do* what I tell you to.'

As these remarks imply, the question 'What shall I do?' is not normative. Nor can this question be, as Nowell-Smith claims, 'the fundamental question of ethics'. The fundamental question is: 'What *should* I, *ought* I, or *must* I do?' Moral philosophy, or other people, might help us to answer *this* question.

Nowell-Smith considers this objection, and replies:

> My reason for treating the 'shall' question as fundamental is
> that moral discourse is practical. The language of 'ought' is

intelligible only in the context of practical questions, and we have not answered a practical question until we have reached a decision.

Though moral discourse is practical, that does not imply that its fundamental question is about what we *shall* do, rather than what we *ought* to do. We may have already decided that we shall do, or shall try to do, whatever we conclude that we ought to do. In answering such moral questions, we would then be answering Nowell-Smith's question, by deciding what to do.

Like the other people from whom I have quoted, Nowell-Smith might now reply that, when we are trying to decide what to do, it would not help to form some belief about what we ought to do, since no such true *belief* could answer our question.

Such claims provide the third main argument for Non-Cognitivism. This argument extends two earlier claims. According to the Naturalist Argument for Non-Cognitivism:

> (A) Since all facts are natural, there could not be any normative truths.

Some Non-Cognitivists add

> (B) Even if there were such truths, no truths could answer normative questions.

Remember next that, in arguing against Naturalism, we can claim:

> (C) Natural facts could not be normative.

Non-Cognitivists, as I have said, accept (C). Some of them add

> (D) Even irreducibly normative facts would not really be normative.

(B) and (D) provide what we can call *the Normativity Argument for Non-Cognitivism*.

This argument is often stated in surprisingly self-undermining ways. When discussing Moore's alleged normative truths, for example, Nowell-Smith writes:

> No doubt it is all very interesting. If I happen to have a thirst
> for knowledge, I shall read on . . . Learning about 'values' or
> 'duties' might well be as exciting as learning about spiral
> nebulae or waterspouts. But what if I am not interested? Why
> should I *do* anything about these newly-revealed objects?
> Some things, I have now learnt, are right and others wrong;
> but why should I do what is right, and eschew what is wrong?

When words are 'used in the ordinary way', Nowell-Smith goes on to say, such questions would be absurd. But they 'would not be absurd if moral words were used in the way that intuitionists suppose'. In 'ordinary life there is no gap between "this is the right thing for me to do" and "I ought to do this"'. Nowell-Smith then objects that, if 'X is right' were taken to mean that X 'had the property' of being right, we *could* sensibly deny that we ought to do what is right.

There is an obvious reply. As well as asking which act would be right, we can ask what we ought to do. On Nowell-Smith's objection, if 'X is what we ought to do' were taken to mean that X had the property of being what we ought to do, we could sensibly deny that we ought to do what we ought to do.   That is not so.

Williams similarly writes that, if the claim that we ought to do something

> just tells one a fact about the Universe, one needs some
> further explanation of why [we] should take any notice
> of that particular fact.

Suppose that we knew another such fact, since we also knew why we should take notice of this fact about what we ought to do. On Williams's objection, we would still need some further explanation of why we should take any notice of this fact.   That is not so.

Hare similarly writes that, if it is merely a fact that some possible act has 'the moral property of wrongness, why should we be troubled by that?' But suppose we knew why we should be troubled by this act's wrongness. On Hare's objection, this would merely be another fact. Though we knew why we should be troubled, we could still sensibly ask why we should be troubled.   That is not so.

Korsgaard similarly writes:

> If it is just a *fact* that a certain action would be good, a fact that you might or might not apply to deliberation, then it seems to be an open question whether you *should* apply it.

But suppose that you *should* apply this fact to your deliberation. On Korsgaard's objection, since this would be just another fact, it would still be an open question whether you should apply this fact to your deliberation. That is not so. If it is a fact that you should do something, it is not an open question whether you should do it.

According to the writers that I have been discussing, normativity has nothing to do with truth. We can next consider some of Korsgaard's arguments for this view.

There are, I have claimed, some irreducibly normative truths. Korsgaard calls this view *normative realism*. Normative realists, Korsgaard argues, cannot help us to decide 'what, if anything, we really ought to do', nor can they *justify* the claim that morality makes on us.   Suppose, she writes:

> you are being asked to face death rather than do a certain action. You ask the normative question: you want to know whether this terrible claim on you is justified. Is it really true that this is what you *must* do? The realist's answer to this question is simply 'Yes'. That is, *all* he can say is that it is *true* that this is what you ought to do.

Practical reasoning, Korsgaard also claims, is not about what we should *believe*, but about what we should *do*. Realists misunderstand this difference. These people mistakenly assume that, when we ask 'practical normative questions . . . there is something . . . that we are trying to find out.' On their view, 'our relation to reasons is one of seeing that they are there or knowing truths about them.' Realism fails, Korsgaard claims, because no knowledge of truths about reasons could answer normative questions.

Korsgaard's objections to normative realism seem to be these:

> Realists discuss the wrong question.

> Realists may not be able to convince us that some answer to our question is really true.

> Even if our question had some true answer, that would not solve our problem. Ours is not a question to which some truth could be the answer.

These objections do not, I believe, succeed. If Korsgaard's question could not be answered by some truth, this question could not be normative. If we cannot convince some people that some answer is true, that is no objection to realism. If there are answers to normative questions, these answers would have to be truths. If there were no truths about what we have reasons to care about, or to do, we could not make better or worse decisions. We might as well act on impulse, toss coins, or do nothing. But there *are*, I believe, such truths. No disagreement could be deeper.

Return to Korsgaard's imagined doubter, who in some crisis asks

> Q1: Is it really true that this is what I must do?

Korsgaard discusses several ways of understanding this question, of which I shall here consider only one. Korsgaard's doubter might be asking:

> Q2: Do I have decisive reasons to act in this way?

Realists might answer 'Yes'. And they might convince this person that their claim is true, since this person really does have decisive reasons to act in this way. But Korsgaard's doubter could then ask

Q3: Why should I do what I have decisive reasons to do?

To this question, Korsgaard claims, realists would have no answer. Decisive reasons, if understood in a realist way, would not have any normative force. Realists 'cannot provide a coherent account of rationality'. According to these people, Korsgaard writes:

> rationality is a matter of conforming the will to standards of reason that exist independently of the will, as a set of truths about what there is reason to do . . . The difficulty with this account . . . exists right on its surface, for the account invites the question why it is rational to conform to those reasons, and seems to leave us in need of a reason to be rational.

Like the other writers quoted above, Korsgaard presents this objection in a surprisingly self-undermining way. According to what Korsgaard calls normative realism, when we know the relevant facts, we are rational if we want, and do, what we have decisive reasons to want, and do. So Korsgaard here claims that, if realism were true, we would need a reason to want, and do, what we knew that we had decisive reasons to want, and do. That is clearly false.

This may not, however, be what Korsgaard means. She continues:

> To put the point less tendentiously, we must still explain why the person finds it *necessary* to act on these normative facts, or what it is about her that makes them normative *for her*.

Suppose this person truly believes that there is something that she must do, in the decisive-reason-implying sense. Realists must still explain, Korsgaard writes, why this person *finds it necessary* to act on this normative fact, by doing what she believes that she must do. Korsgaard might be asking why this person believes it to be *normatively* necessary to do what she believes that she must do. But realists might answer that question. In believing truly that she must do something in the decisive-reason-implying sense, this person would be believing that this act is normatively necessary; and realists might explain this person's reasons for having this true belief.

Korsgaard may instead mean that realists must still explain why this person finds it *psychologically* necessary to do what she believes that she must do. When this person acts on these normative facts, Korsgaard writes, we must explain what makes these facts 'normative *for her*.' Korsgaard seems to be asking here what makes this person's normative belief *motivate* her. As Korsgaard goes on to write

> We must explain how these reasons *get a grip* on the agent.

If Korsgaard is using 'normative for her' to mean in part 'motivates her', she would be giving an account of decisive reasons, and of practical necessity, of the kind that Falk and Williams give. On this account, some act is practically necessary, or is what we must do, when there are facts belief in which would irresistibly move us to act in this way. Korsgaard would add that such practical necessity involves, or is created by, our will.

We have returned to one of our main questions: how we should understand normativity. Korsgaard would be right to claim that, when realists appeal to facts about what is normatively necessary, or about what we must do in the decisive-reason-implying sense, these people do not thereby explain how we are *motivated* to act in these ways. That is an objection to normative realism if, like many Naturalists and Non-Cognitivists, we assume that normativity is, or consists in, some kind of actual or hypothetical motivating force. But realists reject that assumption. When realists claim that we have decisive reasons to act in certain ways, they are not making claims about how, even in ideal conditions, we would be motivated or moved to act. On this view, as I have said, normativity is wholly different from, and does not include, motivating force.

There is a powerful objection, Korsgaard also claims, to any realist view. Realists face an infinite regress from which they cannot escape. When Korsgaard presents this objection, however, she ignores the replies that realists would make. She writes, for example:

> I ask you why you are doing some ordinary thing, and you
> give me your proximate reason, your immediate end. I then
> ask why you want that, and most likely you mention some
> larger end or project. I can press on, demanding your reason
> at every step, until we reach the moment when you are out
> of answers.

But Korsgaard also writes

> You have shown that your action is calculated to assist you in
> achieving what you think is desirable on the whole, what you
> have determined that you want most.

Korsgaard here assumes that, in judging something to be desirable, we
are judging that this thing is what we want most. If that were what we
meant by 'desirable', Korsgaard would be right to claim that we would
soon run out of answers. We would soon reach some desire for which
we could give no further desire-based justification. But Korsgaard's
realists are Objectivists about Reasons. Our aims are desirable, these
realists believe, when these aims have features that give us reasons to
have these aims, and to try to achieve them. If we have decisive or
sufficient reasons to have our aims, we would not, as Korsgaard claims,
run out of answers. We would answer by appealing to these reasons.

Korsgaard then supposes that we have adopted the maxim:

> 'I will do this action, in order to get what I desire.'

She comments:

> According to Kant, this maxim only determines your will if
> you have adopted another maxim that makes it your end to
> get what you desire. This maxim is:
>
> > 'I will make it my end to have the things that I desire.'
>
> Now suppose that I want to know why you have adopted this
> maxim. Why should you try to satisfy your desires?

This question could be used to challenge Subjectivists, who accept some desire-based theory about reasons. But as realist Objectivists, our maxim isn't to satisfy our desires. We respond to the facts that give us reasons to have our desires. Our maxim might be:

> I will make it my end to achieve whatever I have most reason to try to achieve, because these are the ends that are most worth achieving.

Korsgaard's question would then become:

> Why should you try to achieve what you have most reason to try to achieve?

Since 'Why?' asks for a reason, this would mean

> What reasons do you have to try to achieve what you have most reason to try to achieve?

This question answers itself.

Korsgaard also writes:

> We are here confronted with a deep problem of a familiar kind. If you can give a reason, you have derived it from some more fundamental maxim, and I can ask why you have adopted that one. If you cannot, it looks as if your principle was randomly selected. Obviously, to put an end to a regress like this, we need a principle about which it is impossible, unnecessary, or incoherent to ask why a free person would have chosen it.

As before, Korsgaard ignores the realist's view. Any reason, she assumes, must be derived from some maxim, or principle, which we have *adopted*. To solve her problem, Korsgaard claims, we must find some principle about which we cannot or need not ask why we have *chosen* it. But realists try to find truths about what we have reason to want, and to do. These truths would not be principles that we *adopt* or *choose*. We *believe* truths. And if we both believe such truths, and know why we ought to believe them, that would end Korsgaard's justificatory regress. Though it would not be impossible or incoherent to ask why we ought to believe these truths, this question would be unnecessary, since we would know the answer.

In trying to answer the normative question, Korsgaard adds, we are engaged in what Kant called 'the search for the unconditioned'. We are looking

> for something which will bring the reiteration of 'but why must I do that?' to an end . . . The realist move is to bring this regress to an end by *fiat*: he declares that some things are intrinsically normative . . . .

It isn't *realists* who end this regress by *fiat*. A *fiat* is an imperative, or command like 'Do that!' or 'Let that be done!' Unlike Korsgaard, realists do not believe that we can make something normative by commanding or willing that to be so.

Nor do realists merely *declare* that certain truths are normative. Realists believe that, as Korsgaard writes, when we ask normative questions 'there is something . . . that we are trying to find out.' On their view, such questions can have true answers.

On Korsgaard's view, even if there were such truths, they could not answer normative questions. To end the justificatory regress, we must appeal to motivational necessity, and to our own will. That, I have argued, is not so. Motivational necessities are not reasons, nor are they normative. And Korsgaard's regress could not be ended except in the way that she rejects. If we knew both *that* and *why* we must do something, we could not sensibly ask 'But why must we do it?'

There is something right in Korsgaard's view. Our practical reasoning should not end with such normative beliefs. To be fully practically rational, we must also respond to practical reasons or apparent reasons with our desires and acts. But only normative truths can answer practical questions. Normativity is not created by our will. What is normative are certain truths about what we have *reasons* to want, or will, or do.

If there were no such truths, there would be no point in trying to make good decisions. Nothing would matter, and there would not be better or worse ways to live.

30

Normative Truths

105 Disagreements

To introduce what follows, I shall now make some personal remarks.
Though I became a philosopher so that I would have more time to think
about what matters, much of this book is about other questions.   It
may be worth explaining why.

One reason is that, when we ask what matters, part of the answer is
obvious.   As Nagel writes:

> There are so many people one can barely imagine it . . . what
> happens to each of them is enormously important, as
> important as what happens to you. . . . what happens to
> anyone matters the same as if it had happened to anyone
> else . . . the elimination of the worst sufferings and
> deprivations matters most . . . The alleviation of misery,
> ignorance, and powerlessness and the elevation of most of
> our fellow human beings to a minimally decent standard of
> existence, seem overwhelmingly important.

These aims *are* overwhelmingly important.

When we ask what else matters, the answer is less obvious. Some of
my first thoughts were about which futures for humanity would be
better or worse. If the quality of future people's lives would be lower,
for example, could that be outweighed by the fact that there would be
more people who would live? I came across some puzzling problems

which I failed to solve. I also thought about some metaphysical questions whose answers might make a difference to our concerns, and to our reasons for concern.   I had what seemed some false beliefs about what is involved in my continuing to exist, and in its being true that various future experiences will be mine, or true that I shall be dead.   It seemed likely that many other people have similar false beliefs.   We may therefore misunderstand which are the facts that give us reasons to care about our future, and misjudge the strength of these reasons.   Since my thoughts about persons and personal identity had been influenced only by certain Western philosophers, I was encouraged to learn that Buddha seems to have reached similar conclusions.   We may also have false beliefs about the nature and rational significance of time.   We do not, I believe, have reasons to care more about the future than about the past.   What has happened is just as real as what will happen.   Nor is the past less real than the present.   Though people who are dead do not exist now, that is merely like the fact that people who live elsewhere do not exist here.   And time's passage is an illusion.

After starting to discuss these questions in my first book, I intended to think about them further.   As the contents of this new book show, that is not what happened.   I became increasingly concerned about certain differences between my views and the views of several other people. We seemed to disagree not only about what matters, but also about what it would *be* for things to matter, and about whether anything *could* matter.

I might have ignored these disagreements, and tried to answer my own unanswered questions.   But when other people's beliefs conflict with ours, that challenges our beliefs.   As Sidgwick writes:

> if I find any of my intuitions in direct conflict with an intuition
> of some other mind, there must be error somewhere: and if I
> have no more reason to suspect error in the other mind than
> in my own, reflective comparison between the two intuitions
> necessarily reduces me . . . to a state of neutrality.

Such disagreements give us reasons to doubt that we are the people whose beliefs are true.   These disagreements may also give us reasons to doubt that any of these conflicting beliefs are true.   Perhaps none of us is right, because our questions have no answers.

When we disagree with other people, we often have reasons to believe that we are the person who is more likely to be right.   Our opinions may be based on better evidence.   Those with whom we disagree may have earlier been less good in judging what the evidence gave them reasons to believe. And these people may be more likely to have deceived themselves, or to have been misled by some other distorting influence.

In some cases, however, no such claims are true. Those with whom we disagree may be responding to the same evidence, their judgment in other cases may have been as reliable as ours, and they may not be more likely to have been misled. Such people we can call our *epistemic peers*. When we disagree with such people, we should ask whether we have sufficient reasons to assume that it is our beliefs that are more likely to be true. If we conclude that we have no such reasons, we could not rationally keep these beliefs.

In such cases, we can often justifiably believe that we do have one such reason. Even if someone else's judgment has earlier been as good as ours, we now believe that this other person is making some mistake. Since we now believe that this person's judgment is less good than ours, we can justifiably believe that, in this disagreement, we are more likely to be right.

Such reasoning may seem question-begging, since it assumes the very belief whose truth we are trying to assess. But we can have reasons to believe that those with whom we often disagree have worse judgment than us, as is true, for example, of people who believe in astrology, or other superstitions. Since we can justifiably believe that those with whom we *often* disagree are less likely to be right, we can also justifiably have such beliefs even when we have only *one* such disagreement.

Enoch draws a helpful distinction here. Suppose we believe that two thermometers are equally reliable, or that two other people are epistemic peers. If we learn that these thermometers give conflicting readings, or these people have conflicting beliefs, we should believe that each is equally likely to be right. In such cases, there is complete symmetry. But when *we* disagree with someone else, there is always an *asymmetry*.

Since we believe that this other person is making a mistake, we can justifiably regard this person as less reliable than we earlier believed.

This asymmetry, however, may not be deep. In some of these cases, we should continue to give considerable weight to this other person's judgment. Given our new disagreement, we should regard *both* of us as less reliable than we earlier believed, and the difference is only that we should lose more confidence in this other person, whom we should now regard as somewhat less reliable than ourselves. We could not rationally be confident that we are right unless there seems to be some other asymmetry, which explains why it is this other person who is mistaken.

I believe very strongly, for example, that no one could ever deserve to suffer. Of the people in whose moral judgment I have most confidence, some disagree. When some wrong-doers suffer, these people believe, this suffering is in itself good, or at least not in itself bad. Though this belief seems to me mistaken, I would be greatly relieved if I could explain why these people are making this mistake. This may be one of the cases in which an evolutionary explanation helps to undermine what it explains. This retributive belief may seem to justify certain natural reactive attitudes, such as an angry desire to hurt, or the withdrawal of good will. These attitudes are like some simpler emotions that are had by the animals that are most like us. If evolution can explain why many people have these reactive attitudes, that might give some support to the view that these attitudes, and the widely held belief that such attitudes are justified, are not responses to reasons.

There are some other deep disagreements. Subjectivists believe that all practical reasons derive their force from certain facts about our present desires or aims. Objectivists believe that there are no such reasons, since all reasons derive their force from the facts that give us value-based reasons to have particular desires or aims. We ought, I have argued, to reject Subjectivism. Since there are many highly intelligent and rational Subjectivists, this disagreement disturbs me.

The deepest disagreements are about normativity. There are, I believe, some irreducibly normative, reason-involving truths. That is denied by Naturalists, Non-Cognitivists, and Nihilists. Since I disagree with these other people, there must be error somewhere. I cannot rationally keep my beliefs unless I can rationally assume that I am more likely to be right. Since I believe that these other people are mistaken, there is one asymmetry between us. But I cannot rationally have much confidence in my beliefs unless there seems to be some other asymmetry, which would explain why it is these other people, and not me, who have made mistakes.

There are often, I believe, such other asymmetries. My main example here will be the person from whom, in several disagreements, I have learned most. Williams was the most brilliant British moral philosopher whom I have known. If there were no other asymmetries between us, I could not rationally believe that it was I, rather than Williams, who was more likely to be right.

106 On How We Should Live

In Plato's *Republic*, Socrates asks:

> How should we live?

As Williams writes, Socrates did not mean 'How ought we morally to live?' Socrates meant

> Which kind of life is best? How do we have most
> reason to live?

This question leaves it open whether, as Plato believed and tried to show, 'a good life is also the life of a good person'.

Socrates asks which kind of life is *intrinsically*, or *in itself*, best. If we call something

> *intrinsically* good, we mean that this thing has intrinsic
> features or properties that make it good, or in which its
> goodness consists.

Of the things that Socrates, Plato, or others believe to be intrinsic goods, some examples are justice, happiness, benevolence, knowledge of important truths, trustworthiness, and love.

After discussing some of Plato's arguments, Williams suggests that we should 'give up the unrewarding idea of intrinsic goodness'. Williams's objections to this idea seem surprisingly superficial. If some things are intrinsically good, Williams writes, these things 'will have other properties' and their goodness 'will be explained by those properties'. Williams then asks:

> But what is the nature of the a priori guarantee . . . that such
> an explanation cannot refer to something else: for instance,
> that it might not be *improved* by referring to something else?
> Might it not be improved, for instance, by relating these
> properties to things that we value?

There *is* such a guarantee, which is implied by the concept of intrinsic goodness. Such goodness can only be explained by referring to something's *intrinsic* properties. We could not improve this explanation by referring to *something else*. If we claim that something is good because its intrinsic properties are related to other things that we value, we would be claiming that this thing is *extrinsically* or *derivatively* good. We might, for example, claim that justice, happiness, and knowledge are extrinsically good when they have good effects. But we can plausibly believe that these things are also intrinsically good. Williams's questions do not challenge this belief.

Williams also writes that, if there were such intrinsic goods, these would be things

> whose goodness was to be explained in advance of any
> human valuation.

Such goodness, he remarks, would be 'inexplicable'. In the phrase just quoted, Williams means that, if certain things were intrinsically good, we could not explain the goodness of these things by claiming that we valued them, or by referring to any of our other values. Our explanation would have to be the other way round. We would have to claim that we valued these things because of the ways in which they were good.

When Williams calls this kind of goodness 'inexplicable', he does not say what we would be unable to explain. In his only other directly relevant remark, Williams writes:

> There is a danger that if trustworthiness (or anything else) is
> regarded as having an intrinsic value, it will be supposed that

there is nothing else to be said about its valuableness — it is
good because it is good, and that is all there is to be
said about it.

We could also say, however, that any such thing has other properties
that make it good. On Plato's view, for example, what makes justice
good is, in part, that justice involves harmony between the different
parts of a city, or a soul.

Williams has a deeper objection to such claims. We have returned to
the disagreement between Objectivism and Subjectivism about reasons.
When we call something

intrinsically good in the *reason-implying* sense, we mean that
this thing has intrinsic properties that would or might give
us or others strong reasons to respond to this thing in some
positive way, such as wanting, choosing, or trying to achieve
this thing.

As a Subjectivist, Williams believes that there are no such *object-given*
reasons, since all reasons are provided by certain facts about our present
desires or values. This is why Williams finds the idea of intrinsic
goodness 'inexplicable'.

If we give up this idea, as Williams recommends, that would make a
great difference. The ancient Greeks had various beliefs about what
would make some life 'rationally desirable', in the sense of being a life
that we have reasons to want to live. Williams believes that nothing
could be in this sense desirable.   Suppose again that, in

Early Death, unless you take some medicine, you will later
die much younger, losing many years of happy life. Though
you know this fact, and you have deliberated in a procedurally
rational way on this and all of the other relevant facts, you are
not motivated to take this medicine.

Williams claims that you have no reason to take this medicine. It would
make no difference even if, by avoiding this early death, you could give

yourself one of the best and most rationally desirable lives. You have no reason to want to give yourself such a life.

Moral philosophy, Williams admits, can best *start* with Socrates' question. But philosophers have made progress since the ancient Greeks, and we should now turn to a simpler question.   Socrates asked

> Q1: Which kind of life is best? How do we have most reason to live?

Williams suggests that each of us should ask instead

> Q2: What do I basically want?

When he discusses Socrates' question, Williams writes:

> The answer . . . might be: the best way for me to live is to do at any given time what I most want to do at that time.

This is roughly the answer that Williams himself accepts. When we are deciding what to do, Williams believes, we need not ask which aims, acts, or outcomes would be intrinsically better or worse in the reason-implying senses. Nothing could be in these senses better or worse. It is enough to ask certain questions about what we want.

'The aims of moral philosophy,' Williams also writes, 'and any hopes it may have of being worth serious attention, are bound up with the fate of Socrates' question'. If Socrates' question should become Q2, moral philosophy would have to give up these hopes. And non-philosophers would have no reason to try to decide what matters, or what they had reasons to care about. We would never have any such reasons. So it may matter greatly whether, as Williams claims, we should give up the idea that some ways of living are intrinsically better than others.

107 Misunderstandings

When Williams makes claims about reasons for acting, he may seem to be using the phrase 'a reason' in the indefinable normative sense that we can also express with the phrase 'counts in favour'. That is how Scanlon interprets Williams's view.   This view, Scanlon writes,

> does not reflect skepticism about reasons in the standard normative sense . . . Williams seems to be offering a substantive, normative thesis about what reasons we have.

This interpretation is, I believe, mistaken. Williams did not understand this concept of a reason.

That remark is not, as it may seem, arrogant and rude. Williams uses the phrase 'a reason' in a different, *internal* sense, which he explicitly defines. When we say that someone has a reason to do something, Williams claims, we mean roughly that, after informed and procedurally rational deliberation, this person would be motivated to act in this way. Williams often claims that he does not understand the alleged *external* sense of the phrase 'a reason', which Scanlon calls the 'standard normative sense'. And Williams might be right, since there might be, as Williams claims, no such intelligible external sense. There would then be nothing that Williams failed to understand. I shall return to the question whether that is true.

When I have earlier claimed that Williams did not understand this external concept of a reason, some people have urged me to be more *charitable*. These people suggest that, like Scanlon, I should assume that Williams had this concept, and was merely making different claims about which facts give us reasons. But this assumption would, I believe, be *less* charitable. If Williams *did* understand the external normative sense, why does he so often call this sense mysterious and obscure? Though many of us misunderstand our own thoughts, I find it hard to believe, given his brilliance, that *Williams* could have been so muddled or confused. And, if Williams understood the idea that certain facts might count in favour of certain acts, some of his remarks would be baffling. It would be baffling, for example, why he claims that, in *Early Death*, you have no reason to take your medicine. How could Williams believe that though, as you know, taking your medicine would give you many more years of happy life, this fact does not count in favour of your acting in this way? It would also be baffling why Williams finds the idea of intrinsic goodness inexplicable. Williams rejects this idea, I believe, because this kind of goodness is reason-involving, and Williams thinks of reasons, not as facts that *count in favour* of our having some desire or acting in some way, but as facts that might *motivate* us. That is why Williams suggests that, to explain something's goodness, we should describe how this thing is related to what we want or value.

Williams of course knew that, when we say that someone has a reason to act in some way, we may be using this phrase in some sense that is not internalist, because it implies nothing about this person's motives. But such remarks, Williams writes, are not really claims about this person's reasons, but are something else 'misleadingly expressed'. If we claimed that you had a reason to take your medicine, for example, we might mean that this act would be better for you, and better for others. Williams would accept these claims, because he does not use 'better for' in a reason-implying sense. Williams had also read Scanlon's claim that, to explain what we mean by 'a reason', we can say only 'a fact that counts in favour'. Williams would have agreed that, if taking your medicine would save your life, we could intelligibly claim that this fact counts in favour of this act. But this use of 'counts in favour', Williams assumed, would merely express our pro-attitude toward this act. Though we would want you to take your medicine, we should not claim that our pro-attitude is a reason for you. Since you are not motivated to save your life, Williams denies that you have any reason to act in this way. Such remarks show, I believe, that Williams did not understand the distinctive concept of a non-psychological *purely normative* reason.

For another example, we can turn to Williams's claims about his imagined man who treats his wife cruelly. This man is at fault, Scanlon claims, in failing to recognize that various considerations give him reasons to treat his wife better. Williams agrees that, 'if we think of this as a deficiency or fault of this man, then we must think that in some sense these reasons *apply* to him'.   But that does not show, Williams writes,

> that these considerations are already the defective agent's
> reasons; indeed the problem is precisely that they are not.

This remark misinterprets Scanlon. When Williams claims that these considerations are not already this man's reasons, he means that these considerations are not related in certain ways to what this man wants or values. That is a psychological claim. Scanlon is making a quite different, normative claim.   Williams also writes:

> *He ought to have done it* . . . hopes to say that he had a
> reason to do it. But this may well be untrue: it was not,
> in fact, a reason for him.

When Williams writes, 'this may well be untrue', he assumes that he is denying what this claim 'hopes to say'. That is not so. If we claim that some consideration gave someone a decisive reason to act in some way, it is irrelevant to reply 'But this was *not in fact* a reason for him.' Williams means that this consideration did not motivate this person. Our claim was not about this person's motives.

In a similar passage, Williams writes:

> The usual function of 'I should . . . but I am not going to', is to
> draw attention to some special class of reasons, such as ethical
> or prudential reasons, which are particularly good as reasons
> to declare to others . . . but which are not, as it turns out, the
> strongest reasons for me now; the strongest reason is that I
> desire very much to do something else.

When Williams writes that certain reasons are not, as it *turns out*, 'the strongest reasons for me now', that is not a normative claim.

Williams might reject my last remark, since he believes that some psychological claims are also normative.   If I claim that you have a reason to act in some way, Williams remarks, I would not mean only that you are *already* motivated to act in this way.   But I might mean that

> (A) if you knew a certain fact, you *would* be motivated
> to act in this way.

If we give people information that would motivate them, that is enough, Williams writes, to make such claims normative. Williams here uses the word 'normative' in a weak sense.   (A), I believe, is merely a psychological prediction.   After making some claim like (A), I might add that you don't have the slightest reason to act in this way.   In several other passages, some of which I quote in a note, Williams ignores or dismisses the idea of a purely normative reason, and assumes that claims about reasons are, fundamentally, psychological.

Other people make similar assumptions.   As we have seen, subjective theories imply that

> (B) the nature of agony does not give us any reason to want to avoid future agony.

When I have asked Subjectivists whether they really believe (B), some of them answer Yes.   But I use (B) to mean that

> (C) when we remember what it is like to be in agony, what we remember does not count in favour of our wanting, and trying, not to be in agony again.

I doubt that these people really believe (C). These people seem to use the phrase 'a reason' in some other, Subjectivist sense. Some Subjectivists explicitly define some other sense. Like Williams, for example, Falk defines a reason as a fact belief in which would motivate us.   And Korsgaard writes:

> we might define a reason as a cause of a belief or act that has been endorsed by the person who believes or acts.

These senses of the phrase 'a reason' do not even partly overlap with Scanlon's and mine.   If you endorsed the desire for revenge that led you to kill your enemy, that endorsement would not make your desire what Scanlon and I would call a reason. Many other writers seem to use the phrase 'a reason' in some motivational sense.   Allison, for example, writes

> it is the value placed on a desire or inclination by an agent that gives it its 'motivational force', its status as a reason to act.

And rather than referring to normative reasons, Kant nearly always refers to *motivating grounds*.

We can now return to Williams's suggestion that the phrase 'a reason' does not *have* any intelligible, purely normative sense. If that is true, there would be nothing that Williams failed to understand.

When people assume that they have some concept with which they can state intelligible beliefs, these people may be mistaken. One example are certain beliefs about time travel. Suppose I claim that it might have been true that I had caused myself to exist, because I had travelled back in time and had earlier brought it about that my parents met, married, and had me as their first child. If you replied that my claim was not fully intelligible, you would be right. Other examples are some beliefs about time's passage. It can seem meaningful to say that we are moving through time into the future, or that nowness, or the quality of being present, is moving down the series of events from earlier to later, or that, every day, our death is getting closer. But such remarks, though they can seem deeply true, make no sense. There is nothing that could be intelligibly claimed to be what is moving through time. Nor could we explain what it would be for anything to move, not through space during some period of time, but just through time. Though our death is closer now than it was twenty years ago, that is merely like the fact that New York is closer to Washington than Boston is. This comparison may help us to see the *stillness of time*.

Though we are sometimes right to believe that other people's claims make no sense, such disagreements involve an asymmetry. If you believe that you have some concept with which you think intelligible thoughts, this belief is about *your own* mental states. If I believe that you have no such concept, my belief is about *someone else's* mental states. In this disagreement, I am in one way less likely to be right than you. We are less well placed than others to form true beliefs about these other people's mental states. This asymmetry is clearest when we hear someone else state some belief in some language that is unknown to us. We are then very badly placed to judge whether this person is stating some intelligible belief. Similar remarks apply when some speaker of our language says something that we don't understand.

I believe that I use the phrase 'has a reason', in a purely normative sense. Williams doubts that there is any such intelligible sense. In this disagreement, for the reason that I have just given, it is Williams who is less likely to be right. So I can rationally assume that Williams did not fully understand my beliefs about reasons.

We are also asking whether these beliefs are true. Suppose that you fully understand some view, and I only partly understand this view. If I believe this view to be false, I might be right. But I would be, in one way, less likely to be right than you. As before, there is an asymmetry. When people disagree about whether some view is true, those who fully understand this view are, in one way, better qualified to answer this question.

Some ways of living are, I believe, intrinsically better than others, in the reason-implying sense. And I believe that, in *Early Death*, you have a decisive reason to do what would give you many more years of happy life. Because Williams did not have the concept of a purely normative reason, he calls the idea of intrinsic goodness 'inexplicable', and he denies that you have any reason to give yourself this happy life. In this second disagreement, for the reason that I have just given, Williams is less likely to be right. If Williams had fully understood these beliefs about intrinsic goodness, and about reasons, he might have decided that these beliefs were true. I wish that I could ask him whether he would.

108 Naturalized Normativity

Williams assumed, I believe rightly, that normativity is best conceived as involving reasons or apparent reasons. Since Williams's concept of *a reason* is psychological, and is at most weakly normative, so are his other normative beliefs and claims.

Some examples are Williams's beliefs about what he calls *practical necessity* and *moral incapacity*. Suppose that, after anguished deliberation, I say:

I *must* keep my promise to my wife. I *cannot* let her down.

Williams writes that, when we make such claims, we are using 'must' and 'cannot' in something close to their ordinary predictive senses. On this view, though my claim may be partly normative, I am predicting that I will be psychologically compelled to keep my promise, and that I would not be able, intentionally, to let my wife down.

These remarks again show that Williams and I use different concepts. In this imagined case, my claim would be purely normative. If I later gave into temptation, and broke my promise to my wife, Williams might say:

> You were mistaken. As you found out, you didn't *have* to keep your promise. You *could* let her down.

But these remarks would be irrelevant. When I said 'I can't let her down', I didn't mean that I would be unable to let my wife down. I meant that I had decisive reasons not to act in this way, or that this act would be very wrong.   These claims could have been true whatever I later did.

Williams's claims are about *first-person* uses of 'must' and 'cannot'. When each of us applies these words to other people, Williams writes, 'there is room for a split between the predictive and the normative'. If my wife said

> You can't let me down,

this claim would not imply that I won't let her down. When we tell other people that they can't act in some way, Williams writes, that is not a prediction. We mean 'that the relevant reasons tell overwhelmingly against the action'.

These remarks may suggest that, on Williams's view, such claims would be purely normative. But that is not so. On Williams's assumptions, my wife's claim would imply that

> (D) I have overwhelming reasons not to let her down,

and this claim would be psychological. I might be able to inform my wife that she has false beliefs about the strength of my reasons not to let her down.   Quoting Williams, I might truly say:

> These reasons are not, as it turns out, the strongest reasons for me now; the strongest reason is that I desire very much to do something else.

Similar remarks apply to other normative claims.   If my wife said

You *ought* to keep your promise,

this claim would imply that

(E) I have at least some reason to keep this promise.

On Williams's assumptions, (E) is another psychological claim, which might also be false. It might be true that, even after fully informed and procedurally rational deliberation, I am not even slightly motivated to keep my promise. Since the fact that I made this promise would not then be a reason for me, my wife would be wrong to claim that I ought to keep my promise. On Williams's view, such claims could not state purely normative truths. Since *should* and *ought* imply *has a reason*, and facts about reasons are psychological, so are facts about what people should or ought to do.

Williams admits this feature of his view. When we consider someone who doesn't care about his obligations, we may claim that this person ought to care about them.   But this claim, Williams writes,

does not ultimately provide any more 'hold' over the agent . . . this critic deeply wants this *ought* to stick to the agent; but the only glue . . . is social and psychological.

In trying to provide normative glue, we might tell this person that he has an *external* reason to do what he ought morally to do. Such a claim, Williams writes

would seek to 'stick' the *ought* to the agent by presenting him as irrational if he ignored it.

Williams comments:

I doubt very much . . . whether this proposal does capture what the ordinary moral consciousness wants from the *ought* of moral obligation . . . But if this were what was wanted, there would be good reason to see moral obligation as an illusion.

Williams may be right to claim that, when we consider people who don't care about their obligations, most of us would not believe that these people are being irrational. But the most important questions are not about rationality, but about reasons. Most of us believe that, since these people ought to fulfil their obligations, they have reasons to fulfil them. That is part of what 'the ordinary moral consciousness wants'. On Williams's view, these people may have *no* reasons to fulfil their obligations. We cannot criticize or blame people for failing to do what we believe that they have no reason to do. Since Williams assumes that *ought* implies *has a reason*, but also believes that all reasons are internal, Williams concludes that the *ought* of moral obligation, when applied to such people, is an illusion.

This view has unwelcome implications. On Williams's view, we cannot claim that there are some things that it would be wrong for anyone to do. We cannot even claim that it would be wrong for anyone to torture other people for his own amusement. Given some sadist's motivations, this man may have no internal reason act differently. On Williams's assumptions, this man's sadistic acts would not then be wrong. We may blame such people, Williams writes, but when these people have no reason to act differently, the 'institution of blame is best seen as involving a fiction'. Williams here defends one form of Moral Nihilism.

We can now return to questions about what matters. To illustrate such questions, Williams discusses conflicts between the well-being of human beings and animals of other species. We use insecticides, for example, to protect the plants we eat. Such policies are justified, we may believe, because we are more important than the insects that we kill, or because our well-being matters more. If we make such claims, Williams objects, we are supposing that human beings are more important in some *absolute* sense, by mattering more from a 'cosmic point of view'. Williams claims that, since there is no such cosmic point of view, the idea of absolute importance is another illusion. There is only importance *to us*. When our interests conflict with the interests of some other species of animal, the only serious question is 'Which side are you on?'

If we had to choose between the survival either of human beings or of some kind of beetle, our survival *would*, I believe, be more important. This is not, however, the belief that Williams considers and rejects. What Williams calls *absolute* importance is really just another kind of *relative* importance. We would have such absolute importance, Williams claims, if we were important not only to ourselves, but also to the Cosmos, or Universe. And Williams is discussing *psychological* importance. We cannot matter from a cosmic point of view, Williams assumes, because the Cosmos does not have a mind, and therefore cannot care about us.

When I claim that something matters, or is important, that is not a relative, psychological claim, but an absolute, normative claim. If I could save some trapped animal from a painful death, that would be more important than throwing a pebble into the sea. The pain of this animal would matter more, in the sense that we would all have more reason to prevent this pain, if we could. Williams's concepts lead him to ignore this kind of importance.

I also believe that, if human beings flourished, that would be in itself much better than if some species of beetle flourished. That would be better, not because *we* are human beings, but because what is good in the best human lives is much better than anything in any beetle's life. Williams rejects such claims.   In his words, it cannot be

> *just better* that one sort of animal should flourish rather than another . . . This is simply another recurrence of the notion we saw off a while ago, absolute importance.

Though Williams often criticizes Consequentialism, he never considers the kind of view that Consequentialists like Sidgwick accept. When such Consequentialists make claims about how it would be best for things to go, they are using the word 'best' in the impartial-reason-implying sense. Since Williams does not use or understand this sense of 'best', he assumes that Consequentialists use 'best' in what he calls the 'absolute' sense that we 'saw off a while ago'. This use of 'best', Williams assumes, mistakenly implies that some things matter to the Cosmos, or Universe.

Though Williams denies that any outcome could be *just better*, he agrees that, if we flourished, that would be *better for us*. But this claim is only weakly normative. As his claims about *Early Death* show, Williams believes that we have no reason to do what would be best for us. That is why he rejects the question 'How would it be best for me to live?', suggesting that we should ask instead 'What do I basically want?'

109 Sidgwick's Intuitions

The ancient Greek philosophers hoped to find out how it would be best to live. These hopes have gone, Williams writes, since the 'world to which ethical thought applies is now irreversibly different'.

One difference is in our beliefs about Nature, the Universe, or God. Aristotle believed that everything has some natural purpose. Many other people have believed that God gives everyone a purpose. Williams assumes that these beliefs are false. But in our normative thinking, he writes, no one has yet found a good way of doing without such beliefs.

That is not so. We don't need to appeal to these metaphysical or religious beliefs.   Some philosophers, Williams writes,

> would like to be able to go back now to Socrates' question and start again.

This is what we can and should do. We should ask what we have reasons to care about, and to try to achieve. The world has not relevantly changed. If there are better and worse ways to live, as I believe, that is as true now as it was in ancient Greece. To justify the claim that certain kinds of life are best, we don't need to appeal to the purposes of Nature. And rather than claiming that certain acts are wrong because God forbids them, many theists more plausibly claim that God forbids such acts because they are wrong. Normative truths do not have to be grounded in claims about Nature or God. Nor could all such truths be so grounded.

If we are asked how we can recognize such truths, we should appeal, as Sidgwick claims, to our intuitions.   Williams writes

> The model of intuition in ethics has been demolished by a succession of critics, and the ruins of it that remain above ground are not impressive enough to invite much history of what happened to it. . . .

But Sidgwick's view is not in ruins, nor was this view demolished, or even discussed, by any of the critics whom Williams cites.

Williams also states some criticisms of his own. Intuitionists, he writes, 'failed to explain how an eternal truth could provide a practical consideration'. This criticism needs to be explained. Williams may mean that

> (F) if it were merely an eternal truth that some fact provides
> a normative reason to act in some way, Intuitionists could
> not explain how this truth, or fact, could provide a practical
> consideration.

Sidgwick would reply that, if some fact gives us a reason, by counting in favour of some act, this fact would be, or provide, a practical consideration. If Williams intends to reject this claim, he must be using these words in some other sense.

Intuitionism also failed, Williams writes, because this view 'was wrong in assimilating ethical truths to necessities'. On Williams's assumptions about reasons, ethical truths cannot be necessities, since we cannot even claim that these truths apply to all actual people. Given some people's motives, moral *oughts* do not apply to them. But if we have normative object-given reasons, as most Intuitionists believe, there could be necessary truths about such reasons, and about which acts are wrong.

Williams also rejects the Intuitionist's partial analogy with our beliefs about other necessary truths, such as those of mathematics. He remarks that, if such other truths

> were seemingly denied by informants from another
> culture, one would naturally look in the first instance
> for a better translator, but the situation with ethical
> beliefs is not at all like that.

This situation, I have argued, *is* like that. Williams claims that, in *Early Death*, you have no reason to take the medicine that would give you many more years of happy life. This claim would be *seemingly* denied by informants from the *same* culture, since Sidgwick and I would both claim that you have a decisive reason to take this medicine.

But Williams's claim would not *in fact* be denied by Sidgwick or me. As in Williams's imagined case in which someone seemed to deny some obvious mathematical truth, we need a better translator. When Williams claims that you have no reason to take your medicine, he means that, after informed and procedurally rational deliberation, you are not motivated to take your medicine. Sidgwick and I would accept that claim.

Williams adds:

> the appeal to intuition as a faculty explained nothing.   It
> seemed to say that these truths were known, but there was
> no way in which they were known.

Williams rejects this explanation even when applied to the necessary truths of logic or mathematics. He may be intending to deny that any such beliefs can be intuitively grounded, in the sense that our justification for having these beliefs is provided by their content, or what we are believing. This denial would, I believe, be mistaken. Williams may instead be rejecting the view that intuition is a special quasi-sensory faculty which gives us some kind of mysterious contact with mathematical or normative entities or properties. But, as I shall argue later, Intuitionists need not appeal to any such view.

Williams also rejects Sidgwick's intuitions. According to one of Sidgwick's intuitive beliefs, which we can call

> *the Axiom of Temporal Impartiality*: What happens at each
> time is equally important.

In Sidgwick's words, we should have 'an impartial concern for all parts of our conscious life'.   Discussing this axiom, Williams writes:

> almost everybody who agrees with it finds it completely
> self-evident. However, the trouble is that the world also
> contains a group of people, distinguished perhaps from the
> first on grounds of temperament, who find it to an equal
> degree self-evidently false.

The distinction between these groups of people is not, however, temperamental. In another statement of his axiom, Sidgwick claims that

> (G) if some possible experience would be further in the future, this would not be 'a reasonable ground' to care about it less.

We would have no reason, for example, to postpone some ordeal if we knew that this postponement would only make this ordeal more painful. Williams does *not*, as he asserts, find this claim self-evidently false. To find some claim self-evidently false, we must understand this claim, and (G) uses 'a reasonable ground' in the normative sense that, as Williams says, he does not understand.

According to another of Sidgwick's intuitive beliefs, which we can call

> *the Axiom of Personal Impartiality*: What happens to each person is equally important.

In Sidgwick's words,

> the good of any one individual is of no more importance from the point of view (if I may say so) of the Universe than the good of any other.

As before, Williams objects that nothing is important to the Universe. But Sidgwick could have referred instead, as he does elsewhere, to the judgments that we ought to make when we consider events from an imagined impartial point of view.

Williams rejects appeals to what some imagined impartial observer ought to choose, or would have most reason to choose. If this imagined person, Williams writes,

> is not given some motivation in addition to his impartiality, there is no reason why he should choose anything at all; and unless that motivation is benevolent . . . he might as well choose to frustrate as many preferences as possible.

As before, because Williams does not have the concept of a purely normative reason, he assumes that no one has any reason to care about anything.

Williams also criticizes the belief 'that one can look at all one's dispositions from the outside, from the point of view of the universe, and that so doing is embodied in a cool hour of personal reflection'. This model, Williams writes,

> implies an extremely naïve conception of what is going on in the cool hour itself. It is assumed that it is the cool activity of theorizing that will display to oneself the true value of one's own dispositions, where I mean by their 'true' value, the value that they really have for one.

Williams here assumes that, when we ask what is something's true value, we are asking whether we really care about this thing. That is not what Sidgwick means.

Williams suggests some other arguments, which I shall consider later. I shall first discuss my main conclusion about how Williams's views differ from Sidgwick's, and from mine.

110 The Voyage Ahead

Though Williams and I used the same normative words, we used them in different senses. We were not really, as we assumed, disagreeing.

Other people use these words in such different senses. One example is Mackie, who also defends a form of Nihilism, claiming that there are no objective values. In describing the moral beliefs that he rejects, Mackie often uses language that seems purely normative. He talks of 'action-guidingness', 'intrinsic to-be-done-ness', and 'the categorical quality of moral requirements'. But these phrases are misleading. Like Williams, Mackie uses normative language to make psychological claims.

Mackie best explains his view when discussing one of Hume's arguments. Hume claims:

> (A) Reason cannot by itself influence our acts, since reason can only produce beliefs, and our beliefs cannot influence our acts without the help of some passion or desire.

(B) Moral judgments do by themselves influence our acts.

Therefore

Morality cannot be based on reason.

If we are moral rationalists, Mackie writes, we might respond to this argument by denying premise (B).   We might claim that

(C) when we judge that some act is right, this judgment does not by itself 'tend to make' us act in this way, since we must 'also *want* to do whatever is right'.

Mackie then writes that, in claiming (C), we would be denying the 'intrinsic action-guidingness' of moral judgments. We would have to admit that, on our view, there are no 'objective requirements or categorical imperatives', and our use of words like 'right' and 'wrong' would not have any 'prescriptive force'. All we could mean, Mackie suggests, is

(D) 'X is right and Y is wrong, but of course it is entirely up to you whether you prefer what is right to what is wrong.'

Such claims *would* have little force. But Mackie does not explain why he believes that, if we deny (B) and assert (C), our moral judgments would cease to be action-guiding and prescriptive, since they would become claims like (D).

Mackie's belief can, however, be explained. Normativity, Mackie assumes, is one kind of motivating force. When Mackie claims that there are no *objectively prescriptive* values, he means that there are no normative beliefs that would *necessarily motivate* anyone who accepts them.   For example Mackie writes that, on Plato's view,

knowledge of the good . . . provides the knower both with a direction and an *overriding motive*; something's being good both tells the person who knows this to pursue it and *makes him pursue it*.

Several other people make similar claims. On Locke's view, Darwall writes, 'obligation consists in conclusive motives raised through (practical) reasoning', and such motives are conclusive in the *de facto* sense 'by winning a contest of strength'. On Falk's view, when we say that we *ought* to do something, we mean that we feel impelled to do this thing. Such an impulse is *rationally necessary*, thereby meeting Kant's criterion of normativity, if this impulse is 'unavoidably stronger than all opposing motives'.   Kant himself writes:

> the good (the law) . . . which objectively, in its ideal conception, is an irresistible incentive,
>
> *ought* indicates that it is not natural to the will, but that the agent has to be coerced,

Wittgenstein similarly writes:

> the absolute good . . . would be one which everybody, independent of his tastes and inclinations, would *necessarily* bring about or feel guilty for not bringing about.

If this is how we think of objective values, or moral requirements, that may lead us to become skeptics, who deny that there *are* any such values or requirements.   Wittgenstein, for example, adds:

> No state of affairs has, in itself, what I would like to call the *coercive power* of an absolute judge.

Mackie similarly writes:

> The objective values which I am denying would be action-directing absolutely, not contingently . . . upon the agent's desires and inclinations.

In calling the values that he denies *action-directing*, Mackie does not mean that such values would *tell us what we ought to do*. He means that such values would by themselves *cause us to act*. Mackie assumes that, when we believe that some act is categorically required, or is intrinsically *to-be-done*, we are believing that this act has some property awareness of which would be guaranteed to make anyone do it, if they can. On Mackie's view, since no act could have any such property, these normative beliefs are false. There cannot be anything that is, objectively, what we ought to do.

Since Mackie claims to be an Error Theorist, who believes that ordinary moral thinking is mistakenly committed to non-natural moral properties and truths, we might expect him to give a *normative* account of these alleged properties and truths. As I have just said, Mackie does not do that. His claims are about how we might be motivated to act. When Mackie writes that moral judgments do not have *prescriptive force*, he means that our acts and preferences are 'up to us', since we are not psychologically compelled to do what is right.

As these various quotations show, Williams and Mackie, do not use the normative concepts that I and other Non-Naturalists use. Nor does Gibbard. As we have seen, Gibbard writes:

> Thinking what I *ought* to do is thinking *what to do*. . . . When I speak of concluding 'what to do', understand this to mean coming to a choice.

That is not how Non-Naturalists think. When these people conclude that they *ought* to do something, that is quite different from their choosing to do it.   Gibbard also writes:

> Why as I keep asking, does what we *ought* to do matter for *what to do*? Non-naturalism . . . offers no answer.

Given what Non-Naturalists mean by 'ought', Gibbard's question is easy to answer. If we know what we *ought* to do, because we know what we have *decisive reasons* to do, we thereby know *what to do*.

Many other people use such normative words in other senses. Anscombe, for example, claims that, when used by atheists, the phrase 'ought morally' has 'mere mesmeric force', and does not express any 'intelligible thought'. Hare claims that, when we say that something matters, we have not said anything that might be true. Nothing could matter, because ' "matters" isn't that sort of word'. Korsgaard claims that truths about reasons could not answer normative questions. If these people used the words 'ought morally', 'matters', and 'reasons' in the senses that Non-Naturalists use, they would not make these claims, since their claims would then be clearly false.

In a famous passage, Hume describes the 'wretched condition' which his philosophical thinking has left him in. Hume has reached various skeptical beliefs which conflict deeply with the beliefs of other human beings.   He is, he writes,

> affrighted and confounded with that forlorn solitude, in which
> I am placed in my philosophy, and fancy myself some strange
> uncouth monster, who not being able to mingle and unite
> in society, has been expelled all human commerce, and left
> utterly abandoned and disconsolate. Fain would I run into
> the crowd for shelter and warmth . . . I call upon others to
> join me . . . but no one will hearken me. . . . All the world
> conspires to oppose and contradict me.

My predicament is partly similar. Most philosophers seem to reject my meta-ethical and other meta-normative beliefs. In one way, my predicament is worse than Hume's. Many of these other people don't even understand what I believe. When I talk to these people, we can't even disagree. It took me some time to realize the state that I am in. Given the range, subtlety, and depth of Williams's writings about normative questions, I assumed for many years that Williams had some purely normative beliefs. I failed to see that Williams's claims about reasons, and about what we ought to do, are really psychological claims about how we might be motivated to act. I also failed to understand Mackie's similar claims. Since I knew both these people well, I am puzzled and disturbed by our failures to understand each other.

My state is, in two ways, better than Hume's. I am not alone, since some other people have beliefs like mine. Nor am I a skeptic, whose reasoning has led me to 'nothing but doubt and ignorance'. I believe that some things matter, and that we often have decisive reasons. But it was a shock to realize that when Williams, Mackie, and several other people seemed to be denying these beliefs, they were not really doing that, since they never even considered whether these beliefs are true.

Hume also writes:

> before I launch out into those immense depths of philosophy which lie before me, I find myself inclined to stop a moment in my present station, and to ponder the voyage that I have undertaken, which undoubtedly requires the utmost art and industry to be brought to a happy conclusion.

When Hume wrote these words, he was in his late 20's. Hume had many years in which, after launching out into these immense depths, he could try to bring his voyage to a happy conclusion. I am now 67. To bring my voyage to a happy conclusion, I would have to resolve the misunderstandings and disagreements that I have partly described. I would need to find ways of getting many people to understand what it would be for things to matter, and of getting these people to believe that certain things really do matter. I cannot hope to do these things myself. But in these last few chapters I shall try to explain why I hope that, with art and industry, some other people will be able to do these things, thereby completing this voyage.

111 Rediscovering Reasons

In a notorious passage, Hume writes:

> (A) Where a passion is neither founded on false suppositions, nor chooses means insufficient to the end, the understanding can neither justify nor condemn it.

> (B) 'Tis not contrary to reason to prefer the destruction of the whole world to the scratching of my finger . . .

> (C) 'Tis as little contrary to reason to prefer even my own acknowledged lesser good to my greater, and have a more ardent affection for the former than the latter.

> (D) A trivial good may, from certain circumstances, produce a desire superior to what arises from the greatest and most valuable enjoyment. . . .

> (E) In short, a passion must be accompanied with some false judgment, in order to its being *unreasonable*; and even then 'Tis not the passion, properly speaking, which is unreasonable but the judgment.

When Hume claims that these preferences are not contrary to reason, he may be using the word 'reason' to refer to the mental abilities that lead us to have true beliefs. Hume may mean that, as he reminds us elsewhere, such preferences cannot be false. But that would not be enough to justify these claims.

As claim (A) shows, Hume is asking whether passions and preferences can be *contrary to reason* in the normative sense of being unjustified. Hume has told us earlier that he will be asking whether we *ought* to oppose those motives that conflict with reason. (C) claims that, in this normative sense, it is not contrary to reason to prefer our own acknowledged lesser good to our greater good. To support this claim, (D) points out that we may have this preference. But if we claim that some preference is contrary to reason, or unreasonable, we are not claiming that no one ever *has* this preference. When Hume supports (C) by claiming (D), he is mistakenly conflating normative and psychological claims.

Since Hume is asking whether preferences can be reasonable or unreasonable, he should have remembered that we can have reasons either to have, or not to have, some preference. When we prefer our lesser good to our greater good, we may be preferring what we have no reasons to prefer, and strong reasons not to prefer. Hume should be discussing whether that is true. Hume often refers elsewhere to preferences that we have reasons to have, and ought to have. He writes, for example:

> we seek reasons upon which we may justify . . . the passion.
> I shall have a good reason for my resistance . . . and ought to prefer that which is safest and most agreeable.

Such claims are about our object-given value-based reasons to prefer what is intrinsically better.   As Hume himself writes:

> So little are men govern'd by *reason* in their sentiments
> and opinions, that they always judge more of objects by
> comparison than from their *intrinsic worth* and *value*.

When Hume talks of our preferring our own acknowledged lesser good to our greater good, he is probably referring to our tendency to prefer lesser goods in the near future to greater goods that would be more remote.   Discussing this bias towards the near, Hume writes

> There is no quality in human nature which causes more fatal
> errors in our conduct.

That is a very strong criticism. As these and other remarks show, Hume believed that, when we prefer such lesser goods, we are failing to be *governed by reason*. Such preferences are in this sense contrary to reason. So when Hume claims, in the passage quoted above, that such preferences are *not* contrary to reason, he is forgetting, or mis-stating, his normative beliefs. We should distinguish between Hume's *stated* view and his *real* view.

  Given Hume's greatness, Hume's passage has done great damage, since Hume's claims have seemed to support the view that preferences cannot be unreasonable, or irrational. Hume makes other misleading claims, as when he writes: 'Reason is and ought only to be the slave of the passions.' When Hume claims that preferences cannot be contrary to reason, he sometimes means that, since reason produces only beliefs, reason cannot by itself motivate us. In such passages, Hume again conflates normative and psychological claims. He assumes that, when we ask whether some desire is *opposed* by reason in the sense of being unreasonable, we are asking whether reason has the causal power to defeat this desire.   That is not so.

In her defence of Hume's stated view, Baier writes:

> How could one's intention be contrary to reason if one
> acknowledges what reason tells one, that one is sacrificing
> one's greater good, and that very likely one will regret it?

Reason has had its say—its voice has not been silenced. The intention to invite later regrets, to sacrifice one's greater good to one's present pleasure . . . incorporates what reason informs one of; it is the sort of intention that only a rational being with foresight could form. We deplore it when people form such intentions, but not because we are more influenced than they are by our reasoning. We are simply differently influenced.

We deplore such people's intentions, I believe, because we have strong reasons to deplore them, and these people have strong reasons not to form them. Adolescents have strong reasons, for example, not to intend to start smoking, with the predictable result that they will become addicted and will be likely to die much younger. When these adolescents fail to respond to their awareness of these reasons, they are not merely *differently influenced*. If Hume had remembered his real view, he would have rightly called such intentions a *fatal error*, and deplored these people's failure to be *governed by reason*.

Baier adds that, if we prefer the destruction of the world to the scratching of our little finger, and this preference does not rest on false beliefs, we can be criticized for being imprudent, vicious, and callously indifferent. 'Contrary to reason', Baier writes, 'is not the strongest criticism'. Blackburn similarly writes:

The knave is already odious. We already have the word
to express our contempt: it does not add anything except
rhetoric also to call him irrational.

Compared with 'vicious', 'callous', and 'odious', the word 'irrational' may express a weaker criticism. As I have said, however, the more important questions are not about rationality, but about reasons. Suppose again that you fail to be motivated to take the medicine that you know would give you many more years of happy life. If we are Subjectivists, we can call you short-sighted and imprudent. But we must admit that, on our view, you have *no reason* to take your medicine. When cruel people make others suffer, we can call these people vicious, odious, and callous. But on subjective desire-based theories, some of these people have no reason *not* to make others suffer. These other criticisms become much weaker if we must admit that, on our view, these people have no reason to act differently. We may even have to admit that, in harming themselves or others, these people are doing what we believe that they have *most reason* to do, and what they *ought* in the reason-implying sense to do. We may also have to admit that, on our view, these people have no reason to care about the fact that they are being imprudent, or that they are vicious and callous. Why should these people care about these criticisms if, as we believe, they have no reason to care?

Hume is often claimed to be a Subjectivist about Reasons. This claim, I believe, makes two mistakes. All reasons for acting, Subjectivists claim, depend on various facts about our desires or other motivating states. Hume's *stated* view is not Subjectivist, since Hume never discusses whether we have reasons for acting. Nor is Hume's *real* view Subjectivist. As many of his remarks show, Hume really believed that, as well as having reasons for acting, we have value-based object-given reasons to have particular desires, preferences, and aims.

These facts give me some reason to hope that these disagreements might be resolved, so that my voyage might be brought by others to a happy conclusion. As these facts remind us, there is often a difference between what people think they believe and what they really believe. That is especially likely in the case of those who have original ideas. As Hume writes:

> Men of bright fancies may in this respect be compared to
> those angels whom the scripture represents as covering their
> eyes with their wings.

If even Hume was really an Objectivist about reasons, that might be true of other Humeans.

Some Humeans already claim to be Objectivists. These people use normative language to express their attitudes towards certain kinds of act, and some of them claim to believe in reasons that are object-given, rather than desire-based. Blackburn is one example. When Humeans are Expressivists, Blackburn writes, their view can be

> as demandingly categorical as possible. A Humean can issue the injunction to avoid cruelty—whether you want to do so or not. He is forbidding a class of actions, and warning that wanting to perform them counts as no excuse.

Blackburn claims that, in this way, he can use a 'Hume-friendly' version of the concept of an object-given reason. Return to Williams's imagined man who is being cruel to his wife.   Blackburn might tell this man

> (F) You have a decisive reason to treat your wife better, whether you want to or not.

To be able to say such things, Blackburn would have to withdraw some of his other claims. He distinguishes elsewhere between two kinds of reason. There are ordinary, everyday reasons, such as the reason stated by the claim 'I wanted it'.   Something much grander, Blackburn writes,

> would be a reason that everyone must acknowledge to be a reason, independently of their sympathies and inclinations. I shall call that a Reason, with a capital letter. It would armlock everyone. You could not ignore it or discount it, just because you felt differently.

If people have a Reason, Blackburn writes, 'and they shrug it off . . . their very rationality is in jeopardy'. Blackburn objects that, as Hume claimed,

> There are no Reasons . . . just the wills or desires of particular persons.

If there were no Reasons, however, there would be no object-given reasons, and Blackburn's (F) would be false. Blackburn could at most say:

> (G) You have a reason to treat your wife better. But you don't have to acknowledge this to be a reason, independently of your sympathies or inclinations. You could ignore this reason, just because you felt differently.

To defend (F), Blackburn might revise his view, claiming:

> (H) There *are* object-given Reasons. There are some reasons
> that everyone must acknowledge, whatever their sympathies
> and inclinations.

With this revision, Blackburn would be closer to Hume's real view.

Mackie is another Humean who might have come to accept Hume's
real view.   Mackie writes:

> the way a piece of red-hot iron feels when I touch it is
> just a contingent fact about me . . . but it is nonetheless a
> pretty powerful reason for me to take my hand away as
> quickly as I can.

When Mackie calls this feeling of pain a powerful reason, he may mean
only that

> (I) the way the red-hot iron feels strongly motivates me to
> move my hand away.

If this is what Mackie means, he is an Analytical Subjectivist, whose
claims about reasons are merely psychological. This is likely to be what
Mackie means, since this psychological account fits the Metaphysical
Naturalism to which he often appeals. But if Mackie had considered
the distinctions I have drawn, he might have changed his view. Mackie
might have come to believe that

> (J) the way the red-hot iron feels counts strongly in favour of
> my moving my hand away.

If he had believed (J), Mackie would have started to use the concept of
a purely normative reason.   Mackie also writes

> moral approval and disapproval seem to reflect objective
> features in a way that the feeling of pain does not.

There is no such distinction here. Though pain is subjective in the
sense of being a mental state, it is an objective fact what it is like for
someone to be in great pain, by having a sensation that this person

intensely dislikes. And though (J) is a claim that is only about what one person has a reason to do, this claim states an objective, irreducibly normative truth.

Suppose next that Mackie is not now in pain, but that a red hot iron is slowly approaching Mackie's hand. Mackie might then have believed that

> (K) the way the red-hot iron *would* feel, if it touched my hand, counts strongly in favour of my moving my hand away.

If Mackie had believed (K), he would have ceased to be a Subjectivist about reasons. (K) does not refer to any of Mackie's present desires. As (K) claims, the nature of this possible future pain gives Mackie an object-given value-based reason to try to avoid this pain. Mackie also writes:

> A categorical imperative . . . would express a reason for acting which was unconditional in the sense of not being contingent upon any present desire of the agent.

Since (K) describes a reason that is not conditional on any fact about Mackie's present desires, (K) states what Mackie calls a *categorical imperative*. In believing (K), Mackie would have abandoned his Error Theory. The reason-involving badness of Mackie's future pain is an *objective value* of the kind whose existence Mackie denies.

There are two kinds of reason-involving badness here. Mackie might have believed that

> (L) this pain would be *bad for me* in the sense that the way this pain would feel gives me a self-interested or prudential reason to try avoid this pain.

Mackie might also have believed that

> (M) the way my pain would feel gives *anyone* a reason to try to prevent my pain, if they can.

Since there is nothing special about Mackie's pain, Mackie might then have believed that

(N) anyone's pain is *impersonally bad* in the sense that everyone has impartial reasons to try to prevent anyone's pain, if they can.

As Nagel writes:

the pain can be detached in thought from the fact that it is mine without losing any of its dreadfulness . . . suffering is a bad thing, period, and not just for the sufferer . . . *This experience* ought not to go on, *whoever* is having it.

Of these ways in which Mackie's views might have changed, much the greatest would have been the move from Analytical Subjectivism to the belief that

(J) the way that Mackie's pain feels counts strongly in favour of his trying to reduce this pain.

In believing that he had this purely normative reason, Mackie would be abandoning Metaphysical Naturalism. It would be easier to make the further moves to believing (K), (L), (M), and (N).

We can respond to reasons, I have claimed, without knowing that this is what we are doing. When Hume asked whether our desires or preferences could be contrary to reason, he forgot his belief that we can have reasons either to have, or not to have, particular desires or preferences. But that did not affect Hume's life, since he responded well to such reasons. Adam Smith called Hume 'as perfectly wise and virtuous . . . as perhaps the nature of human frailty will permit'.

Similar remarks apply to many other people. Unlike Hume, some of these people never make claims, or think conscious thoughts, that use the concept of a purely normative reason. But these people respond to such reasons, and they often do that better than Rationalists like me. Williams may have been one such person. If such people are not aware of their responses to reasons, that is not surprising. We often don't know how our minds work. When Mozart was asked how he composed his music, he is reported to have said 'I have nothing to do with it'. There are also Moral Nihilists who are very conscientious. Mackie was one such person.

Since people can respond so well to reasons without knowing what they are doing, such knowledge may seem to have little practical importance. But that is not, I believe, true. It matters whether people believe that some things matter. Of the Non-Cognitivists and Nihilists who respond so well to reasons, many, I suspect, earlier believed that there are some normative, reason-involving truths. Such people's past beliefs may have continuing effects on what they care about and do. If other people have never had such normative beliefs, they are likely to do less well. When these people are young, for example, they would be more likely to start smoking, drive dangerously, and make the lesser, non-lethal mistakes that Hume calls fatal errors.

When we are deciding how to live, or we are making other lesser decisions, we should not follow Williams's advice, by asking 'What do I basically want?' We should ask what we have most reason to want, and to try to achieve. I do not mean that, when making these decisions, we should always compile a list of positive and negative reasons, or *pros* and *cons*, and then try to compare their strengths. In many kinds of case, that is the best procedure. But in many other important cases, we should make our decisions in less calculating and conscious ways. The heart has reasons, Pascal said, of which reason knows nothing. Since the heart merely pumps blood, it would be better to say that our mind goes through some processes of reasoning of which we, as conscious thinkers, know nothing. When we need to make some important decision, we should start by thinking carefully about the various facts that might give us reasons for choosing different aims or acts. But we should then let these facts sink in. We would often later find, perhaps after a night's sleep, that we have already made the right decision, and know what to do.

There are other ways in which, if people understand and think about object-given value-based reasons, things would go better. As Keynes remarked, many politicians act in ways that show them to be the slaves of some dead economist. Many economists, we can add, think in ways that show them to be the slaves of some dead philosopher. Like most of the sciences, economics grew out of philosophy. When Welfare Economics began in the late nineteenth Century, economists knew that wealth is only imperfectly correlated with happiness, and that, of these two, it is happiness that matters. For much of the twentieth Century, economists forgot these truths. Many economists even believed that interpersonal comparisons of well-being make no sense. Many also believed that, in their professional work, they should be concerned only with facts, not values. Remember the remark: 'That's not a value judgment. Everyone accepts it.' Economists are not chiefly to blame for having these beliefs, since it was philosophers who first claimed that reasons are given only by desires, that all rationality is instrumental, and that no values are facts, because there are no normative truths. Given our increasing powers to destroy or damage the conditions of life on Earth, we need to lose these beliefs. It is not wealth that matters, or mere preference-fulfilment, but happiness, justice, and the other things that can make our lives worth living.

Even if we understand the view that some things matter in the reason-involving sense, we may reject this view. When Mackie denies that there are any objectively prescriptive values, or categorical moral imperatives, he gives other arguments. Our belief in such values, Mackie claims, is open to strong metaphysical and epistemological objections. Nor can we defensibly believe that there are objective moral truths, given the fact that that there has been widespread moral disagreement, and given the cultural origin of many moral beliefs. Williams makes similar claims, as do many other people. In the next four chapters I shall consider these objections.

31

Metaphysics

112 Ontology

In believing that some things matter, I am believing that there are some irreducibly normative truths. That is denied by most of the people whose views I have been discussing. These people are Metaphysical Naturalists, who believe that all properties and facts must be natural properties and facts. Irreducibly normative truths, these people assume, are incompatible with a scientific world-view.   Gibbard, for example, writes:

> If this is what anyone seriously believes, then I simply want to debunk it. Nothing in a plausible, naturalistic picture of our place in the universe requires these non-natural facts.

To non-philosophers, Gibbard adds, claims like mine 'sound fantastic'. In several other recent books, such views are dismissed in a paragraph or two. Jackson thinks it worth explaining why he even bothers to discuss such views. When Field mentions the belief that there are some non-natural normative properties, he calls this belief 'crazy'. Even if there were such properties and truths, these people add, there is no intelligible way in which we could know about them.

These metaphysical and epistemological objections raise some deep and difficult questions. Blackburn writes: 'there is precious little surprising left about morality: its meta-theory seems to me pretty well exhaustively understood.' This meta-theory seems to me very far from being understood. When we consider either morality or practical and epistemic reasons, there are several fundamental questions that we haven't answered. Some of these questions are about normativity. Others are wider questions about the nature and status of necessary truths, whether and in what way such truths must have truth-makers, and whether and how we might understand and recognize such truths. There are also, I assume, some relevant and important questions that we haven't even asked. Before we understand these questions better, we cannot claim to know that there cannot be any irreducibly normative, reason-involving truths.

If there are no such truths, nothing matters. Since I want things to matter, I cannot consider these questions with the 'disinterested curiosity' that Sidgwick recommends. But some desires are fulfilled. Though we are in the dark, we can, I believe, see dimly how there can be such truths, and how we might know some of these truths.

We can start with the metaphysical objections. Irreducibly normative truths, Mackie writes, would involve 'curious metaphysical objects', 'entities of a very strange sort', which are 'too queer' to be part of the 'fabric of the Universe'. Such objections can, I believe, be answered. In suggesting one such answer, I shall mostly be discussing questions that are not normative. If you are not worried by these metaphysical objections, you might jump to Chapter 32.

When *ontologists* think about the nature of reality, some of them ask:

Q1: What is there? Which are the kinds of thing, or entity, that exist?

Consider, for example:

A: Rocks, stars, human beings, the Universe.

B: Facts, meanings, laws of nature, nations, wars, famines, overdrafts, symphonies, fashions, numbers, and reasons.

C: The Average American, spherical cubes, statements that are both wholly true and wholly false.

Most of us believe that the items in List A exist, and we would also believe, after a little thought, that the items in List C don't exist. But we may be doubtful about some of the items in List B. We may also be unclear what we are asking. What would it be for some fact, law of nature, number, or reason to *exist*?

According to

Fundamentalism: All that exists are the ultimate constituents of reality.

On one such view:

(A) All that exists are sub-atomic particles.   There are no atoms, rocks, or stars.

Such views are implausibly and pointlessly extreme. We should claim instead that

(B) many physical objects are *composite*, in the sense that these objects are made up of smaller components.

Stars, for example, consist of atoms, and atoms consist of sub-atomic particles.   We can add

(C) Though many composite objects exist, these objects do not exist *separately* from their components, since their existence consists in the existence and interrelations of their components.

Some people claim:

(D) What exists in the *fundamental ontological* sense are the ultimate constituents of reality. Composite objects, such as atoms, rocks, and stars, exist only in a *superficial* sense.

Since the Universe is a composite object, (D) implausibly implies that, in the fundamental sense, the Universe does not exist. And if we have claimed (B) and (C), there seems no need to add (D).

As well as claiming that there are physical objects, such as particles and stars, we should claim that there are events and processes, such as a flash of lightning, and the collision of two galaxies. Though events are said in English to occur rather than exist, we can here ignore this fact, and regard occurring as one way of existing.

On one widely held view, often called

> *Actualism*: To be, or to exist, is to be actual, so there cannot be anything that is merely possible.

For something to exist, in the relevant *tenseless* sense, it is enough that there is some time at which this thing exists. We can here ignore the ontological status of things that do not now exist, though they did or will exist at other times. I shall often use 'exist' to mean 'exist at some time'.

We ought, I believe, to accept a different view. According to what I shall call

> *Possibilism*: There are some things that are never actual, but are merely possible. There are some things that might happen but never actually happen, and some things that might exist but never actually exist.

Of the philosophers who discuss questions about what is actual or possible, many ignore this view. Stalnaker, for example, claims that if we believe that there are some things that are merely possible, we shall believe that these possible entities are just as real as entities that are actual. Fine writes that 'especially in its more extreme forms', possibilism 'offends against what Russell has called "our robust sense of reality"'. But Possibilists like me need not believe that merely possible entities are real. Loux defines Actualism as the view 'that only what actually exists is real'. But Possibilists can agree that only what is actual and real is actual and real. We are Possibilists because we believe that there are also some things that are merely possible, rather than being actual and real. These writers do not explain why they ignore this view.

If Actualism were true, much of our thinking would be undermined. For example, we could never choose between different possible acts, or compare their possible outcomes, since there couldn't be any merely possible acts or outcomes. Nor could we ever have reason to regret having acted as we did, since it could never be true that there was something else that we could have done instead.

When we claim that there was some other possible act, we need not mean that, even with things exactly as they were, this other act would have been *causally* possible. The relevant sense of 'could' is the hypothetical sense which is compatible with causal determinism. It is enough that we could or would have acted differently *if* we had chosen to. Actualism implies that, even in this sense, there are no such possible acts.

Some Actualists claim that, if we believe that there are such acts, we are being misled by our language.   Consider first the claim that

(E) there are some impossible objects, such as spherical cubes.

This claim might seem to imply that there are some spherical cubes. To avoid suggesting that there are such things, we could restate (E) as

(F) There could not possibly be objects of certain kinds, such as spherical cubes.

In the same way, some Actualists claim, when we say

(G) There was something else that we could have done,

we may seem to be referring to some merely possible act. To avoid suggesting that there are such acts, these people claim, we should restate (G) as

(H) We could have acted differently.

But (G), I believe, is not misleading, nor does it help to restate (G) as (H). Unlike (F), which explicitly denies that there are spherical cubes, (H) does not deny that there are merely possible acts. Though (H) does not explicitly assert that there was something else that we could have done, (H) is merely another way of saying that there was such a possible act.

Though we can truly claim that there are no impossible objects, such as spherical cubes, we cannot truly claim that nothing ever happens. Actualists should admit that some things happen, and what happens are events. If we could have acted differently, this event was not actual, but was merely possible. Since Actualists deny that there are any such events, their view implies that we could never have acted differently.

Some Actualists claim that, though there are no merely possible events, we can choose how we shall act.   We can truly believe that

> (I) it might either be true that we shall choose to act in one way, or be true that we shall choose to act in some other way.

But (I) implies that there are different alternatives, between which we choose. When we choose to make one alternative actual, the other alternative will be merely possible. Actualists must deny that there are any such alternatives, so their view implies that we cannot ever choose how we shall act. Of those who claim to be Actualists, however, some misdescribe their real view. I defend these claims further in Appendix J.

Many Actualists assume

> *the Single Sense View*: The words 'there are' and 'exist' must always be used in the same single sense.

As before, I believe, we ought to accept a different view.   According to

> *the Plural Senses View*: There is one wide, general sense in which we can claim that there are certain things, or that these things exist. We can also use these words in other, narrower senses. For example, if we say that certain things exist in what I shall call the *narrow actualist* sense, we mean that these things are actually exist as concrete parts of the spatio-temporal world.

In defending Possibilism, I shall also be defending this view. As we shall see, these views have other implications. If there are some things that are merely possible, and there are different senses in which things can exist, we can justifiably believe that many more kinds of thing exist.

To illustrate their view, Possibilists might truly claim

> (J) There was a palace designed by Wren to replace the burnt Palace of Whitehall, but this palace was not built and never actually existed.

If the Single Sense View were true, (J) would mean

> (K) There existed such a palace designed by Wren, but this palace was not built, so that, in the same sense of 'exist', this palace never existed.

This claim is a contradiction, which could not possibly be true. But (J) does not mean (K).   (J) could be more fully stated as

> (L) There was, in the wide sense, a possible palace designed by Wren, but this palace was not built and never existed in the narrow actualist sense.

Actualists might next say that, even if (J) is coherent, such claims are all false. On this view, it is in no sense true there was such a possible palace designed by Wren. But that is not so. Any historian who denied (J) would be making a plain mistake.

Some Actualists would accept that (J) is true, but would claim that (J) is metaphysically misleading.   It would be better, these people claim, to say:

> (M) There was an architectural design by Wren for such a palace, though no such palace ever existed.

This claim is better, these Actualists would say, because unlike a merely possible palace, this architectural design actually existed.

This objection to (J) is not, however, justified. Though (J) claims that there *was* in the wide sense a possible palace designed by Wren, (J) explicitly denies that this palace ever actually existed.   (J) is not in any way misleading.

Other Actualists claim:

> (N) There cannot exist things that do not exist, nor can there *be* certain things if there are no such things.

But Possibilists would accept (N). There cannot have been some possible palace, Possibilists would agree, unless there was such a possible palace.

But this truth does not imply that this possible palace was ever built, and actually existed.

When Quine rejects Possibilism, he objects that we cannot refer to *particular* possible things, because we could not distinguish between these things.   In his words:

> Take, for instance, the possible fat man in that doorway; and, again, the possible bald man in that doorway. Are they the same possible man, or two possible men? How do we decide?

Quine gives up too quickly. We cannot always distinguish between *actual* particular things. And we often can distinguish between particular possible things. Suppose, for example, that I am playing some game of chess. After my opponent has made some move that puts my King in check, there might be only three particular moves that the rules of chess allow me to make. I might choose to make one of these possible moves actual, by moving my King to a certain square. Some observer might then truly claim that one of my other two possible moves would have been better, since it would have led to my victory. We can refer to many other particular possible acts, such as the knock that I should have knocked before opening your bedroom door.

Some people claim that, when we refer to some possible act, we can refer only to a *kind* of act, which might take many different forms, thereby being different *particular* acts. On this view, I couldn't refer in advance to a particular act of moving my King to a certain square, because I don't know how fast I would carry my King through the air, or how high above the chess board my hand would go. But we should deny that every particular act or other event must be precisely as it is. I would be making the very same move in chess, by placing my King on a certain square, however fast I carried my King through the air. And we should not claim that, if some soldier had acted differently during the First World War, this particular war would never have occurred, since it would have been a different war which occurred instead. We can add that, when we have beliefs about particular possible acts, or other events, we don't need to refer to these events in this kind of identifying way. We can often truly believe that, if some event hadn't occurred, there is some other particular event, unknown to us, that would have occurred instead.

Similar claims apply to possible persisting entities, such as buildings or people. We can refer to the particular palace that would have actually existed if the palace designed by Wren had been built. And we might refer to the particular person who would exist if some actual ovum and sperm cell were united, and this fertilized ovum were successfully implanted in some woman's womb. We can add that, to make some true claims about particular possible entities, we don't need to refer to them in such identifying ways. Return to *Jane*, my imagined 14-year-old girl who intends to have a child. We might tell Jane that, if she has some child now, she would give this child a worse start in life than she could give to any child that she might later have, when she is mature. These are intelligible claims, which might be true, about the possible children that Jane might have. These claims could not be true unless it is in one sense true that

> (O) there are many possible children whom Jane might
> later have.

Though we can't identify these possible children, these are not *kinds* of children. Any child that Jane later had would be a *particular* child.

As before, some Actualists would say that, though (O) is in one sense true, this claim is metaphysically misleading, since (O) suggests that there actually exist such entities as merely possible people. But (O) could be more fully stated as

> (P) There are, in the wide sense, many possible children whom
> Jane might later have, most of whom will never actually exist.

Such claims are not misleading, since they explicitly deny that such merely possible people ever actually exist. We ought, I conclude, to accept both Possibilism and the Plural Senses View.   I defend these views further in Appendix J.

If Actualists become Possibilists, they must give up some of their claims. But these people might defend a different view. According to what we can call

Actualist Foundationalism: There are, in the wide sense, many possible entities that never actually exist, and many possible events that never actually occur. But these truths about what is possible all depend on truths about what is actual.

If Possibilism could be given such an Actualist foundation, that would have great importance, since it would help to explain how there can be such truths about what is merely possible. Of the impressive arguments with which some people have defended Actualism, several could be revised so that they support this other view.

Return now to a fuller version of

List B: Facts, meanings, laws of nature, the Equator, philosophical theories, nations, wars, famines, overdrafts, prizes, constellations, metaphors, symphonies, fictional characters, fashions, literary styles, problems, explanations, numbers, logical truths, duties, and reasons.

According to some Actualists, we should deny that there are any things of all or most of these kinds. What exists, these people claim, are only such things as rocks, stars, and human beings. But if we believe truly that there are some merely possible things, such as possible events or people, we cannot plausibly deny that there can be such things as meanings, laws of nature, and philosophical theories. Unlike rocks and stars, these things are not physical objects. But merely possible events are not physical objects. And unlike things that are merely possible, most of the items in List B might be actual. Our words can have actual meanings, and there can be actual laws of nature, philosophical theories, famines, symphonies, and fashions.

When we think about ontology, some people assume, our main task is to consider lists like B, and to try to decide which items in such lists might exist. This assumption is, I believe, mistaken. When we consider physical objects, it is worth claiming that some of these objects may have a special ontological status, by being the fundamental or ultimate components of all larger composite objects. But we should not then try to decide which kinds of composite objects might exist. We should believe that there can be atoms, molecules, rocks, stars, constellations, galaxies, super-galaxies, and the whole physical Universe. Similar remarks apply to the items in List B. If we try to decide which of these kinds of things might exist, we cannot avoid drawing arbitrary distinctions, and we shall make it harder to discuss the various kinds of thing whose existence we have denied. As Aristotle said, 'the question is not *whether* such things exist but *how* they do.' We should claim that, unlike impossible objects such as spherical cubes, things of all these kinds might exist, and we should then try to describe the philosophically important differences between these kinds of thing.

As well as distinguishing between what is actual and what is possible, and between composite objects and their components, we should make other ontological claims. Some things ontologically depend on others, not by consisting in them, but in other ways. On one view, for example, thoughts depend on thinkers, and experiences depend on *subjects*, or the conscious beings who have these experiences. We can next distinguish between *concrete* things or entities, such as physical objects or mental states and events, and *abstract* entities, such as numbers, meanings, and valid arguments. There are also some entities and properties that are *mind-dependent*, in the rough sense that their existence depends on certain facts about some people's mental lives. These distinctions are not sharp, and often overlap. It is sometimes claimed that entities are abstract if they do not exist in space or time. But some abstract entities, such as the Equator, are spatially located, and some others, such as the Eroica Symphony, come into existence at a certain time. Nor can we neatly divide what exists into these different categories. Many things are hybrids, being partly concrete and partly abstract, or being only partly mind-dependent. Nation-states, for example, may be wholly abstract, but nations, tribes, and armies consist, in part, of human beings. When armies or regiments are disbanded, they cease to exist, but the soldiers of which they were partly composed may continue to exist. Nation-states are wholly mind-dependent, as are criminal laws, symphonies, and literary styles. But nations and armies are only partly mind-dependent, as are wars, performances of symphonies, and constellations.

We can also distinguish between the different ways in which various kinds of entity exist. When certain entities or properties are mind-dependent, or are created by us, we can more easily explain what their existence involves. We can explain how there are such things as fashions, fictional characters, or the Eroica Symphony. And we can explain what is involved in the existence of entities or properties that are normative or evaluative in the rule-involving or response-dependent senses. We can describe in naturalistic terms what it is for something to be a crime, a spelling mistake, a breach of etiquette, a joke, or a work of art.

There are other abstract entities and properties that are not mind-dependent, or created by us. Though novelists invent fictional characters, and composers create symphonies, mathematicians and scientists *discover* proofs and laws of nature. It is harder to explain what is involved in the existence of such entities and properties, and how we can know truths about them. Reason-involving normative properties are, I believe, of this independent kind. In defending the belief that some things have these properties, I shall first discuss the debate about whether numbers and some other abstract entities exist. Though numbers and their properties are not normative, their existence, and our knowledge of them, raise some similar questions.

113 Non-Metaphysical Cognitivism

Platonists and *Nominalists* both believe that, if there are numbers and certain other purely abstract entities, these entities do not exist in space or time. We cannot see or touch numbers, or detect them with our scientific instruments. But Platonists claim that such entities exist in some other way, or in some other part of reality. Nominalists reject this claim. Quine for example, once wrote:

> We do not believe in abstract entities. No one supposes that abstract entities . . . exist in space-time; but we mean more than this. We renounce them altogether.

We can ask: '*What* more does Quine mean? What is he renouncing or denying?'

The answer, Quine suggests, could not be simpler. We all understand the question 'What is there?' When we claim that certain things exist, or that there *are* such things, we always use these phrases in the same, familiar sense. We know what it is for rocks or stars to exist. If numbers exist, though they are not in space or time, they exist in the very same sense.

When Nominalists accept this view, they can be led to extreme conclusions. Field, for example, claims that there is no sense in which numbers or other abstract entities exist.   If we said

(A) There are prime numbers that are greater than 100,

this claim would be about nothing. Partly for this reason, Field concludes that such mathematical claims cannot be true, though they may be useful fictions.

Quine qualifies the Single Sense View. He concedes that in a 'popular' but 'misleading manner of speaking' we can allow ourselves to say that there are numbers, such as prime numbers greater than 100. But such 'casual remarks', he writes, 'would want dusting up when our thoughts turn seriously ontological'. When we speak seriously, we should claim that, in the 'literal and basic' sense, numbers do not *really* exist. Many other writers make such claims. Dorr, for example, distinguishes between the *superficial* and *fundamental* senses of the phrases 'there are' and 'there exist'.

Given this distinction, we can redescribe this disagreement. We can ask

Q2: Do numbers really exist in a fundamental, ontological sense, though they do not exist in space or time?

Platonists answer Yes.   Nominalists answer No.

These are not the only possible views. According to a third view, Q2 is too unclear to have an answer. We can call this the *No Clear Question View*. Of those who claim to be Nominalists, some may really accept this third view. These people may doubt that there is any fundamental ontological sense in which some things might or might not exist, though not in space or time. But if we have such doubts, we are not Nominalists.

If Q2 is too unclear to have an answer, we should not claim this answer to be No.

In explaining this third view, we can distinguish two kinds of unclarity. Consider first

(B) There are some colourless green ideas which sleep furiously.

Though (B) is in one sense meaningless, or nonsensical, there is another sense in which (B)'s meaning is clear enough.   We might claim

(C) There could not possibly be any ideas which are colourless, green, or sleep furiously.

Since (C) makes sense, and is true, (B) makes sense, and is false. Another such claim is

(D) There are some headaches which are correct, and others which are mistaken.

I claimed earlier that we could not defend (D), because we could not explain what it would *be* for some headache to be correct, or mistaken. In denying (D), however, I was not claiming that (D) makes no sense. (D) makes sense, and is clearly false. No headache could be correct or mistaken.

It might be objected that, compared with (C) and (D), it makes *more* sense to claim

(E) Numbers really exist in the fundamental ontological sense, though not in space or time.

But this objection, I believe, misdescribes the difference between these claims. Rather than claiming that, compared with (C) and (D), (E) makes more sense, we should say that (E) is closer to being a claim that might be true. (E) is closer to being such a claim because it is *less clear* what (E) means. We cannot imagine coming to understand how there might be some colourless green ideas which sleep furiously, or be some headaches which are correct, and others which are mistaken. When

Platonists assert (E), we can more easily imagine that these people might be able to explain or restate their view so that we can understand how this view might be true. (E), however, needs to be further explained. It is not yet clear enough in what sense it might be true, or might be false, that numbers really exist in a fundamental ontological sense, though not in space or time.

Several people have tried to explain (E).   Dorr, for example, writes:

> There are no numbers. There are no properties. When I utter these sentences, I mean to be using them in the fundamental way. I mean, if you like, that numbers and properties are not part of the ultimate furniture of reality . . . there are, in the final analysis, no such things.

When Dorr refers to the ultimate furniture of reality, he might seem to be referring to the ultimate constituents of what exists in the spatio-temporal Universe. But Dorr would not then be rejecting Platonism, since Platonists do not believe that numbers exist in space or time. Since Dorr cannot be using 'reality' to refer only to the spatio-temporal Universe, his remarks do not sufficiently explain what Platonists assert, and Nominalists like Dorr deny.

Fine writes that, when some people deny 'that numbers really exist', these people mean that

> there is no realm of numbers 'out there' to which our talk corresponds.

As before, since Platonists do not believe that numbers exist in space, it is too unclear what the phrase 'out there' means. Fine also suggests that, rather than asking what exists, we should ask what is *real*, and is 'a genuine constituent of reality'.   In his words:

> we can now define an object to be real if, for some way the object might be, it is constitutive of reality that it is that way . . . the numbers 1 and 2 would be real on this account, for example, if it is constitutive of reality that 2 is greater than 1.

Though we would nearly all believe that 2 is greater than 1, most of us would be puzzled by the question whether this truth is *constitutive of reality*. As Fine remarks, such claims need more explanation.

My claims so far have been negative. According to

the No Clear Question View: Numbers are not a kind of entity about which it is a clear enough question whether, in some ontological sense, they exist, or are real, though they are not in space or time.

We can now turn to some other, more positive views. We are *Cognitivists* about some kind of claim if we believe that such claims can be, in a strong sense, true. Many such claims have metaphysical or ontological implications. In trying to decide whether these claims are true, we must answer some questions about what exists, in an ontological sense. That is true, for example, of claims about concrete entities, such as rocks, stars, philosophers, and bluebell woods. And it may be true of all claims about the natural properties of what exists in the spatio-temporal world. When we believe that claims of these kinds can be in a strong sense true, we are *Metaphysical Cognitivists* about such truths.

When we consider some other kinds of claim, we may accept views of a different kind, which we can call *Non-Metaphysical Cognitivism*. On such views:

(F) There are some claims that are, in the strongest sense, true, but these truths have no positive ontological implications.

(G) When such claims assert that there are certain things, or that these things exist, these claims do not imply that these things exist in some ontological sense.

Some examples, I suggest, are mathematical truths. Nothing could be truer than the truths that 2 is greater than 1, that $2 + 2 = 4$, and that there are prime numbers greater than 100. Not even God could make these claims false. For such claims to be true, there must be a sense in which there are numbers, or in which numbers exist. But in deciding which mathematical claims are true, we don't need to answer the question whether numbers really exist in an ontological sense, though not in space or time. Similar remarks apply to some other abstract entities, such as logical truths and valid arguments. In deciding whether certain claims state such truths or arguments, we don't need to ask whether these truths or arguments exist in an ontological sense.

This view might be confused with a different view. Of those who believe that there are some abstract entities, some have claimed

> (H) Concrete and abstract entities do not exist in the same sense.

Such claims are hard to defend. If we are Non-Metaphysical Cognitivists about abstract entities, we should accept the Plural Senses View, and we should therefore reject (H).   On our view:

> (I) There are both many concrete entities, such as rocks and stars, and many abstract entities, such as numbers and logical truths.

> (J) When we claim that there are entities of both these kinds, we are using the phrase 'there are' in the wide sense.

> (K) Concrete entities also exist in the narrow actualist sense, as actually existing concrete parts of the spatio-temporal world. Abstract entities do not exist in this actualist sense.

I have claimed above that

> (L) though there are, in the wide sense, many merely possible entities, these entities do not exist in this actualist sense.

When we discuss such possible entities, it is enough to claim that these entities exist only in the wide sense. But when we discuss abstract entities, it is worth introducing and using another, narrower sense. We can say

> (M) Some abstract entities can be plausibly claimed to exist, not only in the wide sense, but also in a distinctive, non-ontological sense.

When we claim that there are some things that are merely possible, we must admit that, compared with things that are actual, such merely possible things have a lesser ontological status. That is why it matters, for example, whether good or bad possible events will also be actual, and real. But when we consider certain abstract entities, such as prime numbers and logical truths, these distinctions do not apply. These numbers and truths are not *less* actual, or real, than stars, or human beings. These abstract entities have *no* ontological status. They are not, in relevant senses, either actual or merely possible, or either real or unreal. When we are trying to form true beliefs about numbers or logical truths, we need not answer ontological questions. As one way to sum up these claims, we can say that, though there are these numbers and truths, these entities exist in a non-ontological sense.

We can add that

> (N) it can be a difficult and important question whether
> there *are* certain things in the wide sense, and in this
> non-ontological sense.

We can ask, for example, whether there is some number that has certain properties, or whether there is some undiscovered proof of some theorem. There may be no such number, or proof. We can have several reasons to deny that there are certain abstract entities of these and some other kinds. When we try to refer to such entities, for example, we may fail, because our concepts are too unclear, or indeterminate. Our description of such entities may be in some way inconsistent, or lead to some contradiction. In such cases, we should deny that there are such entities. There is, for example, no number that is both odd and even. Nor is there a set that contains all and only those sets which do not contain themselves, since the claim that such a set exists would involve a contradiction. And when we claim that abstract entities of these kinds have certain properties, these claims may be false. But if our claims avoid these and similar objections, these claims could not be false if and because these entities do not exist in some ontological sense.

Here is another way to illustrate and defend these claims. Like many people, I believe that

(O) it might have been true that nothing ever existed: no living beings, no stars, no atoms, not even space or time.

I discuss this possibility in Appendix D.   Someone might object:

(P) It could not have been true that nothing ever existed. If that had been true, there would have been the truth that nothing existed.   So your alleged possibility is self-contradictory.

This objection, I believe, fails. (O) is a claim about all of the kinds of entity that might exist in an ontological sense.   We can claim that, like numbers,

(Q) truths are not a kind of entity about which it is a clear enough question whether they exist in some ontological sense.

We can also defend a form of Non-Metaphysical Cognitivism. Most truths are true only because things of some other kind exist, in an ontological sense. But truths themselves do not have to exist in such a sense.   Truths need only be true.   We could admit that

(R) if it had been true that nothing ever existed, there would have been this truth.

But there is no contradiction here.   We could add that

(S) though there would have *been* this truth, this truth would have existed only in the wide sense and the non-ontological sense.

Similar claims apply, I believe, to many other abstract entities. Even if nothing had ever existed, there would have been prime numbers greater than 100. It would also have been true that things like rocks, stars, and living beings might have existed. Since these things would have been possible, there would have been these possibilities. And since there might have been rocks that were hard, stars that were hot, and living beings that were in pain, there would have been these and many other uninstantiated properties. But all these things would have existed in the non-ontological sense.

When van Inwagen considers the suggestion that the word 'exist' can have such different senses, he remarks that he knows of no argument for this view 'that is even faintly plausible'. But he comes close to suggesting the argument that I have just given.   Van Inwagen writes:

> I will assume that at least some abstract objects — numbers, pure sets, 'purely qualitative' properties and relations, possibilities, possible worlds themselves — exist in all possible worlds. I do not think that the question that people have actually intended to ask when they ask why anything at all should exist could be answered by pointing out . . . that the number 510 would exist no matter what . . . if the only objects were abstract objects, there is an obvious and perfectly good sense in which there would be nothing at all, for there would be no physical things, no stuffs, no events, no space, no time, no Cartesian egos, no God. When people want to know why there is anything at all, they want to know why that bleak state of affairs does not obtain.

Here is one way to explain such claims. When people ask whether it might have been true that nothing ever existed, these people have in mind all of the kinds of thing that might exist in an ontological sense. They are not asking whether it might have been true that there weren't even such abstract entities as truths, or possibilities, or numbers. These people ignore such abstract entities because, if there are such things, they exist in some non-ontological sense. Such people may not have explicitly considered the difference between these two senses. But they are right to assume that, even if there would have been such abstract entities, it might have been true that, in a different and 'perfectly good sense', there would have *been nothing at all.* Even if these abstract entities would have existed in some non-ontological sense, there might have been nothing that existed in any ontological sense.

Van Inwagen would reject this interpretation of these claims. And he argues that the word 'exist' cannot have two such senses. But I believe that, as I try to show in Appendix J, no such argument could succeed.

We can next compare these claims:

> (T) There are various abstract entities and truths, though these things do not exist in space or time.

> (U) God exists, though not in space or time.

Non-Metaphysical Cognitivism can be plausibly applied to (T), since we can plausibly believe that these abstract entities exist in the non-ontological sense. But this view applies less plausibly to (U). On most people's views, and as I shall here assume, God could not be a purely abstract entity. Partly for that reason, it must be a metaphysical question whether (U) is true. In our beliefs about God, we cannot be Non-Metaphysical Cognitivists. If God exists, that would have to be true in some ontological sense.

When we consider (U), we might appeal to a version of the No Clear Question View. We might believe that, though it makes sense to claim that God exists *in* space and time, it is not clear enough what it would be for God to exist, though not in space and time. For (U) to be true, God would have to exist in some non-spatio-temporal part of reality, like the Platonic realm in which, on Plato's view, there exists the Form of the Good. We may find it hard to understand this claim. As before, however, there is a difference between (T) and (U). When we consider numbers, we can plausibly appeal to a version of the No Clear Question View. We can claim that, since numbers are abstract entities, there is no clear enough sense in which it might be true, or be false, that numbers exist in some non-spatio-temporal part of reality. Since God could *not* be a purely abstract entity, we should make a different and weaker claim about whether God might exist, though not in space or time. We can vaguely understand the possibility that space and time are not metaphysically fundamental. It makes sense to suppose that there is some entity that is more fundamental, and that both space and time metaphysically depend on this other entity. When they discuss the Big Bang, some physicists suggest hypotheses of this kind, and many people make such claims about God. We should admit that (U) might be made clearer, and that this clearer claim might be true or false. I discuss such views further in Appendix D.

We can now return to one of Dorr's remarks about the fundamental sense in which, as Platonists claim and Nominalists deny, numbers exist. Dorr writes:

> it is not an analytic truth that there are numbers, since it is not an analytic truth that there is anything at all. As Hume and Kant maintained in criticizing the standard a priori arguments for God's existence, denials of existence — when taken in the fundamental sense — cannot be self-contradictory.

We should agree, I believe, that *God's* existence cannot be proved merely by appealing to our concepts. According to one such argument, the concept of God is the concept of the most perfect being, and since such a being would be more perfect if this being exists, God must exist. This argument is unsound, as is suggested by the atheist's reply: 'God is so perfect that He doesn't even need to exist'.

Such claims do not, I believe, apply to numbers, or to some other kinds of abstract entity. It cannot follow merely from the concept of a number that there are numbers. But we may be able to prove that there are numbers by appealing to our concepts, and giving some argument. Such a proof may be possible partly *because* it is not true that numbers exist in an ontological sense. We can accept Dorr's claim that there could not be a priori arguments which showed that anything exists in such a sense. But this sense of 'exists' is not, I have claimed, the only important sense. If nothing had ever existed in any ontological sense, there would not have been any stars or atoms, nor would there have been space, or time, or God. But it would have been true that nothing ever existed. As we can also claim, there *would have been* the truth that nothing existed in an ontological sense. This truth would have *existed* in a different *non*-ontological sense. And there would have been many other truths, such as the truths that there are prime numbers greater than 100, and that stars, atoms, and living beings might have existed.

There would also have been some irreducibly normative truths. Compared with nothing's ever existing, it would have been much better if blissfully happy beings had existed, and it would have been much worse if there had existed conscious beings whose lives involved unrelieved suffering. Many people claim that such normative truths are metaphysically too queer to be compatible with a scientific world view. In response to such objections, we should appeal to another form of Non-Metaphysical Cognitivism.   On this view:

> (V) There are some claims that are irreducibly normative in the reason-involving sense, and are in the strongest sense true. But these truths have no ontological implications. For such claims to be true, these reason-involving properties need not exist either as natural properties in the spatio-temporal world, or in some non-spatio-temporal part of reality.

Though some of these normative claims are about acts or other entities that are merely possible, other such claims are about acts or entities that occur or exist in the spatio-temporal world. Two examples are the claims that, in invading Russia, Napoleon acted wrongly, and did what he had decisive reasons not to do. But though this act was an event in the spatio-temporal world, this act's wrongness wasn't a natural property. This is like the way in which a series of symbols written on some page may be a valid proof of some theorem.   Though these symbols exist in the spatio-temporal world, their property of being a valid proof is not, I shall claim, a further natural property of this world.   This proof's validity is not itself a normative property.   But this validity has the non-natural normative property of giving us a decisive reason to accept this proof.   As Nagel writes, such normative claims 'need not (and in my view should not) have any metaphysical content whatever.'

If we accept (V), we might call ourselves *Non-Metaphysical Non-Naturalist Normative Cognitivists*.   But since our main claims are about reasons, I shall call us *Rationalists*.   Those who reject Rationalism I shall here call *Naturalists*.   Though some of these people are not Normative Naturalists but Non-Cognitivists or Nihilists, these people are nearly all Metaphysical Naturalists.

Rationalists, Korsgaard suggests, claim to have 'spotted' some normative entities, as it were 'wafting by'.   This suggestion assumes that Rationalists are Actualists, who believe that there is nothing except the concrete entities that actually exist in the spatio-temporal world. But Rationalists should not be Actualists.   As I argue further in Appendix J, we should be Possibilists, and we should accept some form of Non-Metaphysical Cognitivism.   Actualists deny that there is anything that is merely possible.   This view implies that we can never choose between different possible acts, nor could we ever have reason to regret anything we did, since there could never be anything else that we could have done instead.   We should reject these claims. There are, in the wide sense, many events and other things that are merely possible, since these things are never actual.   These merely possible things are not observable features of the spatio-temporal world.   But all of our practical thinking, and much of our thinking about the world, essentially involves the belief that there are such things.   And there is, I believe, no decisive metaphysical objection to such beliefs. When we claim that there are things that we *could* have done, these claims don't commit us to the existence of strange entities as parts of reality.

Just as there are some things that we *could* have done, there are some things that we *should* have done.   And there are some things that we have reasons to believe, and to want, and to do.   These claims, we can add, do not conflict with what Russell called our *robust sense of reality*.   Unlike entities that are merely possible rather than actual, such normative properties and truths do not have a *lesser* ontological status. Like numbers and logical truths, these normative properties and truths have *no* ontological status.   These properties and truths are not, in relevant senses, either actual or merely possible, or either real or unreal. In asking whether there are such normative truths, we need not answer ontological questions. There are, I believe, some such truths, which are as true as any truth could be.

Naturalists give other objections to this view. As well as claiming that there could not *be* any such non-natural properties and truths, some Naturalists claim that we could not have any reason to *believe* that there are such truths.   We ought, I shall argue, to reject these claims.

32

Epistemology

114 The Causal Objection

According to what we can call

> *the Causal Objection*: Since non-natural normative properties
> or truths could not have any effects, we could not have any
> way of knowing about them.

To have such knowledge, many Naturalists claim, we would need some
mysterious kind of quasi-perceptual contact with these non-natural
properties. Gibbard writes that, according to Rationalists like Sidgwick
and Moore,

> among the facts of the world are facts of what is rational
> and what is not. A person of normal mental powers can
> discern these facts. Judgments of rationality are thus
> straightforward apprehensions of fact, not through sense
> perception but through a mental faculty analogous to
> sense perception.

There could not, Gibbard assumes, be any such faculty. But Gibbard's
description is misleading. His remarks suggest that, according to these
Rationalists, we can be aware of facts about what is rational in something
like the way in which we can feel the heat of the Sun or see the craters
on the Moon. Most Rationalists do not hold such views. We can
form true normative beliefs, these people claim, in something like the
way in which we can form true logical and mathematical beliefs. This

way of forming beliefs does not involve any faculty that is like sense perception.

In suggesting how we can form true normative beliefs, Rationalists can first explain why we don't need to have any such quasi-perceptual faculty. When we have beliefs about the world, these beliefs are mostly about facts or truths that are *contingent*, in the sense that they might have been false. The Sun might have been hotter, and the Moon might have had no craters. We cannot discover whether such beliefs are true merely by thinking about them. We must have perceptual experiences in which we are causally affected by these features of the world, or by causally related features. That is why, to know that there are craters on the Moon, we must use our telescopes.

No such claims apply to *necessary* truths, such as logical or mathematical truths. It is not a contingent feature of our world that $2 + 2 = 4$. This claim would be true in every possible world. Though it is natural to say that we can *see* that $2 + 2 = 4$, this metaphor is misleading. When some truth is not contingent, we have no reason to assume that our way of knowing this truth must be like perception, by involving causal contact with what this truth is about. We often *can* discover logical or mathematical truths merely by thinking about them.

Similar remarks apply to normative truths. We don't need to discover that ours is a world in which we have reasons to believe that $2 + 2 = 4$. Nor do we need to discover that ours is a world in which we have reasons to care about certain things. Mackie writes that, according to Rationalists, we must

> ascertain which of various possible worlds . . . is the actual one — for example, whether the actual world is one in which pain is *prima facie* to be relieved, or one in which, other things being equal, pain is to be perpetuated . . . [The] moral thinker has, as it were, to respond to a value-laden atmosphere that surrounds him in the actual world.

We should reject these claims. Fundamental normative truths are not about how the actual world happens to be. In any possible world, pain would be in itself bad, and *prima facie* to be relieved rather than perpetuated. Similarly, even if the laws of nature had been very different, rational beings would have had reasons to do what would achieve their rational aims. As in the case of logical and mathematical truths, we can discover some normative truths merely by thinking about them.

Logical and mathematical truths are often claimed to be *analytic*, in the sense that they are true by definition, or their truth follows directly from what they mean. I shall not discuss such views here. Even if such views could fully explain our knowledge of logic and arithmetic, which I and many others doubt or deny, these views could not fully explain our knowledge of normative truths. Some normative truths may be analytic. One example may be the truth that, if some man was punished for some crime that he is known not to have committed, this man's punishment could not be just. But that is not a positive, substantive normative truth. There are at least some such truths that are not analytic. The badness of pain, for example, does not follow from the meaning of the words 'bad' and 'pain'. I believe that, like truths about what exists in an ontological sense, *no* such normative truths could be analytic. But I shall not defend this belief here.

When Sidgwick calls our knowledge of some normative truths *intuitive*, he is not referring to any special faculty. Sidgwick means that we can recognize the truth of some normative beliefs by considering only the content of these beliefs, or *what* we are believing. These beliefs do not need to be inferred from other beliefs. Sidgwick also calls some of these beliefs *self-evident*. In using this word, Sidgwick does not mean that such beliefs are infallible. These beliefs, he claims, may need careful reflection, and they may be false. Such beliefs may merely *seem* to be self-evident. These beliefs may also be *indubitable*, or *intrinsically credible*. Such credibility is a matter of degree. I shall return to the relations between these properties.

Though we find some beliefs intrinsically credible, we form most of our true beliefs in other ways. We know some beliefs to be analytic truths, and we form many other true beliefs by responding to reasons, which may be logically conclusive, or decisive in weaker ways, or merely sufficient. Consider, for example:

(A) $1 + 1 = 2$.

(B) $2 + 2 = 4$.

(C) $163 + 228 = 391$.

(D) There are craters on the Moon.

(E) Some human beings will be alive in the year 3000.

For some of us, (A) is true by definition, since we were taught that '2' is the name of the number that we get by adding 1 to 1. Most of us would find (B) intrinsically credible, but would believe (C) only after a calculation which gave us conclusive reasons to have this belief. There are no sharp distinctions here. (B) is close to being true by definition. We could also do a very brief calculation that gave us conclusive reasons to believe (B), though few of us would need to do that. Some mathematicians would find (C) intrinsically credible. When we form beliefs about the world, such as (D) and (E), we seldom have conclusive reasons to have these beliefs. But we have decisive reasons to believe (D), and the facts that are known to us give us sufficient reasons to believe (E).

Since we could justify beliefs like (B) by describing our reasons to have these beliefs, there may seem no need to call such beliefs intrinsically credible. But we may have some beliefs that are not true by definition, or more broadly analytic, but whose justification can be given only by our understanding of their content. To allow for such cases, I shall say that some of our beliefs can be justified either by their intrinsic credibility, or by our reasons for having them, or both. But when this distinction does not matter, I shall use 'epistemic reasons' in a wide sense, which covers intrinsic credibility.

In discussing some of our beliefs, we need the *modal* concepts *necessary*, *possible*, and *impossible*. We can use some modal concepts to define others. Some statement is necessary, for example, or *must* be true, if this statement could not possibly be false. Like normative concepts, however, this group of modal concepts cannot be helpfully explained in other terms. The most fundamental necessary truths are certain logical laws, such as

Non-Contradiction: No statement or proposition could be both wholly true and wholly false.

Some of these laws describe valid arguments, or forms of reasoning. One such law is

> *Modus Ponens*: If it is true both that *P* and that *If P, then Q*, it must be true that *Q*. For example: If I am a man, and my being a man implies that I shall die, it must be true that I shall die.

Such arguments are *valid* in the sense that, if their premises are true, their conclusions must be true. Though these logical truths are not themselves normative, they are closely related to some normative truths. When we know that some argument is valid, and has true premises, we have decisive reasons to accept this argument's conclusion.

Given these similarities between these kinds of necessary truths, our claims to know such truths can be challenged in similar ways. We can next look more closely at one such challenge. Platonists claim that, though numbers are abstract entities which do not exist in space or time, we have many true beliefs about them. Field objects that, since we could not be causally affected by such abstract entities or their properties, Platonists cannot explain how mathematicians could have so many true mathematical beliefs. This correlation, Platonists must admit, would involve some

> massive coincidence . . . We should view with suspicion any claim to know facts about a certain domain if we believe it impossible to explain the reliability of our beliefs about that domain.

Other writers make similar claims about our alleged ability to recognize non-natural normative truths. Street for example writes that, though we might, by a sheer coincidence, have beliefs that matched such truths, this would be 'extremely unlikely'. We can call this *the Massive Coincidence Objection*.

This objection can, I believe, be answered.   We can reply that

> (F) we can form true mathematical and normative beliefs without being causally affected by what these beliefs are about,

and that

> (G) we can sufficiently explain how we came to have
> these abilities.

To illustrate (F), we can use a simpler example. We can design computers whose internal circuitry and software programs enable them to operate in ways that correspond to valid forms of logical or mathematical reasoning. Though these computers do not have beliefs, or any other mental states, that is irrelevant here. These computers can reliably produce true answers to mathematical questions, without being causally affected by numbers or their mathematical properties.

Similar claims apply to us. God might have designed our brains so that, without such causal contact, we can reason in ways that lead us to reach true answers to mathematical questions. We might have similar God-given abilities to respond to reasons, and to form true beliefs about these reasons. These abilities overlap if, as I believe, we form many true mathematical beliefs by responding to epistemic reasons.

As the case of computers shows, such abilities need not involve any quasi-perceptual faculty. When some fact has the property of *being* or *giving us* a reason, we cannot be causally affected by this normative property. But we can respond to such properties in other ways. We respond to reasons when we are aware of facts that give us these reasons, and this awareness leads us to believe, or want, or do what these facts give us reasons to believe, or want, or do. I shall later describe more fully the sense in which, without causal contact, we are *responding* to these normative properties.

Though Field admits that God might have given us the ability to form true mathematical beliefs without being causally affected by numbers or their properties, Field assumes that we can dismiss this possibility, since our brains were not designed by God. Is there some other way in which we might have developed such abilities?

Field assumes the answer to be No. In rejecting Platonism, Field writes:

> mathematical entities as the Platonist conceives them exist
> outside of space and time and bear no causal relations to us

or anything we can observe; and there just don't seem to be
any mechanisms that could explain how the existence of and
properties of such entities could be known.

There is another possibility, however, which Field surprisingly ignores.
Though not intentionally designed by God, our brains may have been
unintentionally designed by evolution, through a process of natural
selection. It may be true that, just as cheetahs were selected for their
speed, and giraffes were selected for their long necks, human beings
were selected for their rationality. That may be how we became able to
reason validly, and respond to reasons.

Of the ways in which human beings differ from other animals, two of
the most fundamental are that we use language, and respond to reasons.
Of these two, I suggest, it is our rationality that is more fundamental.
We are members of the species homo *sapiens*, the humans that are
clever or intelligent in their thoughts and acts, though they may not
be wise. Though our use of language has immense importance, we can
respond to reasons in non-linguistic ways. Language enabled us to have
much greater numbers of more precise and complex thoughts, and to
share these thoughts. Many animals can form true beliefs about what
is happening, or will soon happen, in their immediate environment.
Because we can respond to epistemic reasons, we are able to form many
other kinds of true belief, especially beliefs about the further future, and
the possible effects of different possible acts. The ability of early humans
to form such true beliefs had evolutionary advantages, by helping them
to survive and reproduce. Natural selection slowly but steadily gave later
humans greater cognitive abilities. Just as the faster cheetahs and taller
giraffes tended to survive longer and have more offspring, who inherited
similar qualities, so did the humans who were better at reasoning validly
and responding to reasons.

When Nagel discusses the view that natural selection explains our
rationality, he calls this view 'laughably inadequate'. But Nagel is rejecting more ambitious, reductive versions of this view. As Nagel points out,
evolutionary theories cannot explain normativity itself, or what *it is* to
have reasons to have certain beliefs or desires, or to act in certain ways.
Nor can such theories justify our responses to reasons. In Nagel's words:

> Whatever justification reason provides must come from
> the reasons it discovers, themselves. They cannot get
> their authority from natural selection . . . I follow the rules
> of logic because they are correct — not merely because I am
> biologically programmed to do so.

Nor could evolutionary theories explain how it is possible for there to be animals that respond to reasons. Natural selection does not create any of the possible forms that living beings can take, but merely makes some of these possibilities actual.   As Nagel claims, such selection

> may explain why creatures with vision or reason will survive,
> but it does not explain how vision or reason are possible.

Nagel also suggests, however, that natural selection cannot explain how we became able to respond to reasons. We ought, I believe, to reject this suggestion. If there can be animals who can see, or think rationally, natural selection can do more than explain why such animals will survive. Natural selection can explain how these animals became able to see, or to think rationally. When Nagel discusses 'the advanced intellectual capacities of human beings', he calls these 'extremely poor candidates for evolutionary explanation'. This claim underestimates, I believe, what natural selection can achieve.

How most animals developed vision is now fairly well understood. Random mutation gave a few early animals slight sensitivity to light. These animals had a slight advantage over their contemporaries with no such sensitivity, and were therefore slightly more likely to have surviving offspring, whose genes would give them the same sensitivity to light. After many millions of years of similar small improvements, some of the results were the superbly effective eyes of animals like eagles, hawks, and young human beings.

Consider next:

> *Three Roads*: While using its sense of smell to chase its quarry,
> some dog reaches a place from which there are only three
> exits, or roads. This dog goes down the first road, sniffs, and
> comes back. It then goes down the second road, sniffs, and
> comes back. It then runs down the third road *without sniffing*.

When a Greek Stoic learnt of this event, he conceded that humans may not be the only animals whose thinking can involve some kind of reasoning. This dog might have realized, even if only unconsciously, that its quarry must have gone down the third road. Early humans reasoned in similar ways, thereby forming many advantageous beliefs, such as beliefs about how they could trap some mammoth, or use the properties of fire. They also acquired some useful mathematical abilities. Some early human might have saved his life by thinking:

> Since three lions went into my cave, but only two lions have
> come out, one lion is still in the cave.

Though there are vast differences between such simple abilities and the genius of Euclid, Newton, or Gödel, these are in part differences of degree, not of kind. These much greater abilities, we can plausibly believe, could have been produced by the natural selection, during many thousands or millions of years, of those humans or pre-humans whose rational abilities were slightly greater.

Nagel also suggests that, if natural selection explained our ability to respond to reasons, this fact would cast doubt on this ability. In his words:

> Without something more, the idea that our rational capacity
> was the product of natural selection would render reasoning
> far less trustworthy . . . There would be no reason to trust its
> results in mathematics and science for example.

When Nagel writes 'without something more', he may mean 'without the justification that reason itself provides'. We should accept this claim, so understood. But this justification would not be undermined or weakened, as Nagel may assume, if our rational abilities were the product of natural selection. Since this process merely selects between different possibilities, it does not undermine, or make untrustworthy, what it selects.

In defending Rationalism, my claims so far have been these. When some fact gives us a reason to have some belief, this normative property of being reason-giving is not an empirically discoverable feature of the natural world. Nor could we be causally affected by such normative properties. But natural selection might explain how, without any such causal contact, our ancestors became able to respond to such reasons, because that enabled them to form many true beliefs about the world, some of which helped them to survive and reproduce. If natural selection explains how early humans acquired this ability to respond to reasons, it would not be a coincidence that these humans could form these many true beliefs. Nor would it be surprising that, with their steadily improving rational abilities, and their curiosity, later humans became able to form many other true beliefs, such as beliefs about prime numbers greater than 100, or about black holes and neutron stars, or valid proofs and epistemic reasons. When applied to our ability to form such true beliefs, this evolutionary account provides, I believe, a good enough answer to the Massive Coincidence Objection. We can call this *the Darwinian Answer*.

We can next make a positive suggestion, running this argument the other way. Of our reasons to believe in mathematical truths, it is often said, some are provided by the ways in which scientists use mathematics to predict and understand many features of the natural world. We can suggest a similar defence of the view that we have epistemic reasons. Unlike other animals, we form many true beliefs about what we cannot see, hear, touch or smell, such as beliefs about possibilities, and the further future. We have this ability, we can claim, because we can respond to epistemic reasons. If we were not responding to such reasons, our ability to form so many true beliefs would involve a highly implausible coincidence. We can call this *the Reverse Coincidence Argument*.

This argument could not be a proof. Natural selection has given some animals remarkable abilities to respond in other ways to various features of the world. Some animals navigate, for example, by responding to the Earth's magnetic field, or by recognizing the patterns of stars that move around the celestial pole. Many non-rational animals have specialized cognitive abilities that we cannot yet explain. But human beings have much wider and greater cognitive abilities. And when we ask how we can know as much as we do about logic, mathematics, and the world, the best answer may be that we can respond to valid arguments and epistemic reasons.

115 The Validity Argument

In developing and defending these claims, I shall first give an argument against Metaphysical Naturalism. Because Field assumes both that only God could have given us the ability to form so many true mathematical beliefs, and that God does not exist, Field concludes that these beliefs are not true, and are at best useful fictions. Some other people draw the opposite conclusion. Like Field, Plantinga believes that there could not be any naturalistic explanation of our mathematical abilities. But Plantinga claims that, to solve this and similar problems, we should conclude that these and similar abilities *were* given to us by God.

Most Naturalists would deny that we face any such problem. These people assume that

(H) we are able to form true mathematical beliefs without being causally affected by numbers or their properties,

and that

(I) there is some explanation of these mathematical abilities that is wholly naturalistic, in the sense that it does not appeal to any non-natural properties or truths.

These Naturalists also assume that

(J) there is some naturalistic evolutionary explanation of how we came to have these abilities.

I shall now defend the claim that

(K) though we have the mathematical abilities described by (H), and we can understand how natural selection could have given us these abilities, these facts could not be explained in wholly naturalistic ways.

In defending (H), I have appealed to the abilities of some computers to produce many true answers to difficult mathematical questions. Though these machines cannot be causally affected by mathematical properties, they produce these true answers because they calculate in ways that correspond to valid mathematical reasoning.

When we ask how these computers work, there are two kinds of event or fact that we need to explain. At the *micro-level*, there are many physical changes in the chips, circuits, and other small components of these computers. These events can each be fully explained by the laws of physics.   But we can also argue:

> (L) The laws of physics cannot explain the *higher level* fact that these computers reliably produce many true answers to difficult mathematical questions.

> (M) This fact needs to be explained, since it would otherwise involve a highly implausible coincidence.

> (N) These computers have these abilities only because their calculations correspond to valid reasoning.

Therefore

> (O) These abilities can only be causally explained by appealing to the validity of such reasoning.

We can call this *the Validity Argument*.

Unlike computers, we are conscious rational beings, who can know that we are reasoning in valid ways, and that we can thereby form true mathematical beliefs. It is much less clear what our mathematical abilities involve, since our mental processes differ in several ways from the calculations of computers. But the Validity Argument also applies to us. It may be true that, at the micro-level, the neurophysiological events in our brains can each be fully explained by the laws of physics. But these laws cannot explain how we can form so many true mathematical beliefs.   We can claim that

> (P) these abilities can only be causally explained by the ways in which our mental processes correspond to, or involve, valid reasoning. We can recognize that, if certain beliefs are true, certain other beliefs must be true. We can form these many true mathematical beliefs only *because* we are reasoning in these valid ways. Since we cannot be causally affected by the

validity of these kinds of reasoning, our abilities involve what
we can call a *non-causal* response to this validity.

Though many people assume that all non-random physical processes
can be fully explained by physical laws, that is not so. Many physical
processes must also be causally explained in other ways. That is why
physics is only one of many natural and social sciences. Evolutionary
explanations do not appeal to the laws of physics, nor do the explanations
given by the social sciences, such as demography, or economics. Any
active human brain is much more complicated than a lifeless galaxy,
and many of the processes in our brains, and the acts to which they
lead, could not possibly be explained by physical laws. We form many
of our beliefs by reasoning in valid ways, and validity is not a physical
property. But these non-physical explanations are *compatible* with
physical laws. We can understand how the physical processes in our
brains might correspond to valid reasoning. Though these abilities
involve *non-causal* responses to the validity of such reasoning, these
responses are not *contra*-causal, or miraculous, as the simpler abilities
of computers show.

We can next note that even if, at the neurophysiological level, the
mental processes in our brains are fully causally determined, that does
not threaten the belief that we can reason in valid ways, and can respond
to epistemic reasons. There is a contrast here with practical and moral
reasons, to which we respond with our acts. It can seem plausible that,
to be moral agents, our decisions and acts must involve some kind of
contra-causal libertarian freedom. Though Kant claimed that we must
also have such freedom in our theoretical reasoning, this claim is *not*
similarly plausible. When we form beliefs by reasoning in valid ways,
freedom is irrelevant. If we believe the premises of some argument that
is clearly valid, and we are epistemically rational, we *must* believe this
argument's conclusion. Since this response is *rationally* necessary, it
can also be *causally* necessary at the neurophysiological level. These
two necessities can be, and should be, aligned. We can often truly claim
that we believe some argument's conclusion *both* because the matter in
our brains has conformed to the laws of physics, *and* because we have
responded to some valid argument.

We can now ask whether, if these claims are true, they give a *naturalistic* explanation of our abilities to reason in such valid ways, and of the simpler abilities of our computers. Properties or facts are natural, it is often claimed, when they are of kinds that are investigated or discussed by people who are working in the natural or social sciences. Many scientists use mathematical reasoning, whose validity they discuss. These facts may seem enough to make validity a natural property.

In the sense of 'natural' that is relevant here, however, that is not so. When we call some argument valid, we mean that, if this argument's premises are true, this argument's conclusion must be true. The necessity of these truths is not part of the causal fabric of the world. When Metaphysical Naturalists reject Platonism, these people rightly deny that we could be causally affected by abstract entities or properties. Validity is one such property. Since this explanation of our abilities must appeal to the fact that our reasoning is valid, which is not a natural fact, this explanation is not wholly naturalistic.

Because some Naturalists realize that our mathematical knowledge cannot be explained in wholly naturalistic terms, they conclude that we have no such knowledge. I shall assume that these views are mistaken. As well as being intrinsically very credible, or reached by valid reasoning, many mathematical beliefs are strongly supported by their use in well-confirmed scientific theories. Some of these Naturalists therefore try to show that we can restate the mathematical parts of these scientific theories in ways that do not refer to non-natural abstract entities, such as numbers. Though these attempts are impressive, it seems very doubtful that they could succeed.

Other Naturalists, such as Quine, have been led to change their view. Though Quine first denied the existence of abstract entities on metaphysically Naturalist grounds, he later came to believe that many physical facts could only be explained by scientific theories which refer to certain abstract entities, such as numbers or sets. Quine also assumed that

(Q) if there are important facts which can only be explained
in ways that refer to certain abstract entities, we can justifiably
believe that such entities exist.

Quine therefore concluded that we can justifiably believe, and ought to believe, that there are such entities as sets. This change of view is, I believe, more significant than Quine assumed. If there can be purely abstract entities of any kind, even a kind as minimal as sets, this fact undermines the main arguments for denying that there can be abstract entities of other, less minimal kinds. It does not help to say, like the unmarried lady's maid in an old Punch cartoon, 'Please, Ma'am, it's a very *small* baby'.

To explain our mathematical abilities, it is not enough to admit that there are some abstract entities. We must also appeal to the validity of the reasoning that enables us to form so many true mathematical beliefs. Even to explain the simpler abilities of our computers, as I have argued, we must appeal to truths about what is valid reasoning. Validity is not a natural property, and truths about valid reasoning are not natural facts. So we should reject Metaphysical Naturalism.

In rejecting Naturalism, however, we need not make the Platonist claims that Naturalists have found mysterious or incredible. Our view can be a form of Non-Metaphysical Cognitivism. As I have suggested, and argue further in Appendix J, when we claim that there are some truths about what is valid reasoning, we need not claim that these truths and this validity both *exist* in some ontological sense. And though our mathematical abilities can only be causally explained by appealing to such truths, this causal explanation need not involve any mysterious form of quasi-causal contact with validity or other such abstract properties. Though we form true mathematical beliefs only *because* our reasoning is valid, our response to this validity is non-causal, and compatible with physical laws.

We can now return to the Rationalist view that there are some irreducibly normative epistemic truths, such as truths about the intrinsic credibility of some beliefs, and about epistemic reasons. According to the Causal Objection, since such non-natural properties or truths could not have any effects, we could not have any way of knowing about them. As the Validity Argument shows, this objection fails. We can form true mathematical beliefs by reasoning in valid ways. Computers calculate in valid ways because of the complicated structures of their circuits and software programs, and our much greater abilities can be explained by the much more complicated structures in our brains.

What is harder to explain is how our brains came to be structured in these ways. Just as we know how to design computers so that they can calculate correctly, God would know how to design our brains so that we can reason in valid ways. But we are supposing that our brains were unintentionally produced by natural selection, which is a mindless process, and knows nothing. It is clear, however, that we *are* able to respond, without any causal contact, to the validity of some kinds of reasoning. And we can, I believe, sufficiently explain how natural selection could have given us these abilities.

We have similar abilities, I believe, to respond to epistemic properties. We form many true beliefs because these beliefs are intrinsically credible, or because we are aware of facts that give us reasons to have them. The mental processes in our brains may non-causally correspond to such epistemic properties and truths, and natural selection could have given us these abilities. It makes no relevant difference that, unlike validity, these properties and truths are *normative*.

116 Epistemic Beliefs

Though natural selection may explain how we can respond to valid arguments and epistemic reasons, that does not show that truths about such reasons are irreducibly normative, and that we can know such truths.   I shall now try to defend these claims.

We can first distinguish between two uses of words like 'probable', 'likely' and 'certain'. When we claim that some belief is probably true, or certainly true, we may mean that we have strong or decisive normative reasons to have this belief, or that we ought to have this belief. We also use such words in non-normative senses, to make claims about what is statistically probable or likely, or what is logically certain or definitely true. For reasons that I give in a note, I shall here use the words 'probable', 'likely', and 'certain' only in these non-normative senses, which I shall call *alethic*.

There are several views about the relations between normative and aleth-ic concepts, properties, and truths. According to *Analytical Naturalists*, epistemic normative concepts can be explained in alethic terms, and refer to alethic properties. According to *Epistemic Rationalists*, these concepts are irreducibly normative, and refer to irreducibly normative properties. According to *Non-Analytical Naturalists*, though these concepts are irreducibly normative, they refer to alethic properties.

Consider, for example, the claim that

> (A) when we know that certain facts imply that P is true, these facts give us a decisive reason to believe P.

Schiffer calls (A) 'about as analytic as anything can be'. The truths that are most analytic are those that are true by definition. Schiffer gives, as one example: 'Every widow was once married'. Such analytic truths Schiffer calls 'trivial', and he doubts whether (A) is a normative claim. These remarks suggest that Schiffer accepts one form of Analytical Naturalism.   On this view, when we claim that

> (1) certain facts give us a decisive reason to believe P,

that is another way of saying that

> (2) these facts imply that P is true.

Schiffer would be right to say that, if we use (1) and (2) to mean the same, we ought not to regard (A) as a substantive normative claim. So understood, (A) would be trivial, since (A) would be a concealed tautology, which told us only that when certain facts imply that P is true, these facts imply that P is true.

Analytical Naturalism does, I believe, correctly describe how some people think about epistemic reasons. But we are discussing normative reasons. The alethic concept *implies the truth of* is quite different from the normative concept *gives us a decisive reason to believe*. According to Rationalists, these concepts refer to different properties, and (1) and (2), when they are true, state different facts.   Rationalists would restate (A) as

> (B) when we know that certain facts have the alethic property of implying that P is true, that makes these

facts have the different, normative property of giving
us a decisive reason to believe P.

According to *Non*-Analytical Naturalists, though (1) and (2) have
different meanings, these claims, when they are true, refer to the same
property, and state the same fact. These Naturalists would reject (B),
claiming instead that

(C) when we know that certain facts imply that P is true,
that's *what it is* for these facts to give us a decisive reason
to believe P.

Similar remarks apply to other epistemic reasons. Many people would
accept that

(D) when we know that certain facts make it likely that P is
true, these facts give us some reason to believe P.

Analytical Naturalists would regard this claim as another concealed
tautology.   Rationalists would claim that

(E) when we know that certain facts make it likely that P is
true, that makes these facts have the different, normative
property of giving us some reason to believe P.

Non-Analytical Naturalists would reject (E), claiming instead that

(F) when we know that certain facts make it likely that P is
true, that's *what it is* for these facts to give us some reason
to believe P.

We ought, I believe, to reject this form of Naturalism, for reasons
similar to those I gave in Chapters 25 to 27, when discussing Practical
and Moral Naturalism.

In defending Epistemic Rationalism I shall first say some more about
the distinction between normative and alethic concepts and claims.
Return to the claim that

(G) some argument is valid.

Some people would call this claim normative. But I am using 'normative' in a narrower, reason-implying sense. When we call some argument valid, most of us mean that

> (H) if this argument's premises are true, its conclusion must be true,

and this claim is not normative in this reason-implying sense. What is normative are the claims that

> (I) if we know that some argument is valid, and has true premises, these facts give us a decisive reason to accept this argument's conclusion,

and that

> (J) we ought rationally to accept this conclusion.

Similar remarks apply to

> (K) two plus two must equal four.

This use of 'must' is not normative. (K) does not mean that two plus two have decisive reasons to equal four, or that these numbers ought rationally to equal four. What is normative is not (K) itself, but the claim that we have decisive reasons to believe (K).

Consider next the logical truths that are involved in valid reasoning. My examples are:

> *Modus Ponens*: If P implies Q, and P is true, Q must be true.

> *Non-Contradiction*: No statement could be both wholly true and wholly false.

We can ask:

> Q1: Why do we believe such truths?

> Q2: Are these beliefs justified, and, if so, how?

After describing some logical truths as obviously true, Quine writes:

> A sentence is obvious if (a) it is true and (b) any speaker of the language is prepared, for any reason or none, to assent to it without hesitation . . .

When some belief is in *this* sense obvious, that is a merely psychological fact, and does not justify this belief. Nor would this fact explain why people have this belief. When Horwich discusses our beliefs in such logical truths, he claims that such beliefs are rational in the sense that they are 'innate and irremovable'. As before, these psychological facts would neither explain nor justify these beliefs.

Gödel writes that some logical axioms

> force themselves upon us as being true.

It is not clear what Gödel means. Like Horwich, Gödel might mean that such beliefs are irresistible, or psychologically necessary. This fact would not answer our questions. Gödel might instead mean that these beliefs *must* be true, or are *logically* necessary. This fact, in contrast, may seem both to explain and justify these beliefs.

That is not, however, so.   Consider

(L) $278694573 + 823572198 = 1102266771$.

We know that, *if* (L) is true, this truth is necessary. But this fact doesn't help us to know *whether* (L) is true. To answer that question, most of us would need to do a calculation. Our mathematical beliefs are all, if they are true, necessarily true, but that doesn't tell us *which* of these beliefs are true. Similar remarks apply even to such logical laws as *Non-Contradiction* and *Modus Ponens*. To explain why we believe these laws, it is not enough to point out that these laws state necessary truths. That is not how these truths differ from truths like (L).

When Gödel writes that some beliefs force themselves upon us as true, Gödel may instead mean that these beliefs are

> *self-evidently* true, in the sense that, if we fully understand these beliefs, we can recognize that they are, or must be, true.

That would justify these beliefs. Such beliefs are sometimes called *conceptual* truths. But this word may be misleading. Analytic truths could be called conceptual, since these truths are implied by the concepts that they involve. It follows from the concept of a widow, for example, that any widow was once married. But some claims may be self-evidently true, not because their truth is implied by the concepts they involve, but because it is so obvious that these claims are, or must be, true. Remember next that, when some belief *seems* to us self-evidently true, we may be mistaken. Such beliefs may be false.

When some belief is self-evidently true, this belief may also be

> *psychologically indubitable* in the sense that no one who fully understood this belief would be able to doubt its truth,

and

> *normatively indubitable* in the sense that no one who fully understood this belief, and was free from distorting influences, could rationally doubt its truth.

If some belief *could* not be doubted, there may seem no point in claiming that this belief *should* not be doubted. But some beliefs are indubitable only in the normative sense.   Consider, for example,

> (M) $7 + 5 = 12$.

Someone who was bad at arithmetic might doubt this claim. But no one who both understood and thought carefully about (M) could rationally doubt that (M) is true.

Though (M) is indubitable, we could also defend (M) by giving an arithmetical proof which gave us decisive reasons to believe (M). We can give valid arguments for many other mathematical beliefs, such as the belief that there is no greatest prime number. But we cannot give helpful arguments for *Non-Contradiction* or *Modus Ponens*, nor could we have any direct reasons to believe these truths. These and some other logical truths are too fundamental to be supportable in such ways. There is little point in arguing for these truths, because such arguments would have to assume some of the truths that we were trying to prove. But our belief in such truths can be fully justified.   We can claim that, when

(N) some belief has the alethic property of being self-evident,

that makes it true that

(O) this belief has the normative property of being indubitable.

Many people do not distinguish between these properties, or assume that *being self-evident* is a normative property. This distinction is hard to draw because these properties are so closely related. When it seems to us clear that some belief must be true, we could not rationally doubt this belief.

Other such distinctions are easier to draw. For example, we can claim that, when

(P) certain facts make some belief statistically likely to be true,

that makes it true that

(Q) these facts give us a reason to have this belief.

The alethic property of *making likely to be true* is different from the normative property of *giving us a reason to believe*.

When some normative truth like (Q) is *made* to be true by some alethic truth like (P), we can say that (P) states (Q)'s *alethic ground*. We can also claim that

(R) normative epistemic beliefs are true when, and because, their alethic grounds are true.

According to Epistemic Rationalists, since the concept of a reason is not natural, but irreducibly normative, claims like (Q) can state irreducibly normative truths. Naturalists object that there could not be any such non-natural properties and truths. In defending Non-Metaphysical Cognitivism, I have tried to answer this objection.

Naturalists also object that, since we could not be causally affected by such non-natural properties and truths, we could not have any way of knowing about them. I have claimed that, just as we can respond non-causally to the validity of some kinds of reasoning, we can respond non-causally to intrinsic credibilities and epistemic reasons. And natural selection might explain how we became able to respond to reasons. I shall now try to show that, as well as being able to respond to reasons, we can justifiably believe that there are such normative reason-involving epistemic truths.

33

Rationalism

117 Epistemic Reasons

Whether our beliefs are justified depends on why we have them. Our beliefs may be formed in ways that make them likely to be true. Some examples are beliefs about the world, or what I shall call *worldly beliefs*, which are based on our perceptual experiences. Other beliefs are formed in ways that are unreliable, such as wishful thinking, or hypnosis. When we look for deeper explanations of some of our beliefs, or ways of forming beliefs, the answers may be partly given by natural selection. We may have come to have certain beliefs, or cognitive abilities, because these were evolutionarily or reproductively advantageous, by helping early humans to survive and reproduce. In considering beliefs of some kind, we can distinguish four possibilities:

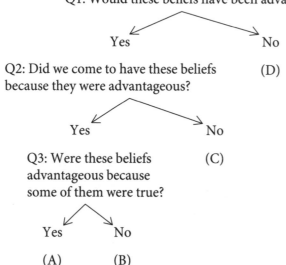

Q1: Would these beliefs have been advantageous?

    Yes   No

Q2: Did we come to have these beliefs   (D)
because they were advantageous?

    Yes   No

Q3: Were these beliefs   (C)
advantageous because
some of them were true?

  Yes   No

  (A)   (B)

Our perceptually based beliefs are of type (A), and natural selection explains how we became able to form such beliefs in these reliable ways. These beliefs were advantageous only because they were often true. Similar claims may apply to our logically and mathematically based beliefs. It might have helped my early human to realize that, since three lions entered his cave and only two had left, one lion was still in the cave.

When some Naturalists discuss our normative epistemic beliefs, these people argue that these beliefs are of type (B). In stating these arguments, I shall use the words 'we' and 'us' to refer to most human beings and to some of the earlier pre-humans from whom we inherited most of our genes.   These Naturalists claim:

> (1) Such normative beliefs were often advantageous, by causing us to have true worldly beliefs which helped us to survive and reproduce.

> (2) Because these normative beliefs were advantageous, natural selection made us disposed to have them.

> (3) These beliefs would have had the same effects whether or not they were true.

Therefore

> (4) These beliefs would have been advantageous whether or not they were true.

Therefore

> (5) Natural selection would have disposed us to have these beliefs whether or not they were true.

> (6) We have no empirical evidence for the truth of these beliefs.

> (7) We have no other way of knowing whether these beliefs are true.

Therefore

> We cannot justifiably believe that these beliefs are true.

We can call this the *Naturalist Argument for Normative Skepticism.*

This argument applies most plausibly to those of our normative epistemic beliefs that are grounded on beliefs about what is certain or likely to be true in the non-normative alethic senses. These are the only normative epistemic beliefs that I am here discussing.

When we consider these beliefs, we can plausibly assume that (3) is true. We can assume that, if these normative beliefs caused us to have certain other beliefs, it would be our *having* these normative beliefs, not their *truth*, that had these effects. We should then accept both (4) and (5). If we were disposed to have certain normative beliefs because these beliefs were advantageous, and these beliefs would have been advantageous whether or not they were true, we would have been disposed to have these beliefs whether or not they were true. Natural selection would have been a distorting influence, since this cause of these beliefs would have been unrelated to their truth. That would give us reasons to doubt that these beliefs are true.

We can next ask whether, as (1) claims, these normative epistemic beliefs were often advantageous.   When we believe that

(A) certain facts make it likely that some worldly belief is true,

we may also believe that

(B) these facts give us a normative epistemic reason to
have this belief.

When Nozick discusses evolutionary explanations of our rationality, he suggests that early humans were often helped by believing that they had such epistemic reasons, and that such normative beliefs would have been advantageous whether or not they were true. Street makes similar claims. Early humans came to believe that they had such normative reasons, Street writes, not because they really *did* have such reasons, but because this belief

guided the formation of [their] beliefs in ways that turned out to be advantageous . . . because it got them to believe things that turned out to be true.

As one example, Street claims that, if some early humans believed it to be likely that

(C) the next tiger that they met would be carnivorous,

it would have helped these humans if they also believed that

(C)'s likelihood of being true gave them a reason to believe
that (C) was true,

since this normative belief would have helped these humans to believe that (C) was true.

Few early humans, we can reply, would have needed such help. Such normative beliefs would have seldom been advantageous. In most cases, it is enough to have the alethic belief that some worldly belief is likely to be true. If we believe that some tiger is likely to be carnivorous, most of us would fear this tiger. Some rash people may have no such fear. But few such people would be helped by believing that (C)'s likelihood of being true gave them a reason to believe (C). Most rash people who ignore such risks would also ignore such epistemic reasons.

Consider next cases in which we believe that

(D) certain facts imply that some belief must be true.

In such cases, we may also believe that

(E) these facts give us a decisive reason to have this belief.

Such normative beliefs are even less likely to have been advantageous. When we believe that some belief *must* be true, we nearly always believe that this belief *is* true. There are some exceptions. We sometimes know that some belief must be true, without really believing this truth, as is shown by our continuing to think and act as if this belief were false. Some examples might be cases in which we have just come to know that someone whom we love must have died, or that we ourselves will soon die. In such cases, if we believe that we have decisive reasons to believe what we know must be true, that might help us really to believe these truths. But few cases are of this kind. It is nearly always enough to believe that some belief must be true. For similar reasons, it hardly ever helps us to believe that some belief is indubitable. We never think: 'Since no one could rationally doubt this belief, it must be true.'

We can sum up these claims as follows. To form many true worldly beliefs, we need to have true alethic beliefs about the likelihood that these worldly beliefs are true. But when we believe that some worldly belief is likely to be true, or must be true, we seldom need to have the normative belief that we have a strong or decisive reason to have this worldly belief. The normative fact that we have this reason doesn't give us a *further* reason to have this worldly belief. Nor do we need to believe that we have more reason to believe what is more likely to be true.

These remarks may seem to conflict with some of my earlier remarks. I claimed that, just as cheetahs were selected for their speed, and giraffes for their long necks, we were selected for our rationality, which mostly consists in our ability to respond to reasons. We respond to epistemic reasons when our awareness of certain facts causes us to believe what these facts give us reasons to believe. By responding to these reasons, we could form many true worldly beliefs, some of which were reproductively advantageous. I have now claimed that our normative epistemic beliefs were seldom advantageous. But these claims do not conflict.   Though I believe that

(F) it was advantageous to respond to such epistemic reasons,

that does not imply that

(G) it was advantageous to believe that we had such normative epistemic reasons.

To be able to respond to epistemic reasons, early humans did not need to have the concept of a normative reason, nor did they need to have normative beliefs about such reasons.

Normative skeptics might now revise premise (1). These people might claim that

(H) these normative beliefs were *sometimes* advantageous.

That might be enough to justify the claim that

(2) natural selection made us disposed to have these normative beliefs.

Natural selection often involves the combined effects of many slight advantages. That was how cheetahs became able to run so fast, and how giraffes developed such long necks.

To assess this reply, we must ask in what sense premise (2) claims that natural selection made us *disposed* to have these normative beliefs. (2) might mean that

> (I) natural selection gave us the cognitive abilities which led us to form such normative beliefs.

But this claim would not support the skeptical argument that we are now discussing, by casting doubt on the truth of these beliefs. Natural selection gave us abilities to form many true beliefs. For premise (2) to support this argument, these skeptics must claim that

> (J) natural selection produced these normative beliefs in the stronger sense of determining their *content*, or *what* we believed.

That might be true if

> (K) we became disposed to have these normative beliefs, not because they were true, but because our having these beliefs was advantageous.

Only these claims would challenge these beliefs.

Though these claims raise very difficult questions, we can plausibly assume that they can at most be partly true.   We can claim that

> (L) these normative beliefs were at most partly produced by natural selection.

In defending (L), we can first question the analogy with the evolution of bodily organs. We can understand how, with millions of years of small genetic changes that were slightly advantageous, natural selection could produce our superbly effective eyes. No such claim applies to our normative epistemic beliefs.   Return to the belief that

> (M) when certain facts imply that some belief must be true, these facts give us a decisive reason to have this belief.

Beliefs like (M) could not have been entirely produced by any such series of small genetic changes. As well as being hardly ever advantageous, such normative beliefs appeared late in the history of human beings, when some of us asked whether and how our other beliefs can be justified. In Hegel's phrase, the owl of Minerva spreads its wings only as dusk falls.

If such normative beliefs were even partly produced or influenced by natural selection, because they were advantageous, this fact would challenge these beliefs. As this skeptical argument rightly claims, natural selection would be a distorting influence. Since these beliefs would be advantageous whether or not they were true, this cause of these beliefs would be unrelated to their truth. But this argument needs to assume that this distorting influence has not been outweighed.

That is what is claimed by this argument's other premises. These skeptics claim that

(6) we have no empirical evidence for the truth of these beliefs,

and that

(7) we have no other way of knowing whether these beliefs are true.

If we are Rationalists, we should admit that (6) is true. On our view, since these beliefs are irreducibly normative, they are not about entities or properties that are part of the causal fabric of the world. Since such normative truths could not have any observable effects, or help to explain what we can observe, we could not have any empirical evidence supporting our belief in these truths.

We should also admit the plausibility of (7). When Street defends this premise, she writes

there is no reason to think that natural selection, *or for that matter any other causal process*, would shape us in such a way that we would be able to track such truths.

These objections can, I have claimed, be answered. Since our fundamental normative beliefs are not about contingent features of the world, we don't need to have empirical evidence for their truth. Nor do we need to be causally affected by these normative truths. We can know some other necessary truths, such as logical and mathematic truths, by responding in non-causal ways to the validity of some kinds of reasoning. We may respond in similar ways to some epistemic properties and truths.

It may help to look more closely at this analogy. These various beliefs are about what *must* be true, in the strong sense that applies to every possible world. One example is the belief that $2 + 2 = 4$. I shall call these our *modal* beliefs. As I have said, we are often claimed to have empirical evidence for the truth of some mathematical beliefs, which is given by the ways in which scientists use these beliefs to make many confirmable predictions. But these facts provide no evidence for the *modal* status of mathematical truths. Such facts could show only that these mathematical beliefs are always in fact true, given the actual laws of nature, leaving it open whether these beliefs must be true.

The skeptical argument that we are now discussing could be applied to these modal beliefs. Modal skeptics might first claim that these beliefs were advantageous.   I have claimed that, when we have believed that

(N) some belief must be true,

it would have seldom helped us to believe that

(O) we had a decisive reason to have this belief.

But though we didn't need to have normative beliefs like (O), we may have been helped by having modal beliefs like (N). When we believe that some belief must be true, this may usefully strengthen this belief. And such modal beliefs may have helped us to form other true beliefs. Arithmetic provides one example. We might learn from experience that two plus two always in fact equals four, that two plus three always in fact equals five, and that two plus four always in fact equals six. But this way of forming such mathematical beliefs would be limited, and slow. To gain most of our mathematical knowledge, we may have needed to believe, even if only at an unconscious level, that mathematical beliefs are necessarily true, and that we could reach other such true beliefs by certain kinds of valid reasoning.

Modal skeptics might also claim that

> (2) because these modal beliefs were advantageous, natural
> selection made us disposed to have them,

and that

> (4) these beliefs would have been advantageous whether
> or not they were true.

We might object that these beliefs could not have failed to be true, since two plus two would equal four in every possible world. But modal skeptics could defend (4) in a different way. When such modal beliefs were advantageous, by helping us to form true beliefs about the actual world, it was irrelevant whether these beliefs applied truly to other possible worlds. It would have been just as advantageous to believe that, in the actual world, given the actual laws of nature, two plus two always equals four. Nor does our logical reasoning need to involve such modal truths. Rather than using arguments that are

> *modally* valid, in the sense that, if their premises are true,
> their conclusions must be true,

it would be enough if these arguments were

> *factually* valid, in the sense that, if their premises are true,
> their conclusions are always in fact true.

If these modal beliefs were partly produced by natural selection, that would provide one challenge to these beliefs. Modal skeptics might claim that

> (5) natural selection would have disposed us to have these
> modal beliefs whether or not they were true.

We must also admit that, as premise (6) claims, we have no empirical evidence for the truth of these beliefs. We cannot have any evidence about the many possible worlds in which the laws of physics, or other laws of nature, would have been different.

As before, however, this argument needs another premise. Modal skeptics must claim that

(7) we have no other way of knowing whether these
beliefs are true.

And we can reject this claim. Our cognitive abilities, we can assume, were partly produced by evolutionary forces. But these abilities later ceased to be governed by these forces, and had their own effects. Natural selection gave us wings, but when we could fly, we soared into the sky. We used these cognitive abilities to discover some new kinds of truths. Nagel gives, as one example, our understanding of arithmetical infinity. It would have been advantageous to form true arithmetical beliefs about various small numbers, such as how many lions have entered and left our cave.   We discover infinity, Nagel writes:

> when we ask whether these numbers . . . are all there is . . .
> It is like stepping into what looks like a small windowless hut
> and finding oneself suddenly in the middle of a vast landscape
> stretching endlessly out to the horizon.

Just as we could discover infinity, though this discovery was not advantageous, we could discover necessity. We could see that, if X implies Y, and X is true, Y must be true.

This use of 'see' does not imply that we have some quasi-perceptual faculty. Such metaphors refer to the kind of rational insight that is involved in every step of valid reasoning. This ability is sometimes claimed to be mysterious. But when it seems to us clear that some belief must be true, there is nothing in our cognitive experience that is more transparent and intelligible, or less mysterious. The mystery could be only how we became able to have these clear beliefs about these necessary truths.

Even if we cannot yet explain how we came to have this ability, we can justifiably believe that we can recognize such necessary truths. For this skeptical argument to succeed, this argument must have premises which are more plausible than the modal beliefs which it claims to undermine.   Two such beliefs are:

(P) Two plus two must equal four,

and

(Q) No statement could be both wholly true and wholly false.

This argument must assume that

(R) we have no way of knowing whether such modal beliefs are true.

Of these three claims, much the least plausible is (R). If (R) were true, we could not know whether

(S) it might have been true that two plus two equals three, or five, or ninety nine.

Nor could we know whether

(T) it might have been true that our beliefs were both wholly true and wholly false.

Since we can have no empirical evidence for modal truths, our modal beliefs raise deep and difficult questions. But we *do* know that two plus two must equal four, and that our beliefs could not be both wholly true and wholly false. We can know some things even if we don't yet know how we know them. Most earlier humans knew many truths about what they could see, hear, touch, and smell, though they didn't know how they knew these truths.

Similar remarks apply to our normative epistemic beliefs.   Two such beliefs are:

(U) When certain facts imply that some belief must be true, these facts give us a decisive reason to have this belief,

and

(V) When certain facts imply that some belief is very likely to be true, these facts give us a strong reason to have this belief.

When normative skeptics challenge these beliefs, their arguments must assume that

(W) we have no way of knowing whether such normative
beliefs are true.

Of these three claims, much the least plausible is (W). If (W) were true,
we could not know whether

(X) we ever have any reasons to have any beliefs.

But we do know that we sometimes have such reasons. When we are
aware of facts that make some belief certainly true, or very likely to
be true, these facts give us a reason to have this belief. These skeptical
arguments cannot succeed, since they have one premise which is much
less plausible than the normative beliefs which they claim to undermine.

These arguments have another feature.   According to these skeptics:

We have decisive reasons to believe that

(Y) we have no way of knowing whether we
have any reasons,

and we ought to believe that

(Z) there is nothing that we ought to believe.

Such arguments are self-defeating. If (Y) were true, we couldn't have
decisive reasons to believe (Y), and if (Z) were true, it couldn't be true
that we ought to believe (Z).

Normative skeptics might revise their claims.   They might argue that

if we could know whether we had any reasons, we
would know that we could have no such knowledge,

and that

if there was anything that we ought to believe, what
we ought to believe would be that there was nothing
that we ought to believe.

These arguments succeed, these people might say, *by* being self-
defeating. Such arguments would not be *damagingly* self-defeating.
But there are, I believe, no such successfully self-defeating arguments.

These skeptics might merely assert their view. Such views are now widely held. Quine suggests that we should abandon normative epistemology. Instead of asking whether and how our beliefs can be justified, or what we have normative reasons to believe, we should merely study how people do in fact form their true beliefs. As Quine writes, 'Why not settle for psychology?' Another great Naturalist, Wittgenstein, also rejects normative epistemology. On Wittgenstein's view, though our reasoning is based on logical laws, such as *Non-Contradiction* and *Modus Ponens*, we cannot defensibly claim that these laws are indubitable, or self-evident, or that we are justified in believing them. We have reached bed-rock, and we can say only that our spade is turned, or *this is what we do*. When we follow the rules of inference, we follow them *blindly*. Non-Cognitivists make similar claims. Gibbard denies that any beliefs could have the property of being rational. There is, he claims, no such property, and when we call some belief rational, we are merely expressing our acceptance of some imperative. Field writes that, though we can call some beliefs reasonable, we should be *non-factualists*. When we call some belief reasonable, we should not take ourselves to be claiming anything that might be true.

There have been other skeptical suggestions. Our beliefs about the world, some people say, may nearly all be false. These beliefs may have been produced by some evil demon, or we may be brains in some vat in the laboratory of some extra-terrestrial being. The world may have been created only five minutes ago, with apparent traces of an unreal past, so that most of our apparent memories are illusions. Normative skepticism is in one way less extreme, since these skeptics do not suggest that our beliefs about the world may nearly all be false. These people claim only that no beliefs could ever be justified. These people may happily admit that, on their view, they cannot justifiably claim that we have any reason to accept their view.

We may not be able to prove that our normative epistemic beliefs are not illusions. We may also be unable to prove that we are not brains in a vat, or being deceived by some demon. But if we claim less than absolute certainty, we can justifiably reject such skeptical views. In arguing that we can know some normative epistemic truths, we must appeal to some of these truths. We must claim that we have sufficient reasons to believe that we are able to respond to reasons. Such arguments are in one way circular, but that does not make them fail. Any justification must end somewhere. Justifications of beliefs can best end with intrinsic credibilities and decisive or at least sufficient epistemic reasons. We do not have to show that we have further reasons to believe that we have these reasons, and further reasons to believe that we have these further reasons, and so on for ever. Some beliefs seem indubitable, and we seem to have decisive reasons to accept many other beliefs. Nor do we seem to have any strong reason to doubt that we do have such reasons. Given these facts, if we can understand how it *might* be true that we are responding to such reasons, we can justifiably believe that we *are* responding to such reasons. We can justifiably believe that there are some truths about what we ought to believe, and that we know some of these truths.

Nagel writes:

> there is a real problem about how such a thing as reason is possible. How is it possible that creatures like ourselves, supplied with the contingent capacities of a biological species whose very existence appears to be radically accidental, should have access to universally valid methods of objective thought?

He also writes:

> If the natural order can include universal, mathematically beautiful laws of fundamental physics of the kind we have discovered, why can't it include equally fundamental laws . . . that we don't know anything about, that are consistent with the laws of physics and that render intelligible the development of conscious organisms some of which have the capacity to discover by prolonged collective effort some of the fundamental truths about that very natural order?

We do, I suggest, know something about these other fundamental laws. These laws include the necessary truths of logic and mathematics, and normative truths about credibilities and epistemic reasons. It is by reasoning in valid ways, and responding to these credibilities and reasons that we have discovered so much about the natural world. And natural selection can explain how, in Nagel's phrase, 'the existence of reason need not be biologically mysterious.'

118 Practical Reasons

We can now turn from epistemic to practical reasons, and to questions about what matters. These questions are harder and more important. It is sometimes said that, just as our beliefs are aimed at the truth, our desires and acts are aimed at the good. But unlike the concept *good*, the concept *true* is not normative. And truth and falsity are simpler than what matters, in something like the way in which white, grey, and black are simpler than the chromatic colours. No one doubts that there are non-normative truths, such as truths about the world, or about logic and mathematics. And there is little fundamental disagreement about which are the kinds of fact that give us epistemic reasons. But many people doubt that there are normative truths, and there is much disagreement about what matters.

When they discuss our practical and moral beliefs, some skeptics argue:

(1) These normative beliefs were often advantageous, by leading us to act in ways that helped us to survive and reproduce.

(2) Because such beliefs were advantageous, natural selection made us disposed to have them.

(3) These beliefs would have had the same effects, by leading us to act in the same ways, whether or not these beliefs were true.

Therefore

(4) These beliefs would have been advantageous whether or not they were true.

Therefore

> (5) Natural selection would have disposed us to have
> these beliefs whether or not they were true.

Therefore

> We cannot justifiably believe that these beliefs are true.

We should accept premise (3). When our normative beliefs lead us to act in certain ways, these beliefs would have these effects whether or not they were true. We should therefore accept both (4) and (5). As before, if natural selection made us disposed to have certain normative beliefs, this fact would challenge these beliefs. Natural selection would be a distorting influence, since this cause of these beliefs would be unrelated to their truth.

Before we discuss this argument's other premises, we can note some relevant facts. As well as being epistemically rational, in ways that enable us to form many true beliefs, we are practically rational, in ways that enable us to achieve many of our aims. Such practical rationality is, however, less impressive, and easier to explain. To act successfully, we must be motivated to achieve certain aims, we must form true beliefs about which bodily movements would achieve these aims, and we must move our bodies in these ways. Of these three components of our successful acts, the first and third are not remarkable. Many non-rational animals are motivated to achieve certain aims, and move their bodies in ways that achieve these aims. What is remarkable is our ability to act successfully in a great variety of deliberate, ingenious, and well-planned ways. But this ability involves not practical but *epistemic* rationality, since it chiefly consists in our forming true beliefs about which ways of acting might achieve our aims.

We can be practically rational in other ways. Unlike other animals, we can be rational in our choice of aims. We often have aims that are good, and rational, in the sense that these aims have intrinsic properties that give us reasons to have them. I shall return to these reasons, and to our beliefs about them. But we can first ask which aims and acts would have been reproductively advantageous, so that it might be natural selection, and not our response to reasons, that motivated early humans to act in these ways.

When some act is in this sense advantageous, that is not the same as this act's being advantageous *for us*. Some way of acting is *reproductively* advantageous when such acts contribute to spreading the genes that make us more likely to act in this way. It might be very bad for us, or for other animals, to act in some of these ways. In many species, for example, the males that most effectively spread their genes have brief and stressful adult lives, and many humans, especially women, have been burdened by having too many children.

Our genes cannot give us the aim of acting in whatever ways would most effectively spread these genes, since that is a highly complicated aim, which we have only recently become able to describe. But our genes can motivate us in other, simpler ways. We can be motivated to act in ways that make us more likely to survive. Early humans, their graves and monuments suggest, were fearfully aware of death. Our genes could give us various other desires, and the instrumental motivation to do what would fulfil these desires. Such advantageous motivation often takes *hedonic* forms. Natural selection gave us bodies and brains that often make us feel pleasure or pain when we act in ways that have good or bad effects on our health, or our children's health, or when we act in various other ways that promote or prevent the spreading of our genes. We can therefore claim that

> (A) it was advantageous for early humans to be motivated to
> act in ways that would lead them to have children, and would
> promote the survival and hedonic well-being of themselves
> and their children.

We can now return to the skeptical argument sketched above. When defending premise (1), some normative skeptics claim that

> (B) it was often advantageous for early humans to believe
> that they had reasons to promote the survival and hedonic
> well-being of themselves and their children.

This claim, I believe, is false. We can object that

(C) to be motivated to act in these ways, early humans didn't
need to believe that they had such reasons.

Many other animals are strongly motivated to act in similar ways,
without having any such normative beliefs. We inherited from our pre-
human mammalian ancestors strong motivations to act in these ways.

There is a further point. Early humans did, I believe, have reasons to
promote the survival and well-being of themselves and their children.
But we can also claim that

(D) to be motivated to act in these ways, these humans did not
need to respond to reasons.

I claimed earlier that, just as cheetahs were selected for their speed, and
giraffes for their long necks, we were selected for our ability to respond
to reasons. That was a claim about *epistemic* reasons. We differ from
other animals by having a great number of true beliefs about the world,
and about the possible effects of different possible acts. To be able to
form so many true beliefs, we needed to respond to epistemic reasons
to have these beliefs. Out of the vast range of possible beliefs, we needed
to be *directed* to the particular beliefs that were true.

Early humans did not, in contrast, differ from other animals by having
a great number of different rational aims. These humans mostly acted in
ways that promoted the survival and well-being of themselves and their
children, or in ways that gave them pleasure or avoided pain. We cannot
similarly claim that, to be able to be motivated to act in these ways, these
humans needed to respond to practical reasons. Many other animals
are motivated to act in these ways, without responding to reasons.

I have rejected the claim that

(B) it was often advantageous for early humans to believe
that they had reasons to promote the survival and hedonic
well-being of themselves and our children.

To be motivated to act in these ways, early humans did not need to have
such beliefs.   Normative skeptics might reply that

(E) though these normative beliefs were not themselves
advantageous, they were indirectly produced by natural

selection. Early humans came to have these aims, and to act in these ways, because these aims and acts were advantageous. Later humans then came to believe that they had reasons to have these aims, and to act in these ways.

We should agree that (E) might be true. If we have some aim, that sometimes leads us to believe that we have reasons to have this aim. But when these skeptics turn from (B) to (E), that weakens their argument. Consider, for example, the belief that

(F) the nature of agony gives us a strong reason to want to avoid being in agony.

It would be significant if these skeptics could claim that

(G) natural selection caused us believe that we have this reason because this belief was advantageous, by motivating us to avoid agony.

These people could then claim that

(H) since this belief would have been advantageous whether or not it was true, this belief was caused in a way that was unrelated to its truth.

If (H) were true, that would cast doubt on the truth of (F). But these skeptics cannot plausibly appeal to (G). We would have been strongly motivated to avoid agony whether or not we believed that we had this reason.   These skeptics might claim that

(I) we believe that we have this reason because natural selection made early humans strongly motivated to avoid agony, and our having this motivation led later humans to believe that we have this reason.

But this claim merely asserts that this motivation led us to believe that we had this reason. And since this belief was not advantageous, we have less reason to assume that we would have formed this belief whether or not it was true.   In these ways (F) is like

(J) when we know that some belief must be true, we have a decisive reason to have this belief.

I have claimed that

(K) it would seldom be advantageous to believe that we had such decisive epistemic reasons. We seldom need to believe that we have reasons to believe what we know must be true.

We can now claim that

(L) when we remember what it is like to be in agony, we seldom need to believe that we have practical reasons to want to avoid such agony.

If we ask *why* we believe that we have these epistemic and practical reasons, the answer, I suggest, is that these beliefs are obviously true.

We have other practical and moral beliefs, many of which, unlike (F), affect what we care about, and do. Some of these beliefs have been claimed to be advantageous, in ways that might challenge these beliefs. But, as before, we can claim that

(K) these normative beliefs were at most partly produced by natural selection.

This skeptical argument therefore needs other premises. These skeptics might claim that

(6) we have no empirical evidence for the truth of these beliefs,

and they must claim that

(7) we have no other way of knowing whether these beliefs are true.

When Street presents her version of this argument, she defends both these claims. Street claims to be, not a Normative Nihilist, but a 'constructivist anti-realist' who accepts a desire-based response-dependence theory. On her view, our desires can make their objects, in one sense, good. We can have true normative beliefs because such beliefs are about what, in certain conditions, we would believe, or want. Such truths *depend* on such facts about us. Things matter, for example, in the sense that they matter to us. But Street denies that there are any *independent* normative truths, such as truths about what matters, and about what is good or bad, in the reason-implying senses. These are the kinds of normative truth in which Rationalists like me believe. Street denies that we could have any way of recognizing such truths. She concedes that, if there were any such truths, we might, by chance, believe these truths. But this possibility, she claims, would be extremely unlikely. In her words:

> the independent normative truth could be *anything* . . . what's ultimately worth pursuing could well be hand-clasping, or writing the number 587 over and over again, or counting blades of grass.

Street then asks

> what are the odds that our values will have hit, as a matter of sheer coincidence, on those things which are independently really worth pursuing?

Street here assumes that, in forming our beliefs about what is worth pursuing, we cannot be responding to the intrinsic credibility of these beliefs, or to our reasons to have them. If we were responding to such credibility, or to such reasons, it would not be a sheer coincidence if these normative beliefs were true. When Street discusses this possibility, she admits that we have some normative intuitions, and what she calls the power of 'rational reflection'. Most of us would strongly believe that, compared with a life of hand-clasping, counting blades of grass, or unrelieved suffering, a happy and productive life would be much better, and more worth pursuing. But such intuitive beliefs, Street claims, are wholly unreliable.   If we trust such beliefs, she writes, we accept

> a strange form of religion—a religion stripped clean of everything except the bare conviction that there are independent normative truths that one is capable of recognizing.

Street gives various arguments for her claim that we could not be able to recognize any such truths. One argument appeals to the fact that we could not be causally affected by non-natural normative properties. This objection can, I have claimed, be answered. We can respond non-causally to the validity of certain arguments, though validity is not a natural property. We can form true modal beliefs, though we have no empirical evidence for these beliefs. We can have similar ways of forming true normative beliefs.

In other passages, Street claims that

> (L) though the power of rational reflection might lead us towards such independent normative truths, this power would be too weak.   In this conflict, the evolutionary forces would win.

In defending (L), Street claims that rational reflection must start with certain normative premises, which she calls our 'starting fund of evaluative judgments'.   Street then argues:

> If we believe that there are such independent normative truths, we should admit that, since our our first normative judgments were produced by the evolutionary forces, which 'bear no relation' to such truths, these judgments were 'thoroughly contaminated with illegitimate influence'. We should expect these judgments to have been 'mostly off track' and 'badly mistaken'. We cannot justifiably believe that rational reflection would enable us to correct these faults, so that we could recognize these independent normative truths.

We can reject these claims. On Street's account, the evolutionary forces caused us to have certain reproductively advantageous normative beliefs. We were led to believe that pain and injury are bad, and that we have strong reasons to promote the survival and well-being of ourselves and our children. I doubt that these beliefs *were* produced by natural selection. But we can reply that, even if they were, these beliefs are *not* badly mistaken, but correspond to some of the independent normative truths. Pain *is* bad, and we *do* have strong reasons to promote the survival and well-being of ourselves and our children. So even on Street's account, our normative thinking would have started with some true normative beliefs. The power of rational reflection could then have led us to believe other such truths.

When Street considers a similar reply, she objects that it takes for granted

> the very thing called into question by my argument — namely
> that we are not hopeless as normative judges. The reply
> trivially assumes that we are *correct* to think that staying alive,
> developing one's capacities, family and friendship, and so on,
> are independently worth pursuing.

To answer her argument, Street then writes, we must show that the evolutionary forces have led us to form true normative beliefs, and we must defend this claim without making any assumptions about which normative beliefs are true. What Street here requires us to do is impossible. Some whimsical despot might require us to show that some clock is telling the correct time, without making any assumptions about the correct time. Though we couldn't meet this requirement, that wouldn't show that this clock is not telling the correct time. In the same way, we couldn't possibly show that natural selection had led us to form some true normative beliefs without making any assumptions about which normative beliefs are true. This fact does not count against the view that these normative beliefs are true.

Street might now return to her claim that, though we may find it intuitively plausible that such things as our survival and well-being are, in the independent senses, good and worth pursuing, we should not trust such intuitive beliefs, which are produced by evolutionary forces. On this objection, our normative intuitions were 'thoroughly contaminated' in a different way. Rather than being too *weak* to be able to defeat the evolutionary forces, our power of rational reflection has been too *influenced* by these forces. Since these normative beliefs were produced by evolution, we cannot defensibly claim that these beliefs correspond to any *independent* normative truths.

119 Evolutionary Forces

This objection assumes that

> (O) these normative beliefs were mostly produced by
> evolutionary forces.

We should agree that, if (O) were true, that would count strongly against the view that we can respond to the intrinsic credibility of such normative beliefs, and to our reasons to have such beliefs. But there is, I believe, no strong evidence for the truth of (O), and much evidence against (O).

In a full assessment of (O), we would need to consider several difficult historical and scientific questions. I cannot do that here. But I can mention some of the relevant considerations.

We can first note, that, when Street and others make claims about the effects of evolutionary forces, these writers are not referring only to *genetic* evolution. Just as certain genes became more widespread when people with these genes were more likely to survive and pass on these genes to their children, certain beliefs became more widespread when communities of people with these beliefs were more likely to be successful, in ways that preserved and spread these beliefs. So we should ask which normative beliefs would have been advantageous either reproductively, or at the social or cultural level. I shall return to the significance of this distinction.

If our normative beliefs were mostly produced by evolutionary forces, we would expect that we would have beliefs that were reproductively advantageous, by making it likely that we would have more descendants. If we ask which normative beliefs would be most likely to have this effect, there are some obvious answers. We would believe that we have strong reasons to try to have as many surviving children as we can, as an end in itself, and not merely because having children would promote our own well-being. But most people do not believe that they have such reasons. When people have become able to use artificial birth control, most of them have chosen to have fewer children. We can similarly claim that, if our moral beliefs were mostly produced by evolutionary forces, we would expect people to believe that they have a duty to have and raise as many children as they can, and that deciding not to have children would be wrong. But this is not what most people have believed. Those who decide to have no children have often been revered or admired. If our normative beliefs were selected to maximize the number of our descendants, and of other people who have our genes, these various facts would be hard to explain.

There have, of course, been many widely held beliefs that were reproductively advantageous. It has been widely believed that, if we do have children, we ought morally to promote their survival and well-being. It has also been widely believed that we have reasons to want to avoid pain and injury, and to promote our own well-being, and reasons to act in ways that would be most likely to achieve our aims. But though these beliefs help us to survive and have surviving children, that does not show that we came to have these beliefs *because* they were reproductively advantageous. We may have formed these beliefs by responding to their intrinsic credibility, or to our reasons to have them.   As Dennett writes:

> The very considerations that in other parts of the biosphere
> count *for* an explanation in terms of natural selection of an
> adaptation—manifest utility, obvious value, undeniable
> reasonableness of design—count *against* the *need* for any
> such explanation in the case of human behaviour.

When people argue that our normative beliefs were partly produced by natural selection, they need to cite beliefs that were both reproductively advantageous, and less easy to explain in other ways. Suppose that it was widely believed that men ought to rape women, and commit adultery, as often as they can. We might have good reason to believe that *these* beliefs were produced by natural selection. But these beliefs have not been widely held. These ways of spreading our genes have been widely believed to be wrong. It has also been widely believed that we ought to care for our aged parents, and refrain from harming other old people, though such acts do nothing to spread our genes. In these cases, our moral beliefs seem not to be produced by but to oppose the evolutionary forces.

As Street and others might reply, we can imagine evolutionary explanations of the beliefs that rape and adultery are wrong, and that we ought to care for our aged parents. But the plausibility of this reply does not *strengthen* but *weakens* the arguments for (O). We can often imagine plausible evolutionary explanations for either of two conflicting normative beliefs. This fact counts against both these explanations. Things are different when we consider many biological facts. When such facts raise a problem for evolutionary theory, as is true, for example, of the origin of sexual reproduction, it *may* be enough if we can imagine some fairly plausible evolutionary explanation. We have strong reasons to believe that such facts have some such explanation. No such claim applies to most of our normative beliefs. Since these beliefs can be plausibly explained in other ways, it is not enough to suggest how these beliefs might have been produced by evolutionary forces.

There is one moral belief whose acceptance can most plausibly be claimed to have an evolutionary explanation. It has been widely believed that incest is wrong, even in the least problematic case of incest between brothers and sisters. Siblings who grow up together are also seldom sexually attracted to each other. These facts may both be explained by the biological fact that incestuously conceived children are more likely to have genetic disorders or diseases. But though incest has been widely believed to be wrong, this belief does not have much importance. More important are beliefs in the wrongness of such acts as lying, stealing, and breaking promises, and in some other deontological prohibitions. Unlike the belief that incest is wrong, these beliefs do not have any distinctive evolutionary explanation. Though these beliefs may not have been disadvantageous, they do not help to support the view that our normative beliefs were produced by evolutionary forces.

We have other moral beliefs that would not have been advantageous, and which seem to count against this evolutionary view. One example is the Golden Rule, which was independently proclaimed and accepted in several of the world's earliest civilizations. As several Darwinians point out, natural selection can explain how we and some other animals became *reciprocal altruists*, who benefit those other members of our group who respond by benefiting us. We scratch other people's backs, and help them in other ways, when and because we believe that these other people have done, or will do, similar things for us. Such behaviour is advantageous, because reciprocal altruists are more likely to be helped by others. If we follow the Golden Rule, however, we do not help only those other people who will reciprocate, by helping us. We treat other people only in ways in which we would be willing to be treated by others, whether or not these others treat us in these ways. To use some other Darwinian phrases, if we are reciprocal altruists, we are *grudgers*, who do not benefit those other people who are *cheats*, since they do not benefit us in return. The Golden Rule, in contrast, tells us to be *suckers*, who benefit everyone, including cheats. As Darwinians point out, compared with being a grudger, it is much less advantageous to be a sucker. So natural selection cannot easily explain humanity's early acceptance of the Golden Rule. Natural selection might explain why, of those who have accepted the Golden Rule, most have often failed to do what this rule requires. But we are discussing explanations of our normative beliefs, not our motivation to act on these beliefs.

We can now return to the complication mentioned above. When Street and others claim that our normative beliefs were mostly produced by evolutionary forces, these writers are in part referring to cultural evolution. Some normative beliefs became more widely spread when and because communities of people with these beliefs were more likely to be successful. It is much less clear how we should assess the claim that certain normative beliefs were in this way, not *reproductively*, but *socially* or *culturally* advantageous. It is less clear, for example, whether and how such explanations of our normative beliefs should be assumed to *debunk* or undermine these beliefs. When the acceptance of certain normative beliefs made some community or culture more likely to survive and flourish, this fact does not as such cast doubt on the truth or plausibility of these beliefs. Such explanations of our normative beliefs do not obviously, in Street's phrase, *contaminate* these beliefs. Some examples are beliefs about the wrongness of lying, breaking promises, and stealing. Though the acceptance of these beliefs might help communities to survive and flourish, this fact does not debunk these beliefs.

These debunking arguments would have most force when they are applied to the normative beliefs that have helped some communities to destroy, conquer, or exploit others. Some examples might be the beliefs that, rather than following the Golden Rule, we ought to give, or may give, strong priority to the well-being of people who are members of our tribe, nation, or race, or followers of the same religion. These beliefs may have been evolutionarily advantageous, not only at the genetic but also at the social or cultural level. Such beliefs have also been widely held. Some people have believed that they were permitted or even required to give *no* weight to the well-being of strangers, or members of other tribes, nations, races, or religions.

These facts also help to show, however, that our normative beliefs have not been mostly produced by evolutionary forces. When we consider how people's moral beliefs have changed over many centuries, we find slow but accelerating progress towards the beliefs that everyone's well-being matters equally, and that everyone has equal rights. Most of us have come to believe that slavery is wrong, and to reject racist and sexist beliefs. And more of us are coming to believe that we should not inflict pain on animals. Like the Golden Rule, these beliefs are clearly *not* the product of evolutionary forces. These facts support an alternative to (O).   We can plausibly claim, I believe, that

> (P) though humanity's earliest moral beliefs were in several ways distorted by evolutionary forces, those distortions are being overcome, so that true moral beliefs are becoming more and more widely held.

These remarks do not refute (O) or establish (P). But on balance, I believe, there is strong evidence against the view that our normative beliefs have been mostly produced by evolutionary forces.

Like many other skeptics, Street also argues:

> (Q) For our normative beliefs to be justified, we must have some empirical evidence for their truth.

> (R) If our normative beliefs are about these alleged independent normative truths, we could not have such evidence.

Therefore

> We cannot justifiably believe that any such beliefs are true.

We should accept premise (R). When we consider beliefs about the world, we often have empirical evidence for the truth of these beliefs. These beliefs can help to explain observable facts, and can provide testable predictions. But when we consider beliefs about what we have reasons to care about, and to do, we have no such evidence. For example, from my claim that we have reasons to want to avoid being in agony, no testable predictions follow. And premise (Q) is plausible. We normally assume that we need some evidence for the truth of our beliefs. This argument therefore seems to have great force.

I believe, however, that we can justifiably reject (Q). We have other true beliefs that are not about observable features of the world. Some examples are modal beliefs about necessary truths, such as mathematical and logical truths. As I have claimed, we cannot have any empirical evidence for such modal truths. But our modal beliefs can be justified. We have these beliefs because they seem to us very credible, or we seem to have decisive reasons to have them. We are responding, we can say, to *apparent* epistemic reasons. We can justifiably assume that, in our mathematical and logical reasoning, this way of forming beliefs often leads us to the truth. Nothing could be clearer than the truths that two plus two must equal four, and that if X implies Y, and X is true, Y must be true.

When I claim that these beliefs are justified, that is not a modal but a normative claim. I am stating the normative view that many of these apparent epistemic reasons really are reasons. We don't need independent evidence for the view that we have these reasons to have these modal beliefs. We can justifiably believe that we have these reasons because we have strong apparent reasons to have this belief, and no strong contrary apparent reasons.

We are now discussing our beliefs about practical and moral reasons. Such beliefs, as Sidgwick writes,

> relating as they do to matter fundamentally different from that with which physical science or psychology deals, cannot be inconsistent with any physical or psychological conclusions. They can only involve errors by being shown to contradict one another.

This last claim is too strong. There can be general arguments for the view that such normative beliefs cannot be true, or justified. Some examples are the metaphysical and epistemological objections that I have been discussing. But Sidgwick rightly claims that there cannot be any non-normative facts, such as physical or psychological facts, that directly conflict with our beliefs about practical and moral reasons.

We form some of these beliefs by responding to apparent epistemic credibilities and reasons. Since our response to such credibilities and reasons is a fairly reliable way of forming beliefs about many other subjects, we have strong reasons to assume that at least some of these normative beliefs are true.

This assumption might be questioned. Some people are good judges only when they are judging certain things. A good mathematician may be a bad psychologist, and vice versa. It might be similarly claimed that, though our responses to apparent reasons enable us to form many true beliefs about many other subjects, including true beliefs about what we have reasons to believe, we cannot reliably form such true beliefs about what we have reasons to care about, and to do.

In considering this claim, we can first note one difference between these beliefs. When we have apparent epistemic reasons to believe that we have epistemic reasons, these apparent reasons are, in a way, about themselves. When we have such reasons to believe that we have *practical* and *moral* reasons, these apparent epistemic reasons are not about themselves. It might be suggested that, just as it may take a thief to catch a thief, our apparent epistemic reasons may be more trustworthy when they are reasons to have beliefs about themselves. Our beliefs about such reasons might be more reliable precisely because they are beliefs about how we can reliably form true beliefs.

This suggestion does not, I believe, survive reflection. We have apparent reasons to have beliefs about a great variety of other things, such as mathematics, atoms, stars, evolution, history, languages, and metaphysics. These apparent epistemic reasons are not less trustworthy because they are apparent reasons to have beliefs about things that are not themselves epistemic reasons.

We have similar apparent reasons to believe that we can have practical and moral reasons. Nor, I believe, do we have any strong conflicting apparent reasons. We can therefore justifiably believe that, just as we have reasons to have various beliefs, we have reasons to have various desires and aims, and reasons to act in various ways. Compare, for example,

> (S) We have reasons to believe that, if we touch a red hot iron, that would cause us great pain,

and

> (T) We have reasons to want and to try to avoid such pain.

We have no strong reason to believe that, though (S) is true, (T) *isn't* true. Justifications for beliefs must end somewhere, and they can best end with what seem to be decisive epistemic credibilities and reasons. It seems intuitively clear that we have practical reasons to want to avoid great pain. Discussing the view that we have no such reasons, Nagel writes:

> There is nothing self-contradictory in this proposal, but it seems nevertheless insane. Without some positive reason to believe there is nothing in itself good or bad about having an experience you intensely like or dislike, we can't seriously regard the common impression to the contrary as a collective illusion.

It seems similarly clear that we have reasons to have many other aims or ends, such as the survival and well-being of ourselves and our children. And just as we can have reasons to believe that

> (U) certain acts are the best or only ways to achieve our aims,

we have reasons to believe that

> (V) we have reasons to act in some of these ways.

We have no strong reason to believe that, though (U) is true, our belief in (V) is another illusion.

According to premise (Q) of the argument we are now discussing, for such normative beliefs to be justified, we must have some empirical evidence for their truth. This premise seems more plausible than it really is. In most areas of our thinking, if we have no such evidence for the truth of some set of beliefs, this fact counts strongly against these beliefs. No such claim applies to these normative beliefs. When we ask whether we have reasons to have certain aims, and reasons to try to achieve these aims, we are not asking questions about natural features of the world. Though we could not possibly have empirical evidence *for* these beliefs, we also could not have such evidence *against* these beliefs. When we ask whether we can have practical and moral reasons, nothing is relevant except our normative intuitions. If it seems to us to be clearly true that we can have such reasons, and we seem to have no strong reason to believe that we can't have such reasons, we can justifiably believe that we can have such reasons.

To defend such beliefs, however, there is one more objection that we must consider. When Street claims that we cannot trust our intuitive normative beliefs, she assumes that we and others have deeply conflicting beliefs. Since we can have no empirical evidence for the truth of such beliefs, our beliefs *would be* seriously challenged if these beliefs conflicted deeply with other people's normative beliefs.

When we are considering some questions, it may be fairly unimportant whether we and other people have conflicting beliefs. We may justifiably believe, for example, that those with whom we disagree have poor judgment, since it is our beliefs that have been shown, in earlier cases, to be true. Or we may justifiably believe that these people have miscalculated, or made some recognizable mistake, or that we have better evidence for the truth of our beliefs. But we are now considering normative beliefs that cannot be defended in such ways. Everything here depends on whether we can trust our ability to form some true normative beliefs, by using what Street calls our power of rational reflection. For such beliefs to be justified, it is not enough that these beliefs seem to us intrinsically very credible, or that we seem to have strong reasons to have them. We must also justifiably believe that we are able to recognize, and assess, the credibility of these beliefs and these apparent reasons. In such cases, it makes a great difference whether we and others disagree, and whether and how we can explain these disagreements. We cannot merely assume that, in such disagreements, it is *we* who are the people who have got things right.

34

Agreement

120 The Argument from Disagreement

We cannot rationally believe that there are moral truths, it is often argued, given the facts of deep and widespread moral disagreement, and the cultural origin of many moral beliefs.

To introduce this argument, I shall sum up some of my claims.

(A) There are some irreducibly normative reason-involving truths, some of which are moral truths.

(B) Since these truths are not about natural properties, our knowledge of these truths cannot be based on perception, or on evidence provided by empirical facts.

(C) Positive substantive normative truths cannot be analytic, in the sense that their truth follows from their meaning.

Therefore

(D) Our normative beliefs cannot be justified unless we are able to recognize in some other way that these beliefs are true.

We do, I believe, have this ability. We have reasons to have certain normative beliefs, and we can respond to these reasons. Normative beliefs can also be self-evident, and intrinsically credible. One such belief is

(E) Torturing children merely for fun is wrong.

There are similar non-normative beliefs, such as

(F) No statement can be both wholly true and wholly false.

Since our normative beliefs are neither caused by what we believe, nor based on empirical evidence, we need another word to refer to our way of forming these beliefs.   On the view that I have called

Intuitionism: We have *intuitive* abilities to respond to reasons
and to recognize some normative truths.

Though it is intuitively clear that certain acts are wrong, most of our moral beliefs cannot depend only on such separate intuitions. We must also assess the strength of various conflicting reasons, and the plausibility of various principles and arguments, trying to reach what Rawls calls *reflective equilibrium*. This kind of intuitively-based reflective thinking is not only, as Scanlon writes,

the best way of making up one's mind about moral matters . . .
it is the only defensible method.

We have similar abilities to recognize truths about what is rational, and about what we have reasons to believe, and want, and do.

Many recent writers reject such claims. Schiffer, for example, doubts that moral intuitions are worth discussing, and Field and Boghossian call the idea of rational intuition 'obscurantist' and 'a mystery'. But these criticisms are aimed at the view that intuition is a special quasi-perceptual faculty. That is not the view that I am defending here. When I use the word 'intuitive', I mean what Boghossian means when he describes one of his claims as 'intuitively plausible' and 'intuitively quite clear'.

Intuitionism can also be challenged with claims about disagreement. When Boghossian denies that beliefs can be intrinsically credible, or self-evident, he points out that

(G) different people might find conflicting beliefs self-evident.

If we claim that we have some ability, however, it is no objection that we might have lacked this ability. Different people might have conflicting visual experiences, which were like dreams and hallucinations, and were not a source of knowledge. But that is not in fact true. Different people's visual experiences seldom conflict, and believing what we seem to see is a fairly reliable way of reaching the truth. It may be similarly true that, after careful reflection, different people would seldom find conflicting beliefs self-evident. Believing what seems self-evident, after such reflection, may be another fairly reliable way of reaching the truth.

When Schiffer argues that there are no moral truths, he claims that

(H) even in ideal conditions, when everyone knows the
relevant facts and is reasoning equally well, we and others
could rationally disagree about any moral question.

For example, Schiffer claims that, though we could rationally believe that

(E) torturing children merely for fun is wrong,

it would be equally rational to reject this belief. This claim assumes that we cannot have decisive reasons to have our moral beliefs. If we had such reasons to believe (E), it would not be equally rational either to have or to reject this belief. What Schiffer calls his *error theory* might be true, since we might never have decisive reasons to have any moral belief. But Schiffer cannot support this theory by claiming that we and others could rationally disagree about any moral question, since this claim assumes that we have no such reasons. Nor could we reject Schiffer's theory merely by claiming that we and others could *not* rationally disagree. When we are trying to decide whether we have decisive reasons to have certain beliefs, we cannot usefully appeal to claims about whether, when considering these beliefs, we and others could rationally disagree.

There is another way to challenge Intuitionism. Rather than claiming that we and others *might* disagree about normative questions, or *could rationally* disagree, Anti-Intuitionists might claim that

> (I) even in ideal conditions, we and others *would in fact* disagree.

These people might then argue:

> Since there would always be such normative disagreements, we cannot justifiably or rationally believe that our normative beliefs are true, nor can we rationally believe that any normative beliefs might be true.

We can call this *the Argument from Disagreement*. If (I) were true, this argument would have great force. If we had strong reasons to believe that, even in ideal conditions, we and others would have deeply conflicting normative beliefs, it would be hard to defend the view that we have the intuitive ability to recognize some normative truths. We would have to believe that, when we disagree with others, it is only we who can recognize such truths. But if many other people, even in ideal conditions, could not recognize such truths, we could not rationally believe that we have this ability. How could *we* be so special? And if none of us could recognize such normative truths, we could not rationally believe that there *are* any such truths.

To answer this argument, Intuitionists must defend the claim that, in ideal conditions, we and others would not have such deeply conflicting beliefs. According to what we can call this

> *Convergence Claim*, or *CC*: If everyone knew all of the relevant non-normative facts, used the same normative concepts, understood and carefully reflected on the relevant arguments, and was not affected by any distorting influence, we and others would have similar normative beliefs.

Unlike the claims that different people might disagree, or could rationally disagree, CC is an *empirical* claim. Though it is a normative question what would count as ideal conditions, it is a psychological question whether, in these conditions, people would have similar normative beliefs.

When Intuitionists claim that we have intuitive abilities to respond to reasons, and to recognize some normative truths, they should admit that we are fallible. Even in ideal conditions, some people would make mistakes, and there would be some disagreements. There may be some normative questions about which, given our present abilities, we would all make mistakes. To answer the Argument from Disagreement, it would be enough to defend the prediction that, in ideal conditions, we would *nearly* all have *sufficiently similar* normative beliefs. Even mathematicians sometimes disagree, but they can recognize mathematical truths. We may also make mistakes about whether and when the ideal conditions would have been met. There may be relevant facts or arguments, or distorting influences, of which we are not yet aware. Our normative thinking is still in its childhood.

For CC to be a significant claim, our concept of a distorting influence must be purely procedural. When someone's normative beliefs have been influenced in some way, we should not claim this influence to be distorting merely because it leads this person to have some normative belief that we reject. That would make it trivial to claim that, if no one was affected by any distorting influence, we and others would not disagree. We must have other reasons to believe that an influence of some kind is likely to distort our own and other people's normative beliefs. One such distorting influence would be our knowledge that, if other people accepted and acted on some normative belief, that would give special benefits to us.

In trying to decide whether CC is true, we must consider various historical and psychological questions. We must ask how much and how deeply people have disagreed, and how such disagreements can be best explained. We cannot hope to reach more than very partial answers to these questions. Given these answers, we must then try to predict whether, in ideal conditions, these disagreements would be sufficiently resolved.

In asking whether the Convergence Claim is true, I have just said, we cannot appeal to our own normative beliefs. We should also set aside our meta-ethical or meta-normative beliefs. Unlike most of us, for example, Schiffer denies that

(E) torturing children merely for fun is wrong.

But this disagreement does not count against the Convergence Claim. Schiffer calls such acts *abhorrent*, and he rejects (E) only because he believes that there are no moral truths. Schiffer would agree that, if there were any moral truths, (E) would be one such truth. Schiffer also calls it puzzling that rational adults use the concept *morally wrong*, since he believes that moral beliefs are best regarded as one kind of desire. As we have seen, many people make such claims. When we ask whether, in ideal conditions, we would all have similar moral beliefs, we should use the phrase 'moral belief' in a meta-ethically neutral sense, which allows that such beliefs might merely be, or be expressions of, such moral sentiments. Like such other Sentimentalists as Hume and Blackburn, Schiffer has what are close enough to moral intuitions.

We cannot assume that everyone has such moral beliefs, sentiments, or intuitions. That seems not to be true of those who are now called *psychopaths* or *sociopaths*. On one estimate, the proportion of such people is 1% of women, and 3% of men. Since these people have no real moral beliefs or intuitions, we cannot claim that, in ideal conditions, their moral beliefs would be similar to ours. But this fact does not threaten the claim that we have the intuitive ability to recognize some moral truths. That claim does not apply to people who have no moral beliefs or intuitions.   Most of us can see, though some of us are blind.

Intuitionism *would* be challenged if it were true that, even in ideal conditions, there would be many deep disagreements between people who clearly *do* have moral beliefs, sentiments, or intuitions. There would be no such disagreement about the wrongness of torturing children merely for fun. But there are many other, more controversial moral questions. Intuitionists need not claim that, in ideal conditions, these disagreements would all be completely resolved. But they they must defend the claim that, in ideal conditions, there would not be deep and widespread moral disagreements.

121 The Convergence Claim

When we discuss normativity, it is a mistake to consider only morality. So we can first return to the question whether, as Intuitionists claim, we can recognize some epistemic normative truths. I believe that

> (J) when some fact implies that some belief must be true,
> this fact gives us a decisive reason to have this belief.

Though Schiffer denies that there are any moral truths, he accepts (J). As I have said, Schiffer calls (J) 'about as analytic as anything can be'. The truths that are most analytic are those that are true by definition. Schiffer's examples are:

> (K) Every widow was once married,

and

> (L) We ought not to do what is wrong.

If (J) were like (K) and (L), by being true by definition, we could not appeal to (J) in defending the Convergence Claim. (J) would not then be a substantive normative truth, but what Schiffer calls a 'trivial truism'. Nor could our belief in (J) help to show that we have the intuitive ability to recognize some normative truths. To recognize that some claim is true by definition, we don't need any normative intuition.

On some uses of the phrase 'a reason', (J) may be true by definition. But I use (J) as a normative claim, which could be restated as

> (M) when some fact implies that some belief must be true, this
> fact counts decisively in favour of our having this belief.

This truth, I believe, is very different from trivial truths like (K) and (L). To explain how those other claims are true, it is enough to say that the word 'widow' means 'a woman who was married to someone who has died', and that, in saying that we ought not to do something, we mean that this act is wrong. We cannot similarly claim that, when we say that

> (N) some fact implies that some belief must be true,

we mean that

> (O) this fact counts decisively in favour of our having this belief.

(N) and (O) have quite different meanings. (N) is not a normative claim. (M) states the substantive normative belief that (N)'s truth would make (O) true.

When Schiffer discusses truths like

> (K) Every widow was once married,

he calls these truths

> *conceptual* or *concept-based* in the sense that no one could fully understand these claims without believing that they are true.

Schiffer might claim that (M) is also a conceptual truth. This use of the phrase 'conceptual' may, I have said, be misleading. If we could not fully understand some claim without believing that this claim is true, the explanation may not be that this claim's truth is based on the concepts with which this claim is stated. We might be unable to disbelieve such a claim because this claim is so obviously true.

(M) is not, however, a conceptual truth in Schiffer's sense. I believe that

> (M) when some fact implies that some belief must be true, this fact gives us a decisive epistemic reason, by counting decisively in favour of our having this belief.

But since (M) is an irreducibly normative claim, (M) states an irreducibly normative, non-natural truth. Some Metaphysical Naturalists understand (M) but reject this claim, because they believe that there cannot be any such truths.

In asking whether the Convergence Claim is true, we should set aside such meta-ethical disagreements. Though I believe that (M) states an irreducibly normative truth, we should ask whether everyone would accept (M) understood in a vaguer, meta-ethically neutral sense. The answer, I believe, is Yes. When so understood, (M) is a substantive normative claim that, in ideal conditions, everyone would accept.

It might be objected: '(M) cannot state a *normative* truth. Norms must be able to be breached or contravened. It would be impossible to know that some belief must be true without also having this belief.' This objection is, I believe, mistaken. People sometimes know that some belief must be true, without really believing this truth, because they continue to think and act as if this belief were false. It is a normative claim that what these people know gives them a decisive epistemic reason to have this belief. My claims about (M) could, however, be applied to other normative epistemic truths. One example is

> (P) If we know that, given what we know, there is a chance
> of 99 in 100 that some belief is true, this fact gives us a strong
> epistemic reason, by counting strongly in favour of our having
> this belief.

(P) is a substantive normative claim that, in ideal conditions, nearly everyone would accept.

Consider next

> (Q) The nature of agony gives us a reason to want to avoid
> future agony.

This claim is not, I believe, a conceptual truth. It does not follow from the meaning of the word 'agony' and the phrase 'a reason' that we have such an object-given reason to want to avoid agony. (Q) is another example of an intuitively recognizable normative truth. I believe that, as Nagel claims, (Q) is intrinsically more plausible than any argument that we might give in (Q)'s defence. Many people either do not have the concept of a purely normative, object-given reason, or believe that there could not be any such reasons, or normative truths. But if we set aside such meta-ethical disagreements, and another distorting influence to which I shall return, few people who understood (Q) would seriously doubt that they have such a reason to want to avoid being in agony.

We can now turn to moral disagreements. When we discuss moral beliefs, we cannot hope to show that the Convergence Claim is true. Nor, however, could skeptics show that this claim is false. We can reasonably predict or hope that, in ideal conditions, we would nearly all have sufficiently similar moral beliefs. Though there have been many moral disagreements, most of these disagreements do not, I believe, count strongly against this prediction. In most cases, some of the ideal conditions are not met.

First, when different people have conflicting moral beliefs, that is often because these people have conflicting non-moral beliefs, or because they do not know all of the relevant non-moral facts.

Some examples are disagreements about distributive justice. There have been many conflicting beliefs about people's property rights, or the inheritance of wealth, or whether some people ought to be paid much more than others, or about which areas of land, natural resources, or man-made goods ought to be privately or publicly owned. These disagreements are often ignored by moral theories. But compared with many questions about which acts are right or wrong, such as questions about when it is right to lie or break some promise, it is more important to ask which inequalities in wealth and income can be morally justified. These inequalities have much more significant effects on people's lives. Disagreements about these questions often depend on people's having conflicting beliefs about human nature, and about the likely effects of different policies or institutions. Similar remarks apply to many other moral disagreements, such as many disagreements about sexual morality, or about our obligations to our close relatives, or about which acts should be illegal, and when and how people ought to be punished. When such disagreements depend in part on conflicting non-moral beliefs, it may be true that, if we all knew the relevant non-moral facts, we would come to have similar moral beliefs.

Many other moral disagreements depend on people's having conflicting religious beliefs. Such disagreements cast little doubt on the Convergence Claim. Most of us would agree, for example, that if the

Universe was created by an omniscient, omnipotent, and wholly good God, we ought to obey this God's commands.

In many other cases, our moral beliefs are affected by distorting influences. That is often true when we have conflicting interests. If we ask whether people should be paid much higher salaries when their innate abilities make them more productive, our answer may depend on whether we ourselves have such abilities. If we ask how much of their income the world's rich people ought to give to those who are poor, our answer may depend on whether we are rich or poor. When our moral beliefs are affected by our knowing such facts about ourselves, we are more likely to make mistakes. These facts ought not to influence us, since they are irrelevant to the truth of these moral beliefs. There are other distorting influences. Many disagreements cannot be ended, for example, because some people become committed to their beliefs, and are unwilling to admit that they have been mistaken.

In another large class of cases, moral disagreements are superficial, since they are about different ways of applying some more fundamental principle. When Mackie defends his error theory, he appeals to the fact that people in some societies believe in monogamy, but people in others believe in polygamy. This disagreement is not disturbing. Consider next the belief that parents have special obligations to care for their children. Since this belief is almost universal, it does not support the Argument from Disagreement. But even this belief is not, for most of us, fundamental. That is shown by how we would respond if we considered those actual or imagined communities, such as some Israeli kibbutz or Plato's Republic, in which children are communally reared. We would not believe that, in such communities, parents were simply acting wrongly in failing to care for their own children. Most of us would believe that (1) people ought to play their part in whatever, in their society, is the established system of bringing up the next generation, and that (2) in the best system parents would care for their own children. Any disagreements about (2) would mostly depend on people's having conflicting non-moral beliefs.

There are other ways in which people may only seem to disagree. In some cases, people use words like 'ought' and 'wrong' in different senses. Sidgwick, for example, claims that he ought not to prefer his own lesser good to the greater good of others. This may suggest that, on Sidgwick's view, he would be acting wrongly if he saved his own life rather than the lives of several strangers. Most of us would reject that view. But Sidgwick seems to be using 'ought' in what I call its *impartial-reason-implying* sense. He seems to mean that, if he assessed his reasons from an impartial point of view, he would have more reason to prefer the greater good of others.   We would not reject that claim.

Some other moral disagreements are not about *which* acts are wrong, but about *why* these acts are wrong, or what *makes* them wrong. Different answers are given by different systematic theories, such as those developed by Kantians, Contractualists, and Consequentialists. Such disagreements do not directly challenge the view that we are able to recognize some moral truths. In defending this view, it is enough to defend the claim that, in ideal conditions, there would be sufficient agreement about which acts are wrong. Though we also have intuitive beliefs about why many acts are wrong, and about the plausibility of different systematic theories, we would expect there to be more disagreement about these other questions. As I have also argued, however, when the most plausible systematic theories are developed further, as they need to be, these theories cease to conflict. If that is true, these theoretical wars would end.

Many other disagreements are about borderline cases. Such disagreements do not count against the view that there are some moral truths. Even when we all agree that acts of some kind are wrong, we should expect that we would sometimes disagree about which acts are of the relevant kind. We may agree, for example, that it is wrong to kill innocent human beings, but disagree about the status of a human embryo or foetus. There are two main ways in which we can use the phrase 'a human being'. On one use, a fertilized ovum counts as a living member of the species *homo sapiens*, and is therefore a human being. This is like the claim that, when the first green shoot emerges from an acorn, this acorn is already an oak tree. We may instead use different concepts of a tree and a human being, claiming that such a sprouting acorn is not yet an oak tree, and that a fertilized ovum or embryo is not yet a human being. When people's concepts differ in this way, that may lead them to disagree about the wrongness of abortion. It is a difficult question whether and how this disagreement could be resolved. But since this disagreement is about borderline cases, it does not cast doubt on the view that it is wrong to kill innocent human beings. There are similar disagreements about which acts count as killing someone, or merely as a failure to save someone's life.

These cases illustrate another kind of disagreement. When we ask whether acts of some kind are wrong, many people assume that the answer must be all-or-nothing. In many cases, however, the morally relevant facts are matters of degree. If an embryo or foetus turns slowly into a human being, the moral objection to an abortion may similarly grow in strength. Nor should we give equal weight to the saving of each person's life. Compared with giving someone fifty more years of life, it is very different to give someone else only a single extra month, or one extra week, or day. Return next to the question of what we rich people ought to give to those who are very poor. If we assume that wrongness is all-or-nothing, we shall be most unlikely to agree on how much we ought to give. And it is hard to believe that there could be a definite answer here, so that what is wrong might be giving less than a tenth of our income, or less than a fifth, or less than half. For most of us, the truth is rather that we shall be acting less wrongly the more we give. When people have conflicting moral beliefs because they mistakenly assume that wrongness cannot be a matter of degree, these disagreements do not count against the Convergence Claim. If these people gave up this assumption, that would end such disagreements.

Many people also fail to see that, in many cases, normative truths are imprecise. One example is the question of how it would be best for someone's life to go. When we are making decisions that will greatly affect the rest of our lives, such as choosing between two possible careers, or deciding whether to have children, the truth is often that neither of these possible futures would be better for us, or would make our lives more worth living. We should not assume that, when neither of two possible lives would be better, these lives must be precisely equally good. Two very different lives could not, I believe, have such precisely related values. These lives would be only *imprecisely equally good*, and this imprecision would often be great. Similar claims apply when we ask which people are worse off than others, in morally relevant senses. People in very different circumstances could not be precisely equally well off. But these questions have answers, since some lives are more worth living, and some people are better off than others. These differences are matters of degree. One life might be *somewhat* better than another, which is *much* better than a third, and one of two people might be either *somewhat* worse off, or *much* worse off. Such comparisons involve what we can call *imprecise cardinal comparability*.

It is easy to think about such cases in ways that lead us astray. When some things can be better or worse than others, and by more or less, it is natural to use what we can call *the Linear Model*. The goodness of these things, we may assume, involves a *dimension*, which we can think of as if it were a line, or scale of value. Something's goodness corresponds to its position on this line. Suppose next that, of two things, X is now worse than Y, and is therefore lower down on the line that represents our scale of value. X starts to get better in some gradual way, and ends up higher on this line than Y, thereby being better than Y. If that is how we think about such cases, we cannot help believing in precision. Since X has moved up this line from being lower than Y to being higher, there must have been a time when X was at the same point as Y, thereby being precisely equally good. In most important cases, that conclusion would be false. Suppose, for example, that X and Y are Shakespeare's drafts of two new plays. Because Shakespeare knows that one of these drafts is worse, he rewrites more than a thousand lines, thereby turning the worse play into the better play. There would be no point, during this rewriting, when these two plays were precisely equally good.

To understand these cases, we must reject this Linear Model, which unavoidably implies precision. Nor should we think in terms of numbers, since these would also imply precision. It would not be enough to use the idea of a *range* of value, by saying, for example that, rather than having a value of 90, something's value ranges from 85 to 95. Such a thing would be only slightly worse than something else whose value ranges from 86 to 96. When we think about cases that involve imprecise cardinal comparisons, we should deliberately avoid thinking in either spatial or numerical terms—except as a form of shorthand that we should remember to be seriously misleading.

A scientific analogy may be helpful here. Before Einstein's great discoveries, many people thought of time as if it were a line, with each moment having some position on this line. On this view, if neither of two events occurs before the other, these events must be simultaneous. No third possibility makes sense. Einstein discovered that, given the surprising ways in which time is related to space and to the speed of light, we must cease to think of the different moments of time as if they all had some position on a single line. When two events occur in sufficiently distant places, if neither event occurs before the other, that does not imply that these events are simultaneous. These events are related in a third way, which is sometimes called being in each other's *elsewhere*.

This analogy is only partial, since Einsteinian space-time involves relations that are precise. But it may help to remember the fact that, for many centuries, it seemed to many people to be certain that time could be represented as a line. This assumption, we have learnt, was a mistake. It may now seem similarly certain that, when some things can be better than others, and by more or less, such differences in value can be represented as if they involved different positions on a line, or scale of value. When such differences are imprecise, as they very often are, this assumption is also a mistake.

It is sometimes claimed that, to persuade people that differences in value can be imprecise, we can show these people that they already recognize this truth in making some of their decisions. Suppose that you have been offered two jobs, A and B, which would involve very different kinds of work, and would involve living in very different cities. You find it hard to choose between these offers, which seem to you equally good. The salary for job B is then significantly raised, making this offer seem much better than it was before. But this improvement doesn't solve your problem, since you still find it hard to choose between job A and this better version of B. Your continuing indecision may seem to show that you earlier believed that jobs A and B were only *imprecisely* equally good. It may seem that, if you had earlier believed that A and B were precisely equally good, you would have decided that this improved version of B must be better than A. But this reasoning is mistaken. You may have earlier assumed that, though there must be some precise truth about the relative goodness of A and B, you knew only very roughly how good these jobs would be. That would be enough to explain how, when B is improved, that does not solve your problem. This improvement may be well within your assumed margin of error.

There are other ways to defend the view that there can be such imprecise differences in value. Consider first comparisons of a different kind. Suppose that someone asks whether Einstein or Bach was a greater genius, or had greater achievements. We may think this a pointless question, since we cannot possibly compare the greatness of scientists and composers, or their achievements. But this response would be a mistake. Einstein was clearly a greater genius than any untalented fifth-rate composer, and Bach was clearly a greater genius than any incompetent fifth-rate scientist. As this shows, there *are* truths about the relative greatness of scientists and composers, and their achievements. If we had earlier believed that there could not be *any* such truths, it would be implausible to move now to the opposite extreme, believing not only that there are such truths, but also that such truths must be precise. Given the very great differences between music and physics, it could not be true, I believe, that Bach and Einstein, or their achievements, were precisely equally great. Nor could it be true that either was slightly greater than the other. Though there can be differences in the greatness of achievements of such very different kinds, these differences must be imprecise.

Since these claims about greatness are evaluative, we can next point out that there is similar imprecision in many non-evaluative and non-normative facts. If we are comparing two very different pieces of mechanical equipment, for example, there may be no precise truth about which of these pieces of equipment is more unwieldy, or awkward to use. And there would often be no precise truths about which of two rooms is more untidy, or which of two theories is more complicated, or which of two mountains it would be harder to climb.

Similar claims apply to the goodness of outcomes. Suppose we believe that it would be in one way better if some group of people received a greater sum of benefits, and in another way better if these benefits were more equally distributed between these people. There would often be no precise truths either about which of two sums of benefits would be greater, or about which of two patterns of distribution would be less unequal. Nor could there be precise truths about the relative importance of how great the sum of benefits would be, and how equally these benefits would be distributed. In such cases, the truth would often be that (1) neither of two outcomes would be better, and that (2) these outcomes would be very far from being precisely equally good. Though we can call such outcomes equally good, it is clearer to say that neither would be better.

Similar claims apply to questions about the wrongness of acts, and about what we ought to do, or have most reason to do. There are often no precise truths either about which acts would do more good, or about the relative importance of other moral considerations, or reasons for acting. There are no such truths, for example, about the relative strengths of our reasons to keep some promise, or to help some stranger who is in distress.

When different people have conflicting beliefs about which of two outcomes would be better, or which of two acts would be wrong, that is often because these people mistakenly assume that such normative truths are more precise than they really are. If these people realized that many such truths are very imprecise, they would often cease to disagree. These people would come to see that neither of two outcomes would be better, or that neither of two acts would be wrong.

There is another way in which these facts about imprecision support the view that there are some normative truths. If such truths had to be precise, it would often be hard to believe that there *are* such truths. It would be hard to believe, for example, that one of two possible lives could be 23.7% more worth living, or that one of two people could be, in some morally relevant sense, 3.16 times better off. When we see that such truths would be very imprecise, it is easier to recognize that some lives are more worth living than others, and that some people are better off.

We can next briefly consider another, similar, but more puzzling kind of case. Some questions may be *indeterminate*, in the sense that they have no answer. That is sometimes true, for example, of the question 'Is he bald?' If some man has no hair, he is bald. If some man has a full head of hair, he is *not* bald. But we cannot plausibly assume that, in all cases between these two extremes, any man must either *be*, or *not* be, bald. In many cases, though it is not true that some man is bald, it is also not true that this man is *not* bald.

Similar claims might apply to normative questions. One example is the wrongness of abortion. Suppose that

(R) it is not true that there is any moral objection to
early abortion.

This may seem to imply that

(S) there is no moral objection to early abortion.

But that may not be so. When it is *not* true that some man is bald, we cannot conclude that it *is* true that this man is *not* bald. In the same way, we might be right to believe both (R) and

(T) it is not true that there is no moral objection to
early abortion.

It might not be true either that there *is* a moral objection to early abortion, or that there *isn't*. There are other difficult moral questions, such as some questions about the ethics of population or the morality of war, which may have no answer.

It may seem a trivial fact that, when we ask whether someone is bald, this question may have no answer. But when we ask normative questions, this possibility can be more puzzling, and disturbing. We may find it hard to give up the assumption that, if it is not true that some act is wrong, this act must be morally permitted. We may think that, if it *isn't* true that some act is wrong, it must be true that this act *isn't* wrong. But if every act must either *be*, or *not* be, wrong, must it not be similarly true that every man must either *be*, or *not* be, bald? And that is not true.

Cases of this kind raise several difficult questions, which partly overlap with questions about imprecision. It is sometimes claimed, for example, that indeterminacy is entirely linguistic or conceptual. On this view, though our words or concepts may be vague, reality could not be vague, and we could always make our concepts more precise so that we could give fuller descriptions of the facts. But this view is too simple. There are indeed many cases of this kind. There are always precise truths, for example, about how many hairs there are, at any time, on some man's head. Though the concept *bald* is vague, we could introduce a more precise concept, which referred to these numbers of hairs. Questions that used this revised concept might all have answers. But there are many other cases to which this view does not apply. In such cases, there is no acceptable way of making some concept precise, since such revised precise concepts would lead us to draw distinctions and make claims which don't fit the facts. These concepts and claims would treat these facts as being more precise than they really are. This is Sen's objection, for example, to all of the criteria that economists have proposed about the relative badness of different patterns of economic inequality. Similar remarks apply to claims about which lives are more worth living, or about the relative strength of many conflicting reasons. If we tried to make such claims more precise, that would often make these claims false. As before, similar remarks apply to non-normative claims. We might, for example, truly claim that one of two theories was about twice as complicated, or that one of two mountains was about twice as hard to climb. But if we said that this theory was 2.17 times as complicated, or that this mountain was 2.17 times as hard to climb, these claims could not possibly be true.

There are also some powerful arguments against most accounts of indeterminacy. We may assume, for example, that if some man is not bald, no removal of any single hair could make this man bald. But that seems to imply that, even if we removed every hair from this man's head, one by one, we could not thereby make this man bald. That conclusion is clearly false. It is highly controversial how we should respond to such *sorites arguments*. These are like Zeno's arguments, in ancient Greece, for the impossibility of motion. These were excellent arguments, which were answered only several centuries later when mathematicians reached a better understanding of infinite sequences. But even before these arguments were answered, the ancient Greeks rightly assumed that these arguments must be unsound. It is clear that some things move. Similar claims may apply to sorites arguments, and to other arguments against the possibility of indeterminacy.

If some normative questions are indeterminate, having no answer, this would provide another explanation of some normative disagreements. When people disagree about whether some act is wrong, they may mistakenly assume that this act must either be, or not be, wrong. If these people gave up this assumption, they might often cease to disagree.

Such indeterminacy may also partly solve another problem. Return to the question of how much we rich people ought to give to those who are very poor. Now that each of us can so easily save so many other people from death, disablement and painful diseases, all plausible moral views require us to give a great deal. These views may seem too demanding. If I am regularly giving substantial amounts to some aid agency, I may think that I am doing well enough. *But I could save some young mother's life, at very little cost to myself. And save another's, and save another's.* We can be knocked over or pulled apart by such thoughts. For most readers of this book, this will be their greatest moral challenge. Most of us will not give enough, and will fail in one of two ways. We may have defensible moral beliefs, but only at the cost of breaking the link between our moral beliefs and our intentions. We must then admit that we intend to act wrongly. Or we may keep this link, intending never to act wrongly, but only at the cost of having indefensible moral beliefs. There is, however, another possibility. If we give to the world's poorest people one hundredth of our income, that is too little, and we are acting wrongly. If we gave nearly everything, that would be enough, and we would not be acting wrongly. But this question may sometimes have no answer. If we give certain proportions of our income, such as one tenth, or one quarter, it may not be true that we are *not* acting wrongly. But it may also not be true that we *are* acting wrongly.

The Argument from Disagreement is sometimes claimed to have most force when it appeals to history. As Nietzsche writes:

> because our moral philosophers . . . were poorly informed and
> not even very curious about different peoples, times, and past
> ages — they never laid eyes on the real problems of morality;
> for these emerge only when we compare *many* moralities.

It is true that, in the more distant past, people held moral beliefs that conflict more strongly with our present beliefs. This fact would count against the view that we all have moral knowledge, since everyone's conscience infallibly tells us which acts are wrong. But that view is clearly false. Even in ideal conditions we might all make some mistakes. Our claim should be only that, in ideal conditions, we would nearly all have sufficiently similar moral beliefs. This Convergence Claim is not threatened by the fact that, in earlier ages, people held moral beliefs that conflict more strongly with our present beliefs. On the contrary, this fact *supports* this claim. As Nietzsche admits, the earliest known moral concepts and moral codes were primitive and crude. When we look at the history of morality, we do not find mere variation, or a jumble of different moralities. We find a series of challenges to established beliefs, which lead to plausible revisions, and to greater agreement.

One example are beliefs about the scope of the moral community. In many of the earliest moralities, this community excluded slaves and people in other tribes or cities, and gave a lesser status to serfs, peasants, people in lower castes, or women. As I have said, there has been slow but accelerating progress towards the beliefs that everyone's well-being matters equally, and that everyone has equal moral claims.

I have now described many ways in which, when different people seem to have conflicting normative beliefs, these cases may not involve pure normative disagreements. These people may be considering borderline cases, or they may not know all of the relevant facts, or they may have conflicting non-normative or meta-ethical beliefs, or they may not understand the relevant arguments, or they may be using different concepts, or be affected by some distorting influence, or they may fail to realize that many normative truths are matters of degree, or that many of these truths are very imprecise, or that some normative questions may not have answers. We can also plausibly believe that, partly by learning from these disagreements, we are making normative progress. These facts do not show that, in ideal conditions, we would nearly all have sufficiently similar normative beliefs. But when we consider most actual disagreements, these disagreements do not, I believe, count strongly against this Convergence Claim.

We can next note that, when we consider some important questions, we *already* have sufficiently similar normative beliefs. With some fairly trivial exceptions, Williams assumes that we cannot claim to have made moral progress, and that there are no moral truths. In defending this skeptical view, Williams appeals to the fact that there have been deep moral disagreements. At one point, Williams writes:

> No doubt there are some ethical beliefs, universally held
> and usually vague . . . that we can be sure will survive at
> the reflective level. But they fall far short of any adequate,
> still less systematic body of ethical knowledge . . .

As Williams himself points out, however, ethical knowledge does not have to be *systematic*. Williams rightly criticizes Sidgwick for making that assumption. It *would* matter if, as Williams claims, the universally held beliefs that survived reflection would not even give us an *adequate* body of ethical knowledge.   But that is not, I believe, true.

When Williams concedes that there are some vague, universally held moral beliefs, his example is

(U) One has to have a special reason to kill someone.

We can make this claim less vague. It has long been almost universally believed that

> (V) except in certain special cases, it is wrong to kill
> any innocent human being who is a member of our
> moral community.

It is now almost universally believed that

> (W) this community at least includes all human beings.

There is some disagreement about which are the special cases in which it is *not* wrong to kill some innocent human being. There are also disagreements about what counts as a living human being, about which human beings are, in the relevant sense, innocent, and about what counts as a killing. But these are all disagreements about borderline cases. Many thousands of innocent people are intentionally killed each year. In nearly all these kinds of case, if everyone knew the relevant facts, we would nearly all agree about whether these acts are wrong. Similar claims apply to many other kinds of act. There are several other important moral beliefs that are nearly universal. Many people act in ways that we nearly all believe to be wrong, and such acts would be much more common if they were not believed to be wrong. Though these beliefs are vague, and there is disagreement about borderline cases, we can justifiably believe that most of these acts *are* wrong.

122 The Double Badness of Suffering

There are some other normative beliefs which are *not* vague, and on which we have already reached sufficient agreement. Few people have denied that

> (A) it is in itself bad to suffer.

All suffering is, in this sense, bad *for the sufferer*. Of those who believe that events can be *impersonally* bad, or bad, *period*, few have denied that

> (B) it is bad when people suffer in ways that they do not deserve.

These claims describe what we can call the *double badness* of suffering. Though suffering is always *in itself* bad, some suffering has good effects which may make it on the whole good, as when the pain that is caused by some injury prevents us from acting in ways that would increase this injury.

Some people believe that

> (C) suffering is in itself impersonally good, or is at least not in itself bad, when and because this suffering is deserved.

This belief does not conflict with (A), since such suffering is thought to be deserved as a punishment, which it could not be if it was not, at least in one way, bad for the sufferer.

Though some people have seemed to deny the double badness of suffering, these people were either not really denying (A) or (B), or they were under the influence of some distorting factor, or both. The Stoics, for example, wanted to believe both that

> (D) everything is for the best,

and that

> (E) those who were virtuous and wise would have a kind of happiness that did not depend on luck, or on how these people were treated by others.

These claims could not be true if it is bad to suffer. The Stoics therefore claimed that suffering is not bad, and that a wise and virtuous man would be happy even while he was being tortured on a rack.

Though they made such claims, the Stoics did not really deny that it is bad to suffer. These people distinguished two kinds of badness, or disvalue, to one of which they gave a misleading name. Pain and suffering were called *dispreferred indifferents*. Though these states were called *indifferent* in the sense that they had no disvalue of the more important kind, they were called *dispreferred* in the sense that a wise man would try to avoid these states, when such attempts were compatible with virtue. When the Stoics called pain and suffering *dispreferred*, they really meant that these states were *dispreferable*, or non-morally bad in the reason-implying sense. That is why a wise man would try to avoid these states. As Williams points out, there was another tension in the Stoic view. If pain and suffering are not bad, why is cruelty, as the Stoics claimed, a vice?

Many later thinkers have claimed, mostly as one part of a theistic view, that everything is for the best. On one version of this view, held for example by Albertus Magnus, the concepts *real*, *good* and *created by God* are quite different, since these concepts are expressed by words with quite different meanings, but these concepts all refer to the same property. This view is a fine precursor of Non-Analytical Naturalism. Of these three concepts, the concept *real* is the one that most clearly refers to a property that we can recognize, and that we know some things to have. When we are in great pain, for example, we know what it is for our painful sensation to be real. We also know that some innocent beings suffer in ways that are undeserved, as is true when a trapped fawn is burnt by some forest fire. This fawn's suffering cannot be bad, Albertus Magnus would have claimed, since this suffering is real and is therefore good. But on this view, when we have claimed that this fawn's suffering is real, we cannot claim that this suffering has the *different* property of being good, since there is no such different property. Since this view denies that there are any such independent normative properties, it does not seriously challenge the belief that undeserved suffering is bad. On a closely related view, the *privation theory*, evil is claimed to be merely the absence of good. Undeserved suffering is bad only in the sense that being in agony is not better than being unconscious.

When people make these implausible claims, they are trying to explain why an omniscient, omnipotent, and wholly good God allows what seem to be pointless evils. If undeserved suffering is bad, it is hard to understand why God allows such suffering to occur. Since these people deny that such suffering is bad because this denial seems to them the only solution to this *problem of evil*, these are not clear cases of undistorted disagreement with the view that suffering is bad. Discussing the many weaknesses and errors in our philosophical and other theoretical beliefs, Hume writes

> two thousand years with such long interruptions and under
> such mighty discouragements are a small space of time to give
> any tolerable perfection to the sciences.

It is one such interruption to our moral thinking that, for many centuries, many people have believed that everything must be, in some way, good.

Of those who hold such views, as I have said, some use normative words in unusual and irrelevant senses. Another example is Kant's early defence of Alexander Pope's claim 'Whatever is, is right'. This claim was mistranslated into German as: 'Whatever is, is good'. Schneewind writes:

> Kant . . . takes perfection to be the relation between the
> conscious desire to bring some state of affairs into being and
> the existence of a state of affairs that fully realizes this
> desire . . . it is plain that . . . Pope's thesis is true, since

whatever is, is as a result of God's willing and so is perfect by definition . . . The problem of physical evil [or the badness of pain] is resolved: there simply is none.

Kant's definition does not, however, provide a solution. The problem of evil is in part that

(F) God seems to will the existence of a world in which there are some things that are in themselves bad, such as undeserved suffering.

If Kant claimed that such suffering was good or perfect in his special sense, he would mean only that

(G) undeserved suffering that is willed by God is willed by God.

This claim cannot show that such suffering is not bad. Though Kant elsewhere warns that concealed tautologies are trivial, he forgot that here.

There is another way in which, when people deny that suffering or pain is bad, they may not be using words like 'bad' in relevant senses. Kant was not doing that, for example, when he later defended the Stoic view that physical pain is not bad. Kant meant only that such pain is not morally bad, in the sense in which people and their acts can be bad. Kant is not denying that physical pain is bad in the non-moral sense of being a state that we have reasons to want not to be in. Ross uses 'bad' in another irrelevant sense. When Ross denies that his own pain is bad, he means only that his pain is not something that he has a prima facie duty to prevent.

There are some other people who seem to deny that suffering is bad. One example is Nietzsche. But as I argue in the next chapter, this is not really Nietzsche's view. There are also some meta-ethical skeptics, whose doubts are irrelevant here. I know of no one who has both understood the claim that suffering is doubly bad, in the reason-implying senses, and also in an undistorted and unbiased way rejected this claim. The double badness of suffering is already, I believe, very close to being a universally recognized truth.

Though my examples have involved physical pain, these claims also apply to mental suffering. Such suffering can be much worse than much physical pain. Of those who have never been severely depressed, for example, many do not realize how awful this state of mind can be. And many of those who kill themselves are not trying to avoid physical pain. When we ask which things can be very bad, the only plausible answers are: great suffering and morally bad people, mental states, and acts. There are many things that may be in themselves good, but the absence of these things is not in itself bad. Friendship, love, knowledge, and various achievements may be in themselves good, but solitude, ignorance, and inactivity are not in themselves bad. False beliefs have been claimed to be bad, but they could not be, in themselves, great evils. And when Moore claims that it is in itself very bad to enjoy looking at ugly things, that is mere aesthetic snobbery.

Though I have claimed only that

(B) undeserved suffering is in itself impersonally bad,

I believe that

(H) no one could ever deserve to suffer,

so that

(I) all suffering is in itself both bad for the sufferer and impersonally bad.

Unlike (B), however, (H) and (I) are not yet universally recognized truths. And unlike those who believe that everything is for the best, some of those who have rejected (H) have not been obviously affected by some distorting influence. I can only hope that, in ideal conditions, these people would accept both (H) and (I). There may be some undiscovered argument by which, at last, such people will be convinced.

35

Nietzsche

123 Revaluing Values

Though we nearly all believe in the double badness of suffering, that does not answer the Argument from Disagreement, since there are other normative questions on which many people have conflicting beliefs. We can justifiably reject this argument if we can justifiably believe that, in ideal conditions, we would nearly all reach sufficient agreement. According to this

> *Convergence Claim*: If everyone knew all of the relevant non-normative facts, used the same normative concepts, understood and carefully reflected on the relevant arguments, and was not affected by any distorting influence, we would have similar normative beliefs.

I cannot hope to prove that, in these ideal conditions, we would have sufficiently similar beliefs. Nor, however, could others prove that we would *not* have such beliefs. We can at most hope to answer particular challenges to these predictions.

I shall here discuss one such challenge. Nietzsche seems to disagree deeply with some of the normative beliefs on which I predict that most of us would agree. It may seem implausible to claim that, in ideal conditions, we and Nietzsche would have agreed. Nor can I simply ignore Nietzsche, since he is the most influential and admired moral philosopher of the last two centuries. Though Sidgwick tells us more of the truth, Nietzsche has been read by about a thousand times as many people. So I shall briefly defend my view that Nietzsche's claims and arguments do not count strongly against my prediction. If you do not admire Nietzsche, being in this way unlike me, you may prefer to skip this chapter.

Nietzsche sometimes claims that pain and suffering are good. In most cases, Nietzsche means only that pain and suffering are necessary parts of what is on the whole good, either as causes or as effects. He writes, for example, that 'profound suffering makes noble', and is the source of all great achievements. Such suffering would be *instrumentally* good, by having good effects. That is compatible with the view that all suffering is *intrinsically* or in itself bad. But in some passages Nietzsche seems to reject this view. For example, Nietzsche writes that 'pain does not count as an objection to life', and he suggests that pain and suffering 'are not only necessary but also desirable for their own sake'. These claims seem to conflict deeply with what most of believe.

There is, however, no deep disagreement here. Nietzsche first accepted Schopenhauer's pessimistic view that, given the suffering of human beings and other animals, it would be better if the Universe did not exist. Though Nietzsche later rejected this view, and tried to believe that suffering is not bad, he did not succeed.

When Nietzsche claims that suffering is in itself good, he is defending the wider view that *everything* is good.   In his words:

> everything actually happens *as it should happen* . . . every kind
> of 'imperfection' and the suffering that result are also part of
> the *highest desirability.*

In defending this view, Nietzsche claims that we can make any event good by *affirming* or welcoming this event. He even suggests that, if we welcome anything that happens, we thereby make *everything* that happens, or the whole history of the Universe, as good as it could possibly be.   If we say Yes to a single moment, Nietzsche writes,

> we have said Yes to all existence . . . in that one moment
> of our saying Yes, all eternity was welcomed, redeemed,
> and justified.

This thrilling claim is clearly false. More cautiously, Nietzsche elsewhere writes:

> My formula for greatness in a human being is *love of fate*: that one wants nothing other than it is, not in the future, not in the past, not in all eternity.

Though he rejected the Buddhist advice that we should try to reduce our suffering by having fewer desires, Nietzsche here implausibly suggests that we should try to have only one desire, by wanting the whole of reality to be just as it is.

Like theistic versions of the view that everything is for the best, Nietzsche's claims about welcoming reality do not strongly challenge the belief that suffering is bad. Nietzsche seems to concede this point when he calls his view 'the *pessimism* of strength', and refers to his 'attempt to acquiesce in the world as it is'.

Of Nietzsche's reasons for making this attempt, one was the fact that his bad health gave him frequent, prolonged, and intense pain. When he tried to believe that everything is good, including all his suffering, this was in part what Nietzsche calls a rational response to his condition, by making his suffering easier to bear. This response was rational *because* Nietzsche's suffering was bad.

Nietzsche also claims that we should change our view about our responses to the suffering of others. To give a brief description of post-Kantian German ethics: Schopenhauer rejected Kant's moral theory, appealing instead to the value of compassion, and Nietzsche rejected Schopenhauer's theory, by denying the value of compassion.

Since Nietzsche makes some harsh and brutal claims, we can first note that he was highly compassionate, in a way that he feared would disable him. In Nietzsche's words:

> my greatest dangers lie in pity . . . I imagine the sufferings of others as far greater than they really are . . . I only need to expose myself to the sight of some genuine distress, and I am lost.

When Nietzsche collapsed into madness in a street in Turin, he was putting his arms around a tired cart horse to protect it from a further beating.

In denying the value of pity or compassion, Nietzsche nearly always means that this attitude or emotion, and the acts to which it leads, have bad effects.   For example, Nietzsche writes:

pity increases the amount of suffering in the world.

Some of Nietzsche's claims are plausible, as when he writes that misery is more contagious than happiness. When someone else's depression makes us deeply depressed, that is in itself bad, and makes us less able to help this other person. But Nietzsche makes some other, implausible claims.   For example, he claims that pity and compassion

involve a *tremendous danger to man* . . . . mankind is in danger of perishing through an ideality hostile to life.

In explaining this danger, Nietzsche writes:

That the sick should *not* make the healthy sick . . . should surely be our supreme concern on Earth; but this requires above all that the healthy should be segregated from the sick,

and he urges us

to grasp in all its profundity—and I insist that this matter requires *profound* understanding—how it cannot be the task of the healthy to nurse the sick and make them well.

These claims are not profound. Nietzsche is not referring here to contagious physical illness. He had no reason to believe that, if the healthy spend some time nursing the sick, that would disable these healthy people.

Nietzsche also had eugenic worries about the degeneration of the species man, or *homo sapiens*. By caring for the weak and the sick, Nietzsche feared, we shall bring 'evolution to a standstill' and 'thwart natural selection'. But such fears cannot explain the strength of some of Nietzsche's claims, as when he writes that 'a philosophy of pity . . . would destroy us, and in a very short time'.

Nietzsche's claims are best explained, I suggest, as responses to his own sensitivity to suffering. To live cheerfully and with a good conscience, Nietzsche claims, each of us needs to have some *horizon* around ourselves. Though our immediate surroundings can be bright, the rest of the world must seem dark to us. If instead we were fully aware of the sufferings of others, we would be 'overwhelmed by compassion', and would not want to live. As these remarks show, Nietzsche's claims about pity did not involve indifference to the suffering of others. Nietzsche feared that, after losing belief in God, Europeans would become pessimistic Buddhists; but in one of his brief lists of virtues, Nietzsche includes the two supreme Buddhist virtues: insight and compassion.

As well as denying that pain is bad, Nietzsche sometimes seems to deny that pleasure and happiness are good. Describing a kind of person whom he admires, Nietzsche writes that this person

> doesn't give a damn about whether he will achieve
> bliss — he has no such interest in happiness in any form
> whatsoever.

But this remark is misleading. There are many passages in which Nietzsche's claims imply that some kinds of joy and happiness are great goods. His ideal human beings would have, he writes, an 'extraordinary happiness' and 'the highest and most illustrious human joys'. Since Nietzsche makes many conflicting claims, it is never enough to quote a few remarks. Nietzsche did express contempt for some pleasures, and he claimed that pain is not an objection to life. But in most of what he writes, Nietzsche assumes that pain and suffering are bad, and that joy and happiness are good. In one of his last notebooks, for example, Nietzsche describes existence as being 'blissful enough to justify even monstrous suffering'.

Nietzsche gives many other descriptions of his ideal human beings. Some of his words and phrases are:

> having the highest power, the glory of life and force, the
> greatest magnificence, splendour, inexhaustible fruitfulness,
> creative, healthy, rich, noble, enterprising, profound,
> independent, brave, strong, triumphant, aggressive,
> destructive, overthrowing, capable of arousing fear.

What is most distinctive here is Nietzsche's emphasis on what he calls 'manly and warlike virtues'.

Some of Nietzsche's claims have been widely misunderstood. Of those who know something of Nietzsche's views, many would be surprised to learn that he detested both militarists and anti-semites, and proposed that, after its victory over France, the new German Empire should unilaterally disarm. When Nietzsche seems to be glorifying physical power, or war, that is sometimes not what he is doing. He uses metaphors of physical strength and struggle to describe the efforts that are needed to make scientific or philosophical discoveries, or to create great works of art.

There are, however, many other claims which are not metaphorical. Some of these claims are not serious, as when Nietzsche suggests, as a promising remedy for the weaknesses of 'tame domestic men':

> universal military service, with real wars and no more joking.

Other claims *are* serious. When explaining why he opposes the virtues of compassion and the relief of suffering, Nietzsche writes:

> Nothing would be more expensive than virtue: for in
> the end it would give us the Earth as an infirmary, and
> 'Everyone to be everyone else's nurse' would be the pinnacle
> of wisdom. True, the much-desired 'peace on Earth' would
> have been achieved! But how little 'good will among men'!
> How little beauty, exuberance, daring, danger! How few
> 'works' for whose sake it would still be worth living on the
> Earth! And oh! absolutely no more 'deeds' whatsoever! All the
> *great* works and deeds which have remained standing and not
> been washed away by the waves of time—were they not all, in
> the deepest sense, great immoralities?

Nietzsche cannot be thinking here of the great works of writers, composers, and artists. Most of these works were not, and did not depend upon, great immoralities.

Some of Nietzsche's claims may be as harmless as Siegfried's declaration, when leaving Brunnhilde, that he is off to perform some *new deeds*. Siegfried's hope may be only to find another dragon whom he can kill.

Nietzsche recommends that we live dangerously, by building our cities on the slopes of a volcano. Such pointless risk-taking might not involve great immorality.

Nietzsche also welcomes the prospect of future wars. This attitude was common when Nietzsche wrote, since no long European war had been fought for 70 years, and Europeans had learnt little from the horrors of the American Civil War. The outbreak of the First World War was later widely greeted with joy. War was welcomed because it would allow men to display the virtues of heroism, idealism, and comradeship. William James therefore argued that we need some moral equivalent of war, in which these virtues could be used in better ways.

What Nietzsche welcomes, however, is the prospect of 'the greatest and most terrible wars'. And he writes:

> Think of what is owed to Napoleon: almost all the higher
> hopes of this century . . . . For a similar prize one would have
> to wish for the anarchic collapse of our whole civilization.

Though Nietzsche would not have regarded Hitler as a similar prize, there is too little difference between these two aggressive warlords, for whose glory millions died.

Nietzsche makes other ominous claims. He hopes that there will be

> a master race, the future 'masters of the earth' — a
> new, tremendous aristocracy built upon the harshest
> self-legislation, in which the will of philosophical
> men of violence and artist tyrants is made to last for
> thousands of years.

He also writes:

> A masterful race can only grow up out of dreadful and
> violent beginnings. Problem: where are the *barbarians* of
> the twentieth century?

> I know my fate. One day there will be associated with my
> name the recollection of something frightful.

Nietzsche's name is rightly associated with some events that are, in some ways, even worse than two terrible world wars. When Nietzsche writes that churches have 'the bad odor of death chambers', that phrase is a grim coincidence. But he makes some other, appalling claims. In most books about Nietzsche, these claims are either ignored, or presented or described as less monstrous than they really are. Safranski writes that, on Nietzsche's view, it is

> permissible to use mankind as material for the production of genius, masterpieces, or even the Ubermensch.

But Nietzsche does not merely write 'use'. A healthy aristocracy, he writes,

> accepts with good conscience the sacrifice of untold human beings who, for its sake, must be reduced and lowered to incomplete human beings, to slaves, to instruments.

Safranski continues:

> And if the masses are more of a hindrance, space has to be created—by getting rid of the 'degenerates', if necessary. Even in his fantasies of annihilation, however, Nietzsche was still a highly sensitive soul and hence more amenable to the option that the 'misfits' could offer to 'sacrifice' themselves willingly.

Though Nietzsche *was* a highly sensitive soul, that is not shown by the remark that Safranski quotes. When he carried out Hitler's order that millions of people be killed, Himmler would have preferred it if these people had willingly sacrificed themselves. Foot similarly writes that some passages in Nietzsche 'seem to license injustice', and Schacht writes that he has chosen to ignore Nietzsche's 'rhetorical excesses'. But Nietzsche refers to 'the *remorseless* destruction of all degenerate and parasitic elements', and he claims that, 'in order to shape the man of the future through breeding', we should be ready to

> annihilate millions of failures, and not to be overcome by the suffering that we create, though nothing like it has ever existed!

These claims are not mere rhetorical excesses, nor do they merely seem to license injustice. Nietzsche also writes:

> The weak and the failures shall perish: first principle of
> *our* love of man. And they shall even be given every
> possible assistance.

That second sentence could be Hitler speaking. When we encourage people to read Nietzsche's books, we should admit that Nietzsche made some utterly appalling claims.

Anscombe writes that, if someone accepts Sidgwick's moral beliefs, 'I do not want to argue with him; he shows a corrupt mind'. Given some of the claims that I have just quoted, Nietzsche's mind may similarly seem too corrupt for his beliefs to be worth considering. But that response would be a mistake. When we ask whether normative disagreements count decisively against the view that there are some normative truths, we cannot simply ignore some of the people with whom we disagree. We should ask why these people hold their views, and whether and how we and they might reach agreement. Anscombe's view provides one example. Anscombe believed that certain acts would always be wrong, whatever their consequences. It would be wrong, for example, either to convict and execute some person whom we knew to be innocent, or to commit adultery or sodomy, even if we knew that our act would prevent some nuclear war that would kill millions of people. Some people would ignore these beliefs as too obviously mistaken. But if instead we consider Anscombe's view, we discover how we might resolve this disagreement. Anscombe believed that such acts are wrong because they are forbidden by God. If we and Anscombe had the same beliefs about God, we might then have the same moral beliefs.

Similar remarks apply to Nietzsche's views. Rather than simply ignoring these views, we should ask why Nietzsche held them. I have quoted James's remark:

> Sidgwick displayed that reflective candour that can at times be
> so irritating. A man has no right to be so fair to his opponents.

We cannot be *too* fair to our opponents. But our main aim is not fairness, but to reach the truth. Nietzsche was a brilliant thinker, who made many claims that are original, important, and true. We should ask whether our disagreements with Nietzsche give us reasons to doubt our own views.

The appalling claims that I have quoted give us no such reasons. Our problem is only to explain why, given Nietzsche's sensitivity to the suffering of others, he made such claims, and had such murderous fantasies. Since Nietzsche made these claims in his last productive years, they may be the first signs and effects of his approaching madness. There seem to be other such effects. In *Ecce Homo*, for example, Nietzsche writes:

> I am mild and benevolent towards everyone . . . It is my fate
> to have been the first *decent* human being . . . I am a *bringer of*
> *good tidings* such as there as never been . . . only after me is it
> possible to hope again.

But he also writes:

> I am by far the most terrible human being there has ever
> been . . . a fearful explosive material from which everything
> is in danger. . . . I know joy in destruction . . . and am the
> *destroyer par excellence* . . . I promise a tragic age.

When Nietzsche made these extreme and conflicting claims, his mind was starting to disintegrate, thereby freeing what he earlier called

> the savage beast which, locked in the cellars beneath the
> foundations of culture, howls and rages.

Nietzsche also makes some remarks which seem to exult in cruelty. For example:

> Let us not be gloomy as soon as we hear the word 'torture' . . . .
> Today, when suffering is brought forward as the principle
> argument *against* existence . . . one does well to recall the

ages in which the opposite opinion prevailed, because men were unwilling to refrain from *making suffer* and saw it as an enchantment of the first order.

When referring to the Greek God whom he most admired, Nietzsche writes: 'Dionysus: sensuality and cruelty'. And when describing 'the oldest festal joys of mankind', Nietzsche lists 'three principal elements: sexuality, intoxication, cruelty'. These passages suggest that Nietzsche had sadistic sexual fantasies. Such fantasies are had by some highly considerate and conscientious people. Nietzsche does not endorse these fantasies, and he writes:

> We should regard men who are cruel as stages of earlier
> cultures which have remained behind . . . they show us
> what we all were, and fill us with horror.

In listing Nietzsche's descriptions of his ideal man, I left out two words. Nietzsche calls this man *wicked* and *evil*. He also claims that 'everything evil, terrible, tyrannical in man . . . serves the enhancement of the species', and he describes one of his books as 'pouring its light, its love, its tenderness upon nothing but evil things'.

These claims are intended to be shocking. Though Nietzsche tried hard to reach the truth, he also had other, conflicting aims. Nietzsche says many things for the sake of paradox, as when he inverts the claim that a good cause can justify even war, declaring instead that a good war justifies any cause. That could be a witticism by Oscar Wilde. Nietzsche also describes himself as *reversing* Christian values. He claims to be seeking

> everything strange and questionable in existence, *all that has
> hitherto been placed under a ban by morality,*

and he writes

> I recognize virtue by . . . its doing precisely everything that is
> otherwise *forbidden.*

If we merely praise *whatever* Christian morality condemns, we cannot hope to reach the truth. We would be relying, not on our ability to get things right, but on the ability of Christian moralists to get things wrong. Describing the new philosophers whom he hopes to inspire, Nietzsche similarly writes:

> it must offend their pride, also their taste, if their truth is supposed to be a truth for every man. One must shed the bad taste of wanting to agree with many. 'Good' is no longer good when one's neighbour mouths it.

When we ask what is good, we cannot aim both at the truth and at disagreeing with our neighbour. Our neighbour's beliefs might be true.

These remarks illustrate a wider point. I am asking whether, in ideal conditions, we and Nietzsche would have had sufficiently similar normative beliefs. When Nietzsche is not aiming only at the truth, these ideal conditions are not met. Nietzsche often has other aims. When he writes 'Not for a single hour of my life have I been a Christian', Nietzsche must have remembered that this claim was false. After calling some of Wagner's music 'the greatest masterpiece of the sublime I know', Nietzsche claims that Wagner wrote 'perhaps the worst music ever written'. He calls Germans 'this utterly irresponsible race which has on its conscience all the great disasters of civilization'. And he writes 'Let us remove the highest goodness from the concept of God: it is unworthy of a god.' These are not the claims of someone who always asks, when a thought occurs to him, 'Is that really true?'

Nietzsche admits that he is not always aiming at the truth. He calls his reversal of Christian morality 'playful' and 'an act of willfulness, and pleasure in willfulness'. Discussing those whom he calls *we immoralists*, Nietzsche writes:

> we would gain power and victory even without truth. The magic that fights for us, the eye of Venus that ensnares and blinds even our opponents, is the magic of the extreme, the seduction that every extreme exercises . . . *we* are extreme.

Nietzsche tried to combine

> a bold and exuberant spirituality that runs *presto* and a dialectical severity and necessity that never takes a false step.

We should expect that, in some cases, Nietzsche achieves only the first of these aims. Nietzsche himself writes that, when we cease to be Christians,

> for a while we don't know which way to turn. We rush
> headlong into the opposite valuations.

In other passages, rather than claiming that his ideal man would always do whatever Christian morality claims to be evil, Nietzsche proposes a less implausible view. His ideal man, he writes, would be *beyond* good and evil, in the sense of ignoring these moral categories. This allows Nietzsche to make claims about what is good or bad in other, *non-moral* senses. Many of the same acts, Nietzsche claims, ought to be done, but for other, non-moral reasons. So we can now turn to Nietzsche's rejection of morality, and his proposed alternatives.

124 Good and Evil

'What defines me', Nietzsche writes, '. . . is that I have *unmasked* Christian morality.' Nietzsche claims that God is dead, by which he means that Europeans are ceasing to believe that God exists. Without the support of this belief, Nietzsche argues, morality as understood by Europeans will not be able to survive. Before I discuss that argument, I shall comment briefly on some of Nietzsche's other arguments.

Though Nietzsche's main target is Christian morality, he rejects all moralities, including those of atheists, or the ancient Greeks. 'As the Sophists claimed', he writes, 'it is a swindle to talk of moral *truths*'. He also writes:

> Moral judgments are . . . never to be taken literally: so
> understood they contain mere absurdity.

> There are no moral facts, only moral interpretations
> of the facts.

> I deny morality as I deny alchemy, that is, I deny what
> they presuppose.

One such presupposition, Nietzsche claims, is that we are morally responsible in ways that can make us guilty, and deserve to suffer. Nietzsche denies that we have the kind of freedom that such responsibility requires. In his words:

> the history of the moral sensations is the history of an
> error, the error of responsibility, which rests on the error
> of free will.

Nietzsche is right, I believe, to deny that we can deserve to suffer. Many people accept Nietzsche's claim that, without such responsibility, morality is undermined. That is why Kant argues that, since we have moral duties, we must have some kind of incomprehensible freedom in a timeless noumenal world. But as Sidgwick and others claim, Nietzsche's claim is a mistake. Even if no one could ever deserve to suffer, we can have moral duties, and our acts can be right or wrong.

Nietzsche also argues that morality presupposes a false psychology. We act morally, Nietzsche assumes, only when we act on some purely altruistic desire, or we are moved purely by the belief that some act is our duty. Nietzsche claims that there are no such acts. In his words

> this whole species of intentions and actions is imaginary; the
> world to which alone the moral standard can be applied does
> not exist at all—there are neither moral nor immoral actions.

Nietzsche's psychological claims are, I believe, false, and even if they were true, morality would not be undermined. Morality does not presuppose any such psychology.

Nietzsche makes some fascinating claims about the origins of morality, especially Christian morality, and he sometimes suggests that these claims undermine morality. But as Nietzsche himself points out, that is not so. When we learn about the origins of morality, or of many other features of human life, we learn very little about the present state, or value, of these things. In Nietzsche's words, 'The more insight we possess into an origin the less significant does the origin appear.'

Nietzsche's rejection of morality also depends in part on his awareness of the differences between the moralities of different cultures and ages.

'The real problems of morality emerge', Nietzsche writes, 'only when we compare *many* moralities.' But Nietzsche does not discuss what such moral disagreements show. He does not, for example, consider and criticize the view that we are resolving our disagreements, and making moral progress.

What is most relevant here is another way in which Nietzsche was led to assume that there are no moral truths. In all English translations of Kant's *Groundwork*, Kant is presented as claiming that

> (A) all imperatives, or commands, are expressed
> with an 'ought'.

This claim is false, since *no* imperatives could be expressed with an 'ought'. But Kant did not make this claim. All imperatives, Kant writes in German, are expressed with the word 'sollen'. That is slightly inaccurate. What Kant could have truly claimed is that

> (B) all imperatives in German *could* be expressed with the
> word 'sollen'.

This German word can be used like the English words 'shall' or 'shalt' in commands like

> (C) Thou shalt not kill!

which means the same as

> (D) Don't kill!

But the word 'sollen' has another sense. This word can also be used like the English word 'ought' in normative claims like

> (E) You ought not to kill.

Unlike commands such as (C) and (D), which could not be either true or false, claims like (E) might be true or false. (C) and (E) have quite different meanings, even if we believe that God's command 'Thou shalt not kill!' makes it true that we ought not to kill. Unlike the German word 'sollen', the English word 'ought' cannot be used both to express commands and to state normative claims. Nor does any other English word have this double use, or these two senses. This fact makes it impossible to translate Kant's German sentence into English, except as a sentence like (B) which is about the word 'sollen'.

The facts that I have just mentioned may seem unimportant, except for those who are translating certain German sentences into English. But that is not so. Though German-speakers can understand the difference between commands and normative claims, this double use of 'sollen' makes it easier to overlook this distinction. Some Germans have been led to assume that moral claims are commands. And that assumption can make a great difference. We cannot ask whether commands are true or false. When people in positions of authority tell us to act in certain ways, we may then be more likely to obey these commands, because we cannot believe that such obedience would be wrong. In German history between around 1850 and 1945, this failure to distinguish between commands and normative claims had many bad effects. (Germany is quite different now.)

This double use of 'sollen' also had some bad effects on post-Kantian German moral philosophy. When moral claims are taken to express commands, that encourages the view that morality essentially depends on God. Kant rightly rejects this view. When Kant first states his Formula of Universal Law, he may mean that we *ought* to act only on maxims that we could rationally will to be universal. But Kant nearly always states his formula as an unambiguous command, the Categorical Imperative.

For more than half a century, Schopenhauer writes,

> ethics has been reclining on the comfortable cushion that Kant had arranged for it, namely the categorical imperative of practical reason. In our day, however, this imperative is often introduced under the name of 'the moral law', which is less ostentatious but smoother and more current. Under this name the imperative slips unobserved into the house after making a slight bow to the faculty of reason and experience; but when once in, there is no end to its orders and commands, without its ever being further called to account.

Schopenhauer elsewhere uses the word 'sollen', which I shall here mistranslate as 'ought', so that we can see more clearly what difference it makes that the word 'sollen' can also express commands. Schopenhauer writes:

> Who tells you that there are laws to which our conduct *ought* to be liable? . . . What justification have you for forcing on us, as the only possibility, a system of ethics framed in the legislative *imperative* form?

> Every *ought* derives all sense and meaning simply and solely in reference to threatened punishment or promised reward . . . the concept of *ought*, the *imperative* form of ethics, applies solely to theological morality, and . . . outside this it loses all sense and meaning.

Since Schopenhauer does not believe that there is a God who makes commands backed up with threats and promises, he concludes that there is nothing that we ought morally to do. Rather than discussing such *oughts*, Schopenhauer claims, philosophers should aim to understand how people are motivated to act morally, and to describe the place of morality in human life.

On Kant's view, Schopenhauer also writes,

> a moral law ought to imply 'absolute necessity'. But such necessity is everywhere characterized by the inevitability of the resulting effect. Now how can we speak of absolute necessity in the case of these alleged moral laws, as an example of which he mentions *Thou shalt not lie*? For as we know and as he himself admits, they remain frequently, indeed as a rule, ineffective.

These remarks assume that, if we claim it to be morally necessary not to lie, we are claiming that no one ever tells lies. Schopenhauer here fails to distinguish between normative and psychological claims.

Like Schopenhauer, Nietzsche both assumes that morality depends on God, and denies that God exists. Nietzsche therefore writes:

there is no 'ought' any more. Morality . . . has been destroyed
by our way of reflection every bit as much as religion.

Some of the English, Nietzsche remarks, have a different view. These
people

believe that they know 'intuitively' what is good and evil . . .
and they therefore suppose that they no longer require
Christianity as the guarantee of morality.

Nietzsche here correctly describes what some of his English contemporaries believed.   An acquaintance of George Eliot writes

I walked with her once in the Fellows' Garden . . . on an
evening of rainy May . . . taking as her text . . . the words
God, Immortality, Duty — she pronounced with terrible
earnestness, how inconceivable was the *first*, how unbelievable
the *second*, and yet how . . . absolute the *third*.

Moral philosophers like Mill and Sidgwick also denied that God exists.
These English moralists, Nietzsche writes,

continue to believe in good and evil, and feel the victory of the
good and the annihilation of the evil to be a *task*.

Nietzsche calls this view *naïve*.   Morality cannot survive, he writes,

when the sanctioning God is gone . . . The 'hereafter' is
absolutely necessary if belief in morality is to be upheld.

Nietzsche here assumes that, without God's threats of punishments in
a future life, people would not be motivated to act morally. The English
moralists had such fears. But as they rightly claimed, we can have other
motives for acting morally, some of which do not depend on belief
in God.

   There are other ways in which morality might depend on God. If
the moral use of 'ought' expresses God's commands, morality would
directly depend on God. In Dostoyevsky's phrase, if God does not exist,
everything is permitted. Nietzsche also writes that, when our conscience
speaks,

> an authority speaks — who speaks?   One may forgive human
> pride if it sought to make this authority as high as possible . . .
> Therefore — God speaks!

Only God, Nietzsche assumes, would be a *high* enough authority. If
morality merely expressed the commands of our society, or ancestors, or
tradition, we would not have sufficient reason to obey these commands.

   The English moralists would reject these claims, since these people
deny that morality consists of commands. When these people claim that
we ought to act in certain ways, they are stating what they believe to be
moral truths. Nor do Nietzsche's claims about authority apply to such
truths. This point may be clearer with non-moral normative truths. If I
claim that you ought to believe Darwin's theory, or that you ought to
stop smoking, you could not object that I do not have the authority to
issue these commands.   These claims aren't commands.

In one passage, Nietzsche writes:

> This morality is by no means self-evident: this point has to be
> exhibited again and again, despite the English dimwits . . . For
> the English, morality is not yet a problem.

Since it is only beliefs that could be self-evident, this remark seems to
allow that moral claims state beliefs, which might be true. But Nietzsche
does not try to show that no such beliefs are true. Nietzsche's aims are
to describe our existing moral beliefs, to explain their origin, and to
assess their effects.   Like Schopenhauer, Nietzsche writes

> To determine what *is*, what it's *like*, appears unutterably high-
> er and more serious than any 'it *ought* to be'.

There is another passage in which Nietzsche may seem to be discussing
whether there are moral truths.   Schopenhauer appeals to

> a fundamental principle on which all teachers of ethics really
> agree, though they state it in different ways: *Harm no one, help
> everyone when you can.*

In one such different statement:

We ought not to harm people, and we ought to help them
when we can.

Nietzsche rejects this principle, calling it 'insipidly false and sentimental'. But this use of 'false' is misleading. Nietzsche does not
ask whether it is *true* that we ought not to harm people, and that
we ought to help them when we can. Frivolously, Nietzsche merely
writes:

> whoever has once felt deeply how insipidly false and
> sentimental this principle is in a world whose essence is
> will to power, may allow himself to be reminded that
> Schopenhauer, though a pessimist, *really*—played the flute.
> Every day, after dinner; one should read his biography on
> that. And incidentally: a pessimist, one who denies God and
> the world but *comes to a stop* before morality—who affirms
> morality and plays the flute—the *harm no one* morality—
> what? Is that really—a pessimist?

There are hints of two arguments here. As before, Nietzsche assumes
that morality depends on God. He also suggests that, since our deepest
motive is a will to power, it is sentimental to be morally opposed to acts
that harm other people. For this objection to be good, Nietzsche would
have to assume that, given our nature, we would seldom be able to
refrain from harming other people. That assumption would be clearly
false.

I am asking whether, in ideal conditions, we and Nietzsche would
have had sufficiently similar normative beliefs. That question applies
only when we and Nietzsche use the same normative concepts. Since
Nietzsche assumes that moral claims express commands, he seldom if
ever uses the concept that we can express in English with the phrase
ought morally. So Nietzsche's claims cannot straightforwardly conflict
with our beliefs about what we ought morally to do.

There can be disagreements of less straightforward kinds, since different normative concepts and beliefs may partly overlap. Given some
of Nietzsche's claims, we can try to predict whether, if we and

Nietzsche had used the same concepts, and the other ideal conditions were met, we would have had similar normative beliefs.

The 'herd-morality' that Nietzsche rejects has, he claims, two main doctrines: *pity for all that suffers* and *equality of rights*. As we have seen, Nietzsche objects that pity increases the amount of suffering in the world. We would agree that, if that implausible claim were true, pity would have bad effects. There is no normative disagreement here.

When Nietzsche rejects equality of rights, this disagreement is, in part, normative. Since Nietzsche gives supreme weight to the greatest creative achievements in art, science, and philosophy, he also gives supreme value to the existence and well-being of the few people who are capable of these achievements. Nietzsche believes that these few people, whom we can call the *creative elite*, should be given special rights. When he makes such claims, Nietzsche may seem to be denying that everyone's well-being matters equally. That would be a deep disagreement with what most of us now believe.

This disagreement is, however, less deep than it seems. Though Nietzsche's main concern is for these creative achievements, and the conditions that make them possible, he believes that other, uncreative people can benefit from these achievements. 'The artist creates his work', Nietzsche writes, 'for the good of other men.' Since Nietzsche fears that such great achievements will become impossible in an egalitarian society, he predicts that our happiness will soon have to depend on the glorious works of art that we have inherited from the past. In such a world, Nietzsche gloriously writes,

> the sun would have set, but the sky of our life would still glow with its light.

These claims do not give less weight to the well-being of uncreative people.

Nietzsche also believes that, though his creative elite should be given special privileges, such as leisure and freedom, such inequalities are, in a way, unfair, and impose responsibilities on this elite. In his words:

This freedom is in fact a heavy debt which can be discharged
only by means of great deeds. In truth, every ordinary son
of the earth has the right to regard with resentment a man
favoured in this way.

To justify their privileges, the elite must create the works and produce
the achievements that will benefit others. Only then, Nietzsche writes,
could these creative people say

Look after me, for I have something better to do, namely to
look after you.

Though Nietzsche makes some rude and dismissive remarks about
people who are mediocre, he also writes:

Hatred of mediocrity is unworthy of a philosopher . . .
Precisely because he is the exception, he must take the rule
under his wing, and must help everything average to keep up
its faith in itself.

When the exceptional human being treats the mediocre more
tenderly than himself and his peers, this is not mere courtesy
of the heart — it is simply his duty.

Nietzsche often refers to the 'extent to which to live and to be unjust
are one and the same thing'. Discussing inequalities of wealth, he
writes:

What is needed is not a forcible redistribution but a gradual
transformation of the mind: the sense of justice must grow
greater in everyone, the instinct for violence weaker.

When we interpret Nietzsche, as I have said, nothing can be proved
by quoting a few claims. Nietzsche makes some other, strongly anti-
egalitarian claims. But these quotations show that Nietzsche had some
strongly egalitarian beliefs. There is no straightforward disagreement
here.

Nietzsche, I suggest, was an egalitarian about the badness of suffering.
He does not seem to believe that suffering is in itself less bad when it is

endured by mediocre human beings. Nietzsche also claims that, when we consider the lives of non-rational animals, we should be 'profoundly indignant' about their 'senseless suffering'.

Most of us believe that, even if the suffering of other animals can be as bad as ours, what is best in human lives has much greater value. When Mill discusses such value, he distinguishes between lower pleasures and those pleasures that involve our higher mental faculties. Mill also claims that, if we know what both kinds of pleasures are like, we would not give up such higher pleasures, even if they involved great discontent, for the sake of *any* amount of the lower pleasures. We would regard these higher pleasures as having infinitely greater value. Mill therefore writes

> It is better to be a human being dissatisfied than a pig satisfied; better to be Socrates dissatisfied than a fool satisfied.

Nietzsche similarly claims that, when compared with mediocre pleasures, what is best in the lives of his creative elite has such infinitely greater value. Mill is a utilitarian egalitarian, and Nietzsche is a perfectionist anti-egalitarian. But as these quotations show, these views are much closer than these labels suggest. There is no deep disagreement here.

Though Nietzsche often expresses contempt for Utilitarians, there are some other striking similarities between these people's views. Nietzsche writes:

> Nowadays there is a thoroughly erroneous moral theory which is celebrated especially in England: it claims that judgments of 'good' and 'evil' sum up experiences of what is 'useful' and 'unuseful'; that what is called good preserves the species while what is called evil harms it. In truth, however the evil drives are just as useful, species-preserving, and indispensable as the good ones — they just have a different function.

Nietzsche fails to see that this English theory overlaps with Nietzsche's own view. Like Nietzsche, Bentham, Mill, and Sidgwick challenged conventional morality, arguing that some acts and motives that are claimed to be bad are in fact good, because they have good effects. These

Utilitarians would accept Nietzsche's claim that, when what are called *evil drives* are just as useful, these drives are not evil, but good.

Nietzsche's main questions, he writes, are these:

> Under what conditions did man devise these value-judgments
> good and evil? And what value do they themselves possess?
> Have they hitherto hindered or furthered human prosperity?
> Are they a sign of distress, impoverishment, of the
> degeneration of life?

Utilitarians similarly ask whether these value-judgments have hindered or furthered human happiness. Nietzsche refers, not to *happiness*, but to *prosperity*. But he is not referring to material wealth, for which he often expresses contempt, and he also mentions *distress*. So there is little difference here.

There are other similarities. Nietzsche believes that no one could deserve to suffer. Utilitarians agree. Nietzsche denies that our acts have supreme value when we act for duty's sake, or act with purely altruistic motives. Utilitarians agree.

Since many people believe that we *can* deserve to suffer, we have not yet reached agreement on this question. But we can reasonably hope that, in ideal conditions, we would all have sufficiently similar normative beliefs. When Nietzsche defends his belief that no one can deserve to suffer and to be punished, he expresses one such hope. Nietzsche describes

> one of the greatest ideas that mankind can have, the idea
> of progress to excel all progress. Let us go forward a few
> thousand years together, my friends. There is a *great deal* of
> joy still reserved for mankind of which men of the present
> day have not had so much as a scent! And we may prom-
> ise ourselves this joy . . . only provided that the evolution of
> human reason *does not stand still*! One day we shall not be
> able to find it in our heart to commit the logical sin that lies
> concealed in wrath and punishment . . .

I am more optimistic. We can hope to reach such agreement, I believe, in fewer than a thousand years.

We can now turn from morality to reasons. Nietzsche refers to 'the Socratic equation of reason, virtue, and happiness'. He means, presumably, not that

reason = virtue = happiness,

but something like:

> If we respond to reason, by doing what we have most reason
> to do, we shall achieve both virtue and happiness.

Sidgwick qualifies this equation, since he believes that, without God and a future life, happiness and virtue do not always coincide. In such cases, Sidgwick believes, reason gives us no guidance.

Nietzsche rejects the Socratic equation in a more sweeping way, calling it 'the most bizarre of all equations'. The acceptance of this equation, Nietzsche writes,

> resulted in the creation of a degenerating type of man — the
> good man, the happy man, the wise man. Socrates is a moment
> of the deepest perversity in the history of men.

Nietzsche seems here to disagree deeply with nearly everyone. We nearly all believe that it would *not* be degenerate, or bad, to be good, happy, and wise.

As before, however, Nietzsche makes conflicting claims. He earlier wrote:

> Socrates had the wisdom full of roguishness that constitutes
> the finest state of the human soul . . . I admire the courage
> and wisdom of Socrates in everything he did, said, and did
> not say.

When Nietzsche later discusses 'whether instinct has more value than reasoning', he writes that Socrates 'naively placed himself on the side of reason'. On this rationalist view,

> one must imitate Socrates and counter the dark appetites with
> a permanent daylight — the daylight of reason . . . One must

be clever, clear, bright at any price: any concession to the
instincts, to the unconscious, leads *downward* . . .

Nietzsche comments:

all this too was a mere disease . . . To have to fight the instincts,
that is the formula of decadence: as long as life is *ascending*,
happiness equals instinct . . . All that is good is instinct — and
hence easy, necessary, free.

But Nietzsche earlier wrote that, if we merely follow instinct or tradition,
we thereby

flee into the dark precisely when reason ought to be taking as
clear and cold a view as possible!

A good philosopher is 'reason-thirsty', thinks with the rigour of a
scientist, and wants to live in 'clear', 'bright, transparent, electric air',
with sunlight around him. Discussing 'religion-founders', Nietzsche
objects that they do not ask 'Was my reason bright enough?' We should
prepare the earth, Nietzsche writes,

for the production of the greatest and most joyful
fruitfulness — a task for reason on behalf of reason!

He even writes

The only happiness lies in reason: all the rest of the world
is dismal.

When he made these earlier, better claims, Nietzsche could have agreed
that, we should not follow reason at *any* price. We can have reasons
to make some concessions to our instincts. But reason should govern
our dark appetites, and may tell us to investigate the unconscious
sources of these appetites, as Nietzsche's admirer Freud rationally
tried to do.

Though Nietzsche makes several claims that contradict what most of us
believe, Nietzsche himself contradicts these claims. When he disagrees
with himself, he does not clearly disagree with us.

Nietzsche and Sidgwick were both greatly disturbed by their loss of belief in God. Nietzsche remained more religious. The most fundamental questions, Nietzsche assumed, were not about what we ought to do, or what is good or bad, but about *why* we exist, and whether the answer can give *meaning* to our lives.

125 The Meaning of Life

In asking what is good or evil, Nietzsche writes, we are asking

> why mankind is here, its goal, its destiny. That means wanting
> to know that mankind *has* a goal, or destiny.

If we were created by God for some purpose, Nietzsche assumes, the meaning of our life would be given by the goal that God gave to us. But we are now losing our belief in God, and in what Nietzsche calls 'a moral world order'. This raises 'a terrifying question: *Has existence any meaning at all?*' We no longer know

> what this tremendous process was *actually* for . . . A new
> What for? — that is what mankind needs.

We shall otherwise 'tip over into nihilism', believing that nothing matters.

Nietzsche struggled to find 'a new What for?' He writes:

> *One* interpretation has perished, but because it was regarded
> as *the* interpretation, there now seems to be no meaning at all
> in existence, everything seems to be *in vain.*

There are, he suggests, other possibilities. If we were created by *Life*, or *Nature*, to achieve some purpose, that would give a meaning to our lives. Life's purpose in creating us might also give a meaning to our suffering. Nietzsche then claims that

> consciousness is just a tool . . . our becoming conscious is
> only one more means in Life's unfolding and the expansion
> of its power.

Since Life gave us consciousness as a means, Nietzsche argues, we have 'no right' to regard any kind of desirable or undesirable consciousness as having value or disvalue as an end. In Nietzsche's words:

> A kind of means has been misunderstood as an end:
> conversely, life and the enhancement of its power have
> been demoted to a means . . . agreeable or disagreeable
> feelings are just a means!

If we condemn Life because our lives involve suffering, we are assuming that this 'disagreeable means' is more important than the end. We are thinking:

> How can it be a good end that makes use of such a means!

Such reasoning, Nietzsche objects, mistakenly presupposes that Life or Nature's end or purpose must exclude the use of pain and suffering as a means. We ought instead to look for an end to whose achievement our pain and suffering would be a necessary means. We would then understand that our pain and suffering are not bad.

In these and similar passages, Nietzsche makes two mistakes. First, we should not assume that either Life or Nature *has* any end or purpose. Second, even if Life or Nature did have some end or aim, this fact would not imply that *we* should also have this aim. Perhaps we ought to have some aim if this aim were given to us by a good God. But Nietzsche recognizes what he calls 'Nature's magnificent *indifference* to good or evil'.

Nietzsche also suggests that Life is, fundamentally, *the Will to Power*, and that this fact both gives us our aim, and determines what has value. In his words:

> What is the objective yard-stick of *value*? Only the quantum
> of *enhanced and organized power*.

Nietzsche sometimes claims that our aim *must* be given by the Will to Power. Since we are a part of Life, or Nature, we must have Life's aims, and do what the Will to Power commands. Nietzsche even claims that we must do what this Will commands 'because we *are* this commandment'. Nietzsche concludes:

> There is nothing to life that has value except the degree
> of power . . . The animal functions are a million times
> more important than all beautiful states and heights of
> consciousness . . . What has been called 'body' and 'flesh'
> is unutterably more important: the remainder is just a
> minor accessory.

Kant memorably wrote that two things filled his mind with ever-increasing reverence and awe: the starry heavens and the moral law. Nietzsche replies, 'Digestion is more venerable'.

As before, we should reject these claims. There is no such Will to Power whose commandments we are forced to obey, or ought to obey. Nor should we regard our bodies as, in themselves, unutterably more important than our conscious minds. Compared with our most valuable conscious states and activities, our animal functions, such as digestion or excretion, do *not* matter a million times more.

Darwin's champion Huxley saw things more clearly here. The cosmic process of natural selection is wholly amoral, and causes great suffering. Given this fact, Huxley writes:

> Let us understand, once for all, that the ethical progress of
> society depends, not on *imitating* the cosmic process . . . but
> in *combating* it.

Nietzsche sometimes saw that we cannot appeal to any aim or purpose had by Life or Nature.   As he remarks:

> This is still the old religious way of thinking and wishing, a
> kind of longing to believe that in *some way or other* the world
> does, after all, resemble the beloved old . . . creative God.

> What these ideas have in common is that the process aims to
> *achieve* something—and now it is realized that this process
> aims for *nothing*, and achieves *nothing* . . . the world has no
> goal and no final state . . . we have sought in everything a
> 'meaning' that it doesn't contain.

In a note to himself, Nietzsche asks whether we ourselves could *give* the cosmic process meaning. In his words:

> Question: once morality becomes impossible, does the pantheistic affirmative stance towards all things become impossible as well? After all, fundamentally it's only the moral God that has been overcome. Does it make sense to conceive of a God 'beyond good and evil'? Would a pantheism in *this* sense be possible? Can we remove the idea of a goal from the process and then affirm the process in spite of this?

In some passages, as we have seen, Nietzsche answers Yes. By welcoming or affirming the cosmic process, Nietzsche suggests, we can make this process good. In his words:

> To redeem the past and to transform every 'It was' into an 'I wanted it thus' — that alone I would call redemption.

But this claim expresses an incoherent fantasy. We cannot now bring it about that we *did* want every past event to happen, nor could such desires make everything good.

In other passages, Nietzsche returns to the aim of *revaluing* all values. We need, he claims, *new* values. But Nietzsche says little about these values. In his last published attempt to revalue values, *The Anti-Christ*, Nietzsche merely returns to attacking Christian values. Nietzsche hopes for 'a new nobility', whose 'formula for happiness' would be 'a Yes, a No, a straight line, a goal'. That is not a helpful formula. Nietzsche also writes:

> We need an affirming race which grants itself every great luxury — strong enough not to need the tyranny of the virtue-imperative, rich enough not to need thrift and pedantry, beyond good and evil; a hot-house for strange and exquisite plants.

That is not an inspiring ideal.

Nietzsche's problem is, in part, that he does not have the reason-implying concepts of what is in itself non-morally good or bad. In this respect he is too influenced by Kant. On Kant's view, we do not have non-moral reasons to promote our own well-being. The principle of prudence is a merely *hypothetical* imperative, which applies to us only if, and because, we want to be happy. Normativity takes two main forms: the categorical imperatives of morality, and the hypothetical imperatives of instrumental, desire-based or aim-based rationality. Since Nietzsche starts with similar assumptions, but rejects morality, he is left with nothing but instrumental rationality. The rejection of morality, Nietzsche assumes, undermines *all* values.   In his words:

> He who unmasks morality has thereby unmasked the
> valuelessness of all values which are or have been
> believed in.

On this view, nothing is in itself good or bad. All value must derive from us. Nietzsche writes:

> Whatever has *value* in our world does not have value in itself,
> according to its nature — nature is always valueless — but has
> rather been *given* value, and we were the givers.

He also writes:

> Knowledge and wisdom have no value as such; nor does
> goodness: one must always first have a goal that confers value
> or disvalue on these qualities.

Moral philosophers, Nietzsche claims, have two tasks. Lesser philosophers should describe people's values, and assess their effects. Another, much smaller group have a much greater task, since they must create new values. Nietzsche writes:

> the real philosophers command and legislate, they say: This is
> how it *shall* be! It is they who determine the *Where to* and the
> *What for* of man.

We cannot, however, *make* things good by commanding or willing that they be good. Though we can sometimes change people's evaluative beliefs, that is not a way of creating new values. Nor can we make anything matter. When something matters *to us*, in the sense that we care about this thing, that is a merely psychological fact. Something *matters* only when, and in the sense that, we have object-given *reasons* to care about this thing.

In some passages, Nietzsche seems to see that we cannot create values. He writes:

> Looked at more subtly, 'That is wrong' really means only, 'I feel nothing of myself in it', 'I don't care about it' . . .

When we evaluate, Nietzsche suggests, we are merely expressing our desires or preferences. 'Every kind of action', Nietzsche writes, 'is identical in value.' If that were true, there would be no point in trying to decide what to do. He also writes:

> A man as he *ought to* be, that sounds as preposterous to us as 'A tree as it ought to be'.

> The world has equal value at every moment . . . in other words it has no value.

As a result,

> everything seems to be *in vain* . . . Mistrust of our previous valuations intensifies until it arrives at the question 'Are not all "values" just decoys that prolong the comedy without getting any closer to a denouement?' Continuing with an 'in vain', without aim and purpose, is the *most paralyzing* thought, especially when one realizes that one is being fooled.

We believe we are important, but that is only how we feel:

> if we could communicate with the mosquito, we would learn that it floats through the air with the self-same importance, feeling within itself the flying center of the world.

Nietzsche concludes:

> One should at last put human values nicely back in the corner
> where alone they have any right to be: as personal little values.
> Many species of animal have already disappeared: if man
> disappeared as well, nothing would be lacking in the world.
> One must be enough of a philosopher to admire even this
> nothingness.

In his early essay 'A Free Man's Worship', Russell claims that, though we
were not created for any purpose, we can truly judge that some parts of
the world are bad, and others good, and we should try to make the lives
of conscious beings go better. Russell's essay, Williams writes, involves

> the kind of muddle that is called sentimentality. Nietzsche by
> contrast got it right when he said that once upon a time there
> was a star in a corner of the universe, and a planet circling that
> star, and on it some clever creatures who invented knowledge;
> and then they died, and the star went out, and it was as though
> nothing had happened.

Nietzsche got things right, Williams assumes, because Nietzsche saw
that nothing is in itself good or bad. Nothing matters. Nietzsche's
struggle to avoid Nihilism failed.

I shall now summarize some of these claims. Nietzsche first assumed
that, to know what is good or evil, we must know *why* humanity exists,
since that would tell us what to do, and would also give our lives
meaning. In Nietzsche's words:

> Just this I seek, some reason for it all.

When Nietzsche concluded that we were not created for some purpose
by either God or Nature, he feared that our lives are meaningless, and
have no value. He therefore struggled to find values which could give
our lives meaning.

Nietzsche's normative concepts made this aim harder to achieve.
Nietzsche's conception of normativity we can call *imperatival*, or
command-implying. He seldom if ever uses the concept of what we

ought morally to do. Nietzsche assumes that morality consists of commands. And he believes that, since God does not exist, there is no commander whose authority is high enough for us to have reasons to obey. Nor did Nietzsche have the concept of what is intrinsically good or bad, in reason-implying senses. Nietzsche assumed that new non-moral values could be created by valuings, which he took to involve commands. In a Godless world, we need new philosophers to create values, by willing '*Thus shall it be!*' Since Nietzsche's normative concepts were command-implying, rather than reason-implying, it is not surprising that his attempt to find values failed.

In response to the Argument from Disagreement, I have claimed that, in ideal conditions, we would nearly all have sufficiently similar normative beliefs. I have mainly discussed beliefs that involve the concept *ought morally*, and the reason-implying concepts *good* and *bad*. Since Nietzsche seldom if ever uses these concepts, he seldom disagrees directly with these beliefs. I have also asked whether, if Nietzsche had used these concepts, his normative beliefs would have been, in ideal conditions, sufficiently like ours. We have, I believe, several reasons to think that the answer would have been Yes. Though Nietzsche makes some normative claims that most of us would strongly reject, some of these claims are not wholly sane, and others depend on ignorance or false beliefs about the relevant non-normative facts. And Nietzsche often disagrees with himself, making other conflicting claims that we would accept. Our disagreements with him are less clear and deep than they seem.

In one of his brilliant early books, Nietzsche writes:

> Of two very exalted things — measure and moderation — it is best never to speak. A few people know their significance and power . . . they revere in them something divine . . . the rest hardly listen when they are spoken of, and confuse them with boredom and mediocrity.

A good thinker, he also writes,

> knows that the talent for having ideas . . . must be rigorously curbed by the spirit of science. Not that which glitters, shines,

excites, but often insignificant-seeming truth is the fruit he
wishes to shake down from the tree of knowledge.

Nietzsche changed. In his last few books, the sun of Nietzsche's life
began its accelerating journey downward into night. These books gave
Nietzsche most of his astonishing posthumous influence and fame. But
they are also what Mann calls 'snow-covered peaks of grotesque error',
some of whose appalling claims show the disintegration of his noble
mind.

Of the false ideas that merely glitter, shine and excite, one example is
Schopenhauer's idea that the whole of reality, is, fundamentally, *the Will
to Existence*. Nietzsche called this idea 'a mythology' and 'a disaster for
science', which results from 'the philosopher's rage for generalization',
and promotes 'all kinds of mystical mischief'. But Nietzsche himself
later wrote:

> Do you know what 'the world' is to me? . . . this, my
> Dionysian world of the eternally self-creating, the eternally
> self-destroying, this mystery world of the twofold voluptuous
> delight, my 'beyond good and evil' . . . *This world is the Will
> to Power*—and nothing else!   And you yourselves are also
> this Will to Power—and nothing else!

Similar remarks apply.

Nietzsche earlier predicted how a great thinker might change in such
a way. When this person comes to believe himself to be a genius,
he ceases to criticize himself. He considers himself 'permitted to pro-
mulgate decrees rather than demonstrate'.   This thinker

> drifts imperceptibly into so wretchedly close an
> approximation to the excesses of priests and poets that one
> hardly dares to remember his wise and rigorous youth, the
> strict intellectual morality he then practised, and his . . . dread
> of inspirations and fantasies. When in earlier years he
> compared himself with other, older thinkers, it was so as to
> seriously measure his weakness against their strength and to

grow colder and freer towards himself: now he does it only so
as to intoxicate himself in his own delusions.

Nietzsche here describes his own earlier years. This older thinker,
Nietzsche adds,

has come to a halt . . . he is past the peak of his powers and is
very weary, very close to the setting of his sun.

Given his father's early death, Nietzsche often feared that he did not
have long to live, and he sometimes feared the madness into which he
fell.   Nietzsche also writes:

A thoughtful man, if he is sure of his reason, can profit by
going among fantasists for a decade and within this torrid
zone surrendering himself to a modest degree of folly.

Nietzsche's journey did not go well, since he lost his reason before he
could return from the torrid zone and free himself from his fantasies
and follies.

Wondering how he will die, Nietzsche writes:

will I have my storm in which I perish? . . . Or will I go out like
a light that no wind blows out, but that grew tired and sated
with itself—a burned-out light? Or will I blow myself out lest
I burn out?

Nietzsche describes how a thinker's life could best end.   He would reach

a high, wide mountain plateau wafted by a fresh breeze,
above it a clear cloudless sky which gazes down all day
and into the night with the same unchanging gentleness:
the time of harvest and the heartiest cheerfulness—it is the
autumn of life.

Addressing himself, he writes:

the same life that has its summit in old age also has its
summit in wisdom, in that gentle sunshine of a continual

spiritual joyousness; both of them, old age and wisdom, you will encounter on the same mountain ridge of life . . . Then it is time, and no cause for anger, that the mists of death should approach.   Towards the light—your last motion; joyful shout of knowledge—your last sound.

He should have had such an end.

36

What Matters Most

126 Has It All Been Worth It?

The badness of suffering casts doubt on the goodness of the world. Despite making some brutal claims, Williams writes, Nietzsche had

> a hyper-sensitivity to suffering. It was linked to a total refusal to forget, not only the existence of suffering, but the fact that suffering was necessary to everything that he and anyone else valued. 'All good things come from bad things' is one of his fundamental tenets.

On this view, since

> the world's achievements and glories — art, self-understanding, nobility of character — cannot in common honesty be separated from the knowledge of the horrors that have been involved in bringing these things about . . . there is a question that cannot, Nietzsche supposed, simply be ignored: whether it has all been worth it.

In asking whether human history has been worth it, we are asking whether the horrors and the suffering have been outweighed, so that human history has been, on the whole, good.

Pessimists answer No. On their view, human existence is on the whole bad, or worse than nothing. Buddha's *first noble truth* is that life is mostly suffering, and Silenus said 'It is best not to be born'.

Nietzsche sometimes makes such claims. If someone had full knowledge of the conscious lives of others, Nietzsche writes, he would 'despair of the value of life' and 'collapse with a curse on existence'. Williams similarly writes that, if we had such knowledge, this would be

> an ultimate horror, an unendurable nightmare . . . if for a
> moment we got anything like an adequate idea of it . . . and
> we really guided our actions by it, then surely we would
> annihilate the planet, if we could: and if other planets
> containing conscious creatures are similar to ours in the
> suffering they contain, we would annihilate them as well.

Nietzsche later struggled to avoid this form of Pessimism. One of Nietzsche's responses was his attempt to make the world good, by saying Yes to everything.

In other passages, Nietzsche claims instead that we cannot intelligibly ask whether it has all been worth it. In his words:

> Judgments of value concerning life, for it or against it, can
> never be true . . . *the value of life cannot be estimated*. Not
> by the living, for they are an interested party . . . not by the
> dead, for a different reason.

Nietzsche here assumes that, if we try to estimate the value of our lives, our judgment would be distorted by self-interest. That may sometimes happen. When Nietzsche tried to believe that suffering is good, so that his own suffering would be easier to bear, Nietzsche's judgment was distorted by self-interest. But when we believe that suffering is bad, our judgment is not distorted in this way.

The world, Nietzsche also writes,

> has no value at all, for there is nothing against which it
> could be measured and in relation to which the word
> 'value' would have meaning. The total value of the world
> is unevaluable, consequently philosophical pessimism is
> among the comical things.

This argument assumes that, when we ask whether something's existence is good, we can only compare this thing's existence with the existence of something else, and ask which is better. That is not so. We can ask whether something's existence is in itself good. Such judgments are comparative only in the minimal sense that we compare this thing's existence with its non-existence, which we can regard as nothing and as having no value. Something's existence is in itself good if it is better than nothing, and bad if it is worse than nothing.

We can also reach such judgments with a series of comparisons. If someone dies a slow and painful death, it would have been both better for this person, and impersonally better, if this person's life had ended earlier. The last part of this person's life was worse than nothing, or in itself bad. We can reach similar conclusions about the whole of someone's life. If someone's life contains much prolonged suffering, and nothing or little that is good, it would have been both better for this person, and impersonally better, if this person's life had ended just after it started. Things may be in one way different if we suppose instead that this person's life had never even started. Perhaps we could not claim that this alternative would have been better for this person. But when we ask which alternative would have been impersonally better, there is little difference between these two comparisons. Since it would have been better if this person's life had stopped just after it started, it would also have been better if this person's life had never started. In other words, it would have been impersonally better if this wretched person had never existed. And since such claims make sense when applied to one person, they also make sense when applied to all conscious beings, or to the whole of reality.

In considering such wider claims, we can first ask

Q1: Has the past been in itself worth it?

To focus on this question, we can imagine learning that some massive asteroid will soon hit the Earth, thereby ending human history. We can then ask whether, compared with what has actually happened, it would have been either better or worse if human history had never occurred, because no human beings had ever existed.

Of those who have asked Q1, some Optimists believe the answer to be clearly Yes, since these people are confident that human history up to now has been in itself good, or better than nothing. Some Pessimists believe the answer to be clearly No. To some of us, including me, the answer seems less clear.

According to Hedonistic Utilitarians, the past has been in itself good if there has been, in the lives of all conscious beings, a positive total sum of happiness minus suffering. To explain such claims, we must explain the sense in which some amount of happiness might be *greater* than some amount of suffering. This sense of 'greater' is normative, in a way that is often overlooked. We can first consider brief pleasures and pains. Some pleasure would be in itself greater than some pain if the nature of these two experiences would on balance give us reasons to choose to have both rather than neither. It might, for example, be worth enduring intense cold on some mountain's summit for the sake of seeing a sublime view. When some pleasure is in this sense *greater* than some pain, these experiences would together give us a positive sum of pleasure minus pain, or as we can say more briefly a *net* sum of pleasure. Such claims need more explanation, and should be qualified in various ways. The relative value of such experiences would be very imprecise. Despite these facts, we can often truly believe that some pleasure is greater than some pain. In some longer part of our life, or our life as a whole, we might similarly have a positive sum of happiness minus suffering. That would be true if it would be worth enduring this suffering for the sake of this happiness.

We can next ask whether some group of people might together have some net sum of happiness. It may help to suppose that a single person could have a series of experiences that were just like all of the experiences in these different people's lives, and we can ask whether this person would have sufficient reasons to endure the suffering in this super-life for the sake of the happiness. If the answer is Yes, this sum of happiness would again be greater than this sum of suffering.

This question is in one way misleading. If we imagine that a single person would have all the experiences in these many lives, we may be led to ignore the distinctions between these lives, or the *separateness* of persons. When we ask whether human history has been in itself worth it, or on the whole good, we should also consider questions about distributive justice. When someone suffers, this person's suffering cannot be straightforwardly *compensated* by benefits to other people. If human history had involved a net sum of happiness which was equally distributed between different people, there would also have been a net sum of happiness within each person's life, and this might have made human history in itself good. But, as we know, this distribution has been very unequal. There have been some people whose lives contained more suffering than happiness, and this fact may have made these people's lives worse than nothing. Some Pessimists have been Utilitarians who believed that the sum of happiness has been clearly smaller than the sum of suffering. But other Pessimists appeal to claims about the world's injustice. These people might believe that, though most people's lives have been well worth living, and the sum of happiness has been greater than the sum of suffering, history has been on the whole bad, because there has been uncompensated suffering in lives that were worse than nothing. As Schopenhauer writes:

> that thousands had lived in happiness and joy would never do
> away with the anguish and death-agony of one individual.

The suffering in these people's lives, these Pessimists may believe, would be decisive. These Pessimists may not be Hedonists. They might believe that even if most people's lives contained great non-hedonic goods, these goods could not outweigh the badness and injustice of some people's uncompensated suffering. On this view, it would have been in itself better if no one had ever lived.

Such views, I believe, are too extreme. To consider a simpler example, suppose there have been many wretched people whose lives were worse than nothing, but whose lives were not *very* bad, since they did not involve long periods of intense suffering. Suppose next that, for each one person who has lived such a life, there have been at least a hundred people whose lives were very well worth living. The answer to Q1 would then, I believe, be Yes, since the past would have been in itself worth it. The uncompensated suffering of the unfortunate minority would have been outweighed by the much greater happiness, and other non-hedonic goods, had by these many other people.

We have other reasons to doubt these Pessimistic views. Though it might be true that past suffering has not been outweighed, such truths are very imprecise. We may also know too little about what has happened. Great suffering was necessary, Nietzsche claims, for all of the things that are good, and all the world's great achievements and glories. That is an overstatement. The building of St Petersburg involved much suffering, and the building of the Pyramids may have involved much more. But such claims may not apply to the building of the Parthenon or Venice, and they clearly do not apply to much of the greatest music, art, or literature, such as that produced by Mozart, Monet, and Goethe, or, we can plausibly assume, Bach, Rembrandt, and Shakespeare. When I consider the parts of the past of which I have some knowledge, I am inclined to believe that, in Utilitarian hedonistic terms, the past has been worth it, since the sum of happiness has been greater than the sum of suffering. But I also believe that, when we ask how well history has gone, these hedonic sums are not all that matter, and that the badness of uncompensated suffering cannot be easily outweighed. I am weakly inclined to believe that the past has been in itself worth it. But this may be wishful thinking.

Human history, however, is not yet over.

127 The Future

We can ask

> Q2: Will the future be worth it?

> Q3: Will human history have been, on the whole, worth it?

Even if the past has been in itself bad, the future may be in itself good, and this goodness might outweigh the badness of the past. Human history would then be, on the whole, worth it. We could also truly claim that the past was worth it, not in itself, but as a necessary part of a greater good. On this view, the past would be like an unhappy childhood in some life that is on the whole worth living.

It would be worth enduring this childhood for the sake of the rest of this life.

No such claim, we can note, applies to the future. If what happens later will be in itself bad, this bad future could not be worth it as a part of the whole of history, since this bad future would not be a necessary part of this larger whole. It would be better if history ended now. In the same way, unlike a wretched childhood, a wretched old age could not be worth it as a necessary part of a life that is on the whole worth living.

In another way, however, the analogy with a single life fails. It might be worth enduring a wretched childhood for the sake of the rest of a good life, since our past suffering might be fully compensated by this good future. The people who suffered in the past, however, would not be compensated by what is good in the lives of future people. We might therefore believe that, even if the future will be in itself very good, this fact could not outweigh the badness of the past.

Though we know little about most of the past, we know even less about the future. If we are doubtful whether the past was in itself good, we may find it hard to predict or even guess whether the future is likely to make history, on the whole, worth it. When we ask whether the existence of human beings will have been, on the whole, good, we may not believe that either answer is more likely to be true. Given what some animals endure, we may have similar doubts about whether it is good that there are other conscious beings on this planet. We don't yet know whether there is conscious life elsewhere. We may thus have no idea whether the existence of the Universe is on the whole good.

This ignorance, however, would have little practical importance. Our practical question is

Q4: What ought we to do?

To answer this question, we don't need to know either whether the past was worth it, or whether the whole of history will have been worth it. Suppose that the past was in itself so bad that, even if the future will be very good, human history will not have been worth it. If that were true, it would have been better if human beings had never existed. But that truth would have no practical implications. If the future would be worth it, we should not give up now.

As before, the point is clearer within one life. If my past life has been worse than nothing, my future may not be good enough to make my life as a whole worth living, and it would then be true that it would have been better if I had never existed. But it might be better if I continue to exist from now on. Even if my past has not been worth it, and my life as a whole will not have been worth it, my future *may* be worth it.

If we were trying to decide whether the existence of conscious beings will have been on the whole good, we would need to compare the past and the future. For practical purposes, however, we can ignore the horrors of the past. It is enough to ask some questions about the future.

It might be objected that we should not ignore these past horrors, by thinking only about how we might help to give humanity a good future. That may seem like building a dance hall or comedy theatre on the site of Auschwitz, or of some other massacre. But of the people who have suffered in lives that were worse than nothing, many suffered in attempts to help to give humanity a good future. These people would have wanted us to try to achieve their aims; and, if we succeed, some of their suffering may not have been in vain.

In deciding what we ought to do, we don't need to know whether the future will be worth it, or is likely to be worth it. It may be enough to ask

Q5: Might the future be worth it?

It may even be enough to ask

Q6: Will the *near* future be in itself worth it?

This second question is easier to answer. If the answer is Yes, we need not ask whether the rest of the future might be, or is likely to be, worth it. We could leave those questions to our descendants.

Suppose instead that the near future will *not* be in itself worth it, but will be worse than nothing. That might become true, for example, if we inflict great damage on the biosphere, by global overheating or in some other way, so that, for this and the next few generations, life would be bleak. We would then need to ask whether the rest of the future might be worth it. If the answer was No, it would be best if human history ended soon. We would not need, in Williams's phrase, to annihilate the planet. It would be enough if none of us had children.

It is clear, however, that the further future might be worth it. Partly for this reason, even if the near future would be very bleak, we should not end human history. It might be claimed that, if our children's lives would be likely to be worse than nothing, we ought not to impose such burdens on them. But that is not, I believe, true. Even if our children's lives would be worse than nothing, they might decide to bear such burdens, as many people have earlier done, for the sake of helping to give humanity a good future. We could justifiably have children, letting them decide whether to act in this noble way, rather than making this decision on their behalf, by never having children.

If I believed only that the further future might be worth it, I might not make these claims. But we can also ask

Q7: Might the future be, on the whole, very good?

When Pessimism was most discussed, in the late nineteenth century, some Pessimists claimed that hardly anyone could have a life that was worth living. Some of these people assumed that their personal experience gave them sufficient evidence for this claim. That is not so. The evidence more plausibly supports the view that, though many people have such wretched lives, many others have lives that are well worth living.

Schopenhauer gives some arguments for his Pessimistic view, but these arguments are weak. Just as the privation theory claims that evil is merely the absence of good, Schopenhauer claims that most pleasure and happiness is merely the absence of pain. That is not true. And Schopenhauer makes two curiously inconsistent claims about the wretchedness of human existence. We can object, he claims, both that our lives are filled with suffering which makes them worse than nothing, and that time passes so swiftly that we shall soon be dead. These are like Woody Allen's two complaints about his hotel: 'The food is terrible, and they serve such small portions!'

Many Pessimists assumed that the nature of human life is fixed, so that what is true now will always be true. For the earliest Pessimists, such as Buddha and some ancient Greeks, that may have been a reasonable assumption. By the mid nineteenth Century, however, it should have been clear that human existence could be radically transformed. Though the world started to become uglier, anaesthetics were discovered. We shall soon be able to prevent most human suffering.

We live during the hinge of history. Given the scientific and technological discoveries of the last two centuries, the world has never changed as fast. We shall soon have even greater powers to transform, not only our surroundings, but ourselves and our successors. If we act wisely in the next few centuries, humanity will survive its most dangerous and decisive period. Our descendants could, if necessary, go elsewhere, spreading through this galaxy.

Compared with the possible future, the past is very short. I remember hearing Bertrand Russell describe his memories of his grandfather, who was born in 1792. Known history is a mere six or eight thousand years. The Earth may remain inhabitable for at least a billion years. What has occurred so far is at most a tiny fraction of possible human history. Nor should we restrict this question to the lives of future human beings. Just as we had ancestors who were not human, we may have descendants who will not be human. We can call such people *supra-human*. Our descendants might, I believe, make the further future very good. But that good future may also depend in part on us. If our selfish recklessness ends human history, we would be acting very wrongly. Such acts might be worse for no one; but, as I have argued, that fact could not justify these acts.

Williams doubts whether it has all been worth it. He contrasts two attitudes to 'Western ethical experience'. According to *progressivists*, who include Plato, Aristotle, Kant, and Hegel:

> the universe or history or the structure of human reason can,
> when properly understood, yield a pattern that makes sense
> of human life and human aspiration . . . somehow or other, in
> this life or the next, morally if not materially, as individuals
> or as an historical collective, we shall be safe; or, if not safe, at
> least reassured that at some level of the world's constitution

there is something to be discovered that makes ultimate sense of our concerns.

Sophocles and Thucydides, by contrast, are alike in leaving us with no such sense. Each of them represents human beings as dealing sensibly, foolishly, sometimes catastrophically, sometimes nobly, with a world that is only partially intelligible . . . [and not] well adjusted to ethical aspirations.

These more pessimistic Greeks, Williams believes, were right. But I believe that, if we recognize certain truths about reasons, we can make sufficient sense of our concerns.

There is one concern of which we can easily make sense. We can try to prevent or relieve suffering, and that is enough to give our lives some meaning. As Nagel writes:

There is a great deal of misery in the world, and many of us could easily spend our lives trying to eradicate it . . . one advantage of living in a world as bad as this one is that it offers the opportunity for many activities whose importance can't be questioned.

Here is one way in which you could do something to relieve suffering. You could form a group of friends who commit themselves to give to some aid agency, like Oxfam, some proportion of their future income. Once each year, this group's newsletter would report whether everyone was still making contributions. It would be hard to admit to the others that you had stopped contributing, so by forming or joining such a group you would make it easier to live up to your ideals. You and the others would need to decide how much of your income you commit yourselves to give. If you aim too high, this plan would be more likely to fail. I suggest one tenth — or, more cautiously, one twentieth.

Nagel also writes:

But how could the main point of human life be the elimination of evil? Misery, deprivation, and injustice

prevent people from pursuing the positive goods which life
is assumed to make possible. If all such goods were pointless
and the only thing that really mattered was the elimination of
misery, that really *would* be absurd. The same could be said of
the idea that helping others is the only thing that really gives
meaning to life. If no one's life has any meaning in itself,
how can it acquire meaning through devotion to the
meaningless lives of others?

These claims are, I believe, too strong. If all that really mattered was
preventing suffering, our lives could all have meaning, since we could
all devote our lives to this aim. Nagel's claim should instead be that, if
there were no great positive goods which could outweigh the suffering
in people's lives, it would not be worth continuing human history.
There would be another, more effective way to prevent suffering. We
should all have no children. For it to be worth our staying alive and
having children, we and they must be able to have lives that are not only
meaningful, but good.

That is clearly possible. Life can be wonderful as well as terrible, and
we shall increasingly have the power to make life good. Since human
history may be only just beginning, we can expect that future humans,
or supra-humans, may achieve some great goods that we cannot now
even imagine. In Nietzsche's words, there has never been such a new
dawn and clear horizon, and such an open sea.

In these chapters I have defended the view that

(A) there are some irreducibly normative reason-involving
truths.

Most recent writers reject such views, appealing to metaphysical and
epistemic objections, or to normative disagreements. I have suggested
how we might answer these objections. Such normative truths, I have
claimed, are not about entities or properties that exist in some ontological sense. Natural selection could explain how, without being causally
affected by any such normative properties, we are able to understand
and recognize such truths. And we can reasonably believe that, in ideal

conditions, we would nearly all have sufficiently similar normative beliefs.

I have also claimed that

> (B) we could not have reasons to believe that there are no irreducibly normative truths, since the fact that we had such reasons would itself have to be one such truth.

This claim does not imply that there *are* such truths. But we can add that

> (C) if we ought to have some belief about this question, this is what we ought to believe.

If we believe that there are some irreducibly normative truths, we might be believing what we ought to believe. If there *are* such truths, one of these truths would be that we ought to believe that there are such truths. If instead we believe that there are no such truths, we could *not* be believing what we ought to believe. If there were no such truths, there would be nothing that we ought to believe. Since

> (D) it might be true that we ought to believe that there are some irreducibly normative truths,

and

> (E) it could not be true that we ought *not* to have this belief,

we can conclude that

> (F) we have unopposed reasons or apparent reasons to believe that there are such truths,

so that

> (G) this is what, without claiming certainty, we ought rationally to believe.

If there were no such normative truths, nothing would matter, and we would have no reasons to try to decide how to live. Such decisions would be arbitrary. We would not be the animals that can understand and respond to reasons. In a world without reasons, we would act only on our instincts and desires, living as other animals live. The Universe would not contain rational beings.

Some things, I have claimed, matter, and there are better and worse ways to live. After many thousands of years of responding to reasons in ways that helped them to survive and reproduce, human beings can now respond to other reasons. We are a part of the Universe that is starting to understand itself. And we can partly understand, not only what is in fact true, but also what ought to be true, and what we might be able to make true.

What now matters most is that we avoid ending human history. If there are no rational beings elsewhere, it may depend on us and our successors whether it will all be worth it, because the existence of the Universe will have been on the whole good.

APPENDICES

Why Anything? Why This?

Why does the Universe exist? There are two questions here. First, why is there a Universe at all? It might have been true that nothing ever existed: no living beings, no stars, no atoms, not even space or time. When we think about this possibility, it can seem astonishing that anything exists. Second, why does *this* Universe exist? Things might have been, in countless ways, different. So why is the Universe as it is?

These questions, some people believe, may have causal answers. Suppose first that the Universe has always existed. Some believe that, if all events were caused by earlier events, everything would be explained. That, however, is not so. Even an infinite series of events cannot explain itself. We could ask why this series occurred, rather than some other series, or no series. Of the supporters of the Steady State Theory, some welcomed what they took to be this theory's atheistic implications. They assumed that, if the Universe had no beginning, there would be nothing for a Creator to explain. But there would still be an eternal Universe to explain.

Suppose next that the Universe is not eternal, since nothing preceded the Big Bang. That first event, some physicists suggest, may have obeyed the laws of quantum mechanics, by being a random fluctuation in a vacuum. This would causally explain, they say, how the Universe came into existence out of nothing. But what physicists call a vacuum isn't really nothing. We can ask why it exists, and has the potentialities it does. In Hawking's phrase, 'What breathes fire into the equations?'

Similar remarks apply to all suggestions of these kinds. There could not be a causal explanation of why the Universe exists, why there are any laws of nature, or why these laws are as they are. Nor would it make a difference if there is a God, who caused the rest of the Universe to exist.   There could not be a causal explanation of why God exists.

Many people have assumed that, since these questions cannot have causal answers, they cannot have any answers. Some therefore dismiss these questions, taking them to be not worth considering. Others conclude that they do not make sense, assuming that, as Wittgenstein wrote, 'doubt can exist only where there is a question; and a question only where there is an answer'.

These assumptions are, I believe, mistaken. Even if these questions could not have answers, they would still make sense, and they would still be worth considering. Such thoughts take us into the aesthetic category of the *sublime*, which applies to the highest mountains, raging oceans, the night sky, the interiors of some cathedrals, and other things that are superhuman, awesome, limitless. No question is more sublime than why there is a Universe: why there is anything rather than nothing. Nor should we assume that answers to this question must be causal. And, even if reality cannot be fully explained, we may still make progress, since what is inexplicable may become less baffling than it now seems.

1

One apparent fact about reality has recently been much discussed. Many physicists believe that, for life to be possible, various features of the Universe must be almost precisely as they are. As one example of such a feature, we can take the initial conditions in the Big Bang. If these conditions had been more than very slightly different, these physicists claim, the Universe would not have had the complexity that allows living beings to exist. Why were these conditions so precisely right?

Some say: 'If they had not been right, we couldn't even ask this question.' But that is no answer. It could be baffling how we survived some crash even though, if we hadn't, we could not be baffled.

Others say: 'There had to be some initial conditions, and the conditions that make life possible were as likely as any others. So there is nothing to be explained.' To see what is wrong with this reply, we must distinguish two kinds of case. Suppose first that, when some radio telescope is aimed at most points in space, it records a random sequence of incoming waves. There might be nothing here that needed to be explained. Suppose next that, when the telescope is aimed in one direction, it records a sequence of waves whose pulses match the number π, in binary notation, to the first ten thousand digits. That particular number is, in one sense, just as likely as any other. But there *would* be something here that needed to be explained. Though each long number is unique, only a very few are, like π, mathematically special. What would need to be explained is why this sequence of waves exactly matched such a special number. Though this matching might be a coincidence, which had been randomly produced, that would be most unlikely. We could be almost certain that these waves had been produced by some kind of intelligence.

On the view that we are now considering, since any sequence of waves is as likely as any other, there would be nothing to be explained. If we accepted this view, intelligent beings elsewhere in space would not be able to communicate with us, since we would ignore their messages. Nor could God reveal himself. Suppose that, with some optical telescope, we saw a distant pattern of stars which spelled out in Hebrew script the first chapter of Genesis. On this view, this pattern of stars would not need to be explained.   That is clearly false.

Here is another analogy. Suppose first that, of a thousand people facing death, only one can be rescued. If there is a lottery to pick this one survivor, and I win, I would be very lucky. But there might be nothing here that needed to be explained. Someone had to win, and why not me? Consider next another lottery. Unless my gaoler picks the longest of a thousand straws, I shall be shot. If my gaoler picks that longest straw, there would be something to be explained. It would not be enough to say, 'This result was as likely as any other.' In the first lottery, nothing special happened: whatever the result, someone's life would be saved. In this second lottery, the result *was* special, since, of the thousand possible results, only one would save a life. Why was this special result *also* what happened? Though this might be a coincidence, the chance of that is only one in a thousand. I could be almost certain that, like Dostoyevsky's mock execution, this lottery was rigged.

The Big Bang, it seems, was like this second lottery. For life to be possible, the initial conditions had to be selected with great accuracy. This *appearance of fine-tuning*, as some call it, also needs to be explained.

It may be objected that, in regarding conditions as special if they allow for life, we unjustifiably assume our own importance. But life *is* special, if only because of its complexity. Even a squirrel's brain is more complicated than a lifeless galaxy. Nor is it only life that requires this fine-tuning. If the Big Bang's initial conditions had not been almost precisely as they were, the Universe would have either almost instantly recollapsed, or expanded so fast, and with particles so thinly spread, that not even stars or heavy elements could have formed. That is enough to make these conditions very special.

It may next be objected that these conditions cannot be claimed to be improbable, since such a claim requires a statistical basis, and there is only one Universe. If we were considering all conceivable Universes, it would indeed be implausible to make judgments of statistical probability. But our question is much narrower. We are asking what would have happened if, with the same laws of nature, the initial conditions had been different. That provides the basis for a statistical judgment. There is a range of values that these conditions might have had, and physicists can work out in what proportion of this range the resulting Universe could have contained stars, heavy elements, and life.

This proportion, it is claimed, is extremely small. Of the range of possible initial conditions, fewer than one in a billion billion would have produced a Universe with the complexity that allows for life. If this claim is true, as I shall here assume, there is something that cries out to be explained. Why was one of this tiny set *also* the one that actually obtained?

On one view, this was a mere coincidence. That is conceivable, since coincidences happen. But this view is hard to believe since, if it were true, the chance of this coincidence occurring would be below one in a billion billion.

Others say: 'The Big Bang *was* fine-tuned. In creating the Universe, God chose to make life possible.' Atheists may reject this answer, thinking it improbable that God exists. But God's existence is much less improbable than the view that would require so great a coincidence. So even atheists should admit that, of these two answers to our question, the answer that invokes God is more likely to be true.

This reasoning revives one of the traditional arguments for belief in God. In its strongest form, this argument appealed to the many features of animals, such as eyes or wings, that seem to have been designed. Paley's appeal to such features much impressed Darwin when he was young. Darwin later undermined this form of the argument, since natural selection can explain this appearance of design. But natural selection cannot explain the appearance of fine-tuning in the Big Bang.

This argument's appeal to probabilities can be challenged in a different way. In claiming it to be most improbable that this fine-tuning was a coincidence, the argument assumes that, of the possible initial conditions in the Big Bang, each was equally likely to obtain. That assumption may be mistaken. The conditions that allow for complexity and life may have been, compared with all the others, much more likely to obtain. Perhaps they were even certain to obtain.

To answer this objection, we must broaden this argument's conclusion. If these life-allowing conditions were either very likely or certain to obtain, then — as the argument claims — it would be no coincidence that the Universe allows for complexity and life. But this fine-tuning might have been the work, not of some existing being, but of some impersonal force, or fundamental law. That is what some theists believe God to be.

A stronger challenge to this argument comes from a different way to explain the appearance of fine-tuning. Consider first a similar question. For life to be possible on the Earth, many of the Earth's features have to be close to being as they are. The Earth's having such features, it might be claimed, is unlikely to be a coincidence, and should therefore be regarded as God's work. But such an argument would be weak. The Universe, we can reasonably believe, contains very many planets, with varying conditions. We should expect that, on a few of these planets, conditions would be just right for life. Nor is it surprising that we live on one of these few.

Things are different, we may assume, with the appearance of fine-tuning in the Big Bang. While there are likely to be many other planets, there is only one Universe. But this difference may be less than it seems. Some physicists suggest that the observable Universe is only one out of many different worlds, which are all equally parts of reality. According to one such view, the other worlds are related to ours in a way that solves some of the mysteries of quantum physics. On the different and simpler view that is relevant here, the other worlds have the same laws of nature as our world, and they are produced by Big Bangs that are broadly similar, except in having different initial conditions.

On this *Many Worlds Hypothesis*, there is no need for fine-tuning. If there were enough Big Bangs, we should expect that, in a few of these, conditions would be just right to allow for complexity and life; and it would be no surprise that our Big Bang was one of these few. To illustrate this point, we can revise my second lottery. Suppose my gaoler picks a straw, not once, but very many times. That would explain his managing, once, to pick the longest straw, without that's being an extreme coincidence, or this lottery's being rigged.

On most versions of the Many Worlds Hypothesis, these many worlds are not, except through their origins, causally related. Some object that, since our world could not be causally affected by such other worlds, we can have no evidence for their existence, and can therefore have no reason to believe in them. But we do have such a reason, since their existence would explain an otherwise puzzling feature of our world: the appearance of fine-tuning.

Of these two ways to explain this appearance, which is better? Compared with belief in God, the Many Worlds Hypothesis is more cautious, since its claim is merely that there is more of the kind of reality that we can observe around us. But God's existence has been claimed to be intrinsically more probable. According to most theists, God is a being who is omniscient, omnipotent, and wholly good. The uncaused existence of such a being has been claimed to be simpler, and less arbitrary, than the uncaused existence of many highly complicated worlds. And simpler hypotheses, many scientists assume, are more likely to be true.

If such a God exists, however, other features of our world become hard to explain. It may not be surprising that God chose to make life possible. But the laws of nature could have been different, so there are many possible worlds that would have contained life. It is hard to understand why, out of all these possibilities, God chose to create our world. What is most baffling is the problem of evil. There appears to be much suffering which any good person, knowing the truth, would have prevented if he could. If there is such suffering, there cannot be a God who is omnipotent, omniscient, and wholly good.

To this problem, theists have proposed several solutions. Some suggest that God is not omnipotent, or not wholly good. Others suggest that undeserved suffering is not, as it seems, bad, or that God could not prevent such suffering without making the Universe, as a whole, less good.

We can ignore these suggestions here, since we have larger questions to consider. I began by asking why things are as they are. Before returning to that question, we should ask *how* things are. There is much about our world that we have not discovered. And, just as there may be other worlds that are like ours, there may be worlds that are very different.

2

It will help to distinguish two kinds of possibilities. *Cosmic* possibilities cover everything that ever exists, and are the different ways that the whole of reality might be. Only one such possibility can be actual, or be the one that *obtains*. Local possibilities are the different ways that some part of reality, or *local world*, might be. If some local world exists, that leaves it open whether other worlds exist.

One cosmic possibility is, roughly, that *every* possible local world exists. This we can call the *All Worlds Hypothesis*. Another possibility, which might have obtained, is that nothing ever exists. This we can call the *Null Possibility*. In each of the remaining possibilities, the number of local worlds that exist is between none and all. There are countless of these possibilities, since there are countless combinations of possible local worlds.

Of these different cosmic possibilities, one must obtain, and only one can obtain.   So we have two questions: Which obtains, and Why?

These questions are connected. If some possibility would be easier to explain, that may give us more reason to believe that this possibility obtains. This is how, rather than believing in only one Big Bang, we have more reason to believe in many. Whether we believe in one or many, we have the question why any Big Bang has occurred. Though this question is hard, the occurrence of many Big Bangs is not more puzzling than the occurrence of only one. Most kinds of thing, or event, have many instances. We also have the question why, in the Big Bang that produced our world, the initial conditions allowed for complexity and life. If there has been only one Big Bang, this fact is also hard to explain, since it is most unlikely that these conditions merely happened to be right. If instead there have been many Big Bangs, this fact is easy to explain, since it is like the fact that, among countless planets, there are some whose conditions allow for life. Since belief in many Big Bangs leaves less that is unexplained, it is the better view.

If some cosmic possibilities would be less puzzling than others, because their obtaining would leave less to be explained, is there some possibility whose obtaining would be in no way puzzling?

Consider first the Null Possibility, in which nothing ever exists. To imagine this possibility, it may help to suppose first that all that ever existed was a single atom. We then imagine that even this atom never existed.

Some have claimed that, if there had never been anything, there wouldn't have been anything to be explained. But that is not so. When we imagine how things would have been if nothing had ever existed, what we should imagine away are such things as living beings, stars, and atoms. There would still have been various truths, such as the truth that there were no stars or atoms, or that 9 is divisible by 3. We can ask why these things would have been true. And such questions may have answers. Thus we can explain why, even if nothing had ever existed, 9 would have been divisible by 3. There is no conceivable alternative. And we can explain why there would have been no such things as immaterial matter, or spherical cubes. Such things are logically impossible. But why would *nothing* have existed? Why would there have been no stars or atoms, no philosophers or bluebell woods?

We should not claim that, if nothing had ever existed, there would have been nothing to be explained. But we can claim something less. Of all the cosmic possibilities, the Null Possibility would have needed the least explanation. As Leibniz pointed out, it is much the simplest, and the least arbitrary. And it is the easiest to understand. It can seem mysterious, for example, how things could exist without their existence having some cause, but there cannot be a causal explanation of why the whole Universe, or God, exists. The Null Possibility raises no such problem. If nothing had ever existed, that state of affairs would not have needed to be caused.

Reality, however, does not take its least puzzling form. In some way or other, a Universe has managed to exist. That is what can take our breath away. As Wittgenstein wrote, 'not how the world is, is the mystical, but *that* it is'. Or, in the words of a thinker as unmystical as Jack Smart: 'That anything should exist at all does seem to me a matter for the deepest awe.'

Consider next the All Worlds Hypothesis, which claims that every possible local world exists. Unlike the Null Possibility, this may be how things are. And it may be the next least puzzling possibility. This hypothesis is not the same as — though it includes — the Many Worlds Hypothesis. On that more cautious view, the many other worlds have the same elements as our world, and the same fundamental laws, and differ only in such features as their constants and initial conditions. The All Worlds Hypothesis covers every conceivable kind of world, and most of these other worlds would have very different elements and laws.

If all these worlds exist, we can ask why they do. But, compared with most other cosmic possibilities, the All Worlds Hypothesis may leave less that is unexplained. For example, whatever the number of possible worlds that exist, we have the question, 'Why *that* number?' That question would have been least puzzling if the number that existed were *none*, and the next least arbitrary possibility seems to be that *all* these worlds exist. With every other cosmic possibility, we have a further question. If ours is the only world, we can ask: 'Out of all the possible local worlds, why is *this* the one that exists?' On any version of the Many Worlds Hypothesis, we have a similar question: 'Why do just *these* worlds exist, with *these* elements and laws?' But, if *all* these worlds exist, there is no such further question.

It may be objected that, even if all possible local worlds exist, that does not explain why our world is as it is. But that is a mistake. If all these worlds exist, each world is as it is in the way in which each number is as it is. We cannot sensibly ask why 9 is 9. Nor should we ask why our world is the one it is: why it is *this* world. That would be like asking, 'Why are *we* who we are?', or 'Why is it *now* the time that it is?' Those, on reflection, are not good questions.

Though the All Worlds Hypothesis avoids certain questions, it is not as simple, or unarbitrary, as the Null Possibility. There may be no sharp distinction between worlds that are and are not possible. It is unclear what counts as a kind of world. And, if there are infinitely many kinds, there is a choice between different kinds of infinity.

Whichever cosmic possibility obtains, we can ask why it obtains. All that I have claimed so far is that, with some possibilities, this question would be less puzzling. Let us now ask: Could this question have an answer?   Might there be a theory that leaves nothing unexplained?

3

It is sometimes claimed that God, or the Universe, make themselves exist. But this cannot be true, since these entities cannot do anything unless they exist.

On a more intelligible view, it is logically necessary that God, or the Universe, exist, since the claim that they might not have existed leads to a contradiction. On such a view, though it may seem conceivable that there might never have been anything, that is not really logically possible. Some people even claim that there may be only one coherent cosmic possibility. Einstein suggested that, if God created our world, he might have had no choice about which world to create. If such a view were true, everything might be explained. Reality might be the way it is because there was no conceivable alternative. But for reasons that have been often given, we can reject such views.

Consider next a quite different view. According to Plato, Plotinus and others, the Universe exists because its existence is good. Even if we are confident that we should reject this view, it is worth asking whether it makes sense. If it does, that may suggest other possibilities.

This *Axiarchic View* can take a theistic form. We might claim that God exists because his existence is good, and that the rest of the Universe exists because God caused it to exist. But in that explanation God, *qua* Creator, is redundant. If God can exist because his existence is good, so can the whole Universe. This may be why some theists reject the Axiarchic View, and insist that God's existence is a brute fact, with no explanation.

In its simplest form, this view makes three claims:

(1) It would be best if reality were a certain way.

(2) Reality is that way.

(3) (1) explains (2).

(1) is an ordinary evaluative claim, like the claim that it would be better if there was less suffering. The Axiarchic View assumes, I believe rightly, that such claims can be in a strong sense true. (2) is an ordinary empirical or scientific claim, though of a sweeping kind. What is distinctive in this view is claim (3), according to which (1) explains (2).

Can we understand this third claim? To focus on this question, we should briefly ignore the world's evils, and suspend our other doubts about claims (1) and (2). We should suppose that, as Leibniz claimed, the best possible Universe exists. Would it then make sense to claim that this Universe exists *because* it is the best?

That use of 'because', Axiarchists should admit, cannot be easily explained. But even ordinary causation is mysterious. At the most fundamental level, we have no idea why some events cause others; and it is hard to explain what causation is. There are, moreover, non-causal senses of 'because' and 'why', as in the claim that God exists because his existence is logically necessary. We can understand that claim, even if we think it false. The Axiarchic View is harder to understand. But that is not surprising. If there is some explanation of the whole of reality, we should not expect this explanation to fit neatly into some familiar category. This extra-ordinary question may have an extra-ordinary answer. We should reject suggested answers which make no sense; but we should also try to see what might make sense.

Axiarchy might be expressed as follows. We are now supposing that, of all the countless ways that the whole of reality might be, one is both the very best, and is the way that reality is. On the Axiarchic View, *that is no coincidence*. This claim, I believe, makes sense. And, if it were no coincidence that the best way for reality to be is *also* the way that reality is, that might support the further claim that this was *why* reality was this way.

This view has one advantage over the more familiar theistic view. An appeal to God cannot explain why the Universe exists, since God would himself be part of the Universe, or one of the things that exist. Some theists argue that, since nothing can exist without some cause, God, who is the First Cause, must exist. As Schopenhauer objected, this argument's premise is not like some cab-driver whom theists are free to dismiss once they have reached their destination. The Axiarchic View appeals, not to an existing entity, but to an explanatory law. Since such a law would not itself be part of the Universe, it might explain why the Universe exists, and is as good as it could be. If such a law governed reality, we could still ask why it did, or why the Axiarchic View was true. But, in discovering this law, we would have made some progress.

It is hard, however, to believe the Axiarchic View. If, as it seems, there is much pointless suffering, our world cannot be part of the best possible Universe.

4

Some Axiarchists claim that, if we reject their view, we must regard our world's existence as a brute fact, since no other explanation could make sense. But that, I believe, is not so. If we abstract from the optimism of the Axiarchic View, its claims are these:

> Of the countless cosmic possibilities, one both has some
> very special feature, and is the possibility that obtains. That
> is no coincidence.   This possibility obtains because it has
> this feature.

Other views can make such claims. This special feature need not be that of being best. Thus, on the All Worlds Hypothesis, reality is *maximal*, or as full as it could be. Similarly, if nothing had ever existed, reality would have been *minimal*, or as empty as it could be. If the possibility that obtained were either maximal, or minimal, that fact, we might claim, would be most unlikely to be a coincidence. And that might support the further claim that this possibility's having this feature would be *why* it obtained.

Let us now look more closely at that last step. When it is no coincidence that two things are both true, there is something that explains why, given the truth of one, the other is also true. The truth of either might make the other true. Or both might be explained by some third truth, as when two facts are the joint effects of a common cause.

Suppose next that, of the cosmic possibilities, one is both very special and is the one that obtains. If that is no coincidence, what might explain why these things are both true? On the reasoning that we are now considering, the first truth explains the second, since this possibility obtains because it has this special feature. Given the kind of truths these are, such an explanation could not go the other way. This possibility could not have this feature because it obtains. If some possibility has some feature, it could not fail to have this feature, so it would have this feature whether or not it obtains. The All Worlds Hypothesis, for example, could not fail to describe the fullest way for reality to be.

While it is necessary that our imagined possibility has its special feature, it is not necessary that this possibility obtains. This difference, I believe, justifies the reasoning that we are now considering. Since this possibility must have this feature, but might not have obtained, it cannot have this feature because it obtains, nor could some third truth explain why it both has this feature and obtains. So, if these facts are no coincidence, this possibility must obtain *because* it has this feature.

When some possibility obtains because it has some feature, its having this feature may be why some agent, or some process of natural selection, made it obtain. These we can call the *intentional* and *evolutionary* ways in which some feature of some possibility may explain why it obtains.

Our world, theists claim, can be explained in the first of these ways. If reality were as good as it could be, it would indeed make sense to claim that this was partly God's work. But, since God's own existence could not be God's work, there could be no intentional explanation of why the whole of reality was as good as it could be. So we could reasonably conclude that this way's being the best explained *directly* why reality was this way. Even if God exists, the intentional explanation could not compete with the different and bolder explanation offered by the Axiarchic View.

Return now to other explanations of this kind. Consider first the Null Possibility. This, we know, does not obtain; but, since we are asking what makes sense, that does not matter. If there had never been anything, would that have had to be a brute fact, which had no explanation? The answer, I suggest, is No. It might have been no coincidence that, of all the countless cosmic possibilities, what obtained was the simplest, and least arbitrary, and the only possibility in which nothing ever exists. And, if these facts had been no coincidence, this possibility would have obtained because—or partly because—it had one or more of these special features. This explanation, moreover, could not have taken an intentional or evolutionary form. If nothing had ever existed, there could not have been some agent, or process of selection, who or which made this possibility obtain. Its being the simplest or least arbitrary possibility would have been, directly, why it obtained.

Consider next the All Worlds Hypothesis, which may obtain. If reality is as full as it could be, is that a coincidence? Does it merely happen to be true that, of all the cosmic possibilities, the one that obtains is at this extreme? As before, that is conceivable, but this coincidence would be too great to be credible. We can reasonably assume that, if this possibility obtains, that is *because* it is maximal, or at this extreme. On this *Maximalist View*, it is a fundamental truth that being possible, and part of the fullest way that reality could be, is sufficient for being actual. That is the highest law governing reality. As before, if such a law governed reality, we could still ask *why* it did. But, in discovering this law, we would have made some progress.

Here is another special feature. Perhaps reality is the way it is because its fundamental laws are, on some criterion, as mathematically beautiful as they could be.   That is what some physicists are inclined to believe.

As these remarks suggest, there is no clear boundary here between philosophy and science. If there is such a highest law governing reality, this law is of the same kind as those that physicists are trying to discover. When we appeal to natural laws to explain some features of reality, such as the relations between light, gravity, space, and time, we are not giving causal explanations, since we are not claiming that one part of reality caused another part to be some way. What such laws explain, or partly explain, are the deeper facts about reality that causal explanations take for granted.

There would be a highest law, of the kind that I have sketched, if some cosmic possibility obtained because it had some special feature. This feature we can call the *Selector*. If there is more than one such feature, they are all partial Selectors. Just as there are various cosmic possibilities, there are various *explanatory* possibilities. For each of these special features, there is the explanatory possibility that this feature is the Selector, or is one of the Selectors. Reality would then be the way it is because, or partly because, this way had this feature.

There is one other explanatory possibility: that there is *no* Selector. If that is true, it is random that reality is as it is. Events may be in one sense random, even though they are causally inevitable. That is how it is random whether a meteorite strikes the land or the sea. Events are random in a stronger sense if they have no cause. That is what most physicists believe about some features of events involving sub-atomic particles. If it is random what reality is like, the Universe not only has no cause. It has no explanation of any kind. This claim we can call the *Brute Fact View*.

Few features can be plausibly regarded as possible Selectors. Though plausibility is a matter of degree, there is a natural threshold to which we can appeal. If we suppose that reality has some special feature, we can ask which of two beliefs would be more credible: that reality merely happens to have this feature, or that reality is the way it is because this way has this feature. If the second would be more credible, this feature can be called a *credible Selector*. Return for example to the question of how many possible local worlds exist. Of the different answers to this question, *all* and *none* give us, I have claimed, credible Selectors. If either all or no worlds existed, that would be unlikely to be a coincidence. But suppose that 58 worlds existed. This number has some special features, such as being the smallest number that is the sum of seven different primes. It may be just conceivable that this would be why 58 worlds existed; but it would be more reasonable to believe that the number that existed merely happened to be 58.

There are, I have claimed, some credible Selectors. Reality might be some way because that way is the best, or the simplest, or the least arbitrary, or because its obtaining makes reality as full and varied as it could be, or because its fundamental laws are, in some way, as elegant as they could be. Presumably there are other such features, which I have overlooked.

In claiming that there are credible Selectors, I am assuming that some cosmic and explanatory possibilities are more probable than others. That assumption may be questioned. Judgments of probability, it may again be claimed, must be grounded on facts about our world, so such judgments cannot be applied either to how the whole of reality might be, or to how reality might be explained.

This objection is, I believe, unsound. When we choose between scientific theories, our judgments of their probability cannot rest only on predictions based on established facts and laws. We need such judgments in trying to decide what these facts and laws are. And we can justifiably make such judgments when considering different ways in which the whole of reality may be, or might have been. Compare two such cosmic possibilities. In the first, there is a lifeless Universe consisting only of some spherical iron stars, whose relative motion is as it would be in our world. In the second, things are the same, except that the stars move together in the patterns of a minuet, and they are shaped like either Queen Victoria or Cary Grant. We would be right to claim that, of these two possibilities, the first is more likely to obtain.

In making that claim, we would not mean that it is more likely *that* the first possibility obtains. Since this possibility is the existence of a lifeless Universe, we know that it does not obtain. We would be claiming that this possibility is intrinsically more likely, or that, to put it roughly, it had a greater chance of being how reality is. If some possibility is more likely to obtain, that will often make it more likely that it obtains; but though one kind of likelihood supports the other, they are quite different.

Another objection may again seem relevant here. Of the countless cosmic possibilities, a few have special features, which I have called credible Selectors. If such a possibility obtains, we have, I have claimed, a choice of two conclusions. Either reality, by an extreme coincidence, merely happens to have this feature, or — more plausibly — this feature is one of the Selectors. It may be objected that, when I talk of an extreme coincidence, I must be assuming that these cosmic possibilities are all equally likely to obtain. But I have now rejected that assumption. And, if these possibilities are *not* equally likely, my reasoning may seem to be undermined.

As before, that is not so. Suppose that, of the cosmic possibilities, those that have these special features are much more likely to obtain. As this objection rightly claims, it would not then be amazing if such a possibility merely happened to obtain. But that does not undermine my reasoning, since it is another way of stating my conclusion. It is another way of saying that these features are Selectors.

These remarks do show, however, that we should distinguish two ways in which some feature may be a Selector. *Probabilistic* Selectors make some cosmic possibility more likely to obtain, but leave it open whether it does obtain. On any plausible view, there are some Selectors of this kind, since some ways for reality to be are intrinsically more likely than some others. Thus of our two imagined Universes, the one consisting of spherical stars is intrinsically more likely than the one with the dancing stars that are shaped like Queen Victoria or Cary Grant. Besides Probabilistic Selectors, there may also be one or more *Effective* Selectors. If some possibility has a certain feature, this may make this possibility, not merely intrinsically more likely, but the one that obtains. Thus, if simplicity had been the Effective Selector, that would have made it true that nothing ever existed. And, if maximality is the Effective Selector, as it may be, that is what makes reality as full as it could be.   When I talk of Selectors, these are the kind I mean.

5

There are, we have seen, various cosmic and explanatory possibilities. In trying to decide which of these obtain, or are actual, we can in part appeal to facts about our world. Thus, from the mere fact that our world exists, we can deduce that the Null Possibility does not obtain. And, since our world seems to contain pointless evils, we have reason to reject the Axiarchic View.

Consider next the Brute Fact View, on which reality merely happens to be as it is. No facts about our world could refute this view. But some facts would make it less likely that this view is true. If reality is randomly selected, what we should expect to exist are many varied worlds, none of which had features that, in the range of possibilities, were at one extreme. That is what we should expect because, in much the largest set of cosmic possibilities, that would be what exists. If our world has very special features, that would count against the Brute Fact View.

Return now to the question whether God exists. Compared with the uncaused existence of one or many complicated worlds, the hypothesis that God exists has been claimed to be simpler, and less arbitrary, and thus more likely to be true. But this hypothesis is not simpler than the Brute Fact View. And, if it is random which cosmic possibility obtains, we should not expect the one that obtains to be as simple, and unarbitrary, as God's existence is claimed to be. Rather, as I have just said, we should expect there to be many worlds, none of which had very special features. Ours may be the kind of world that, on the Brute Fact View, we should expect to observe.

Similar remarks apply to the All Worlds Hypothesis. Few facts about our world could refute this view; but, if all possible local worlds exist, the likely character of our world is much the same as on the Brute Fact View. That claim may seem surprising, given the difference between these two views. One view is about *which* cosmic possibility obtains, the other is about *why* the one that obtains obtains. And these views conflict, since, if we knew that either view was true, we would have strong reason not to believe the other. If all possible worlds exist, that is unlikely to be a brute fact. But, in their different ways, these views are both *non-selective*. On neither view do certain worlds exist *because* they have certain special features. So, if either view is true, we should not expect our world to have such features.

To that last claim, there is one exception. This is the feature with which we began: that our world allows for life. Though this feature is, in some ways, special, it is one that we cannot help observing. That restricts what we can infer from the fact that our world has this feature. Rather than claiming that being *life-allowing* is one of the Selectors, we can appeal to some version of the Many Worlds Hypothesis. If there are very many worlds, we would expect a few worlds to be life-allowing, and our world is bound to be one of these few.

Consider next special features of another kind: ones that we are not bound to observe. Suppose we discover that our world has such a feature, and we ask whether that is no coincidence. It may again be said that, if there are many worlds, we would expect a few worlds to have this special feature. But that would not explain why that is true of *our* world. We could not claim—as with the feature of being life-allowing—that our world is bound to have this feature. So the appeal to many worlds could not explain away the coincidence. Suppose, for example, that our world were very good, or were wholly law-governed, or had very simple natural laws. Those facts would count against both of the unselective views: both the All Worlds Hypothesis and the Brute Fact View. It is true that, if all worlds exist, or there are very many randomly selected worlds, we should expect a few worlds to be very good, or wholly law-governed, or to have very simple laws. But that would not explain why our world had those features. So we would have some reason to believe that our world is the way it is because this way has those features.

Does our world have such features: ones that count against the unselective views? Our world's normative or evaluative features seem not to count against these views, since they seem the mixture of good and bad that, on the unselective views, we should expect. But our world may have two other special features: being wholly law-governed, and having very simple laws. Neither feature seems to be required in order for life to be possible. And, among possible life-containing worlds, a far greater range would not have these features. Thus, for each law-governed world, there are countless variants that would fail in different ways to be wholly law-governed. And, compared with simple laws, there is a far greater range of complicated laws. So, on both the unselective views, we should not expect our world to have these features. If it has them, as physicists might discover, that would give us reasons to reject both the All Worlds Hypothesis and the Brute Fact View. We would have some reason to believe that there are at least two partial Selectors: being law-governed and having simple laws.

There may be other features of our world from which we can try to infer what reality is like, and why. But observation can take us only part of the way. If we can get further, that will have to be by pure reasoning.

6

Of those who accept the Brute Fact View, many assume that this view must be true. According to these people, though reality merely happens to be some way, the fact *that* reality merely happens to be some way does not merely happen to be true. There could not possibly be an explanation of why reality is the way it is, since there could not be a causal explanation, and no other explanation would make sense.

This assumption, I have argued, is mistaken. Reality might be the way it is because this way is the fullest, or the most varied, or obeys the simplest or most elegant laws, or has some other special feature. Since the Brute Fact View is not the only explanatory possibility, we should not assume that it must be true.

When supporters of this view recognize these other possibilities, they may switch to the other extreme, claiming that their view's truth is another brute fact. If that were so, not only would there be no explanation of reality's being as it is, there would also be no explanation of there being no such explanation. As before, though this might be true, we should not assume that it must be true. If some explanatory possibility merely happens to obtain, the one that obtains may not be the Brute Fact View. If it is randomly selected *whether* reality is randomly selected, and there are other possibilities, random selection may not be selected.

There is, moreover, another way in which some explanatory possibility may obtain. Rather than merely happening to obtain, this possibility may have some feature, or set of features, which explains why it obtains. Such a feature would be a Selector at a higher level, since it would apply not to factual but to explanatory possibilities. This feature would determine, not that reality be a certain way, but that it be determined in a certain way how reality is to be.

If the Brute Fact View is true, it may have been selected in some such way. For example, of the explanatory possibilities, this view seems to describe the simplest, since its claim is only that reality has no explanation. This possibility's being the simplest may make it the one that obtains. Simplicity may be the higher Selector, determining that there is no Selector between the ways that reality might be.

Once again, however, though this may be true, we could not assume its truth. There may be some other higher Selector. Some explanatory possibility may obtain, for example, because it is the least arbitrary, or is the one that explains most. The Brute Fact View has neither of those features. Or there may be no higher Selector, since some explanatory possibility may merely happen to obtain.

These alternatives are the different possibilities at yet another, higher explanatory level. So we have the same two questions: Which obtains, and Why?

We may now become discouraged. Every answer, it may seem, raises a further question. But that may not be so. There may be some answer that is a necessary truth. With that necessity, our search would end.

Some truth is logically necessary when its denial leads to a contradiction. It cannot be in this sense necessary either that reality is a brute fact, or that there is some Selector. Both these claims can be denied without contradiction.

There are also non-logical necessities. The most familiar, causal necessity, cannot give us the truth we need. It could not be causally necessary that reality is, or isn't, a brute fact. Causal necessities come lower down. Similar remarks apply to the necessities involved in the essential properties of particular things, or natural kinds. Consider next the metaphysical necessity that some writers claim for God's existence. That claim means, they say, that God's existence does not depend on anything else, and that nothing else could cause God to cease to exist. But these claims do not imply that God must exist, and that makes such necessity too weak to end our questions.

There are, however, some kinds of necessity that would be strong enough. Consider the truths that undeserved suffering is bad, and that, if we know that some argument is valid and has true premises, we ought rationally to believe this argument's conclusion. These truths are not logically necessary, since their denials would not lead to contradictions. But they could not have failed to be true. Undeserved suffering does not merely happen to be bad.

When John Leslie defends the Axiarchic View, he appeals to this kind of non-logical necessity. Not only does value rule reality, Leslie suggests, it could not have failed to rule. But this suggestion is hard to believe. While it is inconceivable that undeserved suffering might have failed to be in itself bad, it is clearly conceivable that value might have failed to rule, if only because it seems so clear that value does *not* rule.

Return now to the Brute Fact View, which is more likely to be true. If this view is true, could its truth be non-logically necessary? Is it inconceivable that there might have been some Selector, or highest law, making reality be some way? The answer, I have claimed, is No. Even if reality is a brute fact, it might not have been. Thus, if nothing had ever existed, that might have been no coincidence. Reality might have been that way because, of the cosmic possibilities, it is the simplest and least arbitrary. And as I have also claimed, just as it is not necessary that the Brute Fact View is true, it is not necessary that this view's truth be another brute fact. This view might be true because it is the simplest of the explanatory possibilities.

We have not yet found the necessity we need. Reality may happen to be as it is, or there may be some Selector. Whichever of these is true, it may happen to be true, or there may be some higher Selector. These are the different possibilities at the next explanatory level, so we are back with our two questions: Which obtains, and Why?

Could these questions continue for ever? Might there be, at every level, another higher Selector? Consider another version of the Axiarchic View. Reality might be as good as it could be, and that might be true because its being true is best, and that in turn might be true because its being true is best, and so on for ever. In this way, it may seem, everything might be explained. But that is not so. Like an infinite series of events, such a series of explanatory truths could not explain itself. Even if each truth were made true by the next, we could still ask why the whole series was true, rather than some other series, or no series.

The point can be made more simply. Though there might be some highest Selector, this might not be goodness but some other feature, such as non-arbitrariness. What could select between these possibilities? Might goodness be the highest Selector because that is best, or non-arbitrariness be this Selector because that is the least arbitrary possibility? Neither suggestion, I believe, makes sense. Just as God could not make himself exist, no Selector could make itself the one that, at the highest level, rules. No Selector could settle *whether* it rules, since it cannot settle anything unless it does rule.

If there is some highest Selector, this cannot, I have claimed, be a necessary truth. Nor could this Selector make itself the highest. And, since this Selector would be the highest, nothing else could make that true. So we may have found the necessity we need. If there is some highest Selector, that, I suggest, must merely happen to be true.

Supporters of the Brute Fact View may now feel vindicated. Have we not, in the end, accepted their view?

We have not. According to the Brute Fact View, reality merely happens to be as it is. That, I have argued, may not be true, since there may be some Selector which explains, or partly explains, reality's being as it is. There may also be some higher Selector which explains there being this Selector. My suggestion is only that, at the end of any such explanatory chain, some highest Selector must merely happen to be the one that rules.   That is a different view.

This difference may seem small. No Selector could *explain* reality, we may believe, if it merely happened to rule. But this thought, though natural, is a mistake. If some explanation appeals to some brute fact, it does not explain this fact; but it may explain others.

Suppose, for example, that reality is as full as it could be. On the Brute Fact View, this fact would have no explanation. On the Maximalist View, reality would be this way because the single highest law is that every local possibility is actual. If reality were as full as it could be, this Maximalist View would be better than the Brute Fact View, since it would explain reality's being this way. And this view would provide that explanation even if it merely happened to be true. It makes a difference where the brute fact comes.

Part of the difference here is that, while there are countless cosmic possibilities, there are few plausible explanatory possibilities. If reality is as full as it could be, that's being a brute fact would be very puzzling. Since there are countless cosmic possibilities, it would be amazing if the one that obtained merely happened to be at the maximal extreme. On the Maximalist View, this fact would be no coincidence. And, since there are few explanatory possibilities, it would not be amazing if the Maximalist highest law merely happened to be the one that rules.

We should not claim that, if some explanation rests on a brute fact, it is not an explanation. Most scientific explanations take this form. The most that might be true is that such an explanation is, in a way, merely a better description.

If that were true, there would be a different defence of the kind of reasoning that we have been considering. Even to discover *how* things are, we need explanations. And we may need explanations on the grandest scale. Our world may seem to have some feature that would be unlikely to be a coincidence. We may reasonably suspect that this feature is the Selector, or one of the Selectors. That hypothesis might lead us to confirm that, as it seemed, our world does have this feature. And that might give us reason to conclude either that ours is the only world, or that there are other worlds, with the same or related features. We might thus reach truths about the whole Universe.

Even if all explanations must end with a brute fact, we should go on trying to explain why the Universe exists, and is as it is. The brute fact may not enter at the lowest level. If reality is the way it is because this way has some feature, to know *what* reality is like, we must ask *why*.

7

We may never be able to answer these questions, either because our world is only a small part of reality, or because, though our world is the whole of reality, we could never know that to be true, or because of our own limitations. But as I have tried to show, we may come to see more clearly what the possible answers are. Some of the fog that shrouds these questions may then disappear.

It can seem astonishing, for example, how reality could be made to be as it is. If God made the rest of reality be as it is, what could have made God exist? And, if God does not exist, what else could have made reality be as it is? When we think about these questions, even the Brute Fact View may seem unintelligible. It may be baffling how reality could be even randomly selected. What kind of *process* could select whether, for example, time had no beginning, or whether anything ever exists? When, and how, could any selection be made?

This is not a real problem. Of all the possible ways that the whole of reality might be, there must be one that is the way reality actually is. Since it is logically necessary that reality be some way or other, it is necessary that one way be picked to be the way that reality is. Logic ensures that, without any kind of process, a selection is made. There is no need for hidden machinery.

Suppose next that, as many people assume, the Brute Fact View must be true. If our world has no very special features, there would then be nothing that was deeply puzzling. If it were necessary that some cosmic possibility be randomly selected, while there would be no explanation of why the selection went as it did, there would be no mystery in reality's being as it is. Reality's features would be inexplicable, but only in the way in which it is inexplicable how some particle randomly moves. If a particle can merely happen to move as it does, reality could merely happen to be as it is. Randomness may even be *less* puzzling at the level of the whole Universe, since we know that facts at this level could not have been caused.

The Brute Fact View, I have argued, is not necessary, and may not be true. There may be one or more Selectors between the ways that reality might be, and one or more Selectors between such Selectors. But as I have also claimed, it may be a necessary truth that it be a brute fact whether there are such Selectors, and, if so, which the highest Selector is.

If that is a necessary truth, similar remarks apply. On these assumptions, there would again be nothing that was deeply puzzling. If it is necessary that, of these explanatory possibilities, one merely happens to obtain, there would be no explanation of why the one that obtains obtains. But as before, that would be no more mysterious than the random movement of some particle.

The existence of the Universe can seem, in another way, astonishing. Even if it is not baffling that reality was made to be some way, since there is no conceivable alternative, it can seem baffling that the selection went as it did. Why is there a Universe at all? Why doesn't reality take its simplest and least arbitrary form: that in which nothing ever exists?

If we find this astonishing, we are assuming that these features *should* be the Selectors: that reality should be as simple and unarbitrary as it could be. That assumption has, I believe, great plausibility. But, just as the simplest cosmic possibility is that nothing ever exists, the simplest explanatory possibility is that there is no Selector. So we should not expect simplicity at both the factual and explanatory levels. If there is no Selector, we should not expect that there would also be no Universe. That would be an extreme coincidence.

The Fair Warning View

Even if no one deserves to be punished, that does not imply that all punishment is wrong. Since the word 'punishment' is sometimes used in a retributive sense, I shall here use the more neutral word 'penalty'. We can plausibly believe that, when certain acts have been made illegal, so that these acts are crimes, our community can be morally justified in imposing certain penalties on those who knowingly commit these crimes.

Such penalties, we can admit, need to be morally justified, since they impose burdens on people, and such burdens are not deserved. But of the people who believe in retributive justice, nearly all believe that we are sometimes justified in imposing undeserved penalties. That is true, for example, in cases that involve strict liability. There are various penalties that people can be justifiably required to pay, even if they have not knowingly committed any crime, nor been negligent or to blame in other ways. Some examples are the fines or damages that some people are required to pay for harms that were caused by their young children.

In most kinds of case, we can plausibly claim that

> (W) though penalties cannot be just or unjust in the
> desert-implying retributive sense, such penalties can
> be *fair* or *unfair*.

When people knowingly commit some crime, or break some other rule or regulation, it may be fair to impose some penalties on these people, which may be either imprisonment or fines. Such penalties are, in some ways, like the prices that we know that we shall have to pay if we act in certain ways. In many cases, for example, we cannot reasonably expect to be permitted to take away someone's property unless we pay some price, in a free exchange, so that this property first becomes ours. In such cases, if we steal someone's property, and we are caught, we cannot reasonably object to paying some greater price, which would here be imposed on us as a penalty. The extra payment would be intended in part to cover the costs of our being caught and convicted, and in part to deter similar future crimes. Even if such penalties are not deserved, they may not be unfair, since they are the penalties that these people knew would be imposed on them if they commit these crimes, and they are caught and convicted. If these penalties would also do enough good, by deterring other crimes, these facts may be enough to make these penalties justified.

These claims do not apply to people who have not committed any crime. Since these people have not chosen to act in some way for which they knew that penalties would be imposed, it would be unfair to impose any great penalties on them. This unfairness provides a strong moral objection to imposing such penalties. And unless these people were falsely believed to have committed some crime, these penalties would also do nothing to deter future crimes. These facts would always, or nearly always, make such treatment wrong.

When we claim that it would be unfair to treat people in certain ways, we are not claiming that such treatment would be retributively unjust. This distinction is clearer in cases that don't involve any penalty or reward. If you were made to pay for something that you hadn't bought, or for some service that you hadn't received, that treatment would be *unfair*, though you don't *deserve* not to be treated in this way.

This account of justified punishment could be called the *Fair Warning View*. To illustrate this view, we can consider the importance of avoiding mistaken convictions. Suppose we knew that, if we had much stronger legal safeguards in the procedures of criminal trials, it would be true both that

> somewhat fewer innocent people would be mistakenly
> convicted and punished for murder,

and that

> many murderers would not be convicted, and many people
> would not later be deterred from committing murders.

We might be able to predict that, for each innocent person who is not mistakenly punished, at least two innocent people would later be murdered.

It is often claimed that, if we believe in retributive justice, we shall give more weight to avoiding mistaken convictions, and less weight to deterring later murders. But that may not be true. If we are Retributivists, we shall believe it to be bad when any innocent person is punished, since this person is not then being treated as he deserves. But we shall also believe it to be bad when any guilty person is *not* punished, since this person is also not being treated as he deserves. If we have stronger legal safeguards, so that many fewer murderers are punished, we may on the whole be less successful in treating people as we believe that they deserve to be treated.

If we are not Retributivists, we do not believe it to be in itself bad when murderers are not punished. Though we believe that innocent people do not deserve to be punished, we also believe that *guilty* people do not deserve to be punished. On our view, all punishment is in itself bad. We therefore have less reason for regret if, as one result of reducing the risks of mistaken convictions, we punish fewer murderers. We may also have a different reason to reduce these risks. On the Fair Warning View, it is in itself bad, because unfair, when anyone is punished for some crime that he or she has not committed.

Even if these views gave similar weight to avoiding mistaken convictions, our attitudes to punishment, and to the people who are punished, would be transformed by disbelief in retribution. We often have more reason to be sorry, not for the victim of some crime, but for the criminal. Compared with their victims, criminals have often lived more deprived and wretched lives. When we imprison such people, in order to deter future crimes, we should greatly regret what we are doing. We should regard these criminals as like people who are quarantined, because they have some dangerous and infectious disease. Any criminal's well-being matters just as much as ours.

Some of Kant's Arguments for his Formula of Universal Law

1

In the second section of the *Groundwork*, Kant writes:

> (A) All imperatives command either *hypothetically* or *categorically*. The former represent the practical necessity of a possible action as a means of attaining something else that one wills (or might will). The categorical imperative would be one which represented an action as objectively necessary of itself, without reference to another end. (G 414)

Kant here asserts that there are only two kinds of claim about what is practically necessary, or what we are required to do. Imperatives are *hypothetical* if they require us to do something as a means of achieving some end whose achievement we have willed. Imperatives are *categorical* if they require us to do something, not as a means of achieving any other end, but as an end, or for its own sake.

These are not, as Kant asserts, the only two kinds of imperative. Kant's remarks draw two distinctions, which combine to give us four possibilities. Some imperative may require us to act in some way either

	as a means of achieving some end,	or	not as a means, but as an end or for its own sake
and either			
if we will this act or the achievement of this end,	(1)		(2)
or			
whatever we will	(3)		(4)

All imperatives, Kant claims, are of types (1) or (4). Kant ignores (2) and (3). It does not matter if we ignore imperatives of type (2), which require us to do something for its own sake, if and because we will this act. It matters greatly, however, if we ignore imperatives of type (3). Categorical imperatives are unconditional, in the sense that they apply to us whatever we want or will. All such imperatives, Kant's remarks imply, require us to act in some way, not as a means of achieving some end, but only as an end, or for the sake of acting in this way. That is not true. Of the imperatives which apply to us whatever we want or will, some might require us to act in some way as a means of achieving some unconditionally required end.

At one point, Kant seems to acknowledge that there might be such imperatives. He writes:

> What serves the will as the objective ground of its self-
> determination is an *end*, and this, if it is given by reason
> alone, must hold equally for all rational beings . . . The
> subjective ground of desire is an *incentive*; the objective
> ground of volition is a *motive*, hence the distinction
> between subjective ends, which rest on incentives, and
> objective ends, which depend on motives, which hold
> for every rational being. (G 427–8)

Kant here claims that, while some ends are subjective, there are also *objective ends*, which reason gives to all rational beings. Some of these might be ends in the ordinary sense: something that we might try to achieve. These are what Kant calls *ends-to-be-produced*. Since Kant distinguishes between such objective ends and merely subjective ends, we would expect that, after describing a class of imperatives which are hypothetical, because they appeal to our subjective ends, Kant would describe a class of imperatives that are categorical, because they give us objective ends-to-be-produced. But Kant claims instead that all categorical imperatives declare some act to be necessary of itself, without reference to another end. This claim implies that there are no objective ends-to-be-produced given by reason to all rational beings. And in both the *Groundwork* and the *Second Critique*, Kant assumes that there are no such ends. Kant's formal Categorical Imperative may *indirectly* require us to try to achieve certain ends, as when Kant argues that his Formula of Universal Law implies that we are required to develop our talents. But that does not make this formula an imperative of type (3). Only ten years later, in his *Metaphysics of Morals*, does Kant claim that there are two such ends: our own perfection and the happiness of others.

Since Kant later claimed that there are two such objective ends-to-be-produced, it may seem not to matter that, in the *Groundwork* and the *Second Critique*, Kant assumes that there are no such ends. But this does matter. Kant's assumption makes a great difference to his arguments in these earlier, more important books.

To help us to assess these claims and arguments, we can next distinguish various senses in which Kant uses two of his most important terms: 'material' and 'formal'. These senses partly overlap with Kant's uses of 'hypothetical' and 'categorical'. In his most explicit definition, Kant writes:

> Practical principles are *formal* when they abstract from
> all subjective ends; they are *material* when they are
> grounded upon subjective ends, and hence on certain
> incentives (G 427–8).

Some imperative or principle 'abstracts' from our subjective ends, if this principle applies to us, or requires something from us, whatever we want or will. We can call such principles *normatively formal in sense 1*. Other principles apply to us only if we have certain desires, or subjective ends. We can call such principles *normatively material in sense 1*.

When some principle is in this sense normatively material, we can be *moved* to act on this principle, Kant assumes, only by a desire to achieve some subjective end. So we can also call such principles *motivationally material*. But when some principle is normatively formal in sense 1, because it applies to us whatever we want or will, our acceptance of this principle can move us to act, Kant claims, without the help of any the ordinary desires that Kant calls 'incentives'. We can call such principles *motivationally formal*.

We can call principles *teleological* if they require us to act in certain ways as a means of achieving some end. Kant sometimes uses the word 'matter' to refer, not only to subjective ends, but to any end-to-be-produced. Thus he defines the 'matter' of an action as 'what is to result from it' (G 428). Since teleological principles have a 'matter' in this wider sense, we can call such principles *normatively material in sense 2.*

There are also principles which are not teleological. Since these principles are *not* normatively *material* in sense 2, we can call them *normatively formal in sense 2.* These principles are *deontological* if they require us to act in some way as an end, or for its own sake, rather than as a means of achieving some other end. Two examples might be requirements not to lie, and not to injure anyone as a means of benefiting others.

Some principles are neither purely teleological nor purely deontological, since these principles require us to act in certain ways partly as an end, or for its own sake, and partly as a means of achieving some other end. That is true, for example, of the principles that require us to keep our promises, and pay our debts. Such principles are often called 'deontological' in a different sense that means 'not *purely* teleological'.

There is another kind of non-teleological principle. Rather than requiring us to act in certain ways, some principles impose some merely formal constraint on our decisions and our acts. One example is Kant's Formula of Universal Law, which requires us to act only on maxims that we could will to be universal laws. We can call such principles *normatively formal in sense 3.*

Principles that are *not*, in this sense, normatively formal we can call *substantive*, or *normatively material in sense 3.* Deontological principles, we should note, are in this sense material, since they require us to act in certain ways. Kant claims that his formula requires 'mere conformity to law as such, without appeal to any law that requires acting in certain ways' (G 402). Deontological principles *are*, precisely, laws that require us to act in certain ways.

We have, then, three normative senses of both 'formal' and 'material', and one motivational sense. When applied to principles, these senses can be summed up as follows:

motivationally material:	*motivationally formal*:
motivates us only with	motivates us all
the help of some desire	by itself
normatively material in	*normatively formal in*
sense 1, or *hypothetical*:	*sense 1*, or *categorical*:
applies to us only if	applies to us
and because there is	whatever we
something that we	want or will
want or will	
normatively material in	*normatively formal*
sense 2, or *teleological*:	*in sense 2*:
tells us to act in a certain	not teleological
way as a means of	
achieving some end	
normatively material in	*normatively formal*
sense 3, or *substantive*:	*in sense 3*:
tells us to act in	imposes only a
a certain way	general constraint
	on our maxims
	or our acts.

2

We can now turn to some of Kant's arguments for his Formula of Universal Law, which Kant also calls his *Formal Principle*, as I shall sometimes do below.

One of Kant's arguments, in *Groundwork 2*, assumes one of the claims that I have already discussed.   Kant writes:

> all imperatives command either hypothetically or
> categorically. The former represent the practical necessity of
> a possible action as a means of achieving something else that
> one wills (or might will). The categorical imperative would be
> one which represented an action as objectively necessary of
> itself, without reference to another end. (G 414)

Kant later writes:

> we want first to enquire whether the mere concept of a
> categorical imperative may not also provide its formula
> containing the proposition which alone can be a categorical
> imperative . . . When I think of a *hypothetical* imperative in
> general I do not know before hand what it will contain . . . But
> when I think of a *categorical* imperative, I know at once what
> it contains. For since the imperative contains, beyond the law,
> only the necessity that the maxim be in conformity with this
> law, while the law contains no condition to which it would
> be limited, nothing is left with which the maxim of the action
> should conform but the universality of a law as such, and this
> conformity alone is what the imperative properly represents
> as necessary. Hence there is only one categorical imperative,
> and it is this: Act only in accordance with that maxim through
> which you can at the same time will that it become a universal
> law. (G 420–1)

In these passages, Kant argues:

> (1) All principles or imperatives are either *hypothetical*,
> requiring us to act in some way as means of achieving some
> end that we have willed, or *categorical*, requiring us to act in
> some way as an end, or for its own sake only, rather than as a
> means of achieving any other end.

> (2) Categorical imperatives impose only a formal constraint
> on our maxims and our acts, since these imperatives require
> only conformity with the universality of a law as such.

Therefore

> There is only one categorical imperative, which
> requires us to act only on maxims that we could will
> to be universal laws.

This argument fails. Kant's premises are false, and even if they were
true, Kant's conclusion would not follow.

Both of Kant's premises, as we have seen, overlook those categorical imperatives which are teleological, requiring us to try to achieve some objective end-to-be-produced.

Kant's second premise also overlooks those categorical imperatives which are deontological, requiring us to act in some way partly or wholly for its own sake. Two examples would be requirements to keep our promises and not to lie. Such imperatives do not impose only a formal constraint.

As several writers note, Kant's conclusion involves a third mistake. Kant assumes that, if some imperative imposes only a formal constraint, this imperative must be his Formula, which requires us to act only on maxims that we could rationally will to be universal laws. That is not true, since there are other possible formal constraints. One example is a requirement to act only in ways in which we believe that it would be rational for everyone to act. This requirement is quite different from Kant's Formula. If we are Rational Egoists, for example, we shall believe that everyone is rationally required to try to do whatever would be best for themselves, though we could not rationally will it to be true that everyone acts in this way.

This mistake might be reparable. Kant might argue that, of the possible formal constraints, only his Formula of Universal Law meets some further requirement that any acceptable principle must meet. But this argument's other premises cannot be repaired. There is no hope of showing that, if some imperative is categorical, it must impose only a formal constraint.

Why did Kant make these mistakes? He may have had in mind, but failed to distinguish, the three senses in which imperatives can be normatively formal. If Kant had distinguished these senses, he would have seen that his argument assumes that being formal in sense 1 implies being formal sense 2, which implies being formal in sense 3. Kant could not have believed that these inferences are valid. The first inference assumes that, if some imperative applies to us whatever we want or will, it cannot require us to act in some way as a means of achieving some required end. That is obviously false. The second inference assumes that, if some imperative does not require us to try to achieve some end, it cannot require us to act in certain ways, but must impose only a formal constraint. That is also obviously false. Kant's failure to notice these points may be due to his preference for thinking at the most abstract level. Only that could explain how, in giving this argument, Kant overlooks the possibility of both teleological and deontological categorical imperatives. Kant thereby overlooks most of the moral principles that other people accept.

We can turn next to *Groundwork 1*. Consider first these remarks:

> an action from duty has its moral worth . . . in the principle of volition in accordance with which the act is done without regard for any object of the faculty of desire . . . For the will stands between its a priori principle, which is formal, and its a posteriori incentive, which is material, as at a crossroads; and since it must still be determined by something, it must be determined by the formal principle of volition if it does an action from duty, since every material principle has been withdrawn from it . . . [Hence] mere conformity to law as such, without having as its basis some law determined for certain actions, is what serves the will as its principle, and must so serve it if duty is not to be everywhere an empty delusion . . . (G 399–402)

Kant's argument here is this:

(1) An act has moral worth only when the agent's motive is to do his duty.

(2) Such an agent acts on a principle which is not material, since it does not appeal to any of his desires.

(3) Such a principle must be formal, requiring mere conformity to law as such.

Therefore

(4) This requirement is the only moral law.

In explaining his first premise, Kant compares two philanthropists (398). The first helps other people out of sympathy, or because he wants to make them happy. The second helps others because he believes that to be his duty. Of these people, Kant claims, the first is lovable, and deserves praise, but only the acts of the second have moral worth.

This may be Kant's least popular claim, damaging his reputation even more than his claim that we should not lie to prevent a murder. Kant's view about moral worth has, however, been well defended. And we don't need to consider such defences, since Kant's argument need not appeal to Kant's view about moral worth. Kant's first two premises could become

(5) When we act in some way because we believe this act to be our duty, we are acting on some principle which does not appeal to our desires.

With some qualifications which we can here ignore, this claim is true.

According to this argument's other premise, if some principle does not appeal to our desires, it must require what Kant calls mere conformity to law. That is not true. Such a principle might require us either to try to achieve some end, or to act in certain ways. Kant's argument again overlooks all teleological or deontological principles.

Why did Kant assume that, if some principle does not appeal to our desires, it must require mere conformity to law? He may again have been misled by his failure to distinguish between his different uses of the words 'material' and 'formal'. The will, Kant writes:

must be determined by the formal principle of volition if it does an action from duty, since every material principle has been withdrawn from it . . .

Kant here assumes that, if some principle is not normatively material in sense 1, because it does not appeal to our desires, this principle must be normatively formal in sense 3, imposing only a formal constraint on what we will. That is not true. Though such a principle must be normatively formal in sense 1, it might not be normatively formal in either sense 3, or sense 2. Kant's use of the word 'formal' blurs these distinctions.

There is another way in which Kant may have gone astray. In the same passage, Kant writes:

> the purposes we may have for our actions, and their
> effects as ends and incentives of the will, can give no actions
> unconditional and moral worth . . . In what, then, can this
> worth lie . . . ? It can lie nowhere else than in the principle of
> the will without regard for the ends that can be brought about
> by such an action. (G 399–400)

In the first sentence here, Kant's use of the word 'ends' must refer to our subjective or desire-based ends. An act's moral worth lies, Kant claims, not in the agent's subjective end, but in the agent's motive, which is to do his duty. But when Kant later writes 'without regard for the ends that can be brought about by such an action', he seems to shift, without noticing this, to the wider use of 'end' that would cover all possible ends-to-be-produced, including ends that are objective, or categorically required. This may be why Kant mistakenly concludes that the moral law must be formal in the sense of having no 'regard for the ends' that our acts might bring about.

Groundwork 1 suggests another argument.   Kant writes:

> . . . an action from duty is to put aside entirely the influence
> of inclination and with it every object of the will; hence there
> is left for the will nothing that could determine it except
> objectively the law and subjectively pure respect for this
> practical law . . . But what kind of law can that be, the
> representation of which must determine the will, even without
> regard for the effect expected from it . . . ? Since I have
> deprived the will of every impulse that could arise for it from
> obeying some law, nothing is left but the conformity of actions
> as such with universal law, which alone is to serve the will as
> its principle, that is: I ought never to act except in such a way
> that I could also will that my maxim should become
> a universal law. (G 400–2)

Kant here argues:

(1) When our motive in acting is to do our duty, we must be acting on some principle whose acceptance motivates us without the help of any desire for our act's effects.

(2) For some principle to have such motivating force, it must be purely formal, requiring only that our acts conform with universal law.

(3) Such a principle must require that we act only on maxims that we could will to be universal laws.

Therefore

(4) This requirement is the only moral law.

Kant's first premise here is true. Humeans might claim that, when our motive in acting is to do our duty, we must be moved by a desire to do our duty. But even if that were true, we would not be being moved by a desire for our act's effects.

Premise (2), however, is false. Return to Kant's philanthropist who promotes the happiness of others, not because he wants to make them happy, but because he believes this act to be his duty. Kant's argument implies that, since this person is not moved by a desire for his act's effects, he must be acting on some principle which is purely formal, requiring only that our acts conform with universal law. That is not so. This person might be acting on a principle that requires us to promote the happiness of others.

Premise (3), as we have seen, is also false, since a principle could be purely formal without requiring that we act on universalizable maxims.

Though premise (3) might be repaired, nothing can be done with premise (2). There is no hope of showing that, when our motive is to do our duty, we must be acting on some principle which is purely formal.

Why did Kant make this assumption? When our motive is to do our duty, this motive is purely formal in the sense that it does not involve, or abstracts from, the *content* of our duty. This feature of our *motive* Kant may have mistakenly transferred to the *principle* on which we act. Jerome Schneewind writes that, on Kant's view, a moral agent acts on principle, and that the only principle available, because she is not moved by the content of her action, must be formal. The agent of good will must therefore be moved by the bare lawfulness of the act.

Though such a person may be, in one sense, moved by 'the bare lawfulness' of her act, this sense is only that this person's motive is to do her duty. That leaves it open what this person believes her duty to be. She may be acting on some principle which is *not* formal, since it requires her either to try to achieve some end, or to act in some way for its own sake.

Kant may also be again misled by overlooking his distinctions between different kinds of end. In another summary of Kant's argument, Nelson Potter writes:

All action to which we are determined by some subjective end . . . is action whose maxim is without 'moral content' . . . So the maxim of action from duty must be a maxim which is determined by no such end . . . The only other thing which could determine us to action would be some 'formal' principle, i.e. a principle containing no reference to any end.

As Potter fails to note, there is here a fatal slide from the claim that acts from duty must not be determined by *subjective* ends, to the claim that such acts must be determined by a principle which does not refer to *any* end, not even an objectively required end-to-be-produced. Schneewind similarly writes:

Given Kant's claim that means-ends necessity is inadequate for morality, it is plain that he must think there is another law of rational willing, and so another kind of 'ought' or 'imperative'. The kind of 'ought' that does not depend on the agent's ends arises from the moral law . . . [This law] Kant holds, can only be the form of lawfulness itself, because nothing else is left once all content has been rejected.

There is here the same unnoticed slide. If some law does not depend on the agent's ends, it may still have *content*, requiring more than the mere form of lawfulness. And this law might require the agent to try to achieve some end. Mary Gregor similarly writes:

> [if] principles of reason based on a desire for some end are all
> conditioned principles, the unconditioned necessity of duty
> implies that the principle prescribing duty must be a merely
> formal principle . . . it follows . . . that this principle says
> nothing at all about our ends. It neither commands nor
> forbids the adoption of any end, but merely sets a limiting
> condition on our actions . . .

These claims assume that, if some principle does not appeal to our desire for some subjective end, it cannot say anything about our ends, and can neither command nor forbid the adoption of any end. That does not follow.

It may be suggested that, in making these remarks, I have misinterpreted Kant. When Kant claims that moral principles must be purely formal, he may not mean that these principles cannot be material in the sense of requiring us to try to achieve certain ends. Kant may be making some other point. Consider, for example, these remarks in the *Second Critique*:

> a free will must find a determining ground in the law but
> independently of the *matter* of the law. But besides the
> matter of the law, nothing further is contained in it than
> the lawgiving form. (CPR 29)

Kant may seem here to assume that any practical law *has* matter, which is what this law tells us to try to achieve. His point may seem to be only that, though any law is, in this sense, 'material', our motive in following this law—or the determining ground of our will—should be provided not by this law's matter, but by the fact that it has *the form of a moral law*. And this may seem to be Kant's point, in the *Groundwork*, when he discusses his unsympathetic philanthropist. When Kant claims that, to act out of duty, we must be moved by a principle's law-giving form, he may mean only that we must be moved by our belief that our act is a duty. That could be true of Kant's philanthropist even if this person is acting on a principle which has 'matter' in the sense that it requires him to promote the happiness of others.

This suggested reading seems to me doubtful. Nor could this suggestion repair Kant's arguments. After discussing this philanthropist, Kant takes his argument to show that his Formal Principle is the only moral law. That could not be shown if Kant meant only that this man is moved by a belief that his act is a duty.

Consider next another passage in the *Second Critique*:

> The matter of a practical principle is the object of the will.
> This is either the determining ground of the will or it is not.
> If it is the determining ground of the will, then the rule of
> the will is subject to an empirical condition . . . and so is not
> a practical law. Now if we abstract from the law everything
> material, that is, every object of the will (as its determining
> ground), all that remains is the mere *form* of giving universal
> law. Therefore, either a rational being cannot think of his . . .
> maxims, as being at the same time universal laws, or he must
> assume that their mere form, by which they are fit for a giving
> of universal law, of itself and alone makes them practical
> laws. (CPR 27)

When Kant refers here to 'the mere *form* of giving universal law', he cannot mean 'the mere form of a moral law'. His point cannot be that, if principles have the form of a moral law, that alone makes them practical laws. Kant takes this argument to show that, since we must 'abstract from the law everything material', we ought to act only on maxims that we could will to be universal, because only these maxims 'are fit for a giving of universal law'. Kant must be referring here to his Formula of Universal Law.

In the paragraph just quoted, Kant comes close to seeing that his argument is invalid. The *Second Critique* was the fastest written of Kant's major works, and this paragraph shows the speed with which Kant wrote. What Kant calls the 'matter' of a principle, or the 'object of the will', is the object or aim which this principle tells us to try to achieve. This object would be the will's 'determining ground' if we were moved to act upon this principle by a desire to achieve this object.

After remarking that this object either is *or is not* the will's determining ground, Kant claims that, if we abstract from the law every object of the will which is its determining ground, we are left only with the mere form of giving universal law. That is not so, as Kant's earlier remark implies. We may be left with some object of the will which is *not* the will's determining ground. One such object might be the happiness of others. We might be moved to try to achieve this object, not because we want to make others happy, but out of duty and our belief that the happiness of others is a categorically required end. We would not then be acting on a principle that was purely formal. So Kant's argument again fails to support his conclusion.

Consider next Kant's summary of his view:

> The sole principle of morality consists in independence
> from all matter of the law (i.e. a desired object) and in the
> accompanying determination of choice by the mere form of
> giving universal law which a maxim must be capable of
> having. (CPR 33)

Kant here forgets the difference between his two uses of the phrase 'the matter of the law'. On Kant's narrower use, this 'matter' is a desired object. On Kant's wider use, a law's 'matter' is whatever this law tells us to try to achieve, which might be some categorically required end. Kant assumes that, if some moral principle does not have 'matter' in his narrower sense, it cannot have 'matter' in this wider sense. This leads him to conclude that, if some moral principle does not appeal to a desired object, it must require the mere form of giving universal law. That is not true. As before, Kant overlooks all substantive categorical principles.

3

Near the end of *Groundwork 2*, Kant reviews all possible alternatives to his Formula of Universal Law. Some of these principles Kant calls 'empirical' in the sense that they appeal to our desires. Other principles he calls 'rational' in the sense that they appeal to 'grounds of morality' which are 'based on reason'. Kant gives, as one example, a principle that requires us to promote our own perfection.

Kant defends his Formula by arguing against all other principles. The concept of perfection, he objects, is too vague. But Kant could not claim that *all* principles which are 'based on reason' must be too vague; so he must give some other argument against these other principles. At this critical point, Kant writes:

> I believe that I may be excused from a lengthy refutation of all these doctrines. That is so easy . . . that it would be merely superfluous labour. (G 443)

Kant's 'refutation' of all other principles takes only one paragraph. This begins:

> Whenever an object of the will has to be laid down as the basis for prescribing the rule that determines the will, there the rule is none other than heteronomy; the imperative is conditional, namely: *if* or *because* one wills this object, one ought to act in such or such a way; hence it can never command morally, that is, categorically. Whether the object determines the will by means of inclination, as with the principle of one's own happiness, or by means of reason directed to objects of our possible volition in general, as with the principle of perfection, the will never determines itself *directly*, just by the representation of an action, but only by means of an incentive that the anticipated effect of the action has upon the will . . . (G 444)

Kant here claims that all other principles can provide only hypothetical imperatives. To defend this claim, Kant first repeats his distinction between the two ways in which we can be moved to act on these other principles. When we are moved to act on these principles, Kant writes, our will may be determined either by means of inclination, as in the case of empirical principles, 'or *by means of reason*', as in the case of rational principles. But Kant then forgets this second possibility, since he goes on to claim that, in both these cases, our will would be determined by means of an 'incentive' which the anticipated effect of our act had upon our will. Kant distinguished earlier between *incentives*, which he defines as the 'subjective grounds of desire', and *motives*, which he defines as 'objective ends' or 'grounds of volition', which are 'given by reason alone' to all rational beings. So, when Kant claims that it can be only some *incentive* which moves us to act on these rational principles, he is inconsistently denying that, as he has just conceded, we could be moved to act on such principles not by an inclination but by reason.

Kant's argument requires him to deny that, when acting on such a rational principle, we could be moved by reason. To justify this denial, Kant might claim that reason does not give us any objective ends-to-be-produced. But though Kant's arguments in the *Groundwork* assume that reason gives us no such ends, Kant says nothing that supports this claim. And if some rational principle requires us to try to achieve such an objective end, we could act upon this principle in the same reason-provided way in which we can act upon Kant's Formula of Universal Law.

The *Second Critique* contains another version of Kant's 'refutation'. Kant writes:

> If we now compare our *formal* supreme principle of pure
> practical reason . . . with all previous *material* principles of
> morality, we can set forth all the rest, as such, in a table in
> which all possible cases are actually exhausted, except the one
> formal principle . . .
>
> Practical Material Determining Grounds in the principle of
> morality:

	Subjective	
External		*Internal*
Education (Montaigne)		Physical feeling (Epicurus)
The civil constitution (Mandeville)		Moral feeling (Hutcheson)
	Objective	
External		*Internal*
Perfection (Wolff and the Stoics)		The will of God (Crusius and others)

Those in the first group are without exception empirical and obviously not at all qualified for the universal principle of morality. But those in the second group are based on reason. . . . the concept of perfection in the *practical* sense is the fitness or adequacy of a thing for all sorts of ends. This perfection, as a characteristic of the human being . . . is nothing other than talent and . . . skill. The supreme perfection in *substance*, that is, God . . . is the adequacy of this being to all ends in general. Now, if ends must first be given to us, in relation to which alone the concept of *perfection* . . . can be the determining ground of the will; and if an end as an *object* which must precede the determination of the will . . . is always empirical; then it can serve as the Epicurean principle of the doctrine of happiness but never as the pure rational principle of the doctrine of morals . . . so too, talents and their development . . . or the will of God if agreement with it is taken as the object of the will without an antecedent practical principle independent of this idea, can become motives of the will only by means of the happiness we expect from them; from this it follows, *first*, that all the principles exhibited here are *material*; second, that they include all possible material principles; and, finally . . . that since material principles are quite unfit to be the supreme moral law . . . the formal practical principle of pure reason . . . is the *sole* principle that can *possibly* be fit for categorical imperatives . . . (CPR 39–41)

In this passage, Kant argues:

There are only two material principles which might be objective and based on reason: the principles of perfection and of obedience to God's will.

The concept of *perfection* is the concept of something's fitness or adequacy as a means of achieving ends. God is supremely perfect because he is an adequate means to every end.

Since the idea of perfection cannot move us to act unless we have some end to which this perfection is a means, and since all such ends are empirical, or given by our desires, the principle of perfection cannot be moral, but can serve only as the Epicurean principle of pursuing our own happiness.

The principle of obeying God's will also cannot move us to act except through the expectation of our own happiness.

Therefore

These principles are material, and are the only possible material principles.

Material principles cannot be moral laws.

Therefore

Kant's Formula is the only moral law.

Kant's premises are all false; and even if they were true, Kant's conclusions would not follow. Kant writes, rather charmingly, that his table 'proves visually' that there are no other possible objective material principles; but 'possible' does not mean 'shown in Kant's table'. Perfection is not all instrumental. God's perfection could not be that of an ideal Swiss army knife, or all-purpose tool. It is not true that all of our ends are given by our desires, since we can have objective ends that are given to us by reason. If we act on some principle either of perfection or of obedience to God's will, our motive can be something other than a desire for our own happiness. Even if our motive would have to be this desire, that would not show that these are the only possible material principles. It is not true that material principles cannot be moral laws. And even if that were true, Kant's Formula is not the only formal principle, so this argument could not show that Kant's Formula is the only moral law.

Kant gives some other arguments for his Formula of Universal Law. These other arguments, I believe, also fail. But that does not matter. Moral principles can be justified by their intrinsic plausibility, and by their ability to support and guide our other moral beliefs. I have argued that, with some revisions, Kant's Formula provides a remarkably successful version of Contractualism, which Kant could defensibly, though not undeniably, claim to be the supreme moral law.

Kant's Claims about the Good

The Latin language has a defect, Kant writes, since it uses the words *bonum* and *malum* in two senses, which German distinguishes. Kant's claims can also be applied to the English words *good* and *bad*. When widened in this way, Kant's claims would be these. Where Latin has to use the same word *bonum*, and English has to use the same word *good*, German distinguishes between *das Gute* and *das Wohl*. And, where Latin has to use *malum*, and English has to use *bad*, German distinguishes between *das Böse* and *das Übel* (or *das Weh*). (CPR 59–60)

These claims are mistaken. Latin and English have words whose meaning is similar to 'das Wohl'. Two such words in English are 'well-being' and 'happiness'. And Latin and English have words whose meaning is similar to 'das Übel' and 'das Weh'. Three such words in English are 'ill-being', 'suffering', and 'woe'. The language which is impoverished is not, as Kant claims, Latin, or English, but Kant's own version of German. Kant uses 'Gute' and 'Böse' to mean only 'morally good' and 'morally bad'. In English and other versions of German, we can express the thought that, if someone suffers, that is both bad for this person, and a bad event. Kant's version of German cannot express such thoughts, and Kant seems not to understand them.

Consider, for example, Kant's remarks about the Latin sentence:

> *Nihil appetimus nisi sub ratione boni, nihil aversamur nisi sub ratione mali,*

or, in English,

> We want nothing except what we believe to be good, and we try to avoid nothing except what we believe to be bad.

Kant complains that, given the ambiguity of the words 'boni' and 'mali', this 'scholastic formula' is 'detrimental to philosophy'. This formula, Kant writes,

> is at least very doubtful if it is translated as:

>> we desire nothing except with a view to our well-being
>> or woe,

> whereas if it is translated:

>> we will nothing under the direction of reason except insofar
>> as we hold it to be morally good or bad,

> it is indubitably certain and at the same time quite clearly
> expressed.

Kant's translations are both incorrect. This 'scholastic formula' does not use 'boni' and 'mali' to mean 'well-being' and 'woe'. Nor does it use these words to mean only 'morally good' and 'morally bad'. This formula rightly assumes that we want many things because we believe them to be either morally or *non*-morally good. On Kant's second proposed translation, this formula would not be, as Kant claims, 'indubitably certain'. It would be seriously mistaken. That is well shown by the case of woe, or suffering. On Kant's proposal, for us to have a reason to want ourselves not to suffer—or, in his words, for us to 'will' this 'under the direction of reason'—our suffering would have to be morally bad. Since suffering is not morally bad, Kant's view implies that we have no such reason.

It might be suggested that I am misreading Kant, since Kant may use 'das Böse' in a way that covers non-moral badness. The word 'evil' is so used in many discussions of the problem of evil, since most theologians rightly regard suffering as part of this problem. My reading, however, seems to be correct. Kant continues:

> . . . good or evil is, strictly speaking, applied to actions, not to
> the person's state of feeling . . . Thus one may always laugh
> at the Stoic who in the most intense pains of gout cried out,
> 'Pain, however you torment me, I will still never admit that

you are something evil (*kakon, malum*)', nevertheless, he was
right. He felt that it was something bad, and he betrayed that
in his cry; but that anything evil attached to him he had no
reason to concede . . . (CPR 60)

As Irwin notes, Kant misunderstands this Stoic claim. This Stoic didn't
mean that the pains of gout aren't morally bad, in the sense that
applies only to agents and to acts. That claim would be trivial, since no
one believes that pain is in that sense bad. The Stoic was making the
controversial claim that his pain isn't even *non-morally* bad for him, or
a bad state to be in.

Consider next Kant's remarks about Hedonism. Kant writes that,
since good and evil must

always be appraised by reason and hence through concepts,
which can be universally communicated, not through mere
feeling . . . a philosopher who believed that he had to put a
feeling of pleasure at the basis of his practical appraisal would
have to call that good which is a means to the agreeable, and
evil that which is a cause of disagreeableness and of pain; for
appraisal of the relation of means to ends certainly belongs to
reason. (CPR 58)

Kant's thinking here is close to Hume's. Kant assumes that, since
pleasure and pain are feelings, they cannot be appraised by reason,
and judged to be good or bad. The most that hedonists could claim,
he says, is that things are good if they produce pleasure, and bad
if they produce pain, since reason is capable of judging that one
thing produces another. Kant understates the implications of this
view. If pleasure cannot be in itself good, hedonists could not call
something good because it produces pleasure. For something to be
good because of its effects, its effects must be good. Hedonists could
at most claim that some things are good, because they are effective,
as a *means* of producing pleasure. But Hedonists would have to admit
that other things are in the same sense good as a means of producing
pain. So, on Kant's view, no form of normative Hedonism would
make sense.

Why does Kant believe that, since pleasure and pain are feelings, they cannot be appraised by reason?   Kant writes:

> the usage of language . . . demands that good and evil be
> judged by reason and thus through concepts which alone
> can be universally communicated and not by mere sensation
> which is limited to individual subjects and their
> susceptibility. (CPR 58)

This remark suggests that we could not rationally judge that it was bad to be in pain, since such a judgment would have to be made with public and communicable concepts, and not with a private sensation. But when we judge that pain is bad, that judgment is not a sensation. It is a judgment *about* a sensation, made with the communicable concepts *pain* and *bad*. Nor could Kant be assuming that, since the word 'pain' refers to a private sensation, this word has no communicable meaning. Kant does not deny that we can refer to pain. Kant's point must be that the concept *bad* cannot be applied to a sensation. As he explicitly claims,

> good or evil is, strictly speaking, applied to actions, not to the
> person's state of feeling. (CPR 60)

Kant seems to make this claim because he either lacks, or rejects, the concept of something's being in itself non-morally good or bad. If we believe that events or states can be non-morally bad, we have no reason to deny that it can be bad to be in pain. Nothing is more clearly bad, in this non-moral sense, than being in great agony.

Kant's views about what is good or bad may be in part explained by the fact that he makes little use of the concept of a normative reason. Kant's main normative concepts are *required*, *permitted*, and *forbidden*. These concepts cannot express the thought that some things are in themselves good, or worth achieving, and others are in themselves bad, or worth avoiding or preventing. Kant says that he uses 'good' to mean 'practically necessary'. That is not what 'good' means. Something can be good, even though some available alternative would be even better. To understand this kind of goodness, or badness, we must be able to have the thought that certain properties or facts give us reasons, by counting in favour of our having some desire, or acting in some way. Pain is bad in the sense that its nature gives us reasons to want and to try to avoid being in pain.

Kant may, at certain points, have such thoughts. Thus he writes:

> What we are to call good must be an object of the faculty of desire in the judgment of every reasonable human being, and evil an object of aversion in the eyes of everyone. (CPR 61)

And he writes:

> Someone who submits to a surgical operation feels it no doubt as an ill, but through reason he and everyone else pronounces it good. (CPR 61)

Kant is unlikely to mean that such an operation is morally good, and he may not mean only that this operation is, like a murderer's poison, good as a means. Kant may mean that this operation has effects which are good in the non-moral sense, since it saves this person's life. And in writing 'feels it . . . as an ill, but through reason . . . pronounces it good', Kant seems to suggest that, in being an ill, this pain is bad. But despite such passages, Kant often claims that 'good' or 'evil' cannot be applied to states of feeling, and that well-being and woe cannot be in themselves good or bad. Thus he writes:

> The end itself, the enjoyment that we seek, is . . . not a *good* but a state of *well-being*, not a concept of reason but an empirical concept of an object of feeling . . . (CPR 62)

This feature of Kant's view is well shown by his claims about the principle of prudence. Kant often calls this principle a merely hypothetical imperative, assuming that it applies to us only because we want to promote our own future happiness. In its only important form, the principle of prudence is *not* hypothetical. According to this principle, even if we don't care about some act's likely effects on our future happiness—as some young smokers don't care about the cancer they may cause themselves to have in forty years—we have reasons to care, and we ought rationally to care. Dying early from lung cancer is not morally bad. But such deaths, and the suffering they cause, are in themselves bad for people, and impersonally bad. In much of his writing, as I have said, Kant seems not to have recognized these kinds of badness, and our non-moral reasons to care about them, and to prevent them if we can. This creates a huge gap in Kant's view. Practical reason, Kant suggests, makes only two kinds of claim. At one extreme, there is moral duty; at the other, instrumental rationality. There is little but a wasteland in between. If we are taught such a view, but we then cease to believe in moral duty, we shall believe only in instrumental rationality. That is the only kind of rationality in which many people now believe.

Autonomy and Categorical Imperatives

The moral law, Kant claims, is a categorical imperative. We are subject to this law, Kant also claims, only if we give it to ourselves. If these claims are taken seriously, they cannot both be true.

Kant writes:

> If we look back upon all previous efforts that have ever been made to discover the principle of morality, we need not wonder why all of them had to fail. It was seen that the human being is bound to laws by his duty; but it never occurred to them that he is subject only to laws given by himself but still universal and that he is obligated only to act in conformity with his own will . . . I shall call this basic principle the principle of the autonomy of the will in contrast with every other, which I accordingly count as heteronomy . . . (G 432–2)

According to this 'basic principle', which we can call Kant's

> *Autonomy Thesis*: We are subject only to principles that we give to ourselves as laws, and obligated only to act in conformity with our own will.

There are two other relevant possibilities. According to Nihilists, we are not subject to any principles, even if we give them to ourselves as laws. We can ignore that possibility here. According to what we can call

> *The Heteronomy Thesis*: We are subject to certain principles, and obligated to act in conformity with them, whether or not we give these principles to ourselves as laws, and whatever we will.

Though Kant does not explicitly refer to this thesis, he says that he will 'count as heteronomy' all principles which are not compatible with his Autonomy Thesis, and the Heteronomy Thesis is what all such other principles have in common.

We are *subject* to some principle when this principle applies to us. So we can call principles

> *autonomous* when they apply to us only if we give them to ourselves as laws,

and

> *heteronomous* when they apply to us whether or not we give them to ourselves as laws.

I shall return to the question of what Kant means by our *giving* ourselves some principle *as a law*.

As we have seen, Kant draws another, partly similar distinction. Principles are

> *hypothetical* imperatives if they require us to act in some way as a means of achieving some end whose achievement we have willed,

and

> *categorical* imperatives if they require us to act in some way whether or not we have willed the achievement of some end.

Hypothetical imperatives, Kant also writes, say that

> I ought to do something *because I will something else*. The moral and therefore *categorical* imperative in contrast says: I ought to do something even though I have not willed anything else. (G 441)

Kant's second sentence is ambiguous. He may mean that a categorical imperative applies to us unconditionally, whatever we have willed. But this sentence could be read more literally. Kant may instead mean that, though a categorical imperative applies to us only because we have willed that to be so, this imperative applies to us even if we have not *also* willed something *else*.   On this reading, unlike hypothetical imperatives, a categorical imperative applies to us even if we have not also willed the achievement of some end.

With these distinctions we can describe four kinds of imperative.

	Some imperative may apply to us either	
	only if and because we have willed that to be so	or whether or not we have willed that to be so
and either		
only if and because we have willed the achievement of some end	strongly hypothetical	weakly hypothetical
or		
whether or not we have willed the achievement of some end	weakly categorical	strongly categorical

According to Kant's Autonomy Thesis, we are subject only to principles or imperatives that we give to ourselves as laws, and obligated only to act in conformity with our own will.   This thesis implies that

> (1) hypothetical imperatives are strongly hypothetical, since these imperatives apply to us only if and because we have both willed them to apply to us, and willed the achievement of some end,

and that

> (2) categorical imperatives are weakly categorical, since these imperatives apply to us only if and because we have willed that to be so.

According to the Heteronomy Thesis, we are subject to certain principles or imperatives, and obligated to act in conformity with them, whether or not we give these imperatives to ourselves as laws. This thesis implies that

> (3) hypothetical imperatives are weakly hypothetical, since these imperatives apply to us only if and because we have willed the achievement of some end,

and that

> (4) categorical imperatives are strongly categorical, since these imperatives apply to us unconditionally, whatever we have willed.

We can now return to Kant's claim that the moral law is a categorical imperative. If Kant means that the moral law is a *strongly* categorical imperative, Kant must reject his Autonomy Thesis. As we have just seen, only *heteronomous* imperatives can be strongly categorical.

Kant may instead mean that the moral law is a *weakly* categorical imperative. But as I shall now argue, we ought to reject this claim, because we ought to reject Kant's Autonomy Thesis.

Kant writes:

> reason commands what ought to happen (G 408).

> reason alone . . . gives the law . . . (G 457)

> we stand under a discipline of reason, and in all our maxims we must not forget our subjection to it, or . . . detract anything from the authority of the law . . . (CPR 82)

Such remarks conflict with Kant's Autonomy Thesis. If reason alone gives the law, and we are subject to reason's laws, we are not subject only to laws that we give to ourselves.

Kant saw no conflict here. He assumes that, just as each of us has a will, each of us has, or is, *a reason*. He writes, for example, 'one cannot possibly think of a reason that would consciously receive direction from any other quarter with respect to its judgments . . .' (G 448). Kant therefore claims

> The law by virtue of which I regard myself under obligation
> . . . proceeds from my own pure practical reason, and in being
> constrained by my own reason, I am also the one constraining
> myself. (MM 418)

Such claims, I believe, are indefensible. Consider first the laws that govern theoretical reasoning. Such reasoning, it is sometimes said, should obey the laws of logic. But we need a distinction here. Consider, for example, two logical laws:

> *Non-Contradiction*: No proposition can be both true and false.

> *Modus Ponens*: If it is true both that *P* and that *If P, then Q*, it must be true that *Q*.

These laws are not normative, nor could our reasoning obey these laws. What we can obey are two closely related epistemic principles or laws. According to

> *the Non-Contradiction Requirement*: We ought not to have contradictory beliefs.

According to

> *the Modus Ponens Requirement*: We ought not to believe both that *P*, and that *If P, then Q,* without also believing *Q*.

Kant claims that, since reason is subject only to laws which it gives to itself, reason must regard itself as the source or author of such requirements. We can accept these metaphorical claims if Kant means only that these laws are rational requirements.

According to Kant's Autonomy Thesis, I am subject to these requirements because I give them to myself as laws. I, Derek Parfit, give myself the law that requires me to avoid contradictory beliefs. Only a madman could think that. Nor would it help to say that it is *my reason* which requires that I avoid such beliefs. Kant's phrase 'my reason' could refer only to my rationality. My epistemic rationality is my ability to be aware of epistemic reasons and requirements, and to respond to both of these in my beliefs. There is no sense in which these abilities could be the source or author of these reasons and requirements. Nor could I or my rationality be the source or author of practical imperatives, such as the moral law.

It may be objected that, in making these remarks, I am not discussing Kant in his own terms.   For example, Kant writes:

> to think of a human being who is accused by his conscience
> as one and the same person as the judge is . . . absurd . . . a
> human being's conscience will, accordingly, have to think
> of *someone other* than himself (i.e. other than the human
> being as such) as the judge of his actions . . . This requires
> clarification, if reason is not to fall into self-contradiction.
> I, the prosecutor and yet the accused as well, am the same
> *human being* (numerically identical). But the human being
> as the subject of the moral lawgiving which proceeds from
> the concept of freedom and in which he is subject to a law
> that he gives himself (*homo noumenon*) is to be regarded
> as another (of a different kind) from the human being as a
> sensorily affected being endowed with reason, though only
> in a practical respect . . . (MM 438 and note)

In this passage, Kant claims that the human being both *is* and *is not* one and the same person or human being as his inner judge and prosecutor, since as a sensorily affected being endowed with reason he both *is* the same as—but ought also to be regarded (though only practically) as being *not* the same as—his noumenal self. A philosopher who could make such claims might seem likely to dismiss as quibbling my claim that I am not pure reason.

Kant, I believe, would not have responded in this way. Kant was rightly proud of having created what he called 'the critical philosophy'; and such philosophy, he writes, 'must proceed as precisely . . . as any geometer in his work' (CPR 92). Given Kant's great originality, and the difficulty of many of the questions which he tried to answer, it is not surprising that he often failed to be precise. And the answers to some of Kant's questions could not be precise. But to take Kant seriously in his own critical terms, we should try to state his ideas, and to assess his arguments, as clearly and carefully as we can.

Kant would not have believed that I, Derek Parfit, am pure reason. So, if pure reason gives me certain laws, I do not give myself these laws. And in being subject to these laws, I am not subject only to laws which I give myself. These truths, which Kant would have accepted, contradict Kant's Autonomy Thesis.

Some writers suggest that, when Kant talks of our *giving* ourselves some law, he uses 'give' in a different sense from that in which he claims that 'reason alone . . . gives the law'. Kant could then without contradiction claim that we give ourselves the laws that, in a different sense, reason alone gives. On the most plausible suggestion of this kind, when Kant talks of our giving ourselves some law, he means only that we *accept* this law, believing it to be a rational or moral requirement. Hill, for example, writes:

> The sense in which the principles of autonomy are 'imposed on oneself by oneself' is puzzling, but at least it is clear that Kant did not regard this as an arbitrary, optional choice but as a commitment that clear thinking reveals, implicit in all efforts to will rationally, the way one may think that commitment to basic principles of logic is implicit in all efforts to think and understand . . . a will with autonomy accepts for itself rational constraints independently of any desires and other 'alien' influences.

Korsgaard similarly writes:

> you might pay your taxes . . . because you think everyone should pay their share, or because you think that people should obey laws made by popular legislation. These would be, in an ordinary sense, examples of autonomy—of giving the law to yourself because of some commitment to it or belief in it as a law.

On this reading, Kant's Autonomy Thesis could be restated as

> *The Endorsement Thesis*: We are subject only to principles that we ourselves accept.

According to this version of Kant's view, there are some principles which reason gives to us as laws, in the sense that these principles are rational requirements. But we are *subject* to such principles, and obligated to think and act in conformity with them, only if and because we accept these principles, or believe them to be true.

This version of the Autonomy Thesis, though more modest, has striking implications. On this view, when applied to Korsgaard's example, people ought to pay their share only if they themselves believe that they ought to pay. If we don't accept Kant's Formula of Universal Law, this formula does not apply to us. And if we accepted no moral principles, we would have no obligations, nor could any of our acts be wrong.

These would be unacceptable conclusions. The moral law, Kant claims, is a categorical imperative. I suggested earlier that, if Kant keeps his Autonomy Thesis, he might claim that the moral law is at least *weakly* categorical. We are subject to Kant's Formula, he might say, if we accept this formula. But Kant's Formula would not then be a *categorical* imperative. Moral laws, Kant claims, apply to all rational beings. If Kant's Formula did not apply to those rational beings who don't accept this formula, this formula could not be a moral law.

Kant might reply that everyone accepts his formula. This formula, Kant claims, 'is the sole law which the will of every rational being imposes on itself' (G 444). Since this claim cannot be an empirical generalization, Kant must mean that all rational beings *necessarily* accept this formula.

In what sense might it be necessary that everyone accepts Kant's Formula of Universal Law? At one point, Kant asks

> But why, then, *ought* I to subject myself to this principle?
> (G 449)

Kant then writes that, unless we can answer this question, we shall not have shown the moral law's 'validity and the practical necessity of subjecting oneself to it'. These remarks suggest that, for Kant's Formula to be valid, it must be *normatively* necessary that we accept this formula.

Given Kant's Autonomy Thesis, this suggestion raises two problems. First, even if we ought to accept Kant's Formula, that does not imply that we *do* accept this formula. And on both readings of the Autonomy Thesis, if we don't accept Kant's Formula, it does not apply to us.

Second, if we don't accept Kant's Formula, Kant's Autonomy Thesis undermines the claim that we *ought* to accept, or are *required* to accept, this formula. According to Kant's Thesis, we are required to accept Kant's Formula only if we ourselves accept this requirement. If we do not accept this requirement, it does not apply to us. Nor would it help to claim that we are required to accept this requirement to accept Kant's Formula. That could not be true unless we accept this second requirement, and so on for ever. There is an infinite regress here, of the kind that is vicious rather than benign.

Given these problems, Kant might appeal instead to some kind of *non-normative* necessity. Return to the principles that govern theoretical reasoning, such as the Non-Contradiction and Modus Ponens Requirements. On Kant's Autonomy Thesis, if we did not accept these requirements, they would not apply to us. But Kant might reject this counterfactual, on the ground that what it requires us to suppose is too deeply impossible. As Hill suggests and Kant might claim, all thinkers necessarily accept these requirements, since their acceptance is necessarily involved in, or in part constitutes, thinking. If we didn't believe that we ought not to believe both *P* and *not P*, we couldn't even count as *believing* P. In believing something, we are committed to disbelieving the negation of our belief. Similarly, if we really believed both *P* and *If P, then Q*, we couldn't fail to believe that we ought either to believe Q, or give up one of these other beliefs.

Kant might make similar claims about the principles that govern instrumental rationality, such as the general Hypothetical Imperative that requires us not to will some end without at the same time willing what we believe to be the necessary means to this end. If we didn't accept this requirement, Korsgaard suggests, we couldn't even count as willing some end. The acceptance of such principles may be necessarily involved in being an agent.

This defence of Kant's Autonomy Thesis would, however, undermine this thesis. According to the rival, Heteronomy Thesis, we are subject to various requirements whether or not we accept these requirements. To use the same examples, we are rationally required to avoid contradictory beliefs, and to take the necessary and acceptable means to our ends, and these requirements do not depend on our acceptance of them. For Kant's view to be different from the Heteronomy Thesis, and to be an assertion of *autonomy*, Kant must claim that these requirements, or their normativity, in some sense derive from or depend on us. He might claim that, if we did not accept these requirements, they would not apply to us. But as I have said, that would be very implausible. On the suggestion we are now considering, we can ignore this possibility, since the acceptance of these requirements is necessarily involved in our even being thinkers and agents. If that is true, however, there is no sense in which these requirements, or their normativity, could be claimed to derive from us.

There is another problem. These claims could not be applied to Kant's Formula of Universal Law. There is no hope of showing that, if we didn't believe that we ought to act only on universalizable maxims, we couldn't be agents, since we would be unable to act. There are many successful agents who have considered and rejected Kant's Formula.

Kant might claim that, even if we reject his formula, and believe it to be false, there is some other sense in which we do accept this formula, and give it to ourselves as a law. But when applied to us as human beings, this claim would either be false, or would have to be given some sense which made it trivial. Kant might claim instead that we all necessarily accept his formula as noumenal beings in a timeless world. But such a claim would be open to decisive objections. Since Kant cannot defensibly claim that everyone *does* accept his Formula of Universal Law, Kant's claim could at most be that, *if we were fully rational*, we would all accept this formula.

According to Kant's Autonomy Thesis, if we do not accept Kant's Formula, it does not apply to us. To defend his view that his formula applies to all rational beings, Kant must revise his thesis. And as I have just argued, Kant's claim could at most be that we are subject only to those principles or requirements that we either do accept, or would accept if we were fully rational. We would be subject to these requirements even if, because we were not fully rational, we did not accept them.

Kant's Thesis, so revised, would cease to make any distinctive claim. On the rival, Heteronomy Thesis, we are rationally or morally required to have certain beliefs and to act in certain ways, and these requirements apply to us whether or not we accept them. Heteronomists could agree that, if we were fully rational, we would accept these requirements. If we did not accept these requirements, we would be failing to respond to our reasons for accepting them. So the difference between these views would disappear.

There is, I conclude, no defensible and non-trivial version of Kant's Autonomy Thesis. Kant claims, I believe rightly, that there are some categorical imperatives. We are often rationally or morally required to have certain beliefs, or to act in certain ways. And such requirements are unconditional, since they apply to us whether or not we accept them, and whatever we want or will. So we should reject what Kant calls his 'basic principle', according to which morality is grounded in the autonomy of the will.

In arguing against Kant's Autonomy Thesis, I have ignored one complication. In many passages, including some from which I have quoted, Kant uses the word 'heteronomy' in a different sense. When Kant talks of self-*legislation*, he means in part self-*determination*. Reason gives a law, Kant writes, when it determines the will (CPR 31). Since Kant often identifies reason with the will, he often assumes that, when reason determines the will, the will is determining itself. Kant also assumes that, since we are rational beings, it is our reason, or our will, which is our authentic self, or what is most truly us. So Kant believes that *we* are autonomous, or self-determining, when our acts are motivated by our reason, or our will. This can be called *motivational autonomy*.

There is *heteronomy* in this motivational sense when our acts are motivated by something other than our reason, or our will. That is true, Kant claims, when our acts are motivated merely by some desire. Kant claims that, since our desires are non-voluntary products of our natural constitution, they are alien to our true self. In his words, when we merely try to fulfil some desire,

> the will does not give the law to itself, but an alien impulse
> gives it by means of the subject's nature (G 444).

When our acts are motivated merely by our desires, rather than by our reason or our will, we can call these acts *motivationally heteronomous*.

Kant's claims about motivational heteronomy contain, I believe, some important truths. But this other use of 'heteronomy' can cause confusion.   For example, Kant writes:

> if the will does not give itself the law . . . heteronomy
> always results . . . only hypothetical imperatives become
> possible (G 441).

Our will does not give itself some law when our will is subject to some law that is not given by itself. That is so when we are subject to some valid imperative which is strongly categorical. When we act on some moral imperative, Kant claims, our reason can by itself motivate us without the help of any desire, so our act is *motivationally autonomous*. In the sense in which this claim is true, it would apply to our acting on imperatives which are strongly categorical, and in that sense *normatively heteronomous*. When we act on such imperatives, our acts need not be heteronomous in the quite different sense of being motivated by our desires. And when we are subject to strongly categorical heteronomous imperatives, we are not subject only to hypothetical imperatives. So Kant should not claim that, when there is *normative* heteronomy, only hypothetical imperatives are possible. By using the word 'heteronomy' in both normative and motivational senses, which he fails to distinguish, Kant conflates two very different things: motivation by desire, and strongly categorical requirements.

Like many other people, Kant often conflates normative and motivational claims. This has regrettable effects, some of which I discuss in Appendix I.

Kant's Motivational Argument

1

Near the start of *Groundwork 2*, Kant defines imperatives as

> *hypothetical* when they 'represent the practical necessity of a possible act as a means of achieving something else that one wills (or might will)',

and

> *categorical* when they 'represent an act as objectively necessary of itself, without reference to another end' (G 414).

If we claim some act to be necessary as a means of achieving some end, we may mean only that this act is a causally necessary means. And Kant later writes that hypothetical imperatives say 'what one must do in order to attain some end' (G 415). But when Kant defines these imperatives as representing some act's 'practical necessity', this necessity may be partly normative, since Kant may mean that we are rationally required to take the means to our ends. And when Kant defines categorical imperatives as claiming some act to be 'necessary of itself', this necessity seems purely normative. These imperatives, we can assume, are unconditional requirements. Unlike hypothetical imperatives, which apply to us only if and because we will the achievement of some end, categorical imperatives apply to us whatever we want or will.

After defining these two kinds of imperative, Kant asks how such imperatives are possible. Hypothetical imperatives, he answers, need no explanation or defence. If we know some act to be the only means of achieving some end, it is analytically true that we cannot fully will this end without willing this necessary means, 'insofar as reason has decisive influence on us'. Surprisingly, Kant then writes:

(1) On the other hand, the question of how the imperative
of morality is possible is undoubtedly the only one needing
a solution . . . It cannot be made out by means of any example,
and so empirically, whether there is any such imperative at
all, but it is rather to be feared that all imperatives which seem
to be categorical may yet be in some hidden way hypothetical.
For example, when it is said 'you ought not to promise
anything deceitfully', and one assumes that . . . an action of
this kind must be regarded as in itself evil and that the
imperative of the prohibition is therefore categorical: one
still cannot show with certainty in any example that the will
is here determined merely through the law, without any other
incentive, although it seems to be so; for it is always
possible that covert fear of disgrace, perhaps also obscure
apprehension of other dangers, may have had an influence on
the will . . . In such a case . . . the so-called moral imperative,
which as such appears to be categorical and unconditional,
would in fact be only a pragmatic precept that makes us
attentive to our advantage . . . (G 417)

These remarks are puzzling. After asking how there can be categorical
imperatives, Kant turns to the prior question of whether there *are*
any such imperatives. When Kant writes that this question is not
empirical, he might seem to mean that unconditional requirements,
since they are normative, are not empirically observable, as detectable
features of the world around us. Kant then remarks, however, that 'all
imperatives which seem to be categorical may yet be in some hidden
way hypothetical.' For example, there may seem to be a categorical
imperative which forbids lying. But when someone refrains from lying,
Kant points out, we cannot be certain that this person's motives were
purely moral. This person's act may have been partly motivated by
some self-interested fear or desire. In such a case, Kant concludes, the
imperative not to lie, which seemed to be moral and categorical, would
really be only pragmatic and hypothetical.

Suppose that, in stating this conclusion, Kant were using 'categorical'
in the sense that he has just defined.   Kant's claim would then be

> (A) If this person's motive for acting was not purely
> moral, the imperative not to lie would not here be an
> unconditional requirement, since this imperative would
> not apply to this person. Given this person's motives, he
> was not morally required not to lie.

This cannot be what Kant means. Kant did not have the strange belief that, if we conform to some moral requirement for motives that are not purely moral, this requirement does not apply to us. (A) is both clearly false, and inconsistent with many of Kant's other claims. For example, Kant often claims that we can fulfil duties of justice whatever our motive. He did not mean that, when we fulfil some duty of justice for self-interested motives, this duty did not apply to us. Kant's view is only that, if we do our duty for non-moral motives, our act does not have moral worth.

Since Kant cannot mean (A), he seems to have shifted to other senses of 'hypothetical' and 'categorical'. And Kant does use these words in other senses.   Near the start of the *Second Critique*, he writes

> Imperatives themselves, when they are conditional—that
> is, when they do not determine the will simply as will but
> only with respect to a desired effect, that is, when they are
> hypothetical . . .

Imperatives are hypothetical, in the sense Kant here defines, when they determine our will, or motivate us, only with the help of a desire for some effect. Imperatives would be categorical, in a corresponding sense, when they motivate us all by themselves, without the help of any such desire.   As Kant elsewhere writes

> Categorical imperatives differ essentially from [those that
> are hypothetical], in that the determining ground of the
> action lies solely in the law of moral freedom, whereas in
> the others it is the associated ends that bring the action to
> reality . . . (L 486)

Kant defines a 'determining ground' as 'the motivating cause' of an act (L 493, 268, 582). To express these senses, we can call imperatives *motivationally hypothetical* when their acceptance motivates us only with the help of a desire for some end,

and

motivationally categorical when their acceptance motivates us all by itself, or without the help of any such desire.

We can similarly say that, on Kant's other, normative definitions, imperatives are

normatively hypothetical if they require us to act in some way as a means of achieving something that we want or will,

and

normatively categorical if they require us to act in some way unconditionally, or whatever we want or will.

We can now suggest another reading of the end of passage (1). Kant imagines someone who conforms to the moral imperative not to lie, but who acts for some non-moral motive, such as fear of disgrace. Kant then comments that, if

(B) this person's act was not motivated by his acceptance of this imperative,

it would be true that

(C) this imperative was not, as it seemed, categorical.

If Kant meant that this imperative would not be *normatively* categorical, or an unconditional requirement, Kant's comment would, as I have said, be baffling. But Kant may mean that this imperative would not be *motivationally* categorical. (C) would then be another way of stating (B).

Though this suggestion would explain this part of passage (1), it would give us another problem. Shortly before this passage, Kant has presented and discussed his normative definitions of 'hypothetical' and 'categorical'. Near the start of (1), Kant asks

Q1: Are there any categorical imperatives?

On the definition that Kant has just given, this should mean

> Q2: Are there any unconditional requirements? Are we
> required to act in certain ways, whatever we want or will?

But what Kant then discusses is

> Q3: Are there any requirements whose acceptance motivates
> us all by itself, or without the help of a self-interested desire?

Why this sudden, unexplained shift?

On what we can call the *conflationist* reading, Kant takes Q3 to be
another way of asking Q2. Though Kant uses 'categorical' in both
a normative and a motivational sense, he fails to distinguish these
senses. Kant assumes that, if some imperative motivates us all by itself,
that's what it is for this imperative to be an unconditional normative
requirement.

Though there are some passages in which Kant seems not to draw
this distinction, it is hard to believe that he was not aware of it. So we
might next suggest another, *non-conflationist* reading of passage (1).
Kant may assume that

> (D) if no one ever acted for purely moral motives, no one
> would be subject to categorical moral requirements.

On this view, moral imperatives must have the power to motivate us
all by themselves. Passage (1) might be a misleading statement of (D).
Kant claims that, if his imagined person did not act for purely moral
motives, this person had no duty not to lie. But this may not be what he
intended to say. He may have intended to claim that, if *all* cases were of
this kind, there would be no categorical imperatives.

When we consider only passage (1), this suggestion seems fairly
plausible.   A few pages earlier, however, Kant explicitly claims that

> (E) even if no one has ever acted for purely moral motives,
> obedience to the moral law would still be 'inflexibly
> commanded by pure reason'.

(D) and (E) cannot both be true.

We might next suggest, however, that (E) is not really Kant's view. Though Kant claims that we can never know that anyone has acted for purely motives, he also writes:

> the pure thought of duty . . . has by way of reason alone . . . an influence on the human heart [that is] much more powerful than all other incentives (G 410–11).

If Kant thought it possible that no one has ever acted for purely moral motives, it is hard to see how he could also believe that the pure thought of duty is much more powerful than all other motives. So Kant may assume that, since we *can* act for purely moral motives, we are subject to categorical requirements.

We have other reasons to believe that Kant assumes (D). There are many passages in which Kant seems to assume that

> (F) we cannot be subject to a categorical imperative unless this imperative motivates us all by itself.

Return for example to Kant's question 'How are all these imperatives possible?' Kant says that he is asking

> (2) how the necessitation of the will, which the imperative expresses . . . can be thought . . . We shall thus have to investigate entirely a priori the possibility of a categorical imperative, since we do not here have the advantage of its reality being given in experience, so that what would be necessary would not be to establish this possibility but merely to explain it. (G 420)

The reality of a categorical imperative, Kant seems here to assume, might have been given in experience, in which case this reality would have needed only to be explained. Kant seems to mean, by this imperative's 'reality', its ability to motivate us all by itself. He goes on to write

> (3) . . . how such an absolute command is possible, even if we know its tenor, will still require special and difficult toil, which, however, we postpone to the last section.

In the last section of the *Groundwork*, Kant argues that pure reason can by itself motivate us, and much of Kant's *Second Critique* has the same aim. In passages (2) and (3), Kant seems either to conflate the normative and motivational senses of 'categorical', or to assume that these two senses go together, since an unconditional moral requirement must be able to motivate us all by itself.

In another passage, Kant writes that moral laws

> must hold not only for human being but for *all rational beings as such*, not merely under contingent conditions and with exceptions but with *absolute necessity* (G 408).

Kant here asserts that

> (G) true moral laws must be both universal and normatively categorical, applying to all rational beings whatever they want or will.

Kant continues

> . . . it is clear that no experience could give occasion to infer even the possibility of such laws. For by what right could we bring into unlimited respect, as a universal precept for every rational nature, what is perhaps valid only under the contingent conditions of humanity? And how should laws of the determination of *our* will be taken as laws of the determination of the will of rational beings as such . . . if they were merely empirical and did not have their origin completely a priori in pure but practical reason?

When Kant claims that moral laws must hold for all rational beings, this claim seems normative. But Kant then turns to motivation. If 'the laws of the determination of our will' were *merely empirical*, Kant writes, we could not assume that the same laws would apply to all rational beings. The laws to which Kant here refers cannot be normative requirements, since such requirements are *not* empirical, and we *could* assume that such normative requirements apply to all rational beings. Kant must be referring to laws about how our wills are determined, or how we can be moved to act. Only such laws might be merely empirical in a way that prevents our assuming that they apply to all rational beings. So, in asking whether there are moral laws which hold for all rational beings, Kant takes himself to be asking whether there are necessary truths about what motivates all such beings.

On the non-conflationist reading, Kant here assumes that

> (H) No principle can be a true moral law unless all rational beings would necessarily be motivated to act upon it.

When Kant claims that reason, or the moral law, must *determine* the will of all rational beings, he does not mean that this law must always *move* these beings, guaranteeing that their do their duty. Imperfectly rational beings can fail to do what morality requires. That is why, unlike God or other beings who are wholly good, imperfectly rational beings have duties. But the moral law, Kant may assume, must at least motivate all rational beings in the sense of making them to *some extent* disposed to do their duty. We can be motivated to do our duty, even when we are not moved to act in this way. ((H), we can note, allows that we can do our duty for non-moral motives, so (H) does not implausibly imply that, when we act for non-moral motives, we are not subject to the moral law.)

Kant elsewhere writes:

> The question is therefore this: is it a necessary law for all rational beings always to appraise their actions in accordance with such maxims as they themselves could will to serve as universal laws? If there is such a law, then it must already be connected (completely a priori) with the concept of the will of a rational being as such . . . since if reason entirely by itself determines conduct (and the possibility of this is just what we want now to investigate), it must necessarily do so a priori. (G 426–7)

When Kant asks whether it is necessary for all rational beings to act only on universalizable maxims, his question again seems to be normative. But Kant then takes his question to be whether reason all by itself can determine conduct. Kant does not say that, to answer his normative question, we must answer another, motivational question. He treats these as a single question. This passage gives some support to the conflationist reading. But Kant may again be assuming here that the moral law cannot be normatively categorical, making unconditional requirements, unless this law is motivationally categorical, motivating us all by itself.

2

In *Groundwork 3* and elsewhere, Kant argues at length that his Formula of Universal Law, which I shall here call Kant's *Formal Principle*, is motivationally categorical. There are two ways to interpret these arguments. On one reading, Kant believes that he has already shown in *Groundwork 2* that, *if* there is a supreme moral principle, this must be Kant's Formal Principle. Kant then assumes that, to show that there is such a supreme principle, we must show that this principle meets one further requirement, by being motivationally categorical.

In many passages, however, Kant seems to suggest a more ambitious argument, which might show in a different way that Kant's Formal Principle is the supreme moral law.   Kant seems to argue:

> (G) True moral laws must be both universal and normatively categorical, applying to all rational beings whatever they want or will.

> (H) No principle could be such a moral law unless the acceptance of this principle would necessarily motivate all rational beings.

> (I) No principle could have such necessary motivating force, and thus be able to be a true moral law, unless this principle can motivate us all by itself, without the help of any desire.

> (J) Only Kant's Formal Principle has such motivating force.

> (K) There must be some moral law.

Therefore

> Kant's Formal Principle is the only true moral law, and is thus
> the supreme principle of morality.

We can call this Kant's *Motivational Argument* for his Formal Principle.
Premise (I) may explain more fully why Kant assumes that, for some
law to be normatively categorical, this law must also be motivationally
categorical. Kant seems to assume that, unless some law motivates us
all by itself, it could not be necessary that this law would motivate all
rational beings, and thereby be able to be a categorical requirement.

One objection to this argument is posed by

> *Moral Belief Internalism* or *MBI*: No one could accept some
> moral principle without being, to some degree, motivated
> to act upon it.

If MBI were true, Kant's argument would be undermined, or made
trivial. Premise (H) lays down a test that every possible principle would
pass. It would be true of every moral principle that its acceptance would
necessarily motivate all rational beings. Kant could not then defend
premise (J), which claims that only Kant's Formal Principle has such
necessary motivating power. Nor would Kant need to argue that his
Formal Principle motivates us all by itself.

  Suppose next that MBI is false. If we could accept moral principles
without always being motivated to act upon them, (H) may seem too
strong. As Kant often says, we are not always fully rational. It may
seem implausible to claim that, for some principle to be a moral law,
there must never be anyone who, even when being irrational, fails to be
motivated by their acceptance of this principle. We might suggest that
Kant should appeal instead to

> (H2) No principle can be a true moral law unless its
> acceptance would necessarily motivate all rational beings
> *insofar as they were rational.*

This is like the claim which, given our imperfect rationality, Kant makes
about hypothetical imperatives. If we will some end, Kant writes, we

would will what we know to be the necessary means 'insofar as reason has decisive influence' on us (G 417).

If Kant rejects MBI and appeals to (H2), however, his argument would face another, similar objection. On some views, even if we are fully rational, we might fail to be motivated to act on our moral beliefs. But this is not Kant's view.   Kant clearly assumes that

> (L) if we were fully rational, we would be motivated to do what we believed to be our duty.

Given (L), if Kant appealed to (H2), his argument would again be trivial. All moral principles would motivate all rational beings, insofar as they were rational. So Kant's argument must appeal to the bolder premise (H). That may be in one way an advantage. Since (H) states a requirement that is harder to meet, there is more hope of defending the claim that only Kant's Formal Principle meets this requirement.

Could Kant defend this claim?   Kant assumes that

> (M) all rational beings accept his Formal Principle, and give this principle to themselves as a law.

For example, Kant writes:

> Common human reason . . . always has this principle before its eyes (G 402).

> Everyone does in fact appraise actions as morally good or evil by this rule (CPR 69).

If all rational beings necessarily accept Kant's Formal Principle, that would provide one sense in which this is the only principle that necessarily motivates all these beings. That would be true even if, as MBI claims, no one could accept any principle without being motivated to act upon it. (M), however, is clearly false. And Kant could not, I believe, defend (M) without assuming that his Formal Principle is the true moral law. Nor could this assumption be one premise of an argument that is intended to show that Kant's Principle is the true moral law.

For Kant's argument to be worth giving, he must reject MBI, claiming that we could accept some moral principles without being motivated to act upon them. But Kant might claim that, while we could accept *false* moral principles without being motivated to act upon them, moral *knowledge* necessarily motivates. This defence of (J) would appeal to we can call

> *the Platonic view*: If some moral principle is true, that gives it
> the power to motivate all rational beings.

If Kant appeals to this view, however, he could not defend (J) except by appealing to his argument's conclusion. If it is a principle's truth that gives this principle such necessary motivating power, Kant could not show that only his Formal Principle has such power except by showing that only his Formal Principle is true.

There is another way in which Kant's argument might support its conclusion. Rather than assuming that a principle's truth gives it the power to motivate all rational beings, Kant might run this inference the other way.   Kant may assume that

> (N) if some principle has the power to motivate all rational
> beings, that makes this principle true.

If Kant could independently defend (N), he could then conclude that his Formal Principle is the one true moral law.

Kant, I suggest, did argue in this way. What is most relevant here is Kant's discussion, in the *Second Critique*, of what he calls 'the method of ultimate moral inquiry'. In such inquiry, Kant claims,

> the concept of good and evil must not be determined before
> the moral law (for which, as it would seem, this concept would
> have to be made the basis) but only (as was done here) after it
> and by means of it (CPR 62–3).

Failure to grasp this truth has led, Kant writes, to

> all the errors of philosophers with respect to the supreme
> principle of morals . . . The ancients revealed this error

> openly by directing their moral investigation entirely to
> the determination of the concept of the *highest good*, and so
> of an object which they intended afterwards to make the
> determining ground of the will in the moral law . . . they
> should first have searched for a law that determined the will
> a priori and directly, and only then determined the object . . .

These claims can be given two readings. On a normative interpretation, Kant's claims are these. When these ancient philosophers asked what was the highest good, they were asking what we had most reason to want, or what was most worth achieving, or something of this kind. Their mistake was to assume that we should first try to decide what is the highest good, and could then conclude that this good end is what we ought to try to achieve. On this reading, Kant claims that we should reverse this procedure. We should start by asking what we ought to do, or what is right, and only then draw conclusions about what is good. In Rawls's phrase, rather than the good's being prior to the right, the right is prior to the good.

What Kant writes, however, is that these philosophers should first have searched for a law that *determined the will*. This seems to mean that, rather than asking

Q4: What is the highest good?

we should ask

Q5: How are rational beings moved to act?

If we can find some law that necessarily determines the will, Kant remark suggests, we could then draw conclusions about both the right and the good. On this reading, rather than morality's being prior to, and thus in one sense determining, the motivation of rational beings, it is the motivation of such beings which is prior to, and determines, morality. The moral law must be founded, not on truths about the highest good, but on truths about motivation.

Kant makes several other claims which seem to express this second view. Thus, after claiming that the concept *good* must not be determined before the moral law, Kant continues:

That is to say: even if we did not know that the principle of
morality is a pure law determining the will a priori, we would
at least have to leave it undecided in the beginning whether
the will has only empirical or else pure determining grounds a
priori . . . since it is contrary to all basic rules of philosophical
procedure to assume as already decided the foremost question
to be decided. (CPR 63)

The 'foremost question', Kant here assumes, is about motivation. And
Kant writes that, on the view that he is rejecting,

. . . it was thought to be necessary first of all to find an object
for the will, the concept of which, as that of a good, would
have to constitute the universal though empirical determining
ground of the will.

Kant claims that, on this mistaken view, the good is whatever empirically
determines the will. On the true view, Kant then writes, the concepts
of *good* and *evil* are 'consequences of the a priori determination of the
will'. Both views, on Kant's account, describe the good in motivational
terms.

Consider next this claim:

Suppose that we wanted to begin with the concept of the good
in order to derive from it laws of the will . . . since this concept
had no practical a priori law for its standard, the criterion
of good and evil could be placed in nothing other than the
agreement of the object with our feeling of pleasure or
unpleasure.

Since this claim is about the criterion of good and evil, it may seem
to be normative. Kant may seem to mean that, if we start by asking
what is good, in the sense of what we have reason to try to achieve, our
answer would have to be: only whatever gives us pleasure. But as the
context shows, Kant's claim is again about motivation. If we start with
the concept of the good, Kant writes,

> then this concept of an object (as a good object) would at
> the same time supply this as the sole determining ground
> of the will.

He also writes

> If the concept of the good is not to be derived from an
> antecedent practical law but, instead, is to serve as its basis,
> it can only be the concept of something whose existence
> promises pleasure and thus determines the causality of the
> subject, that is the faculty of desire, to produce it. (CPR 58)

Kant seems here to claim that, if the concept of the good is not derived from the moral law, we would have to regard the good as whatever motivates us, and our answer would have to be: whatever gives us pleasure. On this account, when hedonists say that pleasure is the only good, their claim is psychological.

Kant's account is too narrow, since Greek Hedonism often took a normative form. When Epicurus claimed that what is best is a life without pain, he meant that having such a life is what is most worth achieving. And when other writers claimed that pleasure is not the only good, they did not mean that things other than pleasure can motivate us.

When Kant claims that the concept of the good should be derived from the moral law, he may mean in part that, in Rawls's phrase, the right is prior to the good. But as these other passages suggest, Kant seems to hold another, more radical view. The 'foremost question', Kant claims, is whether there is some law that necessarily determines the will. If there is such a law, Kant seems to assume, this law will tell us both what is right and what is good. When Kant refers to a law 'that determines the will', Rawls takes this to mean that such a law 'determines . . . what we are to do', i.e. what we ought to do. But this cannot be all that Kant means. When Kant asks 'whether the will has only empirical or also pure determining grounds' (CPR 63), he is asking what motivates us.   And he writes:

> Either a rational principle is . . . in itself the determining
> ground of the will . . . in which case this principle is a
> practical law a priori . . . the law determines the will directly
> and the action is in itself good . . . or else a determining
> ground of the faculty of desire precedes the maxim of the
> will . . . in that case such maxims can never be laws. (CPR 62)

These remarks suggest that, on Kant's view, if there is some principle that necessarily determines the will of all rational beings, this principle's motivating power makes it the true moral law.

3

We can now ask whether Kant's Motivational Argument could succeed. Could Kant show, or give us reason to believe, that only his Formal Principle would necessarily motivate all rational beings?

Kant believed that, when we act on his Formal Principle, our motivation takes a unique form. It is often claimed that, in his account of non-moral motivation, Kant is a psychological hedonist. That claim, however, is misleading. Except when he discusses his Formal Principle, Kant is a hedonist about even moral motivation. Hence Kant's surprising claim that

> all material practical principles . . . are, without exception, of
> one and the same kind and come under the general principle
> of self-love or of one's own happiness (CPR 22).

After noting that we can be happy to have done our duty, Kant writes:

> Now a *eudaimonist* says: this delight, this happiness, is really
> his motive for acting virtuously. The concept of duty does not
> determine his will *directly*; he is moved to do his duty only *by
> means* of the happiness he anticipates. (MM 378)

This is just what Kant claims about how we can be moved to act on all material or substantive principles, such as requirements to promote our own perfection or the happiness of others. Kant writes that, even when our will is determined

> by means of reason . . . as with the principle of perfection,
> the will never determines itself directly, just by the
> representation of an act, but only by means of an
> incentive that the anticipated effect of the action has
> upon the will (G 444).

Though Kant admits that such principles have 'determining grounds'
that are 'objective and rational', he claims that such principles

> can become motives of the will only by means of the happiness
> we expect from them (CPR 41).

We can be moved to act, Kant often says, in only two ways. Either our
will is determined by 'the mere lawful form' of our maxim, since we are
acting on his Formal Principle,

> or else a determining ground of the faculty of desire
> precedes the maxim of the will, which presupposes an
> object of pleasure or displeasure and hence something
> that *gratifies* or *pains* (CPR 62).

He also writes:

> all determining grounds of the will except the one and
> only pure practical law of reason (the moral law) are
> without exception empirical and so, as such, belong to
> the principle of happiness . . . (CPR 93)

> The direct opposite of the principle of morality is the principle
> of one's own happiness made the determining ground of the
> will; and . . . whatever puts the determining ground that is to
> serve as a law *anywhere else* than in the lawgiving form of the
> maxim must be counted in this. (CPR 25)

In these and other passages, Kant assumes that

> (O) when we act on Kant's Formal Principle, reason directly
> and by itself motivates us. In all other cases, our motivation
> takes a hedonistic form.

When Kant claims that 'material principles' are 'quite unfit' to be moral laws, he seems to be appealing to (O). His objection seems to be that, since such principles motivate us in this hedonistic way, they cannot be guaranteed to motivate all rational beings. Even if we all got pleasure from acting—or from the thought of acting—on some material principle, that would be a contingent fact, which depended on our natural constitution. We cannot assume that all rational beings would get similar pleasure, and would thus be motivated to act upon this principle (CPR 34). For some principle to be guaranteed to motivate all rational beings, as is required of any moral law, this principle must motivate us in a different, non-hedonistic way. And that is true, Kant claims, only of his Formal Principle.

Kant did not always assume (O). In one passage in the *Groundwork*, Kant writes:

> In order for a sensibly affected rational being to will that for which reason alone prescribes the 'ought', it is admittedly required that his reason have the capacity to induce a feeling of pleasure or of delight in the fulfilment of duty . . . (G 460)

This remark implies that

> (P) even when we act on Kant's Formal Principle, our motivation must be hedonistic.

Kant seems to be assuming here that, when we accept his Formal Principle, reason always produces in us the needed feeling of pleasure or delight. If we accepted other principles, Kant might claim, reason would not produce in us this feeling. This could be how, compatibly with (P), only Kant's Formal Principle would necessarily motivate all rational beings.

Kant's accounts of motivation are too hedonistic. Even when applied to non-moral motivation, Psychological Hedonism is mistaken. But Kant's distinction could be revised.   He might claim that

> (Q) when we accept his Formal Principle, reason always directly motivates us to act upon it. To act on any other

principle, we must be motivated by some desire, and we may
not have any such desire.

Kant might even allow that all acts are motivated by desires. He could
then claim that

(R) when we accept his Formal Principle, reason always
produces in us a desire to act upon it. When we accept other
principles, we may not have such a desire.

Since these claims are not hedonistic, they are in one way easier to
defend.

Both claims raise the same questions. Does reason by itself motivate
us only when we accept Kant's Formal Principle? If so, why is that
true?

Kant may be right to claim that, when we act on his Formal Principle,
we are motivated by reason, or by our moral beliefs. And he may be
right to distinguish between this kind of motivation and some kinds of
motivation by desire. But Kant's Motivational Argument requires him
to distinguish between two kinds of *moral* motivation. His claim must
be that, if we accept his Formal Principle, our moral beliefs motivate
us in a special and uniquely reliable way. That would be so if it was
only moral knowledge that had such special motivating power, and only
Kant's Formal Principle was true. But as I have said, Kant's argument
cannot assume that his Formal Principle is true, since that is what
this argument is intended to show. For Kant's argument to support
his principle, it must be the *content* of Kant's Formal Principle, not its
truth, which gives this principle its unique motivating power. Kant must
claim that, if we believe that we ought to act only on universalizable
maxims, this belief necessarily motivates us. If we accept any other
moral principle, our moral beliefs would not have such power.

Kant often seems to make this claim.   For example, he writes:

Only a formal law, that is, one that prescribes to reason
nothing more than the form of this universal lawgiving as the
supreme condition of maxims, can be a priori a determining
ground of practical reason (CPR 64).

Kant's defences of this claim are surprisingly oblique. He is more concerned to show that pure reason can be practical, by determining our will. Kant takes it for granted that, *if* pure reason is practical, it moves us to act on his Formal Principle.   He even writes:

> pure reason must be practical of itself and alone, that is, it
> must be able to determine the will by the mere form of a
> practical rule . . . (CPR 24)

Kant here identifies reason's being practical with its determining the will by a rule's mere form. That is a slip, since reason might move us to act on one or more substantive principles.

As this slip suggests, Kant assumes that his claim is uncontroversial. Thus, when introducing his Formula of Universal Law, Kant writes

> The most ordinary attention to oneself confirms that this idea
> is really, as it were, the pattern for the determinations of our
> will. (CPR 44)

We can easily be directly aware, this remark implies, that our acceptance of Kant's formula motivates all our moral acts. That is not, however, true.

Kant's claim, as he often says, cannot appeal to empirically established psychological laws. The Universe may contain non-human rational beings, and we have no evidence about the motivation of such beings. It must be an a priori truth that all rational beings would be motivated by Kant's Formal Principle. And for Kant's argument to succeed, there must be no such truth about any other moral principle.

Kant assumes that there are such a priori truths about the motivating power of the moral law.   For example, he writes:

> we can see a priori that the moral law, as the determining
> ground of the will, must by thwarting all our inclinations
> produce a feeling that can be called pain . . . (CPR 73)

> the moral law . . . in as much as it even strikes down
> self-conceit, that is humiliates it, is an object of the greatest

> *respect*, and so too the ground of a positive feeling that is not
> of empirical origin and is cognized a priori . . . .

Similarly, after mentioning our

> boundless esteem for the pure moral law stripped of
> all advantage . . .

Kant writes

> . . . one can yet see a priori this much: that such a feeling is
> inseparably connected with the representation of the moral
> law in every finite rational being (CPR 80).

But Kant does not defend these implausible claims, nor do they imply that the moral law must be his Formal Principle.

There are other features of Kant's view that may have led him to believe that only his Formal Principle necessarily determines the will. He may again be influenced by a failure to distinguish between his uses of the words 'material' and 'formal'.   Thus Kant writes:

> all that remains of a law if one separates from it everything
> material, that is, every object of the will (as its determining
> ground), is the mere *form* of giving universal law (CPR 27).

> If a rational being is to think of his maxims as practical
> universal laws, he can think of them only as principles that
> contain the determining ground of the will not by their matter
> but only by their form.

These remarks seem to assume that, if some principle is not motivationally material, because it can motivate without the help of a desire, this principle must be normatively formal in sense 3, imposing a merely formal constraint.   As I have claimed, that does not follow.

Kant may also have assumed that, since pure reason determines our will as noumenal beings in the supersensible timeless world, reason must determine our will with some principle which, because it is merely formal, has the abstract purity of that world. Consider, for example, these remarks:

> The will is thought as independent of empirical conditions
> and hence, as a pure will, as determined by the mere form
> of law . . .

> It is a question only of the determination of the will . . .
> whether it is empirical or whether it is a concept of pure
> reason (of its lawfulness in general). (CPR 31)

> Reason takes an immediate interest in an action only when
> the universal validity of the maxim of the action is a sufficient
> determining ground of the will. Only such an interest is pure.
> (G 460 note)

Some passages involve both these assumptions.   Thus Kant writes:

> Since the matter of a practical law . . . can never be given
> otherwise than empirically . . . a free will, as independent
> of empirical conditions (i.e. conditions belonging to the
> sensible world) . . . must find a determining ground in the law
> but independently of the matter of the law . . . The
> lawgiving form . . . is therefore the only thing that can
> constitute a determining ground of the will. (CPR 29)

Kant here argues that, since a moral will must be free from empirical
conditions, and cannot be determined by anything material, such a will
must be determined by Kant's Formal Principle. As before, that does
not follow. Kant was inclined to group together, like opposing armies,
several pairs of contrasting concepts and properties:

material	formal
empirical	a priori
pleasure-based	duty-based
heteronomous	autonomous
phenomenal	noumenal
contingent	necessary
conditional	unconditional
impure	pure

The first of these distinctions, however, is not exhaustive. Some substantive principles are not, in the senses Kant intends, either material or formal. And such principles can be a priori, duty-based, necessary, unconditional, and, in the relevant senses, pure.

When Kant rejects all 'material' moral principles, he gives no example of what is claimed by such principles, saying only that they appeal to such things as happiness, perfection, or God's commands. As we have seen, in giving some of the arguments of the *Groundwork*, Kant seems to overlook those substantive principles that make categorical requirements. For Kant's Motivational Argument to succeed, however, his claims must apply to all such principles. Kant must claim that his Formal Principle differs from all such 'material' or substantive principles in being the only principle that would necessarily motivate all rational beings.

Kant could not defend this claim. Our moral beliefs do not have special motivating force if and because we derive them from Kant's Formal Principle. Compared with substantive moral beliefs — such as the beliefs that it is wrong to kill, or that we have a duty to care for our children — there is no magic in the thought that we should act only on universalizable maxims.

Kant's Motivational Argument, I conclude, cannot support his principle. Since Kant appeals to this argument so often, he seems to have found it especially convincing. It is not easy to explain why. Of Kant's reasons for believing that his Formal Principle is the supreme moral law, one seems to have been his belief that his Formal Principle has unique motivating force. But Kant, I suspect, had this second belief only because he believed that his Formal Principle is the supreme law.

4

Kant's argument is open, I believe, to other objections. This argument assumes that

> (H) no principle can be a true moral law unless its acceptance
> would necessarily motivate all rational beings.

As we have seen, there are two ways to defend this claim. On *the Platonic view*, moral knowledge necessarily motivates. If some moral principle is true, that gives it the power to motivate all rational beings. On Kant's view, it seems, this dependence goes the other way. Rather than assuming that a principle's truth gives it such motivating power, Kant seems to assume that

> (S) if some principle has the power to motivate all rational beings, that makes this principle a true moral law.

This view we can now call *Kant's Moral Internalism*. Remember next that, on my proposed revision of Kant's Formal Principle, acts are wrong unless they are permitted by principles whose universal acceptance *everyone* could rationally will. Though Kant appeals only to what we ourselves could rationally will, that is because he assumes that what each of us could rationally will is the same as what everyone could will. And Kant appeals to 'the idea of the will of every rational being as a will giving universal law' (432). So we can assume that Kant would accept

> (T) moral principles are true only if and because these are the principles whose universal acceptance everyone could rationally will.

This claim is intuitively plausible. We can see how some principle's truth might depend on its acceptability, which might in turn depend on whether we could rationally will it to be true that everyone accepts this principle. Kant's Moral Internalism could instead be stated as

> (U) moral principles are true only if and because their acceptance would necessarily motivate all rational beings.

This claim is much less plausible. Why should a principle's truth depend, not on its acceptability, but on its motivating power? Kant himself writes

> Nothing is more reprehensible than to derive the laws prescribing what *ought to be done* from what *is done* (*First Critique*, A/319/B 375).

We can add, 'or from what moves us to do it'. I have rejected Kant's claim that we are autonomous, in the sense of being subject only to requirements that we give ourselves. We are subject, I believe, to several rational and moral requirements, whose truth and normative force do not in any way derive from us. But I believe that, unlike us, morality *is* autonomous in a sense that is close to Kant's. Moral requirements are not determined from outside, or by something other than morality itself. Morality's autonomy is denied by Kant's form of Moral Internalism. Rather than first asking what is good, Kant claims, we should first search for the law that determines the will of all rational beings. We can then derive, from this motivational truth, truths about what ought to be done. This *heteronomous* account of morality is, I believe, deeply flawed.

One way to bring that out is this. According to what Kant calls the *principle of self-love*, we ought rationally to promote our own happiness. Since Kant believes that all rational beings necessarily want their own happiness, he must agree that this principle would necessarily motivate all these beings. Given Kant's Moral Internalism, he ought to conclude that the principle of self-love is a true moral law.

Perhaps because he sees the problem I have just described, Kant rejects the principle of self-love in a way that is curiously inconsistent with his rejection of other material principles.   Kant claims both that

> (V) these other principles cannot be true moral laws because
> it is *not* a necessary truth that all rational beings would be
> motivated to act upon them,

and that

> (W) the principle of self-love cannot be a true moral law
> because it *is* a necessary truth that all rational beings would
> be motivated to act upon it.

If these objections were both good, we would have to conclude that there cannot be any true moral laws.

Neither objection, I believe, is good. Unlike (V), which assumes Kant's Moral Internalism, (W) goes to the opposite extreme. (W) assumes that, if some principle would necessarily motivate all rational beings, that *disqualifies* this principle from being a true moral law. In rejecting the principle of self-love on this ground, Kant misapplies another, less implausible view. On that other view, since the concept of *duty* is the concept of a constraint, those who would be certain to act in some way, because they had no contrary temptations, could not have a duty to act in this way. Beings who were wholly good, Kant claims, could not have any duties. This view does not imply, however, that the principle of self-love cannot be a moral law. As Kant himself points out, most of us sometimes fail to act on this principle, as when we fail to resist the temptation of some immediate pleasure, at a foreseen and greater cost to our future happiness. So Kant should not reject this principle on the ground that all rational beings would necessarily have *some* motivation to act upon it. Though Kant seems right to say that the principle of self-love is not a true moral law, he must reject this principle with some claim about its content, rather than its motivating power.

The same applies to other principles. Just as Kant should not reject the principle of self-love on the ground that its acceptance *would* necessarily motivate all rational beings, he should not reject other principles on the ground that their acceptance would *not* necessarily motivate all such beings.

When we ask which moral principles are true, or what is right and what is good, we should not follow Kant's proposed 'method of ultimate moral inquiry'. We should not search for some law that necessarily determines the will. Perhaps, as Platonists believe, true moral laws would necessarily motivate all rational beings. But if that were so, it would be a consequence of the truth of these moral laws, and the rationality of these beings. If moral knowledge would necessarily motivate all rational beings, that would not be because it is the power to motivate these beings which makes a principle a true moral law. Motivation is not, in that sense, prior to morality.

In some passages, Kant's Moral Internalism seems to take a more extreme, reductive form. He seems to accept

> (X) If some principle would necessarily motivate all rational
> beings, that does not merely make this principle a true moral

law. Having such motivating power is *what it is* to be a true moral law.

This view is suggested by several of the passages quoted above. Thus, after claiming that moral laws

> must hold . . . for all rational beings as such . . .

Kant continues

> how should laws of the determination of our will be taken
> as laws of the determination of the will of rational beings
> as such . . . if they were merely empirical and did not have
> their origin completely a priori in pure but practical
> reason? (G 408)

Moral laws, Kant here suggests, are not merely the laws *that* necessarily determine the will. They are laws *of* the determination of the will. He also writes:

> the good (the law) . . . which objectively, in its ideal
> conception, is an irresistible incentive.

> . . . So here we lack the ground of duty, moral necessitation;
> we lack an unconditioned imperative, no coercion can be
> thought of here that enjoins immediate obligation. (L 497)

> Such a being has no need of any imperative, for *ought*
> indicates that it is not natural to the will, but that the agent
> has to be coerced. (L 605)

Ideal normativity, Kant here assumes, involves an irresistible coercive incentive. Kant similarly writes that, to prove that there are categorical imperatives, we must show

> that there is a practical law which by itself commands
> absolutely and without all incentives (G 425).

A law commands absolutely, this remark suggests, if this law moves us to act without the aid of other incentives.   As Kant also says

> The practical rule, which is here a law, absolutely and directly
> determines the will objectively, for pure reason, practical in
> itself, is here directly law-giving. (CPR 31)

Reason gives a law, Kant here assumes, by determining the will. Or
consider Kant's remark that moral imperatives

> have no regard either for skill, or prudence, or happiness, or
> any other end that might bring the actions into effect; for the
> necessitation to act lies purely in the imperative alone (L 487).

Though Kant describes necessitation as the relation which is expressed
by 'ought', this remark treats this relation as the *bringing about* of an
act. Consider next Kant's claim that imperatives are categorical when
they assert

> the practical necessity of the action in an absolute sense,
> without the motivating ground being contained in any
> other end (L 606).

This definition conflates normativity and motivation. Similarly Kant
writes:

> Human actions . . . if they are to be moral, have need of
> practical imperatives, i.e. of practical determinations of the
> will to an action. (L 486)

> duty . . . lies . . . in the idea of a reason determining the will by
> means of a priori grounds (G 408).

> Practical good . . . is that which determines the will by means
> of representations of reason . . . (G 413)

> The concepts of *good* and *evil* . . . are . . . modi of a single cat-
> egory, namely that of causality . . . (CPR 65)

On such a view, I believe, normativity disappears.

I have been discussing only some of Kant's claims. Kant himself
distinguishes between normativity and motivating force, as when he
writes:

> Guideline and motive have to be distinguished. The guideline
> is the principle of appraisal, and the motive that of carrying
> out the obligation; in that they have been confused, everything
> in morality has been erroneous. (L 274)

In some passages, Kant seems to forget this warning. But consistency is
not, as Kant claimed, a philosopher's greatest duty. It is more important
to have, as Kant often did, new ideas that take us closer to the truth.

On What There Is

1

Rather than being *Actualists*, who believe:

There is nothing except what actually exists,

we ought, I have claimed, to be *Possibilists*, who believe:

There are some things that are merely possible.

I have also made some conceptual claims. According to

the Plural Senses View: There is one wide, general sense in which we can claim that there are certain things, or that such things exist. We can also use these words in other, narrower senses. For example, if we say that certain things exist in what I call the *narrow actualist* sense, we mean that these things are, at some time, actually existing concrete parts of the spatio-temporal world.

As Possibilists, we should claim:

There *are* in the wide sense some possible things that never exist in this actualist sense.

There are also, I have claimed, some abstract entities, such as some logical and normative truths, which exist in a distinctive, non-ontological sense. I shall here develop and defend these claims. In defending Possibilism, my main aims are to defend the Plural Senses View, and the implications of both views. Possibilism is the thin end of a wider wedge.

Some Actualists say:

Nothing actually exists except what actually exists.

But Possibilists would accept this trivial claim. For Actualism to be a significant view, Actualists must claim:

Nothing exists in any sense except what actually exists.

Many Actualists would deny that there is any other sense in which things might exist.   These people assume

the Single Sense View: The words 'there are' and 'exist' must have only the same single sense.

Plantinga, for example, writes that, when Possibilists say that

(A) there is some entity that is merely possible and never actually exists,

this claim is 'monumentally perplexing', since (A) means that

(B) there 'is a thing such that there is no such thing'.

This remark is surprising, since Plantinga earlier wrote:

What might it mean to say that there are some individuals that do not exist? . . . Perhaps we can say something about what is *not* meant. It is not suggested, of course, that there exist some things that do not exist, 'exist' being taken the same way in each occurrence.

When Plantinga discusses (A), he seems to forget this earlier claim, since he assumes that Possibilists *are* making the contradictory suggestion that there exist some things that, in the same sense of 'exist', do *not* exist.

Few people give arguments for the Single Sense View. When he defends this view, for example, Quine merely writes:

There are philosophers who stoutly maintain that 'exists' said of numbers, classes, and the like and 'exists' said of material objects are two uses of an ambiguous term 'exists'. What mainly baffles me is the stoutness of their maintenance. What can they possibly count as evidence? Why not view ['exists'] as unambiguous but very general . . ?

If there could be no evidence *for* the view that 'exists' can have two senses, there could also be no evidence *against* this view, and Quine should also be baffled by the stoutness with which some people defend the Single Sense View.

There is, however, some evidence for the Plural Senses View. Quine himself writes that, if some word or phrase 'can be clearly true or false of one and the same thing', that is 'the nearest we have to a clear condition of ambiguity'.   Quine's example is the claim that

(C) dark feathers are light.

Since dark feathers are light in weight but not in colour, (C) is in one sense true and in another sense false. As this example shows, the word 'light' is ambiguous, having two senses.   Return next to

(D) There was a palace designed by Wren to replace the burnt Palace of Whitehall.

This claim is also in one sense true and in another sense false. We can truly say

(E) There was such a possible palace designed by Wren, but this palace was not built and never actually existed.

This example shows that, on Quine's proposed criterion, the phrase 'there was' has at least two different senses. There was such a palace in the wide sense, but not in the narrow actualist sense.

Single Sense Theorists might reply:

(F) What makes (D) ambiguous is not the phrase 'there was' but the word 'palace'. This word has two senses, since it can mean either 'possible palace' or 'actual palace'.

On this view, we should replace (E) with

(G) There was such a possible palace designed by Wren, but since this palace was not built, there was no actual palace designed by Wren.

But (F) is implausible, and (G) supports both Possibilism and the Plural Senses View. (G) tells us that there was a palace that was merely possible, because this palace never became actual. That is another way of claiming that there was such a possible palace, though this palace never existed in the actualist sense.

In the passage quoted above, Quine is defending the view that

> (H) material objects and abstract entities can both be claimed to exist in the same 'very general' sense.

It is often assumed that, if we accept (H), we thereby accept the Single Sense View. But that is not so. We could accept both (H) and the Plural Senses View. We could claim

> (I) There are, in the wide sense, both material objects and abstract entities.

But we would add:

> (J) As well as existing in this wide sense, many material objects also exist in the actualist sense, by being actual concrete parts of the spatio-temporal world. Abstract entities do not exist in this narrower sense, nor do material objects that are merely possible.

Quine's remarks provide no argument against this view.

Other writers deny the distinction drawn by (J). Stalnaker writes that, as an Actualist, he believes that

> (K) 'existing and actually existing are the same thing. There exists nothing that is not actual.'

This claim, Stalnaker remarks, should not be understood as 'a restrictive metaphysical thesis'. This remark suggests that (K) does not conflict with any metaphysical view. That would be true if there was a difference between the meanings of the phrase 'there are' and the word 'exist', so that Possibilists could accept (K) but add that

(L) there *are*, in the wide sense, some things that are merely possible, and never actually exist.

Stalnaker also calls (K) 'a trivial consequence of the meaning of the word "actual"'. This remark again suggests that (K) and (L) do not conflict. It could not be a consequence of the meaning of 'actual' that the phrase 'there are' cannot be used in this wide sense.

When Stalnaker calls (K) a *trivial* consequence of the meaning of 'actual', his point may be that 'actually' can be used, like 'truly', in a way that reinforces any indicative statement or assertion, without adding anything to its meaning. Instead of saying 'X', we could always say 'Actually X'. But this fact does not support Actualism. Possibilists could use this sense of 'actually', and restate (L) as

(M) There actually are, in the wide sense, some things that are merely possible and never exist in the actualist sense.

Stalnaker's Actualism seems, however, to be a metaphysical view, so he might reject both (L) and (M). When he claims that (K) is not a restrictive metaphysical thesis, Stalnaker may mean that, though (K) makes a metaphysical claim, there is no other intelligible or coherent metaphysical view. He may assume that

(N) the words 'there are' and 'exist' must have only the same single sense, which means 'actually exist'.

We can call (N) the *Actualist Single Sense View*. If 'there are' must mean 'there actually exist', Possibilists could not coherently claim that there are some things that are merely possible, and never actually exist. Though (N) could not follow from the meaning of the word 'actually', many Actualists assume (N).

Rather than merely assuming the Single Sense View, van Inwagen vigorously defends this view. Van Inwagen rejects the very idea of a merely possible concrete object, such as a merely possible horse, or human being. 'Like "round square",' he writes, ' "non-actual horse" is a contradiction in terms.' But if we say

(O) There was a possible palace that was never actual,

that is not a contradiction. Van Inwagen might reply

(P) Nothing that isn't actual could be a *palace*.

But in the sense in which (P) is true, (P) means that nothing that isn't actual could be an *actual* palace. This claim does not conflict with (O), which isn't a claim about an actual palace.

Like Stalnaker, Van Inwagen seems to assume that

(Q) since the word 'actually' adds nothing to the content of any assertion, we can truly assert that everything that exists actually exists.

But (Q) does not support the Single Sense View. If the word 'exists' can be used in both the wide and actualist senses, we could claim

(R) Everything that exists in the wide sense actually exists in this sense, and everything that exists in the actualist sense actually exists in this sense.

What (Q) shows is that, in explaining the actualist sense, it is not enough to say

Something exists in the actualist sense if this thing actually exists.

That is why I claimed

Something exists in the narrow actualist sense if this thing is an actual concrete part of the spatio-temporal world.

Return now to the claim that

(E) There was a possible palace designed by Wren, but this palace was not built so that it never actually existed.

If the Single Sense View were true, (E) would mean

> (S) There actually existed such a possible palace, but this palace was not built so that, in the same sense of 'exists', this possible palace never actually existed.

This claim is a contradiction, which could not possibly be true. But (E) does not mean (S). If we use my definitions and the redundant sense of 'actually', (E) could be more fully stated as

> (T) There actually existed in the wide sense such a possible palace, but this palace was not built so that it never actually existed in the actualist sense.

Unlike the contradictory (S), this claim is coherent and might be true.

Van Inwagen might object that (E) and (T) are *not* coherent, because the words 'there are' and 'exist' cannot have two such different senses. There are, van Inwagen writes, 'two clear and compelling arguments' for the Single Sense View. According to one of these arguments:

> When we say 'There are some Xs', we mean 'The number of Xs is greater than zero'.
>
> The phrase 'The number of . . . is greater than zero' has only one sense.

Therefore

> The phrase 'There are some Xs' has only one sense.

But if 'there are' has two senses, A and B, we could coherently claim both

> The number of Xs that there are, in sense A, is greater than zero,

and

> The number of Ys that there are, in sense B, is greater than zero.

For example:

> The number of possible buildings that there are in the wide
> sense is greater than zero,

and

> The number of actual buildings that there are in the actualist
> sense is greater than zero.

These claims conform to van Inwagen's second premise, since they both use the phrase 'The number of...is greater than zero' in the same sense. But these claims use the phrase 'there are' in two different senses. So this argument does not show that this phrase has only one sense.

Van Inwagen also argues:

> When we say 'There exists an F' what we mean is equivalent
> to 'It is not the case that everything is not an F'.

> The word 'not' has only one sense.

Therefore

> The phrase 'There exists an F' has only one sense.

We could reply:

> It is not the case that everything is not a possible building, nor
> is it the case that everything is not an actual building. As these
> facts might show, there is one wide sense in which there are
> both possible and actual buildings. But some of the possible
> buildings do not also exist in the actualist sense.

Van Inwagen suggests another argument, which takes the form of a funny story. He is discussing Meinong's view that words like 'there are' and 'exist' can have one sense when they are applied to abstract entities, such as numbers or mythical beings, and can have another sense when they are applied to physical objects, such as buildings or rocks. On this view, we might say that there *are* some abstract objects which do not, in the other sense, *exist*. Van Inwagen's story goes:

> One day my friend Wyman told me that there was a passage
> on page 253 of Volume IV of Meinong's *Collected Works*
> in which Meinong admitted that his theory of objects was
> inconsistent. Four hours later, after considerable fruitless
> searching, I stamped into Wyman's study and informed him
> with some heat that there was no such passage. 'Ah' said
> Wyman, 'you're wrong. There is such a passage. After all,
> you were looking for it: there was something that you were
> looking for. I think I can explain your error; although there *is*
> such a passage, it doesn't *exist*. Your error lay in your failure
> to appreciate this distinction.' I was indignant. My refusal to
> recognize a distinction between existence and being is simply
> my indignation, recollected in tranquillity and generalized.

Though this joke is funny, it does not apply to Meinong's view. Since Wyman accepts Meinong's view, he would not have claimed that there *was* such a passage, in the sense that applies to abstract entities. Such a passage in a printed book would not have been an abstract entity but a sequence of visible marks on a physical object. Wyman would have claimed only that no such passage existed. Van Inwagen's indignation was not justified.

I shall now tell another story, about the view that Plantinga asserts and van Inwagen defends. My story goes:

> As Plantinga leaves the room, he tells me that one actually
> existing state of affairs is that my wife is dead. I am struck with
> horror and grief. Four hours later, when he returns, Plantinga
> says: 'Don't worry. Though this state of affairs actually exists,
> it isn't *actual*. Your wife is alive and well.'

After my needless hours of grief, my indignation *would* be justified. On Plantinga's view, merely possible states of affairs actually exist, and they exist 'just as serenely as your most solidly actual state of affairs'. But these actually existing states are not, Plantinga claims, actual, in the sense of being actualized, or obtaining. Given Plantinga's definitions, his claims are coherent. But when my wife is alive and well, it may be misleading to claim that one actually existing state of affairs is that my wife is dead. Unlike my wife's actual state of being alive, her possible state of being dead is not real, or is at least *less* real, and can therefore be plausibly claimed to exist only in the wide sense. That is why it matters whether someone is actually or merely possibly dead. As Fine writes:

> there is an ontological difference between actual objects and merely possible objects . . . We might call someone who takes actuality seriously an actualist.

Possibilists like me are also, in *this* sense, actualists. We believe that being actual is ontologically very different from being merely possible. That is why we claim that, though there is one wide sense in which there are both actual objects and objects that are merely possible, it is only the actual objects that also exist in the narrower, actualist sense.

There is also an ontological difference between concrete objects, such as rocks and stars, and abstract entities, such as numbers and logical truths. We can therefore defensibly claim that, though both kinds of entity exist in the same wide sense, these kinds of entity also exist in different, narrower senses. I shall return to this claim.

Van Inwagen's arguments for the Single Sense View do not, I conclude, succeed. Nor, I believe, could any such argument succeed. Such arguments could at most show that everything that exists should be claimed to exist in the same wide sense. These arguments could not show that we cannot also intelligibly use other, narrower senses. To illustrate this point, we can turn from the concept *being* or *existing* to the concept *doing*. Consider:

> accidentally killing someone, stumbling over a hidden
> stone, forgetting something, digesting food, growing older,
> contracting measles.

These can all be claimed to be things that, in a wide sense, we *do*. But we can also use the word 'do' in a narrower sense, which applies only to voluntary and intentional acts. The things just listed are *not*, in this sense, things that we do. No argument could show that the word 'do' cannot be intelligibly used in such different senses. Nor could any argument show that the words 'there are' and 'exist' cannot have similarly different senses.

Some Actualists reject Possibilism with surprisingly extreme remarks. Plantinga calls this view 'monumentally perplexing', and Lycan calls it 'literally gibberish or mere noise'. These people may be misled by the fact that

> (U) the word 'actually' adds nothing to the content
> of an assertion.

This fact may suggest that Possibilism is false, since everything that exists *actually* exists. But as Plantinga points out, the word 'actually' can be misleading. (U) could not show that the words 'there are' and 'exist' cannot be intelligibly used in different senses. (U) could show only that

> (V) when something exists in any of these senses, this thing
> actually exists in this sense.

It could still be true that

> (W) though something actually exists in one of these senses,
> this thing does not actually exist in some other sense.

In my example:

> (X) There actually was, in the wide sense, a possible palace
> designed by Wren to replace the Palace of Whitehall. This
> possible palace was not built and therefore never actually
> existed in the actualist sense.

(X) is not 'monumentally perplexing' or 'literally gibberish', but a clear and coherent claim.

2

According to

> Possibilism: There are, in the wide sense, some things that are
> merely possible, and never actually exist.

Since Actualists cannot appeal to the Single Sense View, they cannot reject Possibilism as incoherent, or self-contradictory. But they might claim that Possibilism is false. Actualists might say:

> It could not be in any sense true that there are some things
> that are merely possible.

In discussing this view, we can first consider, not persisting things such as buildings or people, but acts and other events. Many Actualists ignore events. When these people deny that there are any merely possible entities, they often discuss farfetched examples. Quine suggests that, when people claim that there are such entities, their 'main motive' is to be able to make claims about mythical beings, such as the winged horse Pegasus. And Burgess and Rosen write:

> Among wilder metaphysical entities are possibilia,
> unactualized possible worlds and the unactualized possible
> entities that inhabit them.

But such entities include anything that we could have done, such as the knock that we should have knocked before opening someone else's bedroom door. There is nothing mythical or wild in such merely possible events.

Rather than merely ignoring events, some Actualists claim:

> (A) There are no events. There are only persisting things, such
> as people, rocks, and stars.

Some of these people argue:

> (B) We cannot justifiably believe that there are entities of
> some kind unless there are facts that we cannot adequately
> describe except in ways that refer to such entities.

> (C) Whenever someone makes some true claim which seems
> to refer to some event, we can restate this claim, or adequately
> redescribe the relevant facts, without referring to any event.

Therefore

> We cannot justifiably believe that there are any events.

We ought, I believe, to reject (B). Consider, for example, the facts that

> (D) there are some happily married couples, mountain ranges, and clusters of stars.

We could redescribe such facts in ways that referred only to the relations between various people, mountains, and stars. So (B) mistakenly implies that we could not justifiably believe (D).

Though we can truly claim that there are such happy couples, mountain ranges, and clusters of stars, we should admit that these composite entities are not fundamental. Actualists might similarly claim:

> (E) When we describe what fundamentally exists, we need not mention events. It is enough to refer only to persisting things.

If (E) seems plausible, that may be because in ordinary English we do not say that events *exist*. We would not, for example, say that the First World War came into existence in 1914, continued to exist for four years, and then ceased to exist. We would say instead that this war *occurred* during these four years. But there *was* a First World War, and a Second World War, and we can hope that there will not *be* a Third World War.

Nor are events less fundamental than persisting things. When some persisting thing hardly changes, as when some rock stays on the surface of the Moon for a million years, we might call this thing a very boring event. That claim would be a category mistake, since it is really this thing's *history* that is very boring. But such claims provide a different and acceptable way of redescribing some parts of reality. Though the Sun is a persisting object, and the Great Fire of London was an event, we could think of the Sun in a different way, as a much greater and longer lasting fire. When things change, in contrast, we cannot redescribe these changes as persisting things. If I jump into some river and save your life, this act is not remotely like some rock or other unchanging persisting thing. If there were no events, because nothing ever happened, the

Universe would have no history, nor could we exist. We live lives, and each life is a series of events.

In living our lives, and thinking about what happens, we must also think about many possible events. When we are deciding what to do, we must choose between different possible acts, often by considering the possible outcomes of these acts. And there are other ways in which we should try to have true beliefs about many possible events. Without such beliefs, for example, we could not give causal explanations, since such explanations appeal to facts about what would have happened, if things had been in some ways different.

Actualists cannot defensibly deny that there are acts, and other events. To defend Actualism, however, these people must deny that there are any merely possible events. When we are deciding what to do, Possibilists like me believe,

> (F) there are, in the wide sense, different possible acts between which we choose. Since only one of these acts will be actual, the other acts are merely possible.

Actualists must claim:

> (G) There are only actual acts. It could not be in any sense true that there are some acts that are merely possible.

Since Actualists must reject (F), they must give a different account of what is involved when we decide what to do. Some Actualists claim

> (H) There actually exist the possibilities that we shall act in any of several ways, and we choose between these possibilities.

These Actualists might say that, unlike (F), (H) does not assert or imply that there is anything that is merely possible.

There is, I believe, no such difference between (F) and (H). Though (H) claims that there actually exist these different possibilities, these Actualists must admit that only one of these possibilities will be actualized, in the sense of being what actually happens. When we are deciding what to do, we choose which of these possibilities will be what actually happens. The other possibilities will not actually happen, but will remain mere possibilities. Though (F) claims that there are, in the wide sense, some acts that are merely possible, and (H) claims instead that there actually exist these unactualized possibilities, these are different ways of stating the same fact. If those who claim to be Actualists accept (H), these people are not, I shall argue, really Actualists.

Some other Actualists claim

> (I) There actually exist several ways in which we might act, and we choose in which of these ways we shall act.

Similar remarks apply. Of these ways in which we might act, only one will be the actual way in which we act. The unactualized ways in which we might act do not relevantly differ from what Possibilists call merely possible acts.

Other Actualists deny that there exist such abstract entities as possibilities or ways of acting. When these people describe what is involved in our making some decision, some of them claim

> (J) It might be true that we shall act in any of several ways, and we choose which of these things will be true.

Others claim

> (K) We think thoughts about the different ways in which we could act, and we choose which of these actual thoughts will guide our actual future act.

Similar remarks apply. Like (H) and (I), these claims imply that, when we are deciding what to do, we have different possible alternatives. When we choose which alternative will be actual, the other alternatives will be merely possible.

Actualists might reply that, when they say that

> (L) we could act in several different ways,

this claim does not imply that

> (M) there are such *entities* as different possible alternatives.

But there is no relevant difference between (L) and (M). We do not state a different metaphysical view merely by using the verb 'could' and the adverb 'in different ways', rather than the adjective and noun 'possible alternatives'. These alternatives are the different ways in which we could act. If Actualists make any of claims (H) to (L), they cannot defensibly deny that

(N) there are, in the wide sense, such merely possible alternatives.

Since these people cannot deny (N), they should become Possibilists, who believe that

(O) there are, in the wide sense, some things that are merely possible.

It is irrelevant whether we can describe such cases without explicitly referring to such possible alternatives. As Church pointed out, misogynists might adequately describe the world without claiming that there any women, but that would not show that there are no women. We are asking whether, in our thoughts about our lives and other features of the world, it is enough to think only about what *actually* happens or will happen. And that is *not* enough. To make good decisions, or understand what causes what, we should try to form true beliefs about what *might* happen, or what *would* have happened. If there was no sense in which there are such merely possible events, we could not form such true beliefs.

Some Actualists would reply that we can form true beliefs about some things that don't exist.   One such belief is

(P) Pegasus, the winged horse, doesn't exist.

In believing (P), we need not be believing that there exists a winged horse, Pegasus, that doesn't exist. To avoid the appearance of self-contradiction, we could restate (P) as

(Q) There is no such winged horse.

In the same way, these Actualists would say, we can have some true beliefs about merely possible events, even though there are no such events.

This reply overlooks the difference between negative and positive beliefs. When we believe that certain things do *not* exist, this belief could be true even though there are no such things. But for us to have true positive beliefs about certain things, there must *be* such things. We could not truly believe that

(R) some horses run faster than others

unless there are some horses. I have claimed that

(S) when we are deciding what to do, we should try to form true positive beliefs about some events that are merely possible, such as beliefs about the possible outcomes of different possible acts, most of which will not be actual.

We could not form such true beliefs unless there *are*, in the wide sense, such merely possible events.

When we claim that there *are* such events, we do not mean that such events actually occur. As Possibilists, we distinguish between what is actual and what is merely possible. When we are in great pain, for example, our painful conscious state is actual and real. This pain is very different from the merely possible pain that someone who is *not* in pain *might* now be in. This great difference can make Actualism seem undeniably true. There may seem to be no sense in which there could be pain or suffering that is merely possible, rather than actual and real.

There *is*, I am arguing, such a sense. We ought, when we can, to prevent suffering. But we can prevent suffering only if there is a sense in which there is some possible suffering that we are preventing. That is why it could not be true that we have prevented the suffering of some rock. But though there *is* a sense in which there can be possible suffering that we prevent, this sense is very different from the thicker *actualist* sense in which there is actual suffering that we fail to prevent. That is why we should try to *prevent* suffering. Only actual suffering matters.

Suppose next that I let you die, though there was something that I could have done which would have saved your life. We can claim that

(T) though there *was* this possible act, this act did not exist in the thicker sense of being actual.

When we make such claims, we need not mean that, since determinism is false, some other act would have been causally possible. It is enough that I would have saved your life if I had chosen to act in this way. For Actualists to reject our view, they must claim that

> (U) it is never in any sense true that there was something else that we could have done, or any possible suffering that we could prevent, or anything else that might happen, but does not in fact happen.

This claim, I believe, is clearly false.

Of those who accept Actualism, most assume the Single Sense View. These people believe that, when we say that there are certain things, we must mean that these things actually exist. If that were true, Possibilists could not coherently claim that

> (V) there are some events that are merely possible, and never actually exist or occur.

As I have now argued, since this claim uses 'there are' in the wide sense and uses 'exist' in the actualist sense, (V) is coherent, true, and not in any way metaphysically misleading.

Of those who once defended Actualism, some would now reject (U) and accept (V). Though many people still claim to be Actualists, most of these people, I shall argue, misdescribe their real view. When such people cease to be Actualists, they could revise some of their arguments so that these arguments support a partly similar view. According to this view, which I call

> *Actualist Foundationalism*: Though there are some things that are merely possible, and never actually exist, all truths about what is possible are in some way grounded on truths about what is actual.

It is of great importance whether this view is true. Many truths about what is possible *are* grounded, as these people claim, on truths about what is actual. This view could not, I believe, cover all such truths, but I shall not defend this belief here.

3

We can now turn from events to persisting things, which raise some different questions. In some cases, Possibilists could claim

> (A) There is a possible person who would become actual if
> a certain actual ovum and actual sperm cell were united and
> successfully implanted in some woman's womb.

Actualists might reject (A), claiming instead

> (B) There actually exists a pair of reproductive cells which, if
> united, would later become an actual person.

Possibilists could reply that, though this pair of cells actually exists, this person does not actually exist, and that, if these cells are never united, this person will never actually exist. It would then be true, I believe, that there was a merely possible person.

Though such cases support Possibilism, they also support Actualist Foundationalism. This truth about this possible person is grounded on truths about these actual reproductive cells. Such cases are, in this respect, unusual, and misleading. Some writers suggest that

> (C) a possible person is something that is possibly a person.

In cases of the kind described by (A), we might claim that there is indeed such a thing. This pair of actually existing cells, we might say, is possibly a person. But many claims about possible people should not take this form. Suppose that, as members of some community, we are choosing between two energy policies which will have significant effects in the further future. We might then truly claim that

> (D) there are many possible future people whose
> well-being might be seriously affected by our choice
> between these policies.

But we should not, I believe, claim that there are or will be some actually existing entities which are *possibly* these people, or which might become these people. Rather than claiming (C), we should claim that

> (E) a possible person is a person who might be, or become, actual.

Return to Jane, my imagined 14-year-old girl who intends to have a child. We might truly claim that

> (F) if Jane has a child now, she would give to this particular child a worse start in life than she could later give to any of the children whom she might have if she waited for several years before having children.

This claim is about a very large number of possible particular people, who are the many children some of whom Jane might have in the next ten or twenty years. We should not regard Jane's possible children as actually existing entities that are not people but that might be people. Such claims should take a simpler form. We should claim that

> (G) there are many possible children whom Jane might have,

in the sense that,

> (H) of the possible events that might occur, many would involve Jane's having some particular child.

There *are* these possible people in the sense that there might later actually exist one or more of these people. If it is true that

> (I) Jane might have a certain child,

it is true that

> (J) there is this possible child whom Jane might have.

These are two ways of stating the same fact. When we claim that there are many possible children whom Jane might have, or that there are many possible future people whose well-being might be affected by our choice between two energy policies, we mean that there might in the future actually exist such people.

Of those who claim to be Actualists, some would accept (I). Plantinga, for example, claims that, as an Actualist, he believes that 'there are no things that do not exist'. But he also claims that

(K) there *could* exist things that do not actually exist.

Suppose that some woman, *Sarah*, is being treated for infertility, and doctors have obtained from Sarah and her husband an actual ovum and sperm cell. Plantinga would then accept that

(L) there could exist the child whom Sarah would have if this pair of cells were united and successfully implanted in Sarah's womb.

What Plantinga rejects is only the claim that

(M) there *is* this possible child whom Sarah could have.

Someone might now object:

There is no real disagreement here. If we would all agree that this child *could* exist, it is unimportant whether we claim that there *is* this possible child. And if we would all agree that we *could* act in different ways, it is unimportant whether we claim that there *are* different possible acts between which we must choose.

There is, indeed, no real disagreement here. But that is because, though Plantinga claims to be an Actualist, that is not really true. We can first return to Plantinga's view about states of affairs. Possibilists like me claim

(N) There are some possible states of affairs that are never actual.

Plantinga claims

(O) There actually exist some possible states of affairs that are never actual.

These claims do not state significantly different views. Like Possibilists, Plantinga claims that there are some states of affairs that are merely possible, since they are never actual.

Plantinga might reply that he *is* defending Actualism. Unlike Possibilists, Plantinga claims that these merely possible states of affairs *actually* exist. But since we can use the word 'actually' in a sense that does not change the meaning of an assertion, Possibilists could restate (N) as

> (P) There actually are, in the wide sense, some possible states
> of affairs that are never actual.

As this restatement helps to show, (N) and (O) are not relevantly different claims. And Plantinga's use of 'actually exist' may, as I have said, be misleading. If Plantinga claimed that one *actually existing* state of affairs is that the USA has declared war on China, we might take him to mean that the USA has actually declared war on China. Since Plantinga accepts that there are some states of affairs that are possible but are never actual, he is really a Possibilist about such states of affairs. We cannot defend Actualism by saying that such merely possible states of affairs actually exist.

We can now return to possible people. On Plantinga's view, the word 'actual' has different meanings when applied to states of affairs and persisting things. While states of affairs can be actual in the sense that they *obtain*, persisting things can be actual in the different sense that they *exist*. Plantinga therefore claims that, though we should believe that

> (Q) there actually exist some states of affairs that are never
> actual in the sense that these states never obtain,

we cannot coherently believe that

> (R) there actually exist some persisting things that are never
> actual in the sense that these things never exist.

There cannot be such merely possible persisting things, Plantinga assumes, because claims like (R) imply that there 'is a thing such that there is no such thing'. I have argued that, since Plantinga accepts (Q), he is really a Possibilist about states of affairs. But Plantinga might reply that, since he rejects (R), he is an Actualist about persisting things.

This hybrid view is not, I believe, defensible. In the case described above, Plantinga would accept that

> (S) if some pair of actually existing cells were united and successfully implanted in Sarah's womb, a certain child would be conceived and come into existence.

Suppose next that Sarah will never actually have this child. Plantinga would then accept that

> (T) there is a possible state of affairs in which this child would exist, but this state of affairs will never be actual, in the sense that it will never obtain.

This claim does not relevantly differ from the Possibilist claim that

> (U) there is a possible child whom Sarah might have, but this child will never actually exist.

These claims are both about some possible child, and tell us that this child will never actually exist. We cannot defensibly accept (T) but reject (U).

Plantinga would reject (U) because he believes that such claims involve a contradiction. The words 'there are' and 'exist', he assumes, both have only the same single sense. If that were true, and we use the word 'actually' in the sense that adds nothing, we could restate (U) as

> (V) There actually exists a possible child whom Sarah might have, but in the same sense of 'actually exist' this child will never actually exist.

This claim would indeed be a contradiction. As I have argued, however, we should reject the Single Sense View. If we use my definitions, and add the word 'actually', (U) could be more fully stated as

> (W) There actually is, in the wide sense, a possible child whom Sarah might have, but this child will never be actual, by existing in the actualist sense.

Such claims are coherent, and in this imagined case (U) and (W) would be true.

Of those who claim to be Actualists, some would reject Plantinga's view that there exist such abstract entities as merely possible states of affairs. If they considered Sarah's possible child, many of these people would use one of the following phrases:

> It might be true that such a child will exist,
> There might exist such a child,
> Such a child might exist,
> Possibly: Such a child will exist,
> It is possible that such a child will exist,
> There could be such a child,

adding:

> But there will actually be no such child.

But these are not ways of avoiding the Possibilist claim that there are some things that are merely possible. These are merely other ways of stating the fact that

> (U) there is a possible child whom Sarah might have, but this child will never actually exist.

The difference is only that, instead of using the non-modal verb 'is' and the modal adjective 'possible', these other claims use the modal verb 'might', or the modal adverb 'possibly', or the modal phrase 'It is possible that'. These claims would all be about the possible event in which Sarah has this child, and would tell us that this possible event will not occur, so that this possible child will not actually exist. To defend Actualism, we would have to defend the claim that

> (W) it is in no sense true that there is such a possible event, and such a possible child whom Sarah might have.

And (W) would be clearly false. There would be, in the wide sense, both such a possible event and such a possible child.

There are other ways in which, in our abstract thinking, we can be misled by such grammatical differences. When we discuss normative reasons, for example, we can say that certain facts *are* reasons to act in some way. This way of talking treats these facts as having the *property* of being reasons. We can also say that these facts *give* us reasons to act in this way, thereby treating reasons as *entities* which are distinct from the reason-giving facts. We can also say that these facts *count in favour* of acting in this way, thereby treating reasons as *activities*, or as what facts *do* when they count in favour of some act. But we need not ask whether reasons really are properties, or entities, or activities. These are merely different ways of making the same claims. Just as it makes no difference whether we say that certain facts are reasons, or give us reasons, or count in favour of some act, it makes no difference whether we say that it *might* be true that certain people will exist, or that there *are* these possible people. These are two ways of stating the same Possibilist view.

Though we should often try to be more precise, and draw new distinctions, we should also try to avoid distinctions which are merely linguistic. We should not think, like the English speaker: 'The French call it a *couteau*, and the Germans call it a *messer*, but we call it a *knife*, which is, after all, what it *really is*'. Nor should we think: 'When others say that there *is* some possible child whom Sarah might have, we say that there *could* be such a child, which is what is *really* true.' We should not mistake these differences in wording for differences in meaning, and differences in the beliefs that these different words express.

4

I have defended Possibilism for several reasons. First, if we are Actualists, that may lead us to fail to recognize, or to deny, some important truths. I have claimed that

> (A) when we are deciding what to do, we should try to form true beliefs about our different possible acts, and their possible effects.

Though Actualists deny that there are any such merely possible acts and other events, (A) is so obviously true that Actualists are unlikely to be led astray. Things are different, however, when we turn from possible events to possible people. Scanlon writes:

> . . . the beings whom it is possible to wrong are all those who do, have, or will actually exist.

Many other writers make such claims. These claims may suggest that

> (B) our acts cannot be wrong unless there is or will be, at some time, some actual person whom we have *wronged*, and to whom we *owed* it not to act in this way.

And many people have believed that

> (C) we cannot be acting wrongly if we know that there will never be any actual person whom our act will affect for the worse, or whose rights our act would violate.

These claims are, I believe, mistaken. As I have argued:

> (D) When we are making certain choices that will have effects in the further future, such as choices between two energy policies, we should consider the possible effects of our different choices, not only on actual future people, but also on the many possible people who, if we had acted differently, would have later existed.

And we should believe that

> (E) our choice of one of two policies may be wrong, because it will greatly lower the future quality of people's lives, even though we know that, because our choice will affect who it is who later lives, this choice will never be worse for any actual future person.

If people in every generation chose such policies, the quality of future lives would steadily decline. The world would be slowly wrecked.

To recognize that, in choosing such policies, we have acted wrongly, we must consider the ways in which, if we had acted differently, our acts would have affected some people who never actually exist, but were merely possible. It will be easier to ignore such facts if we are Actualists, since we shall then believe that

(F) there is no sense in which there *are* any such merely possible people.

If there was *no* sense in which there are such people, we couldn't think about them, since such thoughts would be about nothing.

Possibilism, I have also claimed, is the thin end of a wider wedge. As the arguments for Possibilism help to show, we should reject the Single Sense View. And if we believe that there are, in the wide sense, some merely possible entities and events, we should believe that there are entities of many other kinds. Some examples are:

words, meanings, philosophical theories, nations, human needs, overdrafts, symphonies, courage, fictional characters, literary styles, problems, explanations, numbers, logical truths, duties, and reasons.

Since such entities are abstract, they do not exist in the narrow actualist sense as concrete parts of the spatio-temporal world. But unlike entities that are merely possible, some of these abstract entities can be claimed to be actual in another, wider sense. There are, for example, many actual words, with actual meanings, and many actual philosophical theories, nations, and symphonies.

When people cease to be Actualists, they might turn to another view. According to what we can call

Alethic Realism: There cannot be anything that is not part of reality. Nor can any claim be true unless there is some part of reality to which this claim corresponds, and which makes this claim true.

Alethic Realists can believe that there are some abstract entities of the kinds just mentioned. These entities are created by us, or depend on the activities of human beings. By using language, we make it true that there are certain actual words, with actual meanings. And there are some actual symphonies, theories, and nations because some people have composed these symphonies, developed these theories, or lived together in certain ways. These facts are enough to make these abstract entities part of reality. Alethic Realists can also claim that, since we know how we create these entities, and what their existence involves, these entities are not metaphysically mysterious. There is nothing puzzling in the existence of these words, meanings, symphonies, and nations.

Alethic Realism can also be applied to some entities and events that are merely possible. It may seem that, since these entities and events never actually exist or occur, they cannot be in any sense part of reality. But that is not so. What actually happens depends in part on what might have happened. If I lose some game of chess, for example, by failing to make some move that would have won this game, my mistake was a part of reality. Since my actual move was a mistake only because I could have made a different, winning move, the fact that such a move was possible can also be claimed to be a fact about reality.

Compared with Actualism, Alethic Realism covers more of the truth. But we ought, I believe, to reject this view. In cases of the kind just mentioned, facts about what is possible depend on facts about what is actual. I could have made some winning move only because the rules of chess allowed such a move, given the actual position of the chess pieces on the board. Similar remarks apply when there is some merely possible person who would have existed if some actual ovum and sperm cell had been successfully united. But there are countless other ways in which things could have gone differently, so that different people and other entities would have existed, and these possibilities cannot all depend on facts about what is actual. There are also countless other more remote possibilities. Reality might have contained entities of very different kinds, and the laws of nature might have been very different. These facts about how reality might have been cannot all depend upon, or be made true by, facts about how reality actually is.

Nor can Alethic Realism be defensibly applied to some other kinds of abstract entity, and to some necessary truths, such as certain logical, mathematical and normative truths.   One example is

(G) there are prime numbers greater than 100.

Though we created the phrase 'prime number', and the meaning of this phrase, we did not create prime numbers, nor did we make (G) true. Even if we had never existed, there would have been prime numbers greater than 100.   Similar remarks apply to:

(H) No proposition can be both wholly true and wholly false.

(I) If P implies Q, and P is true, Q must be true.

(J) If we know both that P implies Q, and that P is true, we have decisive reasons to believe Q.

(K) We have reasons to prevent or relieve the suffering of any conscious being, if we can.

We did not create these truths, nor does their truth in any way depend on us.

Since we did not create these necessary truths, or make them true, these truths raise some deep and difficult questions. But these truths are not, I believe, *metaphysically* mysterious. When we claim that there are such truths, we can use the phrase 'there are' not only in the wide sense, but also in a narrow *non-ontological* sense. On the view that I believe we should accept, which I call

> *Non-Metaphysical Cognitivism*, these necessary truths are not made to be true by there being some part of reality to which these truths correspond. Since any truth can be said to be really true, there is a trivial sense in which these truths can be said to be about reality. But these truths are not about *metaphysical* reality, since they do not imply that certain things exist in some ontological sense.

This form of Cognitivism cannot conflict with what Russell calls our 'robust sense of reality', since these claims are not about metaphysical reality. When some view has no metaphysical implications, it cannot be open to metaphysical objections.

Alethic Realists may object that the words 'there are' and 'exist' cannot be used in any such relevant non-ontological sense. If we say that *there are* certain truths, but we deny that these truths exist in any ontological sense, our claim may seem to be a contradiction. In considering this objection, it may help to compare Alethic Realism with two other similar views.   According to

> *Spatialism:* Nothing can exist that is not in space.

On this view, there can't *be* any thing that isn't anywhere. But that is not so. Though the Eroica Symphony was composed in Vienna, and has been performed in many places, this symphony itself, as an abstract entity, couldn't be anywhere. Nor could many other abstract entities, such as the meanings of our words, philosophical theories, jokes, overdrafts, or the rhyme scheme of a Petrarchan sonnet. These entities could not exist anywhere in space. But there *are* such entities, since there are, in the wide sense, many actual words, meanings, symphonies, and many abstract entities of many other kinds.

According to

> *Temporalism*: Nothing can exist that is not in time.

As Temporalists could point out, though most abstract entities could not exist anywhere in space, some of these entities do exist only at certain times. Symphonies exist only after they have been composed, and before there were any language users, there were no words, or meanings. Other abstract entities, Temporalists might claim, exist at all times. If we use a language with tensed verbs, such as English, we may assume that Temporalism must be true. Temporalists might say that, when we claim that there are prime numbers greater than 100, we must mean that there are *now* such prime numbers, though we can add that these numbers always have existed, and always will.

We ought, I believe, to reject this view. We cannot defensibly claim that, though many abstract entities could not exist in space, all such entities must exist in time. When we claim that there are prime numbers greater than 100, we should use 'there are' in a tenseless and timeless sense. Mathematical claims are not about what is always true. We should not, for example, claim that we know some facts about the future, because we know that there will always be prime numbers, and that two plus two will always equal four.

Return now to Alethic Realism.   I have claimed that

> (L) there are, in the wide sense, certain necessary truths,
> such as those stated by (G) to (K). Though such truths
> are about certain abstract entities and properties, they have
> no ontological implications. These truths are not about
> metaphysical reality.

Alethic Realists might object:

> (M) When you claim that there *are* these necessary truths, that
> must be a claim about reality.   To be is to be real.

If they are Nominalists, these Realists might claim:

> (N) Since such truths and abstract entities could not exist in
> space or time, there cannot be any such truths.

Some Platonists would reply:

> (O) These truths and entities exist in some part of reality that
> is not in space or time.

When they make such claims, these Platonist Realists are, I believe, too
close to their Nominalist opponents. These truths and entities don't have
to exist in any part of reality, not even a special non-spatio-temporal
Platonic realm. These truths are real only in the trivial sense that they are
really true. And, since these truths are necessary, they do not have to be
made true by there being some part of reality to which they correspond.
This dependence goes the other way. It is reality that must correspond
to these truths.

End Notes

Some of these notes can be read on their own, since I quote enough of the passages to which these notes apply. In other notes I quote the first words of some block of text and some relevant later words. I give references in a later set of notes.

156 *I have learnt a great deal from Allen Wood's fascinating books.* And from the many comments that, with great generosity, he has given me. I shall here discuss only the Kantian part of Wood's commentary.

158 *This claim is another version of my Kantian Contractualist Formula.* My version of this formula appeals, not to what it *would be* rational for everyone to choose, but to what everyone *could* rationally choose. It would be harder to defend the claim that there is some set of principles that it would be uniquely rational for everyone to choose, so that this choice would be rationally required.

174 *As these and many other passages together show*... Herman herself elsewhere writes: 'On a Kantian account, we say that an action is contrary to duty when its maxim cannot be willed to be a universal law' (Herman (1993) 89).

190 *If we appeal. . 'Then I am not a Kantian'.* I am grateful to Herman for correcting several mistakes in an early draft of this chapter. Herman's commentary makes several other very interesting, subtle, and plausible claims. I do not attempt to discuss these claims, in part because they are not directly relevant to my claims and arguments.

193 *Case One involves*...*So Scanlon's view implies, implausibly*... When Scanlon discusses this example, he suggests that, just as White could reasonably reject any principle that permitted Grey not to give his organ to White, Grey could reasonably reject any principle that required him to make this gift. If that were true, Scanlon writes, there would be 'a moral standoff', in which there was 'no right answer' to the question of what Grey ought to do (138). This claim, I have argued, understates the problem raised by this example. There would not be a moral standoff, since White could appeal to the Greater Burden Claim, and on Scanlon's assumptions Grey would have no reasonable reply.

198 *the Telic Priority View*... According to Telic Egalitarians, inequality is in itself bad. When benefits come to people who are worse off, that is in one way better because it reduces the inequality between different people. This view is open to the *Levelling Down Objection*, which I discuss in Parfit (1991). Suppose that those who are better off suffer some misfortune, and become as badly off as everyone else. Telic Egalitarians must admit that, on their view, these events would be in one way a change for the better, because there would no longer be any inequality, even though these events would be worse for some people and better for no one. Many people find that hard to believe. The Priority View avoids this objection. Because this view does not assume that inequality is in itself bad, this view does not imply that it would be in any way better if those who are better off became as badly off as everyone else. When they consider the Levelling Down Objection many people conclude that they were not, as they assumed egalitarians, since their real view is that benefits or burdens matter more when they come to people who are worse off.

200 *Because Utilitarians believe... And, as Scanlon now agrees, we ought to reject these conclusions.* Scanlon writes: 'where the base line is equal, benefiting only Blue seems objectionable, because all have the same claim to some benefit' (in Stratton-Lake (2004) 131).

... *These cases show, I believe, that Scanlon ought to drop his Individualist Restriction.* My claims apply only to cases in which both (1) the baseline is equal and (2) we can give much greater benefits to some people than to others. If the baseline is equal, and we could give equal benefits to each person, as is often true, no one could reasonably reject a principle requiring us to give everyone such benefits. But cases in which (1) and (2) are true, though they are much less common, help us to see more clearly the implications of Scanlon's Individualist Restriction.

202 *In his book, however...* Scanlon imagines a case in we have to choose between these outcomes:

	Future months of pain	
	for A	for B
(1)	61	0
(2)	60	2

Scanlon then writes: 'the way in which A's situation is worse strengthens her claim to have something done about her pain, even if it is less than could be done for someone else' (WWO 227). Since he refrains from saying that we *ought* to give A her lesser benefit, though A's situation is much worse than B's, Scanlon here gives very little weight to distributive principles.

212 *We can next ask whether... we would all have stronger reasons to want to be given many more years of life.* It might be objected that the burden of

acting wrongly, if we were in Grey's position, would outweigh the burden of not receiving the many more years of life if we were in White's position. But this principle would not *impose* on us the burden of acting wrongly. We could avoid that burden by giving away our organ, and thereby losing a few years of life. That would be a smaller burden than White's loss of many years of life.

214   *Scanlon now accepts that his Contractualist theory should take some such form.* He writes: 'I should have avoided describing Contractualism as an account of the property of moral wrongness . . . This claim . . . can be dropped from my account without affecting the other claims I make for Contractualism' (Stratton-Lake (2004) 137). He also writes: 'The fact that an action would cause harm may make it reasonable to reject a principle that would permit that action, and thus make that action wrong in the Contractualist sense I am describing. It is also true that an action's being wrong in this sense makes it morally wrong in the . . . general sense of that term' (Stratton-Lake (2004) 136). For a longer discussion, see Scanlon (2007B).

222   *In considering these effects . . . And all of the children who will be conceived will be born and become adults.* To avoid irrelevant complications, we can also suppose that, if we cancel Program A, the children who could have been cured would not later know this fact.

224   *the Pareto Principle . . . This principle implies . . .* This problem is in one way like the *Paradox of Voting.*   According to

> *the Majority Criterion*: It is wrong to follow some policy
> when some other policy is preferred by a majority of the
> relevant people.

When we are choosing between three or more policies, this criterion can fail.   Suppose that

> one third of us prefer A to B and B to C,
> another third prefer B to C and C to A,
> and another third prefer C to A and A to B.

Two thirds of us prefer A to B, another two thirds prefer C to A, and another two thirds prefer B to C. The Majority Criterion therefore mistakenly implies that, whichever policy we follow, we shall be acting wrongly, since some other policy is preferred by a majority of the relevant people. As such examples show, we should reject the Majority Criterion, which cannot be a fundamental moral principle. (Arrow later widened this conclusion with his famous *Impossibility Theorem*, but this shows only that there is no good way to choose our social policies if we ignore almost all the relevant facts.)

. . . These are unacceptable conclusions . . . we must revise this view, so that it ceases to have these implications. There is another way to avoid such conclusions. We might claim that, if some act would indirectly cause someone to exist who would have a life worth living, this act would thereby benefit this person. I defend this claim in RP, Appendix G. According to what we can call

> the *Wide Person-Affecting View*: Other things being equal, one
> of two acts would be wrong if it would benefit people less.

If causing someone to exist can benefit this person, this view rightly implies that, in *Case Four*, our three possible acts are morally equivalent. The benefits to Tom and Dick of our doing A would be equal to the benefits to Tom and Harry of our doing B, which would be equal to the benefits to Dick and Harry of our doing C.

Though the Wide Person-Affecting View provides one fairly plausible answer to the Non-Identity Problem, this view is irrelevant here. First, if we appealed to this view, we would not be revising but be abandoning the Two-Tier View. The Wide Person-Affecting View has the same implications as the No Difference View. This view implies both that, in *Case One*, the two medical programs are equally worthwhile, since both programs would give the same sum of benefits to future people, and that, in *Case Two*, we ought to choose Program B, since this program would give greater benefits to future people.

Second, we are here discussing Scanlonian Contractualism, which appeals to the principles that no one could reasonably reject. Suppose that, in *Case Two*, we choose Program A, thereby failing to give these greater benefits to these future people. We cannot claim that any principle that permits this choice could be reasonably rejected by these people. The people who might have received these greater benefits would never actually exist. Scanlon's Formula condemns some act only when, if we acted in this way, there would be some actual person who could reasonably reject any principle that permits such acts. In *Case Two*, if we chose Program A, there would be no such people.

228 *As I explain in a note . . .* If we do A rather than B, Bernard would lose 50, and there would be an impersonal gain of only 10, so Bernard's personal loss would not be outweighed. In the same way, if we do B rather than C, Charles would lose 40, and there would be an impersonal gain of only 30, so Charles's personal loss would not be outweighed. But if we do C rather than A, there would be an impersonal loss of 40 and *no* personal gain, so this *impersonal* loss would not be outweighed. The Two-Tier View therefore implies that, whatever we do, we shall be acting wrongly.

230 *On some other versions . . . who would live for 65 and 35 years.* Suppose that our alternatives are these:

A	Adam lives for 70 years	Bernard lives for 40 years	—	—
B	—	Bernard lives for 80 years	Charles lives for 20 years	—
C	—	—	Charles lives for 65 years	David lives for 35 years

If we do A, Bernard will have a complaint of 40, if we do B Charles will have a complaint of 45, and if we do C no one will have any complaint. The impersonal totals are: A: 110, B: 100, C: 100. If personal complaints count for only a third as much as impersonal losses, the deducted totals would then be: A: 97, B: 85, and C: 100. So Temkin's view would imply that we ought to choose C.

234 *Scanlonians cannot, however, make such claims . . .* Nor would it help to appeal to the non-comparative account of benefits and burdens. On this account, A and B would be morally equivalent, since cancelling either program would impose on equal numbers of people the burden of living for only 40 years. Nor would it help to appeal to people's rights.

236 *General people are not individuals . . . .* Kumar suggests that, to solve the Non-Identity Problem, Scanlon should appeal to claims about what could be reasonably rejected, not by particular people, but by a *type* of person, which Kumar defines as a normatively significant set of characteristics (Kumar (2003) 111). But *sets of characteristics* can't reject principles, nor could we *owe* anything to them.

   . . . there is no sense in which our doing A was worse for Dick. This point is even clearer when we consider cases in which different numbers of people might exist. Scanlon includes, among the acts that his formula condemns, irresponsible procreation. He may be thinking only of cases like that of Jane, who chooses to have a child when she is too young to give this child a good start in life. But he may also have in mind some of those poor people who have many children, with the result that their children are very badly off. We may believe that it would be better if, instead of having ten children, some couple had only two or three children. But if this couple have ten children, we should not claim that it would have been, in any relevant sense, *better for these ten children* if there had been only two of them.

240 *We ought . . . to choose Program B.* And not merely because of the bad effects on others of there being many people who die at 40 rather than many others who die at 80.

259 *There may be other cases . . .* Another example is Murphy's view about the demandingness of morality. When he asks what we rich people ought to

give to those who are very poor, Murphy argues that we ought to give our fair share, which is roughly the proportion of our wealth or income that it would be best for people like us to give (Murphy (2000)). On this view, we are not morally required to give more than our fair share, merely because other rich people fail to give what they ought to give. This view is more easily defended if we appeal, not to the principles whose general acceptance would make things go best, but to the principles that no one could reasonably reject. Even if we could make things go better by giving much more than our fair share, the principle of fair shares, we can plausibly argue, could not be reasonably rejected.

265 *Some of these people are Nihilists, or Error Theorists* . . . Though these people are often called 'Cognitivists', that name is misleading. The word 'Cognitive' refers to knowledge, and these people believe that we have no normative knowledge. These people are *Semi-Cognitivists* in the sense that they accept a Cognitivist account of the meaning of normative claims.

266 *(2) this act maximizes happiness* . . . This claim uses the word 'happiness' in some naturalistic sense which involves no normative judgment, such as the judgment that egoists or sadists cannot be truly happy.

267 *I shall argue later that we ought to reject Metaphysical Naturalism.* In Sections 112, 113, 115, and Appendix J.

268 *This, I shall argue* . . . *My claims would not then be normative in the reason-implying sense.* There are other claims which use normative concepts, but are not in this sense normative. One example is the claim that acts are right if they are not wrong. This claim merely tells us how these concepts are related, and neither states nor implies that anyone has any reason to act in some way. Though in one sense normative, this is not a *substantive* normative claim.

269 *On Williams's account* . . . *we often mean something like* . . . As Williams writes, 'I think that the sense of a statement of the form 'A has a reason to do X' is given by the internalist model' (Williams (1995) 40, with 'do X' in place of 'phi'). See also 'Internal and External Reasons', in Williams (1981). These articles contain many similar remarks. In some passages I shall later quote, Williams discusses how we should define the term 'reason' and what claims about reasons mean. He also writes: 'What are we saying when we say that someone has a reason to do something? . . . we do have to say that in the internal sense he indeed has no reason to pursue these things . . . . if we become clear that we have no such thought, and persist in saying that the person has this reason, then we must be speaking in another sense, and this is the external sense . . . What is that sense? . . . In considering what the external reason statement might mean . . . .' See also the endnote below about page 437.

270 *These we can call the external senses . . .* If we used 'external' merely to mean 'not internal', there might be other external senses of the phrase 'has a reason'. Some of these might be naturalistic senses. If Analytical Naturalists were Hedonistic Rational Egoists, for example, they might claim that, when we say that we have decisive reasons to act in some way, we mean that this act would maximize our own happiness. But such senses are seldom proposed, and have little importance. I shall use 'external reason' in the indefinable, irreducibly normative sense.

280 *Whenever some natural fact gives us a reason . . .* The same distinction applies when some normative fact, such as the fact that some act is unjustifiable to others, gives us a reason.

294 *Williams's objection should instead be that, as he often says, he doesn't understand such claims . . .* See also Sections 107–8 below.

295 *Most Naturalists assume that, if there are any moral properties and facts, these would have to be natural properties and facts.* I use the word 'property' in the wide non-metaphysical sense with which we can restate any claim that is, or might be, true. Whenever someone ought to act in some way, for example, we could say either that this act has the property of being what this person ought to do, or that this person has the property of being someone who ought to act in this way. We can similarly say that some fact has the property of being, or giving someone, a reason. For an account of such claims, see Schiffer (2003).

296 *This Co-extensiveness Argument . . .* For one version of this argument, see Jackson (1998) 122–129.

297 *being the only even prime number cannot be the* same *as being the positive square root of 4 . . .* When Jackson gives this argument, he claims that, since triangles are *equilateral* just when they are *equiangular*, these concepts refer to the same property. When applied to this example, Jackson's view has some plausibility. These triangles have a single shape that can be described in these two ways. But no such claim applies to the concepts of *being the only even prime number* and *being the positive square root of 4.* These concepts don't refer to a single property which could be described in both these ways.

298 *This claim would use a normative concept . . .* This concept is normative because it refers to the property that makes acts *right.* If this concept were not normative, (G) would not be a normative claim, as (G)'s restatability as (F) shows it to be.

300 *These claims are, I believe, seriously mistaken . . .* When certain natural properties of acts would make these acts right, the rightness of these acts is often claimed to *supervene* on these natural properties. Mental states, it is similarly claimed, supervene on states of the brain. Though these two kinds of supervenience are in some ways similar, they also differ greatly, I believe, in other ways. Normative supervenience should be considered on its own.

304 *since identity is a symmetrical relation . . .* It is worth noting that, though identity is a symmetrical relation, claims about the identity of some property often involve an *asymmetrical* relation. When we claim that heat is the same as molecular kinetic energy, we can add that, when the molecules in some object move more energetically, that's *what it is* for this object to be hotter. It is less plausible to claim that, when some object is hotter, that's *what it is* for the molecules in this object to move more energetically. Moral Naturalists might appeal to this asymmetry in answering some objections to their view.

307 *There is another, more straightforward reason . . . Since Wide Naturalists would accept this claim, their views do not seriously conflict with Non-Naturalist Cognitivism.* Some Wide Naturalists might claim that, though normative facts are irreducibly normative, they are like other natural facts in being contingent, empirically discoverable facts about the world. This view, which *would* seriously conflict with Non-Naturalist Cognitivism, I shall not consider here.

309 *Some legal theorists . . . claim . . . that acts cannot be illegal if the law that forbids such acts is morally unacceptable.* And some laws may be partly stated in moral terms.

311 *It will be enough to consider Searle's claim that (B) implies (C).* One claim *implies* another when, if the first claim is true, so is the second. When some argument's premises imply its conclusion, we can *derive* this conclusion from these premises.

313 *Searle's argument. . If we believe that promises create obligations, but that such sworn oaths do not, this would have to be a substantive moral view, which could not be true by definition.* There are other, similar rule-involving social practices. When British children are out walking, and they see a shining conker from a chestnut tree, the first child who points and says '*Bags I that*' thereby acquires ownership of this conker. Similar remarks apply to adults, as when Columbus said something that meant 'Bags I this continent for the King of Spain', or when explorers in the early American West staked out claims to a plot of land. In the case of British children it is also true by definition that, when some parent says, 'All of you should help with the washing up', the first child who says, '*Fains I do that*' thereby escapes this obligation. Adults might say 'You can't escape such an obligation merely by saying "Fains I do that" '. Act Consequentialists could similarly say 'You can't give yourself an obligation merely by saying "I promise to do that" '.

314 *But (G) is not a normative claim.* As I argue on pages 505–6 below. *(G) may be in Searle's sense 'evaluative'; but this sense, as I explain in a note, is irrelevant here.* Searle has in mind the sense of 'evaluative' in which, when we say that some knife is sharp or that some poison is effective, we may be evaluating this knife or poison. When we know which non-normative

properties would make something relevantly good, we can recommend this thing by claiming that it has these properties. That does not make such claims normative.

321 *... the non-normative fact that is stated by (S).* When I claim that this fact is not normative, I do not mean that this fact is unimportant. Non-normative facts can have great importance. But we should distinguish between (S) itself and the normative fact *that* (S) is important.

323 *The Injustice Argument may seem to be of this kind ... Similar remarks apply, I believe, to all such arguments.* Things would be different if we had no thin, or purely normative concepts, such as the concepts *wrong* or *a reason*. We could not then claim that, though some thick concept applies to some act, that does nothing to show that this act is wrong, or that we have some reason not to act in this way. This may be why Anscombe recommends that we stop using such thin concepts (Anscombe (1958) 13–14).

324 *... justice could not be — as some Pythagoreans were said to have believed — the number 4.* But they chose the right number, as when we speak of a *square deal.* No one could have believed that justice was the number 13.

327 *Like Non-Naturalists ... Non-Cognitivists believe that normative claims are in a separate, distinctive category, so that natural facts could not be normative.* This is how Moore's famous argument against Naturalism led several people to accept, not Moore's Non-Naturalist view, but various forms of Non-Cognitivism.

334 *Such analogies can seem to support the view that some form of Naturalism is true.* These analogies can at least be claimed to show that some form of Naturalism *might* be true, since these analogies suggest that normative concepts might refer to natural properties. As I have said, however, we don't need to appeal to such analogies to defend this claim. It is enough to cite the normative concept of *the natural property, whichever it is, that makes acts right.* And, as I have argued, this claim, though true, does not support Naturalism.

337 *In the referential sense, (J) and (K) state the same fact ... numerically identical to himself.* It might be objected that, even in the referential sense, (J) and (K) state different facts, since only (K) ascribes to Shakespeare the property of being the writer of Hamlet. But when we use the referential criterion for the identity of facts, we regard the phrase 'the writer of Hamlet' as merely one way of referring to Shakespeare, and we ignore the other information that this phrase gives us.

349 *If we learnt that there was only one property here ... it could not be a positive substantive claim about what we ought to do.* My objections to these views may seem to assume that, for some claim to be substantive, it *must* tell us about the the relation between different properties. I am not

making that assumption. Some claims are substantive, though they tell us only that some things have a certain property.   Two examples are:

(1) There are some acts that are forbidden by God,

(2) There are some acts that are wrong.

These claims are substantive, as is shown by the fact that atheists would reject (1), and Moral Nihilists would reject (2).   Another such claim is:

(3) There are some acts that are disallowed by the only set of principles whose universal acceptance everyone could rationally choose.

Some people would reject (3) because they believe that there are no such principles.   Another example is:

(4) There are some acts that would maximize happiness.

Some people would reject (4) because they believe that interpersonal comparisons of hedonic well-being make no sense. Since these people deny that some people can be happier than others, they believe that there could not be any truths about which acts would maximize the sum of happiness that would be had by different people.

Consider next

(5) Wrong acts are wrong.

This claim, I earlier wrote, is not substantive, but trivial. But if (5) were taken to imply that some acts are wrong, this claim would be in one way substantive.   (5) is wholly trivial only if (5) means

(6) If certain acts are wrong, these acts are wrong.

Though Nihilists deny that any acts are wrong, they would accept (6).

Return now to the Utilitarian Naturalist claim that

(C) being an act that would maximize happiness is the same as being what we ought to do.

If (C) is intended to imply that there are some acts that would maximize happiness, this claim is in one way substantive. As I have just said, some people deny that any acts could have this property. But this disagreement is irrelevant here. Of those who are neither Utilitarians nor Naturalists, many believe that some acts would maximize happiness. We are asking whether, if we already have that belief, (C) might give us further information, thereby stating a substantive normative view.

353 *Since (C) can easily seem informative, we can call this the Single Property Illusion.*   The previous note is again relevant here.

367 *These remarks do not imply . . . plausible and important claims.* As I have said, some Naturalists also give plausible accounts of facts that are normative in other senses, such as the rule-implying sense, or some response-dependent attitudinal sense.

379 *Moral Subjectivists . . .* Hume, for example, writes: 'when you pronounce any action or character to be vicious, you mean nothing but that . . . you have a feeling or sentiment of blame' (*A Treatise of Human Nature*, Book III, Part I, Section I). (Hume is unlikely to have meant this literally.)

On this view, acts can be right or wrong in the kind of way in which apples can be red or green . . . As Hume also writes, 'Vice and virtue, therefore, may be compared to sounds, colours, heat and cold, which . . . are not qualities in objects, but perceptions in the mind' (Book III, Part I, Section I).

381 *Moral convictions cannot be beliefs . . .* As Hume writes: 'Morals excite passions, and produce or prevent actions. Reason of itself is utterly impotent in this particular. The rules of morality, therefore, are not conclusions of our reason' (*Treatise*, Book III, Part I, Section I). (Hume's own argument was aimed only at those Moral Rationalists who believed that morality was entirely derived from reason. Though many Non-Cognitivists appeal to this argument, Hume's view seems to have been, not Non-Cognitivist, but a form of Moral Intersubjectivism.

389 *Gibbard also claims . . . you wouldn't need to believe that this is the window through which you ought to jump.* Gibbard might reply that, when we are tempted not to do what we have planned, we shall be more likely to act on our plan if we believe that this is what we ought to do. But this reply would not help Gibbard to explain the concept *ought* by appealing to the idea of adopting plans.

397 *Blackburn tries to avoid . . . When other Non-Cognitivists say that there are no moral truths, they are not making the moral claim . . . They are making the quite different meta-ethical claim . . .* In defending his partly similar version of Non-Cognitivism, Timmons well describes the relation between these moral and meta-ethical claims. Timmons writes: 'the two most obvious perspectives from which to judge the correct assertibility of moral statements are what we can call the *detached* perspective and the *engaged* perspective . . . Given my irrealist story about moral discourse, when one judges from a morally detached perspective, and thus simply in the light of semantic norms, moral statements are neither correctly assertible nor correctly deniable, and so they are neither true nor false' (Timmons (1999) 150–1).

429 *Enoch draws . . . we can justifiably regard this other person as less reliable than we earlier believed.* From the other person's point of view, there is a similar asymmetry the other way. That is how, judged from any neutral,

third point of view, there may still be symmetry between us and the person with whom we disagree.

433 *Q2: What do I basically want?* The ancient Greeks were concerned, Williams writes, with 'questions of what life it is worth one's leading and of what one basically wants' (2003, 45). Though Williams uses the word 'questions' here, he often insists that, in discussing how we should live, the Greeks were concerned with a *single univocal* question.

437 *This claim predicts... Williams ignores or dismisses...* For example, Williams writes:

> I do not deny... that sentences of the form 'A has a reason
> to do X'... are used in ways that do not satisfy the internalist
> condition. My claim is, first, that when they are so used... the
> speaker intends some roughly specifiable other thing which
> does not mean the same in general as 'A has a reason to do X',
> such as, 'We have a reason to want A to do X'... and second,
> that there is no principled and convincing way of distinguishing
> the basic sense of 'A has a reason to do X' from these other
> things other than an internalist interpretation... we are still
> owed an account of what is being said when the reason claims
> are directed to people who are known not to have internalized
> the practice, or to be insufficiently responsive to it... It is much
> too late in the day to suppose that a socially sanctioned reason
> gets a hold on a given agent simply because he finds himself
> within the boundaries of a society in which that reason is widely
> recognized... We need a realistic account, social and
> psychological, of what is going on when seemingly externalist
> claims, referring to a social or institutional reason, are directed
> at recalcitrant or unconvinced agents. (Williams (2001) 93–5)

As these remarks show, Williams thinks of reasons in psychological, motivational terms. Discussing the claim that his imagined man has an external reason to treat his wife better, Williams writes:

> What is the difference supposed to be between saying that the
> agent has a reason to act more considerately, and saying one
> of the many other things we can say to people whose behaviour
> does not accord with what we think it should be? As for instance
> that it would be better if they acted otherwise? (IROB 39–40

The difference is precisely that, as we are claiming, this man *has a reason* to act in this way. There are certain facts which this man should regard as counting in favour of this act. We are not making a claim about what might motivate this man, or have a *hold* on him.

Williams elsewhere writes that, if everyone had the same desires and other motivating states, 'the distinction between externalism and internalism would fade away' (Williams (2006) 114). Williams here assumes that, even according to Externalists, what we have reasons to do depends on our desires and other motivating states. That is not so. Externalists can believe that, even if everyone has certain desires, no one has any reason to fulfil these particular desires.

Williams often claims that he does not understand such non-psychological uses of the phrase 'has a reason'. He writes, for example, 'reasons theorist *may* want me to say this: one of the mysterious things about the denial of internalism lies precisely in the fact that it leaves it quite obscure when this form of words is thought to be appropriate . . . I do not believe . . . that the sense of external reason statements is in the least clear . . .' (1995) 39 – 40. And he claims that externalists do not 'offer any *content* for external reasons statements' (1995B) 191.

There are some passages which suggest that Williams did have the concept of a normative, external reason. He writes, for example: ' "You can't kill that, it's a child" is more convincing as a reason than any possible reason that might be advanced for its being a reason' (ELP 81). But such passages are rare.

438 *When people assume . . . But such remarks, though they can seem deeply true, make no sense.* Or so I now believe. I hope to think further about this question.

443 *just better . . .* He also writes: 'if any evolutionary development is spectacular and amazing, it is the proliferation and diversification of insects . . . they are truly wonderful' (2006) 141. Though insects are wonderful, it is amazing that Williams believes them to be more wonderful than Plato, Shakespeare, Bach, and Einstein.

454 *As claim (A) shows . . . Hume has told us earlier . . .* Hume writes: 'Every rational creature, 'tis said, is obliged to regulate his actions by reason; and if any other motive or principle challenge the direction of his conduct, he ought to oppose it, till it be entirely subdued, or at least brought to a conformity with that superior principle . . . the supposed pre-eminence of reason over passion' (*Treatise*, Book II, Part III, Section III). Hume also writes: 'we come to a philosopher to be instructed how we shall choose our ends, more than the means for attaining these ends' ('The Skeptic', in Hume's *Essays*).

455 *Such claims are about our object-given value-based reasons . . .* There are many other such remarks. For example, Hume writes: "tis easily conceived how a man may. . have reason to wish that, with regard to that single act, the laws of justice were for a moment suspended' (*Treatise*, Book III, Part II, Section II); 'all these reasons led men to prefer the son of

the late monarch . . . These reasons have some weight' (III, II, X);' Cyrus pretended a right to the throne . . I do not pretend that this reason was valid' (II, II, X); 'But this, in my opinion, is not a sufficient reason for excluding them from the catalogue of virtues' (III, III, IV); 'provided you can give me any plausible reason, why such a falsehood is immoral . . . But the same person . . . has no reason to complain . . . to give a reason why truth is virtuous and falsehood vicious' (Appendix); 'which seems to me a sufficient reason for abandoning utterly that dispute . . . . yet a little reflection will show us equal reason for blaming their antagonists . . . ' (I, IV, V); 'For which reason, I think it proper to give warning. .' (I, III, XIV); 'For which reason, it may be proper in this place. .' (I, III, XV); 'For which reason, we must turn our view. .' (II, II, II). These claims all refer to normative reasons.

'*So little are men govern'd by reason . . .* ' (my emphases, II, II, VIII.) Hume also writes that we mistakenly 'desire objects more according to their situation than their intrinsic value' (III, II, VII).

460 *Since (K) describes . . . of the kind whose existence Mackie denies.* Mackie notes that we sometimes claim that people have categorical reasons to avoid future pain. Commenting on such claims, Mackie writes: 'Our established concept of personal identity through time is here functioning analogously to an institution like promising, introducing a requirement for attention to the future well-being of what will be the same human being' (Mackie (1977) 78). Mackie also writes that, if we say that we have reasons to relieve the pain of other people, we are 'bringing in the requirements of something like an institution: an established way of thinking, a moral tradition, demands that I show some concern for the well-being of others.' Since Mackie is unimpressed by appeals to the requirements of social institutions, he denies that we have any reasons to want to prevent our own or other people's future pain. Such reasons, I agree, could not be given by institutional requirements. The truth is simpler, and is expressed by (K) to (N).

465 *We can start with the metaphysical objections . . . 'entities of a very strange sort'. . . .* There may seem to be a simple way to avoid this objection. Rather than saying that certain natural facts *give* us reasons to have certain beliefs or desires, we can say that these facts *are* reasons to have these beliefs or desires. On this account, normative reasons are not strange entities, since such reasons are natural facts. Or we might say that certain natural facts *count in favour* of our having certain beliefs or desires. But these are merely different ways of saying the same thing. And though these facts are natural, their property of *being a reason*, or *counting in favour*, and the fact that they have this property, are both irreducibly normative. Naturalists deny that there can be such properties and facts.

467 *These writers do not explain why they ignore this view.* In another defence of Actualism, Lycan doesn't even mention Possibilism. He assumes that,

if we reject Actualism, we must be *Concretists* who believe that possible worlds are just as concrete as the actual world (Lycan (2002) 307). Lycan later accepted Possibilism.

468   *When we claim that there was some other possible act . . . The relevant sense of 'could'. . .* I defend this claim in Section 38.

474   *As well as distinguishing . . . thoughts depend on thinkers.* . This view is, I believe, mistaken, as I argue in Parfit (1999). But some claims of this kind are true.

476   *When Nominalists accept this view . . .* Field (1980). Such versions of Nominalism are hard to defend. Field also writes: 'the Nominalistic objection to using real numbers was not on the grounds of their uncountability . . . the objection was to their abstractness: even postulating *one* real number would have been a violation of Nominalism as I'm conceiving it' (1980, 31). These claims are about uncountability, abstractness, and Nominalism. Since these would also be abstract entities, Field's view implies that these claims are also about nothing, and cannot be true. Field might accept this conclusion, since he argues that arithmetic, though not true, is a useful fiction. He might say the same about his Nominalist view.

482   *(S) though there would have been this truth . . .* As these remarks imply, we might combine Non-Metaphysical Cognitivism with the No Clear Question View. We might believe that (1) entities like truths and numbers exist in a non-ontological sense, and that (2) it is not clear enough whether these entities might also exist in some ontological sense. If Platonists can explain some such sense, we might then come to believe that these entities exist in both these senses.

491   *Since we could justify beliefs like (B) . . . some of our beliefs can be justified either by their intrinsic credibility, or by our reasons for having them, or both.* If we find some belief intrinsically credible, and we know that what we find intrinsically credible is more likely to be true, our finding this belief credible may give us an indirect reason to have this belief, and help to make it justified.

494   *Of the ways in which . . . two of the most fundamental . . .* In both cases, there is no sharp distinction here, since some animals have something close to a limited language, and can respond to certain reasons. . . . *Natural selection . . . gave later humans greater cognitive abilities.* The cognitive abilities that we owe to natural selection are in several ways fallible, and sometimes lead us away from the truth. There are also some advantageous false beliefs. But these facts do not undermine the general claims that we are much better than other animals at forming true beliefs about the world, and that we came to have these abilities because they helped early humans to survive and reproduce.

503   *For reasons that I give in a note . . .* I shall be considering arguments for the view that no epistemic truths are irreducibly normative, since

such truths are also alethic truths. These arguments do not appeal, and could not usefully appeal, to the partly normative senses of words like 'probable', 'likely' and 'certain'. These senses are in some ways like thick normative concepts, such as *courageous, rude,* and *chaste,* and raise similar complications. It is clearer to discuss the relations between purely normative epistemic concepts, such as the concept of *an epistemic reason,* and non-normative alethic concepts.

504 *Analytical Naturalism does, I believe, correctly describe*... This Naturalistic concept of an epistemic reason can be usefully compared with what Williams calls the concept of an *internal* practical reason. There are several differences. When we claim that someone has an internal practical reason, that is a claim about this particular person's motivational states. When Analytical Naturalists claim that someone has an epistemic reason to have some belief, that claim is not about this person's motivation, but is about whether this person is aware of facts that either entail some belief, or make this belief likely to be true. These properties are not psychological but alethic. But, like the concept of an internal practical reason, this reductive concept of an epistemic reason is not normative.

505 *that's what it is for these facts to give us a decisive reason*... Though the people who hold this view often claim to be Naturalists, *implying the truth of* is not, in the relevant senses, a natural property.

508 *... because it is so obvious that these claims are, or must be, true.* For example, when I think, 'This is the thinking of a thought, so at least some thinking is going on', I could not understand this thought without believing it to be true. But that does not make this a conceptual truth.

normatively indubitable. . and was free from distorting influences... As Srinivasan has said, nearly all beliefs could be rationally doubted in certain special cases, such as when we believe that we are dreaming, or that we have been given some mind-scrambling drug.

509 *But we cannot give helpful arguments for Non-Contradiction or Modus Ponens*... As Boghossian claims, however, it may be worth showing that such logical truths are not self-undermining, but are in a circular way self-supporting (Boghossian (2000) 229–254)... *nor could we have any direct reasons to believe these truths.* But we might have indirect reasons, given by the facts that (1) these beliefs seem to us indubitable, and that (2) we can justifiably put some trust in our ability to recognize the intrinsic credibility of such beliefs.

519 *... factually valid, in the sense that, if their premises are true, their conclusions are always in fact true.* I claimed earlier that, to explain how our computers can produce so many true answers to difficult mathematical questions, we must appeal to the fact that these computers calculate in ways that correspond to valid reasoning. That was, in one way, an overstatement.

It would be enough if these computers calculate in ways that correspond to reasoning that is *factually* valid. This point did not affect my argument, since we could not be causally affected by this property of factual validity.

528 *Many other animals are motivated to act in these ways, without responding to reasons.* There is a similar difference between our mathematical beliefs and our beliefs in the few fundamental logical truths. We cannot form true mathematical beliefs merely because such beliefs were advantageous, since we could not merely happen to form so many true mathematical beliefs. But we might have merely happened to form the few logical beliefs that were reproductively advantageous, by enabling us to reason in valid ways, thereby forming true beliefs about the world.

529 *Later humans then came to believe. .* This is what Street claims in Street (2006) Section 4. It might be similarly claimed that, after we had come to use the concept of a practical reason, it would have been advantageous to believe that we had reasons to act in these ways. If we believed that we had no such reasons, that might weaken our motivation to act in these ways.

535 *When people argue . . . these beliefs have not been widely held . . .* For actual examples of this kind, Street might suggest the beliefs that homosexuality and birth control are wrong. But when we ask why these beliefs have been widely held, the explanations do not, I believe, give strong support to (O).

537 *natural selection cannot easily explain humanity's early acceptance of the Golden Rule.* As Fitzpatrick suggests, we can imagine an evolutionary explanation for our becoming unconditional altruists (Fitzpatrick (2008) Section 2.2). This disposition might have been advantageous if early humans lived in small enough communities. As before, however, if natural selection could explain both conditional and unconditional altruism, we have less reason to accept either explanation.

541 *. . . our belief in (V) is another illusion.* Street might claim that, even on her constructivist view, we have reasons to do what will achieve our aims. But as I argue in Sections 84 and 96, such claims are trivial unless they state normative truths of a kind that, as a Naturalist, Street denies.

553 *In another large class . . . We would not believe that . . . these parents were simply acting wrongly . . .* Sidgwick suggests another example which may lead us to doubt whether it is a fundamental truth that parents ought to give priority to their own children. He writes: 'If, however, we consider the duty of parents by itself, out of connection with this social order, it is certainly not self-evident that we owe more to our own children than to others whose happiness equally depends on our exertions. To get the question clear, let us suppose that I am thrown with my family upon a desert island, where I find an abandoned orphan. Is it evident that I am less bound to provide for this child as far as lies in my power, the means of subsistence, than I am to provide for my own children?' (ME 346–7).

564 *We can next note . . . With some fairly trivial exceptions . . .* The exceptions
are the truths which use thick normative concepts, such as the truth that
some woman is unchaste, or that some man's act is unpatriotic. Williams
recognized, I believe, that such truths have little importance. That is
why he writes that, for those who know such truths, 'reflection destroys
knowledge' ((1985) 148, 167). Since most of us believe that there are moral
truths, Williams writes, 'ethical thought has no chance of being everything
it seems' (135). Nor can philosophers usefully discuss whether morality
can be objective. All that is left of that issue now is the anthropological
question of 'the degree of ethical resemblance' between human beings in
different cultures.

   Williams seems not to regret these Nihilist conclusions. When we
discuss normative questions, Williams writes, 'We do not need the idea
of an ultimately objective answer'. It is enough to find answers to which
different people 'could honourably agree'. This view, Williams remarks,
reverses Platonism.   For Platonists,

> the aim is ultimate truth or rationality, and the powers that
> could lead us to it merely need to be protected from interference
> by persuasion. The present picture is rather of a world in which
> everything is, if you like, persuasion, and the aim is to encourage
> some forms of it rather than others. ('Saint-Just's Illusion' in
> Williams (1995).

Our aim can only be persuasion, Williams writes, because we have given
up the fantasy of 'ultimate ethical truth'.   But this view, he adds, is *not*

> a product of despair, a mere second-best for a world in which
> the criteria of true objectivity and ethical truth-seeking have
> proved hard to find. To recognize how we are placed in this
> respect is, if anything, an affirmation of strength (1995B 148).

If we are indeed in such a world, we might show strength by recognizing
and facing up to this fact. But that does not imply that, compared with
objectivity and ethical truth, mere persuasion is not a 'second-best', but is
just as good.

   If we are disappointed, Williams writes, this problem comes from the
idea that 'what we would really like to have' is a 'vindicatory history' of
our beliefs, one which shows these beliefs to be justified. Williams claims
that, when we realize that we could not possibly justify our beliefs, we
shall cease to regret this fact.

   Other people make such claims. Timmons, for example, writes that,
when we consider morality from a neutral meta-ethical perspective, we
should conclude that there are no moral truths, and no moral knowledge
(Timmons (1999) 144). But this fact is *less interesting*, Timmons adds,

than the fact that, when we speak from some morally engaged perspective, we can talk *as if* we had moral knowledge. This attitude, I suggest, is sour grapes. Timmons prefers the pretense of moral knowledge only because he assumes that we can't have the real thing.

565 *There is some disagreement . . . In nearly all these kinds of case . . .* The main exceptions are cases that arise during the fighting of a war, and capital punishment.

596 *Nietzsche and Sidgwick were both greatly disturbed . . . Nietzsche remained more religious.* But in a letter to Tennyson's son (HSM 540–1) Sidgwick wrote:

'Wordsworth's attitude towards Nature was one that, so to say, left Science unregarded . . . But for your father the physical world is always the world as known to us through physical science: the scientific view of it dominates his thoughts about it; and his general acceptance of this view is real and sincere, even when he utters the intensest feeling of its inadequacies to satisfy our deepest needs. Had it been otherwise, had he met the atheistic tendency of modern Science with more confident defiance, more confident assertion of an Intuitive Faculty of theological knowledge, overriding the result laboriously reached by empirical science, I think his antagonism to these tendencies would have been far less impressive.

I always feel this strongly in reading the memorable lines:

> If e'er when faith had fallen asleep,
>   I heard a voice 'believe no more',
>   And heard an ever-breaking shore
> That tumbled in the Godless deep;
>
> A warmth within the breast would melt,
>   The freezing reason's colder part,
>   And like a man in wrath the heart
> Stood up and answered 'I have felt'.

At this point, if the stanzas had stopped here, we should have shaken our heads and said 'Feeling must not usurp the function of Reason. Feeling is not knowing. It is the duty of a rational being to follow truth wherever it leads'.

But the poet's instinct knows this; he knows that this usurpation by Feeling of the function of Reason is too bold and confident; accordingly in the next stanza he gives the turn to humility in the protest of Feeling which is required (I think) to win the assent of the 'man in men' at this stage of human thought:

> No, like a child in doubt and fear:
>   But that blind clamour made me wise;

> Then was I as a child that cries,
> But, crying, knows his father near;
>
> And what I am beheld again,
>   What is, and no man understands;
>   And out of darkness came the hands
> That reach through nature, moulding men.

These lines I can never read without tears. I feel in them the indestructible and inalienable minimum of faith which humanity cannot give up because it is necessary for life; and which I know that I, at least so far as the man in me is deeper than the methodical thinker, cannot give up'.

These lines I can seldom read without being close to tears.

602 *the kind of muddle* . . . Williams (2006) 138 . . . . *Nietzsche, by contrast, got it right* . . . Williams seems here to think it important that, after human history ends, and the sun goes out, it will be as though none of us had ever existed. But this could be true only in the sense that we had left no traces of our existence. And that would not matter. Though Russell's essay is sentimentally expressed, he understood time better. 'The Past', Russell writes, has 'the enchanted purity of late autumn, when the leaves, though one breath would make them fall, still glow against the sky in golden glory. The Past does not change or strive . . . the things that were beautiful and eternal shine out of it like stars in the night'. These things, though beautiful, were not eternal. But they did not need to be. Though what is past is not real now, what is distant is not real here. These are not ways of being less real.

611 *As Schopenhauer writes* . . . (1966) 576. Schopenhauer weakens his point by adding 'and just as little does my present well-being undo my previous sufferings'.

617 *I suggest one tenth — or, more cautiously, one twentieth.* You may be helped by looking at www.givingwhatwecan.org

653 *Kant here claims. . . . Only ten years later, in his Metaphysics of Morals, does Kant claim that there are two such ends . . .* Though Kant assumes, in the *Groundwork*, that there are no such objective ends-to-be-produced, that does not explain his claims in passage (A) quoted above. Kant here writes that all imperatives either *represent* some act as a necessary means to some subjective end, or represent some act as necessary in itself. This claim is about the content of possible imperatives. (A) cannot be read as claiming that, though some imperatives represent some act as a necessary means to some objective end-to-be-produced, no such imperatives are valid, because there are no such ends. So in this passage and in his later arguments, Kant seems to overlook this kind of imperative. Given Kant's

love of taxonomies which are exhaustive in the sense of covering every possibility, Kant's overlooking of these imperatives is a mystery. I suggest one possible explanation in the second note below about page 655.

655   *There are also principles . . . and not to injure anyone as a means of bene-fiting others.* The phrase 'for its own sake' can be used, we should note, in a slightly different sense. Our acts have moral worth, Kant claims, only when we act *'from* duty', or for the sake of duty. When we act on some deontological principle, such as a requirement not to lie, we may both be acting in some way for its own sake rather than as a means of producing some effect, and be doing our duty for its own sake. But we might also act from duty on some purely teleological principle, such as one that requires us to do what would benefit others. Though we would then *do our duty* for its own sake, our duty would be to *act* in this way, *not* for its own sake, but as a means of benefiting others.   (See Korsgaard (2008) 178–9.)

. . . *normatively formal in sense 3.* . . . We can now suggest one way in which Kant may have overlooked the possibility of categorical teleological imperatives. Kant may have had in mind three of the distinctions that I have just drawn. When considering imperatives that require us to act in some way, Kant may have seen that any such imperative must either

motivate us only with the help of some desire,	or	motivate us all by itself,

and must either

apply to us only if we have some desire,	or	apply to us whatever our desires,

and must either

tell us to act in some way as a means of achieving some end,	or	tell us to act in some way for its own sake only.

If Kant did not distinguish clearly between these distinctions — as is suggested by the fact that he uses 'formal' and 'material' to express all three distinctions — this may explain why he misdescribes the third distinction, claiming that all imperatives tell us to act in some way either for its own sake only, or as a means of achieving some *desired* end. The other two exhaustive distinctions both refer, in their left-hand side, to our desires. By adding this reference to desires, Kant may have drawn the third distinction in a way that is *not* exhaustive, since it overlooks those imperatives that tell us to act in some way as a means of achieving some categorically required end.

658   *Kant's second premise . . . do not impose only a formal constraint.* Premise (2) makes another mistake. Kant has defined imperatives as categorical when they 'represent some act as necessary of itself, without reference to another end'. That description fits some deontological principles, such as

some requirements to keep our promises. But Kant's Formula of Universal Law does not claim certain acts to be necessary in themselves, since this formula imposes only a formal constraint. So, on Kant's definition, Kant's Formula—which he calls 'the Categorical Imperative'—is not a categorical imperative.

668 *Kant's argument . . . in which we can act upon Kant's Formula of Universal Law.* Kant's 'refutation' contains another argument. Kant writes:

> Because the impulse that the representation of an object possible
> through our powers is to exert on the will of the subject in
> accordance with his natural constitution belongs to the nature
> of the subject—whether to his sensibility (inclination and taste)
> or to his understanding and reason, which by the special
> constitution of their nature employ themselves with delight
> upon an object—it would, strictly speaking, be nature that gives
> the law; and this, as a law of nature, must not only be cognized
> and proved by experience—and is therefore in itself contingent
> and hence unfit for an apodictic practical rule, such as moral
> rules must be. . (G 444)

Kant again concedes here that, when some principle gives us some 'object' or end, we might be moved to act upon this principle, not by our inclinations, but by our reason. When applied to such principles, Kant's argument is this:

> (1) If we believed that there was some end that we were required
> to try to achieve, and we were moved to act on this belief by
> our reason, this motivation would depend on our natural
> constitution. It would be a natural feature of us that we were,
> in this way, rational, being able to be moved by our belief in this
> requirement.

> (2) Since our being moved by this belief would depend upon
> our nature, it would really be nature, not reason, which gave us
> this requirement.

> (3) Since natural laws are contingent, but moral requirements
> must be necessary, this requirement could not be a moral law.

Though this argument raises deep and difficult questions, it cannot be sound. We might similarly claim that, since our ability to reason logically depends on our nature, logical laws must be natural and contingent. Kant would rightly reject that claim. And to protect his Formal Principle from this argument, Kant must claim that our ability to act on his principle does *not* depend on our natural constitution. Kant might say that we act on his principle not as natural but as noumenal beings. But even on that assumption, this argument could not show that there are no true substantive principles. As before, if there are such principles, we might act upon them in whatever way in which we can act on Kant's Principle.

699 *We can call this Kant's Motivational Argument . . . and thereby be able to be a categorical requirement . . .* Of Kant's grounds for making this assumption, another may be his view that, for our acts to have moral worth, 'it is essential . . . that the moral law determine the will directly' (C2 71). If no principle could directly motivate us, none of our acts, on this view, could have any moral worth. Suppose, however, that our acceptance of the moral law motivates us, not directly and all by itself, but only with the help of a standing desire to do our duty. It would be implausible to claim that, when we act on this desire, doing our duty because it is our duty, our acts have no moral worth.

722 *This claim, Stalnaker remarks . . .* Stalnaker (2003)

723 *Stalnaker's Actualism . . .* For more discussion of Stalnaker's claims, see my note about page 729 below.

726 *Meinong's view . . .* Meinong might also deny that there is a wide sense in which both concrete and abstract entities exist. That denial would, I have claimed, be a mistake. Meinong's view should at most be that, though there are, in the wide sense, both concrete and abstract entities, concrete entities also exist in one of two narrower senses, and abstract entities also exist in a different narrower sense (which some express with the word 'subsist').

728 *After my needless hours . . . whether someone is actually or merely possibly dead.* Van Inwagen could point out that, just as his story does not apply to Meinong's view, my story does not apply to Plantinga's view. I have concealed the fact that Plantinga uses 'state of affairs' in an unusual sense. When Plantinga introduces this sense, he gives examples like *Socrates' being snubnosed.* But Plantinga treats states of affairs as very like propositions, which can be true or false. If Plantinga had told me that one actually existing state of affairs is that my wife is dead, he would have meant only that there actually exists this false proposition. If I had understood this remark, I would not have been struck with horror and grief. But this does not undermine my claim that being actually dead is ontologically different from being merely possibly dead.

729 *Van Inwagen's arguments . . . cannot also intelligibly use other, narrower senses.* Stalnaker suggests another argument for Actualism. Possibilists claim that

> (1) there are in the wide sense some things that are merely possible and do not actually exist.

Stalnaker claims that, as an Actualist, he believes that

(2) 'existing and actually existing are the same thing. There exists nothing that is not actual.'

Surprisingly, Stalnaker writes that (2) should be understood

not as a restrictive metaphysical thesis . . . but simply as a trivial consequence of the meaning of the word 'actual'.

It is not obvious how it could follow from the meaning of the word 'actual' that the words 'there are' or 'exist' cannot be used in different senses. Stalnaker's point might be that 'actually' can be used like 'truly', in a way that reinforces any declarative statement, without adding anything to its meaning. If Possibilists use this sense, they could restate (2) as

(3) there actually are in the wide sense some things that are merely possible and do not actually exist.

When Stalnaker claims that his (2) is 'not a restrictive metaphysical thesis', he must mean that (2) does not conflict with any metaphysical view. That would be so if the phrase 'there are' can be used in the wide sense, but the word 'exist' can only be used in the actualist sense, which means 'actually exist'. (1), (2), and (3) might then all be true. Since Stalnaker's (2) would not then conflict with Possibilism, it would be misleading to call this view 'Actualism'.

There is, however, another possibility. When Stalnaker describes the kind of view that he defends, he takes the only alternative to be what Lewis calls 'modal realism'. On Lewis's view, everything that is possible exists, and is just as real as anything that exists in the world around us. When Lewis claims that many of these existing things are not *actual*, Lewis means that these things exist in a part of reality that is not spatio-temporally related to the world around us. Stalnaker's point may be that Lewis's use of the word 'actual' is unusual and misleading, since it follows from the ordinary meaning of the word 'actual' that everything that really exists is actual, whether or not these things are spatio-temporally related to us. Since Stalnaker assumes that Lewis's view is the only other possible view, he may not have considered the Possibilist view stated by (1), which uses the word 'actually' in its ordinary sense.

736 *Of those who once defended Actualism, some would now reject (U) and accept (V).* Two such people, they tell me, are Adams and Fine (in correspondence).

737 *Some writers suggest that (C)* . . . Fine, for example, writes: 'Consider now a possible person. Then it is possibly a person' (2005) 216. (But see the next note.)

738 *(E) a possible person is a person who might be, or become, actual.* This may be Fine's actual view. Fine writes: 'If I am right, the difference between

possible and actual objects is not correctly regarded as a difference in kind. It is a difference in what one might call ontological status, or of what it is for the object to be'(Fine (2005) 14). These remarks suggest that possible people are people who might be actual. (On the next page, however, Fine writes: 'In talking of possible objects — of possible people, say, or possible facts — one is talking of actual people or actual facts — but under the rubric of what is possible'. When we talk about some person who might have been actual, but was never actual — -such as the person who would have existed if some actual ovum and sperm cell had been united — we are not talking about an actual person.)

747 *When we claim that there are such truths, we can use the phrase 'there are' not only in the wide sense but also in a narrow, non-ontological sense.* It might seem enough to claim that the wide sense of 'there are' has no ontological implications. But that could not be true unless we could also relevantly use 'there are' in an explicitly non-ontological sense.

748 *When we claim that there are prime numbers greater than 100, we should use 'there are' in a tenseless and timeless sense.* We can use verbs in a tenseless sense even when we are discussing things or events that do exist or occur in time. When historians say, for example, that the Bronze Age *precedes* the Iron Age, they do not mean that the Bronze Age *now* precedes the Iron Age, or that it always did and always will precede this age.

References

These notes refer to the Bibliography. Some of these notes give only the opening words of some block of text, because what follows makes it clear to what some note refers. In references to this book, page numbers in Roman refer to this volume, and page numbers in italics refer to Volume One.

143 *he whom I want to use* . . . G 430.

145 *According to my proposed Harmful Means Principle* . . . *229.*

153 *Kant appeals, for example* . . . G 432.

 the real progress of ethical science . . . ME viii.

156 *Though Wood believes* . . . *Wood calls this the 'least adequate'* . . . Wood (2008) 69. See also his discussion in Wood (1999) Chapter 3.

 Self-appointed defenders of Kant . . . Wood (2006) 372 note 2. These defenders of Kant are 'self-appointed', Wood writes, 'because Kant never tries to use the universalizability test as a general moral criterion in the way they are trying to defend.' That, I believe, is not true, given the passages I cite on 173–4 above (and Volume One *294).*

 desperately seek . . . Wood (2008) 72.

157 *In revising Kant's formula* . . . *some of Kant's claims.* Wood (2008) Preface.

 Kant's Formula of Autonomy, which Kant sums up . . . G 431.

 tells us to think of ourselves . . . Wood (2008) 78.

158 *Wood calls FA 'the most definitive form'.* . . . Wood (2008) 78, 80–4. Wood is quoting Kant's claim that 'one does better in moral judging always to proceed in accordance with the strict method and take as ground the universal formula of the categorical imperative: *Act in accordance with that maxim which can at the same time make itself into a universal law'.* Most commentators assume that Kant is referring here to his Formula of Universal Law. Wood argues that Kant is referring to his Formula of Autonomy. For an earlier defence of this claim, see Wood (1999) 187–190. . . . *But as Wood also claims, FA is not a reliable criterion* . . . What FA gives us, Wood writes, is only 'a spirit in which to think about how to act . . . not a procedure for deducing . . . principles to act on' (Wood (2008) 78).

159 *Wood also discusses . . . Wood ignores this part of Kant's Formula . . .* Wood (1999) 142.

Perhaps the most fundamental proposition . . . Wood (1999) 121.

160 *Kant's project in ethics . . . how morality's demands on us 'make sense'.* Herman (1993) 210, 212.

These claims need . . . All persons, Kant claims . . . Just before this definition, Kant refers to 'the dignity of a rational being' (G 434).

Kantian dignity, many writers assume . . . Herman (1993) 238, Wood (1999) 130, Kerstein (2002) 182, Korsgaard (1996) 125.

161 *our non-moral rationality . . . Wood claims . . .* Wood (2008) 88; and (1999) 114–6, 94–5.

162 *the absolute worth that grounds morality.* Wood (2008) Chapter 5, Section 2.

an inference from the objective goodness . . . Wood (1999) 127.

Wood even suggested . . . Wood (1999) 129.

morality, and humanity . . . G 435.

163 *The unexercised capacity for morality . . .* As Dean writes, 'There is an inherent conceptual difficulty in claiming that a capacity has incomparably high value . . . to attribute some value to a mere capacity implies an even greater value for the realized capacity' Dean (2006) 86.

Wood considers and rejects . . . He reminds us that, on Kant's view . . . G 406. *Wood then writes . . .* Wood (1999) 120.

164 *the moral law commands me . . .* C2 125 and 129.

Wood gives another argument.. This claim, Wood concludes . . . Wood (2008) 40. See also Wood (1999) 20 . . . *Kant's ethics is grounded . . . on what Wood calls . . .* Wood (2008) 94.

165 *When Wood refers . . . he still takes Kant to be claiming . . .* Wood (2008) 91. . . . *Herman similarly writes . . .* Herman (1993) 213.

165 *These claims are not, I believe . . . as Herman notes . . .* Herman (1993) 214.

165 *Failure to assign . . .* Herman (1993) 124.

166 *killing is not wrong because . . .* Herman (1993) 124.

the aggressor acts on a maxim . . . Herman (1993) 129. This sentence continues '(self) by another'. But I am not the same as my agency.

167 *to act morally is always to act . . .* Wood (1999) 116–7.

worry about the injunction . . . Wood (1999) 144.

168 *Kant does claim that respect for a person . . .* C2 78.

169 *In some of her brilliant discussions . . . cannot provide a criterion of wrongness.* This formula, she wrote, can give us 'predeliberative moral knowledge', by showing that there is a moral presumption against acting in certain ways for certain reasons. This task is 'the only one it can perform' (Herman (1993) 147). See also Herman (1993) 112 and 146.

'. . . *no one has been able to make it work.*' Herman (1993) 104, 132.

172 *all duties, just because they are duties, belong to ethics.* MM 219.

173 *Though Herman seems to accept . . . Herman has elsewhere made this claim.* Kant's Formula, she writes, may be intended only to show that there is a 'deliberative presumption' against acting in certain ways for certain reasons (1993) 182. In this commentary, Herman may be making a different, stronger claim. Kant may intend his formula to give us a criterion of when some act is wrong in the motive-dependent sense, even though such acts may *not* be wrong in the sense of being morally impermissible and contrary to duty.

to inform myself in the shortest and yet infallible way . . . G 403.

174 *common human reason, with this compass in hand. . .* G 404.

178 *not all things required . . .* Herman (1993) 34.

180 *I ought never to act except in such a way . . .* G 402.

183 *states of affairs are not possible bearers of value . . .* Herman (1993) 95.

184 *Things that happen . . .* Herman (1993) 94.

There is no point of view . . . Herman (1993) 99.

If everyone killed as they judged useful . . . Herman (1993) 118.

If we accept some desire-based . . . Herman seems to reject . . . She writes, for example, 'Desires do not give reasons for action: they may explain why such and such is a reason for action . . . but the desire itself is not a reason' (Herman (1993) 194–5).

will a world where one's life . . . Herman (1993) 120 (my italics).

185 *Kant himself . . . Kant writes that 'a lie always harms another . . .'* 8 426 (my italics).

since many cases could occur . . . G 423.

187 *To salvage the argument . . .* Herman (1993) 49.

Herman first considers Rawls's proposed solution . . . Rawls claims . . . Rawls (2000) 175.

188 *if either of two conditions holds . . .* Herman (1993) 52.

Herman considers an objection . . . she calls it 'a strength . . . Herman (1993) 54 note 12.

190 *if he lets his maxim of being unwilling . . .* MM 453.

I cannot will that lovelessness should become a universal law . . . LE 233.

On Kant's view, Herman elsewhere writes . . . (1993) 153–5, and 'Leaving Deontology Behind').

Then two of us suffer . . . MM 457.

192 *GBC: it would be unreasonable* . . . Scanlon (1982) and (1997) 272.

194 *We can also call such reasons personal grounds* . . . *Scanlon adds* . . . WWO 212, and elsewhere.

the justifiability of a moral principle . . . WWO 229.

Scanlon also defends this claim . . . Scanlon (1982) and (1997) 267. He also writes that he is one of those 'who look to Contractualism specifically as a way of avoiding Utilitarianism' (1998) 215.

Jones has suffered an accident . . . WWO 235.

195 *Utilitarians reach such unacceptable conclusions* . . . *Scanlon writes* . . . WWO 241.

A contractualist theory . . . WWO 230.

Scanlon qualifies this view . . . *He suggests* . . . WWO 240.

201 *is central to the guiding idea of Contractualism* . . . WWO 229.

202 *our attention is naturally directed first* . . . Scanlon (1982) and (1997) 123.

206 *Scanlon suggests that, rather than saving one person's life* . . . WWO 239–40.

207 *In some cases, as Temkin suggests* . . . Temkin (forthcoming) Chapters 3 and 4.

209 *It is not unreasonable to refuse* . . . Scanlon (2001) 200.

212 *There may, however, be other grounds* . . . *We would instead be claiming that these facts about human nature provide reasonable grounds for rejecting principles that require such acts.* See Nagel (1991) Chapters 1 and 2.

213 *In his book, Scanlon claimed* . . . *This claim, I have argued, was a mistake.* (Volume One, 368–370). I discuss this distinction below on 299–301.

214 *impersonal values are not themselves grounds* . . . WWO 222.

All reasons for rejecting principles . . . *Scanlon believes both that outcomes can be good or bad* . . . WWO 182.

215 *In answering this question* . . . WWO 219.

217 *contractualism provides no reason* . . . WWO 187 . . . *He also writes: 'a restriction to presently existing human beings* . . . WWO 186.

218 *Such bad effects* . . . *As Scanlon writes* . . . WWO 168.

219 *I have called this the Non-Identity Problem.* RP Chapter 16.

226 *Temkin suggests one way in which we might revise the Two-Tier View.* In discussion.

231 *According to Scanlon's Impersonalist Restriction . . . Scanlon writes . . .* in Stratton-Lake (2004) 128.

235 *the particular forms of concern . . .* WWO 219.

238 *impersonal, in Scanlon's sense . . .* WWO 219.

241 *The idea of justifiability to all possible beings . . .* WWO 186–7.

242 *In making these claims . . . As I have claimed elsewhere . . .* In RP sections 124 and Parfit (1986).

253 *most naturally understood . . .* Stratton-Lake (2004) 133.

  Rawls similarly suggests . . . Rawls (1971) 25.

264 *The correct view . . .* Korsgaard (1996) xiii.

268 *On a third conception . . .* Korsgaard (1996B) 85. Korsgaard continues: 'What the argument . . . actually seems to do is to prove that if there were any Utilitarians then their morality would be normative for them'. Korsgaard seems here to mean 'would motivate them'. Anderson (1991) 21. Anderson also writes 'These agents do not find the perspective of quantitative Hedonism to have normative force: upon reflection, they are unwilling to sacrifice the higher pleasures for any of the lower. No [such] agent, on Mill's view, can be moved by quantitative Hedonism'.

270 *Many other writers give. . . . Falk, for example, defines . . .* Falk (1950). Falk discusses these senses of 'ought' and 'should' in many of the articles reprinted in Falk (1986).

  Darwall similarly writes that, on his view, 'the content of the judgment that there is reason for one to do X is simply that were one rationally to consider facts relevant to doing X, then one would be moved to prefer doing X' (Darwall (1983) 128 (with 'A' replaced by 'X')).

  Williams calls this decisive-reason-implying sense of 'ought' 'the practical or deliberative sense', and he writes: 'Since "A ought to do X" in the practical sense is relativized to the agent's set of aims, projects, object-ives, etc . . . it follows that if a given claim of this kind is based on the assumption that A had a certain objective which he does not have, and if there is no sound deliberative route to that objective from objectives that he does have, then the claim is wrong' (1981 120). Williams also writes, 'If A tells B that he ought to do a certain thing, but A is under a misapprehension about what B basically wants or is aiming at, then A's statement, if intended in this sense, must be withdrawn' (1981 124).

  (E) this act would best fulfil . . . This formulation is intended to cover Williams's remark that, when we say that someone has a reason to do X, we mean something like 'A could reach the conclusion that he should do X (or a conclusion to do X) by a sound deliberative route from the motivations he has in his actual motivational set' (1995) 35. Though Williams writes only that A 'has a reason to do X', his later use of 'should do X' shows that

he is discussing a decisive reason, and what he calls the 'practical' sense of 'should' and 'ought'. We need not here discuss Williams's claim that A's motivations must *already* be in A's actual 'motivational set', rather than being motivations that A might acquire while deliberating on the facts, since this part of Williams's view makes no relevant difference to my claims.

271 *When Williams discusses this imagined case* . . . Williams (1995) 104. Williams assumes only that his imagined person needs to take some medicine to preserve his health. I have added that, if you don't preserve your health, you will lose many years of happy life. This further assumption would not alter Williams's view about this example.

272 *When Williams argues that there are no such reasons* . . . Williams gives some other arguments, which I discuss briefly near the end of Chapter 4, and in Parfit (1997). Some of these arguments are aimed at some proposals that Williams makes about what it might mean to claim that someone has an external reason. But these proposals do not describe the indefinable irreducibly normative sense of the phrase 'has a reason' that Scanlon, I, and others believe that we use. If we can use the phrase 'has a reason' in this external sense, our claims about such reasons are untouched by these arguments. I discuss Williams's view further in Chapter 30, especially Section 107.

277 *(C) we ought rationally to do* . . . Darwall (1983) 210–11.

On the view that Darwall describes . . . Darwall (1983) 128. In these quoted passages, Darwall is not describing his own view, which I shall discuss later.

278 *It is essential to any adequate* . . . *Unless a claim to the effect* . . . Williams (1995) 36.

280 *As I have said, such claims are* . . . *we must have the concept of advice.* I follow Scanlon WWO 20.

283 *in what I have called the motivation sense* . . . Falk (1986) 35, 184.

the test of whether a fact is . . . Darwall (1983) 128.

When I consider the fact . . . Darwall (1983) 86. As we shall see, however, Darwall's final version of Analytical *Internalism* is not a form of Analytical *Naturalism*.

285 *These writers point out that* . . . Darwall, for example, makes such claims (in discussion).

290 *that 'I ought' is different from 'I would want* . . . Falk (1950) 80.

291 *Though Falk calls this suggestion* . . . Falk (1986) 48, 62–3.

292 *Falk then suggests* . . . *In Falk's words, we want the hearer* . . . Falk (1986) 66. When Falk discusses a case like *Revenge*, he writes: 'That "causing you hurt will revenge me" may prove a strongly persuasive consideration . . . But this need still not be more than a "bad" or "insufficient" reason for doing

what this consideration is tempting me to do. For it may still be that, if I still made way in my thoughts for a more faithful and less passion-distorted view of the act . . . I would cease to find it choice-influencing altogether. The consideration would be a "bad" reason and an inferior guide for lack of "true" power of influence' (Falk (1986) 93).

It may seem surprising . . . 'too nebulous to be meaningful'. Falk (1986) 34.

293 *Blame rests, in part, on a fiction* . . . (1995B) 16.

294 *The case for internalism* . . . Darwall (1983) 80.

295 *Most of these Naturalists* . . . Smith (1994) 57; Sturgeon (1988) 239; Boyd (1988) 199, reprinted in Darwall (1996) 119.

302 *As I have also claimed, however . . . By appealing to some such functionalist theory, these people argue* . . . For two such arguments, see Smith (1994) and Boyd (1988).

304 I have found, to my surprise . . . *a crude and only partial analogy.* Schroeder rejects this analogy in his (2007) 75–8.

305 *Some Naturalists make claims* . . . Sturgeon (2006). To put this distinction in a different way: While Sturgeon claims that normative facts may be natural facts even if we *cannot* be confident that we shall *ever* be able to restate these facts in non-normative terms, my definition implies that normative facts are not natural if we *can* be confident that we shall *never* be able to restate these facts in these terms. These claims do not conflict. . . . *On this form of Moral Naturalism* . . . Like many Naturalists, Sturgeon seems here to ignore the difference between rightness and the property that makes acts right. To illustrate how Moral Naturalism might be true, it is not enough to suppose that acts are right just when they maximize pleasure. What we are supposing might be true because, when acts maximize pleasure, that makes them have the different property of being right. That would not help to show how rightness might be a natural property.

306 *Sturgeon suggests another sense* . . . Sturgeon (2006) 100.

311 *Searle argues* . . . Searle (1969) Chapter 8.

It will be enough to consider . . . Given these facts, Searle claims . . . Searle writes that, in rejecting this conclusion, we would be 'using words in incoherent ways' (1969), 195). (Searle most often claims that, in accepting (B) we *commit* ourselves to accepting (C), but the idea of committing ourselves seems unhelpfully close to the idea of undertaking an obligation.)

312 *When Searle considers a similar objection . . . Act Consequentialists are free to claim* . . . Searle (1969) 188–9. (Searle makes this claim, not about Act Consequentialists, but about nihilistic anarchists. But this difference is irrelevant here.)

Searle might next reply . . . Searle (2001) 193.

313 *to recognize something* . . . (1969) 186.

319 *If a procedure is one.* . . . Anscombe (1958) 16.

321 *Anscombe refers, for example* . . . Anscombe (1958) 18.

322 *Anscombe uses 'wrong' to mean 'forbidden by God', or 'against divine law'.*
     This is implied, for example, by Anscombe's claims about the meaning of
     'morally wrong' in her (1958) 17–18.

328 *normative concepts are distinct* . . . Gibbard (2006) 323.

335 *Return next to Gibbard's suggestion* . . . Gibbard (2006) 328.

340 *According to Darwall and some other Non-Analytical Naturalists* . . .
     Williams, for example, seems to accept this view, and Darwall explicitly
     accepts it (in conversation).

346 *The properties are one and the same* . . . Gibbard (2006) 329.

     As Moore remarks . . . Moore (1903) 64.

357 *(A) when some fact explains* . . . (A) is implied by what Schroeder calls
     'Biconditional' in Schroeder (2007) 57. Schroeder adds many qualifications
     to this claim, but these are irrelevant here.

     (D) when some fact explains . . . That's what it is for some fact to be a reason.
     This is the claim that Schroeder calls 'Reason' in Schroeder (2007) 59.

359 *If this was Schroeder's only claim . . . that would reduce the 'unintuitiveness'*
     of his view. Schroeder (2007) 95–6.

361 *Schroeder himself writes that 'reasons count in favour . . .'* Schroeder (2007)
     87. See also his v and 65.

363 *For the philosophical naturalist* . . . Darwall (1992) 168. (Darwall's sentence
     continues 'perhaps when the agent's deliberative thinking is maximally
     improved by natural knowledge.') Darwall's claim seems an overstate-
     ment, since these Metaphysical Naturalists might describe some kinds
     of normativity in rule-involving or attitudinal terms. But Darwall may
     be right to assume that, when these people discuss reasons, their most
     plausible move is to identify normative and motivating force.

365 *Sturgeon, for example, writes* . . . Sturgeon (1988). *'there is nothing more*
     'there' . . . Jackson (1998) 124–5. Jackson also writes: 'all there is to tell
     about moral nature can be told in naturalistic terms' (1992) Section 4 . . .
     Railton, for example . . . Railton (2003) xvii–xviii.

368 *Of those who deny . . . but how they are best to be used.'* Brandt (1992) 29.

369 *As one example* . . . I take this example from Gibbard (1990).

370 *similar questions might be raised* . . . Brandt (1979) 144.

372 *we have a choice as moral philosophers* . . . Brandt (1992) 35–6.

376 . . . *it is hard to see how* . . . Jackson (1998) 127.

377 *Though these last two . . . this would be what 'we ought to aim at'.* Jackson (1998) 142.

381 *Some Humeans claim . . . As Nagel argues . . .* Nagel (1970) Chapter 5.

384 *Some of these writers . . . can, in a way, state facts.* Another such writer is R. M. Hare, whose *Universal Prescriptivism* is inspired by Kant. On Hare's view, moral claims are like universal imperatives or commands, which tell everyone to keep their promises and not to lie. In his final statements of his theory, Hare argues that, if we ask which universal commands we can honestly accept, we would all reach the same Utilitarian answers. Since we would reach the same answers, we can claim these answers to be true. Hare's theory can thus be regarded as a version, not of Non-Cognitivism, but of *Kantian Constructivism*. See Hare (1981) and (1997).

384 *The 'key to meaning', Gibbard writes . . .* Gibbard (2003) 194. Moore's main contribution, Gibbard also writes, was to ask 'What . . . is at issue in moral disputes? What does the disagreement consist in?'

On Blackburn's theory . . . Such people disagree, Blackburn claims . . . Blackburn (1998) 69.

385 *Gibbard similarly claims . . .* Gibbard (2003) 74.

the concept of ought just is . . . Gibbard (2003) 184.

The hypothesis of this book . . . Gibbard (2003) ix–x.

If we understand concluding what to do . . . Gibbard (2003) x and 10.

386 *These claims may correctly describe . . . 'what's obvious is to choose life over death'.* Gibbard (2003) 254, 9.

387 *In many cases . . . In response to a similar objection, Gibbard writes . .* Gibbard (2006).

I the chooser don't face . . . Gibbard (2003) 9.

388 *It may be objected, Gibbard notes . . .* Gibbard (2003) 270.

We must count a change . . . Gibbard (2003) 273, 271.

Responding to a similar objection . . . Gibbard (2003) 54.

Gibbard also claims . . . Gibbard appeals to the fact . . . Gibbard (2003) 268–74.

389 *When Gibbard returns . . . 'we need each other's help.'* Gibbard (2006) 77.

These claims do not support . . . what is involved in real normative disagreements. As Gibbard himself writes: 'For anything I've claimed, a convenient interpretation might be no more than a convenient fiction—like the stupidities we attribe to the computers on our desks.' Though convenient fictions can have some uses, they are not relevant here.

Can I ever be mistaken. . ? Gibbard (2003) 17, x.

390 *quasi-realism is trying* . . . Blackburn (1984) 197. Blackburn's quasi-realism, he also writes, attempts to practise alchemy by transmuting 'the base metal of desire into the gold of values' (*Philosophy and Phenomenological Research* July 2002).

   According to Cognitivists . . . as Gibbard concedes . . . Gibbard (1990) 287.

391 *if our attitudes* . . . Blackburn (1998) 309.

   is that of people . . . Blackburn (1998) 49, 275, 90.

   When two desires . . . Blackburn (1998) 118 note 36.

   Of course there is no problem . . . Blackburn (1998) 318 (my italics).

392 *You can't disagree* . . . Gibbard (2003) 65.

   the quasi-realist can . . . Blackburn (1993) 20.

394 *As I have said, however, claims like (F)* . . . This defence of Blackburn's view is open to the Incoherence Objection that I present in Volume One, Section 13.

   there are a number . . . Blackburn (1998) 318.

   We have other reasons . . . would not *be improved.* Blackburn (1998) 117. He elsewhere writes, surprisingly, 'I think this view is confirmed if we ask: could one not work oneself into a state of doubting whether the capacities generating moral attitudes are themselves so very admirable? The answer is that one could, but that then the natural thing to say is that morality is all bunk and that there is no pressure toward objectivity for the quasi-realist to explain' (Blackburn (1993) 20) . . . *These attitudes would be their own judge and jury* . . . I follow Shafer-Landau (2003) 28–9.

395 *when I wonder* . . . Blackburn (1998) 313.

   Egan adds . . . Egan (2007).

396 *Blackburn might instead* . . . Blackburn (1998) 318.

   This internalizing response . . . his disapproving attitude towards such acts. As he writes: 'No, no no, I do not say that we can talk as if kicking dogs were wrong, when 'really' it isn't wrong. I say that it is wrong (so it is true that it is wrong, so it is really true that it is wrong, so this is an example of a moral truth)' Blackburn (1998) 319) . . . *not to his own attitude, but to this suffering* . . . As Blackburn writes: 'The projectivist can say this vital thing: that it is not because of our responses . . . that cruelty is wrong' (Blackburn (1993) 172). He also writes: 'One ought to look after one's young children, whether one wants to or not. But that is because we insist on some responses from others, and it it is sometimes part of good moralizing to do so' (Blackburn (1993) 177). But he could withdraw this claim.

397 *To think that* . . . Blackburn (1993) 129.

   There is no problem . . . Blackburn (1999) 214.

398 *go on to ask* . . . Blackburn (1998) 50.

If some theorist . . . Blackburn (2009) 207 (my italics).

399 *Return now to Blackburn's claim* . . . Blackburn (1993) 4, 20.

401 *what it is for someone* . . . Gibbard (1990) 8.

403 *Gibbard uses the word 'norm'* . . . Gibbard (1990) 70, 46.

As before, Gibbard avoids . . . Gibbard (2003) 9 – 10. More exactly, Gibbard says that 'ought' here adds nothing.

404 *To 'accept a norm'* . . . Gibbard (1990) 68 – 76.

Return now.. Gibbard writes . . . Gibbard (1990) vii.

What is it, then . . . Gibbard (1990) 7.

405 *really are rational* . . . Gibbard (1990) 9.

406 *he seems to be doing* . . . Gibbard (1990) 153.

407 *is part of what has been missing* . . . Gibbard (1990) 172.

To claim authority . . . Gibbard (1990) 173.

As before, Gibbard notes . . . Gibbard (1990) 175.

Gibbard similarly talks . . . Gibbard (1990) 177.

408 *can transform our view* . . . Gibbard (1990) 33.

409 *After claiming* . . . Gibbard (1990) 8.

Can I ever be mistaken. . ? Gibbard (2003) 17, x.

410 *that when we say something matters* . . . Hare (1972) 33 – 4.

411 *I do not understand* . . . Hare (1972) 40.

414 *moral judgments cannot be* . . . Hare (1952) 195.

Many other writers . . . Blackburn (1998) 70. (Blackburn writes 'for any fact'; but, since he is defending Expressivism about normative claims, he must intend his remark to apply to what Realists claim to be normative facts.)

Gibbard similarly claims . . . Gibbard (2003) 98.

just change the subject . . . Gibbard (2003) 15.

415 *Gibbard makes another* . . . Gibbard (2003) 16. Blackburn makes similar claims. See, for example, Blackburn (1998) 87.

Nowell-Smith . . . Nowell-Smith (1954) 319 – 20.

417 *No doubt it is all* . . . Nowell-Smith (1954) 61.

Williams similarly writes . . . Williams (1981) 122. (I have expanded some abbreviations.)

418 *Hare similarly writes* . . . Hare (1981) 217.

Korsgaard similarly writes . . . Korsgaard (2008) 317.

you are being asked . . . Korsgaard (1996B) 38.

419 *Practical reasoning,* . . . Korsgaard (1996B) 44, 41 note 68.

 Korsgaard discusses several ways . . . For a longer discussion of Korsgaard's view, see Parfit (2006). Even there I say little about some of the most original and central features of Korsgaard's rich and complex view, such as her claims about our practical identity.

420 *rationality is a matter* . . . Korsgaard (1997) 240.

421 *We must explain how these reasons* get a grip *on the agent.* Korsgaard (1997) 240, my italics. Korsgaard similarly writes: '. . . a realist account of the *normativity* of the instrumental principle is incoherent. For think how the account would have to work. The agent would have to recognize it, as some sort of eternal normative verity, that it is good to take the means to his ends. How is this verity supposed to *motivate* him?' (Korsgaard (2008) 3150, my italics).

422 *You have shown* . . . Korsgaard (1996) 163–4.

426 *There are so many people* . . . Nagel (1991) 11–13.

427 *if I find any of my intuitions* . . . ME 342.

430 *This question leaves it open* . . . Williams (1985) 5.

431 *But what is the nature* . . . (2003) 129.

 Such goodness . . . Williams (2002) 90.

 There is a danger . . . Williams (2002) 90.

432 *If we give up this idea* . . . SP 44.

 Williams claims that you have no reason . . . Williams (1995) 104.

433 *The answer* . . . *might be* . . . Williams *(1985)* 20.

 'The aims of moral philosophy,' . . . Williams *(1985)* 1.

434 *does not reflect skepticism* . . . WWO 364–5.

435 *that these considerations.* . . . Williams (2001)

436 *He ought to have done it* . . . (1995B) 16.

437 *As we have seen, subjective theories imply* . . . Volume One, Chapter 3.

 we might define a reason . . . Korsgaard (2009) 26.

 it is the value placed . . . Allison (1996) 113.

442 *We can now return* . . . *There is only importance to us.* (1985) 118. Discussing Utilitarianism, Williams writes: 'Luther thought that it did matter to the Universe what happened to mankind, but this view thinks that all that matters to the Universe is, roughly speaking, how much suffering it contains' (2006) 147.

440 *Williams's claims are about first-person uses* . . . (1995B) 53; (1985) 193.

444 *One difference is* . . . *Williams assumes..* (1985) 53.

445 *But Sidgwick's view* . . . Williams cites Toulmin (1950), Hare (1952), and Nowell-Smith (1954).

   were seemingly denied . . . (1985) 94.

446 *almost everybody* . . . (2003) 285.

447 *(G) if some possible experience* . . . ME 381.

   the good of any one individual . . . ME 382.

   is not given some motivation . . . Williams (1985) 84.

448 *implies an extremely naïve* . . . (2003) 291–2.

449 *(C) when we judge* . . . Mackie (1980) 54.

   (D) 'X is right and Y is wrong . . . Mackie (1982) 55. (I have inserted the references to X and Y.)

   knowledge of the good . . . Mackie (1977) 40 (my italics).

450 *Several other people* . . . Darwall (1995) 284 and 19.

   the good (the law) . . . R, Book I, Section II.

   ought indicates.. LE 605

   the absolute good . . . (my italics) Wittgenstein (1965) 7.

   the objective values . . . Mackie (1977) 28.

451 *Why as I keep asking* . . . Gibbard (2003) 184 my italics.

   Many other people . . . Anscombe (1958) 8. Hare and Korsgaard: see 410–11 and 419 above.

452 *affrighted and confounded* . . . Treatise, Book I, Part IV, Section VII.

453 *before I launch out* . . . Treatise, Book I, Part IV, Section VII

   In a notorious passage . . . Treatise, Book II, Part III, Section III.

454 *we seek reasons* . . . Book II, Part II, Section III.

   I shall have a good reason.. Book I, Part IV, Section VII.

455 *So little are men govern'd by reason*.. Book II, Part II, Section VIII

   There is no quality . . . Book III, Part II, Section VII.

   In her defence . . . Baier (1991) 166.

456 *Baier adds* . . . 165

   The knave is already odious.. (1998) 223–4.

457 *Men of bright fancies* . . . Treatise, Book I, Part IV, Section VII.

458 *As demandingly categorical* . . . Blackburn (1998) 258.

   Blackburn claims . . . *an object-given reason.* He calls this the concept of an *external* reason. But that phrase is misleading, since there can be desire-based external reasons, of the kind described on page 289 above.

   would be a reason . . . *There are no Reasons* (Blackburn (2001) 108–134.

459 *the way a piece of red-hot iron feels* . . . Mackie (1980) 34.
     a categorical imperative . . . (1977) 29.

461 *the pain can be detached in thought* . . . Nagel (1986) 161.
     Adam Smith called Hume 'as perfectly wise and virtuous . . . *as perhaps the nature of human frailty will permit'.* Letter from Adam Smith to William Strachan Esq, 1776.

464 *if this is what anyone seriously believes* . . . Gibbard (1990) 154.
     To non-philosophers . . . Jackson (1998) 128 . . . *Field mentions* . . . In Boghossian (2000) 144, and Field (2001) 387.
     These metaphysical . . . Blackburn (1993) 163.

467 *Of the philosophers who have* . . . Stalnaker (1986) 121, Fine (2005) 214–5, Loux (1998) 166.

471 *Take, for instance, the possible fat man* . . . Quine (1951) 2–3.

474 *As Aristotle said.* . . . Corkum (2008) 76, quoted by Schaffer in Chalmers (2009) 352.

475 *We do not believe in abstract entities* . . . Quine (1947).

476 *Quine qualifies* . . . *When we speak seriously* . . . Quine (1969) 98–100. Dorr (2008) 32–36.

478 *There are no numbers* . . . Dorr (2008) 34.
     there is no realm of numbers . . . in Chalmers (2009) 159.
     we can now define an object . . . in Chalmers (2009) 172.

483 *When van Inwagen considers* . . . van Inwagen (2001) 18.
     I will assume that at least some . . . van Inwagen (2001) 57–8.

485 *it is not an analytic truth* . . . Dorr (2008) note 2.

486 *Though some of these normative claims* . . . *As Nagel writes..* in Korsgaard (1996B) 205.
     Rationalists, Korsgaard suggests . . . Korsgaard (1996B) 44.

488 *among the facts* . . . Gibbard (1990) 154.
     There could not . . . *Sidgwick* . . . *explicitly rejects* . . . ME 34–8. *they may be false..* ME 211, 383.

489 *ascertain which* . . . Mackie (0000).

492 *massive coincidence* . . . Field (1998) 396.
     Other writers make . . . *'extremely unlikely'* . . . Street (2006) 122.

493 *Though Field admits* . . . Field (1998) 396.
     mathematical entities . . . Field (1990) 214.

494 *When Nagel discusses* . . . Nagel (1997) 75.

495 *Whatever justification . . .* Nagel (1997) 139, 136.

496 *When a Greek Stoic . . .* This Stoic was Chrysippus, as reported in Sextus Empiricus, *Outlines of Pyrrhonism* 1.69, quoted in Long (1987) 216.

may explain why creatures . . . Nagel (1986) 78.

Without something more . . . Nagel (1997) 135.

498 *In developing and defending . . . Plantinga believes . . .* Plantinga (1993) Chapter 12.

500 *We can next note . . . Kant claimed . . .* Groundwork 3, perhaps in response to Leibniz's view that even God had to respond to epistemic reasons.

501 *Because some Naturalists . . . Some of these Naturalists therefore try . . .* One example is Field (1980).

504 *Schiffer calls (A) 'about as analytic . . .'* Schiffer (2003) 263. *'Every widow was once married..'* Schiffer (2003) 249.

507 *a sentence is obvious . . .* Quine (1975) 206.

When some belief is . . . When Horwich discusses . . . In Boghossian (2000) 168.

Gödel writes . . . Gödel (1947) 484. He is discussing the axioms of set theory which provide the logical basis for much mathematical reasoning.

508 *Such beliefs are sometimes called conceptual truths . . .* See, for example, Schiffer (2003) 249.

513 *When Nozick discusses . . .* Nozick (1993) Chapter IV. Nozick writes: 'I am not suggesting that it is the capacity to recognize independently valid rational connections that is selected for. Rather, there is a factual connection, and there was selection among organisms for that kind of connection seeming valid . . . [and] to lead to certain additional beliefs, inferences, and so on. There is selection for recognizing as valid certain kinds of connection that are factual, that is for them coming to seem to us as *more* than just factual' (108–9). Nozick seems here to be using 'valid rational connections' in a normative sense. And he may include, under what *is more than just factual*, the dispositions to believe that certain inferences are valid, and that such inferences can give us reasons to have certain beliefs. These beliefs might both, he suggests, be merely useful illusions.

guided the formation . . . Street (forthcoming).

517 *there is no reason to think that natural selection . . .* (my italics) Street (forthcoming A) my italics.

520 *when we ask whether these numbers . . . are all there is . . .* Nagel (1997) 72.

there is nothing in our cognitive experience . . . As Bonjour claims (Bonjour (1998) 108).

523 *As Quine writes, 'Why not settle for psychology?'* Quine (1969) 75. Quine suggests that, as epistemologists, we might study 'perceptual norms'. But

his example of such *norms* are merely the different sounds that constitute a spoken alphabet (90*)* . . . *Field writes* . . . In Boghossian (2000) 139.

524   *there is a real problem* . . . Nagel (1997) 4.

If the natural order . . . Nagel (1997) 131–2.

525   *the existence of reason need not be biologically mysterious* . . . Nagel (1997) 136.

When they discuss our practical and moral beliefs, some skeptics argue . . . Street presents different versions of this argument in Street (2006), (A) and (B). Several other people suggest such arguments. For example, Nozick writes that an evolutionary explanation 'threatens to bypass moral rightness or bestness completely . . . This type of explanation. . . . would also seem to show that it is unreasonable to believe that there are any such (objective) evaluative facts' (Nozick (1981) 342).

527   *Such advantageous motivation often takes hedonic forms.* For a discussion of this fact's significance, see Skarsaune (forthcoming).

531   *the independent normative truth* . . . Street (B).

a strange form of religion . . . Street (A). When she makes this claim, Street assumes that we and others often disagree about these alleged normative truths. I shall return to the significance of such disagreement.

532   *If we believe that there are such independent normative truths* . . . Street (B).

We can reject these claims . . . pain is *bad, and we* do *have strong reasons* . . . For excellent discussions, see Enoch (2010), Kahane (forthcoming), Skarsaune (forthcoming), and Fitzpatrick (2008).

533   *the very thing called into question* . . . Street (B).

The very considerations that in other parts . . . Dennett (1995) 487.

538   *These examples also help . . . slow but accelerating progress* . . . See Singer (1981).

539   *relating as they do to matter fundamentally different* . . . ME 213.

541   *There is nothing self-contradictory in this proposal* . . . Nagel (1986) 157–8.

544   *the best way* . . . Scanlon (2003) 149.

Many recent writers . . . Schiffer (2003) 252; Field 'Apriority as an Evaluative Notion' in Boghossian (2000) 119–20 note 6; Boghossian in 'Knowledge of Logic', in Boghossian (2000) 231; and Boghossian (2008) 250 and 223.

545   *(G) different people might find* . . . Boghossian (2000) 239.

For example, Schiffer claims . . . Schiffer (2003) 247–8. In describing his imagined people, Schiffer calls them 'equally intelligent, rational, imaginative, and attentive (please feel free to insert whatever I left out' (243–4).

I have inserted that these people are rational in the sense that they would respond to reasons.

546 *(I) even in ideal conditions, we and others would* in fact *disagree*... This may be what Boghossian means, in claiming (G).

549 *Though Schiffer denies.... Schiffer calls (J)*... Schiffer (2003) 263.

(L) We ought not to do what is wrong. Schiffer (2003) 249. (It might be claimed that (L) is not trivial, because this claim implies that some acts are wrong. But in the sense that makes (L) true by definition, (L) means that, if certain acts are wrong, we ought not to act in these ways. Moral Nihilists could accept (L), but deny that any acts are wrong.

550 *conceptual* or *concept-based*... Schiffer (2003) 249.

But since (M) is... Some Metaphysical Naturalists... Schiffer may be one such person. When Schiffer claims that certain facts give us a reason to have some belief, he may not use the word 'reason' in the irreducibly normative sense that I express with the phase 'counts in favour.' Schiffer says that he doubts whether epistemic reasons are normative.

554 *Many other disagreements... We may instead use different concepts of a tree and a human being*... I discuss these views further in Parfit (2008).

559 *... which of two patterns of distribution would be less unequal.* For an outstanding discussion of this question, see Temkin (1993).

560 *Cases of this kind raise several difficult questions*... For discussions of both kinds of case, see the articles in Chang (1997).

561 *This is Sen's objection*... Sen (1973).

562 *because our moral philosophers*... Nietzsche, BGE.

564 *No doubt there are some*... Williams (1985) 148.

567 *two thousand years*... *Treatise*, Book I, Part IV, Section VII.

Kant... takes perfection... Schneewind (1998B) 496. *... when he later defended the Stoic view.* C2, 60... *When Ross denies that his own pain is bad*... Ross (1939) 272–284. (Ross makes this claims about pleasure, but he intends it to apply to pain.)

569 *Though my examples... When Moore claims*... Moore writes that 'aesthetic appreciation' of 'what is positively ugly... is certainly often positively bad in a high degree' (1903) 239.

570 *I shall here discuss one such challenge. Nietzsche seems to disagree deeply*... My references to Nietzsche will give quotations without the opening words of the paragraphs in which they may be contained.

571 *profound suffering makes noble..* BGE 270... *pain does not count as an objection to life.* EH 100... *are not only necessary but also desirable for their own sake.* LNB 173 (suffering is implied though not mentioned).

everything actually happens... LNB 207.

we have said Yes to all existence . . . LNB 135–6 WP 532–3.

572 *My formula for greatness* . . . EH 68.

the pessimism of strength LNB1 180. *attempt to acquiesce in the world as it is.* LNB 86 WP 527.

my greatest dangers. Letter to Overbeck 1884.

573 *pity increases the amount of suffering in the world.* D 134.

misery more contagious than happiness. AC 573.

involve a tremendous danger to man. LNB p 97, 225; BGE Preface.

That the sick should not make the healthy sick . . . GM 3, 15.

to grasp in all its profundity . . . GM 3, 14–15.

we shall bring 'evolution to a standstill GM 134. *thwart natural selection.* LNB 241 *a philosophy of pity.* D137.

574 *needs to have some horizon..* UM 63. As Williams similarly writes: "It is not an accident or a limitation or a prejudice that we cannot care equally about all the suffering in the world: it is a condition of our existence and our sanity'. Williams 000.

overwhelmed by compassion. In Ansell Pearson (2009) 232.

become pessimistic Buddhists LNB 90.

the two supreme Buddhist virtues: insight and compassion. LNB 69 BG 202.

doesn't give a damn WP 410.

highest and most illustrious human joys . . . *extraordinary happiness.* LNB 48.

blissful enough. LNB 250.

575 *manly and warlike virtues.* WP 78.

with real wars and no more joking. LNB 169.

Nothing would be more expensive. LNB 103–4.

576 *building our cities on the slopes of a volcano.* GS 283.

the greatest and most terrible wars. HH 176.

Think of what is owed to Napoleon . . . *for a similar prize.* LNB 150, 181, WP 469.

a master race, the future 'masters of the earth'. LNB 71.

where are the barbarians of the twentieth century? LNB 208, WP 465.

I know my fate. EH 126.

577 *the bad odor of death chambers.* Z 2, 204.

permissible to use mankind as material . . . Safranski (2002) 269.

accepts with good conscience the sacrifice of untold human beings. BGE 25.

the remorseless destruction. EH 81.

annihilate millions of failures. WP 506. He also writes: 'starting with the annihilation of people who feel contented' (LNB 61).

578 *The weak and the failures shall perish.* AC 2 570.

Anscombe writes . . . Anscombe (1958) 17.

579 *I am mild and benevolent.* EH 124–6.

I am by far the most terrible. EH 82, 88, 126.

the savage beast. HH 195.

Let us not be gloomy. GM 2: 7 , GM 3: 6.

580 *oldest festal joys . . . sexuality, intoxication, cruelty.* D 18, WP 421.

We should regard . . . HH 36.

everything evil, terrible, tyrannical.. BGE 244.

pouring its light, its love, its tenderness. EH 96.

a good war justifies any cause. Z 1:159.

everything strange and questionable. EH Foreword 2.

I recognize virtue . . . LNB 193.

581 *it must offend their pride.* BGE 243.

Not for a single hour. LNB 234.

the greatest masterpiece of the sublime. 112

the worst music. CW.

this utterly irresponsible race. Kaufmann (1954) 653.

it is unworthy of a god. LNB 189.

pleasure in wilfulness. HH 7.

we are extreme. LNB 190.

a bold and exuberant spirituality. BGE 213.

582 *We rush headlong.* LNB 229

for other, non-moral reasons. D 103.

What defines me. EH 131.

it is a swindle to talk of moral truths.. WP 23.

they contain mere absurdity. TI 501.

There are no moral facts. LNB 94, WP 149,

I deny morality as I deny alchemy. D 103.

583 *the history of the moral sensations.* HH 34.

As Sidgwick and others claim . . . ME, Book I, Chapter 5.

this whole species. WP 413

The more insight we possess. D 44.

584 *only when we compare many moralities.* BGE 186.

(A) all imperatives . . . G. 413.

585 *ethics has been reclining on the comfortable cushion* . . . Schopenhauer (1995) Introduction.

586 *Who tells you that there are laws. . . . Every ought derives all sense and meaning* . . . Schopenhauer (1995) 52, 55 (some of the emphases are mine). Kant himself writes, in the First Critique: 'everyone regards the moral laws as commands; and this the moral laws could not be if they did not . . . carry with them promises and threats. First Critique A 811 B 839. Kant continues 'Without a God and without a world invisible to us now but hoped for, the glorious ideas of morality are indeed objects of approval and admiration, but not springs of purpose and action' (A 813 B 841).

a moral law ought to imply . . . Schopenhauer (1995) 53.

587 *there is no ought any more.* HH 34.

believe that they know 'intuitively' what is good and evil. TI 516.

I walked with her once in the Fellows' Garden. F.W.H. Myers 'George Eliot' in the *Century Magazine*, November 1881.

continue to believe in good and evil. LNB 230.

when the sanctioning God is gone . . . LNB 93.

588 *an authority speaks.* WP 157.

For the English, morality is not yet a problem. TI 515.

To determine what is. LNB 133.

a fundamental principle. quoted in BGE, 186.

589 *whoever has once felt.* BGE 186/289.

590 *The artist creates his work.* UM 178.

the sun would have set, but the sky of our life. HH 105.

591 *This freedom is in fact a heavy debt.* UM183.

Look after me. UM 184.

Hatred of mediocrity. LNB 203.

When the exceptional human being. AC 57.

to live and to be unjust. UM 76.

What is needed is not a forcible redistribution. HH 166.

592 *profoundly indignant about their senseless suffering.* UM 157

It is better to be a human being dissatisfied . . . Mill (1861) 260.

Nowadays there is a thoroughly erroneous moral theory. GS Book 1, 4.

593 *Under what conditions did man devise* . . . GM Preface 3.

one of the greatest ideas that mankind can have. HH 183/354.

594 *the Socratic equation . . . the most bizarre of all equations.* TI The Problem of Socrates, 4.

a moment of the deepest perversity. LNB 255, WP 235.

Socrates had the wisdom. HH 86.

naively placed himself. LNB 2.

one must imitate Socrates. TI the Problem of Socrates, 10.

595 *all this was a mere disease.* TI The Problem of Socrates, 11.

flee into the dark. D 107.

reason-thirsty. GS 319.

bright, transparent, electric air. GS 293.

Was my reason bright enough? GS 319.

—a task for reason on behalf of reason! HH 357.

The only happiness lies in reason: all the rest of the world is dismal. Notes 1875.

596 *why mankind is here.* WP 184.

Has existence any meaning at all? GS 357.

A new What for?—that is what mankind needs. LNB 178.

tip over into nihilism. LNB 138.

One interpretation has perished. LNB 117 WP 35.

consciousness is just a tool.. our becoming conscious is only one more means. LNB 29, 198.

597 *A kind of means has been misunderstood as an end . . . How can it be a good end . . .* LNB 198, WP 376.

nature's magnificent indifference to good or evil. LNB 184.

What is the objective yard-stick. LNB 215.

598 *There is nothing to life that has value.* LNB 119.

Digestion is more venerable. LNB 140.

598 *Let us understand . . .* T. H. Huxley 'Evolution and Ethics', in T. H. Huxley and Julian Huxley, *Evolution and Ethics*, 1893–1943, Pilot 1947: 82.

This is still the old religious way. LNB 24.

we have sought in everything a meaning that it doesn't contain. WP 12.

599 *Question: once morality becomes impossible.* LNB 118, WP 36.

To redeem the past. EH 110.

a Yes, a No, a straight line, a goal. TI 44 473.

We need an affirming race. LNB 166–7.

600 *He who unmasks morality . . .* EH 8.

it is on moral judgments. EH 133.

Whatever has value in our world. GS 301.

Knowledge and wisdom have no value as such. LNB 225.

the real philosophers command. LNB 39, WP 510.

601 *Looked at more subtly* . . . LNB 71.

A man as he ought to be, that sounds as preposterous to us as 'A tree as it ought to be'. LNB 226.

The world has equal value at every moment. LNB 212.

601 *everything seems to be in vain* . . . LN 117.

if we could communicate . . . TLNS.

602 *One should at last put human values* . . . LNB 220.

In his early essay 'A Free Man's Worship', Russell (1903).

Just this I seek . . . GS 23/61.

603 *Of two very exalted things—* HH around 273.

knows that the talent . . . HH 125.

604 *the sun of Nietzsche's life. . . .* to use Schacht's fine phrase.

all kinds of mystical mischief. HH 216.

And you yourselves are also this will to power—and nothing else! LNB 38–9.

drifts imperceptibly. D 542.

605 *very weary, very close to the setting of his sun.*

A thoughtful man. HH 262.

will I have my storm in which I perish? GS 315.

it is the autumn of life. HH 375.

606 *your last sound.* HH 135.

607 *a hyper-sensitivity* . . . Williams (2003) 317.

608 *an ultimate horror* . . . Williams (2006) 146–7.

Judgments of value concerning life. TI 474.

philosophical pessimism is among the comical things. LNB 212.

611 *that thousands had lived.* Schopenhauer (1962) 576.

616 *the universe or history* . . . Williams (1993) 163–4.

617 *There is a great deal of misery* . . . Nagel (1987) 217.

623 *Appendix D Why Anything? Why This?* This appendix was first published in *The London Review of Books*, 22 January and 25 February, 1998. I am grateful to *The Review* for permission to republish here.

624 . . . *as Wittgenstein wrote. Tractatus Logico-Philosophicus* 6.5

624 *One apparent fact* . . . In my remarks about this question, I am merely summarizing, and oversimplifying, what others have claimed. See, for example, Leslie (1989).

648 *If we find this astonishing* . . . *That would be an extreme coincidence.* Of several discussions of these questions, I owe most to Leslie (1979) and Nozick (1981); then to Swinburne (1979), Mackie (1982), Unger (1989), and some unpublished work by Stephen Grover.

663 *the only principle available* . . . in Guyer (1992) 325.

All action to which . . . Potter (1998) 40.

Given Kant's claim . . . Schneewind (1998) 318.

664 *[if] principles of reason* . . . Gregor (1963) 78–9.

665 *When Kant refers here* . . . *because only these maxims 'are fit for a giving of universal law'* . . . Thus, after writing that only 'lawgiving form . . . can constitute a determining ground of the will', and commenting on that claim, Kant concludes that 'the fundamental law' is 'So act that the maxim of your will could always hold at the same time as a principle in a giving of universal law' (C2, 29–30.)

668 *The Second Critique contains another version* . . . For an excellent discussion of both these arguments, see Kerstein (2002) Chapter 7. There is much else in Kerstein's book which goes beyond, and may partly correct, my brief claims in this appendix.

674 *As Irwin notes* . . . Irwin (1996) 80.

682 *Kant claims that, since reason is subject* . . . See, for example, 'What is Orientation in Thinking', VIII, 145, 303–4, and G 448.

684 *The sense in which* . . . Hill (1992) 88.

Korsgaard similarly writes.. Korsgaard (1996), 22.

686 *Kant might make* . . . *Korsgaard suggests.*. Korsgaard (1997).

692 *Categorical imperatives differ essentially from [those that are hypothetical]* . . . Kant writes, 'from the problematic and pragmatic', which are his names for the two forms of hypothetical imperative.

694 *(E) even if no one has ever acted* . . . Kant writes 'even if there have never been actions arising from such pure sources, what is at issue here is not whether this or that happened; that, instead, reason by itself and independently of all appearances commands what ought to happen; that, accordingly, actions of which the world has perhaps so far given no example, and whose very practicability might be very much doubted by one who bases everything on experience, are still inflexibly commanded by pure reason' (G 407–8).

700 *Everyone does in fact* . . . Both this and the previous quotation apply to the Formula of Universal Law. This remark refers to the rule: 'ask yourself

whether, if the action you propose were to take place by a law of nature of which you were yourself a part, you could indeed regard it as possible through your will. . . . if you belonged to such an order of things, would you be in it with the assent of your will?

701 *the Platonic view* . . . See Darwall (1992).

702 *These claims can be given* . . . *In Rawls's phrase* . . . Rawls (1971) 30–3.

704 *When Kant claims* . . . *Rawls takes this to mean* . . . Rawls (1999) 524–5.

716 *the good (the law)* . . . *Religion: Book I, II.*

720 *Plantinga, for example* . . . Plantinga (1974) 132.

     What might it mean . . . Plantinga (1974) 121–2.

     There are philosophers . . . Quine (1960) 131.

724 *Like 'round square', he writes* . . . Van Inwagen (2001) 13.

725 *Van Inwagen might object* . . . *There are, Van Inwagen writes* . . . in Chalmers (2009) 482–492.

727 *One day my friend* . . . Van Inwagen (2001) 16.

     After my needless . . . *On Plantinga's view* . . . *'just as serenely* . . . *'* Plantinga (1974) 132.

728 *there is an ontological difference* . . . Fine (2005) 2.

729 *Lycan calls it 'literally gibberish* . . . *'* in Loux (1979) 290. (Lycan may here be rejecting Lewis's view, which is often misleadingly called a form of Possibilism.)

730 *Quine suggests that, when people claim* . . . Quine (1951) 3.

     Among wilder . . . Burgess (1997) 14.

732 *In living our lives* . . . *if things had been in some ways different.* As Williamson argues in his (2007) 141.

744 *have thoughts* . . . *Prichard suggests..* (1947) 93.

     . . . the beings whom it is possible to wrong . . . WWO 186–7.

Bibliography

Allison, Henry (1996) *Idealism and Freedom* (Cambridge University Press).

Anderson, Elizabeth (1991) 'Mill and Experiments in Living', *Ethics* October.

Anscombe, Elizabeth (1958) 'Modern Moral Philosophy' *Philosophy* Vol 33, No 124 (January), reprinted in *Ethics*, edited by Judith Thomson and Gerald Dworkin (Harper and Row, 1968).

Ansell Pearson, Keith (2009) *Companion to Nietzsche* (Wiley Blackwell).

Baier, Annette (1991) *A Progress of Sentiments* (Harvard University Press).

Blackburn, Simon (1984) *Spreading the Word* (Oxford University Press).

—— (1993) *Essays in Quasi-Realism* (Oxford University Press).

—— (1998) *Ruling Passions* (Oxford University Press).

—— (1999) 'Is Objective Moral Justification Possible on a Quasi-Realist Foundation?', *Inquiry*, 42.

—— (2001) *On Being Good* (Oxford University Press).

—— (2009) 'Truth and A Priori Possibility', *Australasian Journal of Philosophy*, Vol 87, issue 2.

Boghossian, Paul (2000) *New Essays on the A Priori*, edited by Paul Boghossian and Christopher Peacocke (Oxford University Press).

Boghossian, Paul (2008) *Content and Justification* (Oxford University Press).

Boyd, Richard (1988) 'How to be a moral realist' in *Essays on Moral Realism*, edited by Geoffrey Sayre-McCord (Cornell University Press).

Brandt, Richard (1979) *A Theory of the Good and the Right* (Oxford University Press).

—— (1992) *Morality, Utilitarianism, and Rights* (Cambridge University Press).

Brink, David (2001) 'Realism, Naturalism, and Moral Semantics' in *Moral Knowledge*, edited by Ellen Frankel Paul, Fred D Miller and Jeffrey Paul (Cambridge University Press,) 157.

Burgess, John (1997) and Gideon Rosen, *A Subject with No Object* (Oxford University Press).

Chalmers, David (2009) *Metametaphysics*, edited by David Chalmers, David Manley, and Ryan Wasserman, (Oxford University Press).

Chang, Ruth (1997) *Incommensurability, Incomparability and Practical Reason*, edited by Ruth Chang (Harvard University Press).

Copp, David (2001) 'Realist-Expressivism: A Neglected Option for Moral Realism', in *Moral Knowledge*, edited by Ellen Frankel Paul, Fred D Miller, and Jeffrey Paul (Cambridge University Press).

Corkum, Phil (2008) "Aristotle on Ontological Dependence", *Phronesis* 53.

Cuneo, Terence (2007) *The Normative Web* (Oxford University Press).

Darwall, Stephen (1995) *The British Moralists and the Internal 'Ought'* (Cambridge University Press).

—— (1983) *Impartial Reason* (Cornell University Press).

—— (1992) 'Internalism and Agency' *Philosophical Perspectives, Vol. 6. Ethics.*

—— (1992B) Allan Gibbard, and Peter Railton 'Toward Fin de Siecle Ethics: Some Trends, *The Philosophical Review*, (January).

—— (1996) *Moral Discourse and Practice*, edited by Stephen Darwall, Allan Gibbard and Peter Railton (Oxford University Press).

Dean, Richard (2006) *The Value of Humanity in Kant's Moral Theory* (Oxford University Press).

Dennett, Daniel (1995) *Darwin's Dangerous Idea* (Penguin).

Dorr, Cian (2008) 'There Are No Abstract Objects' in *Contemporary Debates in Metaphysics*, edited by Theodore Sider, John Hawthorne, and Dean W. Zimmerman (Blackwell).

Egan, Andrew (2007) 'Quasi-Realism and Fundamental Moral Error', *Australasian Journal of Philosophy*, 85:2.

Engstrom, Stephen (1992) 'The Concept of the Highest Good in Kant's Moral Theory', *Philosophy and Phenomenological Research.*

Enoch, David (2005) 'Why Idealize?' *Ethics* 115 (July), and 'Idealizing Still Not off the Hook: A Reply to Sobel' (forthcoming).

—— (2010): 'The Epistemological Challenge to Meta-Normative Realism', *Philosophical Studies.*

—— (forthcoming) 'Not Just a Truthometer' (*Mind*).

Falk, W. D. (1950) 'Morality and Nature', *The Australasian Journal of Philosophy.*

—— (1986) *Ought, Reasons, and Morality* (Cornell University Press).

Field, Hartry (1980) *Science Without Numbers* (Princeton University Press).

—— (1990) 'Mathematics and Modality', in *Meaning and Method*, edited by George Boolos (Cambridge University Press).

—— (1998) 'Mathematical Objectivity and Mathematical Objects' in *Contemporary Readings in the Foundations of Metaphysics*, edited by Stephen Laurence and Cynthia Macdonald (Blackwell).

—— (2001) *Truth and the Absence of Fact* (Oxford University Press).

Fine, Kit (2005) *Modality and Tense* (Oxford University Press).

Finlay, Stephen (2009) 'The Obscurity of Internal Reasons' *Philosopher's Imprint*.

Fitzpatrick, William (2008) 'Morality and Evolutionary Biology' *Stanford Encyclopaedia of Philosophy* (Stanford University).

Gibbard, Allan (1965), 'Rule Utilitarianism: Merely an Illusory Alternative?' *Australasian Journal of Philosophy*, 43.

—— (1990) *Wise Choices, Apt Feelings* (Oxford University Press).

—— (2006) 'Normative Properties' in *Metaethics after Moore*, edited by Terry Horgan and Mark Timmons (Oxford University Press).

—— (2006) 'The Reasons of a Living Being' in *Foundations of Ethics*, edited by Russ Shafer-Landau and Terence Cuneo (Blackwell).

—— (2003) *Thinking How to Live* (Harvard University Press).

Gödel, Kurt (1947) 'What is Cantor's Continuum Problem?' reprinted in Philosophy of Mathematics, edited by Paul Benacerraf and Hilary Putnam (Cambridge University Press, second edition 1983).

Gregor, Mary (1963) *Laws of Freedom*, (Oxford University Press).

Guyer, Paul (2000) *Kant on Freedom, Law, and Happiness* (Cambridge University Press).

—— (2006) *Kant and Modern Philosophy* (Cambridge University Press).

—— (1992) *The Cambridge Companion to Kant*, edited by Paul Guyer (Cambridge University Press).

Hare, R. M. (1952) *The Language of Morals* (Oxford University Press).

—— (1963) *Freedom and Reason* (Oxford University Press).

—— (1972) 'Nothing Matters', in R.M. Hare *Applications of Moral Philosophy* (Macmillan).

—— (1981) *Moral Thinking* (Oxford University Press).

—— (1997) 'Could Kant Have Been a Utilitarian?', in R. M. Hare *Sorting Out Ethics* (Oxford University Press).

Harman, Gilbert (2000) *Explaining Value* (Oxford University Press).

Herman, Barbara (1993) *The Practice of Moral Judgment* (Harvard University Press).

Hill, Thomas E. (1992) *Dignity and Practical Reason* (Cornell University Press).

—— (2000) Respect, Pluralism, and Justice (Oxford University Press).

—— (2002) *Human Welfare and Moral Worth* (Oxford University Press).

Hume, David: *A Treatise of Human Nature*.

Irwin, Terence (1996) 'Kant's Criticisms of Eudaemonism', in *Aristotle, Kant, and the Stoics*, edited by Stephen Engstrom and Jennifer Whiting (Cambridge University Press).

Jackson, Frank (1992) 'Critical Notice of Hurley' *Australasian Journal of Philosophy* vol. 70.

—— (1998) *From Metaphysics to Ethics* (Oxford University Press).

Kahane, Guy (forthcoming) 'Evolutionary Debunking Arguments', *Nous*.

Kant, Immanuel: I use the following abbreviations, and many of my references contain the numbering of the Prussian Academy edition, which are given in most English editions:

C1: *Critique of Pure Reason.*

C2: *Critique of Practical Reason.*

G: *The Groundwork of the Metaphysics of Morals.*

LE: *Lectures on Ethics.*

MM: *The Metaphysics of Morals.*

R: *Religion within the Limits of Reason Alone.*

SRL: *On a Supposed Right to Lie from Altruistic Motives.*

TLNS: *On Truth and Lies in a Non-moral Sense.*

Katz, Jerrold (1998) *Realistic Rationalism* (Bradford, the MIT Press).

Kaufmann, Walter (1954) *The Portable Nietzsche* (Viking).

Kelly, Thomas (2005) 'The Epistemic Significance of Disagreement' in *Oxford Studies in Epistemology: Vol 1*, edited by John Hawthorne and Tamar Gendler-Szabo (Oxford University Press).

Kerstein, Samuel (2002) *Kant's Search for the Supreme Principle of Morality* (Cambridge University Press).

Korsgaard, Christine (1986) 'Skepticism about Practical Reason' *The Journal of Philosophy*, January.

—— (1996) *Creating the Kingdom of Ends* (Cambridge University Press).

—— (1996B) *The Sources of Normativity* (Cambridge University Press).

—— (1997) 'The Normativity of Instrumental Reason', in *Ethics and Practical Reason*, edited by Garrett Cullity and Berys Gaut (Oxford University Press).

—— (2008) *The Constitution of Agency* (Oxford University Press).

Kumar, Rahul (2003) 'Who Can Be Wronged?' *Philosophy & Public Affairs*, Vol 31 no 2.

Leslie, John (1979) *Value and Existence* (Blackwell).

—— (1989) *Universes* (Routledge).

Long (1978) *The Hellenistic Philosophers*, A. A. Long and D. N. Sedley (Cambridge University Press).

Loux, Michael (1979) *The Possible and the Actual* (Cornell University Press).

—— (1998) *Metaphysics* (Routledge).

Lycan, William (2002) 'The Metaphysics of Possibilia' in The Blackwell Guide to Metaphysics, edited by Richard M. Gale (Blackwell).

Mackie, John (1977) *Ethics* (Penguin Books).

—— (1980) *Hume's Moral Theory* (Routledge & Kegan Paul).

—— (1982) *The Miracle of Theism* (Oxford University Press).

Mill, John Stuart (1861) *Utilitarianism*.

Moore, G. E. (1903) *Principia Ethica* (Cambridge University Press).

Murphy, Liam (2000) *Moral Demands in Nonideal Theory* (Oxford University Press).

Nagel, Thomas (1970) *The Possibility of Altruism* (Oxford University Press).

—— (1973) 'Rawls on Justice', *Philosophical Review* (April).

—— (1979) *Mortal Questions* (Cambridge University Press).

—— (1986) *The View from Nowhere* (Oxford University Press).

—— (1991) *Equality and Partiality* (Oxford University Press).

—— (1995) *Other Minds* (Oxford University Press).

—— (1997) *The Last Word* (Oxford University Press).

Nowell-Smith, Patrick (1954) *Ethics* (Penguin).

Nietzsche, Friedrich: I use the following abbreviations, often with the numbers of the section which contains some quoted passage.

AC: *The Antichrist.*

BGE: *Beyond Good and Evil.*

CW: *The Case of Wagner.*

D: *The Dawn.*

EH: *Ecce Homo.*

GM: *The Genealogy of Morals.*

GS: *The Gay Science.*

HH: *Human, All Too Human.*

LNB: *Late Notebooks*, translated by Rudiger Bittner (Cambridge University Press, 2003).

TI: The Twilight of the Idols

UM: Untimely Meditations

WP: The Will to Power

Z: Thus Spake Zarathustra

Nozick, Robert (1974) *Anarchy, State and Utopia* (Blackwell).

Nozick, Robert (1981) *Philosophical Explanations* (Oxford University Press).

—— (1993) *The Nature of Rationality* (Princeton).

Parfit, Derek: RP: *Reasons and Persons* (Oxford University Press, 1984, reprinted with some corrections in 1987).

—— (1986) 'Comments' in *Ethics*, Summer.

—— (1991) 'Equality or Priority?', Lindley Lecture, (University of Kansas), reprinted in *Some Questions for Egalitarians*, edited by M. Clayton and A. Williams (Macmillan, 2000).

—— (1997) 'Reasons and Motivation', *Proceedings of the Aristotelian Society, Supplementary Volume*.

—— (1999) 'Experiences, Subjects, and Conceptual Schemes', *Philosophical Topics*, Vol 26, No 1 and 2.

—— (2006) 'Normativity', in *Oxford Studies in Metaethics Vol 1*, edited by Russ Shafer-Landau (Oxford University Press).

—— (2008) 'Persons, Bodies, and Human Beings', in *Contemporary Debates in Metaphysics*, edited by John Hawthorne, Dean Zimmerman, and Theodore Sider (Blackwell).

Plantinga, Alvin (1974) *The Nature of Necessity* (Oxford University Press).

—— (1987) 'Two Concepts of Modality', in *Philosophical Perspectives 1, Metaphysics*, edited by James Tomberlin (Ridgeview).

—— (1993) *Warrant and Proper Function* (Oxford University Press).

Potter, Nelson (1998) 'The Argument of Kant's Groundwork', in *Kant's Groundwork of the Metaphysics of Ethics, Critical Essays*, edited by Paul Guyer, (Rowman and Littlefield).

Prichard, H.A. (1949) *Moral Obligation* (Oxford University Press).

Quine, W. V. (1947) Nelson Goodman and W.V.Quine 'Steps toward a Constructive Nominalism', *Journal of Symbolic Logic*.

—— (1951) 'On What There Is', *From a Logical Point of View* (Harvard University Press).

—— (1960) *Word and Object* (MIT Press)

—— (1969) *Ontological Relativity* (Columbia University Press).

—— (1975) 'Reply to Hellman' in *The Philosophy of W.V.O. Quine*, edited by L. Hahn and P. Schilpp (La Salle: Open Court).

Railton, Peter (2003) *Facts, Values, and Norms* (Cambridge University Press).

Rawls, John: TJ: *A Theory of Justice* (Harvard University Press, 1971).

—— (1989) 'Themes in Kant's Moral Philosophy', in *Kant's Transcendental Deductions*, edited by E. Foerster (Stanford University Press).

—— (1999) *Collected Papers,* edited by Samuel Freeman (Harvard University Press).

—— (1996) *Political Liberalism* (Columbia University Press).

—— (2000) *Lectures on the History of Moral Philosophy*, edited by Barbara Herman (Harvard University Press).

—— (2001) *Justice as Fairness* (Harvard University Press).

Ross, Sir David (1939), *Foundations of Ethics* (Oxford University Press).

Russell, Bertrand (1903) *A Free Man's Worship.*

Safranski, Rudiger (2002) *Nietzsche*, translated by Shelley Frisch (Norton).

Scanlon, T.M.: WWO: *What We Owe to Each Other*, (Harvard University Press, 1998).

—— (1982) 'Contractualism and Utilitarianism', in *Utilitarianism and Beyond*, edited by Amartya Sen and Bernard Williams (Cambridge University Press), reprinted in *Moral Discourse and Practice*, edited by Stephen Darwall, Allan Gibbard and Peter Railton (Oxford University Press, 1997) and in T.M. Scanlon *The Difficulty of Tolerance* (Cambridge University Press, 2003).

—— (2003) 'Rawls on Justification', in *The Cambridge Companion to Rawls*, edited by Samuel Freeman (Cambridge University Press).

—— (2003B) 'Value, Desire, and the Quality of Life', in *The Difficulty of Tolerance* (Cambridge University Press).

—— (2007) *Common Minds*, edited by Geoffrey Brennan, Robert Goodin, and Michael Smith.

—— (2007B) 'Wrongness and Reasons', in *Oxford Studies of Metaethics Volume 2*, edited by Russ Shafer-Landau.

—— (2001) 'Thomson on Self-Defence' in *Fact and Value*, edited by Alexander Byrne, Robert Stalnaker, and Ralph Wedgwood (The MIT Press).

Schiffer, Stephen (2003) *The Things We Mean* (Oxford University Press).

Schneewind, Jerome (1977) *Sidgwick's Ethics and Victorian Moral Philosophy* (Oxford University Press).

—— (1992) *The Cambridge Companion to Kant*, edited by Paul Guyer (Cambridge University Press).

—— (1998) 'Natural Law, Skepticism, and Methods of Ethics', in *Kant's Groundwork of the Metaphysics of Morals: Critical Essays*, edited by Paul Guyer (Rowman and Littlefield).

—— (1998B) *The Invention of Autonomy* (Cambridge University Press).

Schopenhauer, Artur (1966) *The World as Will and Representation, Volume 2*, translated by E.F.Payne (Dover).

—— (1995) *On the Basis of Morality*, translated by E. F. J. Payne (Hackett)

Schroeder, Mark (2007) *Slaves of the Passions* (Oxford University Press).

Searle, John (1969) *Speech Acts* (Cambridge University Press).

Searle, John (2001) *Rationality in Action* (The MIT Press).

Sen, Amartya (1973) *On Economic Inequality* (Oxford University Press).

Shafer-Landau, Russ (2003) *Moral Realism* (Oxford University Press).

Sidgwick, Henry: ME: *The Methods of Ethics* (Macmillan and Hackett, various dates).

—— HSM: *Henry Sidgwick: A Memoir*, by A.S. and E. M. S (Macmillan).

—— (2000) *Essays on Ethics and Method* edited by Marcus George Singer (Oxford University Press).

Singer, Peter (1981) *The Expanding Circle* (Farrar, Strauss, and Giroux).

Skarsaune, Knut (forthcoming) 'Darwin and Moral Realism: Survival of the Iffiest', *Philosophical Studies*.

Smith, Michael (1994) *The Moral Problem* (Blackwell).

Stalnaker, Robert (1986) *Midwest Studies in Philosophy* edited by French and others, Volume XI.

—— (2003) *Ways a World Might Be* (Oxford University Press)

Stratton-Lake Philip (2004) *On What We Owe To Each Other* (Blackwell).

Street, Sharon (2006) 'A Darwinian Dilemma for Realist Theories of Value' Philosophical Studies 127, no.1 (January).

—— (2009) 'In Defense of Future Tuesday Indifference: Ideally Coherent Eccentrics and the Contingency of What Matters', *Philosophical Issues* vol. 19.

—— (forthcoming) 'Evolution and the Normativity of Epistemic Reasons', *Canadian Journal of Philosophy*.

—— (A) 'Objectivity and Truth: You'd Better Rethink It' (typescript).

—— (B) 'Mind-Independence Without the Mystery: Why Quasi-Realists Can't Have It Both Ways' (typescript).

Sturgeon, Nicholas (1988) 'Moral Explanations', in *Essays on Moral Realism*, edited by Geoffrey Sayre-McCord (Cornell University Press).

—— (2006) 'Ethical Naturalism', in *The Oxford Handbook of Ethical Theory*, edited by David Copp (Oxford University Press).

Swinburne, Richard (1979) *The Existence of God* (Oxford University Press).

Temkin, Larry (1993) *Inequality* (Oxford University Press).

—— (forthcoming) *Rethinking the Good: Moral Ideals and the Nature of Practical Reasoning* (Oxford University Press).

Timmons, Mark (1999) *Morality Without Foundations* (Oxford University Press.

Toulmin, Stephen (1950) *An Examination of the Place of Reason in Ethics* (Cambridge University Press).

Unger, Peter (1984) 'Minimizing Arbitrariness: Toward a Metaphysics of Infinitely Many Isolated Concrete Worlds', *Midwest Studies in Philosophy* IX reprinted in Peter Unger *Philosophical Papers Volume 1.*

van Inwagen, Peter (1998) 'The Nature of Metaphysics', in *Contemporary Readings in the Foundations of Metaphysics*, edited by Stephen Laurence and Cynthia Macdonald (Blackwell).

—— (2001) *Ontology, Identity, and Modality* (Cambridge University Press).

—— (2002) *Metaphysics* (Westview).

—— (2009) 'Being, Existence, and Ontological Commitment', in *Metametaphysics*, edited by David Chalmers, David Manley, and Ryan Wasserman (Oxford University Press).

Weinberg, Steven (1993) *Dreams of a Final Theory* (Pantheon).

Williams, Bernard (1979) 'Internal and External Reasons', in *Rational Action*, edited by Ross Harrison (Cambridge University Press), reprinted in Williams (1981).

—— (1981) *Moral Luck* (Cambridge University Press).

—— (1985) *Ethics and the Limits of Philosophy* (Fontana).

—— (1993) *Shame and Necessity* (University of California Press)

—— (2001) Chapter 4 Postscript, in *Varieties of Practical Reasoning*, edited by Elijah Millgram (MIT).

—— (2002) *Truth and Truthfulness* (Princeton University Press).

—— (2003) *The Sense of the Past* (Princeton University Press).

—— (2006) *Philosophy as a Humanistic Discipline* (Princeton University Press).

Williamson, Timothy (2007) *The Philosophy of Philosophy* (Blackwell).

Wood, Allen (1999) *Kant's Ethical Thought* (Cambridge University Press).

—— (2002) 'What is Kantian Ethics?' in *Groundwork for the Metaphysics of Morals*, Immanuel Kant, edited and translated by Allen Wood (Yale University Press).

—— (2006) 'The Supreme Principle of Morality', in *The Cambridge Companion to Kant and Modern Philosophy*, edited by Paul Guyer (Cambridge University Press).

—— (2006B) 'The Good Without Limitation', in *Groundwork for the Metaphysics of Morals*, edited by Christoph Horn and Dieter Schonecker (Walter de Gruyter).

—— (2002) *Groundwork for the Metaphysics of Morals*, translated by Allen Wood, (Yale University Press).

—— (2008) *Kantian Ethics* (Cambridge University Press).

INDEX

Since pages 1 to 30 contain summaries of my main claims and arguments, I shall not here repeat some of the information in those summaries. This index gives page numbers for (1) my main discussions of various subjects, with numbers below 30 referring to summaries, (2) my scattered remarks elsewhere about these subjects, (3) my brief remarks about some other subjects, and (4) some other people's claims. Some of these entries overlap, either because their subjects overlap, or to reduce the number of entries that merely tell you to see some other entry.

abortion, and the Argument from Disagreement: 554–5, 560

abstract, roughly: not concrete, lacking causal powers and (in most cases) spatio-temporal location: 20–1, 474–87, 492–4, 501–2, 719–47; and see Metaphysical Naturalism

Actualism: nothing exists in any important sense except what actually exists, see Metaphysical Naturalism

Adams, Robert, rejects pure unqualified Actualism, 770

aesthetics: and response-dependence moral theories, 379, 309–10; the aesthetic category of the *sublime*, and one example, 624

aggregation: whether and how it matters what number of people receive benefits or burdens, 4–5, 193–212; whether the concept of the best outcome should answer such questions, 247

agony: see pain

Albertus Magnus and Non-Analytical Naturalism: 566

All Worlds Hypothesis: 629, 631–6, 641

Allison, Henry: 437

analytic truths: 299–300; these could not be substantive truths about what exists, 485; nor be substantive normative truths, 490–1, 504, 549; not the same as self-evident truths, 508; and see conceptual claims and truths

Analytical Naturalism, see Normative Naturalism

Anderson, Elizabeth: 268

anorexia nervosa: 369–70, 375

Anscombe, Elizabeth: the Injustice Argument, 319–24; whether atheists can have moral beliefs, 451; on ignoring people with Sidgwick's beliefs, 578

apparent reasons: we have such a reason when we have some belief whose truth would give us some reason; normativity is best conceived as involving reasons or apparent reasons, 268; we ought rationally to respond to apparent reasons even when these are not real reasons but are merely apparent (Volume One); though we cannot have evidence for the truth of modal and irreducibly normative beliefs, we have strong and unopposed apparent reasons which justify some of these beliefs, 518–24, 539–42

Aristotle: everything has some purpose, 444; we should ask, not *whether* certain things exist, but *how* they exist 474

Arrow's Impossibility Theorem: 748–9

atheism: and morality, 451, 444; and the ontological argument, 485; and the Steady State Theory, 623; and the appearance of fine-tuning, 626

attitudinal conception of normativity, see Normativity

Autonomy Thesis, and categorical imperatives: 29, 678–88

Autonomy, Formula of, Wood's claims about: 156–8

autonomy: respect for, 143, 153; preference for autonomy over welfare, 148–9; autonomy-protecting or -infringing principles, 143–152

Axiarchic View: reality is the way it is
because this way is best, 306–7; and
the existence of God, 632–4; gives an
explanation of reality that is intelligible,
633–4, but could not be complete,
643–4, and seems to be false, 634; other
partly similar explanations, 634–48
Axioms of Temporal and Personal
Impartiality: 446–7
Ayer, A. J. : 'That's what I should have
said', 384

Baier, Annette, defends Hume's notorious
passage: 455–6
baseline, in questions about distributive
justice: 196–7
Bentham, Jeremy: on the suffering of
animals, 167; on conventional morality,
592
Big Bang: may depend on some entity that
is not in space or time, 484; may have
been fine-tuned, 624–30
Blackburn, Simon: 15–16; defends
Non-Cognitivist Expressivism, 384–5,
401; adds Quasi-Realism, 390–400;
appeals to the Improved Standpoint
Criterion; claims that we can internalize
meta-ethical questions, 396–8, which
are pretty well understood, 464; claims
that beliefs could not answer practical
questions, 414; suggests a Humean
Expressivist account of object-given
reasons, 457–9
Boghossian, Paul: rejects appeals to
intuitions, 544–5, 787 (on 546); on
justifying our beliefs in certain logical
truths, 761
borderline cases, and moral
disagreements: 554–5, 564–5
Boyd, Richard, goodness is probably a
physical property: 296
Brandt, Richard: suggests naturalistic
substitutes for normative concepts,
368–376
Bridge: the Harmful Means Principle and
treating people as a mere means,
146–7; an objection to Kantian Rule
Consequentialism, 151–4
Brute Fact View about reality: 637,
639–47; and higher-order Selectors,
647–8
Buddhism: on personal identity, 427; on
desires, 572; the two supreme virtues,

574; Buddha's first noble truth, 607;
and pessimism about the future, 616
Buridan's Ass, who starves because he
cannot choose without a reason: 386
Burning Hotel: and Analytical
Subjectivism, 283–4, 292; and the
Normativity Objection to Non-
Analytical Naturalism, 326–7;
and Gibbard's account of practical
reasoning, 386–9; and whether
normative truths could help us to
decide what to do, 414

cardinal comparability: being better or
worse, and by more or less; such truths
are often very imprecise: 556–9; and
normative disagreements, 559
Causal Criterion of natural facts: 306–7
Close Enough View, and Scanlon's
Individualist Restriction: 203–4
codes of honour: and the rule-involving
conception of normativity, 268; and
natural normative facts, 308–9
Co-extensiveness Argument for
Naturalism: 296–7, 752
Cognitivism: 265–6, Semi-Cognitivism,
why so called, 751 (on 265); and see
Normative Naturalism and
Non-Naturalism
compassion: Schopenhauer, Nietzsche,
Buddhism, 572–4, 590–2; we need to
have some horizon for our concern,
788
computers: can answer mathematical
questions without being causally
affected by numbers or their properties,
493; this fact provides an argument
against Metaphysical Naturalism,
498–503
conative attitudes, or motivating states:
378–9, and response-dependence
theories of normative or evaluative
facts, 379, 309–10; and Non-
Cognitivist, Expressivist theories,
380, 384–5, 390–400
concealed tautologies: 275–6; Analytical
Subjectivism, 276–7, 287–8; and some
of Searle's arguments from 'is' to
'ought', 314; Analytical Naturalism
about epistemic reasons, 504–5; Kant
on the problem of evil, 567–8; and one
form of Scanlonian Contractualism,
213–14

conceptual or concept-based claims and truths: and substantive truths, 275–8, 285–8; and scientific discoveries about natural kinds, such as heat and water, 325; and thick-concept arguments from 'is' to 'ought', 314–24; and what exists, 485; and self-evident truths, 508, 550–1; and see analytic truths, concealed tautologies

concrete, roughly: physical or mental thing or property, located in space-time, which might have causes and effects: 474, 479; and abstract entities, 480; and the narrow actualist senses of 'there are' and 'exists': 469, 480, 722, and see Metaphysical Naturalism

Consent Principle, and the Kantian idea of respect for autonomy: 143–4; actual consent and redirecting the runaway train, 151

Consequentialism: the impartial-reason-implying sense of 'best', 247, which cannot be used by Subjectivists, 443, 447; and both Kantian and Scanlonian Contractualism 244–59; and arguments from 'is' to 'ought', 311–12; and moral disagreements, 553–4; and see the index of Volume One

consisting in, constituting: 299–300

constructivism, 191, 530, 762 (on 541), 779

contingent, not necessary: 307; and the need for evidence and empirical tests, 489, 517

Contractualism: see Kantian Contractualism, Scanlonian Contractualism; and the index of Volume One

Contractualist Priority View: 201–3, 747 (on 202), 207–8

Convergence Claim: an answer to the Argument from Disagreement, 545–6; in ideal conditions, we would nearly all have sufficiently similar normative beliefs: 546–8; some non-moral examples, 549–52, 565–9; many moral disagreements can be explained in ways that do not cast doubt on the Convergence Claim, 552–65; the widely overlooked imprecision of many normative truths, 555–9; some normative questions may have no answers, 559–62

correct or incorrect uses of words, and normativity in the rule-implying and reason-implying senses: 268

credibility: some beliefs are intrinsically credible though we have no direct reasons to have these beliefs, 490–1; when certain beliefs seem to us intrinsically credible, this fact may give us indirect reasons to have them, 760 (on 491); we can respond to such credibility, and to epistemic reasons, in non-causal ways, though such responses are fully compatible with causal laws, 492–3, 502–3

criterion of wrongness: whether Kant's formulas are intended to provide, 173–4, and might provide, 156–8, 169, 188–90

Darwall, Stephen: and Analytical Internalism or Subjectivism, 277, 283–6; on the concept of a reason, 294; on Metaphysical Naturalism, normativity, and motivating force, 363, 778; and Non-Analytical Naturalism, 340, 362–3; on Locke, 450

Darwin, Charles, and the appearance of design in living beings: 627

Darwinian Answer to the Massive Coincidence Objection: 492–7

debunking explanations: when the causes of our beliefs are unrelated to their truth, this fact casts doubt on these beliefs; see Non-Naturalism, evolutionary debunking explanations

Dennett, Daniel, on obvious reasonableness as an alternative to evolutionary explanations: 535

Depleting or Overheating: and the Non-Identity Problem, 218, 221; and Scanlonian Contractualism, 239, 241; and the future, 614

desert: retributive and non-retributive, 316–17; the Injustice Argument: if we deny that certain punishments would be retributively unjust, we show that we do not know what 'unjust' means, 318–24; Scanlonian arguments against retributive desert, 216; deep disagreements about, 429; and the badness of suffering, 565–9; whether retributive desert is presupposed by morality, 583; Nietzsche's prediction,

593; and the Fair Warning View,
   649–51
determination of the will: and Kantian
   autonomy, 688; and Kant's
   Motivational Argument for his
   Formula of Universal Law, 696, 703,
   709–11; and Kant's more reductive
   form of Moral Internalism, 715–18
disagreements, rational significance of:
   427–30, 542–8
dispreferred indifferents, Stoics and the
   badness of pain: 566
Disproportional View: the importance of
   lesser benefits and burdens is less than
   proportional to their size, 206–8
distorting influences on our beliefs: 428,
   513; claims about such influences
   should be purely procedural 546–7;
   one such influence is self-interest, 553;
   another is the belief that everything is
   for the best, 566–7; indubitability and
   skepticism, 508, 761
distributive justice: and Scanlon's
   objections to Utilitarianism, 4–5,
   193–208; and Kantian and Scanlonian
   Contractualism, 245–59;
   disagreements about often depend on
   non-moral disagreements, 552; and
   the separateness of persons, 236,
   610–11
Dorr, Cian: on whether abstract entities
   exist, 476, 478; analytic truths and
   ontological claims, 485
Dostoyevsky, Fyodor, 587
double badness of suffering: 565–9

Early Death: and Analytical Subjectivism,
   270–272, 281–4; and Williams's
   rejection of the idea of an intrinsically
   good life, 432–4, 439, 443–6
Eating Our Car, Naturalism about reasons
   and the Triviality Objection: 360–1
economists: 'that's not a value judgment',
   463; proposed measures of the badness
   of inequality, 561
Egalitarianism: Telic and Deontic, 198;
   and Nietzsche, 590–2
Egan, Andrew: 388
Einstein: on simultaneity, 557; whether
   Einstein's genius was greater than
   Bach's, 558; suggests that reality must
   be as it actually is, 632
Eliot, George: on God, Immortality, and
   Duty, 587

empirical or natural properties and facts:
   307; these include rule-involving but
   not reason-involving normative
   properties or facts, 308–10; nor modal
   properties or facts, 518–19, nor
   validity, 501–2
Endorsement Thesis, an interpretation of
   Kant's Autonomy Thesis: 684–5
Enoch, David: on the significance of
   disagreement, 428–9; on evolutionary
   debunking arguments, 786 (on 532)
epistemic peers: 428

epistemic reasons and the intrinsic
   credibility of certain beliefs, 490–2; to
   be able to recognize some necessary
   truths, by responding to such
   credibilities and reasons, we need not
   be causally affected by these normative
   properties, 489–90; how natural
   selection might have given us such
   abilities, 490–8, 760 (on 494); and
   Metaphysical Naturalism, 498–503;
   normative and alethic epistemic
   concepts, properties, and truths,
   504–10; natural selection and
   normative epistemic beliefs, 511–17;
   our way of knowing some modal truths,
   518–21; skeptical challenges to our
   modal and normative epistemic beliefs:
   the Causal Objection, 488–97; the
   absence of evidence, 517–25, 530,
   539–42; and see Non-Naturalism,
   epistemological objections

equal shares, equal chances, and one
   difference between Kantian and
   Scanlonian Contractualism: 256–8
Error Theories: 265, 273; Mackie's error
   theory, 451; Ayer's response 184; this
   theory's implications when applied to
   Mackie's future pain, 460; Schiffer's
   error theory, 545; and see Nihilism, and
   Non-Naturalism, Arguments against
Ethics Committee, Moral Naturalism and
   the Triviality Objection: 342
etiquette: the rule-involving and
   reason-involving conceptions of
   normativity, 268; and natural
   normative facts, 308–9
evil, problem of: for theists, 567–8,
   628–9; for the Axiarchic View, 632–4;
   suffering rightly regarded as part of the
   problem, 673; can be a distorting
   influence on people's beliefs, 566–7

evils, less varied than goods: 568

evolutionary debunking arguments: see Non-Naturalism, epistemological objections

exist: whether there could be any irreducibly normative, non-natural entities, properties, or truths: see Metaphysical Naturalism

Expressivism: about morality, 380–5, 390–400; about rationality, 401–10; and see Non-Cognitivism

Externalism about reasons: 270–4, 752; and internal reasons, 270–90; the Externalist Subjective Theory, 288–9; since the phrase 'internal reason' should be dropped, normative reasons need not be called 'external', 290

extrinsic goodness: 52, 455 (on 52); 431

facts, referential and informational senses of 'same fact': 337; Analytical Naturalists must use the informational sense, 337–9

Fact Stating Argument against Normative Naturalism (warning, dreary): 336–41

Fair Warning View: 649–651

Falk, David: reasons are facts that would motivate us, 270; Falk's sense of 'ought' would be used to state empirical, psychological facts, 282–3; on Kant's criterion of normativity and rational necessity, 290; conclusive reasons are irresistible motives, 291; the goodness of a reason can be experienced, 292; a purely normative sense of 'ought' would be 'too nebulous . . . to be meaningful', 292

Field, Hartry: 464, rejects Platonism about numbers 476, 760; the Massive Coincidence Objection to the claim that we know many arithmetical truths, 492–4, 498; on normative epistemic beliefs, 523, 544

Fine, Kit: on the reality of numbers, 478–9; rejects pure, unqualified Actualism, 770; on possible people, 770

fine-tuning of the Universe, appearance of: 625–8

Fitzpatrick, William: on evolutionary explanations of moral motives and beliefs, 762 (on 537)

functionalist defences of Naturalism: 302–3, 333–4, 353–6; and see Normative Naturalism, the Normativity and Triviality Objections

future of humanity: 614–16, 612–20

future people: 217–243

gaps waiting to be filled, concepts that have: 302, 353

general people: a useful phrase but not a kind of person, 220; and the choice between the Two-Tier View and the No Difference View, 220–24; Scanlonian Contractualists cannot defensibly appeal to claims about what could be reasonably rejected by general people, 231–2, or by people to whom some description applies, 235–6, or by people who never exist, 239–40

Gibbard, Allan: claims that normative concepts might refer to natural properties, 328; that is true, but not in a way that supports Naturalism, 298–99, 329–332; appeals to the analogy with scientific discoveries, 334–6; suggests the Single Property Defence, 346–53, 464; defends Non-Cognitivism, 384–390; thinking what I *ought* to do is thinking *what to do*, 385–7; on disagreements between plans, 387–9; claims that his Expressivist account of rationality can help us to decide whether there are better and worse ways to live, 401–410; on normativity and truth, 414–15; objections to Non-Naturalism, 451, 464, 488

global warming: and the Non-Identity Problem, 218–19, 221, 239–241; and a bleak future, 614

God: 307, 322–3; and morality, 444, 484–5; and moral disagreements, 553, 578; and the problem of evil 566–8; Nietzsche's claims about: 582, 584–9, 596–9, 603; and the Universe: 623, 626–9, 632–5, 640, 643–4, 646

Godel, Kurt: on axioms that force themselves upon us as true, 507–8

Golden Rule, and evolution: 536–8

goodness, intrinsic: Williams rejects the idea (430–5, 439), but Hume does not (455, 759–60); Nietzsche claims that everything (571–2) and nothing (601–2) is good; reason-involving intrinsic goodness must be denied by Subjectivists, 432–5, 439, 447, and by Constructivists, 422–5, 530–1; and Volume One

Great Risk, whether one of two acts would be wrong may depend on the possible alternatives: 225

Greater Burden Claim, or GBC, and Scanlonian Contractualism: 192–3, 209–10, 212

Gregor, Mary: 664

Hard Naturalism: 365–7; close to Nihilism, 368; and naturalistic substitutes for normative concepts and claims, 368–77

Hare, Richard: denies that anything could matter, 410–11; on normativity and truth, 411–14 (but see 779)

Harmful Means Principle, different from the objection to harming people *merely* as a means: 146–7, 151

headaches, and the Improved Standpoint Criterion: 392–3, 399

heat and molecular kinetic energy, see Normative Naturalism, analogies with scientific discoveries

hedonic values and reasons: 194–5, 206, 610–13, 615–18, 672–7: see also pain; and Volume One

Hedonistic Act Utilitarianism: as an example to help us to decide whether some form of Moral Naturalism might be true: 266–7, 296–306, 330, 334–6, 341–352

Hegel: 517, 616

Herman, Barbara: on Kant's claims about value, 160–1; respecting rational agency, 164–66; and Kant's Formula of Universal Law, 169–90

Heteronomy Thesis, Kant's: whether compatible with Kant's belief in categorical imperatives, 678–81; arguments for and against this thesis, 681–8; and motivational heteronomy, 688–9

Hill, Thomas, on Kant's Autonomy Thesis: 684

Horwich, Paul: 507

how should we live? Williams rejects this question, 430–3; on some views, there could be no true answers, 409, 425, 600–2; and see mattering

human being, different concepts of, and moral disagreements: 554–5, 787 (on 554)

humanity, future of: 614–16, 612–20

Hume: Sentimentalist moral theory, 378–9, 756; Humean Argument for Non-Cognitivism: 381–3; Humean Theory of Motivation: 381–2; Hume's wretched condition, 452; whether his voyage could be brough to a happy conclusion, 453; the notorious passage, 453–4; Hume's stated view about reasons and his real view, 454–7, 461, 758–9; on interruptions to the moral sciences, 567

Huxley, Thomas, Darwin's champion, rejects evolutionary ethics: 598

identity of facts: the referential and informational criteria, 336–7

identity of properties: see Normative Naturalism: analogies with scientific discoveries, and the Single Property Defence

Imagined Cases:
  Bridge: the Harmful Means Principle and treating people as a mere means, 146–7; as an objection to Kantian Rule Consequentialism, 151–4
  Buridan's Ass, who starves because he cannot choose without a reason: 386
  Burning Hotel: and Analytical Subjectivism, 283–4, 292; and the Normativity Objection to Non-Analytical Naturalism, 326–7; and the Triviality Objection, 357–8; and Gibbard's account of practical reasoning, 386–9; and whether normative truths could help us to decide what to do, 414
  Depleting or Overheating: and the Non-Identity Problem, 218, 221; and Scanlonian Contractualism, 239, 241; and the future, 614
  Early Death: and Analytical Subjectivism, 270–2, 281–4; and Williams's rejection of the idea of an intrinsically good life, 432–4, 439, 443–6
  Eating Our Car: Naturalism about reasons and the Triviality Objection: 360–1

Ethics Committee, Moral Naturalism and the Triviality Objection: 342

Great Risk: whether one of two acts would be wrong may depend on the possible alternatives: 225

Jane's child: Jane's future child and general people, 220; giving our children a good start in life, 239; wronging without harming, 242; and whether there are, in the wide sense, some merely possible people, 472, 738

Jones and the football game: Utilitarianism and whether the numbers count, 194–5, 206

Musical Chairs, and the Disproportional View: 208

Revenge, to illustrate psychological and normative concepts and claims: 281–7

Transplant: and which principles would be optimific, 152, 342; and substantive moral beliefs, 342

Tunnel, and autonomy-protecting principles: 148, 151, 153

Two Medical Programs: and the Non-Identity Problem, our choice between the No Difference View and the Two-Tier View, 221–31; and Scanlonian Contractualism, 231–6, 240–1

impartial reasons: and the Kantian Contractualist Formula, 147–50; and Scanlonian Contractualism, 216, 237–243; not the same as reasons that are impersonal in Scanlon's sense, 238

imperative conception of normativity, see Normativity

imperatives: categorical: and the double use of the German word 'sollen', 584, which has had some bad effects, 585–7; and Kant's arguments for his Formula of Universal Law, 28–9, 652–9; whether such imperatives conflict with Kant's Autonomy Thesis, 678–89; their role in Kant's Motivational Argument, 690–699, 716–7; hypothetical imperatives and non-moral object-given reasons, 676–7; can be used by Expressivists, 458; Mackie's claims about, 460–1

impersonal reasons, in Scanlon's sense, 215, not the same as impartial reasons: 238

Impersonalist Restriction, see Scanlonian Contractualism

importance: psychological and reason-involving senses, 601; absolute and relative, 442–3; and see mattering

Impossibility Theorem, Arrow's: 748–9

imprecise comparability: 555–61; the Linear Model, 556; Bach and Einstein, 558; and normative disagreements, 559

Improved Standpoint Criterion, and whether our desires or other conative attitudes can be mistaken: 392–6

inconsistency of plans or desires: 390–2

indeterminacy, and questions that have no answer: 559–62

Individualist Restriction, see Scanlonian Contractualism

indubitability: 490, psychological and normative, 508–9; our belief in the normative property does not help us to reach true beliefs, 514–15; when Metaphysical Naturalists discuss our beliefs in logical truths, some deny the indubitability of these truths, 523–4

informational sense of 'same fact': 336–9

Injustice Argument: 318–324

Internalism about reasons, see Normativity, Subjectivist theories, and Normative Naturalism

internalizing meta-ethical questions: 396–9

intrinsic credibility, see credibility

intrinsic goodness, see goodness

Intuitionism: we can form some true beliefs, such as some logical, modal, and normative beliefs, not in response to evidence, but by responding to their intrinsic credibility, 489–92, 543–5; these intuitive abilities need not involve any mysterious, quasi-perceptual faculty, 488; though we cannot yet fully explain these abilities, that is not a decisive objection to this view, 521; but intuitionist must defend the claim that, in ideal conditions, we would nearly all form sufficiently similar beliefs, 546–8; and see Non-Naturalism

Jackson, Frank: the Co-extensiveness Argument for Naturalism, 296–7, 752; 'there is nothing more "there"', 365; and Hard Naturalism, 368, 376–7

Jane's child: Jane's future child and general people, 220; giving our children a good start in life, 239; wronging without harming, 242; and whether there are, in the wide sense, some possible people, 472, 738

Jones and the football game: Utilitarianism and whether the numbers count: 194–5, 206

justice: see distributive justice, retributive justice, desert

justificatory regress, Korsgaard's claim that normative realists cannot avoid such an infinite regress: 421–5

Kahane, Guy: on evolutionary debunking arguments, 786 (on 532)

Kant and Kantian Contractualism: 1–4, 9–10, 28–9: Kant's claims about consent, and treating people merely as a means, 143–7; whether Kant's ethics is an ethics of value: 159–68; Kant's Formulas of Autonomy and of Universal Law, 156–8, 169–91; Kantian Contractualism and Rule Consequentialism: Wolf's objections to my claims, 147–55, Herman's objections, 182–91; Kantian and Scanlonian Contractualism, 244–59; Kant's early proposed solution to the problem of evil: 567–8; Kant's use of 'sollen', commands and normative truths: 583–6; Kant's Arguments for his formulas: in the *Groundwork*, 652–668, in the *Second Critique*, 665–6, 668–71; his Motivational Argument, 690–718; Kant's claims about autonomy and categorical imperatives: 678–89; and about non-moral goodness, 672–7; his greatness, see Volume One

Keynes, John Maynard, politicians, economists, and philosophers: 462

Korsgaard, Christine: on what will turn out to be the best meta-ethical view, 264; on normativity and motivation, 268, 420–1; truths cannot answer normative questions, 418–19; objections to normative realism, 419–24, 782; on the concept of a reason, 437; normative entities wafting

by, 486; on Kant's claims about goodness, 160; on Kant's Autonomy Thesis, 684; on acting from duty, but with the aim of benefiting others, 766

Leslie, John, and the Axiarchic View: 643, 792 (on 624 and 628)

legal: facts about what is legal or illegal are, in one sense, normative natural facts, 308–9

Linear Model and imprecise comparability: 556

Lost Property Problem, and the Normativity Objection: 345, 359

Loux, Michael: 467

Lycan, William: 729, 763–4

Mackie, John: his Error Theory, 384; on normativity and motivation, 448–452; on reasons, 459–461; on arguments for moral skepticism, 463, 465, 489

Majority Criterion, and the Paradox of Voting: 748

Many Worlds Hypothesis: 628, 631, 640

Massive Coincidence Objection: 492, 497

mathematics: necessary truths, 326; abstract entities, 474; whether and in what sense numbers exist, Platonism, Nominalism, and the No Clear Question View, 475–479, Non-Metaphysical Cognitivism, 479–85; our knowledge of mathematical and logical truths, 488–98, 506–10, 524; these abilities could be explained by natural selection, 494–500, 512; and skeptical objections to modal beliefs, 518–521

mattering: in the normative and psychological senses: 601, 442–4; whether there are better and worse ways to live, 409, 430–3; whether anything matters, 367, 411, 425, 601–2; skeptical arguments or claims, 463–5, 488, 492, 517, 525–6, 538, 546; summary of my replies, 618–19; what now matters most, 607–18, 620

Maximalist View about what exists: 636, 645

maximizing happiness: 194–5; and how this property might be related to the property of being right 266–7, 296–8; the analogy with molecular kinetic energy, see Normative Naturalism, analogies with scientific discoveries; and the Triviality Objection, 341–351, 366–7

merely possible entities and events, see Metaphysical Naturalism

meta-ethics, 263–603: the decisive battlefield, 269; and normative disagreements, 548, 551; how well understood, 464–5; and see Metaphysical Naturalism, Nihilism, Non-Cognitivism, Non-Naturalism, Normative Naturalism, and Normativity (most of the next few pages)

Metaphysical Naturalism: all properties and facts are natural, 465–487, 502, 618, 719–747; this view conflicts with the belief that there are some irreducibly normative, non-natural properties and truths, 464–5, thereby supporting either Normative Naturalism, 295–6, or Non-Cognitivism, 383, or Nihilism, 383

    Actualism and Possibilism: 467–73; 719–25; 729–747

      Actualism: nothing exists in any important sense except what actually exists; Possibilism: there are some things that are merely possible and never actually exist; the Single Sense View, the words 'there are' and 'exists' have only one important sense; the Plural Senses View, these words have one wide sense and other narrower senses, 467–9

      Possibilists should appeal to this second view, claiming that there are, in the wide sense, some things that are merely possible, and never exist in the *narrow actualist* sense, by being concrete parts of the spatio-temporal world: 469

      an example that supports the Plural Senses View, 469–70, 721–2; another example: whether it might have been true that nothing ever existed, 482–3; Quine's rejection of the Plural Senses View, 720–1; though there are, in the wide sense, both material objects and abstract entities, that does not show that

we should reject the Plural Senses View, 722; Stalnaker's appeal to the meaning of 'actual', 722–3, 769; van Inwagen's arguments for the Single Sense View, 723–9

there are, in the wide sense, many merely possible acts and other events, 730–6; there are also many merely possible people, and other persisting things, 737–8; Jane's first child, 220; Quine's possible men in the doorway, 471; we can have beliefs about such possible people, who would be particular people, 472–3; when we are making some decisions, we ought to think about such people, 744–5

those who claim to be Actualists may misdescribe their real view, 739–43; some of these people might move to Actualist Foundationalism, 472–3, 736

Possibilism is the thin end of a wider wedge: if there are, in the wide sense, some things that never actually exist, we should claim that there are things of many kinds, some of which are actual, though not in the *narrow actualist* sense by being concrete parts of the spatio-temporal world, 473–5; we should ask not *whether* such things exist, but *how* they do, 474 many such things are abstract, in the sense of being neither physical nor mental, lacking causal powers and, in most cases, spatio-temporal location, 474; some abstract entities, such as legal systems, the meanings of words, and fictional characters, are mind-dependent or created by us; others, such as the laws of nature, numbers, and reason-involving normative properties and truths, are in neither way dependent on us, 475–6

four views about such entities: Platonism, Nominalism, and the No Clear Question View: 475–9; Non-Metaphysical Cognitivism: 759 (on 465), 479–87, 502; the non-ontological senses of 'there are' and 'exist', 480–3, 745–9

Metaphysical Naturalism: (*cont.*)
the Validity Argument against
Metaphysical Naturalism:
498–502
Naturalist epistemological objections
to the belief in irreducibly
normative truths, see
Non-Naturalism

Mill, John Stuart: morality without God,
587; and Nietzsche, 592
modal properties and truths: necessary
truths, which apply to all possible
worlds, 489–92; the absence of
evidence for modal beliefs, and modal
skepticism, comparison with normative
skepticism, 518–22, 532, 539
Modus Ponens: 492, 506–9, 523, 682,
686
Moral Belief Internalism: 381–3, 699
Moral Expressivism: 380–5, 390–400;
Expressivism about rationality, 401–10;
and see Non-Cognitivism
Moral Subjectivism and Intersubjectivism:
379–80, 384
Moral Naturalism, see Normative
Naturalism
moral progress: 538, 563–4, 584, 593
Moral Sentimentalism, Cognitivist and
Non-Cognitivist: 378–80, 400, 548
moral worth: and the wrongness of acts,
172–3, 175–6; and one of Kant's
arguments for his Formula of Universal
Law, 659–61
motivating grounds: 438, normativity and
motivating force, 717–18
motivational conception of normativity:
see Normativity
motive-independent wrongness and the
Mixed Maxims Objection to Kant's
Formula of Universal Law: 170–2
Musical Chairs and the Disproportional
View: 208

Nagel, Thomas: v; on the Humean theory
of motivation, 381; on the badness of
suffering, 426, 461; on the metaphysics
of normative truths, 486; on rationality
and natural selection, 494–6, 524–5;
on our discovery of infinity, 520; on our
knowledge of normative truths, 541,
551; on whether and how our lives can
have any meaning, 617–8

Narrow Person-Affecting View: 219; and
see the Wide Person-Affecting View,
749
natural selection: might explain our
abilities to do mathematics, to reason
validly, and respond to reasons, 494–7;
might explain some of our normative
beliefs in ways that cast doubt on their
truth, thereby providing evolutionary
debunking arguments: see Non-
Naturalism, epistemological
objections
Naturalism: see Metaphysical Naturalism,
Normative Naturalism
Naturalistic Fallacy: 378; and the Single
Property Defence, 345–56
necessary truths: logical and normative,
and our knowledge of such truths: 326,
445–6, 489–510; and modal truths,
518–525; and the absence of evidence
539–42; and see Non-Naturalism
necessity, normative and psychological:
439–41, 448–51, 690–718
New Kantian Formula, and Herman's
claims about wrongness: 174–9
No Difference View, one answer to the
Non-Identity Problem: 219–33
Nietzsche, Friedrich: 570–608, 612, 618

Nihilism, and error theories: though
positive normative claims are intended
or believed to state truths, such claims
are all false, 263–7, 327; why called
'Semi-Cognitivism', 751 (on 265); the
Naturalist Argument for Nihilism, 383;
some Non-Cognitivists are close to
Nihilism, 384, 410; as are Hard
Naturalists, 368; Williams's form of
Moral Nihilism, 442, which Williams
claims should not be disappointing,
763–4; Mackie's similar view, 448–51;
Schiffer's error theory, 545–6;
Nietzsche's rejection of morality,
587–9, and loss of belief in any values,
or meaning in life, 596–602

Non-Cognitivism: 15–17; Sentimentalism
and Expressivism, 378, 380–1; the
Humean Argument for Non-Cognitivism, 381–3; the Naturalist
Argument, 383–4; Gibbard's defence of
Non-Cognitivism, 384–390; thinking
what I *ought* to do is thinking *what to
do*, 385–7; disagreeing with

plans, 387–9; whether Non-Cognitivists can explain normative mistakes, 389–400, Blackburn's Improved Standpoint Criterion, 392–6; Blackburn's claim that we can internalize meta-ethical questions, 392–6; Hare's denial that anything could matter, since '"matters" isn't that sort of word', 410–12; Expressivist accounts of rationality, and whether there are better and worse ways to live, 401–410; the Normativity Argument: truths could not be normative, or answer normative questions, 413–425

Non-Identity Problem, how our acts can affect future people, and the importance of these effects: 219–33

Non-Naturalism: Normative Non-Naturalist Non-Metaphysical Cognitivism, or Rationalism: 263–603, 618–19
   irreducibly normative, reason-involving or reason-implying concepts, claims, and truths: summaries of claims about: 10–14, 19–21; summaries of objections to beliefs in such truths, and of some replies, 19–25, 618–19; and see Volume One, Part One
   natural and non-natural concepts, claims, and facts: 263–9, 305–10; and see Normative Naturalism
   Arguments against Non-Naturalism:
      doubts about the intelligibility of irreducibly normative concepts and claims: 272–4, 290–4, 434, 754; people who seem not to use such concepts: 290–4, 410–11, 414–18, 434–41, 448–53
      motivational objections: the Humean Argument for Non-Metaphysical Cognitivism, 383–5; the Normativity Argument, truths could not be normative, 413–18; Korsgaard's claims, 418–25; and see Non-Cognitivism
      metaphysical objections: 295–6, 327, 383, 464–5; replies: 759 (on 465), 465–87, 498–503, 719–47; and see Metaphysical Naturalism

epistemological objections: 488–97, 511–69
   the Causal and Massive Coincidence Objections, 488–92; can be answered, as the analogy with computers shows, 492–3, we could respond non-causally to validity, and other modal and normative properties and truths, 498–502; and natural selection could explain how we came to have these abilities, the Darwinian Answer and the Reverse Coincidence Argument, 492–7, 510
   evolutionary debunking explanations of our normative beliefs: when natural selection explains how humans came to form certain beliefs, this explanation may either support or cast doubt on these beliefs, 511–12; such explanations would cast doubt on certain beliefs if we came to have such beliefs because they were reproductively advantageous, and these beliefs would have been advantageous whether or not they were true, 511–12; such explanations have been claimed to cast doubt on our normative epistemic beliefs, 511–13; whether these beliefs were advantageous, 513–17; similar debunking arguments have been applied to our practical and moral normative beliefs, 525–6; whether these beliefs were advantageous, 527–30; whether they were mostly produced by evolutionary forces, 534–8, 786 (on 532)
   the absence of evidence for these normative beliefs, 538–42; we are claimed to have no other way of knowing whether these beliefs are true, 517, 531–3
   the Rationalist's response: 489–98, 503–10, 517–24, 539–45
   we can form some true beliefs, such as some logical, modal,

Non-Naturalism: (*cont.*)
  and normative beliefs, not by
    responding to evidence for the
    truth of these beliefs, but by
    responding to their intrinsic
    credibility, or to our reasons to
    have them, 489–92, 543–5
  though there can be no evidence for
    these normative beliefs, there can
    be no evidence against them; in
    such cases, strong unopposed
    apparent reasons can justify our
    beliefs, 518–24, 538–42
  in the epistemic case, skeptical
    arguments are self-defeating, 522
  to respond to these credibilities and
    epistemic reasons, we do not need
    any mysterious quasi-perceptual
    faculty, as the analogy with
    computers again shows, 502–3;
    though we cannot yet fully explain
    what is involved in these abilities,
    that is not a decisive objection to
    our belief in them, 521
  the Argument from Disagreement:
    427–30, 542–6; to defend their
    view, Rationalists or Intuitionists
    must be able to have the rational
    belief, or hope, that in ideal
    conditions we would nearly all
    form sufficiently similar
    normative beliefs, 546–8; defence
    of this Convergence Claim:
    548–68, 589–95
  and see Normativity

Normative Naturalism: 10–14; 263–377
  Analytical Naturalism: 10–11, 263–7;
    Analytical Subjectivism or
    Internalism about reasons, 267–290;
    Williams on internal and external
    reasons, 269–75; the unimportance
    of internal reasons, 275–88; the
    Externalist Subjective Theory,
    288–90; the phrase 'internal reason'
    is used, confusingly, in two different
    senses, and should be dropped,
    289–90; Analytical Epistemic
    Naturalism, 503–5
  Non-Analytical Naturalism: 11–14
    Moral Naturalism, 295–357
    Non-Analytical Naturalism about
      reasons: 357–65
    making right and being right,
      299–301

  the depth of the disagreement:
    303–5
  Reductive and Wide Naturalism
    305–7
  natural facts that are normative in
    rule-implying, motivational,
    attitudinal, or response-dependent
    senses, 308–10
  Arguments for and against
    Non-Analytical Naturalism:
    appeals to normative or
      rule-involving institutions,
      310–14
    thick-concept arguments, 315–24
    the Co-extensiveness Argument:
      296–7, 752 (on 297)
    the Normativity Objection: 324–7
    analogies with scientific discoveries
      about natural kinds, such as heat
      and water: 298–303, 325, 329–38,
      352–6, 366–7
    the Fact Stating Argument (warning,
      dreary): 336–41
    the Triviality Objection: 341–64,
      566
    the Ethics Committee, 342–3;
    the Lost Property Problem: 345,
      359;
    the Single Property Defence 345–56,
      754–5
  Soft Naturalism, Hard Naturalism, and
    Nihilism 364–77

Normativity:
  normative concepts: 263–8, 290–4;
    Volume One, Chapters 1 and 7;
  reason-involving irreducibly normative
    truths: the sense in which these are
    not natural facts, 305–10; defending
    beliefs in such truths, 464–569
  conceptions of normativity:
    rule-involving: 267–8, 308–9,
      312–14
    attitudinal: 268–9; Cognitivist,
      378–80, 309–10; Non-Cognitivist,
      380–4; Quasi-Realist 390–400
    imperatival or prescriptive: 268,
      291–2, 414, 448–9, 584–90,
      602–3, 779
    reason-involving, purely normative:
      268, 309–10, 326–7
    reason-involving, with motivational
      accounts of reasons, Analytical
      Subjectivism or Internalism,
      10–11, 269–94,

motivational: and Metaphysical
Naturalism, 363; motivational
arguments against Moral Cognitivism, 378, 381–3; against the
belief in irreducibly normative
truths, claiming that no truths or
beliefs could be normative, 413–
425; people who seem not to have
the concept of a purely normative,
non-motivating reason, or of
purely normative moral truths,
290–4, 410–11, 414–18, 434–41,
448–53; normative and motivational heteronomy, 689; Kant's
Motivational Argument,
689–718
practical reasons:
Objectivist or objective theories: such
reasons are given, not by our
desires or aims, but by the facts
that give us reasons both to have
certain desires or aims, and to try
to achieve them, 432, 394, 270;
though some Humeans deny that
we have such object-given
value-based reasons, this was
Hume's real view 455, 758–9;
explaining and defending this
view, 457–63, and see Non-
Naturalism, and Volume One
Subjectivist or subjective theories:
practical reasons all depend on
facts about our present desires or
aims, either those we actually have,
or the desires or aims that we
would now have after informed
deliberation: Analytical
Subjectivists, who give
motivational accounts of reasons,
10–11, 269–94; Non-Analytical
Naturalist Subjectivism, 357–62;
Non-Naturalist Subjectivism,
288–90, 362–3; and see
Normative Naturalism, and
Volume One
the Normativity Objection to
Normative Naturalism, 324–7,
which is accepted by many
Metaphysical Naturalists, 327
the Triviality Objection to Soft
Naturalism: Normative Naturalists
cannot make positive substantive
normative claims, 341–62

conceptual and substantive
normative truths; 275–8, 285–8,
about epistemic reasons, 504–6;
and see concealed tautologies
normative and alethic epistemic
concepts and claims: 502–10, 512,
15, 521–4, 551
normativity and normative
importance: 279–80
mattering: in the normative and
psychological senses: 601, 442–4;
whether there are better and worse
ways to live, 409, 430–3; whether
anything matters, 367, 411, 425,
601–2; skeptical arguments or
claims, 463–5, 488, 492, 517,
525–6, 538, 546; summary of my
replies, 618–19; what now matters
most, 607–18, 620

Nowell-Smith, Patrick, the fundamental
question for ethics is not 'What *should* I
do?' but 'What *shall* I do?': 415–17
Nozick, Robert: suggests evolutionary
debunking explanations of our
normative epistemic beliefs, 513, 785
(on 513), and of our moral and
evaluative beliefs, 786 (on 525)
Null Possibility: 482–5, 623, 629, 630–2,
636, 639
numbers, existence of, see Metaphysical
Naturalism

Objectivism about reasons: see
Normativity, and Volume One
ontological objections to the belief in
irreducibly normative truths, see
Metaphysical Naturalism

pain, agony, suffering: pain in the relevant
sense only when disliked; badness of,
and reasons to want to avoid or prevent:
167, 184, 437, 459–461, 489–90, 541;
evolution and our motivation to avoid,
527–30, 786 (on 527); believed to be
bad by nearly everyone, the main
exceptions being those who don't have
the concept of non-moral badness, or
are under some distorting influence,
551–2, 565–9; Kant's claims,
567–8,

pain, agony, suffering: (*cont.*)
   672–7; Nietzsche's claims, 571–4,
   591–2; and whether it has all been
   worth it, 607–12; and see Volume One
Paradox of Voting: 748
Pareto Principle, the transitivity of *worse
   than*, and unavoidable wrong-doing:
   224–5, 748
Pascal, the heart, and making important
   decisions: 462
Pessimism: Schopenhauer, Nietzsche, and
   Williams, 571–4, 608: Buddhism, 574,
   607; and whether it has all been worth
   it, 610–12; and the future, 615–18
Plantinga, Alvin: on the explanation of
   our mathematical abilities, 498; on
   Possibilism, 720; on actually existing
   states of affairs, 727–9; may not really
   be an Actualist, 739–42
Plato: on intrinsic goodness, 430–2;
   whether normative knowledge
   necessarily motivates 449–50, 701,
   713–15; whether there might be some
   part of reality that is not in space or
   time, 484; and the Axiarchic View, 632
Platonism about abstract entities: 475–8,
   485, 492–3, 501–2
Plotinus: 632
Plural Senses View: the words 'there are'
   and 'exist' have more than one
   important sense, 469; see Metaphysical
   Naturalism
Pope, Alexander: 'Whatever is, is right',
   567
Possibilism about what exists, see
   Metaphysical Naturalism
possible people: Jane's first child, 220;
   Quine's possible men in the doorway,
   471; we can have beliefs about
   particular possible people, 472–3; there
   are, in the wide sense, many merely
   possible people, 737–4; when we are
   making some decisions, we ought to
   think about such people, 744–5; as
   Scanlonian Contractualists, we cannot
   appeal to claims about what could be
   reasonably rejected by people who are
   merely possible, 239–40; and see
   Metaphysical Naturalism
Potter, Nelson: 663
practical necessity, moral incapacity,
   Williams's psychological account of:
   439–41
principles of equal chances and equal
   shares: 257–8, one difference between

Kantian and Scanlonian
   Contractualism
Priority View, Telic and Deontic: 198–9,
   747; the Contractualist Priority View,
   201–3, 747 (on 202), 207–8
privation theory of evil: 567
problem of evil: for theists, 567–8, 628–9,
   673; for the Axiarchic View, 632–4
procedural rationality: 270–1, 281,
   287–8
progress, moral: 538, 563–4, 584, 593
promises: and Searle's main argument
   from 'is' to 'ought': 310–13
property: any characteristic, feature, or
   way that something is: 264, 752
   (on 295)
Proudhon, Pierre-Joseph: on legal
   ownership, 316
punishment, justification of: see
   retributive justice

Quasi-Realists: Non-Cognitivists who
   believe that they can claim all, or nearly
   all, that Cognitivists claim: 384–5,
   39–1, 390–400
quasi-perceptual faculty of knowing about
   non-natural properties and truths: not
   assumed by most Intuitionists, 488–9,
   520, 544, and not needed, 489–92, as
   the analogy with computers shows, 493,
   498–500
Quine, W. V. O. : on possible people, 471;
   renounces abstract entities, 475–6;
   change of view, 501–2; on the
   obviousness of logical truths, 507;
   rejects normative epistemology, 523

Rationality: how we can rationally
   respond to disagreements, 427–30;
   whether wrong-doing is always
   irrational, 441–2; the more important
   questions are not about rationality, but
   about reasons, 442; we choose
   rationally when we make some choice
   because we have beliefs whose truth
   would give us sufficient reasons to
   make this choice; Hume's notorious
   claim that no desire or preference could
   be unreasonable or contrary to reason,
   453–4; not Hume's real view, 455,
   758–9; our abilities to reason validly,
   and respond to epistemic reasons,
   490–2, which might have been
   produced by natural selection, 494–5,

513–15, 525–8; and rational intuitions, 531–3, 543–7; procedural rationality, 270–1, 281, 287–8; Brandt's Naturalist account of rationality: 369–76; Gibbard's Expressivist account, 385, 401–10; Nietzsche's conflicting claims about: 594–5, 600, 619–20; and see Volume One

Rawls-Scanlon Cases: 246–7, 250–1
realism, normative: belief in normative truths that are not response-dependent, mind-dependent, or constructivist; often assumed to make positive ontological claims; the word 'realism' not used by me for this reason
reason: concept of, and other reason-implying concepts, Volume One, Chapter 1; kinds of reason and other claims about reasons: see index to Volume One
reason-involving conception of normativity, see Normativity
referential sense of 'same fact': 336–8
religion: and morality, 444, 585–9; and the meaning of life, Nietzsche assumes that only God or Nature could provide, 596–9, and do not provide, 601–3; and moral disagreements, 552–3, 578
respect: for autonomy, 143, 153; for rational agency or rationality, 164–7; for the moral law and for persons, 168
response-dependence theories of normative or evaluative facts, 379–80; such theories may describe some natural facts that are normative in the attitudinal sense, 309–10
retributive justice and desert: 316–17; the Injustice Argument, 318–24; Scanlonian arguments against retributive desert, 216; deep disagreements about, 429; and the badness of suffering, 565–9; whether presupposed by morality, 583; Nietzsche's prediction, 593; and the Fair Warning View, 649–51
Revenge, to illustrate psychological and normative concepts and claims: 281–7
Reverse Coincidence Argument: 497
rightness, wrongness, and the properties that make acts right or wrong: 299–301, 341–356; Scanlon's claims about, 213–14
rule-involving conception of normativity, see Normativity

Russell, Bertrand: 'our robust sense of reality', 467, which should not be offended by, and provides no objection to, Non-Metaphysical Cognitivism, 487; on normative truths, 602; the shortness of history, 616; and the reality of the past, 765

Scanlon, T. M.: v; rejects Williams's claim that he (Williams) does not understand the concept of an external reason, 434–7
Scanlonian Contractualism: 4–10, 191–259
  Scanlon's Individualist Restriction, 191–6; why Scanlon should give up this restriction, 4–5, 196–212; the Contractualist Priority View, 201–3, 207–8, 255; the Close Enough View, 203–4; whether small pleasures for many people could morally outweigh a single person's severe pain, 194–5; even if the numbers count, the single person might reasonably answer No, 206; but in many cases that involve large numbers, trivial benefits or burdens should not be ignored, 204–6; the Disproportional View, 206–8; Grey's organ and White's life, 208–12
  Scanlon's claims about wrongness, which he has rightly revised, 213–14; Scanlon's Impersonalist Restriction disallows appeals to the goodness or badness of outcomes, 214–15; given Scanlon's claims about wrongness, he cannot now defend this restriction as true by definition, but would have to weaken his theory's claims, which he need not do, 5–6, 214–17
  Scanlonian Contractualism should make claims about what we owe to future people, 217; to answer such questions, we must consider the Non-Identity Problem, and choose between the Two-Tier View and the No Difference View, 6–7, 218–31; whichever view Scanlonians accept, they have strong reasons to give up the Impersonalist Restriction, 7–9, 231–43, 744–5; this revision would not undermine but strengthen Scanlonian Contractualism, 239–43

Scanlonian Contractualism: (*cont.*)
this revised theory, I argued, can be combined with Kantian Contractualism and Rule Consequentialism, 244–6; Scanlon objects that, in what I call Rawl-Scanlon Cases, some people could reasonably reject optimific principles, 246–7; on plausible assumptions, however, these people could rationally choose these principles, 247–51, and could not reasonably reject these principles, 251–5; but Scanlonian Contractualism supports certain principles more strongly than Kantian Contractualism, 255–7; in some other cases, the three parts of the Triple Theory may conflict, but without weakening this theory, 257–9

Schiffer, Stephen: suggests a reductive account of epistemic reasons, which would not be normative, 504; on moral intuitions, 544–5; his error theory, 548–50

Schneewind, Jerome: 567, 662–3

Schopenhauer, Artur: objections to Kant's ethics, 186, 572, 585; assumes that morality consists of commands, and depends on God, 586; on compassion, 572; pessimism, 571, 611, 615; on the argument for God's existence as the Creator, or First Cause, 634

Schroeder, Mark, Non-Analytical Naturalism about reasons: 357–63

Searle, John, arguments from 'is' to 'ought': 310–14, 753

second-order properties: properties that are had by properties: 329–332

Selectors of reality: 637–48

self-evidence: the property of beliefs whose truth we can recognize by considering only their content, such beliefs may be fallible, 490; closely related to indubitability, 508–9; both properties denied by Metaphysical Naturalists, 523; two self-evident beliefs, 544; and intuitions, 544–5

Semi-Cognitivism, why so called, 751 (on 265)

Sen, Amartya: on the imprecision of some normative truths, 561

separateness of persons, and distributive justice: 236, 610–11

Sidgwick: recommends disinterested curiosity, 153; would reject Naturalism, 301–4, 334–6; on the rational significance of some disagreements, 427; Sidgwick's intuitionism criticized by Williams, Gibbard, and Mackie, 443–8, 488–90; though we cannot have evidence for the truth of our purely normative beliefs, we also cannot have evidence against their truth, 539–40; Sidgwick's claims about impartial reasons do not conflict with our moral beliefs, 554; 'he shows a corrupt mind', 578; Sidgwick and Nietzsche, 570, 592, 594, 596; and Tennyson, 764

Single Property Defence of Naturalism, 345–54

Single Sense View, the words 'there are' and 'exist' have only one important sense: 469; see Metaphysical Naturalism

Skarsaune, Knut: on pleasure, pain, and evolutionary debunking arguments, 786 (on 527, 532)

skepticism: 293, 380, 511–42, 552, 564; and see Nihilism, Error Theories

Smith, Michael: 295

Socrates: and Williams, 430–3, 444; and Nietzsche, 594–5

Soft Naturalism: 364–9

Soft Naturalist's Dilemma: 366–7

sollen: the double use of this German word has had some bad effects: 26, 584–6

sorites arguments: 561

Srinivasan, Amia: 761 (on 508)

Stalnaker, Robert: seems to ignore Possibilism, 467; on Actualism and the meaning of 'actual' 722–4, 769

Standard Ought Claim: 355

Steady State Theory: the Universe has always existed, and in a similar form, 623

Stoics: on the badness of pain, 566–8, 673–4

Street, Sharon, epistemological objections to Non-Naturalism: 492, 513–14, 517, 786 (on 525), 530–8, 542

Sturgeon, Nicholas: 295, 305–6, 365, 368

Subjectivism about reasons, see Normativity, Normative Naturalism, and Volume One

substantive normative truths and claims: see Normativity

suffering, see pain
supervenience: 752 (on 300).

tautologies, see concealed tautologies
Telic Egalitarianism: 198; and the
  Levelling Down Objection, 747
Telic Priority View: 198, 201, 248–9,
  254–5
Temkin, Larry: on spreading burdens but
  concentrating benefits, 207–8; on the
  Two Tier View, 226–230, 233
thick normative concepts, and arguments
  from 'is' to 'ought': 315–24, 326
time, its nature and rational significance:
  427, 438, 765
Transplant: and which principles would
  be optimific, 152, 342; and substantive
  moral beliefs, 342
trivial or imperceptible benefits and
  burdens: 204–6; and Parfit, RP,
  Chapter 3 (see the *Harmless Torturers*)
Triviality Objection to Naturalism:
  341–364
Tunnel, and autonomy-protecting
  principles: 148, 151, 153, and Volume
  One
Two Medical Programs, and the
  Non-Identity Problem, our choice
  between the No Difference View and
  the Two-Tier View: 221–31; and
  Scanlonian Contractualism, 231–4
Two-Tier View: 219–33, 241

unjust-world sense of 'ought': 287
Utilitarianism: Utilitarians go astray,
  Scanlon claims, because they add
  together different people's benefits and
  burdens, 193–6; Scanlon's objection
  should instead be that Utilitarians reject
  distributive principles, 196–201;
  Utilitarianism and Contractualism,
  257–8; Hedonistic Act Utilitarianism
  as an example of Moral Naturalism:
  266–7, 296–306, 330, 334–6, 341–352;
  Nietzsche's claims about, 592–3; see
  also Consequentialism

validity, logical: defined, 492; and deriving
  'ought' from 'is', 310–24; validity is not
  a normative property, 314, 492, 506;
  and Metaphysical Naturalism, 480, 486;
  and an argument against Naturalism,
  498–502; non-causal responses to
  validity, 492–4, 498–503; and modal

truths, 519; our knowledge of both
  modal and normative epistemic truths,
  520–25
Van Inwagen, Peter: on whether it might
  have been true that nothing ever
  existed; 483, arguments for the Single
  Sense View, 723–8:

water and H2O, see Normative
  Naturalism, analogies with scientific
  discoveries
welfare economics: 462
what we owe to each other: and what
  Scanlon calls 'impersonal reasons',
  215–17; not the same as impartial
  reasons, 238; and the Non-Identity
  Problem, 241–3
Wide Naturalism: 306–7
Wide Person-Affecting View: 749
Williams, Bernard: 17–18; Williams's
  account of reasons, 269–88, 293–4;
  normativity and truth, 417–8; on how
  we should live, and intrinsic goodness,
  430–3; mutual misunderstandings,
  433–48, 452–3; normative and
  psychological concepts and beliefs,
  434–44; Williams and Sidgwick,
  444–48; on moral disagreements 564;
  on whether we should be disappointed
  by moral skepticism or Nihilism,
  763–4; on the Stoics, 566; on Russell
  and Nietzsche 602; on why we cannot
  care equally about all suffering, 788; on
  whether it has all been worth it, 607–8,
  615–17
Wittgenstein, Ludwig: on the absolute
  good, 450; rejects normative
  epistemology, 523; on unanswerable
  questions, 624; and the Universe, 631
Wolf, Susan: on actual and possible
  consent, 143–4; on treating people
  merely as a means, 144–7; on Kantian
  Rule Consequentialism, 147–55
Wood, Allen: 156–68; on Kant's Formula
  of Autonomy, 156–8; on Kant's
  Formula of Humanity: 158–68; Wood's
  Foundational Thesis, 160–3
wrongness, rightness, and the properties
  that make acts wrong or right:
  299–301, 341–356, 213–14
'wrong': senses of, Volume One,
  Chapter 7

Zeno: 561